D0165133

THE CLASSIC MAYA

In the first millennium AD, the Classic Maya created courtly societies in and around the Yucatan Peninsula, leaving some of the most striking intellectual and aesthetic achievements of the ancient world, at large settlements like Tikal, Copan, and Palenque. This book is the first in-depth synthesis of the Classic Maya. It is richly informed by new decipherments of hieroglyphs and decades of intensive excavation and survey. Structured by categories of the person in society, it reports on kings, queens, nobles, gods, and ancestors, as well as the many millions of farmers and other figures who lived in societies predicated on sacred kingship and varying political programs. *The Classic Maya* presents a tandem model of societies bound by moral covenants and convulsed by unavoidable tensions between groups, all affected by demographic trends and changing environments. Focusing on the Classic heartland but referring to other zones, it will serve as the basic source for all readers interested in the civilization of the Maya.

Stephen D. Houston is the Dupee Family Professor of Social Sciences at Brown University. The author of numerous books and articles, he is also an archaeologist who has excavated and mapped Classic Maya cities for more than twenty-five years. A MacArthur Fellow, Houston is also the recipient of grants from the National Endowment for the Humanities and the National Science Foundation.

Takeshi Inomata is Professor of Anthropology at the University of Arizona. He has conducted archaeological investigations at the Maya Center of Aguateca and at Ceibal in Guatemala. His numerous publications examine Maya political organization, warfare, architecture, households, and social change.

CAMBRIDGE WORLD ARCHAEOLOGY

SERIES EDITOR
NORMAN YOFFEE, *University of Michigan*

EDITORIAL BOARD
SUSAN ALCOCK, *Brown University*
TOM DILLEHAY, *Vanderbilt University*
STEPHEN SHENNAN, *University College London*
CARLA SINOPOLI, *University of Michigan*

The *Cambridge World Archaeology* series is addressed to students and professional archaeologists, and to academics in related disciplines. Most volumes present a survey of the archaeology of a region of the world, providing an up-to-date account of research and integrating recent findings with new concerns of interpretation. Although the focus is on a specific region, broader cultural trends are discussed and the implications of regional findings for cross-cultural interpretations considered. The authors also bring anthropological and historical expertise to bear on archaeological problems and show how both new data and changing intellectual trends in archaeology shape inferences about the past. More recently, the series has expanded to include thematic volumes.

RECENT BOOKS IN THE SERIES

CAMBRIDGE WORLD ARCHAEOLOGY

THE CLASSIC MAYA

STEPHEN D. HOUSTON

Brown University

TAKESHI INOMATA

University of Arizona

CAMBRIDGE
UNIVERSITY PRESS

CAMBRIDGE UNIVERSITY PRESS

Cambridge, New York, Melbourne, Madrid, Cape Town, Singapore,
São Paulo, Delhi, Dubai, Tokyo

Cambridge University Press
32 Avenue of the Americas, New York, NY 10013-2473, USA

www.cambridge.org
Information on this title: www.cambridge.org/9780521669726

First published 2009

Printed in the United States of America

A catalog record for this publication is available from the British Library.

Library of Congress Cataloging in Publication data

Houston, Stephen D.
The classic Maya / Stephen D. Houston, Takeshi Inomata.
    p.   cm. – (Cambridge world archaeology)
Includes bibliographical references and index.
ISBN 978-0-521-66006-8 (hardback) – ISBN 978-0-521-66972-6 (pbk.)
1. Mayas – Mexico – Yucatán (State).   2. Mayas – Mexico – Yucatán (State) – Antiquities.
3. Yucatán (Mexico : State) – Antiquities.   I. Inomata, Takeshi.   II Title.   III. Series.
F1435.H795   2010
972′.6501–dc22   2009020200

ISBN   978-0-521-66006-8 Hardback
ISBN   978-0-521-66972-6 Paperback

CONTENTS

LIST OF FIGURES

PREFACE

The Classic Maya are a fiction from which deeper realities emerge. In all probability, indigenous groups of the Yucatan Peninsula and adjacent zones never perceived themselves as a single "people" during the first millennium. Yet, they can be treated as such for a very simple reason: the Classic Maya lived in ways more alike than unlike. Most spoke related languages, including a prestigious form, now extinct, termed "Classic Ch'olti'an." Some of their thoughts found expression in an elaborate hieroglyphic script, easily the most complex developed in the New World. This script recorded ideas and practices found consistently across the Maya region. Codified symbols, including images freighted with meaning and narrative, reflected much of the same, with conventions and concepts that could be understood from the Isthmus of Tehuantepec to the valleys of western Honduras. Regardless of area, the Classic Maya lived in civic communities of semidivine kings, nobles, farmers, and craftspeople, in daily converse with spirits of sundry origin, location, and influence. Their settlements had similar layouts, their crafts and agriculture related technologies. Scholars can be forgiven, then, for treating the Classic Maya as a single phenomenon, albeit one of a diverse and complex nature.

In part, this book is a new story of the Classic Maya. Over the last two decades, with more generous funding and greater numbers of Mayanists, evidence of who the Classic Maya were and what they did has increased. Large sums of money and other resources – although never enough – have been invested into archaeological digs, but not all of the results have been fully published, nor are there signs of their being published in a timely fashion. The decipherment of glyphic texts and more refined studies of iconography disclose new views on the Maya. Other disciplines, from soil science to biological anthropology, reveal tandem information. The Mayanist can now poach valuable and stimulating ideas from gender or cultural studies, geography, political science, psychology, linguistics, art history, and comparative anthropology. The belief that studies of the Classic Maya should be reduced to any one interpretive approach, be it "processual," "ecological," or "humanistic" archaeology, restricts rather than enhances understanding. This book attests to the futility of maintaining rigid disciplinary boundaries or defending the sanctity of "–isms." The Classic Maya will remain elusive without an eclectic and flexible approach from which scholars can paint a portrait in color rather than monochrome.

A work of synthesis cannot, without becoming a tedious encyclopedia, cover all advances or touch on every theme and archaeological site. Nor can it be a chronicle of historical developments, an approach essayed successfully by others (Martin and Grube 2008). But it can and must chart the most important topics, in fair evaluation of the current state of Classic Maya studies. Progress in research has seldom been uniform. Most archaeological projects take place primarily in the lowland areas, from which the richest epigraphic and iconographic data emerge. As a result, our discussions deal mainly with the lowland Maya at the expense of their highland neighbors and target the southern lowlands more than the northern reaches of the Yucatan Peninsula. This is a weakness we attempt to remedy in part, but the uneven emphasis is unavoidable given the range and availability of present knowledge and authorial expertise.

Synthesis walks in steady pace with analysis. The first combines and balances information, the other dissects and scrutinizes it. A useful line of study is to consider opposed themes, since the conflict and friction between these polarities produce insights into the Classic Maya. This book highlights two such themes. The first is the divide between inside and outside perspectives, what the Classic Maya said about their world and what we, from a vastly different vantage, perceive in their actions and artifacts. The second concerns two overlapping domains of the Classic Maya. One domain involves royal courts as forces for cultural conservatism and innovation. In some respects, the courts and the apparatus of ancestor veneration and god cults housed in temples *were* the Classic Maya city. As collections of palaces, pyramids, plazas, reservoirs, and courtyard residences, the cities served as centers of pilgrimage, worship, and defense; places of patronage for difficult skills; nodes of tribute and redistribution; repositories of the dead; schools for the courtly arts – all features that exerted a powerful attraction to settlement, as part of a continuing spectacle that must have entertained and enthralled Maya communities. In ancient perspective, such activities not only meant spiritual fulfillment but led to material and social consequences. On these hinged the successful continuation of society and the smooth cycling of individual lives. The other domain held the farmers, fishers, hunters, gatherers, and traders who made up the mass of society. Their labor materialized food, shelter, and other substances and objects that made possible the activities of royal courts, as well as the maintenance of society as a whole. These individuals did not merely follow cultural schemes devised by the royal court but actively assisted in the creation of Classic Maya society and worldview. Their value systems assimilated and were assimilated by those of royal courts. In other ways they diverged, if in a manner that remains difficult to decode.

The story of the Classic Maya concerns the convergence and interplay of the two domains, one courtly, the other not. Loosely speaking, the former contained "elites," the second "nonelites." We use these terms with reservations. Our disquiet with a simplistic, two-layered model of Maya society is offset by the need to develop a convincing picture of power relations, one that nonetheless recognizes diverse social roles, statuses, and identities that overlapped and crosscut. The same is true for our categorization of "farmers," "craftspeople," and "traders." Evidence tells us that in most cases these people did not form distinct social groups. A craftsperson who produced exquisite art objects could also engage in royal ceremonies and court intrigue. An artisan who fired large storage vessels might just as easily hold a digging stick in his *milpa*. Our understanding of courtiers, farmers, and craftspeople is directed more toward activities, formalized as "practices," that contributed to survival, political achievement, and social fulfillment.

This book came into existence for several reasons. First, we wished to focus on the Classic Maya per se. Many excellent volumes, including those by Coe (1999b) and Sharer and Traxler (2005), give a rich and satisfying account of the Maya as a whole, from archaic lifeways to the agonies of the Guatemalan civil war (other such volumes include Demarest [2004] and McKillop [2006]). But we felt the Classic Maya deserved their own treatment. Why are there no good volumes on the Greeks, from Mycenae to Perikles and from Lord Byron, promulgator of Greek independence, to King Constantine of Greece and the Colonels who overthrew him? Because too much has changed in that small part of the world, and no scholar would willingly write such an expansive work. So too for the Maya. The only other book on the subject, now translated into English, presents the Classic Maya in discrete slices ("art," "Mayan writing") that do not, for us, meaningfully describe the civilization (Arellano et al. 1999).

Second, we wished to write a book around kinds of people and, where possible, about specific people, without, however, getting mired in the controversial minutiae of Classic history. Donadoni's *The Egyptians* (1997) was a direct inspiration, with its delightful and instructive chapters on "The Dead," "Women," and "The Pharaoh." The congruence of this treatment with "agency theory" or "practice theory" is deliberate and even provocative. In the last decade, it has become perilous to avoid citation of Pierre Bourdieu and Anthony Giddens – although their sway is diminishing somewhat – just as an earlier generation found it necessary to reference Maurice Godelier and Louis Althusser. To what extent does this literature recycle theological concerns with free will (Herzfeld 2001: 149)? How is our interest in the changing pattern of Maya kingship specifically elucidated by the feedback loops of practice and agency theory? The search for compromise is laudable. Theories of human behavior that emphasize individual action must find a balance against those stressing social hedges of the same, just as the physical facts of the human body require conditioning and appraisal by the human mind. This dynamism forms part of the human experience, and no amount of abstract modeling will account for all of its capricious motions.

A third reason stemmed from our wish to present this information in an academic manner. For us, "academic" does not equate to snobbish or showy erudition. Rather, the text is designed for undergraduates, professional colleagues, and other readers who wish to engage the nuances of difficult material, openly acknowledged to be demanding and subject to shifts of interpretation. In our judgment, the undoubted popularity of Maya studies is its own blessing and curse. Mayanists benefit from popular attention that garners jobs, TV spots, and fame, leading even to the recent and, by some lights, lamentable movie *Apocalypto*. That same public distinction can be the scourge of our field. There is an inevitable risk (and temptation) to distort, oversimplify, and sensationalize in a subtle form of marketing that curries yet more attention. At the writing of this book, we are in another such cycle, this one relating to apocalyptic prophecy and the year 2012.

A final motivation for the volume is to allow readers to eavesdrop on a conversation that is only partly resolved. *The Classic Maya* records a dialogue between two very different people who, somehow, have made their way to the Classic Maya. One comes out of art history, epigraphy, and the archaeology of meaning (Houston), the other from settlement analyses, household archaeology, and the study of power relations (Inomata). Both are interested in social science and in deeper stories about people reacting creatively to a stressed but malleable environment. Thus, the book can be said to represent a fusion of two perspectives joined into a whole that is designed not to be seamless but to be sensitive to the contradictions of the Classic Maya. Again, our particular expertise, the southern Maya lowlands, colors the presentation, in part because, with some exceptions, textual data from the northern Yucatan are relatively scarce and problematic.

The narrative we devise also relates to the present, and to the connection between the past and the modern world. In this volume, the explicit focus on people comes from our self-reflection as practitioners of Maya archaeology – a field that, at some points in the past, devoted far more attention to objects than to the individuals and groups who created them. This ought to change. The Classic Maya left cultural and biological heirs who have suffered much over the past few centuries. Writing an account that focuses on people reminds us of the respect due to their descendants. However, this does not imply a blurring of Classic and modern Maya. Classic Maya do not walk on the streets of Santiago Atitlán, in Guatemala, or through the markets of Mérida, Yucatan. They deserve to be seen in context, as beings of their time and place; evidence from them and about them everywhere and always trumps information from later Maya.

To put this another way, the difference between a sacred king of the Classic Maya and a Yucatec *hmen* is surely greater than their similarity. A delicate and challenging antinomy for the students of the Maya is the strain between the ancient legacy of the modern Maya and the plain fact that they, like any other ethnic group, have recreated and modified their culture and society in response to changing natural and human environments. Nor should compassion and respect for the Maya lead to a utopian view of their society. The Classic Maya had their share of social problems and contradictions. For all our admiration of Classic Maya culture, we, as scientists and humanists, necessarily confront the negative aspects of their world. The purpose of this book is not to provide a final word on the Classic Maya and their culture. That will never be possible, nor can all mysteries be clarified from current data. We need many other perspectives, including those prompted by reactions to *The Classic Maya*.

Readers will want a roadmap through this book. The first section, "Setting," begins with Chapter 1, which introduces the Classic Maya and their academic study. Chapter 2 sketches a view of social convergences and dissonances among the Maya; Chapter 3 examines the beginnings of the Classic Maya in the Preclassic, when many themes of the Classic period first appear, if obscurely. Chapter 4 presents the arc of Classic Maya development within its environmental setting, as currently understood and as those milieux changed through time. The second section, "Social Actors," opens with Chapter 5, which turns to the royal courts that served as stages of their interaction, along with their denizens and other features of court-centered settlements. Chapter 6 focuses on the nobles that undergirded and populated the court, and Chapter 7 considers "beings" that the Maya saw as important members of their civic community – deities, supernaturals, and ancestors. Chapter 8 explores the farmers on whom all others depended, and Chapter 9 presents the craftsmen and women who shaped objects of value and utility, trading them on far-flung networks. These people are the most shadowy but crucial to understanding the majority of Classic Maya. The final chapter examines the ruptures within Classic Maya society and, especially, the tumult of the Maya collapse, which sent the Classic Maya into oblivion. Houston was principally responsible for Chapters 2, 5, 6, and 7, along with the Preface, whereas Inomata took the lead for Chapters 3, 4, 8, 9, and 10; they split work on Chapter 1. The spelling of royal names follows Houston's reading of the relevant glyphs, with input from a magisterial book by Martin and Grube (2008); most dates, where exact, derive from historical texts and from the dominant correlation of the Christian and Maya calendar (Lounsbury 1983). The transcription of day, month, and language names tends also to accord with common practice, with the proviso that alternatives exist, some equally valid.

A book comes from the authors' minds and fingers but draws on the hidden encouragement and help of many people. Norman Yoffee commissioned the book for the World Archaeology series and has been most patient with its slow production. His editorial board commented usefully on earlier outlines and drafts, although our idiosyncratic approach may seem out-of-step to some. Kazuo Aoyama, Alfonso Lacadena, Payson Sheets, and David Webster kindly commented on drafts of certain chapters, and Don Rice provided a thoughtful review of our first submitted manuscript. Other input came from Traci Ardren, David Stuart, and Karl Taube; Wyllys Andrews, Kazuo Aoyama, Tim Beach, Michael Coe, Bruce Dahlin, Francisco Estrada-Belli, Barbara Fash, Thomas Garrison, Sue Giles, Charles Golden, Nikolai Grube, Zachary Hruby, Scott Hutson, Sarah Jackson, Justin Kerr, Alfonso Lacadena, Juan Pedro Laporte, Simon Martin, Carlos Pallan, Jorge Pérez de Lara, Werner Rutishauser, Payson Sheets, Joel Skidmore, David Stuart, George Stuart, Karl Taube, Richard Terry, and Mark Zender helped with figures. Bradley Sekedat of Brown University did heroic labors in preparing the manuscript, and at the University of Arizona, Jessica Munson with her superb computer skills improved various illustrations. Our spouses, Nancy Dayton Houston and Daniela Triadan, provided loving homes and partnerships, without which . . . nothing. Financial support for Houston came from the College of Family, Home, and Social Sciences at Brigham Young University, and especially from former dean Clayne Pope and the two chairs of his department, formerly John Hawkins and Joel Janetski, who provided collegial support of the kind available in few other institutions. Dean Pope and Professor. Hawkins were instrumental in awarding Houston a University Professorship named after Jesse Knight, an intrepid miner of Utah's hills and mountains who found gold and gave it to others, especially a struggling university in backwater Provo. More recently, he has benefitted from leaves at Brown University and as the recipient of funds from the Dupee Family Professorship in Social Sciences and fellowships from Dumbarton Oaks, the National Endowment for the Humanities, and the American Philosophical Society, all in the 2007–2008 academic year. At Dumbarton Oaks, Joanne Pillsbury, Emily Gulick, and Bridget Gazzo showed the greatest kindness to Houston, as did the other Pre-Columbian Fellows. For his part, Inomata is grateful for generous leaves from the Department of Anthropology at the University of Arizona during the academic years 2001–2002 and 2006–2007, with thanks particularly to chair John Olsen, the Junior Faculty Professional Development Leave of the College of Social and Behavioral Sciences, and the National Endowment for the Humanities.

PART I

SETTING

CHAPTER 1

INTRODUCTION

THE THRILL OF DISCOVERY

An archaeologist trains for years to frame the right questions. But every now and then comes a flash of unexpected discovery. Takeshi Inomata felt this in the rooms of a ruined building at Aguateca, Guatemala. Scraping through muddy soil, he found a scatter of objects, including pottery, figurines, shells, stone tools, and pieces of jade. Many were of exquisite design and manufacture. Inomata soon discovered that, at Aguateca, after an attack by unknown people some twelve-hundred years ago, nobles or members of the royal family left their treasure, having fled invading enemies or been captured by attackers. At that instant Inomata knew his life would change. His team had uncovered a Pompeii of the Classic Maya, with a privileged glimpse into a lost way of life (Inomata 2003). Houston felt that same thrill when seeing, for the first time, a carved panel at Piedras Negras, Guatemala, a text just emerging from its sheltering earth, or while peering into an infrared TV camera at Bonampak, Mexico, its murals obscured by crust, its meaning laid bare by new technology (Houston et al. 2000; Ware et al. 2002).

The study of the Classic Maya, who flourished in and around the Yucatan Peninsula from about AD 250 to 900, is in a golden age (Figs. 1.1 and 1.2). There are unprecedented numbers of excavations, a flurry of publications facilitated by the web, along with dozens of advanced degrees on Maya subjects or new positions for academics who teach classes on the Maya. A largely deciphered system of writing gives a strong, often surprising voice to the past (Houston 2000). Effective scientific techniques provide new detail on manufacture, agriculture, and imagery (Beach et al. 2006; Dunning et al. 2002). Piqued by popular magazines, TV specials, and Hollywood movies, public interest has reached new heights, as does tourism in sites that are only a few hours away by jet or land vehicle from the United States or metropolitan Mexico, Guatemala, and Honduras (Ardren 2006; Casteñeda 1996; Aimers and Graham 2007). Descendants of Maya who lived at sites like Copan, Palenque,

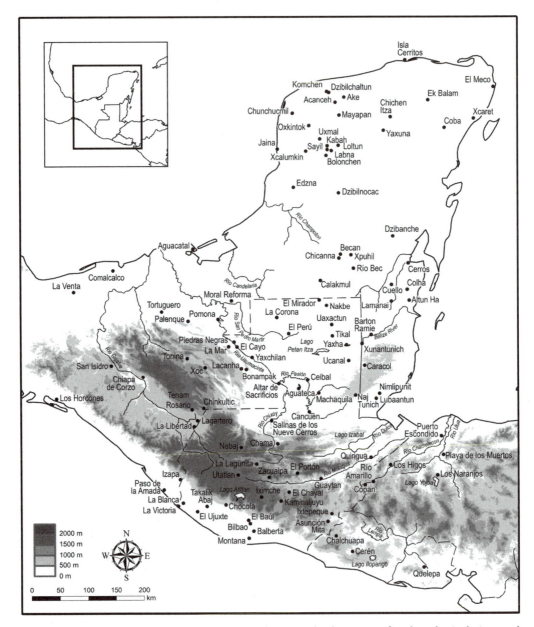

Figure 1.1. Map of Maya region, showing the location of archaeological sites and geographic features.

and Chichen Itza pay attention to the meaning of such cities and, in some circles, wish to have a say in their interpretation and use. This is a rich story of scholarship and reception, with many participants and as many opinions as there are scholars working with Maya materials. In this introductory chapter on finding out who the Classic Maya were, we first present a discussion of the physical Maya setting. We follow this discussion with a history of

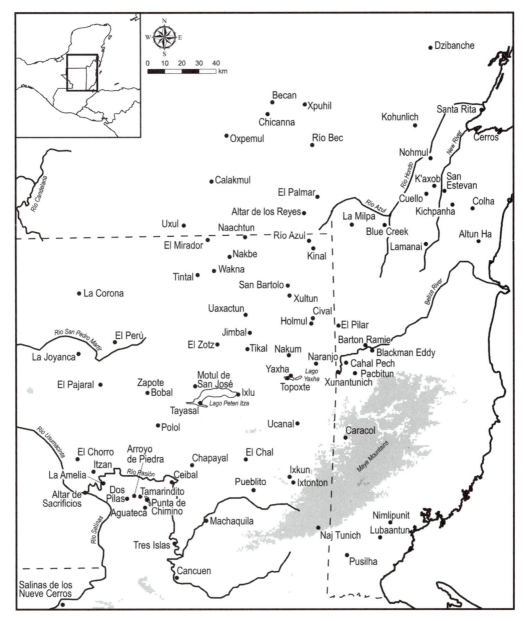

Figure 1.2. Map of the central southern Maya lowlands with the location of archaeological sites.

academic research into the Classic Maya, incorporating views influenced by new information conditioned by larger trends in archaeology and politics. As will be shown, there are many currents that waft through Maya studies. A final section looks at the Maya cultural landscape, which is expressive of indigenous ideas and engineered by royal and nonroyal intention. These set the stage for the drama of Classic Maya life.

THE CLASSIC MAYA AND THEIR WORLD

Who were the Classic Maya? Their ethnic identity is a complex issue with profound historical and anthropological implications. For today's Maya, anthropologists and cultural activists consider language the primary marker of ethnicity (Fischer and Brown 1996). The Maya are, above all, those who speak
Mayan languages. The origin of the term "Maya," however, remains opaque.
The sixteenth-century bishop Diego de Landa (Tozzer 1941: 7) and the
seventeenth-century chronicler Diego López de Cogolludo (1971, I: 65) noted
that certain areas of Yucatan, particularly those around the Postclassic center
of Mayapan, were called "Maya." Yet the notion of the Pan-Maya cultural
identity is a relatively recent historical product shaped by contrasts with groups
of European descent and Ladinos of mixed heritage who exercise economic
and political dominance (Warren 1998). The perception of the "Maya" as a
culturally unified, self-acknowledged population may have been nearly absent
during the Classic period, although a general sense of similarity or relatedness
probably existed in contrast to Central Mexican groups and the residents of
neighboring regions (see Preface).

Excluding the Wastekan branch, a linguistic relative occupying northern
Veracruz, the Maya language family today includes roughly 29 known languages, although the number may change slightly depending on classification (Figs. 1.3 and 1.4). The lowland area, on which this book focuses, was
dominated by the Yukatekan and Ch'olan branches. According to recent epigraphic decipherment, most Classic-period inscriptions were written in Classic
Ch'olti'an, a predecessor of today's Ch'orti (Houston et al. 2000; for another
view, see Wald 2007, which strongly privileges the language of Acalan Chontal of Tabasco, Mexico). In the northern part of the Yucatan Peninsula the
majority of the population most likely spoke an ancestral form of Yukatek,
indicating the coexistence of an elite prestige language and a conversational
language for everyday use. This pattern implies the importance of language
in forming cultural ties that cut across political units, at least for the higher
echelons of the society. Mayan speakers during the colonial period and the
present day have occupied an area encompassing today's Guatemala, Belize, the
western portions of Honduras and El Salvador, as well as the Mexican states
of Chiapas, Tabasco, Campeche, Yucatan, and Quintana Roo.

The Maya area can be roughly divided into the lowlands and highlands, a
geographical division that strongly shaped the courses of historical development (Fig. 1.1). The Maya lowlands consist of thick, horizontal limestone formations. Though flat and uniform on a regional scale, the area often exhibits
topographic and ecological diversity on a smaller level, with well-drained
hills and low-lying wetlands shaped through karstic formations and tectonic
activities. A gigantic meteor hit the peninsula some sixty-five-million years
ago, spewing out ejecta that continue to affect water in the Maya world and

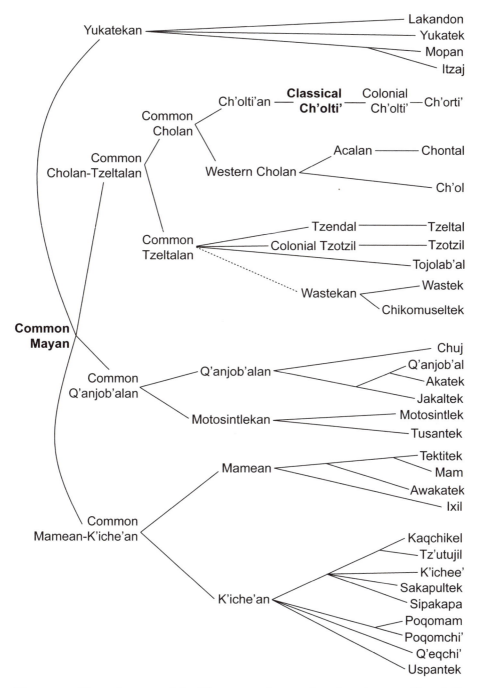

Figure 1.3. Mayan languages (after Houston et al. 2000, for other views, see Campbell 1984, figs. 1, 2).

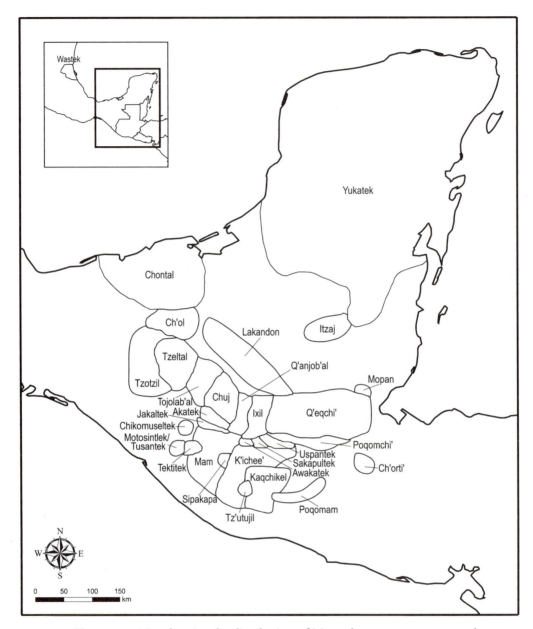

Figure 1.4. Map showing the distribution of Mayan language groups around 1950.

resulting in a crater, the Chicxulub, that influenced the distribution of *cenotes* and water flow to the north. The Maya Mountains in eastern Peten and southern Belize add to the heterogeneity with their rugged topography and igneous rock formations. Rainfall is highest in the southern lowlands, with the annual precipitation ranging from two thousand to four thousand millimeters. It decreases to five hundred millimeters towards the northwestern corner of the Yucatan Peninsula. A large part of the rain concentrates during the rainy season from May to December, with brief dry spells therein that affected

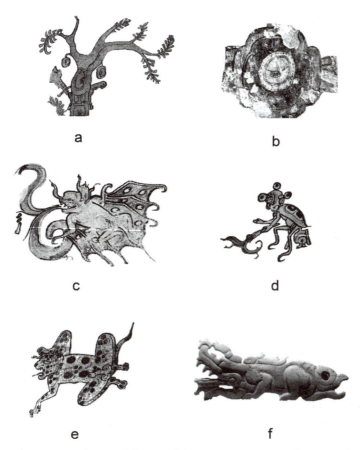

Figure 1.5. Flora and fauna of the Maya region, a selection, all Late Classic period: **a)** mythic tree (K1226, copyright Justin Kerr); **b)** flower (House E, Palenque; photograph by Stephen Houston); **c)** bat (K1080); **d)** firefly (K521); **e)** jaguar (K771); **f)** crocodile (K8750) (copyright Justin Kerr).

human activity. Because of the erosion and dissolution of limestone bedrock, much of the rainfall is quickly lost underground, into the byzantine maze of caves dissolved out of limestone. Surface bodies of water are scarce, particularly in the northern part of the peninsula. Securing water during the dry season was an important concern for the Maya of many areas and led to a technology of water capture from wells to reservoirs of varying size.

Vegetation changes according to the precipitation, from the high tropical jungle in the south to low, thorny shrub forests in the north. The flora and fauna of the lowlands are characterized by the great diversity of species – from jaguar (*Panthera onca*) to tapir (*Tapirus bairdii*) and a variety of fearsome serpents, to still undocumented riches in the arthropod phylum, and, along the coast, fishes that include the *xook*, "shark": many are attested in Classic iconography, and it is possible that English words like "shark" or "cockroach" were of Maya origin (Fig. 1.5; see Jones 1985, also Anderson and Tzuc 2005; Nations 2006; and Schlesinger 2002). Diverse ecological niches, such as high forests in uplands and low vegetation of palms and sedges in seasonal wetlands (*bajos*), may coexist in relatively small areas (Rice 1993). The Maya often used dark, fertile soils of uplands (Rendzina or Rendzina-like soils) for agriculture, sometimes building terraces to reduce soil erosion and to create planting surfaces, a trend that clearly accelerated during the Classic period. Vertisol soils commonly found in *bajo* wetlands shrink and harden drastically during the dry season, but productive wetland agriculture was possible in some areas with adequate drainage systems (Dunning 1996). In contrast to the remarkable biodiversity, the lowlands offered little in terms of mineral resources other than clay for ceramics and limestone as construction material and raw material for lime plaster. A notable exception is the chert found in limestone formations that was used for cutting tools. Concentrations of slate were sometimes employed by Classic Maya for sculptures or tools (Healey et al. 1995), and quartz pebbles and other objects could be collected for ritual purposes, particularly in the enigmatic, copious deposits in caves of Classic Maya date (Brady et al. 2005; Brady and Rissolo 2006). The very notion of a "resource" – from essential, nutritional ones like salt from brine-boiling along the coast or near salt domes inland to hacked-off cave stone for ritual purposes – requires a Maya mind-set that scholars still endeavor to understand (Andrews 1983; McKillop 2002).

The highlands are marked by rugged mountain ranges and deep valleys shaped by rapid-flowing rivers, tectonics, and active volcanoes. Rainfall varies from below one thousand millimeters in the Motagua Valley and the central Chiapas depression to three thousand millimeters in the northern highlands. To a pronounced degree, vegetation varies according to precipitation and altitude, including broadleaf evergreen forests, broadleaf deciduous forests, and coniferous forests (Wagner 1964). The cloud forest of the northern highlands was home to quetzal birds (*Pharomachrus mocinno*), whose bright green feathers were highly valued. The highlands were rich in mineral resources, providing basalt and other igneous rocks for grinding stones and axes, as well as obsidian for cutting tools. Pyrite used for polished mirrors may have been obtained in the Huehuetenango region, and the Middle Motagua Valley is the only confirmed jade source in Mesoamerica (Seitz et al. 2001). Soil types vary widely depending on age, local climate, vegetation, and topography, but volcanic soils of the highlands are in general highly fertile. In highlands and lowlands alike, it is important to remember that patterns in vegetation and climate have shifted over time (see Chapter 3) as a result of rises in sea level, oscillations in rainfall, and human activity – the Maya world was dynamic in its natural and human processes, and the two were intertwined for many millennia (Beach et al. 2008; McKillop 2005).

STUDYING THE CLASSIC MAYA

"Discovery" varies according to point of view. For every archaeologist who claims the first glimpse of this or that site (Bourne 2001), there is a Maya or humble logger or *chiclero* (a tapper of chewing gum sap, from *chicozapote* trees deep in the jungle) who knew of it long before. Recent studies illustrate how at certain sites in the southern lowlands, Maya often visited ruins to supplicate gods and leave objects of reverence (Palka 2005: 258–60). Others were never "lost," especially in northern Yucatan, where some of the first archaeological maps appear in colonial documents (Tozzer 1941: 178). But the eighteenth century is really when Classic Maya cities, especially Palenque and Chiapas, attracted expeditions that influenced scholars and public alike. These expeditions, motivated by the need of the Bourbon monarchs in Spain to understand the farthest reaches of their colonies, did not in fact have an immediate impact, although, ironically, their projects proved destabilizing to the empire they sought to preserve (Dym 2006: 36–42).

The impact of the first expeditions was rather felt through delayed publications, appearing in steady flow from the early nineteenth century on, stirring interest but not, because of indifferent quality, answering many questions (G. Stuart 1992: 4–13). By chance, this was precisely when the Maya lands began to open up to foreign visitors. Spanish control, long allergic to travelers from other lands, gave way to national governments in Mexico and Guatemala that allowed perceptive explorers, most notably John Lloyd Stephens (1805–1852) and his artist Frederick Catherwood (1799–1854), to acquaint the world with Classic-period cities like Copan, Palenque, and others still in Yucatan (Fig. 1.6; Stephens 1841, 1843). Equipped with *camera lucida* (an optical device that facilitates copying), a skilled hand, and a will to master unfamiliar shapes, Catherwood recorded and communicated as never before the aesthetic riches of Classic civilization, although his and Stephens' grasp of the chronology of such pieces remained vague. It was nonetheless Stephens who appended a description of the Maya calendar, by Juan Pío Pérez (1798–1859), and thereby offered an indigenous view of time (G. Stuart 1992: 17; see Section titled "Time").

Soon, and certainly by the decades just prior to the American Civil War, educated readers knew that the Yucatan Peninsula and environs held ruins with palaces, pyramids, and inscriptions. By growing consensus, these remains came from Maya hands, the ancestors of indigenous peoples in and around the peninsula (Houston et al. 2001: 21–3). It took a few more years, however, to see the broader links between Mayan languages and to treat its speakers as historically related peoples, albeit with varying connections to this site or that inscription (Houston et al. 2001: 80–1).

By the late-nineteenth century, individual researchers, often of independent means – Alfred Maudslay (1850–1931), a determined and thorough documenter of sites like Quirigua, Copan, and Tikal, is the exemplary figure (I. Graham 2002) – collected valuable information, to be complemented in the final years of the century by institutions like the Peabody Museum at Harvard. The innovation was not the use of intrepid explorers, as that would continue to the present – until a surprisingly late date, into the 1950s, Maya archaeology had the air of "gentlemen's avocation" (M. Coe 1990). Instead, what changed was the presence of systematic institutional support, including academic and museum positions, providing both the means to undertake work on Classic Maya sites and to hold such people accountable through measures of productivity, from in-house reports to monographs and popular essays. The culmination of this trend, still pursued by the French government through research centers like the *Centre d'Etudes Mexicaines et Centre-Américaines*, was the creation of a research division of the Carnegie Institution of Washington, conceived by Sylvanus Morley (1883–1948), an important student of Maya glyphs, and steered for decades by the doyen of American archaeology Alfred V. Kidder (1885–1963; Givens 1992). Over time, a site-based focus on early (Uaxactun) and late (Chichen Itza) centers shifted to a long-term organization of full-time specialists, such as Ledyard Smith in architecture, Eric Thompson in Maya writing, Edwin Shook in mapping, Tatiana Proskouriakoff in imagery, and a focus on standardized recording (Black 1990; Weeks 2006). This, with work by the University of Pennsylvania at Piedras Negras, and ongoing academic research by Harvard and a few other universities and institutions, such as the Middle American Research Institute at Tulane University, brought coherent form to Classic Maya archaeology (Leifer et al. 2002).

The aging and passing of the original team, along with a shift of priorities at the Carnegie, led to the closing of Mayanist research (Shook 1998). Its synthetic project of winnowing all such research into a comprehensible whole transferred to Tulane, which brought to completion a multivolume *Handbook of Middle American Indians*, even grander than the integrated encyclopedia contemplated by Kidder (Wauchope 1965–1976). There was some attempt to carry on the Carnegie program at research institutes like the New World Archaeological Foundation, now housed at Brigham Young University, but with a focus on phases prior to the Classic period (Ferguson 1956). At this time, Guatemala and Mexico in particular began to sponsor research by first-rate Mayanists, such as Alberto Ruz (1973), excavator of Palenque, and Román Piña Chan, through the creation of two official agencies, the Instituto de Antropología e Historia (IDAEH) in Guatemala and the Instituto Nacional de Antropología e Historia (INAH) in Mexico, with the latter undertaking ambitious full-scale field projects because of greater resources. Research by foreigners has been authorized and controlled by these agencies, with a pattern of ebb and flow according to local attitudes towards nonlocal archaeologists and the countries they come from. By the 1970s, Honduras, Belize, and El Salvador had created similar agencies, in many respects heavily influenced by, or reactive to, Mexican models. Belize and Honduras have increasingly sponsored research at sites of touristic potential, principally at Copan and the surrounding region in the case of Honduras. Likewise Guatemala has sponsored such research at Tikal and in a triangular region of the department of Peten between the large cities of Nakum, Naranjo, and Yaxha (e.g., Castillo 1999).

J. L. Stephens

A. P. Maudslay

J. E. S. Thompson

T. Proskouriakoff

A. Ruz Lhuillier

J. P. Laporte

Figure 1.6. Explorers and archaeologists: John Lloyd Stephens (G. Stuart 1992, fig. 1.11a); Alfred Maudslay (1889–1902, I: pl. 27); J. E. S. Thompson (photograph by Otis Imboden, courtesy George Stuart); Tatiana Proskouriakoff (M. Coe 1992, pl. 29); Alberto Ruz Lhuillier (photograph by Otis Imboden, courtesy George Stuart); Juan Pedro Laporte (photograph by Alfonso Lacadena).

Higher-level education in archaeology has developed gradually, first in Mexico, then Guatemala, Belize, and Honduras, producing hundreds of classicists, with distinguished figures like Juan Pedro Laporte (Laporte and Fialko 1995), Juan Antonio Valdés (1995), Oswaldo Chinchilla (2005), Héctor Escobedo (2004) and Erick Ponciano (2002) in Guatemala, Jaime Awe

(Awe et al. 2005) and John Morris (2004) in Belize, Ricardo Agurcia (2004) and Jorge Ramos (2006) in Honduras, and Antonio Benavides (1997) and Rafael Cobos (2003) in Mexico, along with many others. Outside of Spain and France, where governments support excavation, European classicists tend to concentrate on texts and imagery, in part because of the philological tradition from which many come (but see Isendahl 2002; Prem 2003). This has been accompanied by unprecedented access into Maya language, thought, and history through the decipherments of Maya glyphs, which has accelerated from the late 1950s and culminated in intense progress and often heated debate over the past thirty years (M. Coe 1999a; Houston 2000; Wichmann 2004). At least 10,000 Maya texts reveal something of their content to researchers, ranging from virtually complete decipherment to texts, especially on pots, of the utmost opacity. Nonetheless, a few major Maya cities are still "lost" in the sense of appearing in inscriptions but not as yet tied to any particular site (Grube 2004b).

For the last fifty years, Classic Maya archaeology has evolved from a "colonial" practice done by foreigners in lands under the economic influence of American or European powers to a complex activity involving many institutions, individuals, and government entities. Great visibility comes from the popular media, including *National Geographic* magazine and television specials. Many millions of dollars are at stake in Maya tourism, with strong impact on local populations and their malleable identities (Medina 2003). The growth in the number of academic positions contributes to the creation of field schools for undergraduates, especially in countries where regulations do not prohibit such activities by foreigners. Schools help fund excavations that can be difficult to support, provide training to future archaeologists, justify academic leaves for participating faculty, and inject money into local economies. Yet national sensitivities sometimes perceive the schools in a bad light. By definition, archaeology is destructive, and such programs train foreign students at the expense of another country's patrimony. At the least, most projects in Classic Maya sites are now formally binational, with local and foreign codirectors.

It is likely, however, that the number of projects will decline because of steeply increased costs of doing excavations. Others may trend to less expensive survey, artifactual studies, and museum or archival research. Some of the most valuable work on Classic Maya landscapes comes from the relatively low-cost *Atlas Arqueológico* in Guatemala (e.g., www.atlasarqueologico.com), along with remote sensing sponsored by NASA (Saturno et al. 2007). Private funding may or may not counteract this trend, requiring as it does special contacts and fundraising skills that are seldom taught in graduate programs. Nor are local archaeologists the only constituency. Assertive communities near Classic Maya cities, especially in Guatemala but also in parts of Mexico, lay increasing claim to control over, and even revenues from, ruins. Often, the sites are leverage for local improvements by national governments. In conditions of poverty, land is at a premium, including that of archaeological reserves in countries that can ill afford to police them. Classic Maya archaeology may be in a golden age, but, by a pessimistic view, it ventures into a period of radical restructuring, and perhaps severe reduction, at the very time it bursts with promise and intellectual energy.

Classic Maya ruins have also been at high risk over the last three decades. Remoteness and civil unrest kept many sites in comparatively undisturbed condition. Insurgents tended to look dimly on visitors to regions under their control, and, in turn, the military viewed people in the jungle as potential guerillas. Populations now expand vigorously into ruins, burning to prepare land for agriculture and eventual sale to landowners intent on stock raising. Fueled by demand for marketable goods on the art market, looting has lashed much of the Maya region, although with less activity in the last decade (M. Coe 1993; Paredes 1999). Debate also surrounds the widespread practice of consolidating and, in some cases, reconstructing Maya sites for touristic purposes (Quintana 2000). Such practices are dictated by permits and, with care, can be done in a scholarly fashion to the economic benefit of local communities. The dominant aesthetic demands a telegenic ruin, with removal of vegetation and preparation of neat masonry surfaces, usually unplastered. (Gaudy with red paint, few Classic buildings of any scale would have looked like this originally.) Yet maintenance costs are high in the tropics, and there may be limits to how many structures can be exposed to view. The ironies are many – Classic structures are held together by vegetation yet actively undermined by it; freshly consolidated structures are assaulted and disfigured by seasonal rain and fungus. Greater access invites more wear and tear by tourists. There are no easy solutions to the predicament of Classic Maya ruins in the coming century. "Do no harm," as enjoined on all medical doctors, cannot be applied to archaeologists, who, aside from mapping and remote sensing, reshape forever what they hope to study. One of the most effective solutions has been the removal of important sculptures and building façades at Copan to a regional sculpture museum nearby, thereby reconstituting such mosaics in protected settings to powerful effect (B. Fash 2008).

TIME

From the nineteenth century onwards, and in large account because of deepening study by the Carnegie, Harvard, Penn, and Tulane, a distinction became clear between the buildings, ceramics, imagery, and glyphs of sites clustering near the southern part of the Yucatan Peninsula, on the one hand, and those in the northern part of the peninsula, on the other. The first constituted the "First Epoch" or, as it was called a few years later, the "Old Empire," the second the "Second Epoch" or "New Empire" (e.g., Spinden 1913: 155, 198–9). No "political unity" was implied by a term like "empire," only a certain degree of homogeneity and "common culture," which spread from the southern parts of the peninsula to other regions through a process of "Mayanization" that diffused to "culturally provincial" regions the technologies of writing, fine pottery, and the tendency to settle in large sites (Morley 1947: 50, 72; Morley and Brainerd 1956: 41; cf. Thompson 1940: 129, who questioned the supposed geography of these terms).

Throughout ran a sense of evaluation. One scholar, for example, described a subperiod of the "Old Empire" – its final century, in fact – as the "Great Period" because of its "esthetic heights" (Morley 1947: 54). By 1950, the "Old Empire" was the "Classical Period," a time of "relative peace," "hierachic [priestly] cult, in relative uniformity that existed atop 'divergent local cultures'" (Thompson 1971: 6). The description of periods was generally thought most useful if it could express something intrinsic to that period, a practice also applied to the chronology of other parts of the Americas, such as the Andes (Kubler 1991: 34–5). A few years later, the scholarly framework had shifted to a progression from "Preclassic" or "Formative" to "Classic" to "Postclassic," with overt claims that the stages were developmental, the "Classic stage" being, among the Maya and other groups, a time of "excellence in the great arts, climax in religious architecture . . . [and] the beginning of urbanism": "superlative" is the descriptive adjective (Willey and Phillips 1958: 75, 182–3), along with "stability" and "unchanged" Maya culture (Morley and Brainerd 1956: 436). A "criterion of excellence" supposedly characterized the imagery of the time (Proskouriakoff 1950: 8), passing from an austerely "archaic" style to a "classic" and then a "flamboyant" phase (Thompson et al. 1932: 190). The imagery underwent a gradual devolution from a focus on "religious" or "spiritual" themes to a focus on "physical properties," and then to an emphasis on "dynamic composition" before finally exhausting itself at the end of the Classic period in what has been described as "truly a retrogression" (Proskouriakoff 1950: 181). The decline was thought to be moral in origin. As pointed out in one of the earliest studies of Maya imagery, "any long-continued period of communal brilliancy undermines morals and religion and saps the nerves and muscles of the people as a whole" (Spinden 1913: 198).

At the same time, and despite such claims for qualitative change, the Maya were believed to possess fixed attributes: "unusually honest," "little inclination to leadership," "intensely superstitious" or "fundamentally conservative" (Morley and Brainerd 1956: 32–7; Steggerda 1938). In part, these came from particular friendships between certain archaeologists and Maya, where this or that person was seen to exemplify the whole (Thompson 1950: 13; 1963: 118, 127, 218). Some of the findings appeared in a journal with the sinister title of *Eugenical News*, a "Current Record of Human Genetics and Race Hygiene" (Steggerda 1931). As a concept, "national characteristics" are well-established as a means of describing people, even as self-description – "We French are intellectual; we English are industrious" – but with little factual support in actual assessments of personality (Terracciano et al. 2005). Statements of this sort about the Maya would be made with embarrassment today, and were, in fact, questioned in the mid-twentieth century by those who wondered how similar the "builders of Tikal and Copan" could be to "the culture of present-day Lacandon [Maya]" (Proskouriakoff 1950: 1). Most Mayanists retain a term like "Classic" because of long-standing use, not out of any affection for the label. The steady task of Preclassic specialists has been to show that "Classic" features – writing, corbelled vaults, monumental architecture, rulership – appeared long before Classic times (Coe 1965; Hansen 1998); researchers of the Postclassic strongly and correctly deny that theirs is a period of social or cultural decline or decay (A. Chase and P. Rice 1985: 1). But several features are undeniable: the Classic period offers the most legible and copious texts, with consequences for transparency to scholarship, and, in many areas, the highest amount of population.

Archaeological time is analytical time. It exists because it is useful to scholars, who need it to understand their deposits and the artifacts within them. The usual mode is to rely on ceramics, which change more quickly than other artifact classes, and to group these by periods that establish parameters for excavations – a ceramic of a particular type probably dates a deposit, unless it has been mixed with later materials, a matter for stratigraphy to disentangle (e.g., Sabloff 1975). Archaeologists build chronologies of individual sites or regions by dividing them into units of time called "phases" that correspond to sets of ceramics or "complexes." In rough terms, this works well because many ceramics tend to change stylistically over a span of fifty or more years (related possibly to the working life of a potter or to the tastes of patrons and consumers) and, through broad copying, extend across large parts of the Maya region (Fig. 1.7). Yet all specialists acknowledge that the requirement of placing ceramics in classificatory schemes, especially by surface treatment, is not a sensitive means of discerning changes over time. Much research of this sort remains to be done. With meticulous excavation, chronology can be extraordinarily subtle, as in the microphases of architecture discerned within the deep and complex stratigraphy of places like the North Acropolis at Tikal, the burial place of many rulers at the site (W. Coe 1990). But the dating is relative, a sequence in which something can be said to come before this or that, yet not by how long.

Typically, Classic Mayanists do not infer their absolute dates by "absolute" means. Exceptions include radiocarbon dating and obsidian hydration, which examines the gradual absorption of water to suggest when shaping might have taken place (a thick "rind" expresses great age, a thin one far less time; Freter 1993; Ralph 1965). For the Preclassic period, radiocarbon dating remains the primary basis of chronological studies, along with ceramic cross-dating across different regions. Researchers can calibrate carbon dates to approximate calendrical measures (in this book all dates are calibrated or calendrical), but their effectiveness is hampered by the flattening of the calibration curve between

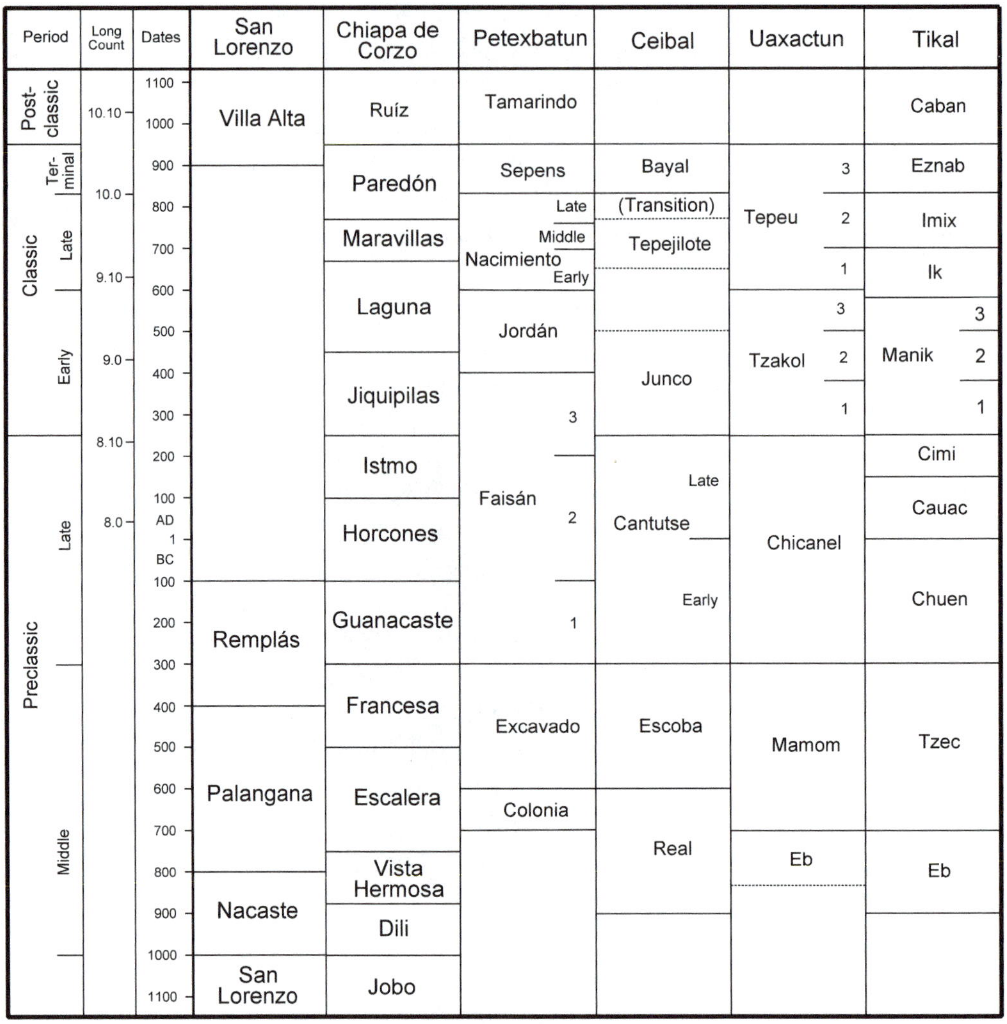

Period	Long Count	Dates	San Lorenzo	Chiapa de Corzo	Petexbatun	Ceibal	Uaxactun	Tikal
Post-classic	10.10	1100 / 1000	Villa Alta	Ruíz	Tamarindo			Caban
Classic — Terminal	10.0	900		Paredón	Sepens	Bayal	3	Eznab
Classic — Late		800			Late	(Transition)	Tepeu 2	Imix
	9.10	700		Maravillas	Middle — Nacimiento	Tepejilote		Ik
		600		Laguna	Early		1	
Classic — Early	9.0	500			Jordán		Tzakol 3	Manik 3
		400		Jiquipilas		Junco	Tzakol 2	Manik 2
	8.10	300			3		Tzakol 1	Manik 1
Preclassic — Late		200		Istmo		Late		Cimi
	8.0	100 AD		Faisán		Cantutse	Chicanel	Cauac
		1 BC		Horcones	2			
		100				Early		Chuen
		200	Remplás	Guanacaste	1			
		300						
Preclassic — Middle		400		Francesa	Excavado	Escoba	Mamom	Tzec
		500						
		600	Palangana	Escalera	Colonia			
		700				Real		
		800		Vista Hermosa			Eb	Eb
		900	Nacaste	Dili				
		1000						
		1100	San Lorenzo	Jobo				

Figure 1.7. Chronological chart of ceramic phases in the Maya lowlands and adjacent areas.

800 and 400 BC, a time-period crucial in terms of Preclassic social change. Readers should know that Preclassic dates may contain substantial error or leeway. For later periods, specialists largely rely on a Maya framework of dates, precise to the day, and link such dates to particular deposits (Fig. 1.8). Not a few inscriptions relate directly to the dedications of stelae, buildings, pyramids, and other features (D. Stuart 1998: 387–93). There are variants of Maya "absolute" determinations, some so stripped down as to puzzle researchers, with only the basic 260-day calendar and another that interlocks with it in 365-day orderings. Together, these create a fifty-two-year cycle. The 260-day period resembles to a striking degree the approximate span of human gestation

Dates	Dzibilchaltun	Belize Valley	Cuello	Kaminaljuyu	Copan	Chalchuapa
1100	Zipche	New Town	Tecep	Ayampuc	Ejar	Matzin
1000						
900	Copo	Spanish Lookout		Pamplona	Coner	Payu
800			Santana			
700		Tiger Run		Amatle		
600						Xocco
500	Piim	Hermitage	Nuevo		Acbi	
400				Esperanza		
300				Aurora	Bijac	Vec
200	Xculul	Floral Park	Cocos	Santa Clara		Late Caynac
100 AD						
1 BC		Mount Hope		Arenal		
100					Chabij	Early
200	Komchen	Barton Creek		Verbena		
300						Chul
400	Late Nabanche	Late Jenny Creek	Lopez	Providencia	Seibito	
500						
600	Early		Bladen		Bosque	Kal
700		Early		Majadas		
800	Ek	Cunil	Swasey	Las Charcas	Uir	Colos
900						
1000						
1100				Arévalo	Gordon	Tok

Figure 1.7 (*continued*)

Figure 1.8. A Maya date in the fifty-two-year calendar, Tonina stucco jamb, Acropolis, AD 708 (photograph by Michael Coe).

and was, in rare cases, used by the Classic Maya to name people, as at Palenque and a few others sites (Earle and Snow 1985). These names probably refer to a person's date of birth within the calendar, in a pattern that recalls an early colonial practice among the Maya (Campbell 1988: 373–86). But the 260-day placements of certain events can be hard to fix in broader time. Presumably, as with many texts, the scribes assumed background information unavailable to present-day readers. Other dates are regional variants, including a Yukatek version that situates time within cycles of twenty years, but with sufficient precision to pinpoint placement. A few Maya sites emphasize the count of twenty-year periods, in anticipation of much later, colonial-era documents that do the same (Bricker and Miram 2002). Pomona, Tabasco, is one such location. It has fragmentary panels that stress long tabulations of twenty-year spans, if always in reference to dynastic officiants (García Moll 2005, lám. 6–4, 6–8, 6–8).

A more ostentatious count specifies the time elapsed from the beginning of a great Maya cycle, comprising thirteen units of *pih* or *pik*, a period of 144,000 days (D. Stuart 2005: 137; Thompson 1950: 147). This is the so-called "Long Count," meaning that it counts an impressive amount of time by use of enumerated quantities of years, months, and days, along with, in rare cases, far higher cycles reaching thousands, even millions of years (Fig. 1.9). A text at Coba is a notorious show-off in this respect, more display than intelligible record of time (I. Graham and von Euw 1997: 22). At the beginning of this period, on August 13, 3114 BC – or so a few texts tell us – new hearths were replaced under godly supervision, although much about these texts continues to perplex experts (Freidel et al. 1993: 61–75).

What is crucial is that the Long Counts represent theological statements about events in the deep past, whereas the Yukatek variant concerns an arithmetical structure of time. The closing of the Long Count, for another act of presumable renewal, takes place in AD 2012. The presence of these dates helps define the Classic period, a time when inscriptions bore such records. Along with these accounts are close or predicted observations of celestial events that involve a surprising number of heavenly bodies, including distant planets barely visible to the naked eye (Justeson 1989: 76–129; Lounsbury 1978). Not a few buildings relate to the calendar or to diurnal movements of the sun. Twin-pyramid complexes at Tikal and a few other sites appear to have been erected at twenty-year intervals, one to the east, another to the west, with plain stelae in front of the eastern pyramid (C. Jones 1969). Similarly, the "E-group" complexes, which go back to the Preclassic period, are oriented to the rise and fall of the sun; the building to the west has four stairways, and a long platform lies to the east, oriented in north-south manner (Aimers and Rice 2006). Other proposed alignments of buildings and celestial features are more speculative (cf. Aveni and Hortung 1986, 1989).

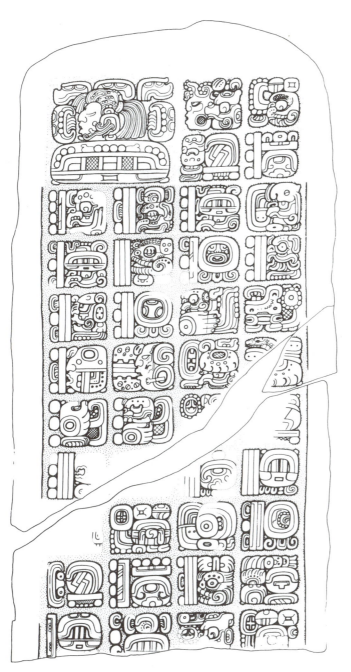

Figure 1.9. A Maya Long-Count date, Dos Pilas Stela 8, AD 727 (drawing by Ian Graham, courtesy of the President and Fellows of Harvard College).

Such features extol abstract, intellectualized time, meshed within intricate cycles that spin in endless progression. They do not concern the "lived" or experienced time that intruded daily into Classic lives (see Golden 2002: 14–103, for discussion; also P. Rice 2004: 56–76). The Classic Maya perceived rulers themselves as embodied time, and their underlings as symbolic bearers of the first days of the year (Fig. 1.10; Houston et al. 2006: 81–9; Schele and Miller 1986, fig. III-12). Other Classic Maya, less concerned with arcane calendars or grandiose self-conception, would also see the passage of the day, the variable coming of the moon, a seasonal calendar of rains and solar heat, wet counterpoised to dry, and hurricanes (Dunning and Houston 2009). Subtle signals, noticeable to most agriculturalists, would tell them when to plant, when to harvest, and when to leave fallow depending on the agronomic technology in use (Chapter 8). And, finally, there were the human cycles of birth, life, death, and that-which-came-after, seen tangibly in the residue of human bone in formal and casual deposits at Classic Maya sites (Chapter 7).

A CULTURAL LANDSCAPE

The landscape of the Maya people was shaped by local experiences of physical space and an imagined world order of distant or mythical places. This universe can be viewed as a layered, concentric space, consisting of the center, the sphere of daily activities, and distant locales, as well as the heaven and underworld. Stone and earth lay below, pierced by caves. The sky arched above, as shown in Classic imagery by a segmented band with signs for celestial elements, ending in the heads of a raptor. The Maya often represented the center with images of the Maize God and *ceiba* trees serving as the *axis mundi*, or "world axis" (Freidel et al. 1993: 39; Taube 1985). This view, however, does not necessarily mean the presence at any one place of the absolute center of the world. In the fragmented political landscape of the Classic Maya, the civic core of each polity and the body of the ruler were probably perceived as pivotal points of the universe, at least in the view of the elite. For the rest of the population, the cores of smaller villages or individual dwellings may have been the centers of their perceived universe. A singular property of Maya beliefs, from early to latest times, was the ability to create microcosms, a small-scale object, even a plate or dish, coming to serve as a token of a vast totality (Houston 1998).

The inner and outer spheres of this concentric order should not be conceived simply in terms of Euclidean three-dimensional space. Images of the broader universe were implicated in the construction of settlements, and the experiences of lived spaces were projected outward to the cosmos. Moreover, such perceptions of spaces were inseparably tied to concepts of time and patterns of cyclic movement (Coe 1965; Berlin and Kelley 1961). The sky and the broad universe were understood in relation to the distant past, including the beginning of the current era, when a "new" or "first hearth-place" was modified in some as-yet-unknown way (Freidel et al. 1993: 59–122), as well as to the daily and seasonal cyclicality dictated by the movements of celestial bodies. The meanings of the landscape were created by association with the

Figure 1.10. Ruler as embodied time, Yuknoom Ch'e'n of Calakmul (after vessel EbI1413 in Museum zu Allerheiligen in Schaffhausen, Switzerland [Prager 2004, fig. 2]).

memories and narratives of distant and immediate ancestors, historical events, and individual experiences.

Besides these rather abstract constructs, it is unclear how the Maya perceived the spatial organization of the Maya area as a whole (cf. J. Marcus 1976). A monument from Altar de los Reyes, Campeche, takes the form of a circular altar – for ancient Maya, the shape of the earth – ringed by the titles of many rulers (Grube 2003, fig. 2; see Chapter 5). The altar itself appears to be labeled as a supernatural "throne" or *tz'am*, perhaps for the local lord, and may tabulate a list of kings that defined the political landscape of the time, as seen from Altar de los Reyes. Royalty and other elites often visited other Maya centers in diplomatic trips, as princesses sent for marriage at foreign courts, and during war campaigns. Clearly, rulers maintained good knowledge of various regions. Recent results of bone chemistry analysis further underscore the considerable mobility of the elite (Buikstra et al. 2004). The Naj Tunich cave in the Classic period and Chichen Itza in Postclassic times attracted pilgrims across political boundaries (Stone 1995). Such mobility was complemented by strong attachment to native places, as reflected in the persistence of many dynasties after defeat. In most cases, ties between people and their homelands prevented victors from usurping the territories of enemies.

Beyond the Maya area, there is evidence of direct contacts with Teotihuacan and other distant cities (see Chapter 5). Such long-distance interactions, however, were most likely limited to a relatively small number of elites. For the majority of Maya these places in the west were more mythic and imagined than not. Claims of connections to the west often served to provide sources of the royal authority (see Helms 1998). The Classic Maya cherished Olmec heirloom objects long after the collapse of the southern Gulf Coast centers (M. Coe 1966), and the rulers continued to use the images of Teotihuacan symbols as representations of royal power after the demise of this Central Mexican metropolis (Stone 1989). Similarly, some elites in Yucatan and the Maya highlands during the Postclassic period claimed descent from ancestors in the west.

At a local level, Restall (2001: 336) demonstrates that the colonial-period Maya in Yucatan conceived their political and social world in concentric form. The center was the patio of the community marked by a *ceiba* tree, which was then encircled by the settlement of the *cah* (municipal community), the territory of the *cah*, and the larger polity, which was a loose political organization of communities subordinate to the center. The outermost layer corresponded to the entire Yucatan peninsula, involving many competing polities. This pattern most likely had its antecedents during the Classic period or even earlier, although the distinction between settlement and surrounding areas was probably less clear before the Spanish forced rural populations to settle in towns (the so-called *congregación* policy). Causeways, or *sakbih*, radiating out from Caracol, Coba, Chichen Itza, and other centers indicate patterns of communication and symbolic connections between core and periphery. An even earlier version of this pattern can be seen in causeways extending from the Preclassic center of El Mirador across wetlands (I. Graham 1967: 40–2; Hansen 1998). Defensive walls are not common at Classic Maya centers, but when present, as in the case of Becan and Chunchucmil, they surround the symbolic core of each community. The rare system of concentric walls at Aguateca appears to contain and define settlement (Fig. 1.11).

A concentric order appears to correlate with the decreasing reach of royal power and increasing distance from the center. One aspect of this pattern is a distinction between the domesticated and the wild. Taube (2003) argues that the civilized world of settlements contrasted with the dangerous forest inhabited by fearsome animals, such as snakes and jaguars. This duality, however, can not be confused with the stark opposition between good and evil in the Judeo-Christian tradition. Many Maya deities combined destructive and productive forces, and, in like manner, the forest was both dangerous and beneficial. It emanated supernatural power, as seen in the prevalence of jaguars

Figure 1.11. Concentric walls at Aguateca, Guatemala.

and snakes in royal symbolism, and provided animals for hunting and plants for gathering (Taube 2003). Moreover, a significant part of forests were probably half-domesticated, in that the Maya tended them to encourage the growth of useful species. Such forests may even have provided refuges where commoners escaped elite coercion, a migration amply attested in colonial times. Although the Maya of the colonial period and the present day typically perceived their communities as bounded space (J. Marcus 1983a; Wisdom 1940: 421–2), it is unclear whether the Classic Maya had comparable ideas. Subtle markers, such as heaps of stone, have yet to be detected at Maya sites. There are, however, walls across valleys in northwestern Peten, Guatemala (Andrew Scherer, personal communication, 2008), and bounded areas of smaller size, known as *solares*, occur throughout the northern part of the peninsula (Barba and Manzanilla 1987; Hutson et al. 2006; Martos López 2002).

Concentric spaces were further ordered by directional concepts that accorded with the passage of the sun and sectors at right angles to it (Vogt 1976: 58). At La Milpa, Belize, researchers detected minor ceremonial complexes at 3.5 km from the civic core, all neatly disposed in cardinal directions (Tourtellot et al. 2002). In the civic layouts of Maya cities, however, directional patterns are not as evident as in the case of earlier La Venta or contemporary Teotihuacan (see Ashmore and Sabloff 2002; M. Smith 2003). The significance of rough orientation to the cardinals is more noticeable in the placement of temples and other buildings (Becker 1971). Various layers of concentric organization may also have broken into smaller spatial units. The Maya area comprised competing polities, and individual kingdoms probably nested within larger sectors called *tzuk* (see Chapter 5; Beliaev 2000; Schele and Mathews 1998: 23).

Another spatial scheme was the mosaic created by natural topography. The karstic landscape of the lowlands consisted of hills and wetlands in small areas, knowledge of which was critically important to Maya farmers (Fedick 1996), shaping their mythical imagination as well. Hills (*witz*) provided well-drained terrain for human occupation, cooled by delicious breezes, and their interiors were considered sources of water, in part because springs often appear near their edges (Stuart 1997a). As the homes of rain deities, caves (*ch'e'n*) in the hills gave access to water – in certain atmospheric conditions, small clouds of mist, tokens of the rain spirit, cluster near the openings of caves. Whereas water nourished humans and plants, it was also tied to the watery world of afterlife, and a common expression of death was *och ha'*, "entering water" (Stuart 1998: 388).

Centers and settlements replicated these features. Pyramids were representations of hills, the dark interiors of their summit temples likened to caves. Temples were also conceived in part as sleeping places (*wahyib*) of gods (see Chapter 7). Plazas in front of them may have been associated with watery domains (Schele and Mathews 1998: 45), providing spacious settings for community performances, many attested on stelae. Even more impressive are the complex and abundant hydraulic systems crafted by the Maya (e.g., Lucero and Fash 2006). Thus, centers and settlements represented both productive and dangerous forces of the world. This notion is most evident in the apparently deliberate placement of some ceremonial buildings over caves (Brady 1997).

The most common type of buildings was obviously the dwelling. Whereas the Maya term *naah* referred to generic buildings, *otoot* meant residential structures, roughly comparable to the Western concept of "home" (Plank 2004).

Most residential complexes, including the humblest huts of poor farmers and ostentatious royal palaces, shared the basic template of an arrangement around a square patio, despite substantial differences in scale and complexity. Residential complexes were primary spaces for the domestic life of the households and at the same time provided stages for political negotiations and social networking with other groups through diplomatic meetings, feasts, and gatherings for kin and local groups. Symbolically, houses were a microcosmos of the Maya world, with their four corners and the hearth mirroring the cardinal directionality and the mythical hearths evoked by the Long Count system. The Maya typically buried their dead under house floors, and these buildings thus served as material representations of kin-group history (however those bonds were understood) and ties to ancestors (McAnany 1995).

For the Maya, the physical world did not consist simply of inanimate, static matter. The sky, hills, bodies of water, and buildings pulsed with spirits, power, and cultural meanings. They formed a dynamic universe, along with the gods, ancestors, animals, plants, material objects, and human beings (*winik*) that inhabited it. People's engagements with these features of the cultural landscape activated and controlled their power. Such engagements took diverse forms, including rituals in caves and on mountain tops, mass spectacles in plazas, fire-entering ceremonies in buildings, agricultural activities, and collections of mineral and other resources. In this setting, with these actions, the Classic Maya flourished for most of the first millennium.

CHAPTER 2

SOCIALITY

CLASSIC MAYA SOCIALITY

Like any people, the Classic Maya lived with pressures that integrated and divided their world. Their unequal society implied the strong operation of cohesive and conflictive forces. Inequality imposed a burden on the poor, the weak, and the unprivileged that had to be obscured, counteracted, or justified in some manner. Without such disguises and counterforces, their society would disintegrate or run the risk of severe disruption insofar as "dominance is always incomplete and monopoly imperfect" (Michael Walzer, cited in I. Morris 1997: 97). Perspectives on how these forces influenced the Maya depend in part on the researcher. Some Mayanists prefer to see Classic societies in more harmonious terms, antagonistic to outsiders but treating members according to a distinctive form of sociality that emphasized covenants or binding, supernaturally sanctioned agreements. Others see the Maya as congeries of factions or interest groups, in continual negotiation and conflict over resources, with elites oppressing and exploiting their social inferiors (Pohl and Pohl 1994). Rather than accepting their fate, those inferiors devised various means of resistance. The truth lies somewhere in between these perspectives. The Classic Maya lived in a vibrant world, affected by centrifugal forces as well as centripetal ones. The two perspectives, one emphasizing harmony, the other internal conflict, correspond to two general models of Maya sociality: the *moral community* and the *divided society*. The tension between the two accounted in large measure for the dynamism and paradoxes of the Classic Maya world.

THE MORAL COMMUNITY

"Morality" is a system of values, of sentiments or principles that are "worthy, desirable, and proper" in a given culture (Klass 1995: 42). Morality takes account of ideas about right and wrong and then influences actions according to those values. Such a system determines which behavior is right and appropriate given a certain set of circumstances – what has been described as "prudential morality" – and according to an ultimate sense of ethical objectives, described as "transcendental morality" (Bailey 1981: 23–24; Fürer-Haimendorf 1967: 226). It lays just as much emphasis on internal, subjective guidance as external, censorious judgment. It also focuses on a "moral object" or an "object of commitment" (Durkheim 1961: 8, 29, 90). A moral object is a focus – always symbolic, sometimes concrete and material – that allows people to channel their purpose in ways that satisfy notions of rightness and propriety. Today, in some circumstances, "morality" implies little more than cant and hypocrisy, but that is a more recent perspective that casts moral judgment into the realm of irrelevance in everyday life. In most societies – and perhaps especially those with weakly developed systems of adjudication and law-making – morality shapes individual behavior to a powerful extent. People tend to believe that the system is not a lie (Durkheim 1965: 14). Moral decision making demands and presupposes commitment to the system. Having decided that there are good and bad acts, a moral actor must respond to that understanding, either positively or negatively, according to an understanding of moral vectors.

Nonetheless, for all its seeming abstraction, morality involves calculations that are intensely personal and self-interested. From this, morality draws special force, for the simple reason that the actor cannot easily escape or ignore those calculations. No two people will use the same reasoning, invoke the same emotions that elicit action, or behave in precisely the same way. Often the choices will be reflexive or automatic, arising from custom and habitual practice (Bourdieu 1990: 53; Mauss 1950: 368–9). But, inevitably, a decision will be made according to what is perceived by the actor to be right or wrong in a process by which the self disciplines itself into a posture of integrity (Lamont 2000: 22–3). That this decision should also be influenced by ideas about sensible, effective, and self- or group-promoting behavior in no way diminishes its strength. Behavior hinges precisely on what is thought to be helpful to the moral actor according to a sense of culturally determined fulfillment. In emotional terms, moral action promotes a sense of well-being – it makes the actor feel content.

As a premise for action, morality nonetheless depends on something more than individual experience and response. Individuals are moral actors in the sense that they make daily decisions about right and wrong conduct. Yet, undeniably, morality develops from social interaction: it does not arise spontaneously, although theologians and a few sociobiologists would find a propensity to moral decision making in human nature. The example and guidance of others allow someone to form an idea of appropriate conduct. By various encouragements or reprimands, members of a society collectively condone some actions and condemn others. This leads to adjustments in individual behavior and guides future practice in a process that begins at infancy and continues until death. Penalties and censure restrain the grossly self-indulgent.

In most societies, immoral thoughts carry no punishments, yet immoral actions do. Ultimately, morality implies, in its breach, parallel notions of deviance and social aberration, the right way existing in uneasy relation to the wrong (Selby 1974: 21–2). Our wish to understand Classic Maya moralities carries with it an obligation to discover what they considered bad and evil. The absence of moral reasoning, especially in societies with undeveloped systems of coercive law or state-imposed fiat, would lead, logically, to anarchy or a Hobbesian condition of unregulated individual desire. No community could long survive this state, nor could any nonsociopathic human exist without some notion of morality. Indeed, the Maya collapse, a time of civic disintegration in some areas, was probably both a material crisis *and* a moral predicament that frayed social contracts.

Morality is a complex part of human existence. The relation between moral values and practice shifts constantly. Individual experience accounts for much of that fluctuation, as does the fact that no system of beliefs is ever entirely consistent (Beidelman 1986: 4). For example, an obligation to kin may outweigh an obligation to a ruler such that the moral actor will need to adjust to a particular situation by weighing alternatives choices (Harman and Thomson 1996: 22). Some actions may be thought desirable in one context, but obligatory or impermissible in another. In addition, different moral systems may co-occur, with peasants employing a moral system that is consciously distinct from that of elites (Giddens 1994: 173; Howell 1997: 4, 7–8; Scott 1976: 165, 167–73).

For modern ethicists the crucial issue is whether moral values are absolute – whether all societies share basic concepts of right and wrong – or whether those values or moral standards pertain only to certain societies (Johnson 1993: 2). Most likely these views are in themselves right and wrong: a concern with right-thinking behavior is surely universal, yet the nature of moral reasoning and "right-thinking" varies enormously. For the Classic Maya lord, it was "right" to torture and humiliate captives, just as some countries today find it "right" to execute criminals or to honor the liberties of "individuals." No disrespect or personal comment is intended in asserting that these notions of rightness exist within and because of particular historical and cultural milieux. A Western "individual" relates to a concept of personhood that has been defined in occidental thinking and jurisprudence over the last two thousand years (Mauss 1985). As we shall see, personhood did not hold the same meaning for the ancient Maya.

Being Moral

Mayan languages express "rightness" in words having to do with just or appropriate behavior. In Yukatek Maya *toh* means "right" and "straight," but also "just thing," "honor," or even "vengeance" (Barrera Vásquez 1980: 800). A similar word appears in most Mayan languages, with the sense, as among Lakan-don Maya, of someone who is a "correct" leader (Boremanse 1998: 69), or, as in Ch'ol Maya, someone who is "responsible" (*tojlel*, Josserand and Hopkins n.d.). Ch'olti' uses *to* for "truth" and assigns, much like English, a positive value to the "right hand," *to-cab* (*tohk'ab*, Ringle n.d.). In Classic Maya imagery, not coincidentally, the viewer's right usually contains higher-ranking figures than those to the left, and distinguished visitors or supplicants sit to the right hand of the central, highest-ranking figure (Houston 1998). In general, then, the disposition of people in spaces of honor follows a pattern of handedness and its moral meanings. Colonial Tzotzil links a cognate term, *toj*, to many virtuous activities, including cleansing, confession, prophecy (*toj-ti'i*, "straight mouth"), and tuning musical instruments – all, to Maya minds, actions that are "straight" and "right" (Laughlin 1988, I: 315–17). The Classic Maya sometimes referred to the concept of "left hand" but always in tandem with the right, and occa-sionally with respect to the sun god: directionality among the Classic Maya seemed to have reflected whether one faced the rising sun (with south being the right hand) or faced as the sun might (with south being the left hand, D. Stuart 2002).

A village, field, house, or pyramid could have irregular outlines, but, con-ceptually, its sides are straight and its alignments direct, as laid out by cords measured according to dimensions intrinsic to the human body (Schele and Mathews 1998: 34–6; Taube 2001). Maya roads or elevated paths, known in Classic times as *sakbih*, are thus, as tokens of "straightness," probable symbols of rectitude and correct, ordered movement, whatever the actual, pragmatic adjustments required by local topography and prior building (Fig. 2.1). (The possibility also exists that such roads represented an important part of mortuary rites, for the reason that death was labeled euphemistically as "road entering," *ochi-bih*.) The same holds true for other alignments noted in Maya architecture (Aveni and Hartung 1986; Harrison 1999: 171–6, 187–91; Hartung 1980), or for the positive value accorded the human definition of perimeters, and house or house-plot boundaries, to the exclusion of the disorderly forest and its untamed denizens (Taube 2003). A more basic term is "good," *uutz*, found in virtually all Mayan languages, a label that may also have the shadings of "just" (Laughlin 1988, II: 578; see also Ulrich and Dixon de Ulrich 1976: 202; Lenkersdorf 1979, I: 353–4), alongside positive adjectives like Kaqchikel terms for "sweet," "thick," and "big," as opposed to "salty," "thin," "small," and "wounded," especially when describing the heart (Hill and Fischer 1999: 323). A negating particle, *ma*, occurs in Maya writing, as in the expression, attested in the Postclassic codices, of *ma (yu)tzil*, "not goodness," or the more direct, if still uncertain, reading of *loob*(?) as "damage, bad thing" (Dresden Codex, page 8a), which could also be applied to the "twisted," untamed, and feral qualities of bush, forests, or caves in Yukatek Maya (Taube 2001). In the codices these terms associate with ominous gods and times of scant food and drink. But they do not reveal the reasoning that discriminates between good or bad.

Morality is seldom reducible to a series of rules or maxims that yield predictable outcomes. Instead, it operates as an imaginative process, a serious kind of play in which the moral actor explores possibilities and then acts on them (Beidelman 1986: 3; Johnson 1993: 2). The basis of such reasoning and action is not so much a series of principles that lead invariably to the "right" decision as it is structured ways of thinking that use *frames* or idealized ways of looking at and connecting things, *metaphors* that link one domain to another, *narratives* that make sense of things by putting them in a story, and *basic emotions*, such as pleasure, pain, and well-being (Johnson 1993: 8–11). For the Classic Maya, a frame would be material or architectural, such as a palace, cave, or temple, or it could be a social encounter, including contact with a ruler in a palace or an enemy warrior on the field of battle. A metaphor would liken humans to the Maize God – in fact, "metaphor" may be too pallid a word to communicate the true transubstantiation involved in this comparison, or the implications such metaphors had for human behavior. A narrative would liken a ruler to the Hero Twin Juun Ajaw; a basic emotion would be the exultation over captives or the joy felt in a crop of fresh maize or the satisfaction taken after a well-performed ceremony. These narratives were pivotal in holding communities together by means of collective parables for right action, much as Homeric poetry provided a central text for much of the ancient Mediterranean, with visual quotes in pottery and many other media (Powell 1991: 207–18).

For a more familiar context – the Middle Ages – Brian Stock refers to such narratives as "physical and mental texts" in that even primarily oral societies have propositions ordered into narratives that are at once public and conventional (Stock 1996: 146–7). The texts may be interpreted and adapted according to time and place. The groups that esteem and review such texts are "textual communities." They fit within a world in which there may be physical texts – the written word and the less explicitly sequenced motifs that come from iconography – but also performances and oral explications of such narratives that serve to bind people into fellowships of joint understanding (Stock 1996: 150). To an uncertain degree, the Classic Maya may have formed such a textual community, if of a more diffuse and heterodox character than, say, observant Jews or Benedictine monks.

Among many Mesoamericans, especially the richly documented Aztec, morality was inculcated through stern upbringing and rhetorical speech that praised and recommended ancestral virtues (Sullivan 1986). It is doubtful that the Classic Maya were any different. A later Maya source points to harsh punishments for children's misbehavior, with an emphasis not on scolding but fierce corporal discipline (Kray 1997: 90–1; Tozzer 1941: 127). A source from colonial Yucatan records the ferocity of priests who punished those who neglected certain rituals (Lizana 1988: 59). The presence at festivals of ritual

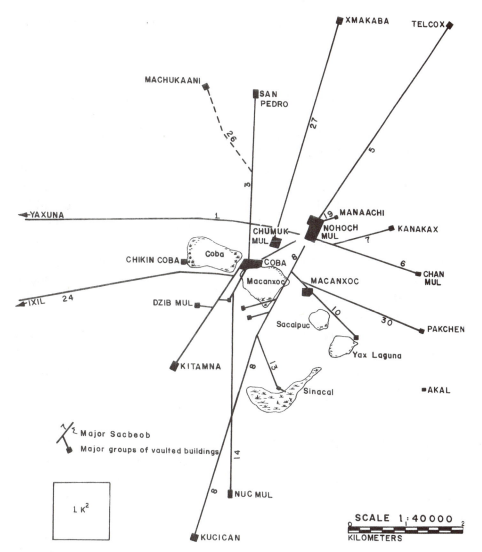

Figure 2.1. Maya roads or *sakbih* in Coba, Quintana Roo, Mexico (Folan et al. 1983, fig. 1.2).

clowns, obscene and discordant, strengthened moral understanding by giving limited scope to comic, mocking displays of immorality (Fig. 2.2, Taube 1988). This was the standard of evil and imprudent conduct that instructed by negative example. The result of such upbringing has been described by one ethnographer of modern Maya as an immutable formalism in which children were expected to reproduce, rather than question or understand, adult or ancestral practices (Watanabe 1992: 99). Such an interpretation is probably too sweeping for the ethnographic Maya and, one suspects, for the Classic Maya as well.

Where did gods fit into this scheme of moral education? To put it plainly, the role of the gods in Mesoamerica clashes with later, occidental notions of deities as flawless and exemplary paragons. Quite the opposite: unlike ancestors, a category discussed in greater detail in Chapter 7, Mesoamerican gods were not so much idealized models of human behavior as forces that existed alongside or outside human judgment. Their very anomaly made them special. Deities might be feared and appeased, but they were not, apparently, regarded as guides for humans to follow. Later sources tell us that gods could be skittish, fickle, and prone to anger. Gods punished offences by inflicting personal illness and destabilizing communities (Monaghan 2000: 34–5). It is less clear, however, whether rulers eschewed divine models for their behavior. The qualities of gods that made them awesome lent themselves naturally to royal appropriation and symbolic transposition. The Sun God was probably regarded as the positive prototype for rulers, just as other gods, gloating over harems of women or stroked by beauties in steambaths, represented, perhaps, a kind of "anti-court," examples of license gone astray (Karl Taube, personal communication, 1995). Most important, some deities established charters for human practices such as births, feasts, and matchmaking (for more on the Maya view of gods and the supernatural, see Chapter 7).

Humans had a different role. They maintained balance between order and chaos by recognizing, with humility and appropriate action, the place of humans in an overall cosmic setting as well as the dependence of humans on other beings (Burkhart 1989: 12, 19, 37–8). "Worthiness," as among the Aztec, attended those who "wept" or were "sad" in acts of reverential deference and solemnity (Hassig 1988: 33). In the harsh Aztec worldview, punishment, likened to a thorn, nettle, or scorpion, caused "someone to be good at last" (Maxwell and Hanson 1992: 173). It is uncertain whether the Maya viewed human misbehavior with quite as much austerity. For them, immorality represented the opposite of all that was right, balanced, and ordered – the festival clowns already mentioned, often depicted in the humble arts of figurine making, came into play here. Of relevance here is that Mesoamericans did not so much have a "religion" per se in the sense of fixed and discrete devotional practices or an orthodox and organized creed. Rather, they had an orientation of "religiosity," an approach to life in which the line between ritual and everyday actions could be difficult to draw. The pragmatic blurred indissolubly with the sacred, and the construction of a house or the planting of a field might be as "ritualized" as the interment of the dead (Monaghan 2000: 30; Vogt 1976: 52–5). Morality or "right" behavior helped people be religious and provided a standard by which to approve or deplore conduct.

Personal salvation, a theological concern brought to later Maya by the Spaniards, meant little in Mesoamerica, since the dead went to places determined by social rank or the manner of death (Burkhart 1989: 90). For the Classic Maya, rulers went not to the realm of the death gods, who embodied disease and reeked of decay and flatulence, but to a flowery paradise (Hill 1992; Taube 2004; see Chapter 7). One suspects that Xibalba, the abode of

Figure 2.2. Maya clowns, Late Classic period (Taube 1989, figs. 24.11b, 24.12c).

death mentioned in colonial sources, awaited some nonelites, although much of this landscape of the afterlife remains unclear to modern eyes. Nonetheless, if humans could not seek any eschatological benefit, they could practice decorum, propriety, and the neutralization of pollution through acts of expiation and "purification" (Burkhart 1989: 87; Monaghan 2000: 33–5).

These acts were, in Mesoamerican and Maya thinking, practical matters. Pollution derived from the very existence of humans, who transgressed daily by the everyday acts of human existence: eating, having sex, being born, dying, and all disordering activities of a serious sort. It is probably no coincidence that some of the few Classic Maya depictions of lovemaking or autoeroticism are found in the liminal, "dark zones" of caves well away from daylight. The filth and disorder that resulted could lead to damaged crops, sickness, deformity, or "twistedness" (Burkhart 1989: 172; Wilson 1995: 152). Certain practices – bloodletting, fasting, abstinence, bathing, sweating, processions, pilgrimages, sweeping, and the Classic Maya treatments of induced vomiting and forced evacuation by enemas – rectified derangements of order by making a person or community "whole" (Hanks 1990: 364; Vogt 1976: 179–89). This meant that such actions had a utilitarian benefit from an indigenous point of view.

Describing these as rituals of purification may be misleading since purification implies a purging or elimination that does not fully describe the process of bodily reconstitution and retuning involved in such complicated procedures. Ritual specialists ensured the effectiveness of these acts by making certain that all was conducted to technical perfection, at the right time and place, and in the right sequence. The calendrical knowledge for which Mesoamerica was

renowned assisted in fixing the timing of ceremonies. Spatial concepts intersected with temporal ones to situate those ceremonies and other activities in
particular places. If undertaken by rulers, acts of ordering potentially extended
the benefits of balance to the community or kingdom (Burkhart 1989: 90). For
the Classic Maya, "religion" could not be compartmentalized from other activities and institutions, a comment that also applies to the complex, historically
accretive religions of ancient Rome (Beard et al. 1998: 43).

In a sense, individual and collective acts promoted, if not always successfully,
a kind of "static dynamism" in Classic society. Dynamism was made inevitable
by human nature and its by-products, the disorder and pollution that, in Maya
thought, necessarily accompanied existence. But it could be checked by human
ingenuity. The community was a kind of social gyroscope that spun and jerked
in balanced equilibrium, one force being met by its opposite. However, the
Maya, along with other Mesoamericans, allowed a role for excess and pollution,
which engendered dangerous emanations that could be manipulated by priests
or rulers (Burkhart 1989: 97–8, 124; Monaghan 2000: 34–5).

Covenants and Responsibility

The moral communities of the Classic Maya can be seen as societies predicated
on a sense of responsibility to gods, kith and kin, living and dead (Monaghan
2000: 36–9). Moreover, there was not one moral community within the Classic
Maya world but many, most more-or-less coterminous with individual kingdoms. To Maya thinking, an evasion of responsibility had real consequences
by undermining health and social stability. It seems likely that, given what is
known ethnographically and historically of the Maya, their moral communities
operated according to the concept of "covenant," a transcendent agreement or
contract binding on all parties (Fischer 2001: 164–6; Monaghan 1995: 222–6;
see Insoll 1999: 9, 208–11, for Islamic parallels). Such contracts did not pre-
cipitate out of thin air, as though a society had decided to form itself and then
promote stability, but as the result of over a millennium of earlier development. The conceptual origins of Classic Maya covenants lay deep in the past
and, indeed, were not devised anew in each generation but built on the very
premise of great antiquity. Their wide diffusion in Mesoamerica hints that this
premise had a real basis (e.g., various studies by Monaghan, especially 1995).

The covenants of Mesoamerica had a heavy supernatural component that
followed from common understandings of the nature and purpose of human
existence. Basic to all was maize, the flesh and food of humans. According
to the K'ichee' epic Popol Vuh, one of the most important resources for
recovering ancient Maya thought, the gods fashioned beings of mud or sticks,
which "walked however they pleased" and did not remember their creators
(Christenson 2000: 49). Later, after destroying or altering their first creations,
the gods made humans out of corn, which, along with other domesticates, had

been discovered under a mountain. These new beings were juicy, blood-filled, and so close to perfection that their keen sight had to be blurred like breath on a mirror. Otherwise they would attain the discernment of the gods (Christenson 2000: 134). The creation of female companions compensated for this loss by gladdening Maya hearts. Many variations on this account exist throughout Mesoamerica, but its essential features again suggest great antiquity. The narrative also laid out, in narrative form, the defining human covenant, that humans owed their flesh to the gods, who in turn subsisted on praise, offerings, and succulent human flesh (Edmonson 1993: 83–4; Monaghan 1995: 223; M. Shaw 1972: 58–61). In a word, humans existed within a *phagiohierarchy*, a chain of beings that eat other beings (Carrasco 1995; Hunt 1977: 89; Monaghan 2000: 37; Read 1998: 132–5). Eventually human flesh returned to the earth as payment for the original loan. The ultimate payment, death, might be deferred through prayer, orations, and sacrificial substitutes, just as, by the same logic, a curer today substitutes a chicken for a patient (Taube 1994: 669–70), the Classic Maya placed offerings as caches within cavities of buildings and platforms (Chase and Chase 1998) or erected altars, known in Ch'ol as *wei'te'*, "food board," for the nourishing of deities (Houston 2001; Josserand and Hopkins 1988). Mythic precedents created obligations that stimulated human interventions to forestall divine will. There was much of human cunning in this, along with the implicit notion that hungry gods were not especially astute or perceptive, particularly the underworld deities whose names recall indigenous terms for disease (Taube 1994: 671).

One pivotal question remains unexplored. Did the Classic Maya truly believe in their gods and their duties to them? This question comes naturally to us today, from a vantage where agnosticism or casual religiosity have become, for better or worse, dominant features of existence. Another way of looking at the question is to ask, what was the nature of nonbelief? Some classicists argue that Greek philosophy was not so much systematic skepticism as doubts about the historicity of Homeric myths: the philosophers did not reject belief but sought to purify it (Price 1999: 126–7; Veyne 1988: 41). Pure atheism was both rare and repugnant to those such as Plato, who saw gods as binding forces of the state. If the Classic Maya had no unified doctrine, no finite number of gods with fixed characteristics, then disbelief would have to occur on a piecemeal basis, or with respect to a certain cult activity. Much the same happened towards the end of the Caste War in Yucatan, in which many Maya neither heeded nor believed the commands of the Talking Cross that otherwise served as a focus of rebellion and indigenous revival (Bricker 1981: 108, 115).

In a world of received wisdom, rooted in ancestral practice, disbelief might have seemed possible in a limited way but inconceivable in general. And if deities had localized aspects and political associations, overt disbelief would border on sedition. Apparent inconsistencies may have been tolerated, much the same way that Medieval Christianity permitted the coexistence of contrary doctrines like free will and divine predestination (MacIntyre 1979: 73). Indeed, it may be a functionalist fantasy to see "culture" or "society" as anything but a dynamic mixture of colliding contradictions or antinomies, held despite their ultimate inconsistency (Clifford 1988: 10, 337–9). Nowhere is this better exemplified than in the inscriptions of Palenque, where an expression meaning "to place in order" (*tz'ak*) alternates with logographs or word signs involving precisely these kinds of contradictions, "sun" juxtaposed with "night," "star" with "moon," "wind" with "water," and "blue-green" with "yellow" – the contrast delimiting a coherent, integrated whole. In terms of moral reasoning, there may have been many narratives among the Classic Maya, some mutually inconsistent in their messages. Ambiguities nurtured a zone of mystery that reminded believers of the limits of human comprehension. It also presented an opportunity for further acts of revelation and crafted a space for new forms of belief. Indeed, the plurality of Classic Maya belief inherently allowed for the assimilation of novel cult practices (cf. similar evidence from Rome, Beard et al. 1998: 62–3, or among the Aztecs, as in Wastek rituals related to the goddess Toci, Durán 1971: 233). Unfortunately, such assimilation is difficult to study in the Maya case. The first mention of a god or of a ritual practice – often a reflection of chance survival in the epigraphic record – is not necessarily the same as its date of introduction. The rites and personages connected with the beginnings of the current "age," set at 3114 BC, would seem to be a Late Classic innovation, but for the fact that a recently discovered text shows its occurrence many generations before (Fig. 2.3).

Most Classic Maya probably followed common practices without much reflection. Mayan terms for "believe" often combine the sense of "recognize," "understand," "know" or even "obey," as though dealing with self-evident or preexisting truths. The Classic Maya most likely operated according to what might be described as situated habit, determined by who they were, what their position in society might be, what they learned as children and in subsequent stages of life, and what might be expected of them in certain fields of activity (Bourdieu 1990: 52–65). The more complex features of Maya belief and practice would have been, one presumes, inherently incapable of wide dissemination. Their very elaboration contributed to a reduced audience and accentuated the value of these arcane ideas as carefully tended and hoarded symbolic capital. Temple summits, with their cramped rooms and difficult access up stairways, helped emphasize the fact that not all features of civic belief and practice were seen or understood by everyone.

Alongside such restricted knowledge and practices was an elite or royal strategy that included rather than excluded people. Most Maya settlements of any size can be understood as settings designed for public rituals (Inomata 2006a). These ceremonies involved many hundreds of people – in fact, close to the full-time population of any given center – within the open plazas and along the processional routes found at most Maya centers. Such rituals continually

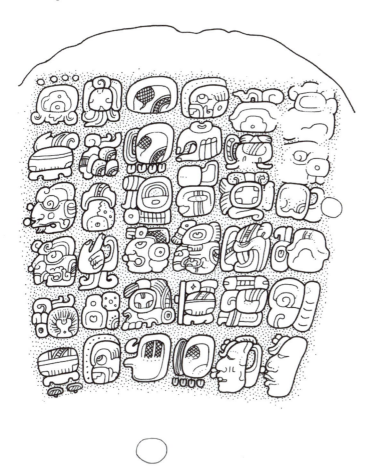

Figure 2.3. Early Classic text relating to 3114 BC, on back of stone mask (drawing by Stephen Houston, provenance unknown).

recreated community and forged solidarity by bringing people together in joint celebrations (Yaeger 2000: 124). The community became something like a congregation, in which members served the gods and leaders operated as ritual adepts (Monaghan 1995: 9). An earlier generation of anthropologists conceptualized Mesoamerican villages and towns as "closed corporate communities" that had joint holdings and protected their economic and political interests against forces of external oppression (Monaghan 1995: 7–9). The closed nature of these communities supposedly defended their integrity against colonial systems of exploitation (Wolf 1955, 1957), although others have discerned these properties well before the time of the conquest (Early 1983; Hill and Monaghan 1987). A congregational view lays greater emphasis on the emotive bonds of symbolic action (Inomata 2006a). By participating in civic ceremonies, people voiced acceptance of appropriate actions, although interpretations of the meanings of those actions might vary, a peasant construing them differently from a courtier (but see Fernandez 1977; Kertzer 1988: 67–8).

Moral Communities

"Communities" would have been defined by an earlier generation of anthropologists as having four qualities: small scale of interaction; similarity of activities and ideas; an economic and political self-sufficiency; and an overt notion that the community differed from others (Kolb and Snead 1997; Murdock 1949; Rapport and Overing 2000: 60; Redfield 1960: 4; Yeager and Canuto 2000: 5–6). A more precise definition might be that a community is both contrastive and symbolic (Rapport and Overing 2000: 62). It exists and defines its boundaries with respect to other communities (Barth 1969), relying on shared meanings that contrast with those of neighbors, no matter what their apparent similarities might be (Cohen 1985: 98).

In most cases the community is "imagined," meaning that it is a subjective invention connecting and emotionally bonding people that will never know their fellow members (Buber 1949: 145; Mandelbaum 2000: 31). The result is a comradeship based on "unselfconscious coherence" (B. Anderson 1991: 6, 16; Bender 1978: 7), but also, if one acknowledges the reality and messiness of human sociality, a desired order that is not always achieved. Such communities are better described as "nascent or emergent" groupings based, as in fourth-century-BC Athens, on "like-mindedness" and ties of mutual obligation (Morris 1997: 96; Mandelbaum 2000: 4, 7). Moral communities might even be said to rest on two communal "myths," in the sense of stylized notions that shape reality but are not in themselves reality. One myth is a belief in voluntary compacts, of willing participation that cannot be imposed coercively; and another is of a depth of integration that weaves the full sum of human experience into the concept of community (Mandelbaum 2000: 33, 36). "Thick" communications – complex, dense messages about the reasons for moral order – are less effective than "thin" ones that can be publically and repeatedly disseminated without distorting their content (Mandelbaum 2000: 54).

Many Classic Maya cities or polities were so small that their members could literally have assembled in public spaces. Faces and identities would become familiar in such contexts. At the same time, relationships became deeper (or "multiplex") because of the density of habitual interaction between a smaller group of people (Cohen 1985: 29). An interlocutor could be a neighbor, kinsman, trading partner, or opponent, but not, generally speaking, a stranger. The constitution of community would have been more challenging in larger cities such as Tikal and Caracol. Dense relationships obviously existed, yet interactions were more likely to be fleeting ("simplex") or uncomplicated by long-standing acquaintance. It could be that, as a means of comfort and practical advantage, the definition of corporate groups was stronger or more pronounced in larger cities than in smaller ones. Larger centers would tend to emphasize groups of manageable size, albeit nested within more unwieldy ones, whereas smaller ones would be more inclined to stress community-level affiliation.

The difference between "thick" and "thin communications" would have been relevant here. The larger the community, the "thinner" the understandings that could be communicated effectively across a larger, more diverse population. "Thick," esoteric knowledge served to separate and categorize people according to their understanding of such intricacies and subtleties. The stories that helped explain and justify the community cohesion – the moral narratives already mentioned – were crucial, for they established the nature of these communities and their "claims of membership"; they "teas[ed] out latitudes and disciplines, simplif[ied] the acts of choice" (Mandelbaum 2000: 77–8). By being told and retold they infiltrated and saturated the ways in which the Classic Maya lived and felt.

As in other parts of Mesoamerica (Kray 1997: 110; Monaghan 1995: 200–1), the sharing of food, drink, and clothing undergirded the Classic Maya notion of community. As among modern Maya, it is probable that to reject an offering of food was to invite or suggest an unresolved quarrel. Commensal feasts are rarely mentioned in hieroglyphic texts (Houston and D. Stuart 2001: 69), yet they commonly appear in depictions of royal courts (Postclassic codices link positive auguries with a hieroglyph for "feast," in which human visages swallow *tamales* and water, Houston and D. Stuart 2001: 69, fig. 3.4). A household supplied the needs of its members by redistribution. The Maya ruler did the same by posing as a generous paterfamilias. He received and distributed the products of his community – *tamales*, meats, chocolate drink and other beverages, and mantles of woven cloth – in commensal feasts consecrated by acts of dancing, a common means in Mesoamerica of summoning spiritual energy (Monaghan 2000: 31). Even images of tribute – the reception of cloth, chocolate beans, feathers, and shells – involved objects, not only of wealth, but of consumption (D. Stuart 1998: 410–14). Thus, the Maya ruler found a model for hierarchy in the inequities of the household.

But it would be a mistake to see these feasts only as arenas for cold-eyed social maneuvering. Instead, they doubtless represented the high-points of the Maya calendar, offering moments of fun, contentment, spectacle, and some respite from what was generally a hardscrabble life for the Maya (Fig. 2.4). In Amazonia, this emotion-laden aspect of sociality has been termed "conviviality," a shared, often jovial sense of amity and play that shapes everyday life and special occasion alike (Overing and Passes 2000: 14–17). Classic Maya feasts may have left evidence in the form of dumps of bone and shattered ceramics near palaces, as at Arroyo de Piedra or Tikal, and sheet middens near ballcourts in Honduras (Fox 1996). Although painted and carved scenes of feasts pertain exclusively to elites, feasts probably involved all levels of the community. Food and drink could have been offered at construction events where

Figure 2.4. Feasting scene on Panel 3, Piedras Negras, from sculpture dating to AD 782 (photograph courtesy of Archives, University of Pennsylvania Museum).

labor was offered in exchange for meals as part of "collective work events." In such events hospitality helped solicit and organize voluntary labor (Dietler and Herbich 2001: 241–2). In other parts of the world, such feasts tend to be lavish, involve many people over a relatively short amount of time, and recruit labor from lower-status groups at the behest of elites. Subsets of the community, such as lineages or households, may have compensated work parties with ad hoc feasts (Tozzer 1941: 96, "The Indians have the good habit of helping each other in all their labors."). To a troubling extent, however, there are no signs of large-scale food preparation in Classic Maya centers. The proposal that royal courts sponsored feasts is not the same as saying that they prepared copious quantities of food and drink. Most Classic Maya palaces contain little evidence of maize grinding or cooking facilities.

THE DIVIDED SOCIETY

A challenge for Classic society, and an instigator of change, came when the moral object – the focus of devotion and commitment – was something other than a ruler or a community deity. The object could be a lineage, extended family, or "house," in the sense of a broader unit of affinity (Gillespie 2000c). It could be a faction at court, a group of master craftspeople, traders, land-owners, warriors, or some other combination of elite and nonelite groups. Objects could shift in their adherents, but real instability ensued when higher-order moral objects gave way to lower-order ones, especially in the hierarchical societies that characterized the Classic Maya. A balance between such objects could, in contrast, lead to greater levels of contentment and a more firmly entrenched commitment to the status quo. Or morality could play no role at all. Self-interest potentially led to agnostic calculations that honored no covenants yet condoned all forms of maneuvering for personal advantage.

Integrated by certain bonds, Classic Maya societies also fluctuated and mutated as competing people or groups vied with each other for resources. At the most basic level of such tensions were individuals motivated by complex vectors of self-interest, including glorification in a society concerned with honor and prestige. The so-called "count of captives," which enumerates an accumulating tally of war prisoners (D. Stuart 1985), exemplifies such self-aggrandizement. At the risk of placing too much importance on labels, thus oversimplifying reality, we can say that societies focusing on matters of honor and personal prestige function as *timocracies*, from the Greek word *timē*, "honor, worth, value," and *kratia*, "power," with the extensional meaning of "rule by"

Figure 2.5. Degraded captive, Dos Caobas Stela 1 (drawing by David Stuart).

(Sykes 1976: 1214; see also Houston et al. 2006: 202–3). Most such societies have been studied in the circum-Mediterranean region, but the general pattern is broadly applicable to other parts of the world, namely, as a preoccupation with personal image and value ("pride") among groups that emphasize face-to-face interaction. In these societies, "the social personality of the actor is as significant as his office" (Peristiany 1966: 11) and claimants to honor "must be granted reputation" or be prepared to silence those who dispute it (Pitt-Rivers 1966: 23–4). Claims to honor or attempts to counter its defilement usually take place within a hierarchical or juridical structure that constrains or, as in the case of Classical Greece, facilitates attempts to buttress personal dignity (Fisher 1992: 498; Pitt-Rivers 1966: 23). Conversely, honor exists within larger group identities, especially pertaining to kin. The degradation of one person's honor affects the honor of others, who must respond to such "pressure of opinion" lest they cease to exist as socially respectable members of a community (Bourdieu 1966: 211). A necessary concomitant of such a system is shame or humiliation (Riesman 1977), as seen so frequently in Classic Maya depictions of contorted captives with exposed genitalia (Fig. 2.5).

The model of the "divided society" proposes that conflict arises from a plain fact: people generally seek to reproduce or improve their position with respect to resources, either tangible or symbolic (Bourdieu 1990: 118–19). The extent to which they succeed or fail partly determines the nature of social inequality. Calculations that reapportion resources often follow a logic of self or group advancement that is, some scholars believe, cross-culturally recognizable. This means that the modern analyst can, without too much difficulty, understand ancient motive from the vantage of "common-sense," as if in response to the prompt, "if I were a Classic Maya. . . ." The haves and have-nots play a large role in dividing society. Elites may have some managerial value, in the sense of coordinating group activities in an efficient or organized manner, but mostly, according to a conflict-oriented perspective, they exploit nonelites (McGuire 1992: 11). In its crudest, most exaggerated form, the model of a divided society rejects the proposition that there is any coherence to human societies, or that, if it exists, such coherence is at all stable (Keesing 1987: 161–3). This view inverts functionalism by seeing social entanglements that are less mutually supportive than dynamic, dysfunctional, and conflictive; strategic alliances may occur, but in a fleeting manner. In all such societies ideas are believed differentially, in a patchwork fashion, and beliefs are always incompletely controlled. Just because elites assert that the world should operate in a certain way does not mean that they succeed in promoting their view (Archer 1988: 2–4; McGuire 1992: 139) – the "dominant ideology" configured to justify and enhance inequality does not always dominate (Abercrombie et al. 1990).

Elites and Nonelites

Titles exist for Classic Maya nobility (see Chapter 6), but there is no explicit labeling of nobles per se, perhaps because their appearance in texts and imagery overtly proclaimed such status without having to specify it more precisely. It is possible that nobles belonged to larger entities that also comprised nonnobles, the difference being determined by acknowledged lordship within the unit and birth-order in a system of titular primogeniture (see the semblant Nahua system of *calpolli*, Lockhart 1992: 16–17). In patrimonial fashion, the K'ichee' Maya called commoners "children" (*al c'ajol*), presumably in the sense of people that needed tending and care (Carmack 1981: 148). Among the Aztec, *calpolli* could be either agglomerative, incorporating outsiders as new members of the community, or represent divisions of preexisting units. Early colonial terms for elites in Mayan languages are revealing. The Yukatek term for nobility, *almehen*, means child of woman *and* man, suggesting a concern with known ancestry on both sides and a genealogical consciousness perhaps lacking in nonnobles (Restall 1997: 88–9). There was a trope of foreign origins for many elites, a practice also seen at Classic centers like Tikal, Guatemala, and Copan, Honduras (see Chapter 6; Roys 1957: 5; D. Stuart 2000). Such consciousness would be buttressed by elite endogamy in the matter of inherited office, as among the Postclassic K'ichee' (Carmack 1981: 150). The Tzotzil expression for nobility, *'atilvinik*, "penis person," vividly emphasizes potency and procreative ability, alongside the morally salient *'utzilvinik*, "good person" (Laughlin 1988, II: 428).

Yet, what these distinguishing terms meant in actual application is opaque, since there is insufficient evidence to decide how the Classic Maya defined the lower reaches of nobility. Someone might have been of "noble" birth – that is, genealogically privileged – but poorly equipped with material resources. By land inheritance, purchase, and other economic maneuvers, others might secure access to goods that point falsely to membership in the nobility. Without texts such people would be exceedingly difficult to identify. The porosity of the membrane between noble and nonnoble status, the degree to which exogamy from these categories was acceptable, remain unclear to recent scholarship (for parallels in early colonial history, see Restall 1997: 92). More likely, a person's status was a complex blend of kin relations, life experiences, rights, rank, and gender (Gailey 1987: 116). This mix varied enormously across the Maya region and according to local circumstances. It would have been compounded by the likelihood, now evident from glyphic decipherment, that elites spoke a very different language from lower-ranking members of their society: such diglossia recalls, among other cases, the pronounced divides between nobility and nonelites in Norman England (Houston et al. 2000).

Resistance among the Classic Maya to such social orders might have involved several options. The most obvious would have been outright revolt. Nonelites could also: (1) depart; (2) abridge tribute and corvée labor by subtle deceits such as withholding produce or by indolent performance in civic duties; (3) commit to other moral objects by, first, focusing on nondynastic cults in distant caves and mountain tops away from elite control, and, second, pledging themselves to alternative devotions in the form of lineage and household "religion" (Borhegyi 1956; Leventhal 1983: 75–6); and (4) express freedom of action by building plaza groups and house mounds in nonconformity with centralized planning. All of these are plausible, even likely, expressions of resistance, but they cannot be confirmed. The plurality of Maya beliefs allowed for the coexistence of moral objects. And the fact that Maya cities exist, seldom with any evidence of large-scale, coordinated planning of residential buildings, points to the reality that, for much of the Classic period, the forces that held communities together superseded those that splintered them.

The option of departure sometimes resulted from acts of resistance. As the old adage goes, people can always "vote with their feet," shifting to zones well away from noxious spheres of elite control (McAnany 1995: 154–6), perhaps through poorly occupied border zones between polities or other areas of scant settlement. Conceivably, this movement would lead to the creation of small hamlets at the peripheries of dynastic polities, the development of settlements occupying remote valleys, rivers, and coastal areas, as in central and southern Belize, or merger into urban populations elsewhere. Or it could have led to urban growth, as at Ceibal, Guatemala, in Late and Terminal Classic times, as people shifted, not to the margins of polities, but to other kingdoms, for a variety of reasons. Most likely, Ceibal's increased size came at the expense of communities in the Petexbatun region devastated by warfare and instability (Demarest et al. 1997; Houston 1987, 1993; Tourtellot 1988b, fig.217, 1990: 99). Historically, it is certainly true that later Maya resisted onerous conditions by leaving for other places, in a process that Farriss has called "drift" (Farriss 1978, 1984: 199; Restall 1997: 174–5; Ryder 1977: 206).

But not all movements were willing ones or statements of resistance. Insecurity brought about by environmental change, economic shifts, and raiding was the most powerful inducement to leave. Few people would stay in an area if they were starving or unprotected from aggression (G. Jones 1982: 291; McAnany 1995: 146). Populations might fill a landscape by searching for arable lands in conditions of demographic growth, deserting their homelands more because of growling stomachs than the irritants and humiliations of hegemonic culture. Settlements lacking large centers or dispersed in distribution should not always be interpreted as refugee zones for "people of refusal," like the Old Believers of Russia or the Maroons of Suriname. Most settlements, even remote ones, built on exceedingly deep roots in their regions, with distinctive trajectories of development, if still interwoven with areas containing dynastic centers and royal courts (E. Graham 1994: 315–33). Functional specializations, such as cacao or salt production, meshed such zones into larger economic systems that still need to be teased out (see Chapter 9). Nominal suzerainty of distant areas might have been acknowledged, as would ownership by distant landlords. Unfortunately, the written sources are mute on these matters.

Such moves were probably more traumatic than joyful. Migration took people away from ancestral places and the bones of honored dead. It deprived them of civically organized contact with community deities, access to goods, services, and opportunities, and the diversion and fulfillment of public ceremonies. A modern anecdote illustrates this feature of civic life: among the Mam Maya, people were said to be "poor and sad" when living in distant villages, far from the center (Wagley 1949: 11). In the later nineteenth and earlier twentieth centuries, Lakandon Maya in Guatemala found themselves in a precarious position because of population shrinkage. They had few choices. They either joined the remaining Lakandon in Mexico, who did not always accept them, or they dissolved as culturally distinct peoples, living on, for a single generation, in isolated farmsteads unable to regenerate themselves (Lee and Hayden 1988: 7; Schwartz 1990: 318). For the Classic Maya, too, separation and isolation might have had short-term benefits yet enduring disadvantages.

The discussion so far has addressed people or groups within the Maya community. Another group existed both within and outside society. These were the enslaved. There is little doubt that this group constituted an important component of pre-Columbian society, although its proportion relative to other groups cannot be determined. Diego de Landa refers to trade in slaves (Tozzer 1941: 94), and Christopher Columbus saw such unfortunates in the trade canoes he encountered near the Maya coast during his fourth voyage (Tozzer 1941: 35). In many instances the ethnohistoric and lexicographical sources make it difficult to distinguish between slaves and a broader category of domestic servants (Carmack 1981: 151). At least there does seem to have been a distinction between slaves and sacrificial captives. The Classic Maya took war captives who were tortured and dispatched in several unpleasant ways: torching by strapping wood to the body, garrotting with sticks twisted around cloth, heart extraction, finger mutilation (rendering warriors unfit for battle), and anything else the sadistic imagination might devise. Some of these victims were of high status. According to Classic Maya imagery, captives made gestures of submission, one hand clasped to shoulder. They brought hand to mouth, perhaps mixing saliva with dirt as a sign of obeisance and sin (Tozzer 1941: 36). They usually kept their names, although the generic epithet accorded to some captives, "torchy macaw," *taj(al) mo'*, suggests that capture could trigger a change of name and stripping of identity (Patterson 1982: 55; Proskouriakoff [1993: 53], speculated that the name corresponded to "invaders from the [Maya] highlands," but this claim has little support). According to later sources, slaves, too, could be taken in war. Others were seized for theft, taken as orphans, given as recompense for crimes, and traded for jade beads and cocoa beans (Las Casas 1909: 616–19; Tozzer 1941: 63, 94, 232). Highland Maya evidence hints that some slaves ("big people," *nimakachi*) were inherited with land, and that they might rise to positions of confidence under rulers (Carmack 1981:1, 56), although this does not discount the possibility that slaves could represent sources of discord – not quite Spartacus, the Roman rebel, but persons of uncertain loyalty. The lone archival source on slaveholding in and before the sixteenth century in Yucatan is the Title of Calkini, which suggests that men were more common slaves than women and tended to be used in the cultivation and clearance of forests (*p'entakk'ax*) or as fisherman along the coast (Restall 2001).

Yucatec laws of the pre-Conquest period seem particularly concerned with the control of both production (the results of labor) and reproduction (the results of procreation). If caught, someone having sexual relations with a slave would lose their freedom, perhaps out of the notion that the conjoining of fluids created affinity, with slave status overriding that of the free (see Tozzer 1941: 232). A common lowland Maya word for "slave" or "enslave," *p'entak*, includes a term for the male member, *p'en*, along with the sense of transformation into a submissive, passive state. The hint of sodomy and wanton licentiousness (Barrera Vásquez 1980: 686–7) emphasizes that the slave's body was not its own, since these practices were otherwise said to be reviled by the Maya. Another pan-Mayan expression, *muun*, may involve the idea of "unripe thing," not yet ready to reproduce, infantile, and disassociated from manly honor (Patterson 1982: 96). The paradox of the slave is insoluble: a person removed from ancestors and descendants but dependent on an exclusive relation to the master, outside and yet encased within social networks, a dependent who is not-kin (Patterson 1982: 5–13). It is striking that captives are often described in glyphic texts by means of a negating particle: the enigmatic term *ch'ahb*, which somehow describes the relation between father and son, is replaced by *ma ch'ahb*, "no *ch'ahb*", when linked to captives (e.g., Tikal Column Altar 1: A4, K8176; David Stuart, personal communication, 1992). The term itself relates somehow to "penance" and "fasting," but in ways that remain mysterious. It may be that the expression places the captive outside the bonds of kinship in some as-yet-unspecified manner. Whether the Classic Maya ever had "slave societies," whole economies based on enslaved labor, is improbable, however. The possession of slaves may simply have bolstered honor and enabled a luxuriant elite existence without placing excessive demands on the free poor (Fitzgerald 2000: 5). The downside might have been the greater opportunities for resistance in the form of escape and the deliberate exercise of household inefficiencies. The increased number of references to warfare in the Late Classic period, although perhaps no more than a stylistic shift in the inscriptions, leads to the suspicion that the economic input of slaves may have grown at that time. If so, it is conceivable, although difficult to show, that a "Maroon" or escaped slave phenomenon influenced the growth of distant settlements, just as many Maya later fled the Spaniards for the refuge of the forest (*ateppecheob*, Acalan Chontal term for "refugee," Smailus 1975: 171).

Group Strife

From this discussion it is clear that there were many cross-cutting sources of discord in the Classic Maya society: nobles versus nobles; rulers versus elites; elites versus commoners; rulers versus intimate members of their family, and so on in a rich drama of strife and negotiation. At a certain point the internal dissensions could be construed as external ones, as feudatories broke away to assert autonomy. Available data suggest that Classic Maya elites had two, almost discrepant qualities: rather like Medieval Japan, they developed and valued a culture of competitive refinement and aesthetic discernment but, again like Medieval Japan, lived within a timocracy based on elaborately developed ideas of honor and glory that could ignite with little prompting. As in Japan, these mores, postures, and attitudes typically operated at elite levels and further distinguished elites from nonelites. An arresting feature among the Classic Maya is the long-term nature of antagonisms in their timocracies and a tenacious memory for aggrievement that borders on vendetta. Rulers extolled glorious acts of captive taking and commemorated these acts with epithets that kept a running tally of captives (D. Stuart 1985). A timocracy and its culture of striving ensured the perpetuation of social abrasion, perhaps according to several kinds of group identity.

Lineage

Terms that approximate the concept of lineage occur in most Mayan languages, albeit with a bewildering variety of forms and meanings: Yukatek, *chibal*; Lakandon, *onen*, an agnatic grouping; colonial Tzotzil, *tasal*; Zinacanteco Tzotzil, *sna*, "house of"; Ch'ol, *pi'öl*, with the connotation of proximate residence and coitus (endogamy?); and K'ichee', *xe'al*, from a term for "root," or the patriline *alaxic*, "be born." The variety suggests that, at this level of existence, there were rough correspondences of these concepts from area to area but pronounced differences in detail. In Yucatan, they could cluster in certain areas or spread thinly across the landscape and into different polities (Restall 1997: 48; Roys 1957: 8), although it must be added that there is no evidence for such macro-groupings at the nonelite level during the Classic period. The only term that appears in Classic-era texts is *naah*, "house," which may relate to the Tzotzil expression. A unique reference at Tamarindito, Guatemala, links the mother and father of the local ruler to different *naah*, "houses," and other evidence shows that they came from different sites, the father from Tamarindito, the mother from *Chak Ha'*, "Red" or "Great Water" (Houston 1993, fig. 4–17, 1998: 521). The references are difficult to explain, as they have no other parallel in the corpus of Maya writing. Yet they do hint that the concept of "house" helped structure social groups.

Family and Household

A "family," although seldom mentioned in later sources and not at all in the glyphs, operated as a corporate unit in Yucatan during colonial times, containing around ten people living in adjacent houses, organized as a four-generation "grandfamily" (Restall 1998: 357, 364). These families included lateral and affinal kin and extended themselves by exogamy, whereas larger corporate units tended to endogamy. Another corporate group might be that of the "household," a social group focused less on descent or fictive kinship than the sharing of activities, such as the production, consumption, and pooling of resources. Most such households are nuclear families, "complex households" that include married offspring or servants and laborers (Blanton 1994: 5), the grandfamilies mentioned before. What groups *do* is thought to be more important than how people are related (Wilk and Netting 1984: 5). In part the household varied in size and composition according to labor requirements (Johnston and Gonlin 1998: 158; R. Rudolph 1992). The concept of a household offers the methodological advantage of focusing on archaeologically visible features. It mutes subjective ideas, such as group identity, that cannot be readily accessed. At the same time, there were probably many different kinds of domestic groups among the Classic Maya, many not reducible to the notion of clustered, organized activities but to other kinds of unions.

House

The concept of the "house" is one way of understanding basic corporate
identities in the Classic period (Gillespie 2000c; Lévi-Strauss 1991). A "house"
is a fetish in the sense of a well-defined thing that embodies and objectifies
corporate identity – it does not so much refer to a particular building as
the identities such buildings represent and configure. The tangibility of the
"house" in this sense is what gives it strength and longevity. By implication, if
the fetish disintegrates, there is some risk of deterioration in corporate identity.
The house harnesses and displays accumulated memories about where the
house came from, who belonged to it, and what its corporate claims might
be. Those claims pertain to landholding or land use, access to labor, and rights
to certain titles, dances, and privileges. As an abstraction, the "house" is also
useful in that it describes the blurred realities of affiliation. Descent and alliance
often crosscut to form a dissonant tangle of conflicting allegiances (Gillespie
2000a: 7–8). The notion of a "house" helps mediate and subdue the pull of
other identities. The fact that it could not do so entirely injects dynamism
into corporate identity. People must work on a continuing basis to maintain
the "house" as a cohesive entity and as a physical object. If they are successful,
the house achieves distinction within the hierarchical societies where such
entities tend to be found (Gillespie 2000b: 51–2). The house can even become
a conveyance that allows certain groups to prosper as corporate aggrandizers
(Waterson 1995: 67–8).

Analytically, the idea of a "house" deflects attention from a fixed adherence
to the consanguineal or "blood" model of kinship systems. This model holds
that terms of affiliation describe actual physical relationships. In several influential works, Schneider has argued that this point of view is naive, that it assumes
a universal application for distinctively Western ideas of inheritance based on
"blood" (e.g., Schneider 1984; but see Scheffler and Lounsbury 1971: 5, who
suggest that kinship is necessarily prior to any statuses derived from it). In fact,
affinity is often reckoned by a variety of means, not only by common descent,
but by marriage alliance, exchange relations, and commensality in the form of
shared food, clothing, and commitments to shared labor (Monaghan 1995: 15,
244–6). Among Tzotzil Maya, appearance rather than blood ties determines
membership in community: "one must dress like one [a Zincanteco], eat like
one, work in the same manner, speak correctly, walk . . . use the same tools as
everyone else. This would be necessary to establish membership; it is essential
to maintain membership" (Devereaux 1987: 99). Nevertheless, members may
still describe their affiliation to a "house" by the language of kinship, which
facilitated the all-important goal of transfer of material and symbolic wealth
across generations (Gillespie 2000b: 27).

Does the "house" concept work for the Classic Maya? The answer is a
qualified "yes." In the first place, there is, as mentioned before, glyphic

evidence for the term. Second, the notion of a "house" accords with the Nahuatl term, *calpolli*, or "big house," and the K'ichee' idea of a *nimja*, "big house" (Lockhart 1992: 16–20; Carmack 1981: 160). Both were units of corporate identity. Among the K'ichee', they were manifested by actual buildings. The Nahuatl *calpolli* tended to control contiguous blocks of land and were in turn divided into wards that contained anywhere from roughly twenty to one hundred households (Lockhart 1992: 17). The Classic evidence could support the view that such units, which hypothetically formed a coherent unit beyond the household, were a median step between households or grandfamilies and polity. Households might have occupied individual plazuelas or adjacent sets of them, where the "house" was a sector or ward of clustered plazuelas, and the polity embraced the sum total of people over whom a holy lord claimed dominion. A mysterious term, *tzuk*, often preceded by a number, may have signaled territorial divisions of a polity or overlapped with social units attached to individual settlements (see Chapters 1, 5; Beliaev 2000). In Yukatek Maya the term refers to "parts," "provinces," "smaller community" (*pueblo pequeño*), and heaps of objects, perhaps in reference to boundary markers (Grube and Schele 1991: 3; Okoshi Harada 1992; Ringle and Bey 2001); the term also occurs in Acalan Chontal as *tzucul*, "neighborhoods" (Smailus 1975: 132). Another rare term links numbers with a glyph that may read *pet* or *peten*, usually "island" in Mayan languages (Nikolai Grube, personal communication, 1992), but also with the meaning of "province." There are, however, no cross-checks with which to test these interpretations.

The embodied, vital nature of the "house" fits well with what is known of Maya ideas about buildings. Physical houses were regarded as living beings that could be fed by ritual means (D. Stuart 1998). Glyphic labels for doorways ("mouth") and other parts of the structure accord explicitly with body terms, the house reciprocally mapping the human body as a kind of building (Houston 1998). Logically, the house imparted resilience to a corporate body whose members were physically ephemeral. The remains of the deceased continued to "live" within the house by being buried under floors and platforms (McAnany 1995). At the same time we see instability in the "house" both as a concrete set of buildings and an abstract pivot of affiliation. Over the long term, the house could fade away by losing competitive struggles with other houses, the house-as-structure falling into disrepair and the house-as-corporate unit drifting into oblivion (Gillespie 2000b: 33).

As always, the overriding and perhaps insuperable problem is matching the archaeology with a conjectural if credible model of society. Advances in physical anthropology may someday make it possible to gauge relatedness among skeletons found within such groups. But even the absence of relatedness could simply mirror the ability of households and "houses" to absorb physically unrelated people. A general inclination of Mayanists is to see diversity in corporate units of the Classic period, with descent groups dominating, say, at Copan, class at Tikal (Haviland 1992: 939; Hendon 1991). The suppleness of what is known of corporate groups does not inspire confidence that this issue can be readily resolved, or that scholars can speak of ephemeral affiliation when only the results of activities remain. Did plazuela groups, the basic unit of Maya settlement, belong to a certain "house"? And how did they reckon membership to this and other corporate units? A prudent response would be that we cannot know from available data. Archaeologists may wish to speak of their finds with ethnographic precision, yet the idiosyncratic histories of plazuelas will always rise to confound them. Another challenge is likening royal courts as "houses" (as implied by Lévi-Strauss' discussion of noble "houses" in Medieval France) to those of other corporate groups in Maya society. In some respects the comparisons are valid in that such groups have similar attributes and modes of interaction. But the comparison also equalizes and conceals what may be deep differences. It is hard to believe that a royal court, the vortex of Maya kingdoms, operated according to the same premises as a group centered on the periphery of a Maya polity.

Land Holdings and Conflict

Another source of discord might have come from the most unseen of factors: the control of labor and access to land of varying quality. There was a possible correlation between such control and group or individual status, leading to countless frictions. The most productive soils, with the most diverse products, would presumably be controlled, directly or indirectly, by elites, who also commanded larger pools of labor. In contrast, thin soils, with limited products, would fall under the sway of the unprivileged. "First settlers," the initial occupants of certain territories, would accrue important advantages in this struggle (McAnany 1995: 96–7). Later occupants would have more limited choices. They could increase their yields only by going farther afield and by aggregating more labor. They could accomplish this by begetting children, seeking wives, and promising reciprocity in exchange for loans of labor. Regrettably, the textual and archaeological sources are silent on these matters. One can guess that the Classic Maya world was frequently in turmoil over land and labor disputes, yet there is no easy way of uncovering the conflicts and stratagems of everyday life. Another problem in interpreting evidence is that landownership was, to judge from ethnohistoric data, variously specified. Some land was held separately by people or smaller groups, other estates were held jointly so as to prevent lands from being divided by inheritance into unproductive and unsustainable economic units (Restall 1998: 369). The clear inequalities in access to resources during Classic times remain at odds with ethnographic evidence that wealth was seen in negative terms. Good fortune could be accumulated through nefarious negotiations with a malevolent Earth

Lord, deepening tensions between the haves and have-nots and leading to witchcraft accusations (Devereaux 1987: 96). Were such disparities any more acceptable in the Classic period, and, if so, why?

Gender

Social tension and friction were conditioned by the notion of gender or local ideas about the nature of males and females. Available evidence indicates that, for the Classic Maya, gender was also an opportunity to celebrate an ideology of complementarity, if qualified by subtle imbalances. Most anthropologists see gender as a cultural construct rather than as an expression of biological universals (Ortner and Whitehead 1981), although physical differences between the sexes cannot be ignored. In a few instances, gender blurred in hermaphroditic or male/female fashion, as seen in the images of the maize god, who combined male and female characteristics (Taube 1985). Another sense of "tandem gender," of both male and female, characterizes a K'ichee' term for religious specialists known as *chuchkajawib*, "mother-fathers," who in many Maya communities are exclusively male (Tedlock 1992: 35). But, on the whole, later sources suggest strong divisions of labor. Women tended to own animals, clothing, some plants, and house plots, men owned and bequeathed agricultural tools (Restall 1995: 587). Only in life-crisis rituals, shamanistic practices, and witchcraft did men and women participate equally, often in connection with locations at the periphery of human settlement (Gossen and Leventhal 1993: 208). In the colonial period men and women rarely undertook collective tasks. Woman bore children and wove clothing, including the cotton mantles that were a crucial item of tribute. Men took responsibility for labor at some distance from the house plot, including forest clearance, boundary marking, cultivation of maize, trade, and tree plantations (Restall 1998: 367). At night, lower-status men and women came together, but ate separately; in the day they parted. But, above all, their identity as male or female coalesced in local terms according to the expectations of particular communities (Devereaux 1987: 99).

Greater numbers of wives could contribute, as among the Aztec, to heightened prosperity in the household (McCafferty and McCafferty 1998: 217–18) as well as ensure the creation of heirs within particular systems of inheritance. Again, as with age, a sense of complementarity pervades Maya discussions of men and women, a complementarity of cosmological wholeness rooted in male-female creator pairs, a balance of social status, and an idealized symmetry of activities (Devereaux 1987: 92). Not a few Maya stelae display males and females on opposite sides of the monument, or on stelae set side-by-side (R. Joyce 2000b: 74–5; J. Miller 1974). Such women often came from more important or larger sites than the males, so their display reflects a sense of pride in their exalted origins. In the Bonampak murals of the Late Classic period, it is noteworthy that women preside over tributary gatherings with men, participate in cross-gender bloodlettings while sitting on thrones, and oversee the display and torture of captives.

Nonetheless, images and texts make it clear that "symmetry" is less apt a label than "hierarchically organized dualism," much like the dominance of the right hand over the left, both of a set yet unequal. "Parity" is doubtless a notion that came uneasily if at all to the Classic Maya. Ethnographic sources indicate that gender ideology among Tzotzil Maya in Chiapas, Mexico, strongly emphasizes a "complementary and formally unranked quality" and as "two necessary parts of a social whole" (Devereaux 1987: 89). Yet it also exposes the asymmetries and real differences between the possibilities available to men and women, the former clearly privileged over the latter (Devereaux 1987: 110). Ethnographically, as among the Lakandon Maya, women deal with such tensions by exercising control over household activities, daughters' husbands, and by the powerful instruments of adultery, gossip, and matchmaking (Boremanse 1998: 53). The archaeological evidence is not entirely clear, although there are suggestions from Tikal that men were increasingly privileged in burial finery and location during Classic times, a pattern that did not seem so pronounced among a diverse group of nonelites (Haviland 1997: 10).

As mentioned before, culture clearly influenced ideas about the meaning of biological differences between men and women, but ultimately this argument may be taking matters too far. Glyphic texts are quite precise about identifying the gender of nobility. This was done by using a term *ix* or *ixik* for females and nothing (Ø or "zero") for men. That is, the absence of *ixik* signaled the presence of a male, the unmarked gender. This is supported by the use of *winik* to mean both "man" and "person." In colonial dictionaries this last term helps explain the otherwise puzzling statements that *winik* refer to "man" and "woman," namely, as rational agents regardless of gender. Still, it seems likely that, for the Classic Maya, *winik* gave nomenclatural primacy to "man" as a general classification for "human," much as anthropologists could, without embarrassment, once write books entitled *Man the Hunter* or *Man in Africa*. In the glyphs some females were described as *ixik . . . winik*, the more precise designation qualifying the more general, unmarked one. Another glyph, read *aj* or, in one dialect, *a*, meant "he of . . . " and necessarily preceded other signs that could record anything from place names to objects made by this person. It is not the case, as has been suggested elsewhere (R. Joyce 2000b: 64–5), that it applied generally to women as well, although rare instances of this usage does occur in later, colonial sources from Yucatan (Clark and Houston 1998: 34).

The issue of gender among the Classic Maya remains controversial when it engages current issues and polemics in feminist and "queer" studies. There have been attempts to dismiss the gender concepts of the Classic Maya as something other than "natural categories" and to suggest that Classic Maya texts did not always specify gender or that they simply viewed it as a fluid category (R. Joyce 2000b: 64, 65). Gender was, in this view, a designation that coalesced through "performance" (Butler 1999: 173, 177), and sexuality in turn involved an act rather than part of a fixed identity (R. Joyce 2000a: 278). These arguments have some merit. There is little doubt that homosexual acts existed among the Maya and that such conduct may have taken place in isolated locations, such as the forest, or in places of sanctioned homosexuality without the necessity of implying permanent sexual identities. A building at San Diego, Yucatan, exhibits sculpted panels of enema insertion, drunken and erratic dances, disheveled hair, and cramped stupor, many with a decided undertone of homoeroticism (e.g., Mayer 1984: pl. 146). The insertion of enemas transparently recalls the act of anal penetration to the extent that the structure at San Diego may have been a young men's house, a place where activities were permitted among youths yet, perhaps, prohibited elsewhere with respect to other age grades. (The wildness of elite youths is one of the central tropes of the Popol Vuh epic, Christenson 2000: 73, 89; a role of warfare may have been to train, test, and, above all, eliminate such destabilizing individuals.) Today, in rural Yucatan, Maya have a fairly relaxed perception of homosexual acts (Karl Taube, personal communication, 2001). These episodes are seen as little more than spasms of physical gratification, without the pervasive negative value assigned categorically to "sodomites" by colonial Spaniards (R. Joyce 2000a: 275–8).

BEING AN ACTOR

How did the Classic Maya understand the nature of a person and its capacity for action? What was their theory of agency? As mentioned before, most scholars agree that "individuals," in the sense of autonomous beings who hold rights to self-determination, are a distinctively Western notion (Dumont 1986; Lukes 1990; Mauss 1985). Nonetheless, there is evidence that traditional societies allow a role for individuals who harbor a contemplative inner life and an ability to change the established order through conscious and unconscious acts (Lienhardt 1985: 43–50). "All human beings are knowledgeable agents" who, when asked, can explain why they do what they do, although the normal course of human behavior is more a matter of habitual conduct than self-conscious, calculated action (Giddens 1984: 281). According to Edmund Leach, such individuals express an essential attribute of humanity: they dislike domination and break rules in a way that leads to new creations, new ways of acting and thinking (Leach 1977: 19–20). The exercise of imagination allows certain people to "go beyond" the current order and persuade others to follow them (Burridge 1979: 116; Rapport and Overing 2000: 4, 7; Sartre 1972: 273). By definition, they are leaders, the people who get things done by influencing others – they are persons with "power" (Giddens 1984: 283). Creative acts are seen as heroic gestures of rebellion and subversion. If generally accepted, those gestures engender new conventions. But this view sits uneasily with the more accepted idea that people everywhere, including unheroic ones, are capable of change through individual acts (Cowgill 2000: 52–3).

Most scholars would also accept that acts are not only susceptible to idiosyncratic or individual impulse but socially and culturally embedded. People respond to antecedent conditions, often without much reflection of conscious decision making. A person who is always making choices in a hyperactive manner represents a caricature of human conduct, which more often than not falls back on habitual decisions (Moore 2000: 260). There can be no truly free agents who operate outside the constraint of preexisting conditions – even Leach would propose that persons react to what came before – nor can those conditions remain unaffected by previous acts. Whether those acts are "rational" is less relevant than whether they are "reasonable" according to local understandings of common sense, logic, and morality (Geertz 1983: 85–92). Self-interest and group-interest will follow those same strictures. Thus, it might be "reasonable" for the Classic Maya to see gods, supernatural beings, and ancestors as part of their civic community. It might be "rational" to believe that both careful weeding and auto-sacrificial bloodletting ensured a good harvest.

To the Classic Maya a person was in part a kind of activated category, "a mortal, transient being . . . [in] a continuing social whole" (La Fontaine 1985: 138–9). We cannot directly access the Classic Maya self – a subjective image developed during the lifetime of an individual – but there is more to be said about their model of categorical personhood, the public projection of "what it means to be a human being: the basic essence, agency, roles, potentialities, and limitations" (Kray 1997: 29). The concept of person-as-category tends to the view that internal motivation and feelings at a particular time were less important than the need to follow prescribed forms, perform preexisting roles, and guide matters to desired ends in a routine manner (Devereaux 1987: 96). Even bodily movement or position, at least as depicted in Maya imagery, was so stylized as to suggest highly disciplined body practices and images, something that can be imagined by the stoicism involved in tooth filing, tattooing, and scarification.

Consider Classic Maya royalty. Through glyphic texts and public imagery their personalities shine with what the present-day observer might see as individualism and transparent motive. Yet evidence from royal names suggests a different notion of identity. In the first place, rulers represented replacements for grandparents, with whom they often shared names. Individual, preaccession names existed (see Chapter 5), including some that might be used after ascension to the throne, but the pattern of repetition in alternating generations dominates at sites like Caracol, Piedras Negras, and Yaxchilan. Although poorly understood, the practice hints that identities transcended generations and superseded personal individuation. Among ethnographic and ethnohistoric Maya of southern Belize, a reason to bury the dead near the living was that souls would recycle into the bodies of newborns (Gillespie 2000: 140; Thompson 1930: 82). Similar beliefs are found among the Tz'utujil and K'ichee' of Guatemala, where life cycles intersect with notions of generational renewal and replacements of grandparents by grandchildren (Carlsen and Prechtel 1991: 26; Mondloch 1980: 9; Warren 1989: 57). For this reason, Tz'utujil males may address their fathers as "child," and a child may be called "parent" (Carlsen and Prechtel 1991: 29). Another pattern occurs at Naranjo, where most kings took the name of some aspect of the Storm God, Chahk, and at Tikal, where rulers often called themselves K'awiil (see Chapters 5 and 7). This pattern points less to alternation of identities than the grouping of rulers into a subset of deities.

Figure 2.6. *Winik* or "person" in Maya texts (Houston et al. 2006, fig. 1.1).

Throughout the Classic period gods and humans alike were described in glyphic texts as *winik*, a category discussed before that translates to "person" as well as "man," "twenty" (the total sum of toes and fingers), and "month" (a conventional period of twenty days used in the Maya Long Count; see Houston et al. 2006: 11–13). Attached to this term were adjectives that tell us precisely what kind of person this might be – where they came from and which attributes they might have (Fig. 2.6). The concept of *winik* is probably the key existential concept for the Classic Maya, although it makes only an infrequent appearance in the texts. A related notion pertains to a glyphic expression **a**, meaning "person," which descends from **-a:'* in Common Mayan, the earliest reconstructible parent of Mayan languages (Houston et al. 2000).

As a label, *winik* suggests a strong connection to what has been described as the dominant spatiotemporal orientation of the Maya person (Monaghan 1998: 140). Here there is greater scope for the idea that the Classic Maya developed under unique circumstances according to historical setting and, it was thought, calendrical influence. This, then, helped form an indigenous theory of individuation that counterbalanced the concept of person-as-category. Historical and ethnographic evidence point to the common belief that people received a destiny when they were born, taking that name as a personal epithet, a practice documented, if somewhat rarely, among the Classic Maya too (Fig. 2.7). This destiny resulted from one's position at birth on the cycle of twenty sacred days and its permutation with a set of thirteen numbers (Tedlock 1992: 107–27). Among the Aztec someone born on the day "Flower" would be artistic and hardworking; a 1 Crocodile person would be fortunate

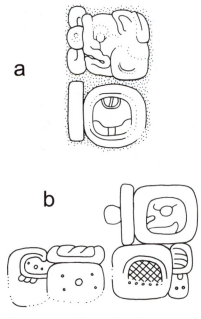

a

b

Figure 2.7. Day sign in personal names at Palenque: **(a)** sculptor, Death Head Monument, Palenque (AD 692); and **(b)** name of possible ruler, Murciélagos Vase (AD 799).

(Furst 1995: 77; Monaghan 1998: 139). People not only possessed attributes assigned by such calendrical associations but, it seems, developed into materializations of those days. (Note that birth, not conception, played a role in personhood, echoing a more general preoccupation with completed rather than incipient acts; similarly, the Maya emphasized moments in time with respect to the larger cycles that encased them, "twelve in its third k'atun" meaning "twelve counted towards finishing the third k'atun [twelve years plus two k'atuns], thus "fifty-two years.") This form of embodiment helps us understand the concept of a person as being linked to the qualities of a day and the fact that the Maya imparted a pronounced physicality to units of time. Much like lords, days of the solar month were "seated," as if in office or attendance, and rulers fused their portraits with those of key calendrical celebrations, especially those of twenty-year periods (D. Stuart 1996). This recalls the practice of ethnographic Maya who treat days as venerable lords (Colby and Colby 1981: 223; Tedlock 1992: 107).

Throughout Mesoamerica, curers claim to evaluate a person's problem according to birth date. The fact that twenty times thirteen equals the span of human gestation underscores the connection between "impersonal" time, divinatory calendars, and human existence (Earle and Snow 1985). However, these auguries were more tendencies or orientations than inflexible predispositions. They were given to many different interpretations and useful, in that flexibility, as a means of eluding inconveniences. The days were useful in distinguishing people, as implied by the K'ichee' Maya term for "destiny" or "character," *wäch*, meaning "face"; of course, a face is the most immediately recognizable, individuating trait of a person (Monaghan 1998: 139; Tedlock 1992: 108). The Classic Maya placed equal weight on the head and especially the forehead as the locus of identity (Houston and Stuart 1998: 83). In Maya representations royal and other names appeared on or above foreheads. This was less of a billboard – following the prosaic idea that such identities would be readily recognizable in the melee of battle or the complex flurry of figures in processions – than a deeper statement about where identity lies. This practice goes back to the time of the Olmec and helped lead to the development of writing as a means of identifying people by icons fused to the head. Only later did such icons physically disassociate from the body and become free-floating.

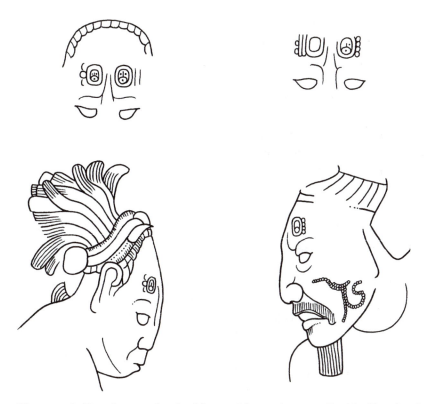

Figure 2.8. Day signs on head of figure, Museo Amparo, Puebla (drawing by David Stuart).

This was the first unambiguous writing in ancient America. One Maya sculpture, most likely from the western Maya lowlands, shows two day signs on the forehead of a ruler and his mother or spouse (Fig. 2.8). Both are Ajaw day signs and, although still poorly understood, may reflect the fusion of day names and their properties with particular individuals.

Personal destiny, though affected by matters beyond human control, could be resisted with sustained effort and guidance, just as certain days or periods could be avoided when the auguries were poor. The five unnamed-days at the end of the 365-day solar calendar were notorious in this regard. Those unlucky enough to be born on these days were considered impotent, worthless, shapeless, and even timeless (Monaghan 1998: 141). Nonetheless, the Classic Maya, who termed this time the "hole of the year" (*u-?-ha'b?*), did perform important activities on the few occasions when such dates are mentioned, as at La Mar, Palenque, and Pomona. Once more, this suggests that negative portents were possibilities rather than certainties, and that a human could counteract a personal leaning through evasive tactics. These decisions might be instigated or strengthened by messages (*muut*, "birds") sent to the figures, usually royalty, who were positioned institutionally to receive promptings from supernatural entities (Houston et al. 2006: 227–51). It may be that in this instance we see a Classic Maya understanding of dreams as meaningful inspirations. Not surprisingly, the Tzotzil Maya also attribute major activities, such as the building of churches, to the influence of certain dreams (Vogt 1969: 352). Other cues doubtless came from Classic Maya practices of divination or prayerful interventions, perhaps those involving crystals, seeds, or beans (Brady and Prufer 1999; Colby and Colby 1981: 46). In such cases decision making was essentially a group activity or, to put it into indigenous terms, a means of discerning divine will so that humans could act on it (Boremanse 1998: 61). Divination was thus a means of clarifying decision making by making its variables transparent or by assigning the impetus for action to a supernatural source.

Here, then, was the scope of flexible personal action. It existed within parameters but also allowed some leeway. One ruler might take advantage of that latitude for action, whereas another less-gifted or fortunate ruler might not. Classic Maya notions of time facilitated this flexibility. The Maya Long Count linked a current date to a starting point in 3114 BC: it recorded elapsed time with respect to a fixed marker, one date having significance only in relation to another. The Long Count, which consisted of at least five progressively larger cycles and sometimes many more, served as an ambitious chronological synthesis. It coordinated cycles, including those on a base-twenty system that recalls the sum of human digits, and included spans of twenty years (the so-called "*k'atun-ajaw*" notations) that were invoked explicitly in tabulating the current life span of rulers. It is possible that this calendar was designed by the Maya or peoples of the Isthmus of Tehuantepec to subordinate cyclic time to linear time, the suggestion being that this mode of time keeping emphasized dynastic succession over the rotation of temporary office (cf. Farriss 1995: 118–19). Long-Count time was linear, particularly if nested within cycles above that of the *bak'tun* or four-hundred-year span. But it also preserved the cyclic quality of more ancient sacred (260-day) and solar (365-day) calendars. Any completion of a major subcycle would be likened to others. Dates on 1 Ajaw might have similar properties, regardless of position within larger frames of time, and so would a one-*k'atun* (20-year) celebration share profound similarities with two-, three-, four-, and five-*k'atun* endings. The overall calendrical system guaranteed that all dates would contrast in absolute terms yet retain fundamental similarities. The Maya recognized that a day and the events taking place on it always resembled, but did not completely replicate, preceding ones. In this sense, days informed and shaped a theory of personality and destiny that connected people to time (Monaghan 1998). Moreover, by invoking a particularly Long-Count date the Classic Maya professed a connection to acts in the remote past. The use of the Long Count reaffirmed a particular view of time and its entanglement with supernatural beings.

It is probable that the Classic Maya, concerned as they were with duty and obligation, conceived of acts as being a kind of "work" or *patan*. Among modern Maya, this term or its analogues apply to acts as varied as the clearance of land for *milpa* (as in Ch'orti' Maya), the fulfillment of a customary task, practice, or calling (*oficio* in colonial dictionaries, Clark and Houston 1998: 34; see also Josserand and Hopkins n.d., *pätch'ujel*), and, to judge from Yukatekan notions of work, the "ritual" labors of a shaman, known in Yukatek as a *hmen*, "he who occupies himself" or "he who engenders or makes" (Hanks 1990: 339, 364; Monaghan 2000: 32). Among Tzotzil Maya, "work" (*'abtel*) is seen as one of two central and acceptable activities, the other being "talk" (*k'op*), which, as prayer or political oratory and gossip, allows people to have a social life and represents theologically the vocalizing capacity that first defined and vitalized humanity (Devereaux 1987: 95; Gossen 1993: 420). In a more subtle comparison, making things is compared to birth in many parts of Mesoamerica, especially in the weaving of textiles (Prechtel and Carlsen 1988: 123). Regrettably, there is no known term for "shaman" in the Classic period, nor is the widespread term for "calendar priest," *aj-k'in*, documented outside of a reference to a god. (The lack of textual salience to such figures is perplexing, particularly for the latter. It may be that "political" figures such as holy lords were ipso facto priests, so no separate identifications or descriptions for ritual specialists were necessary; see Zender 2004b) In Ch'olan languages *patan* is also a term for "tribute" and probably stems from a root, *pat*, meaning "to form" (Kaufman and Norman 1984: 128). *Patan* is evidently spelled only twice in the corpus of Classic inscriptions (*Chakpatan*, "great tribute/work"), once in a highly opaque context on an inscribed shell, the other on Dos Pilas Hieroglyphic Stairway 2, where it appears to refer to the offering of *sakpatan*, "pure" or "artificially made tribute," in connection with a battle against Tikal by Calakmul (Simon Martin, personal communication, 2001). Nonetheless, there may be references to tributaries who enumerate amounts of tribute, as in *3-pa-ta* at Chichen Itza or *18-pa-ta* at Tikal (D. Stuart 1998: 384, fig. 6). These statements do not, however, conform to parallel expressions in Classic script. They remain suggestive but obscure.

There is a strong difference between the acts recorded in Maya imagery and writing and a broader set that must surely have existed. Of everyday activities, such as grinding corn, there is ample evidence in the form of grinding tools (*manos* or pestles, and *metates*, basin-shaped mortars), a few rare images, and no textual references (M. Coe 1982: 49; Simon Martin, personal communication, 2001; Hammond 1982b: 6.2). Activities thought worthy of mention, presumably because grinding was not an elite activity, were quite limited in number, with a tendency to be "summative." What this means is that they refer to an epitomizing action, such as "seize, grab" in the case of captives, but not the acts leading up to it or the events that follow. An act is never wholly new or described in idiosyncratic terms: rather, it conforms to a formulaic category regarded as decorously appropriate for commission to hieroglyphs and imagery. The summative quality of acts is reflected, for example, in depictions of capture. Captives often wear, in advance, the garb of subjugation, a set of perforated and ripped cotton garments donned after battle, not before. To think otherwise presumes an exaggerated kind of "Aztec" flowery war, with predetermined winners and losers, an unlikely scenario for the Maya. This is the same clothing displayed by captives in front of victorious lords or within their palaces. Maya sculptors and painters evidently saw little difficulty in conflating time, merging the act of capture with the act of captive display or presentation.

Acts appearing in the hieroglyphs usually required an accompanying date. The Maya seem to have found timeless events to be a contradiction in terms: action necessitates a temporal frame, just as time involves a concreteness and tangibility that is generally absent from occidental perspectives. Acts also need spatial indicators, such as "this" (*haa'* or *hiin / hina*), or a common toponymic phrase that specifies setting. Expressions such as "he is a captive" may occur without a chronological tether, perhaps because they declare an ongoing state rather than an achievement or change. Another peculiarity of Maya texts is the relative scarcity of active transitives and the ubiquity of passive events. Among the events attested in glyphs, rulers and other elites may arrive from near (*huli*) or far (*tali*) distances, leave (*bixni*), or be forced out (*lok'oyi?*); they may die (*chami?, ochi-bih, och-ha'*) and sit as lords (*chumlaj, chumwani*). In transitive acts, they receive (*ch'amaw*), bury (*butuw*), scatter incense (*chokow*), wrap stones (*k'alaw*), heap stones (*tz'apaw*), give (*ak'aw*), or throw (*alaw*). This is not a complete list of events, but, in the most strenuous and aggressive activities, especially battle, enemies "are captured" or the spears and shields of antagonists simply "fall." And much like a peasant in the field, a ruler might carry a burden (*u-kuchuw ikaatz*) in the sense of discharging a heavy duty, much like a porter carrying a load with a tumpline. This represented, in kernel, his moral obligation to his community. In the cave texts of Naj Tunich, a lord of Caracol records that he "carries" smoke and fire by means of a tumpline glyph (Stone 1995, fig. 7–29). The metaphors of royal work thus derive in part from a vocabulary of more common activities.

SOCIALITY AMONG THE CLASSIC MAYA

The Classic Maya should be approached in their own terms according to indigenous notions of who they were and how they fit into a lattice of social commitment. In practice, limitations of evidence compel researchers to use all the tools at their disposal, including later information and expectations gleaned from the comparative method. Yet, a distillation of these data points to a key, inclusive idea: the Classic Maya lived within a world that balanced community and belief against conflict and self- or group-interest. An entirely objective perspective would limit itself to a study of "living" actors, or at least those that lived in the first millennium. That would be misleading: much like ethnographic Maya, community included supernatural beings and the dead (Bunzel 1952: 270; Gillespie 2000c: 144). The dead continued to occupy the homes and spaces of the living and could be expected to behave as members of a larger, metaphysical community operating by joint interest.

The list of actors in the moral universe of the Classic Maya was long and complex. At its summit were gods, who interacted in Maya thought with humans (see Chapter 7). Ancestors, too, formed a part of the moral community, as did other supernatural beings that were potent but not explicitly identified as deities (see Chapter 7). In royal imagery and text Maya rulers represented the pivot of this chain of being, interceding on the community's behalf with more ethereal beings (see Chapter 5). The reality is that they never achieved a complete claim to monopolize such contact. Serving the ruler, and sometimes in opposition to him, were nobles and lesser members of the royal family. Existentially, they were of a different order from rulers, although the definition of a noble was probably someone of real or fictive royal descent, however remote (see Chapter 6). This left the most mysterious group of Classic Maya – the men and women, the farmers, knappers, weavers, carvers, traders, builders, fishers, and hunters who constituted the bulk of society (Chapters 8 and 9). Much is known about the work they left behind but little about their identity or social organization. Hovering at the margins of the Classic Maya world were outsiders and foreigners (see Chapter 6). The Maya were intensely conscious of cultural differences but did not so much assimilate as encyst such influences, displaying them, when appropriate, in a manner that maintained cultural boundaries.

The idea that a Maya community would consist of seen and unseen beings strikes the present-day observer as illogical. In some respects, this is the predicament of all students of the past, since they bring something of themselves to that encounter. A society conceiving of religion in limited terms would be inclined to view Classic Maya beliefs as elite mystifications or propaganda (Houston 1999). Yet there is no inherent contradiction between beliefs of this sort and self-interested schemes or stratagems, or the presence of "aggrandizers" vying for prestige and social resources. What is needed is a perceptive portrait of the Classic Maya, where spirits interact routinely with humans and sacred postulates seem natural or even inescapable. A noble could seek marriage alliances with the king to improve his personal prospects and those of his lineage. He might be far more reluctant to seek any usurpation of the king's position, since this maneuver would jeopardize a system based on sacred

bloodlines. The maneuver would go too far – beyond the elastic capabil-
ities of the moral community and into the volatile unpredictability of the
fractured society. That the Classic Maya lived with integration and division,
solidarity and discord, is plainly true. Finding out how they did so is the test
before us.

CHAPTER 3

BEGINNINGS

PRECLASSIC HERITAGE

Classic Maya society, like any other grouping, arose from the heritage of its predecessors. Although the "Classic period" refers, as its name implies, to the era of the most sophisticated cultural achievements, the basic elements of its society and culture, including centralized government, social stratification, monumental architecture, and writing, were already present during earlier times. A central question, then, concerns the genesis of lowland Maya civilization: when did it first flourish and how did it lead to what came after? ("Civilization," a label controversial to some scholars, means simply a set of cultural practices and ideas that tend to accompany a society with pronounced centralization and inequality, Cowgill 1991: 256; see Redfield and Singer 1954). During the Preclassic period, lowland Maya civilization, with its shared cultural traits of language, monumental imagery, and architecture, emerged throughout the Yucatan Peninsula and surrounding regions. The spread of similar practices and ideas across space and their continuity through time are notable in comparison to other parts of Mesoamerica, which did not always have the same degree of coherence or fixity. Yet there is considerable evidence, too, for interregional diversity within the Maya lowlands and little proof of a monolithic culture shared by every member of a community. As noted in Chapter 1, the overarching identity of being "Maya" was weakly developed.

The advent of lowland Maya civilization in Preclassic times was coupled with a momentous process in which relatively small, essentially egalitarian groups transformed into larger, internally diverse ones. Such social changes were underwritten by two general trends that relate to the "moral community" and "divided society" discussed in Chapter 2. The first trend was the development of social integration that bound ever-larger populations into political and moral cohesion. This process took place through a shared sense of belonging and a submission to common beliefs and values, as validated by social and ritual practice. The second trend involved increasing internal heterogeneity and subdivision among corporate groups and factions, along with rising social inequalities in power, wealth, and prestige. The development of Maya rulership touched on both themes. Kings became centers of community integration and accelerants of elite domination.

One important aspect of rulership is the effect of ideologies that shaped individual perceptions of social roles and positions (see Gardiner 1992: 65; Therborn 1980: 2). How did people come to accept differences in social status, and how did they abandon what was probably a primordial, egalitarian ethos? Many Maya are likely to have shared certain ideologies that legitimized or tolerated social inequality, but groups and individuals could also have held divergent views of what those ideologies meant (see Abercrombie et al. 1980, 1990). In addressing this question, it is useful to examine how different groups of people, particularly elites and nonelites, changed or maintained diverse practices, not only in relation to governmental institutions but to daily routines at home and in the village. Often, too, shifts and continuities take place across a wide area. A recurrent theme in scholarly debates on the Preclassic Maya is the evaluation of local development in the lowlands against the impact of external influence, particularly from a set of societies known today as the "Olmec." When the lowland Maya had barely begun to establish village life or to make ceramics, the Gulf Coast Olmec already had large settlements with impressive stone monuments. Did the surrounding groups cast a prevailing influence over the lowland Maya, or did the local residents find selective inspiration from neighbors? Discussion of the Classic period focuses of necessity on internal dynamics within lowland Maya society, but this chapter deals extensively with external relations.

NEW WAYS OF LIFE

Early Villages and Ceramics

Pollen analysis indicates that, with the onset of the Holocene, the environment of the Maya area transformed from arid to wetter conditions. Around 10,000 years ago, the southern lowlands were covered by rainforest with tree taxa comparable to today's local vegetation (Leyden 1984).

Study of lake cores shows forest disturbance and maize pollen or phytoliths around 6,000 or 5,000 BC in Panama (Piperno 1989; Piperno and Pearsall 1993) and around 5,000 BC on the southern Gulf Coast of Mesoamerica (Pope et al. 2001). In contrast, the earliest pollen evidence of cultivated maize and manioc in the Maya lowlands, coming from Belize, dates to 3,400 BC (Pohl et al. 1996). The environmental impact of these earlier inhabitants on the Maya lowlands appears to have been relatively small, and substantial deforestation did not occur until 2,400 BC in Belize and around 2,000 BC in Peten (Brenner et al. 1990; Deevey et al. 1979). Thus, long before the appearance of ceramics, the Maya

Figure 3.1. Distribution of early ceramics in the Maya lowlands.

lowlands were probably occupied by a small population that practiced mixed subsistence, including plant cultivation with forest clearance, hunting, and gathering. Although archaeological evidence of such early occupation remains scarce, researchers have identified stone tools possibly used by preceramic populations in Belize and Yucatan, including points for hunting and axes for cutting trees and digging (Alvarez 1982; Iceland 1997; Velázquez 1980).

During the early half of the Middle Preclassic period (1000–300 BC), or possibly slightly earlier, sedentary communities coalesced in various parts of the southern lowlands. This was the time when the foundations of Maya civilization came into being, as most clearly reflected in the appearance and spread of ceramics (Fig. 3.1). Cunil pottery in the Belize River Valley and around Holmul in eastern Peten appears to represent the earliest pottery in the Maya lowlands, with dates of 1,200 to 900 BC (Awe 1992; Awe et al. 1990;

Figure 3.2. Reconstruction drawings of Cunil ceramics (Clark and Cheetham 2002, fig. 8, courtesy of the New World Archaeological Foundation).

Garber et al. 2004). These ceramics have dull red and black slips, and characteristic modes include postslip incisions on horizontally everted rims (Fig. 3.2). Pottery in other parts of the Maya lowlands followed around 1,000 or 900 BC. In northern Belize, the Swasey complex at Cuello and related Bolay ceramics at Colha contain glossy red slips that resemble later Mamom ceramics and lack characteristic attributes of Cunil pottery (Cheetham 2005: 28; Valdez 1987: 233–7). Although the original claim of Swasey dating to the beginning of the Early Preclassic has been refuted (Andrews and Hammond 1990; Hammond et al. 1991: 62), its precise timing is still debated. John Clark and David Cheetham (2003) emphasize its resemblance to Mamom ceramics and place the beginning of Swasey around 850 BC. Rosemary Joyce and John Henderson (2001), however, point out that this complex includes pattern burnished unslipped pottery with micaceous paste, similar to Early Preclassic materials from Puerto Escondido, Honduras. If so, the early facet of Swasey may date to as early as 1100 BC. In the Belize River Valley, Cunil ceramics were followed by the Jenny Creek complex around 900 BC, identified at the site of Barton Ramie.

For the central lowlands, Clark and Cheetham (2003; Cheetham et al. 2003) argue that the early facet of the Eb complex found at Tikal bears some similarities to Cunil in its incisions and red and black slips, suggesting the development of Eb from this predecessor (Culbert 1977: 36; 1993). Comparable ceramics, Ah Pam, are found in the Lake Yaxha and Lake Sacnab Basins (Rice 1979: 13–22; Hermes 1999). The early Ox complex in the Mirador Basin is another point of controversy. Richard Hansen (1998: 55–6; 2005) presents radiocarbon dates between 1,400 and 1,000 BC associated with Ox pottery, which would thrust them long before Eb and Swasey. These ceramics, however, display waxy slips characteristics of later Mamom ceramics, which leads

Figure 3.3. Real-Xe ceramics excavated from Ceibal (photograph by Takeshi Inomata).

Clark and colleagues (2000: 501) to doubt the validity of these results and to suggest a date of around 900 BC. Hansen (2005) counters, pointing to the presence of traits common among the Early Preclassic ceramics of Mesoamerica, including red-rimmed tecomates and finger punctuations.

The earliest ceramics in the Pasión area (Fig. 3.3) are the Xe complex found at Altar de Sacrificios (Adams 1971) and the Real complex at Ceibal (Sabloff 1975), possibly dating to 900 BC. These complexes from the Pasión area have matte red and black slips, and Cheetham (2005) stresses their similarities to Cunil ceramics. In the Xe and Real complexes, however, postslip incisions on horizontally everted rims are relatively rare. Instead, Xe and Real ceramics include a substantial amount of vessels with matte white slips, which are prevalent in the Chiapas highlands and rare in the Cunil and Eb complexes (Bryant et al. 2005). Xe and Real pottery may represent a transitional form between Chiapas and eastern lowland materials. Further down the river, the Chiuaan complex of the middle Usumacinta region closely resembles the Gulf Coast materials, although the residents of this area adopted waxy Maya ceramics during the Late Classic period (Rands 1977, 1987). In the northern lowlands, the reevaluation of the Ek ceramic complex from Komchen identified postslip incisions tied to Cunil ceramics, despite differences in slip colors and vessel shapes. Similar materials were also found at Kiuic in the Puuc region (Andrews et al. 2008). These ceramics were followed by the Nabanche complex at Dzibilchaltun and Komchen and its related pottery in Campeche and Yucatan, all characterized by heavy-walled vessels as well as low-gloss black and variegated buff-to-orange wares (Joesink-Mandeville 1977; Ball 1978).

Our knowledge of these ceramics is still fragmentary, but most researchers agree that the introduction of ceramics correlated with the development of more sedentary modes of life. Pottery betokens a long-term investment in a particular place, where fragile yet heavy objects can be used and stored. Remains of probable residential structures from the early Middle Preclassic period are best documented at Cuello (Cartwright, Gerhardt, and Hammond 1991). These consisted of round or apsidal low platforms with plaster floors and postholes that supported superstructures of perishable materials. Similar buildings have been found at Colha (Potter et al. 1984), K'axob (McAnany and López Varela 1999) and Blackman Eddy (Garber et al. 2004); indeed, all resemble earlier or contemporaneous structures outside the Maya lowlands (e.g., Clark and Blake 1994). Buildings associated with Cunil ceramics at Cahal Pech, however, appear to have been rectangular (Cheetham 1998), hinting at either a wide variety of plans that happen to be incompletely sampled or the early appearance of distinct traditions of vernacular architecture. Excavators at Cuello also identified three structures surrounding a patio, whose layout is similar to patio groups typical of the Classic period (Cartwright, Gerhardt, and Hammond 1991). Most burials were placed under house platforms, again prefiguring practices of the Classic period (Hammond 1999; Robin and Hammond 1991; McAnany et al. 1999). Basic forms of Classic Maya sociality, which linked household organization and ancestor veneration, probably materialized during the early Middle Preclassic period.

Predecessors and Contemporaries in Southeastern Mesoamerica

Social changes in the Maya lowlands did not occur in isolation. The earliest pottery in southeastern Mesoamerica is found on the southern Pacific Coast. These Barra ceramics, dating to 1,800 to 1,700 BC, are fairly elaborate, and Clark and Blake (1994; Clark and Gosser 1995) suggest that people aspiring to high status and control over others employed these novel objects in the course competitive feasting. The ceramics may thus signal a transition from egalitarian societies to ones with hereditary inequality. During the following Locona phase (1,700 to 1,500 BC), an edifice much larger than other buildings nearby was constructed at Paso de la Amada, Chiapas. Clark and Blake (Blake 1991; Clark 1997) interpret this as an elite residence and as evidence of established hereditary inequality, but there remains the possibility that it was a communal structure, perhaps even a men's house (see Lesure 1997; Marcus and Flannery 1996: 90–1). Either way, it is clear that the southern Pacific Coast was several centuries ahead of the Maya lowlands in its ceramic technology and village lifeway. A possible ballcourt appears to have been built at Paso de la Amada around this time, indicating other kinds of collective action (Hill and Clark 1991). Similar social changes were in progress in other parts of Mesoamerica, including the southern Gulf Coast. Ceramics like those of the southern

Pacific Coast appear to have spread through the Isthmus of Tehuantepec to the southern Gulf Coast (Clark and Gosser 1995). Clark et al. (2000) suggest that this distribution corresponds to that of Mixe-Zoquean speakers, although the conjecture is almost impossible to prove. At Copan, Rayo ceramics dating to around 1,500 to 1,200 BC bear some similarities to Isthmian materials (Viel 1993). A possibility, not easily testable, is that the residents of western Honduras also spoke non-Mayan languages (Clark et al. 2000: 452).

Around 1,400 BC, spectacular developments in social stratification and rulership took place on the southern Gulf Coast. Material expressions of this new form of society consisted of enormous platforms, massive stone monuments, and finely crafted portable objects. This "Olmec" civilization is generally considered the first in Mesoamerica. Along with the growth of centers on the southern Gulf Coast, distinctive art styles, including the motifs known problematically as the "were-jaguar" and "fire-serpent," spread throughout Mesoamerica. The use of the term "Olmec" has been confusing and controversial. By the term "Gulf Coast Olmec" we mean the occupants of the area who were responsible for the precocious, near-urban settlements of San Lorenzo, La Venta, and other centers and might have been (but were not certainly) speakers of Mixe-Zoquean languages. Regrettably, there is no internal evidence for this linguistic affiliation in the form of hieroglyphic texts. The links of certain Mixe-Zoquean terms to the Olmec tend to be unpersuasive, pertaining instead to far earlier developments relating to agriculture (Campbell and Kaufman 1976). At the least, Olmec styles and traits reflect specific religious beliefs and elite ideologies, which spread in a wide area from central Mexico, Guerrero, and on to Lower Central America during the Early and Middle Preclassic periods.

The nature of Olmec civilization has been one of the most vigorously debated problems in Mesoamerican archaeology. Some view Gulf Coast society as a "mother culture" (M. Coe 1965). Others believe that such formations resulted from evenly balanced interactions between different regions of Mesoamerica (Demarest 1989; Flannery and Marcus 1994; Grove 1996). Such debates have been shaped not only by available archaeological data but by theoretical predisposition. Until the 1970s, conquest, migration, and diffusion had been major themes of archaeological explanation; thereafter, the popularity of the so-called "processual" archaeology began to lend greater emphasis to internal processes of social change. Recent years have witnessed a reevaluation of interregional movements of people and ideas. Although complex and two-directional interactions must have figured in social changes of the Greater Isthmian region, the relations between the southern Gulf Coast societies and other areas were probably asymmetrical (Stark 2000; Lesure 2004; Pool 2007: 17). There is increasing evidence that the Gulf Coast Olmec had more pronounced social stratification and political centralization, and that the concepts of rulership mirrored in stone monuments in various parts of Mesoamerica were most likely inspired by either direct or indirect contacts with the Gulf Coast Olmec. Recent data on unidirectional moves of ceramics from San Lorenzo to various parts of Mesoamerica provide strong support for this view (Blomster et al. 2005; Neff et al. 2006).

San Lorenzo became a major center around 1,400 BC. Its gargantuan platform was dotted with colossal heads and other stone monuments hauled from distant quarries. Colossal heads seem to have depicted individuals rulers, each identified by preglyphic signs emblazoned on the head. Recent excavations by Ann Cyphers (1999) have revealed possible elite residences, next to which were possible workshops for recarving stone monuments. Finds like these indicate the presence of highly developed social stratification with well-established rulership. Central authorities commanded a large labor force that included craft specialists (Coe 1965a; Lowe 1989). The contemporaneous, water-logged site of El Manatí provides a rare glimpse of the Olmec spiritual world. Offerings of rubber balls, greenstone axes, and wooden sculptures were deposited at a spring (Ortíz and Rodíguez 1999), disclosing the importance of rituals related to water and hills, along with the practice of the ballgame in this early period. A remarkable aspect of the San Lorenzo chronology is the rapidity of social transformation. A span of only three or four centuries separated the appearance of ceramics from the establishment of a large center with centralized administration.

During the Early Preclassic period before 1000 BC, evidence of direct control by the Gulf Coast Olmec in southeastern Mesoamerica confines itself mostly to the middle Grijalva Basin and to the southern Chiapas Coast (Clark and Pye 2000). Although differentially fired black and white wares are sometimes considered markers of Olmec influence, Demarest (1989) argues that these ceramics derived from a common tradition in what is called the Greater Isthmian region, stretching from the southern Gulf Coast to the Guatemalan Pacific Coast and Guatemalan highlands, all the way to western Honduras and El Salvador (see Lowe 1977). Relevant data were recovered at Copan, Honduras. Excavations by William Fash deep under Group 9N-8, a Classic-period residential group, revealed a series of rich, elite burials with so-called Gordon ceramics (1,200–1,000 BC) (Fash 1991: 67–70; Viel 1993). Some ceramic vessels were carved with common Olmec motifs, such as the "flame-eyebrow" and "hand-wing," and Burial VIII-27 contained over three hundred drilled jade pieces. Although Copan later became an important Classic Maya center, during the Preclassic period it had closer ties to the Greater Isthmian region than to the Maya lowlands.

Around 1,000 BC San Lorenzo declined, and La Venta became the preeminent Olmec center. La Venta showed significant innovations in site plans and material culture, which probably reflected further developments in royal ideology. Colossal heads were found at La Venta, but they may have been coeval with San Lorenzo examples. A new, dominant form of stone monument was the stela with bas-relief, and jade figures of supernatural motifs became common, perhaps because of the discovery of new jade sources of exceptional quality and lustrous color in the Sierra de las Minas of present-day Guatemala (Taube et al. 2004). Site planning at La Venta was different from San Lorenzo, in that pyramids, mounds, and plazas defined ceremonial spaces. During the period between 1,000 to 750 BC, rapid changes in architecture, site planning, and monumental art occurred throughout the Greater Isthmian region, including Tabasco (Sisson 1976) and Chiapas (Lee 1989; Lowe 1977). In the southern Guatemalan highlands, the residents of Kaminaljuyu began to construct earthen platforms around 900 to 800 BC (Escobedo et al. 1996; Román 1993), and the nearby center of Naranjo rose to be an important ceremonial locus in the Valley of Guatemala. Recent investigations led by Barbara Arroyo (Arroyo et al. 2007) at the latter site dated a series of plain monuments to 700 to 500 BC. In the northern Guatemalan highlands, earthen platforms similar to those at Kaminaljuyu were built around 850 BC (Sharer and Sedat 1987). About the same time, some centers on the Pacific Coast began to construct large mounds comparable to Pyramid C of La Venta. For example, now-destroyed Mound 1 at La Blanca on the western Guatemalan Coast (Love 1990) was twenty-five meteres high, and the El Trapiche E3–1–2 mound in western El Salvador was twenty meters high (Sharer 1989). Olmec-style stone monuments also began to appear in these areas, including examples from Takalik Abaj on the Guatemalan Coast and the Chalchuapa area in western El Salvador. These shifts in material culture were closely connected to increasing social inequality. At Kaminaljuyu, the first elite burials appeared around 800 BC (López 1993). The placement of pyramids and monuments implies not only a larger investment of material and labor. Buildings such as these imposed new sets of meaning and orderings of space, perhaps with links to emerging social relations and values (Love 1999).

The Maya Lowlands in the Mesoamerican World

The occupants of the Maya lowlands were the last major group in Mesoamerica to adopt pottery (Clark and Cheetham 2003). Why were the use of ceramics and the development of sedentary communities significantly later than here than in surrounding areas with similar elevations and ecology? Were there earlier, as-yet-undetected settlements of great scale in the Maya lowlands? The paucity of archaeological remains in the Maya lowlands dating to the Early Preclassic partly stems from environmental conditions. Soil formation is slow, organic remains seldom endure, and many materials left on the surface wash away with driving, seasonal rains. Most parts of the Maya lowlands lack deep stratigraphy, and early materials mixed with later objects might go unrecognized. Nevertheless, given the large amount of excavation conducted in the Maya lowlands, this scarcity of data probably reflects the exiguous reality of early occupation. Population levels in the Maya lowlands before 1,000 BC were most likely low.

A critical factor in such cultural and social tardiness may have been the nature of maize agriculture. During the Early Preclassic period, maize cobs were quite small and maize cultivation may not have been highly productive. Arnold (2000) suggests that maize did not become an essential part of subsistence on the southern Gulf Coast until the Middle Preclassic period. Stable carbon isotope analysis of skeletal remains from the Pacific Coast of Chiapas and Guatemala by Blake and others (1992) indeed show that maize was only a small part of diet during the Early Preclassic period, but its consumption notably increased around 1,000 BC. Macrobotanical remains of maize from early periods are still limited, but maize cobs may have reached a length of around 6 cm, along with a larger number of rows (Clark et al. 2007: 33). In addition, Taube (2004) notes that maize symbolism in Olmec iconography dates mostly to the Middle Preclassic. The occupants of the southern Gulf Coast and Pacific Coast may have relied significantly on riverine and marine resources during the Early Preclassic period. The Maya lowlands, with the exception of Belize and parts of Tabasco and Campeche, probably did not have comparable natural resources. Opening the rainforest required heavy infusions of labor. Until genetic changes in maize led to sufficient cob sizes, the Maya lowlands may simply not have been a desirable place for agriculturalists (Puleston and Puleston 1971; Willey 1970). It is suggestive that a concentration of preceramic remains has been found in northern Belize, where riverine resources were more abundant and periodic depositions of alluvium allowed sustainable yields with even relatively modest effort. Although preceramic populations in the Maya lowlands engaged in forest cropping and plant cultivation, the development of pottery and sedentary villages corresponds, by one interpretation, to a threshold in subsistence: the time when local Maya committed fully to agriculture centered on maize cultivation.

In making this argument, we do not wish to give an impression of ecological determinism. Our view is that the synergy of cultural and natural forces can bring about varying results in different historical settings. It appears more than a coincidence that the rapid spread of village life with ceramics in the Maya lowlands corresponded to apparent shifts in maize cultivation. If agricultural productivity played a central role in this social change, it was an expression of a historical process shaped by the convergence of various other conditions.

Notably, most early ceramics are found in sites near surface bodies of water, including areas along the Belize River and Pasión River (Ball 1977). In the central lowlands, early sites (and later large centers) are located near *bajos*. Previously, scholars believed that these seasonal swamps were once perennial wetlands or lakes, but there was little supporting evidence for this belief (Harrison 1977). A recent study by Nicholas Dunning and colleagugs (2002) in northern Belize shows from pollen and sedimentation that some of the *bajos* did indeed hold water year-round until the end of the Preclassic period, when soil erosion resulting from deforestation transformed many *bajos*. Similarly, Richard Hansen and colleagues (2002) argue that *bajos* in the Mirador

Basin were perennial marshes until the end of the Preclassic. These permanent bodies of water provided both reliable sources of water and a wide range of ecological resources, including fish, water fowl, and varied vegetation.

The early ceramics from the Maya lowlands were well-developed technically. Clearly, they did not represent independent inventions. Archaeologists have suspected that this technology and all that it implied organizationally were brought by early colonizers who migrated from elsewhere. Some of the Cunil vessels exhibit incised designs comparable to Olmec pottery, including so-called *k'an* crosses, flame eyebrows, and pointed motifs (Cheetham et al. 2003: fig. 6). Garber and colleagues (2004) suggest that the closest similarities are found in Chotepe ceramics from Puerto Escondido, Honduras (Joyce and Henderson 2001). Andrews (1990) suggests that the Xe-Real ceramics were made by Mixe-Zoquean speakers who migrated from Chiapas. In addition, LeRoy Joesink-Mandeville (1970) has suggested that Nabanche ceramics in the northern lowlands are more closely related to the pottery of the Gulf Coast Olmec area than to the southern Maya lowlands, and that they were brought there by migrants. Most archaeologists, including Andrews (1986: 36), believe that there is little clear evidence for such migrations to the northern lowlands, however. Increasing evidence of preceramic occupation compels us to examine the active roles of indigenous lowland populations, who were unlikely to have been passive interlocutors in this process. Cheetham (1998, 2005) has reevaluated early ceramics from the Maya lowlands, contending that scholars overemphasize interregional differences. Clark and Cheetham (2003) also emphasize that there are no clear antecedents of early Maya lowland ceramics in surrounding areas, and they speculate that the indigenous occupants of the Maya lowlands adopted new ceramic technologies from neighboring regions but also applied styles used on local containers made of perishable materials. These observations lead them to argue that the Maya lowlands had been occupied by the Maya since preceramic times and that the early ceramic complexes with prevalent red-slipped vessels developed directly into succeeding Mamom pottery. Again, such direct correlations between ceramic styles and ethnic identities remain tentative. Many specialists of Preclassic Maya ceramics still regard Xe-Real pottery as quite distinct from other contemporaneous Maya ceramics. Overly dichotomized views between migrations and local adoptions are probably misleading. Diverse yet related trajectories of ceramic development in various parts of the Maya lowlands appear to reflect a complex interplay between internal processes and external influence.

The Emergence of a Divided Society

The introduction of pottery and sedentary villages to the Maya lowlands was quickly followed by the establishment of hereditary inequality. Jaime Awe (1992) and Cheetham (1998; Clark and Cheetham 2003) believe that hereditary inequality was already present during the Cunil phase at Cahal Pech, Belize. They point out that Structure B-IV 10a-sub was placed on a high plastered floor and its walls were painted, whereas other buildings sat on lower platforms with earth floors. This large structure was also associated with a large amount of imported goods, such as jade, marine shells, and obsidian. Yet these data were obtained from small test excavations, and their interpretation continues to be debated. There is a possibility that the elaborate structure was a communal building or that the status of its occupants was acquired rather than inherited. Even so, Cahal Pech reflects the presence of leaders who were able to organize the labor and activities of village members. Such organization would have been a direct precursor to the hereditary inequality that followed soon after. Patricia McAnany and Sandra López Verela (1999:155) report that during the early Chaakkax period at K'axob (800–600 BC), status differentiation, possibly gender based, was already notable, and one adult male burial contained more than two thousand shell beads. According to Norman Hammond (1999: 50; see also Wilk and Wilhite 1991), by 650 BC Cuello was a substantial community with a population of five hundred, and differences in burial offerings may reflect emerging hereditary inequality (Hammond 1999). A jade from an early Middle Preclassic (late Bladen 650 BC) child burial resembles pieces from Chacsinkin, Yucatan (see the later section titled "Olmec Connections"; Andrews 1986, 1987). A similar ornament is also worn by a figure in the monument from San Antonio Suchitepequez (Shook and Heizer 1976). At Nakbe by 600 BC there already were differences in access to prestige goods and in sizes of residential structures (Hansen 1998). Cranial deformation and dental inlays were also present. Although these traits do not always signal high status (Krejci and Culbert 1995), they show the beginning of cultural traits that would continue to be used throughout pre-Hispanic times and point to the human body as a field of social display.

The Middle Preclassic occupants of Cahal Pech, Cuello, and Nakbe had access to interregional trade goods, such as *Strombus* shells from the Caribbean and jade from the Motagua River. At Cival, near Holmul, and at Ceibal, celts and other jade artifacts were placed in cruciform caches that closely resembled those found at La Venta, Tabasco, and San Isidro in Chiapas (see section titled "Olmec Connections"). Researchers have also recovered obsidian from the Guatemalan highlands in association with pre-Mamon ceramics. At most sites, including Cahal Pech (Awe and Healy 1994) and Barton Ramie (Willey et al. 1965: 444–5), many of these obsidian artifacts were flakes, although a small number of obsidian blades are reported from the central Peten lakes region (Rice 1984), Cuello (McSwain et al. 1991b), and Ceibal (Aoyama 2006). Obsidian blade technology first appeared at the beginning of the Middle Preclassic in Chiapas, on the Guatemalan Pacific Coast, and in western Honduras (Aoyama 1999; Clark 1987; Jackson and Love 1991). The Maya lowlands caught up with this trend soon after. Clark (1987) argues that blade technology may have required some degree of coordination between quarry specialists at distant obsidian sources and blade producers, thus reflecting more complex political organization or at least long-distance contact (see Awe and Healy 1994; Jackson and Love 1991). Nonetheless, in the Old World, blades appear onwards from the Upper Paleolithic period without such organizational sophistication.

Other artifacts provide equally significant evidence of social and cultural practices. Barkbeaters, a ridged and grooved stone for the production of paper, occur in early Middle Preclassic levels at Cuello (McSwain et al. 1991a: 189–90) and K'axob (McAnany and López Verela 1999: 157) and in the late Middle Preclassic layer at Ceibal (Willey 1978: 55, 80). The Maya may have been making paper for books, but it is possible that the material was used for clothing, decoration, and absorptive, flammable offerings in ritual. Solid hand-molded figurines have been found in small number from the Swasey phase at Cuello (McSwain et al. 1991a) and from the Real-Xe phase at Ceibal (Willey 1978: 9). These figurines were probably related to beliefs and rituals held at household and community levels, although their precise meaning eludes archaeologists.

The emergence of new patterns of social relation and associated beliefs is particularly well reflected in architecture. The residents of Nakbe started to build two-to-three-meter high platforms and associated plazas towards the end of the early Middle Preclassic period (Clark et al. 2000). Some buildings contained thick stucco floors and stone block weighing roughly one hundred kilograms (Hansen 1998: 60). About the same time, a two-meter-high platform, Structure B1–5th, was built at the smaller site of Blackman Eddy in the Belize River Valley (Garber et al. 2004). At Ceibal, excavations in the platform in front of Structure A-24 revealed substantial constructions dating to the early Middle Preclassic period. With no less than fifteen episodes of expansion, this building measured at least five meters in height by the end of the Real-Xe phase. Interestingly, the structure was made of dense clay, with some floors consisting of gravels and what appears to be crushed limestone (Bachand et al. 2005; Schwendener and Inomata 2006). This construction technique contrasts with the masonry buildings of the central lowlands and reflects, along with the associated Real-Xe ceramics, closer affinities to Chiapas and the southern Gulf Coast. These findings suggest that the initial development of monumental construction was already underway in various parts of the Maya lowlands, although details varied considerably.

CRYSTALLIZATION OF LOWLAND MAYA CULTURE

Sharing Practices and Ideas across Regions

The onset of the late Middle Preclassic period around 700 or 600 BC witnessed substantial social changes, marked by the broader sharing of cultural practices

across regions and the increasing institutionalization of social inequality and
political centralization. A ceramic style called Mamom spread in much of the
Maya lowlands (Fig. 3.4, Willey et al. 1967; Forsyth 1999). This tendency
towards ceramic homogeneity culminated in the following Chicanel ceramic
sphere. Mamom ceramics were significantly different from materials found
in neighboring areas. In the Mamom sphere, red and orange ceramics with
waxy slips were dominant, contrasting with the Greater Isthmian materials of
black, white, and differentially fired wares. The ocherous and earthen tones of
Mamom pottery may been both aesthetically and technologically motivated:
Maya buildings tend also to have been slathered with red pigment, perhaps as
a herbicide against fungus (Ray Matheny, personal communication, 1998), a
colorant that muted surfaces in intense sunlight, and a tint associated by later
Maya with blood, intensity, and greatness. The distinctive ceramic traditions
in the Maya lowlands and in the Greater Isthmian region were maintained
throughout the Preclassic period (Andrews 1986; Demarest 1989; Lowe 1978).
The wide distribution of Mamom ceramics represents the emergence of a
lowland Maya cultural sphere.

The origin of Mamom pottery is still poorly understood, but its likely roots
are found in the central to eastern lowlands, including the Mirador Basin
and northern Belize, where the first manifestation of Mamom appears in the
form of glossy to waxy slips. In the Belize Valley, represented by the Jenny
Creek complex, Mamom-like slipped vessels were gradually accepted, but
local types persisted as utilitarian wares (Ball and Taschek 2003). At Ceibal,
however, the transition appears to have been more drastic. The matte slip of
Real-Xe ceramics was quickly replaced by waxy-slipped types. In the northern
lowlands, local Nabanche types seem to have coexisted with newly introduced
Mamom ceramics (Ball and Taschek 2007).

The trend towards ceramic homogeneity was paralleled by changes in architecture. Investigations at Nakbe illustrate that, in the late Middle Preclassic
period, residents created major platforms, pyramids up to eighteen meters
high, and public plazas (Hansen 1998). Builders at Nakbe used even larger
stone blocks of consistent size and form (up to a meter long and half a meter
wide) than in early Middle Preclassic buildings (Hansen 1998: 71). Substantial
Middle Preclassic buildings may also be present at El Mirador, covered by vast
Late Preclassic constructions. Contemporaneous monumental structures were
found in other areas of the southern lowlands, including Tikal, Uaxactun, and
Río Azul, along with evidence of large-scale levelings and abrasions of natural
limestone outcrops (Adams 1999: 40–1; Laporte and Valdés 1993). Recent
investigations confirm that the northern lowlands participated in this trend: at
Yaxuna excavators detected a ten-meter-high building, and comparable constructions were found at Komchen, Acanceh, Xocnaceh, and Poxila (Andrews
et al. 2008; Andrews 1990; Stanton and Ardren 2005).

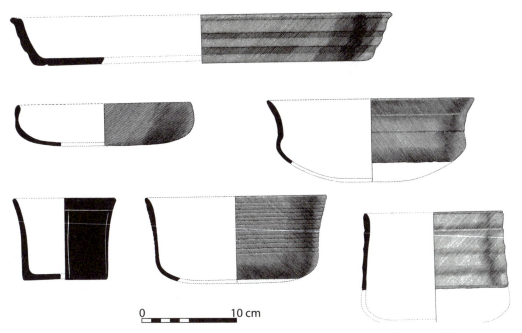

Figure 3.4. Mamom ceramic vessels (Smith 1955, fig. 14, courtesy of the Middle American Research Institute, Tulane University).

Masonry construction became a defining feature of lowland Maya architecture. Earlier and contemporaneous monumental constructions in the Greater Isthmian region, including those at La Venta, La Blanca, Takalik Abaj, and Kaminaljuyu, were primarily of earth, if sometimes covered by stone facings (González 1996; Lowe 1962). At Ceibal the change in ceramics may have been paralleled by the introduction of masonry constructions, with plaster floors in its civic core (Bachand et al. 2005), but many buildings still contained a substantial amount of earth in their fills. In comparison to the rapid change in ceramic at this center, the shift in construction techniques was gradual. At Altar de Sacrificios, where limestone is not locally available, earthen buildings continued to be made (Willey 1973:27). Thus, the choice of building materials was partly affected by availability, partly by cultural decisions.

Prominent forms of public architecture during this period were circular platforms and so-called "E-Group" complexes, first identified in Group E at Uaxactun, hence the name. At Uaxactun four circular platforms measuring thirty to forty centimeters in height and 5.5 to 5.8 meters in diameter were uncovered under the Group E plaza (Ricketson and Ricketson 1937). At Cahal Pech excavators found four circular platforms up to two to three meters in height and nine-and-a-half meters in diameter. Aimers et al. (2000) observe that these were open-air platforms without superstructure and that ample spaces were reserved around them. This suggests that such configurations served as stages of public performance, at which time members of the community aggregated. Aimers et al. (2000) argue that these rituals were tied to ancestor veneration, but it is uncertain whether these buildings were originally intended for mortuary deposits. Excavations at Ceibal revealed a circular structure and a rectangular platform built next to each other on a large platform, suggesting that circular buildings might have been used for diverse purposes. After the Preclassic period, circular platforms seem to have become less important, although their presence is known, if spotty, at a number of sites. At Uaxactun the circular platforms were later covered by an E-Group plaza.

The E-Group complex consisted of a pyramidal building on the western side and an elongated platform on a north–south axis to the east. This building arrangement continued into the Classic period, although later versions often included three temple structures on the eastern platform (Blom 1924; Ruppert 1940: 222). It was suggested that the complex at Uaxactun was oriented to the sun on the solstices and equinox, but Aveni and Hartung (1989: 451–5) have shown that most E-Group complexes at other Maya sites do not exhibit exact solar alignments. The function and symbolism of E-Group complexes are still being discussed, probably not in ways that can ever be resolved (Aimers and Rice 2006). Indeed, it may be a mistake to view them as proto-observatories or as concerned with anything other than general solar orientation. Karl Taube has shown that the iconography of the central pyramid in the example at Uaxactun seems connected with feathered serpents, the course of wind or rain from the east, and cosmic mountains, and other such pyramids may have related but still distinct iconography (Saturno et al. 2005: fig. 17b).

As for dating, an E-Group complex identified by Laporte and Fialko (Laporte and Fialko 1995: 46–7) in the Mundo Perdido complex at Tikal may be the earliest known example in the Maya lowlands (Fig. 3.5). During the late Eb or early Tzec phase (ca. 700 BC), the first version of this group consisted of a three-meter-high western pyramid (5C-54–1) and a forty-two-meter-long eastern platform (5D-84/88–2). E-Group complexes at Nakbe and Wakna in the Mirador Basin may be roughly contemporaneous or slightly later (Hansen 1998: 66). These E-Group assemblages represent the first, uniform monumental compounds in the Maya lowlands and, very loosely, may reflect a new ideology related to hierarchical social order (Hansen 1998; Laporte and Fialko 1995). Although the lack of any real understanding of their meaning and function makes it difficult to evaluate them further, the probability remains that they reproduced and remade the features of a natural landscape, channeling particular rituals that spread cult-fashion across the Maya lowlands and perhaps incorporating monumental plans from non-Mayan areas to the west (see the section titled Olmec Connections). Nonetheless, the concentration of E-Group complexes in central Peten may not simply reflect sampling bias but express precocious social development in the region. During the Late Preclassic period, E-Group complexes showed a broader distribution,

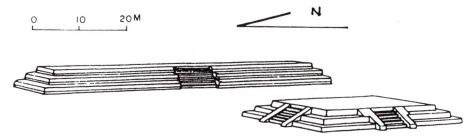

Figure 3.5. E-Group complex at Tikal dating to ca. 700 BC (Laporte and Fialko 1995, fig. 7).

including northern Yucatan, but still with a relatively well-defined clustering in the area from central Peten to southwestern Belize (Chase and Chase 1995: fig. 55; Hansen 1998: 68, tab. 2). Chase and Chase (1995) argue that, at these centers, E-Group complexes were the central foci of site planning and social organization.

Replication of E-Group assemblages in broad areas indicates the presence of centralized decision making in each community, sufficient to adopt such ceremonial templates and to mobilize the necessary labor to express those designs in concrete form. This labor may have been organized not so much through brash commands as by volunteer work parties compensated by feasts and fulfilled by feelings of civic commitment (see Dietler and Herbich 2001). Although E-Group complexes and associated rituals may originally have been of a communal nature, to which no specific groups or individuals lay exclusive claim, the buildings probably continued to evoke the prestige and recognition of those who organized their construction.

Clark and Hansen (2001) propose that large platforms associated with E-Group assemblages served as residential complexes for emerging elites. Groups 18 and 66 at Nakbe, for examples, are square platforms measuring about eighty by eighty meters, with several rectangular buildings on top. Although Clark and Hansen suggest that they were occupied by elites during the late Middle Preclassic period, the hypothesis has yet to be tested by extensive excavation. The A-24 platform at Ceibal also supported multiple structures, probably since the early Middle Preclassic. The excavated structures were linked to dense deposits of ceramics, carbon, and animal bones, perhaps the result of domestic activities. Alternatively, the buildings could have served as communal settings for feasting and other gatherings. A small number of greenstone ornaments found near a late Middle Preclassic structure on this platform may distinguish its residents from other community members, but other artifacts are of common type. The residents' privileged status, if any, appears to have been expressed mainly through the central location of the dwellings rather than through an inventory of rich possessions.

Interestingly, buildings on the A-24 platform at Ceibal were covered by construction fill at the end of the Mamom corresponding phase. At this time the complex was apparently converted into an open, wide platform. Construction of Structure A-24 on the western side of the platform might have started then, too. The building later grew into the largest temple pyramid at Ceibal. Similar processes seem to have happened at other centers, though at different times. At K'axob, the oldest residential group at the center of the community was covered by an open platform associated with a temple during the late part of the Late Preclassic period (McAnany and López Varela 1999; McAnany 2004). A comparable transformation took place in Platform 34 of Cuello at the beginning of the Late Preclassic (Hammond 1991). McAnany (1995) has argued that the lineages of the earliest settlers enjoyed higher status than other community members and that they eventually became ruling elites, at least at some centers. The construction of temple-plaza complexes over residential groups may signify that the domestic rituals and places tied to such groups were elevated to communal significance, leading to the centrality of dynastic ancestor worship in public ceremonies and spaces of the Classic period.

Despite tantalizing signs of greater social division and political centralization, there is only equivocal evidence of rulership during the Middle Preclassic period. The contemporaries of the southern Gulf Coast and the Pacific Coast, as well as later Maya, expressed their notions of rulership in stone monuments. Hansen (Clark et al. 2000) argues that large stone sculptures weighing up to eight tons were erected at centers in the Mirador Basin during the late Middle Preclassic period. At Nakbe, Altar 4, measuring 1.8 meters in diameter, was placed at the base of a platform. Hansen indicates that Nakbe Stela 1, with its elaborate carving of two standing figures, was originally paired with this altar and was reset during the Late Classic period (Hansen 1992b). However, the dating of these monuments, particularly that of Nakbe Stela 1, remains controversial. It is just as unclear whether these monuments were tied to the kinds of rulership attested in later periods. As emphasized in the section "Mountain Builders of the Rainforest," Stela 1 is sure to depict deities, not kings.

Hansen (1994; Clark et al. 2000: 464; Clark and Hansen 2001) notes that one figurine from this period depicts a three-pronged Jester God image, or a symbol of kingship, although this identification is tenuous. He adds that the mat motif, a symbol of rulership in later periods, had made an appearance on ceramics at Nakbe (Clark and Hansen 2001). Mat motifs are also known from a smaller center of Cuello (Hammond 1999: 58). Still conspicuously absent, or nearly absent, are royal tombs. Although the number of excavated burials of this period is generally small, the paucity of known tombs may reflect the reality of mortuary practice. A potential exception is the burial recently excavated at San Bartolo, containing several ceramic vessels and greenstone

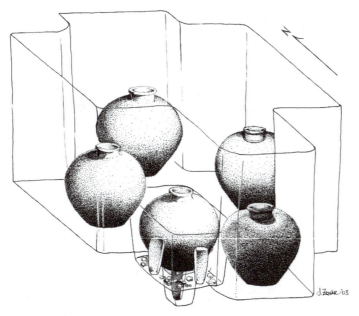

Figure 3.6. Cruciform cache found at Cival (Estrada-Belli 2006: fig. 3, courtesy of Francisco Estrada-Belli).

ornaments (Saturno 2006). The date of this interment, however, needs further study.

Olmec Connections

Did a new, emerging social order develop locally or under influence of foreign groups? Unlike surrounding areas, the Maya lowlands show few Olmec traits. During the early Middle Preclassic, Olmec-style stone monuments were absent, although a relatively small number of portable objects with Olmec motifs passed down into later periods, presumably through the Maya of this time. Incised motifs on Cunil pottery may reflect Olmec iconography, but the following Mamom ceramics exhibit few signs of foreign influence. The most notable evidence of Olmec influence is seen in cruciform caches at Ceibal, with greenstone celts and Real-Xe ceramics (Willey 1978: figs. 90, 91, 104, 105; Smith 1982: 118, 243, figs. 188, 189), and at Cival towards the end of its Cunil-like phase, both in association of E-Group assemblages (Fig. 3.6; Estrada-Belli 2006; Michael Callaghan, personal communication, 2008). Similar caches have been found at La Venta (Drucker 1952: figs. 10b, pl. 8; Drucker et al. 1959: fig. 51), at San Isidro, Chiapas (Lowe 1981), and most recently at Chiapa de Corzo (Bachand et al. 2008). The specific arrangement of the cache indicates that the early Middle Preclassic occupants of Ceibal and Cival shared certain religious beliefs with those of the Chiapas highlands and southern Gulf Coast.

In the northern lowlands, a cache of seventeen Olmec-style jade pieces was found at Chacsinkin, Yucatan (Fig. 3.7). Although they were placed in a Late Classic structure, Andrews (1986) believes them to be imported from the Olmec heartland during the late Middle Preclassic period. He further argues that most of the red pottery at La Venta, 2 percent of the entire collection, is essentially the Maya Joventud Red with a rim shape characteristic of the northern Maya lowlands. These data suggest to Andrews, plausibly so, that there were direct contacts between the Olmec heartland and the northern Maya lowlands.

In terms of architecture, the E-Group complex has generally been considered characteristic of the Maya lowlands (Stanton and Freidel 2003; Valdés 1995). Clark (Clark and Hansen 2001; Clark et al. 2000), following Gareth Lowe (1989) and Andrew McDonald (1983), however, points out that the E-Group complex was a primary component of site planning at La Venta and centers in the Chiapas highlands, including Vistahermosa, Mirador (not to be confused with El Mirador in the central Maya lowlands), San Isidro, Ocozocoautla, Chiapa de Corzo, Finca Acapulco, and La Libertad (Lowe 1989). Tzutzuculi on the Chiapas Pacific Coast and Kaminaljuyu in the Maya highlands also had E-Group assemblages, the latter consisting of a western pyramid and three mounds placed linearly on the eastern side instead of on a long platform (Murdy 1990: 355–6; Valdés 1995: 74). According to Clark, this architectural formation was invented by the Gulf Coast Olmec and then spread to the east. He argues that Chiapas centers copied the overall plan of the La Venta site core, consisting of pyramids, plazas, a royal acropolis, and an E-Group complex, all arranged along a north-south axis. This pattern differs strongly from site-planning designs at lowland Maya centers, which tend to follow east-west directionality. Although orientation and composition need chronological evaluation at each site, it seems unlikely that the occupants of the southern Gulf Coast and Chiapas borrowed a lowland Maya element and incorporated it into a highly standardized overall layout. A more credible scenario is that the lowland Maya selectively adopted an element of the Gulf Coast-Chiapas site plan.

The layout of the Preclassic core area of Ceibal is suggestive. Its arrangement of plazas and large platforms around a possible E-Group complex along the north-south axis is remarkably similar to centers in highland Chiapas. The resemblance parallels the affinity to the west expressed in earthen construction and Real ceramics of the early Middle Preclassic period. The presence of a cruciform cache with greenstone celts in the E-Group plaza suggests that architectural forms did not simply result from casual imitation but, rather, accompanied ritual practices and, possibly, religious ideas comparable to those of Chiapas and the Gulf Coast. In addition, the A-24 platform at Ceibal mentioned above may be comparable to platforms that surround E-Group complexes at Chiapas centers. Excavations at Mound 27 at Mirador and Mound 2

Figure 3.7. Jade offerings from Chacsinkin, Yucatan (Andrews V 1986, fig. 1, courtesy of the Middle American Research Institute, Tulane University).

at La Libertad in Chiapas revealed multiple structures on top of them, associated with middens and subfloor burials, all pointing to functions similar to the example at Ceibal (Agrinier 2000; Clark 1988). Similarities between Chiapas and Ceibal contrast with more diverse spatial arrangements in the central Maya lowlands. Although a cruciform cache was found in the E-Group plaza of Cival, extensive excavations in E-Group complexes at Tikal and Uaxactual failed to detect comparable deposits. Ritual practices in the central lowlands may have been more variable.

Just as telling is the substantial construction of plaza areas at Ceibal during the Preclassic period, with fills measuring two to four meters in thickness. Similar raised plazas are found at La Venta and in Chiapas, but excavations at most lowland Maya sites, including Nakbe, Tikal, and Uaxactun, found relatively thin plaza fills of the Preclassic period. Precise data are not available, but the fill volumes of plazas at La Venta, the Chiapas centers, and Ceibal may surpass the mass of coeval pyramids. Heavy investments of labor in plazas happened not simply because of the local topography or longer occupation history. The plazas were crucial constructions, furnished with extravagant cache deposits, epitomized by the so-called "Massive Offerings" at La Venta with up to fifty tons of serpentine blocks (Drucker et al. 1959). The sequence of constructions, cache deposits, and ritual performances probably made the plazas ideologically charged loci, with strong conceptual links to the Gulf Coast and Chiapas; by contrast, the central Maya lowlands primarily emphasized built forms visible on the surface. These observations hint at the importance of western inspiration, as well as a process of selective adoption by the predecessors of the Classic Maya.

In the Middle Preclassic Chiapas highlands, evidence of marked social inequality in residences and burials is weak, and large stone monuments are scarce. Stelae and other monumental sculptures apparently depicting rulers are mainly found on the Gulf Coast and the Pacific Coast during this time, including Tzutzuculi, Pijijiapan, Takalik Abaj, and Chalchuapa (Clark and Pye 2000), although with a notable exception of Xoc in eastern Chiapas (Ekholm-Miller 1973). If central ideas for some Maya architecture and ritual derived from the Chiapas highlands, the lack of overt expression of political power in the forms of tombs and monuments in the Maya lowlands may relate to similar practices among neighbors to the west.

Despite indications of interaction, there is no clear evidence that the Gulf Coast Olmec migrated into or controlled the Maya lowlands. The common material culture of the lowland Maya remained distinct from surrounding regions. The process was more likely a complex interplay of local invention, variable adoption of foreign elements, and inspiration through direct and indirect contact. As social inequality developed, emergent Maya elites might have borrowed well-entrenched elements of rulership of the southern Gulf Coast. However, it is important to avoid confusion here: descent does not imply equivalence, and notions of why one person, a ruler, would dominate others probably shifted in countless, subtle ways, just as Carolingian kingship drew on, yet differed profoundly from, the Roman notion of rulership.

LATE PRECLASSIC APOGEE

Mountain Builders of the Rainforest

In accord with trends in Mamom pottery, the even more homogeneous Chicanel ceramic sphere spread in a broader area of the Maya lowlands during the Late Preclassic period, probably from about 300 BC on (Forsyth 1999). At many sites where there was a weak Mamom presence, or none at all, evidence of strong Chicanel occupations is found, indicating that overall population had grown significantly. There is a direct continuity from Mamom ceramics to Chicanel materials. Like their predecessors, Chicanel ceramics were characterized by red-slipped monochrome vessels (Fig. 3.8). Homogeneity was both spatial and social. There were no clear differences between ceramics in probable elite residences and those in ordinary households (Clark and Hansen 2001).

During this time, mammoth structures were built at centers in the Mirador Basin. Among them, El Mirador was particularly impressive. During the latter

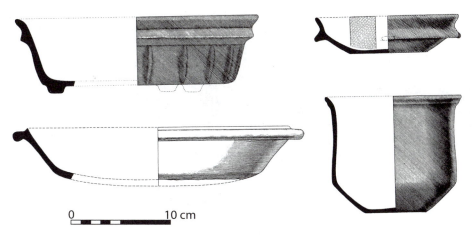

Figure 3.8. Chicanel ceramic vessels (Smith 1955, fig. 16, courtesy of the Middle American Research Institute, Tulane University).

part of the Late Preclassic period, the Danta pyramid was seventy-two meters high from the bottom of the basal platform (Matheny 1986: 20), and the Tigre pyramid in the western part of the center measured fifty-five meters in height (Hansen 1990). Even more remarkable is the construction mass of these buildings. Later Classic-period pyramids tend to be slim and tall, reaching impressive heights over a relatively small base. Preclassic constructions far exceed any Classic-period pyramid in construction mass and thus the labor invested in construction (Fig. 3.9). The base of the Danta complex covered an area of five hundred by three hundred and fifty meters. These gigantic edifices were literally human-made sacred mountains, of a scale unlike most sites in the Maya region. Conspicuous investment of labor also manifested itself in details of the buildings. The Preclassic builders used large stone blocks on the exteriors, which were placed with their longer axis penetrating into the core of the structure. The intent may have been to enhance stability in such massive constructions or to underscore their dominance over recalcitrant materials (the local limestone is quite hard), along with a need to project their truly prodigious control over labor. Classic buildings usually employed much smaller blocks with their longer axis along the surface, thus forming thin veneers, in a general aesthetic or building strategy that emphasized superficial grandeur over solidity of construction. In addition, Preclassic buildings exhibit generous use of stucco. Some stucco floors were twelve centimeters deep, thicker than floors of any other periods. This implies a vast amount of wood for the preparation of stucco since intense heat is needed to produce lime from carbonate rock (Hansen et al. 1997).

Smaller yet similar monumental structures were built at other lowland Maya centers during this period. At Tikal, Structure 5C-54, the western pyramid of the E-Group complex, grew in size and reached eighteen meters in height and sixty meters in width at its base between 200 and 1 BC (Laporte and Fialko

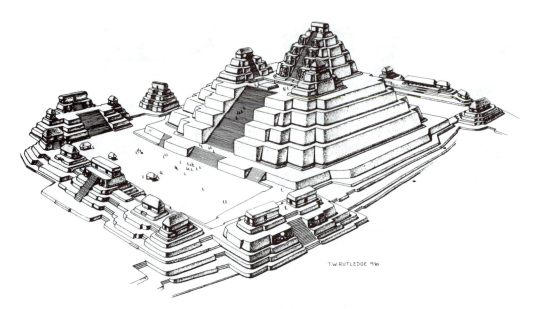

Figure 3.9. Tigre Pyramid, El Mirador (Hansen 1990, ii, drawing by T.W. Rutledge).

1995: 50). The North Acropolis was also built up substantially (Coe 1990). At Lamanai, Structure N10–43 was transformed from a modest residential construction to a pyramid thirty-three meters high (Pendergast 1981: 39–42). At Cerros, a small farming village grew into an important center and the residents built a temple, Structure 5C-2nd (Freidel 1986).

A characteristic architectural arrangement started around 300 BC was the so-called "triadic complex" (Hansen 1990, 1992a, 1998). It consisted of a primary structure flanked by two smaller buildings facing each other on a pyramid or platform. The triadic arrangement became the primary feature of monumental compounds, surpassing the importance of E-Group complexes. Triadic groups occupied the summit of many major architectural complexes at El Mirador and Nakbe. This pattern was also found at Tikal (Coe 1990), Uaxactun (Valdés 1992, 1995), Lamanai (Pendergast 1981), Cerros (Freidel 1986), and Dzibilchaltun (Andrews 1965). The triadic pattern continued to be used during the Classic period, if not clearly with the same meaning.

Along with the triadic complex, architectural sculptures became common. They usually consist of enormous stucco masks of deities that flank the primary stairway of structures. Although some architectural sculptures are known from Middle Preclassic sites in other areas of Mesoamerica, lowland Maya architectural art was essentially a local development. A mask decorating Structure B1–4th of Blackman Eddy may be as early as the end of the Middle Preclassic period (Garber et al. 2004). At Calakmul, excavations directed by Ramón Carrasco Vargas (2005) detected the eight-meter-high Substructure II-c covered by massive Preclassic construction. The building, possibly dating between 400 and

Figure 3.10. Stucco mask found at Cival (Estrada-Belli 2006: fig. 6, courtesy of Francisco Estrada-Belli).

200 BC – to be sure, the dating is debatable – was adorned with elaborate façade sculptures depicting Chahk, the Rain God, in horizontal position flanked by supernatural birds. Somewhat later architectural sculptures have been found at El Mirador (Hansen 1990, 1992a), Nakbe (Hansen 1992b), Tikal (Coe 1990), Uaxactun (Ricketson and Ricketson 1937; Valdés 1992, 1995), Cerros (Freidel 1986), and Lamanai (Pendergast 1981). In Group H at Uaxactun, excavated by Juan Antonio Valdés (1992, 1995), stucco masks decorated the basal platform, whereas a vaulted structure atop it was adorned with sculptures of horizontal figures similar to that of Calakmul. Recent excavations into the triadic group at Cival by Francisco Estrada-Belli revealed well-preserved masks from around 200 BC (Fig. 3.10). At Nakbe, Hansen (1998: 82) believes that the base of Structure 1 was adorned with masks of the Principal Bird Deity, the Preclassic version of Wukub Kaqix described in Popol Vuh. The meaning of these deity masks is, however, unclear, and the possibility remains that some represent mythological locales or royal names (David Stuart, personal communication, 1999).

Iconographic themes that are more confidently tied to rulership become apparent during this period. The carved monuments of El Mirador and Nakbe, mentioned above, would date to this time, if not earlier. Nakbe Stela 1 depicts two figures in elaborate attire, but there are, unfortunately, no glyphic texts.

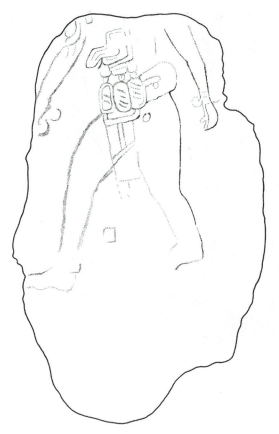

Figure 3.11. Stela 2 of Cival, the Late Preclassic period (Estrada-Belli 2006: fig. 8, courtesy of Francisco Estrada-Belli).

These figures are probably not the "Hero Twins" identified by the excavator but still likely represent deities. Although the sculpture may not depict a historical scene, it indicates that elaborate ceremonial attire comparable to that of Classic times was already in use. The costumes were loaded with symbols tied to the ideology of rulership, and the facial features of the figures resemble those of Olmec imagery. A likely depiction of a ruler is Cival Stela 2, recently unearthed near the cruciform cache (Fig. 3.11). Although its top part is missing, the remaining portion shows a striding figure with a bird-head pectoral with three hanging plaques similar to those worn by rulers on monuments at Kaminaljuyu, Takalik Abaj, and La Mojarra (Estrada-Belli 2006). The small Stela 18 from El Mirador displays a format that becomes standard by Early Classic times. It shows a ruler, much eroded or in a carving that may never have been finished, facing the viewer; an ancestor wreathed in clouds looks down on his descendant (Fig. 3.12; McAnany 1998: fig. 5). Even at the small center of Cuello, a supposed stela, though without glyphs, was erected around AD 100 (Hammond 1982a, 1999).

Among the most spectacular recent finds are the murals at San Bartolo in northeastern Peten. At this medium-sized center, excavations into the Las Pinturas structure by William Saturno revealed exquisite paintings on the north and west walls of a small chamber attached to the back of a pyramid, with carbon dates pointing to a temporal frame of 200 to 100 BC (Saturno et al. 2006b). The north wall shows a Preclassic version of the Maize God with Olmec-like features, standing in front of what Karl Taube calls "Flower Mountain," a paradisical, primeval place (Fig. 3.13). On the west walls were scenes of animal sacrifices with one of the Hero Twins, which colonial-period K'ichee' called Hunahpu, engaged in bloodletting. Also depicted are the Principal Bird Deity perched on the world tree and the Maize God dancing in the underworld. These mythological narratives are surprisingly consistent with those of Popol Vuh and even with the Postclassic Dresden codex. A theme of historical importance is a coronation scene, in which a possible ruler seated on a wooden scaffold receives a crown from another figure (Fig. 3.14). The scene is reminiscent of the scaffold scenes of Classic-period stelae at Piedras Negras and may suggest that the notion and institution of rulership were in place, set in the mythological charter in a manner comparable to the better-known examples from the Classic period. Against this is the overridingly mythic nature of imagery in the murals, which do not clearly specify any historical content. Preclassic murals were also found in Structure 5D-Sub-10–1st beneath the North Acropolis of Tikal, but less is understood of their meaning.

Such representations were accompanied by early hieroglyphic texts. Glyphs painted on the San Bartolo murals possibly narrate the painted scenes and name the figures. In an even deeper level of the Las Pinturas building, excavators discovered a text painted on a wall fragment, with carbon dates pointing to 300 to 200 BC (Saturno et al. 2006a). One

Figure 3.12. Stela 18 of El Mirador, the Late Preclassic period (drawing by Stephen Houston).

glyph may be the sign of *ajaw*, hinting, if read correctly, that the concept of rulership was already present at the beginning of the late Middle Preclassic. At El Mirador, Stela 2 was carved with Preclassic iconographic motifs and glyphs (Hansen 1991). Hansen suggests that some other monuments from the Mirador Basin carried glyphs that were later erased. A relatively rich late Middle Preclassic burial recently discovered at Ceibal contained a worked shell with residues of red pigment, its shape reminiscent of ink pots used by Classic-period scribes. Although the exact function of this object is not clear, it is tempting to tie it to the emerging practice of painting and writing.

Although stelae with inscriptions are still rare, precursors of Classic art and writing can be seen in some portable objects, mostly dating towards the end of the Late Preclassic. A remarkable example is the greenstone pectoral at Dumbarton Oaks, depicting an Olmec deity (Schele and Miller 1986: pl. 31). On the back of this object, the Late Preclassic lowland Maya carved a figure of a ruler

Figure 3.13. Maize God depicted on the north wall of the Las Pinturas structure, San Bartolo (painting by Heather Hurst, courtesy of William Saturno, San Bartolo Archaeological Project).

wearing a Jester-God headband. The accompanying hieroglyphic text possibly records the accession of the ruler. Hieroglyphs are also found on a carved bone from Kichpanha, Belize, and jade earflare from Pomona, Belize (Schele and Miller 1986: pl. 9). A relief sculpture in Loltun Cave, Yucatan, depicts a ruler wearing a Jester-God headdress and a hieroglyphic text. When they appear, such texts tend to have minimal suffixation, offer lists of head signs, display glyph blocks whose outlines equate to single glyphs, and generally display a pronounced degree of variety and an uncertain degree of sign codification (Houston 2000: table 1). The inscriptions are almost completely unreadable, excepting a very few signs. Monumentalism in these texts is nearly absent, as at El Mirador, where the few surviving signs are so tiny as to be visible only at close range. The same pattern holds at San Bartolo.

Given these iconographic and glyphic data, it is puzzling that elite tombs are nearly absent in the Maya lowlands during the early Late Preclassic period or earlier, with the notable exception of the San Bartolo burial mentioned above. Earlier and contemporaneous rich elite tombs have been reported from nearby areas in the Gulf Coast region, the Guatemalan highlands, and Honduras. The

Figure 3.14. The coronation scene depicted on the west wall of the Las Pinturas structure, San Bartolo (painting by Heather Hurst, courtesy of William Saturno, San Bartolo Archaeological Project).

absence of formally excavated elite burials from the Mirador Basin is especially noteworthy and perplexing. Extensive excavations and looter's trenches into triadic groups at El Mirador and Nakbe failed to reveal tombs, intimating that these buildings may not have functioned as mortuary temples (Hansen 1998: 89), although, to be sure, the mass of these structures makes it almost impossible to do a complete probe of their interiors. Looters' trenches into a triadic building at Wakna, Structure 3 did, however, expose a series of possible elite tombs with Chicanel ceramics and reportedly a large amount of jade, if looters' accounts are to be trusted (Hansen 1998: 90–2). Excavations into most parts of the Preclassic layers in the Mundo Perdido complex at Tikal only revealed burials with unimpressive offerings. A small number of richer interments began to appear in the latter half of the Late Preclassic, and the earliest elite burial in the Mundo Perdido complex dates to the Cimi phase (AD 1–250, Laporte and Fialko 1995: 52–3). Contemporaneous tombs were also uncovered in the North Acropolis of Tikal (W. Coe 1990; Krejci and Culbert 1995). Importantly, those early tombs at Tikal were placed under small shrines or in front of buildings, not necessarily along the central axes of ceremonial complexes. Burial 85 in the North Acropolis is among the first examples that established the strong preference of the central lines for elite interments that persisted through the following periods. The vaulted chamber of this tomb contained a body in a seated position accompanied by a greenstone mask with a three-pronged crown.

During the Late Preclassic period, causeways running across *bajos* connected El Mirador and other centers in the basin (Hansen 1998: 75). The earliest causeway may have been constructed during the late Middle Preclassic (Dixon et al. 1994; Hansen 1998: 75), although Arlen Chase and Diane Chase (1995) doubt these early dates. Causeways were also built at other Late Preclassic sites, including Komchen in Yucatan and Cerros. Those in the Mirador Basin probably facilitated communication and political integration between centers. Scarborough (1991: 150) suggests that a causeway at Cerros may also have served as a dike wall for reservoirs. Ringle (1999: 207) correctly emphasizes their performative aspects, pointing out that the causeway of Komchen connected two large structures. One of them, Structure 25O1, was fronted by a broad low terrace, which probably served as a stage for public performance. The causeway connected with this space may have emphasized linear, "correct" movement (see Chapters 2 and 5) and choreographed processions that were conceived as sacral acts with beginning and terminal points. Ringle also notes that a causeway of Cerros led to a ballcourt, a ritual space perhaps related to the later myth of the Hero Twins who defeated the underworld gods. Ballcourts from later periods were commonly associated with causeways, a feature that also points to the ritual and performative functions of causeways or at least to their central position in Maya cities.

Transformation and Continuity in Domestic Life

At El Mirador, ordinary residential structures were built around patios, a pattern resembling that of the Classic period (Demarest et al. 1984). This may reflect social organization at the domestic level in patterns prefiguring those of the Classic period. Although these domestic groups were integrated into larger communities, they may have developed stronger characteristics as corporate groups that coalesced with clearer delimitations of rights, properties, and membership. Despite a certain level of standardization in spatial arrangements, residential groups also emphasized differences among them all the more strongly through the elaboration of domestic buildings (Hendon 1999). At many sites, small Middle Preclassic domestic buildings made of perishable materials on the ground level were partially replaced with more permanent, raised platforms during the Late Preclassic. Conceptually, this must have exerted an impact on local perceptions of rootedness and long-term heritage from preceding generations. At Ceibal, Cerros, and Komchen, large platforms supported multiple buildings (Hendon 1999: 106; Ringle 1999: 190). Such platforms doubtless coincided with perceived demarcations of shared space along with practical commitments to enhanced drainage and the creation of drier living spaces in a land of seasonal downpours.

A signal change involved the drastic decline in the use of figurines at most communities (Clark et al. 2000: 469; Ringle 1999: 193). Figurines dating to the Middle Preclassic period are commonly found associated with domestic remains and are believed to have been used in domestic ritual activities. The disappearance of figurines, then, hints at notable changes in domestic ritual activities and beliefs. During the Middle Preclassic period, evidence of centralized ritual activities was limited at most sites, although their emergent forms can be seen in the early construction of E-Group complexes and other public buildings. The changes in domestic rituals were possibly related to the establishment of a new ideological framework centered around divine rulership and with an emphasis on its connection to the supernatural world. Ringle (1999: 195) notes that, along with the disappearance of figurines, local or minor temples became common. These small pyramidal structures were often associated with domestic residential groups and were widely distributed in centers and their peripheries (Tourtellot 1988b; Wilk and Wilhite 1991: 127). Minor temples may have been dedicated to religious beliefs comparable to those represented by larger pyramids at the core of each center. This may signify that social and religious orders at local and domestic levels mirrored the organization of the larger polity (Ringle 1999: 196). Local and domestic groups were likely to have been internally differentiated in terms of authority and power. Like those of the ruler, the reach and authority of local leaders may have been ideologically sanctioned, particularly through ancestor veneration (McAnany 1995; McAnany et al. 1999).

Much like those of the Middle Preclassic, domestic groups continued to serve as primary foci of economic production. Domestic middens contain numerous materials related to the working of shell and bone objects and lithic tools (Hendon 1999). In other words, productive activities were dispersed over wide residential areas, and there is no clear evidence of centrally controlled production facilities. Community-level specialization occurred when there was a concentration of valued raw materials or unique conditions, including the high-quality chert at Colha, Belize, and salt production at Komchen (Hester 1985). Even in these cases, production activities appear to have been closely associated with other aspects of domestic lives. The elites who established and guided new social orders do not seem to have controlled daily economic activities of the masses to any consequential degree. For a large part of the population, agricultural activities continued to be their economic basis, and these people appear to have remained economically autonomous and essentially self-sufficient. This also means that the economic foundation of large Late Preclassic centers rested on local agricultural production rather than the centrally administered manufacturing industries or the control of trade in large quantities. Yet, this does not imply that the elite neglected economic activities. At Nakbe, Preclassic occupants carried soils from *bajos* to terraces in elevated terrains so as to make viable agricultural fields (Martínez et al. 1999). Such intensive cultivation may have been conducted under the supervision of the elite. At Edzna, in Campeche, Ray Matheny and colleagues (1983) documented an extensive system of canals dating to the Late Preclassic period, which may have been capable of irrigating four hundred and fifty hectares of agricultural lands. Its enormous scale, as well as the fact that canals were connected to circular moat-like features surrounding the central portion of the site, suggests that this hydraulic system reflected initiatives on the part of the elite, much like *sakbih* or causeways but in watery form.

Violence and Conflict

Conflicts between centers and violence within political units are likely to have been integral parts of Late Preclassic life. The central precinct of El Mirador may have been defended by stone walls (unpublished sculptures on display at the site show war captives), and the circular moat-like feature at Edzna probably served a defensive purpose. In addition, the center of Cerros is surrounded by a moat, and defense may have been one of its functions. Webster (1976) demonstrated that large walls and ditches that surrounded the central part of Becan were defensive and likely constructed during the Late Preclassic period. Such defensive features were even more prominent during the Late Preclassic period than during most of the Classic period. Although abundant epigraphic and iconographic evidence attests that the Classic Maya frequently engaged in war, fortifications remained rare until the end of the Late Classic. The presence of substantial defensive features during the Late Preclassic period underscores its nature as a time of intense conflict.

New elites may also have practiced ritualistic forms of violence. Among the lowland Maya, as well as other peoples of Mesoamerica, human sacrifice was an important element related to the supernatural sanction of elite authority and to the exercise and demonstration of dominion. Although direct evidence is limited, the practice of human sacrifice most likely started during the Preclassic period. A decapitated skeleton found in a late Middle Preclassic burial at Cuello may represent human sacrifice, although the possibility of ancestor veneration remains a possibility. During the Late Preclassic period at Cuello, roughly thirty-two individuals were placed over an earlier patio group in a mass sacrificial burial at the time of construction of Platform 34. Another mass burial with twelve individuals was created slightly later (Robin and Hammond 1991). Bound captives are also attested as modeled stucco figures from Río Azul, from the very end of the Preclassic period. Genitalia exposed, hair matted and disheveled, hands bound, the captives are on bent knee (Adams 1999: fig. 3–33) in a thematic presentation that is relatively common in objects from the Late Preclassic–Early Classic transition (Ichon and Arnauld 1985: fig 10).

Name glyphs atop ornaments lashed to their backs probably record their names, although, regrettably, the published drawings are poor and indistinct. There is a tendency for such captives to come in pairs, either on incised shells, disks, or in stone, as on Kaminaljuyu Monument 65. The meaning of this pairing is obscure.

The emerging lowland Maya elite may have emulated the practices of their neighbors. The Gulf Coast Olmec likely started the practice of human sacrifice during the Early Preclassic. At the ceremonial site of El Manatí near San Lorenzo, Ponciano Ortíz and Carmen Rodríguez (2000) found remains of human infants. During the Middle Preclassic, child burials associated with a throne at Chalcatzingo, Morelos, probably result from sacrifice (W. Fash 1987; see also Grove 1981: 58). Middle Preclassic Olmec-style monuments depicting felines over humans may communicate metaphors of human sacrifice (Taube 1995). The most explicit use of such grisly rituals as evocations of elite power comes from late Middle Preclassic and early Late Preclassic Monte Albán. There, more than three hundred stone monuments called *danzantes* depict sacrificial victims. Closer to the Maya lowlands, a Middle Preclassic elite burial with twelve sacrificed victims was found at Los Mangales in the Salama Valley in the northern Maya highlands (Sharer and Sedat 1987: 147). Depictions of human sacrifice became explicit in Late Preclassic monumental art, including Izapa Stela 21, which shows a vivid scene of decapitation with gushing blood, albeit in a probable mythological context. Clearly, human sacrifice was enmeshed in Mesoamerican systems of belief. The practice of auto-sacrifice or bloodletting may have had deeper roots. Pointed objects and imitation stingray spines made of greenstone found at La Venta and other Olmec sites were probably used for bloodletting. The practice of human sacrifice gave elites a combination of supernatural sanction for their authority and intimidation through overt displays of violence.

Competing or Influential Neighbors?

Ideologies associated with divine rulership in the Maya lowlands appear to show some connection to those reflected in Olmec arts. The right figure depicted on Nakbe Stela 1 wears an Olmec-like head in front of his forehead, probably as an early representation of the Jester God. The image of this deity became a conspicuous symbol of kingship for the Classic Maya. It was identified with three prongs on the forehead and was usually worn as a headband. The precursor of the Maya Jester God is seen in Olmec imagery (Fields 1991; Freidel 1990). Taube (1998) argues that the Olmec Jester God conflates the notions of the world tree, the Maize God, and the Principal Bird Deity. Olmec features are also evident in the Maize God of the San Bartolo murals, and the Olmec jade artifacts kept as heirlooms by later Maya rulers hint at memories or invocations of the distant past.

Despite these possible inspirations from the neighbors, the lowland Maya may have expanded to the west during the Late Preclassic, perhaps not in a peaceful manner (Bryan and Clark 1983; Clark et al. 2000: 459). From about 450 to 200 BC there were significant social changes in the Chiapas highlands. Many sites, including La Libertad, were abandoned around 300 BC, and new settlements, such as El Cerrito, were placed in more defensible locations. Chicanel-like ceramics were introduced, and masonry platforms, traits common in the Maya lowlands as opposed to the earthen construction of the area, began to appear. At Chiapa de Corzo, a Maya-like palace complex was constructed, as well as triadic temples reflecting specific Maya elite beliefs (Clark et al. 2000: 473; Lowe 1977: 230; 1995). These changes may have involved actual migrations of Maya speakers and seem also to reflect changes in a broader political balance. On the Gulf Coast, La Venta and other Olmec centers declined while powerful centers emerged in the Mirador Basin. In some areas, local utilitarian ceramics were replaced by Maya types, although Maya influence in central Chiapas is primarily seen in elite culture, such as in monumental architecture and elite ceramics. Overt Maya stimulus at Chiapa de Corzo ended around AD 100, which may have corresponded to the decline of El Mirador (Clark et al. 2000).

The areas to the south – the Maya highlands and Pacific Coast – hold critical information for understanding Late Preclassic developments and transitions to the Classic period in the Maya lowlands. On the southern Pacific Coast during the Late Preclassic period, Olmec-style monuments were replaced by the Izapan art style, which bore close similarities to later lowland Maya monuments. Monuments at the center of Izapa on the eastern Chiapas Coast are generally assigned to the Guillen period (300–50 BC), but their dates are far from certain. They lack hieroglyphic texts, but their iconography is richly narrative. Stela 25 depicts a monstrous bird and a figure with a severed arm. This probably represents a prototype of a mythical story recorded in Popol Vuh in which the Hero Twins defeated a supernatural bird, Wukub Kaqix, though a twin, Hunahpu, lost an arm in the struggle. Taube (1998: 439) points out that Miscellaneous Monuments 6, 8, and 10, which consist of three massive stone balls, may have represented a three-stone hearth, which became an important element in later Maya myths. On the Guatemalan Coast, Izapan-style monuments with texts and Long-Count dates, ranging from the first century BC and the second century AD, have been found at the sites of Takalik Abaj and El Baúl.

Hieroglyphic texts and Long-Count dates are also found in central Chiapas and on the southern Gulf Coast. Stela 2 of Chiapa de Corzo has the date of *7.*16.3.2.13 (36 BC, the asterisks indicate reconstructed numbers in the Long Count), which corresponds to the period of lowland Maya influence in central Chiapas. Texts from the Gulf Coast, belonging generally to the canons of Isthmian script, include Tres Zapotes Stela C, with the date of 7.16.6.16.18

(32 BC), and the Tuxtla Statuette, from 8.6.2.4.17 (AD 162). The majestic La Mojarra Stela 1 records long texts with the dates of 8.5.3.3.5 (AD 143) and 8.5.16.9.7 (AD 156). Justeson and Kaufman (1993) argue that Isthmian script recorded the Mixe-Zoquean language, a reasonable but unproven conjecture given the controversial nature of their decipherment. These writings may have developed from the Olmec iconographic tradition, as indicated by the recent discoveries of the Cascajal block and other forms of early writing on the southern Gulf Coast (Pohl et al. 2002; Rodríguez Martínez et al. 2006). Terminal Olmec monuments, including San Miguel Amuco Stela 1 and La Venta Monument 13, form a probable bridge to Isthmian and southern Guatemalan scripts (Houston 2000: 143).

In the Maya highlands, Kaminaljuyu developed into an important center during the late Middle Preclassic period. The presence of large elite burials signaled social stratification, and the construction of an effigy mound known as the "Serpent Mound" had already started (López 1993; Ortega et al. 1996; Velásquez 1991). The late Middle Preclassic occupants of Kaminaljuyu appear to have invested significant labor in intensive agriculture, as shown by canals drawing water from the now-desiccated Miraflores Lake to agricultural fields nearby (Barrientos 1997; Valdés and Hatch 1996). During the Late Preclassic period, Kaminaljuyu was the most powerful center in the Maya highlands. Social hierarchy with rulership was well established, as demonstrated by two spectacular tombs excavated by Edwin Shook and Alfred Kidder (1952) in Mound E-III-3. "Stela 10" depicts deities as well as hieroglyphic texts of elusive meaning. Jonathan Kaplan (1995) has demonstrated that this was a throne most likely used by the ruler. Monument 65 records rulers sitting on such thrones and facing bound captives, with evidence of name glyphs in place of headdresses.

In the northern highlands, the most powerful center in the Salama Valley seems to have been El Portón. Its Monument 1 has what appears to be a glyphic column, which may be the earliest example of writing in the Maya area, but its date of 400 BC is still being debated. The continuation of a sculptural tradition in the Salama Valley during the Late Preclassic period is exemplified by monuments found at Laguneta, which show affinity to the Izapan style (Sharer and Sedat 1987: 433). In the Chixoy drainage to the west, Alain Ichon (1977) found a number of relief sculptures in the Izapan style at the site of La Lagunita. The transcendent stylistic links between distant areas underscores the vast scale of elite interaction at the time and the ability of artisans to participate intimately in broad networks of meaning and artistic convention. The inclusion of ceramics vessels imported form the highlands in Tikal Burial 85 attests to such interaction (Culbert 1993: fig. 5).

Patterns of interactions within the highlands and the Pacific Coast are suggested by comparative ceramic studies. Arthur Demarest (1986) recognizes two areas with relative ceramic homogeneity during the Late Preclassic period.

The sequential Providencia and Miraflores ceramic spheres include the centers of Kaminaljuyu in the highlands, Bilbao on the Guatemalan Coast, and Chalchuapa in western El Salvador. The Uapala ceramic sphere comprises the sites of Copan and Los Naranjos in Honduras and Quelepa in eastern El Salvador. Although the argument is not yet proved, it is tempting to link the Providencia and Miraflores spheres to speakers of highland Mayan, and the Uapala ceramic sphere to the poorly understood Lenca, a non-Mayan group of northern Central America (Andrews 1976).

INTO A NEW ERA

The end of the Preclassic period was a time of profound social change in the Maya lowlands. El Mirador and other major centers in the Mirador Basin were largely abandoned around AD 200. Hansen (1994: 371) found reconstructible vessels on the last occupation floors, suggesting that abandonment was rapid. This social upheaval probably convulsed surrounding areas too. The palace at Chiapa de Corzo was violently destroyed, and the ceramics of the area returned from pottery with Maya affiliations to the local Isthmian tradition (Lowe and Mason 1965; Clark et al. 2000). In the Guatemalan highlands and on the Pacific Coast, many monuments at Kaminaljuyu and Takalik Abaj may have been destroyed about this time (Schieber de Lavarreda and Orrego Corzo 2001; Hatch 2003). Few monuments were erected in the highlands and on the Pacific Coast in the following period.

Recent geological studies suggest that the Maya area went through pronounced droughts at the end of the Preclassic period (Haug et al. 2003). The analysis of wetland sediment data has led Dunning and colleagues (2002) and Hansen and others (2002) to argue that humans were at least partly responsible for ecological problems. With a substantial population increase, the rate of deforestation accelerated towards the end the Preclassic. Soil erosions changed hydrological conditions, transforming perennial lakes or marshes to seasonal wetlands. If this reconstruction is applicable to the Maya lowlands, the residents of large centers at the edge of wetlands may have been affected profoundly.

Still, some centers, most notably Tikal, survived the Preclassic collapse. Vernon Scarborough (1994) has suggested that, whereas the Preclassic water management was a concave or "bowl-like" system that relied on canals and reservoirs within or at the margins of low-lying terrains, it shifted to a convex one in the Classic by means of reservoirs built in uplands. A successful shift in water management systems might have contributed to the continuity of Tikal (nonetheless, the distinction may be too categorical, as both periods show a preference for settlement on higher ground and with sources of water, both natural and artificial, nearby). The problem in understanding these developments, however, is that the ceramic chronology of the Preclassic-to-Classic transition is fraught with ambiguity. In the Pasión region, southeastern

Peten, and other areas, Chicanel ceramics with waxy slip might have continued into the Early Classic (Lincoln 1985; J. Laporte 1995). If so, the fall of
centers in these regions could have been a few centuries later than that of
the central lowlands. Some sites may not have declined at all. These regional
differences compel us to consider the importance of social and political influences. The Maya of various areas contributed and responded to the large-scale
social changes associated with the demise of El Mirador, although much of
this process remains enigmatic.

THE GENESIS OF LOWLAND MAYA CIVILIZATION

Contrary to the earlier perception that lowland Maya civilization emerged at
the beginning of the Classic period, it is now beyond doubt that most of its
elements were already in place during the Preclassic period. As a cultural block,
the Maya lowlands become recognizable at least by the mid Middle Preclassic
period. From this time on, the area probably continued to be occupied by
the same linguistic and cultural groups until the Spanish conquest, with some
exceptions. During the Preclassic period, these groups shared similar material
culture, culminating in the Chicanel ceramic sphere, which clearly differed
from surrounding areas. In other words, the Preclassic lowland Maya were not
much concerned with expressing differences between lowland groups through
material culture but rather emphasized their distinction from groups nearby
(Ringle 1999: 198). Although more regionalized ceramic styles characterized
the Classic period, the Maya lowlands persisted as a relatively discrete cultural
region. This stability may have been partly aided by its peninsular setting
bordered by mountain ranges, as well as by the presence of a prestige language,
an ancestor of Ch'olti' Maya, that bound diverse elites (Houston et al. 2000).

Among the critical elements of Maya civilization that emerged during the
Preclassic period may have been the notion of rulership along with associated governmental institutions and political symbols. There are two schools
of thought. David Freidel and Linda Schele (1988a) suggest that Maya rulership crystallized rapidly during the first century BC. Favoring that view is the
paucity of royal representation much before that date and the difficulty of reading any texts of the time. There is potentially a grave problem in presuming that
Classic-period meanings were essentially the same in earlier periods and that
titles, narratives, or insignia carried the same connotation, regardless of period:
this is rather like blurring the distinction between an early Irish "king," with
his small fort and herd of cattle, and King Louis XIV of France, both with similar title but very different status. Equally worrisome is the evidence of strong
disruptions at the end of the Preclassic, when continuities in political organization may have come to an end or been thoroughly redefined. Nonetheless,
a second school of interpretation emphasizes deeper roots. Viewed a certain
way, the San Bartolo murals signal that the institution of rulership with related

mythical narratives was already well established around 100 BC. The earlier text containing the *ajaw* sign – again, if correctly identified and understood as to its nuance *at that time* – hints at its origins as early as the third century BC. The common use of Olmec symbols and objects by Late Preclassic Maya rulers also reflect their own historical understanding of royal symbolism going back, perhaps, to the Middle Preclassic. First came social inequality, if of an indeterminate sort, then, by the late Middle Preclassic, the spread of Mamom ceramics and obsidian blades in the Maya lowlands, as well as the construction of E-Group complexes in the central and eastern lowlands. Future research on the period between 700 and 100 BC will be critical in understanding the emergence of Maya rulers.

The cultural uniformity throughout the Maya lowlands and the magnitude of constructions at El Mirador make it tempting to posit a Mirador "state" controlling a large part of the lowlands or even extending its influence over the Chiapas highlands (Clark et al. 2000; Bachand 2006: 539–67). The presence of royal titles and other symbols at smaller centers, such as San Bartolo and Cival, may, however, point to the presence of multiple ruling groups arising at various locations. Given the clues of rulership during this period, it is likely that centralized governmental institutions were in operation. Yet, we know next to nothing about the specific forms and functions of such institutions. Whatever the degree of political unification, the process of interaction was not always peaceful. Substantial fortifications found at Becan, Edzna, and other sites suggest that rivalry between groups in some cases escalated into physical violence.

A fundamental change in this political process was ideological in nature (Clark et al. 2000: 469; Hansen 1990, 1992a). Although still indistinct, a new ideological scheme associated with emerging elites penetrated various layers of society, transforming religious beliefs and ritual practices among the majority of the population. As seen in the disappearance of figurines and the development of minor temples, rituals at the domestic level were integrated into a centralized, hierarchical system of coalescent ideologies. Novel religious beliefs became crucial mechanisms for integrating an increased population at any one center, previously divided into smaller autonomous units. These ideologies served at once to unite growing communities and to divide them into privileged and unprivileged groups.

The establishment of the elite was accompanied by a cultural component best described as "high culture" (Baines and Yoffee 1998). The Preclassic was the time of formation for the cultural and aesthetic values that constituted the core of a civilization. The exclusive access to the knowledge of religion, to supernatural power, and to materials brought from distant places distinguished elites from the rest of society and provided morally defensible and naturalized means of legitimization. Public spectacles in plazas and temples conducted or sponsored by the elite probably brought the members of the community together and helped to propagate elite-centered ideologies and values. Material objects associated with the elite during the Preclassic period appear to have been charged more with symbolic values than economic ones, as there were relatively small differences between elites and nonelites in terms of ceramics, lithics, and other commonly used objects.

Unlike ideological transformations, economic trends may be described as continuous growth without major structural change. Agricultural production grew greatly and promoted increases in population. Each domestic group, however, appears to have engaged in economic activities that persisted from the Middle Preclassic period and consisted mainly of agriculture and craft production in domestic contexts. Economic management may not have been an important part of elite endeavor. Long-distance trade focused on small quantities of prestige goods that distinguished elites and enhanced their prestige, but it had a relatively small effect on overall economic organization. Although the unique concentration of resources and particularly favorable conditions of production stimulated the growth of a few specialized communities, the economy of most large centers was solidly based on local agricultural production. The main concern for elites was not economic regulation but the recruitment of labor and the retention of population in heightened competition between centers (Ringle 1999: 190). This pattern appears to have continued into the Classic period.

This process contrasts with major sites in Mesoamerica like Monte Albán and Teotihuacan. In the Oaxaca Valley a new capital of Monte Albán was suddenly established around 600 BC at the top of a previously unoccupied hill (Marcus and Flannery 1996). In the Valley of Mexico, Teotihuacan grew explosively, amassing 80 to 90 percent of the valley population between AD 1 and 200, just after the destruction of the rival center of Cuicuilco by volcanic eruptions (Sanders et al. 1979). Such drastic changes in settlement patterns in Oaxaca and central Mexico probably reflected strong initiatives of the elite. Whether large populations moved into the new capitals willingly or unwillingly, these processes of displacement detached large populations from their former economic bases and forced them to adjust to dramatically different social and economic orders. Such social transformations in extraordinary magnitudes strongly affected the later course of social development in these areas. Large populations probably became more dependent on elites in terms of economic and political relations, and the power of elites extended more deeply into their societies. In the Maya lowlands, in contrast, a significant transformation was limited mainly to the domain of ideology without dramatic changes in the daily economic practices of a large part of the population.

What is shared in the Maya lowlands, central Mexico, and the Oaxaca Valley is the critical role of monumental construction. All areas experienced a significant increase in construction during relatively early stages of urban growth. Such monumental construction was not only a consequence of increased social complexity but a catalyst for further development. In the Maya lowlands, the most significant disruption in daily activities of most of the population may have resulted from just such construction. As Mendelssohn (1971) has observed for Egyptian pyramids, such construction disconnected the masses from old patterns of life centered around agriculture and entangled elites in the scheduling of labor. Moreover, the pyramids at El Mirador were unprecedented construction projects that surpassed any previous attempts to a large degree, bringing about unforeseen consequences. It is conceivable that, as the construction projects progressed, new forms of administrative organization of labor and of other logistics were required and devised, including novel inducements to voluntaristic work parties and, beyond such parties, to sustained commitments towards active maintenance of such large buildings. Furthermore, the authority of the elite was strongly recognized by the population who participated in such activities. Such large projects for religious purposes gave a rationale for the mobilization of a large labor force without a significant coercive force. When the projects came to a conclusion, elites and nonelites were more dependent on each other, and a web of interaction could then be employed towards other, hitherto unconsidered purposes. Another similarity may be found in the role of conflict and violence. In all these areas, evidence of warfare increased along with the development of the centers, and human sacrifice as a form of ritualized violence became a critical component of elite beliefs and practices: elites may have been increasingly seen as ferocious and, to nonelites, fearsome in the sense that expressions of violence to outsiders nurtured a foreboding threat to insiders (Joyce and Winter 1996).

It is hard to deny the importance of local processes in the Preclassic development of lowland Maya civilization. Yet the lowland Maya could borrow the concepts of hierarchical society, divine rulership, religious beliefs, and accompanying material symbols devised by other groups. A tendency to adaptability and the absorptive inclusion of new ideas facilitated the rapid development of Preclassic lowland Maya civilization. The introduction of foreign elements primarily reflects initiatives on the part of lowland Maya elites rather than impositions from outside. In this process, the lowland Maya became the most loyal followers of the Olmec tradition, which emphasized the glorification of individual rulers legitimized by supernatural power (Clark 1997; M. Coe 1977a); Teotihuacan and Monte Albán may have diverged from this old Mesoamerican tradition, with a less overt emphasis on the personal nature of leadership (Blanton et al. 1996).

For the Classic Maya, however, the stage was now set.

CHAPTER 4

THE CLASSIC PERIOD

POLITICAL HISTORY

Dynastic Origins

Tikal, Guatemala, became a central player in elite politics after the fall of El Mirador and other Preclassic cities nearby. Its earliest known monument, Stela 29, dates to AD 292, but later inscriptions indicate that many other rulers came before. Although such early kings are poorly understood, the dynastic record hints at a founder around AD 90 (Martin 2003: 5). Archaeological data on construction and settlement corroborate the view that Tikal survived severe political turmoil at the end of the Preclassic period, seemingly without major disruption. Its fourteenth ruler, Chak Tok Ich'aak ("Great Misty Claw" [spellings below from Martin and Grube 2008: 28]), is recorded on various monuments and ceramic texts of the late fourth century, underscoring the site's tenacity and the importance of this king.

Other centers began to formalize dynastic rule around the fourth and fifth centuries AD. The dynastic history of Calakmul, Campeche, later to become Tikal's major rival, remains enigmatic, in part because of the poor preservation of its monuments. The center is traditionally associated with the powerful Kan ("snake") dynasty. Various codex-style vessels made in or near the Mirador Basin during the late seventh and early eighth centuries tabulate a long list of rulers, although, contrary to some suggestions, it is not at all certain that those early rulers governed El Mirador as the dynastic seat of this dynasty: other alternatives are more likely (Fig. 4.1, Martin 1997; Martin and Grube 2008: 102). In a puzzling turn, epigraphic evidence first places the Kan dynasty, not at Calakmul, but at Dzibanche, Quintana Roo, some 140 kilometers to the northeast. Calakmul itself was probably governed by a different line of rulers until about AD 630 (Martin 2005).

Other sites are even more grandiose in their historical claims. Naranjo, Guatemala, which has close genealogical ties to Tikal, asserts an early origin to

Figure 4.1. Dynastic vase from the area of Calakmul, Mexico (K6751, copyright Justin Kerr).

its dynasty and, according to one text, a mythical ancestor some 896,000 years in the past. The well-documented history of Naranjo begins with Aj Wosal (a modern nickname), a ruler who took the throne in AD 546, although earlier flesh-and-blood lords are attested in the form of fragmentary texts (Tokovinine and Fialko 2007). Other centers in the central lowlands, including Balakbal, El Zapote, Xultun, Yaxha, and Uaxactun, started to erect monuments in the fourth and early fifth centuries. Further to the west, Palenque also claimed vague descent from deities in ancient times, but its historical origin appears to trace back to one K'uk' Bahlam, who acceded to royal office in AD 431. Such dynasties, with mythic accounts of origin, contrast with a second set of dynasties who have fully historic origins, as in the royal family of Yaxchilan, Mexico, which began to flourish around AD 359 (see Chapters 5 and 7).

The Teotihuacan Connection

The single most important political event of the Early Classic period occurred in AD 378: an enigmatic figure, Sihyaj K'ahk', arrived at Tikal and, on the same day, a local ruler, Chak Tok Ich'aak, "entered the water," a euphemism for death. Sihyaj K'ahk' is also recorded at Uaxactun and, possibly, at Río Azul, suggesting his wide political influence (Fig. 4.2). In the following year, Yax Nuun Ahiin was enthroned as the next ruler of Tikal, and his reign was marked by the abundant use of Teotihuacan symbols and objects, such as Tlaloc images, tripod cylinders, and green obsidian. Glyphic texts note that Yax Nuun Ahiin's father was "Spearthrower Owl," the lord of an as-yet-unknown place. David Stuart (1999) has suggested that this figure was a ruler of Teotihuacan who sent his military captain, Sihyaj K'ahk', to subjugate Tikal and install his young son, Yax Nuun Ahiin, as the new king of a distant center in the Maya region.

Figure 4.2. References to Sihyaj K'ahk', "Born from fire": **(a)** Tikal Marker: G4–H4 (after photograph by Stephen Houston); and **(b)** Bejucal Stela 1:B7 (after photograph by Ian Graham).

A likely resting place of Yax Nuun Ahiin was Burial 10, where numerous ceramic vessels with Teotihuacan motifs were found. Isotope analysis of the skeleton, however, indicates that the occupant of that tomb was born in Peten, Guatemala, not central Mexico (Wright 2005). The nature of the AD 378 event continues to be debated, although further exploration at related sites, like Sufricaya or Bejucal, Guatemala, are likely to elucidate the connection (Braswell 2003; Estrada-Belli et al. 2006).

Contacts with Teotihuacan or related areas certainly started before AD 378. On the Guatemalan Pacific Coast, the presence of a wide range of Teotihuacan-related materials, including "theater" censers (likely to represent mummy bundles prior to cremation, Taube 2000: fig. 10.22), *candeleros*, figurines, tripod cylinder vessels, and green obsidian, suggest that Teotihuacan established its colonies around the first half of the third century (Bove and Medrano 2003). At Altun Ha, David Pendergast (1990: 263–75; 2003) discovered, in Structure F-8 at that site, a tomb capped by a large number of artifacts, including green obsidian and Teotihuacan-related ceramics. The interment dates no later than AD 250. Excavations at the Mundo Perdido complex of Tikal by Juan Pedro Laporte and Vilma Fialko (1995) revealed *talud-tablero* buildings dating to the late third century. This architectural style, consisting of a vertical rectangular panel (*tablero*) supported by a sloped wall (*talud*), is generally considered an indicator of Teotihuacan influence (Fig. 4.3). Laporte, however, argues that *talud-tablero* buildings are widely distributed in Mesoamerica, and their presence at any given site may not necessarily signal direct contacts with Teotihuacan.

After AD 378, Tikal and its Teotihuacan-associated groups may have instigated significant political changes, including the establishment of new dynasties in various parts of the Maya lowlands. A reference to Sihyaj K'ahk' at Río Azul, as well as the presence of green obsidian and tripod cylinder vessels, suggests to Richard Adams that this center was directly controlled by Tikal (Adams 1999: 66–8). But it is at Copan, Honduras, where archaeologists found especially intriguing evidence. Retrospective texts note the arrival of its dynastic founder,

K'inich Yax K'uk' Mo', in AD 427 (D. Stuart 2004a). Excavations under the Acropolis by Robert Sharer and his team have uncovered earthen buildings and tombs dating to the fifth century, many containing rich offerings with Teotihuacan motifs (Bell et al. 2004; Sharer et al. 1999). In particular, the Hunal tomb appears to house the body of the dynastic founder, and its bone isotope signature strongly indicates a distant, lowland origin (Buikstra et al. 2004). Glyphic texts suggest that the nearby center of Quirigua was also founded at the same time (D. Stuart 2004a).

In the Pasión region, excavations by Bruce Bachand (2006) at Punta de Chimino, a small peninsular site on Lake Petexbatun, uncovered a cylinder-shaped crypt that contained a seated body dating to the early fifth century. Burial construction is similar to the Motmot tomb at Copan, from the same period (W. Fash and B. Fash 2000: 443), and comparable examples have also been reported from Chac in the Puuc region (Smyth and Rogart 2004). Although the stone-lined construction at Punta de Chimino is not the same as that of most Teotihuacan burials, the seated position appears to reflect inspiration from that central Mexican city. Soon after the interment, a temple and a monument at Punta de Chimino were ritually destroyed, leading to the near-abandonment of the site (Bachand 2006: 596). At Ceibal, the largest center in the Pasión region, an early ruler, K'an Mo' Bahlam (floruit AD 415), was mentioned in a retrospective text, but the center appears to have been all but abandoned soon after his reign (Sabloff 1975). At the small site of Tres Islas on the Pasión River, where there is little evidence of substantial occupation, three stelae, dating between AD 395 and 475, depict figures in Mexican warrior attire (Tomasic and Fahsen 2004). It is possible that a Teotihuacan-associated group, possibly from Tikal, was partially responsible for the drastic political and social changes in the Pasión region around the fifth century, although this requires further study (Demarest and Fahsen 2003).

In more distant areas, Tikal's involvement is less clear, and of variable nature. In the Guatemala highlands, Kaminaljuyu enjoyed a burst of activity in the Early Classic period, following the social disruption at the end of the Preclassic period. The prominence of Teotihuacan traits during this period, including *talud-tablero* architecture and ceramics, has long been noted (Sanders and Michels 1977). Although Teotihuacan influence may have reached Tikal through Kaminaljuyu (Coggins 1979), investigations in the 2000s indicate that the strong manifestations of Teotihuacan-related traits at this highland center postdate AD 378 (Braswell 2003; Houston et al. 2003). At Los Horcones, Chiapas, researchers have found stone monuments with Teotihuacan iconography and other cultural traits tied to central Mexico, dating mainly to the fifth and sixth centuries. This center probably functioned as an important trade base that connected Teotihuacan and the southern Maya area (García-Des Lauriers 2007). Teotihuacan-related traits have also been noted in the Puuc region

Figure 4.3. Structure 5C-49 with *talud-tablero*, Mundo Perdido complex, Tikal (photograph by Takeshi Inomata).

further to the north, at Oxkintok and Chac (Varela and Braswell 2003; Smyth and Rogart 2004).

The Age of Calakmul

Tikal continued to exert a predominant role during the reigns of Yax Nuun Ahiin's son, Sihyaj Chan K'awiil, as well as during following reigns, while Teotihuacan influence steadily diminished. A turn of fortune came in AD 562 with a defeat delivered probably by the Kan dynasty and Caracol, Belize (Houston 1987b; Martin and Grube 2008: 39). The following "dark age" of Tikal was traditionally considered the Middle Classic "hiatus," but this was in fact the time of prosperity for the Kan dynasty and its ally, Caracol. By defeating Naranjo, the Kan dynasty continued to expand its sway during the reign of "Yuknoom Head" – the name is incompletely deciphered – who appears to have moved the dynastic seat from Dzibanche to Calakmul in the 630s (Martin 2005). The succeeding ruler, Yuknoom Ch'e'n, enjoyed unmatched power in the Maya lowlands. Indeed, he is one of the few Maya kings who could justly be termed an "emperor," meddlesome in many polities, a strategist of the first order (Martin and Grube 2008: 108–9).

The emerging center of Dos Pilas became a new focus of the continuing rivalry between Tikal and the Kan dynasty. Dos Pilas was founded in the early seventh century by Bahlaj Chan K'awiil, a royal prince of Tikal, possibly as part of Tikal's attempt to reestablish its control of the Pasión region (Fig. 4.4; Houston 1993; Guenter 2003). Dos Pilas, however, was soon defeated by Calakmul. Following the battle, Bahlaj Chan K'awiil became Calakmul's ally and waged a series of battles against his brother, Nuun Ujol Chahk, the ruler of Tikal. With the help of Yuknoom Ch'e'n, Bahlaj Chan K'awiil eventually delivered a decisive defeat to the Tikal king in AD 679. The victorious Dos Pilas king sent his daughter, "Lady Six Sky," to Naranjo so as to reestablish, in AD 682, that dynasty as an ally of Calakmul (Houston 1993: 108).

Although the Kan dynasty, now located at Calakmul, was undoubtedly the prepotent power during the seventh century, its grip on the Maya area was incomplete. For example, although Palenque suffered serious defeats at the hands of the dynasty in AD 599 and 611 (Martin and Grube 2008: 161), the following king, K'inich Janahb Pakal, "Pakal the Great," successfully revived the center and drew a certain Nuun Ujol Chahk of Santa Elena, Tabasco, into his fold (note that this person is not the same as the ruler of Tikal). This did not, however, prove to be a long-lived success, and that region soon fell back into other zones of influence (Martin and Grube 2008: 161). In the southeastern area, Copan under the rule of "Smoke Imix" appears also to have been little affected by Calakmul's expansion.

Tikal's Revival and Regional Powers

In AD 695, Tikal regained its strong position through Jasaw Chan K'awiil's victory over the Calakmul king, Yich'aak K'ahk' (Schele and Freidel 1990: 205) – this was Calakmul's Waterloo. His son, Yik'in Chan K'awiil, continued on this path of success by defeating El Perú (Waka') in AD 743 and Naranjo in AD 744 (Martin 1996). The Kan kingdom lost its power, if not its ability to erect more stelae. With a few exceptions, its snake emblem disappeared from Calakmul and foreign references after the 730s. The original bat emblem glyph appears to have returned at Calakmul, a development that may point to the revival of its local dynasty (Martin 2005). The Kan dynasty's close ally, Caracol, also declined, and its elite activities diminished for a time.

Tikal's prosperity is most evident in the form of tall pyramids built during the reigns of Yik'in Chan K'awiil and his successors. These include his father's funerary building, Temple 1, an iconic structure in the modern Republic of Guatemala that embellishes its main unit of currency. The influence of these Tikal rulers, however, may not have had as wide-reaching an impact as that of their ancestors. Many other centers appear to have been preoccupied with political and military battles in their own regions. Dos Pilas, for example, wrenched its focus away from the conflict with Tikal and redirected its energies to the consolidation of its dominance over the Pasión region and nearby areas; this process included the defeat of Ceibal in AD 735 and the foundation of

Dos Pilas' secondary capital at Aguateca. Yaxchilan reached its heyday during the reigns of "Itzamnaaj" Bahlam (Shield Jaguar) and "Yaxuun" Bahlam (Bird Jaguar) from the late seventh century through the mid eighth century (again, note that the two royal names are not fully deciphered and should be viewed with caution). These kings seem primarily to have skirmished with minor or nearby centers, continually affected by a tense rivalry with Piedras Negras, a few dozen kilometers downriver. At Piedras Negras, the *k'atun*-anniversary that its Ruler 4 celebrated with his subordinate lords in AD 749 was a particularly important royal event, narrated on a panel dedicated nearly a half century later (Houston and D. Stuart 2001).

Palenque enjoyed the height of architectural and artistic achievement during the reign of K'inich Kan Bahlam and K'inich K'an Joy Chitam in the late seventh and early eighth centuries. The latter king, however, was captured in a battle with Tonina (Schele and Mathews 1991). The fate of Copan was similar. Its king, Waxaklajuun Ubaah K'awiil, erected a series of magnificent stelae during the early eighth century, but in AD 738 he was captured and killed by a subordinate lord of Quirigua, K'ahk' Tiliw Chan Yopaat. Despite these defeats, the dynastic lines of Paleque and Copan persisted, Copan going on to create the majestic stairway known as Hieroglyphic Stairway 1.

The northern part of the Yucatan Peninsula remained in the shadow of the more powerful and more populous southern lowlands throughout much of the Early Classic period, albeit with massive constructions in sites like Ake.

Figure 4.4. Dos Pilas Stela 9, showing Bahlaj Chan K'awiil of Dos Pilas, AD 682 (Photograph by Ian Graham, courtesy of the Peabody Museum of Archaeology and Ethnology, copyright the President and Fellows of Harvard University).

It was in the Late Classic period that explosive growth took place, yet always with the proviso that, until the later years of the Classic period, historical texts do not fall into reconstructible narratives of any detail or scale. In the Puuc region, Oxkintok, which became an important center during the late Early Classic period, continued its occupation into the Terminal Classic (Carmean et al. 2004). Edzna in Campeche, with a pattern of substantial Preclassic construction, also began to erect monuments in the seventh century. Near the northwestern coast, two major centers, Dzibilchaltun and Chunchucmil, grew during the same time to impressive size and scale.

Chunchucmil, with an estimated population of twenty thousand to thirty thousand, exhibited an unusually decentralized urban plan, with less emphasis on ceremonial buildings than other communities (Fig. 4.5). According to one explanation, this use of space reflected the city's mercantile orientation towards the salt trade and away from dynastic or courtly activity (Dahlin and Ardren 2002). The northeastern zone of the peninsula was apparently dominated by Coba, in Quintana Roo, Mexico. Its architecture shows close affinities with the southern lowlands, and many of its monuments date to the seventh century. The one-hundred-kilometer-long causeway connecting Coba with Yaxuna, the longest in the Maya area, was probably constructed around the seventh century (Stanton and Gallarta 2001). Ukit Kan Lehk, who founded Ek Balam in the eighth century, appears to have had some connection with Coba. Excavations in Structure 1 of Ek Balam by Leticia Vargas and Víctor Castillo (2006) have revealed a sumptuous building with elaborate façade sculptures, along with the tomb of the local lord. In addition to these powerful centers, numerous smaller centers emerged during the Late Classic period. This regional rivalry led to further heightened competitions and the eventual downfall of many centers towards the end of the Late Classic period and during the Terminal Classic (see Chapter 10).

BUILDINGS AND OBJECTS

Architecture

By the beginning of the Classic period, a basic repertory of the Maya architectural forms and techniques was already present. The Classic Maya directed substantial energy to the construction of ceremonial complexes with plazas and temple pyramids (Fig. 4.6). At Tikal, Preclassic temples, including the Mundo Perdido complex and the North Acropolis, received further renovations during the Early Classic, preserving the basic form of a Preclassic pyramid with its wide base. The construction of Temples 5 and 5D-33 at Tikal, erected just at the beginning of the Late Classic period, marked a shift to new temple forms that emphasized height rather than basal mass (the shape may already have been under experimentation at nearby El Zotz, Guatemala). This tradition

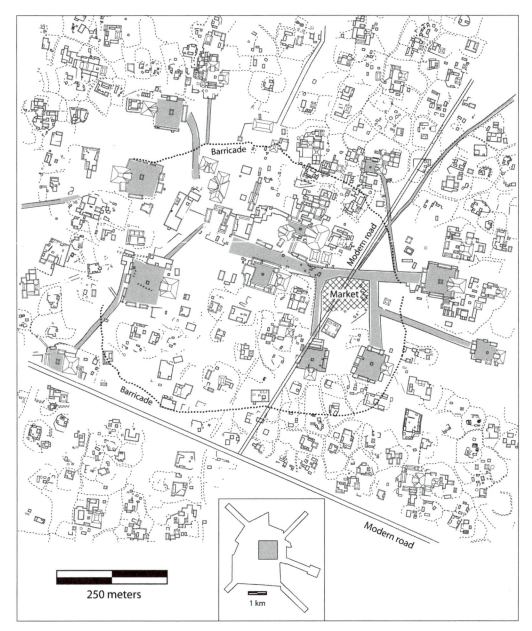

Figure 4.5. Map of Chunchucmil, Yucatan (courtesy of Bruce Dahlin and Scott Hutson).

flourished in a series of mammoth constructions at Tikal, including Temples 1 and 4, measuring forty-seven meters and seventy meters in height, respectively. The style of temples spread to other centers in the central lowlands, such as Yaxha. In addition, Temple 1 at Tikal is the best-known example of temples originally designed as funerary monuments, in worthy company with the celebrated Temple of the Inscriptions at Palenque, tomb of Pakal the Great. The

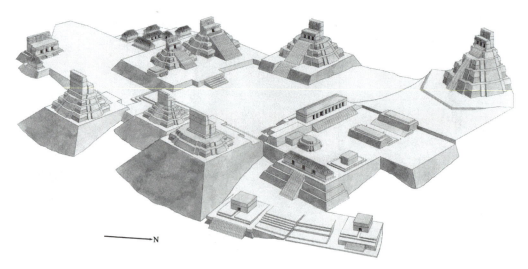

Figure 4.6. Reconstruction drawing of Piedras Negras South Group (drawing by Mark Child).

emphasis on steep pyramidal shape led to a peculiar style in the Río Bec region in the northern part of the central lowlands. The occupants of Becan, Río Bec, and Xpuhil in this area built imitation temples with decorative stairways that were impossibly steep and too narrow to climb (see Chapter 5).

Structure L8–8 at Aguateca, abandoned during construction, provides a unique glimpse into the sequence of temple construction (Fig. 4.7, Inomata et al. 2004). Builders started with the core of its first level by making a series of construction bins. The outer walls of each bin consisted of rough stones stacked in orderly manner and filled with more stones. While the outer layer of the first level was being completed with a "skin" of finely cut stone blocks and mortar, builders turned their attention to the core of the second level. As the pyramid grew higher, builders facilitated access by fashioning a construction ramp with rough stones just behind the building.

Another common type of building was the so-called "palace," typically of multiroom buildings placed on a platform and as epitomized by the Palace of Palenque. The Central Acropolis of Tikal exhibits a long sequence of development, from the Early Classic through Late Classic (Harrison 1999). At Copan the palace of the Early Classic dynastic founder K'inich Yax K'uk' Mo' combined earthen and masonry structures (Sharer et al. 1999). This complex was later covered by a series of masonry buildings, eventually resulting in the Acropolis, a sector with a variety of ceremonial or religious functions. At Uaxactun, in contrast, an Early Classic temple complex was expanded into a large palace complex, called Group A, during the Late Classic period. The configuration of the royal palace at Caracol, called Caana, was unique. It was placed on a massive pyramidal base, merged with a triadic temple complex

Figure 4.7. Structure L8-8 at Aguateca, an unfinished temple (photograph by Takeshi Inomata).

(Fig. 4.8). In a somewhat similar setting, the royal residential complex of Piedras Negras was built on a natural hill.

Many of the complexes that we call palaces were certainly residences of the royal family and other elites, but they also served administrative and ceremonial purposes (Andrews and Fash 1992; Harrison 1999). Some rooms were equipped with a bench as a throne and sleeping area. Excavations of rapidly abandoned buildings at Aguateca have provided detailed data on the use of space in these buildings. The center room usually held a relatively small number of objects and appears to have been used mainly for gatherings and receptions of visitors. Ceramic jars and bowls in these rooms probably contained food and drink for such occasions. The head of the household may also have conducted courtly duties and craft production in the center room. Side chambers generally contained large numbers of objects and were employed for sleeping, food preparation, craft work, and storage (Inomata et al. 2001, 2002). These buildings commonly faced a patio. Political meetings held in a palace structure, often depicted in ceramic paintings, were probably viewed by various participants who occupied the space in front of it. Wide stairways in front of these buildings also served as stages for theatrical acts (M. Miller 1986: 114; Inomata 2001a). When necessary, occupants shielded themselves from outside view by a curtain or some other removable feature. In general, the open nature of some Maya residential complexes is striking, distinguishing them from the more secluded palaces of bronze-age Crete, Ottoman Turkey, historic-period China, and other regions.

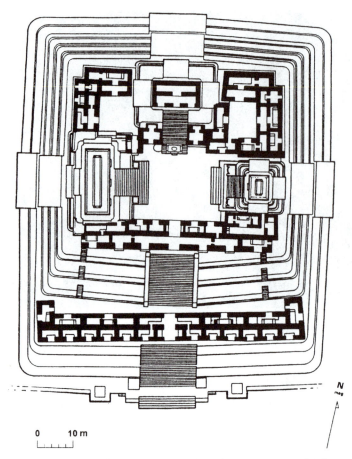

0   10 m

Figure 4.8. Caana Pyramid, Caracol, Belize (courtesy of Arlen and Diane Chase).

Ballcourts occur at most large Maya centers. Many of them consisted of parallel structures with sloping sides facing inwards, but those at Uxmal and Chichen Itza had vertical walls. All were important foci of public and elite ceremonies. Some of them had round, carved ballcourt markers in the playing alley. Differences in the sizes and forms of ballcourts point to diversity and flexibility in the game, with size reaching its maximum in the ballcourt of Chichen Itza, measuring 166 by 68 meters.

Some palaces and temples had wattle-and-daub walls and thatched roofs, whereas others included solid stone walls and masonry roofs with corbelled vaults, built with horizontally stacked blocks, each projecting farther and farther inward until they could be capped by a single stone. There were also pyramids in truncated shapes without structures on top, including the main pyramids of some E-Group complexes and those of the Twin Pyramid Complexes at Tikal. Vaulted roofs necessitated thick walls, and the width of the room was usually limited to three meters. The large stone mass of these buildings,

Figure 4.9. Balamku, Campeche, stucco façade with mythic hills and creatures, Early Classic period (photograph by Karl Taube).

however, kept their rooms relatively cool, even in tropical heat. Some buildings were decorated with "roof combs," vertical ornaments built on the center line of the roof. Floors and in some cases walls were covered with smooth plaster, and many buildings appear to have been painted red. These plastered surfaces, particularly the exteriors exposed to the harsh tropical elements, probably required frequent maintenance.

The tradition of stucco sculptures that decorated Preclassic temples continued into the Early Classic period, with the finest examples found in the Rosalila Temple of Copan, at Kohunlich, and at Balamku (Fig. 4.9). During the Late Classic, this technique was largely replaced by stone mosaic sculpture. The elaboration of stone mosaics culminated in the Puuc region of the Yucatan Peninsula during the Terminal Classic period. The façades of various buildings at Uxmal, Sayil, and other centers exhibited the Principal Bird Deity and sundry geometric shapes. At Palenque, however, architectural stucco ornaments continued to be emphasized. Stucco-sculpture façades also saw a brief revival at Machaquila, Cancuen, and Ceibal in the Pasión region at the end of the Late Classic and during the Terminal Classic periods.

The Maya shared many architectural traits, but regional differences can be pronounced. Limestone was the primary construction material for most of the lowlands, whereas the highland Maya used earth and volcanic stones. Stone blocks in Classic constructions were generally smaller than those of Preclassic predecessors, but a notable exception was the megalithic architecture built in Yucatan during the Early Classic period. At the western center of Comalcalco, where stone materials are scarce, structures were made of mud bricks. Influence from other areas, including *talud-tablero* architecture during the Early Classic and central Mexican architecture at Chichen Itza, also contributed to architectural diversity.

Commoners built their houses on low platforms surrounding a patio, although these typically were smaller and less elaborate than elite compounds. Some of them had features similar to elite residences, including stone walls, benches, and room partitions. Much like the pattern even in elaborate palaces, the most common form of these houses was a rectangle, but residences of elliptical shape were also built in the northern lowlands (Kurjack 1974). Nonelite residences are found both in the core zone of each site and in peripheral areas. Beyond the civic ceremonial core, they show a pattern of dispersed distribution, resulting most likely not from central planning, but from the social and economic necessities of individual households and other groups.

In addition to such individual buildings, the Maya created causeways and reservoirs. Causeways provided important ceremonial spaces for processions and other rituals. At the same time, the practical utility of these flat and well-drained roads is clearly recognizable for those who have experienced the broken karst topography of the Maya lowlands and their muddy terrain during the rain season. Reservoirs were generally built within the central precincts of sites in the central lowlands and served as important sources of water during the dry season. Some of them were converted from depressions that came into existence with quarrying for building materials. Maya cities, however, lacked effective sewage and waste-management systems. Most buildings did not have toilets, except for the rare examples of the Palenque Palace, and the Maya, both elites and commoners, typically tossed their household garbage behind or near their households. Although these middens left convenient sources of information for future archaeologists, the practice was not necessarily beneficial for those who lived there. Like many other preindustrial cities of the world, Maya centers were probably less-than-healthy places.

Monuments and Writing

Stelae and other monuments are the hallmark of the Classic period, although the tradition began earlier. Early Classic stelae typically depicted rulers from the side, although frontal views became more common during the Late Classic period. Some stelae still retain original red paint, and plain stelae without carving may originally have held painted designs. Other forms of carved monuments, including lintels and panels, gained popularity in the latter part of the

Classic period. Although stelae placed in plazas were probably viewed by numerous people, including nonelites, lintels and panels that decorated temples and palaces looked to the elite as their intended audience. This difference is also reflected thematically. Stelae often depict rulers in full ceremonial costumes performing in mass spectacle or dance. In contrast, many lintels and panels represented rulers and other elites engaging in courtly meetings and other events, often in less ostentatious attire.

In large parts of the Maya lowlands, bas-relief carvings were prevalent, but stelae at Copan, Quirigua, and Tonina display more three-dimensional carving (Fig. 4.10). Regional differences also expressed themselves in materials. Limestone was by far the most common material, but sculptors used volcanic tuff at Copan and a gritty and erodible sandstone at Quirigua, Altar de Sacrificios, and Tonina. In rare instances, slate quarried from the Maya mountains was also used (Healey et al. 1995).

Many of those monuments, as well as some ceramic painting, were decorated with hieroglyphic writing. A significant development in glyphic script appears to have taken place during the transition between the Preclassic and Classic periods, with the establishment of a basic scheme that combined logographs and phonetic or syllabic signs of consonant + vowel form (Houston 2000). Much of the Preclassic writing prior to this change resists understanding, in part because of difficulties in accessing the sounds of the script through phonetic elements. The next major change occurred at the beginning of the Late Classic period, with the addition of various new phonetic signs. Late Classic writing was highly phonetic, and modern decipherment has been most successful on these late texts.

Figure 4.10. Tonina Monument 146, AD 787 (photograph by Ian Graham, I. Graham et al. 2006, *Corpus of Maya Hieroglyphic Inscriptions*, Vol. 6, Part 3: 77, reproduced courtesy of the President and Fellows of Harvard College).

Ceramics

Ceramics provide the most common artifact at any Maya site, and it is the rare, extensive dig that does not uncover sherds by the ton. The sequence of change roughly reflects political trends. Highly homogeneous Late Preclassic ceramics led to more regionalized styles with the rise of competing polities during the Early Classic period. In the fragmented political landscape of the Late Classic, ceramics exhibited further regionalization. Utilitarian ceramics, however, tended to be fairly conservative. Large unslipped jars, either plain or striated, were used to store food and water throughout the period. Bowls of large or medium sizes were probably used for soaking maize and cooking.

Changes in painted ceramics are more clearly noticeable, although the chronological sequence for the beginning of the Classic period, sometimes called the Protoclassic, still remains unclear. Some scholars suggested that migrations from the southeastern highlands resulted in the introduction of Protoclassic traits, including wavy line motifs with resist or positive painting (Usulutan decoration), mammiform tetrapods, orange slipped wares, and first polychromes (Gifford 1976: 128). Recent studies, however, discern complex patterns of local development and interregional interaction, as well as the coexistence of so-called Protoclassic traits with Preclassic and Early Classic ones over a long period. Brady and colleagues (1998) suggest that, just around 75 BC, Maya potters from the northwestern peninsula all the way to the Pasión region, the central lowlands, and western Belize began to experiment with gloss orange slip and lighter paste while the waxy slip and darker paste of the Late Preclassic ceramics remained in use. Tetrapods (four-legged ceramics) also appeared during this period. Around AD 150 a kind of glossy orange slip and white-to-buff undersurface, some with polychrome decoration, developed at the same time as large mammiform tetrapods. These features coexisted with other Early Classic traits as late as AD 400. Importantly, waxy Chicanel wares may have persisted instead of, or alongside, these Protoclassic/Early Classic traits until around AD 400 in some areas, including Coba and Dzibilchaltun in the north, the Pasión region, and the southeastern Peten (Laporte 1995; Lincoln 1985).

Tzakol and related ceramic complexes correspond to Early Classic ceramics in the central lowlands, now characterized by new glossy wares (Fig. 4.11). Most polychromes were plates or bowls with ring base and basal flange, decorated with animal or supernatural figures and geometric motifs painted in red and black. During the fourth century, Teotihuacan influence introduced tripod cylinder vessels, often with black slip or stucco painting. In the Late Classic period, Tepeu and related ceramics began to dominate in the central and southeastern lowlands, the Pasión region, and western Belize (Rice and Forsyth 2004) (Fig. 4.12). Common forms included red-slipped, medium-sized jars with a concave bottom, which the Maya used to carry water and other liquids by placing them on the head. (Today, Maya women still use vessels of the identical shape, though most of these containers are now made of plastic.) Miniature bottles contained tobacco powder, pigments, and other materials. Polychrome ceramics of this period often had a creamy underslip that permitted a greater range of color. Their shapes included round-sided bowls and

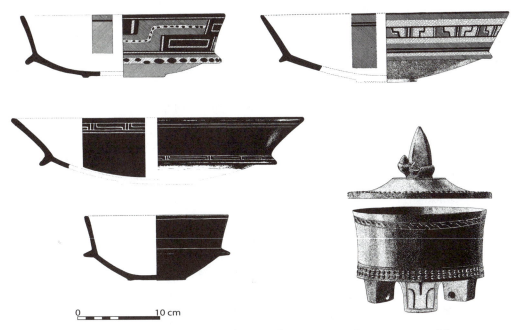

Figure 4.11. Tzakol ceramic vessels (Smith 1955, figs. 10, 20, and 25, courtesy of the Middle American Research Institute, Tulane University).

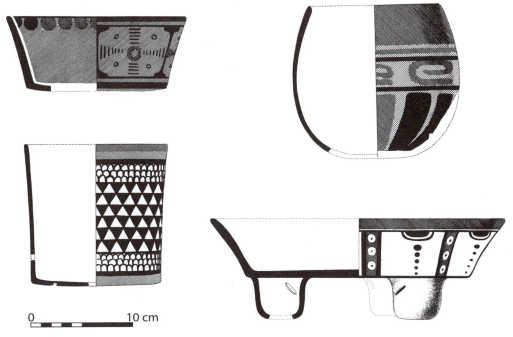

Figure 4.12. Tepeu ceramic vessels (Smith 1955, figs. 33, 39, 55, and 62, courtesy of the Middle American Research Institute, Tulane University).

tripod plates. The height of Maya ceramic artistry occurs as vase paintings on cylinders of the seventh and eighth centuries. Famous examples include polychrome vessels produced at the so-called "Ik" site and the Naranjo region, as well as the "codex-style" vessels with black lines over a cream base made in the Mirador Basin.

In the Late Classic there is clear evidence of growing regional diversity in ceramic styles. At Piedras Negras, for example, potters developed poly-chromes with resist techniques. Areas around Palenque were known for fine paste ceramics of brown and gray colors (Rands 1987). Fine Gray Ware from this area began to be traded into other parts of the lowlands during the eighth century (Foias and Bishop 1997). Copan and the southeastern area maintained its distinct ceramic tradition from the Preclassic period. Their Copador poly-chrome of the Late Classic period lacked the finesse of the central-lowland counterparts, but a specular hematite red imparted a distinct "look" to the ceramics, which glittered in oblique light. The northern lowlands diverged from its southern neighbors by developing a unique tradition characterized by Slate Ware with waxy gray to brown slip.

Stone Tools

In the virtual absence of metal, the Maya made various types of tools from stone. Their types and frequencies reflect variable access to materials by geo-graphical region and social group, as well as local traditions, but their chrono-logical changes are not as noticeable as those of ceramics. The Maya made cutting tools mainly from locally available chert and obsidian imported from the highlands (Fig. 4.13). Use-wear analysis by Kazuo Aoyama (1999) and oth-ers show that their shapes and use do not follow any one-to-one correlation (Fig. 4.14). Many chipped-stone artifacts were multipurpose tools. A common type of chert tool was the oval biface, employed in cutting wood, shaping stone for construction or digging soil for farming. Points may have been used as knives and spear points. Many unretouched flakes also functioned as cutting tools.

A vast majority of obsidian artifacts were prismatic blades, which served as all-purpose cutting tools. The blade technique allowed the lowland Maya to use this imported material with high efficiency. Some blades were probably embedded in wooden or bone handles, but many were held directly in hands. A small number of obsidian points and macroblades, especially those of elaborate shape, such as the so-called "eccentrics," were associated strongly with elites (Fig. 4.15). Basalt, jade, and other hard stones were polished into axe shapes. Attached to wooden handles or used as chisels, they could hew wood or carve stone for elite sculpture.

Every household needed at least one grinding stone (Moholy-Nagy 2003; Rovner and Lewenstein 1997). The common names for the pestle and mortar,

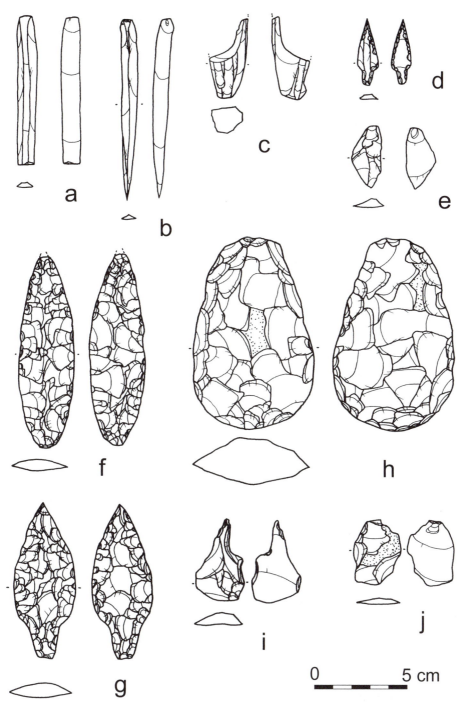

Figure 4.13. Range of lithics from Aguateca: (**a-e**) obsidian; (**a-b**) prismatic blades; (**c**) polyhedral core fragment; (**d**) prismatic blade point; (**e**) percussion flake; (**f-j**) chert; (**f-g**) bifacial points; (**h**) oval biface; (**i**) drill; (**j**) bifacial thinning flake (drawings by Kazuo Aoyama).

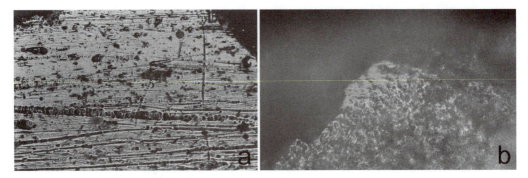

Figure 4.14. Use-wear on stone tools observed under a high-power microscope: **(a)** parallel striations on an obsidian blade from cutting wood; **(b)** polish and parallel striations on a chert bifacial point from cutting bone (courtesy of Kazuo Aoyama).

manos and *metates,* are not the original Maya terms but are later adoptions from Spanish and Nahuatl, the language of the Aztecs and other peoples. Large basin-shape *metates* made of limestone were probably used primarily for grinding maize. *Metates* made of harder imported stone, such as basalt, typically possessed flat grinding surfaces supported by tripods; they tended to be smaller than limestone ones and appear to have been used in grinding food, medicine, pigments, and clay.

Other Artifacts

Hand-molded ceramic figurines were nearly absent during the Early Classic period. A small number of mold-made figurines were limited mostly to elite funerary contexts. During the Late Classic period figurines regained popularity in both elite and nonelite contexts. Many combined techniques of molding and hand-modeling and depicted human and animal figures. A large portion of them were hollow and were to be played as whistles or ocarinas (Triadan 2007). In addition to such whistles, the Maya made various types of musical instruments. Archaeologists have found flutes and multichambered whistles made of ceramics and shell trumpets, but other wind instruments were likely shaped of wood. Drums included smaller, handheld versions made of ceramics and larger ones made of wood. Other instruments could be made of turtle carapaces, bone rasps, and wooden rattles, lending percussion and rhythm to Classic Maya music.

Bone tools included pointed objects generally called awls, which may have been used for textile, basket, and leather working. Some bone needles had an eye for threading. Stingray spines with ragged edges were used in blood-letting, and the Maya also made imitations of such exotic and fragile objects out of bone and jade. Spindle whorls for spinning threads were fashioned of stone, clay, reused ceramic sherds, and possibly other perishable materials,

Figure 4.15. Chert eccentric, Late Classic period, Dumbarton Oaks Research Library and Collections, PC.B.589 (M. Miller and Martin 2004, pl. 82; copyright Dumbarton Oaks, Pre-Columbian Collection, Washington, DC).

including wood. In some cases, the whorls may have served as flywheels for drills (Kovacevich 2007).

An important material for ornaments was jade. The Maya sawed and polished this hard material into statues, pendants representing anthropomorphic and zoomorphic motifs, hanging celts, tubes, and beads. Various greenstones

Figure 4.16. Wooden box, Tortuguero area, Mexico, AD 681; Kislak Collection, Library of Congress (copyright Justin Kerr).

were used for similar purposes. Other ornaments were made of alabaster, pyrite, ceramics, bone, and shell. Ceremonial attire, such as headdresses, often joined durable with perishable materials, including feather, cloth, and leather. Pyrite was also sawn and polished as mosaic pieces that could be fitted into circular or rectangular mirrors. Many other objects made of delicate or organic materials did not survive in the tropical environment, from codices made of bark to a variety of textiles, leather objects, and wooden artifacts and furniture. A small number of wooden statues, wooden bowls, and textile fragments survived in exceptionally rare contexts, including well-sealed or packed tombs, dry caves, and cenotes (Coggins 1992). These give some hint of a disappeared but abundant set of artifacts (Fig. 4.16).

CLASSIC MAYA SOCIETY

Changes in politics and material culture during the transit of the Classic period were closely tied to demographic trends. The pattern in the Early Classic period is still problematic because of uncertainties in ceramic chronology, but in many areas outside of the central lowlands the population appears to have declined from Late Preclassic levels. The political fortune of individual dynasties clearly affected this process. For example, the population at Caracol grew substantially after it (or its allies) defeated Tikal (A. Chase and D. Chase 1989). The Late Classic period witnessed a rapid increase in population throughout the Maya lowlands. Surveys at various sites and in intersite areas show that population growth was exponential. Many previously unoccupied or sparsely inhabited areas were filled in, and numerous new dynasties and other political powers emerged. The absolute population is difficult to estimate, but some studies suggest that, at Tikal, it reached roughly sixty thousand, and the same or larger can be imagined for Calakmul and other first-rank cities (Culbert et al. 1990).

Yet, for all the dynamism of their history and the diversity by region, the Classic Maya maintained cultural continuity over time, sharing practices and ideas across a wide area. The material and historical setting is now in place. The moment has come to "interview" indirectly the people who composed Classic Maya society, its kings and nobility, gods and queens, and, not least, its farmers, traders, and artisans.

PART II

SOCIAL ACTORS

CHAPTER 5

KINGS AND QUEENS, COURTS AND PALACES

KINGS AND GOVERNANCE

For the Classic Maya, kings were highly visible in imagery and texts. If a stela displayed a person, it was likely a ruler; if a pot showed a building, it was almost always a palace, where rulers received gifts and gave commands. The visibility of kings provides an opportunity for scholars, along with a challenge. Detailed records give a sense of personality and intention available for few other people of the time. But, in all likelihood, kings were not the only ones to play a role in governance or decision making. Some kings "governed," others simply "reigned," presiding over events they did not control (Evans-Pritchard 1971: 117; de Jouvenel 1959; Flathman 1980). No amount of unearned, institutional or hereditary authority could compensate for deficits in charisma and ingenuity (Lindholm 1990). Yet the Maya clearly found much to value in hereditary kingship. The limited pool of candidates risked the chance of untalented rulers. The advantage was that, as kings passed away, predictable inheritance offered stability during changes of office, facilitated by a doctrine of sacred, legitimating essence that separated rulers from other beings (Houston and D. Stuart 1996: 295). The physical setting of royal courts assisted that task by providing an enduring and enlargeable infrastructure for the kings and their families, courtiers, and servants.

THE *AJAW*

The basic concept of kingship was an ancient term, *ajaw*, "lord," traceable back to the beginning of Mayan languages (Fig. 5.1). There is a suspicion, not yet confirmed by historical linguistics, that the term arose from an agentive particle, *aj, or "a being connected with," and a term for "shouting," *aaw (Kaufman and Norman 1984: 139; also Houston and Stuart 1996: fn. 3). This calls to mind an oratorical term for rulership in regions like Postclassic central Mexico, where *tlahtoāni*, a title for lordship, also meant "speaker" (Karttunen

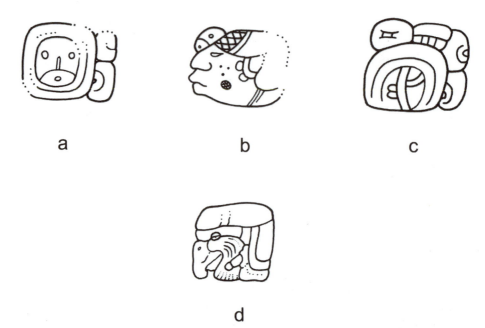

Figure 5.1. Maya glyphs for *ajaw*, "lord": **(a)** El Cayo Panel 1: M16; **(b)** and **(c)** Piedras Negras Panel 2: N1, J'3; and **(d)** Copan Hieroglyphic Stairway, Step XIII (drawing by Stephen Houston).

1983: 266). The sign for *ajaw* appears as early as the third century BC (Saturno et al. 2006: 1282). Whether it held the same meaning as later examples is unproven, however. Preclassic Maya texts can scarcely be read, and only a few inscriptions reveal more than a name or two (Schele and Miller 1986: 119–20; cf. Mora-Marín 2001). By the Early Classic period, at least, *ajaw* becomes more interpretable. It attached to particular places or to stages of life as a means of distinguishing one lord from another: thus, *mutul-ajaw*, "lord of Tikal" or, perhaps, *winik-ha'b-ajaw*, "lord of a 20-year span" (e.g., Tikal Stela 31: I2-J2, I4, C. Jones and Satterthwaite 1982, fig. 51; D. Stuart and Houston 1994: 3, 5). The title was always a noun, the term for "lord," preceded by an adjective of varying sort. Only later, towards the end of the Early Classic, did it acquire a third element, separating the ruler from others who held *ajaw* status. Rulers were now *k'uhul*, "holy" or "sacred" (Houston and Stuart 1996: 295). Perhaps a simple change in rhetoric, the addition could also signal real shifts in the conceptual basis of rule.

Underlying the *ajaw* title was a set of myths that expressed itself clearly by the Early Classic period. These myths were of a young lord with a headband who corresponds to one of the Hero Twins of Maya myth (M. Coe 1989: 167–8). The Hero Twins represented energetic youths of great cunning who bested the lords of death (Fig. 5.2). As such they exemplified the most worthy kind of king: ingenious, tenacious, active, fearless. The young lord with a spot on his cheek – and, more rarely, with three dots connected to the Maya solar deity, a

Figure 5.2. Hero Twins in Late Classic imagery, Boston Museum of Fine Arts (K1892, MFA 1993.565, copyright Justin Kerr).

god connected to rule – embodied dominion over humans, whereas his twin, with jaguar markings on his body, personified lordship over animals (Taube 2003: 472, 487). The widespread use among Classic kings of "theonyms," names acquired on accession that refer to particular deities in motion or state-of-being, underscores the means by which rulers likened themselves to gods, if not quite claiming to be deities themselves (Houston and Stuart 1996: 295; also Colas 2004: 266–77). The fact that rulers had personal names, some of which continued in use after accession, suggests that "tying the headband" (one of several expressions for elevation to the throne) resulted in a redefinition or augmentation of identity: before, purely human (if elite); afterwards, avatars of gods. Their descent from distant founders, some with godly biographies and lifetimes of impossible length, underscored their unique propensity to rule (Martin and Grube 2008: 70; Schele 1992). At Tamarindito, Guatemala, the founder is evidently a lordly star-being, a line of descent presumably not shared with peasants at the site (Houston 1993, figs. 4–5, 4–17).

Many *ajaw* titles correspond to the so-called "emblem glyph," a claim of sacred dominion by one person at any one time over a particular location (Fig. 5.3). In origin, the title was thus toponymic or geographically oriented, although it seemed later to gain a more diffuse or abstract sense of "rule over such-and-such an area." There could be several *ajaw* in one generation, and perhaps this more inclusive category embraced all offspring of rulers. But, with very rare exceptions, only one living person could use a particular emblem title. Occurrences of multiple holders, as at Copan, reflected unusual circumstances. Some of the titles were assigned to deities who "sat" in high office with a human ruler (David Stuart, personal communication, 1998). Others referred to rulers who were probably kin but living at different sites. At places like Palenque and Tortuguero or Tikal and Dos Pilas, each set with joint use of emblems, there were no guarantees that these lords enjoyed good relations. Indeed, quite to the contrary: most were adversaries (Martin and Grube 2008: 165). A few sites with ragged succession, in fraternal line or other arrangements, may accord the "holy lord" title to such brothers, with a hint of corulership or, in less strong form, *primus inter pares* ("first among equals") for the eldest (e.g., Palenque Palace Tablet, L15; Greene Robertson 1985, fig. 259). In much the same way, the later texts and imagery of Caracol, Belize, emphasizes joint, almost equal displays of dynasts (A. Chase et al. 1991: 13). One altar presents the captives of a person using the high title of *bakab* (see Section titled "Emblems and Regional Variety"). More telling, the expression used to record his general age usually appears with kings, not underlings. Yet the very same altar identifies the supervisor of these captures as a living ruler of Caracol. The late date of the sculpture and the surprising emphasis on a secondary figure hint at local fractures in royal authority towards the end of the Classic period (Martin and Grube 2008: 99). This phenomenon, of elites surfacing in monumental displays once reserved for kings, has been widely noted by other scholars (e.g., Webster 2002: 138–9).

There was an intermediate position between a king ruling one site only and those reigning at different sites, despite laying claim to the same title. Attested in areas of relatively open terrain, this pattern developed when a single king reigned over several communities. In the Petexbatun region of Guatemala, the same lord appears at sites like Aguateca and Dos Pilas (Houston 1993: 116–21). The last known king elected to focus on Aguateca alone, perhaps for defensive reasons, as Dos Pilas had, because of topography, poor potential as a redoubt (Inomata et al. 2001). Prior to that time, however, these places may have served as seasonal residences for the king and his court or as special-service locale for particular rituals (Ball and Taschek 2001). It is striking, for example, that Dos Pilas has a ballcourt and Aguateca does not. Another example occurs in and around Pomona, Tabasco, including a hilltop settlement known as Panhale (Anaya Hernández 2002; García Moll 2005: 21–2, fig. 2–1). Several distinct sites show rule by the holy *pakbul* lord, a title associated with what must have been a single kingdom. The impression is that the rulers deliberately selected a variety of terrain for their settlements, some defensive, others less so, or near bodies of water that could be controlled from certain positions. Agricultural studies may eventually show that multiple royal seats of this sort responded to

Figure 5.3. Selection of emblem titles, Copan dynasty, eighth century AD: **(a)** molded pot, area of Quirigua, Guatemala (photograph from Michael Coe); **(b)** and **(c)** blocks from the Hieroglyphic Stairway, Copan (courtesy of the Peabody Museum of Archaeology and Ethnology, copyright the President and Fellows of Harvard University).

a mosaic of potentials for local plant growth or favored foods. An alternative is simply that, through many residences, they extended the royal presence to as many locations as possible, recalling the pattern of peripatetic kingship known in Medieval Europe and as late as Charles V of Spain (Adamson 1999b: 11). The region near Zapote Bobal, Guatemala, is another such area with what may be multiple settlements ruled by one king, the *hix-witz-ajaw* or "feline-hill" lord (Fitzsimmons 2006; D. Stuart 2003). His royal line favored a simple statement of lordship and did not describe itself generally as "holy." This leads to the unanswered question of how such epithets were acquired or assigned and whether they corresponded to some subtle hierarchy of rulers.

EMBLEMS AND REGIONAL VARIETY

Every year, more inscriptions are discovered in the center, margins, and political interstices of the Yucatan Peninsula where the compaction of kingdoms is greatest. Those finds, along with renewed scrutiny of eroded monuments, contribute to a growing list of emblems (Martin and Grube 2008: 19). A few pertain to "lost sites," documented in texts but not yet connected to places (Grube 2004b). Future fieldwork will doubtless fill the gaps, yet the absence of emblems at certain cities in Yucatan, Campeche, and Quintana Roo poses another challenge. Perhaps the holes in coverage express variation in the nature of rulership or distinct notions of what was worth recording. The difficulty in picking one explanation over the other comes from the usual dilemma in archaeology of inferring broad conclusions from a small number of texts or assuming that few inscriptions equate to few or no kings.

Even known emblems display great and often baffling variety. Several titles indicate "holiness" yet fail to specify that someone was an *ajaw*, at least in the main royal epithet (Houston 1986). Others emphasize the *ajaw* title but not the property of sacrality, except for certain rulers. The dynasty of Itzan, Guatemala, had a few kings who boasted of being "holy," others who only labeled themselves as *ajaw* of that kingdom (Houston 2007a). This diversity is particularly pronounced in Yucatan and adjacent areas. A few places, very few given the intensity of settlement, displayed a full emblem. One would be Ek Balam, Yucatan, which had a *k'uhul talol-ajaw*, "holy *talol* lord," but there, too, the use of the title is unpredictable: the same king could also be a mere *talol-ajaw* (Lacadena 2004; also Graña-Behrens 2006). Yucatan clearly had a distinct system of royal titles in that high titles occurred in some of the texts but prior to personal names, a practice that was the reverse order of texts in the southern Maya Lowlands (see below; Lacadena 2000). In contrast, Oxkintok, also in Yucatan, uses an unusual emblem that seems not even to contain an *ajaw* title (García Campillo 1991, 1992). High lords of other sites, such as Xcalumkin, Campeche, go by a noble title, not a royal one, suggesting very different connotations of these titles, depending on region. Scholars are far from sorting out what this variety means and whether it expresses actual diversity of governance.

In fact, increasing evidence points to broad shifts in political landscapes during the Classic period, and not just between regions but within them. At Altar de Sacrificios, not far from Itzan, later kings replaced an early emblem with a new one of wholly different form, as though a dramatic rupture had taken place (Houston 2007a). Similar shifts may occur at Calakmul, Campeche, with consequences for the principal royal title, which went from a bat head to that of a snake, with profound differences in reading (Martin 2005: 7–8). Several examples attest to an historical process by which lords accrued two titles of lordship. This resembles the many labels used by Elizabeth II, who, because of vagaries in empire, reigns as Queen of Great Britain and Queen of Canada, Australia, and so forth. For the Maya Yaxchilan is the clearest analogy. Early lords declared themselves to be *pa'-chan-ajaw*, lords of the "split-sky" place, a location associated with Yaxchilan; they only intermittently added a second, as yet, undeciphered title of lordship (Martin 2004: 6). At times, rulers at the nearby site of Bonampak also employed two separate titles of lordship, along with clear references to their settlement as the "hill of the vulture," *usiij-witz* (David Stuart, personal communication, 2005). Dominion flowed over more than a single location and, in these examples, could extend to multiple kingdoms. Although joined in the person of one king, the kingdoms retained their distinct identities. This applied equally to a shadowy set of regional terms, 7 *tzuk* and 13 *tzuk*, which stipulated broader divisions (*tzuk*) of the Maya world beyond the limits of particular polities (Chapter 1, Beliaev 2000: 76).

Alliances can shift, too, in ways openly acknowledged by Maya rulers, with dramatic evictions of unlucky kings. A vivid if periodically ambiguous case comes from Dos Pilas, Guatemala, as recorded in recently recovered fragments of Hieroglyphic Stairway 2 (Fahsen 2002; Guenter 2003, with emendations by Houston). First, the great dynasty of Calakmul hit hard at the king of Dos Pilas, Bahlaj Chan K'awiil or Ruler 1, who scurried into exile at Aguateca, some few kilometers to the southwest. The Calakmul ruler then assaulted Tikal, a cousin dynasty of Dos Pilas, and entered into contact with the rulers of Cancuen to the south of Dos Pilas. A brief truce ensued, negotiated at a place that may be the same as the large site of Yaxha, in Guatemala. The regional powers did allow Dos Pilas to battle towards the south at a place called Koban (in the Alta Verapaz of Guatemala?) and possibly against Machaquila, where the rulers of Dos Pilas took captives in the process (Ciudad and Lacadena 2006). But the ruler of Tikal clearly did not approve of this entente with Calakmul. According to the text, he attacked the city of Dos Pilas, forcing its Ruler 1 into exile once more and engendering a crucial shift in alliance. The site of Dos Pilas burned, along with some of its allies. The king of Tikal pursued Ruler 1 from place to place yet the hostilities eventually ended: the ruler of Tikal found defeat at a site called Pulil, his "Waterloo," allowing Ruler 1 to return to Dos Pilas. Twenty-three days later there appear, in brutal phrasing, "hills of skulls" and "pools of blood," indicating severe problems, perhaps death, for the lord of Tikal. The king of Calakmul performed a ritual dance attended by Ruler 1, a true survivor who soon commemorated his third *k'atun* (twenty-year) span as ruler. The Stairway projects a view of the king of Dos Pilas as a tenacious and flexible figure, but the overall hero is his overlord, the "king of kings" of the Maya, Yuknoom Ch'e'n (Martin and Grube 2008: 109).

From this and much other evidence it is certain that Classic Maya kings knew of distant rulers. In this respect, the most revealing are two sets of texts at Copan and Ceibal (D. Stuart 1993: 339, fig. 6). At Copan, on Stela A, four lords from Copan, Tikal, Calakmul, and Palenque bear some connection to particular kinds of sky, linked – weirdly – to tails, wood, a deer hoof and an unidentified element; directional signs follow but in unclear relation to the kings. Almost ethereal in content, the inscription concludes with an account of the opening and sealing of holes or caches during a key calendrical rite. In contrast, Ceibal Stela 10, dated more than a hundred years later, to AD 849, mentions the local king and three foreign visitors from Tikal, Calakmul, and the Lake Peten Itza region (Fig. 5.4). Physically present at Ceibal – so the text tells us, anyway – each ruler comes to witness an important calendrical celebration. There is some overlap between the texts at Copan and Ceibal, both of which focus on prestigious kings from far parts of the Maya region. Yet there is little proof that the stelae echo large-scale divisions of the Maya world by quadrant or sector, each presided over by a particular monarch (cf. J. Marcus 1976: 16–8).

An enigmatic and fragmentary text from Altar de los Reyes, Campeche, sketches out yet another ordering of foreign lords, among them the rulers of Tikal, Palenque, Calakmul, Motul de San José, Edzna (as identified by David Stuart), and someone associated with the Mirador Basin, to judge from a title used in that zone (Šprajc 2003). Here, in all probability, the number of lords surpasses ten. Like Copan but unlike Ceibal, the rulers are identified by title rather than personal name, as though the more general designation interested the sculptors, not a precise reference to a particular king. In this, the texts recall the association in Maya texts, especially on pottery, between generally specified rulers and nocturnal, almost sinister aspects of the royal soul. These aspects, called *wahy*, were often composites of violent and dangerous forces or creatures and may have represented an indigenous theory of dreams – the word *wahy* means "sleep" in most Mayan languages – and, perhaps, of royal behaviors motivated by wild, animal-like urges that arise in the thrashings of dreams, when constraints drop and certain principles of the physical world no longer operate (Chapter 7, Houston and D. Stuart 1989; Grube and Nahm 1994). The *wahy* references also avoid any link to specific rulers, leaving the suspicion that rulership at certain sites could be understood in the abstract, without reference to the personalities that occupied the throne. An image from Piedras Negras, in which a ruler sits within a cave and is surrounded by beings much like *wahy*, leads to the suspicion that these beings were also channels for oracular pronouncements and that rulers had to make pilgrimages or short trips to encounter messages from such beings (D. Stuart and I. Graham 2003: 33). The cave of Naj Tunich, Guatemala, clearly served as a place of pilgrimage in Late Classic times and perhaps before, where rulers from many kingdoms visited and one youth, according to a painted text, came to "see the road [*bih*], see the *wahy*," perhaps as some journey of spiritual growth and self-definition (Stone 1995, fig. 8–65d). Other caves, too, have texts that record visits, "arrivals" (*huli*) and "processions" (*ani*) by royalty or the kindling of fire with torches and sprinkling of incense at particular times (Stone 1995, fig. 4–89, 4–96, 4–97; Vogt and D. Stuart 2005: 160). A surprising find is the discovery that, at two different caves, one in Chiapas, another in Guatemala, paired figures celebrated an important calendrical celebration in AD 426, as though part of carefully orchestrated rituals across the Maya region (Houston 2007b). It seems likely that Maya rulers valued and wore jaguar pelts not only because of the ferocity of the creature but because of its identity as a creature of liminality, a nocturnal cat identified with the night sky and one that enjoys water as few felines do (Taube 1994, fig. 6).

There is a natural tendency in Maya studies to assume parity between the holders of *ajaw* titles. In some ritual sense this might have been so in much

Figure 5.4. Ceibal Stela 10 (photograph by Ian Graham, I. Graham 1996, *Corpus of Maya Hieroglyphic Inscriptions*, Vol. 7, Part 1: 32, reproduced courtesy of the President and Fellows of Harvard College).

the way that European kings addressed each other as "brothers" or close kin. But too much literalism can be misleading. A comparison between Tikal and the small settlement of Itzan shows sites ruled by people with emblems. Yet they exist at vastly different scales, Tikal sprawling over many hundreds of hectares, Itzan only a few. The surface of royal rhetoric masks great disparities in the nature of these settlements. A classic study by Martin and Grube (2008) works out the subtleties of unequal relationships during a time when one dynasty, centered at Calakmul, Mexico, maneuvered aggressively to outflank Tikal, its main rival: Hieroglyphic Stairway 2 at Dos Pilas, discussed earlier, is but a small part of the story, which shows great, internal consistency. A holy lord could "belong" to another, in an intensely personal relationship that, as with some subordinate titles, outlasted the life of the overlord (Fig. 5.5; Houston and Mathews 1985, fig. 12; Martin and Grube 2008: 19). Mention of enemies prompted some sculptors and scribes to abridge the emblem. Lords were "holy" at home but only *ajaw* to their foes, without any designation of sacredness (Miller and Martin 2004: 183, pl. 101). Perhaps, in defeat, the act of capture stripped lords of this exalted quality. In reverse process, lords could rise from lower to *ajaw* status. Early in his career, a lord at Lacanha, Mexico, held a subordinate title (Miller and Martin 2004, pl. 34). Within a few decades, a text from the Bonampak murals confirms that he rose to *ajaw* through some undetermined process of promotion. The Maya were keenly aware of such changes. In retrospective accounts at Palenque, rulers who had taken paper or cloth headbands, *hu'n*, a pan-Maya insignia of authority, preceded a sequence of kings with overt claim to lordship, *ajawlel* (D. Stuart 2007a). Again, this could be a minor matter of rhetoric, but it could also indicate a real promotion in status. Some such promotions were simply by claim, with the kings arrogating higher status. But a few examples may show the need for external warrant. At Copan and perhaps at Piedras Negras, rulers state that they voyaged to a building within a distant locale, perhaps Teotihuacan, to receive a legitimating object, the *k'awiil* (see Chapter 7 on this deity; also D. Stuart 2000: 490–4, fig. 15.22; Marc Zender, personal communication, 2007). This recalls the ancient Mexican practice by which kings traveled to illustrious kingdoms to receive emblems of rule (Byland and Pohl 1994: 139–40; Olko 2005: 167–8). Among the Maya, lords may have needed such prestigious objects because they were founders, as at Copan, or because of problems in dynastic succession. A fresh start required powerful symbolic support that had to come from elsewhere.

Such renovations may have been relatively common in periods of great violence between kings. At Palenque, a passage in the Temple of the Inscriptions refers to a time of troubles for the dynasty that culminates in an attack by Calakmul against the center of Palenque (Grube 1996; Martin and Grube 2008: 160–1). The text laments the period in no uncertain language, for it is the time when "holy ladies [perhaps gods?] get lost, lords get lost" (*satayi k'uhul ixik* [?] *satayi ajaw*), after which things, perhaps tribute, are no longer given (*ma'-yak'aw*). But, in AD 615, the dynasty bounces back with the accession of a ruler, K'inich Janahb Pakal, a pivotal king of Palenque. As a broader point, it is likely that many Classic Maya accounts were structured much like the early colonial, Yucatecan count of periods, embroidered with events both good and bad. Pomona, Tabasco, has a comparable listing of periods, spread across different panels, but these in turn probably assembled snippets of information from day-to-day accounts, such as an extraordinary, daily record painted for

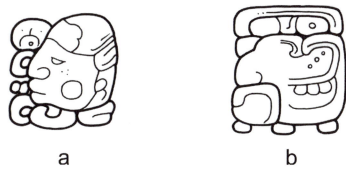

a   b

Figure 5.5. Statements of subordination: **(a)** column, AD 715, St. Louis Museum of Art column, 384:1978; and **(b)** Piedras Negras Stela 12: D16, (D. Stuart and I. Graham 2003, *Corpus of Maya Hieroglyphic Inscriptions*, Vol. 9, Part 1: 62, reproduced courtesy of the President and Fellows of Harvard College).

unknown reasons on an Early Classic wall at Uaxactun, Guatemala (A. Smith 1950, figs. 45, 47). Certain days have no notations, indicating that, for the kings, little of consequence happened on those dates.

References to overlordship show that some Maya kings were more prestigious and influential than others. A rough correlation exists between the prominence of a king and a particular title, read *kaloomte'* although not fully explained. The title is often used at Tikal but only after the arrival of visitors from Teotihuacan, perhaps pointing to some introduction from a foreign source (e.g., Tikal Stela 4: B6). The title, too, has expansive geographical referents, with linkages to the four directions, *lak'in* (east), *ochk'in* (west), *xaman* (north), and *nohool* (south). Through time, it diffused in Maya inscriptions, as did an expression *bakab*, which appears to have meant "head of the earth" or even "hilltop" (Houston et al. 2006: 62–3). Exalted at first, both titles diminished in exclusivity through wide use. For example, by the later years of the Late Classic, the comparatively small site of Aguateca used it, perhaps to distinguish itself from a minor relative at an even smaller site, La Amelia (Houston 1993, fig. 4–24). The symbolic weight of this title may have continued in Yucatan, however: a king mentioned at Ek Balam, but from another unknown city, is called the "north *kaloomte'*" (Lacadena 2004). The northerly reference accords neatly with the actual location of Ek Balam towards the top of the Yucatan Peninsula.

A title that does not lose its cachet is an epithet used by the later kings of Calakmul, *yuknoom*, "shaker." In Maya texts, *yuk*, the verb in this title, describes the motion of earthquakes and, presumably, the tremors induced by strong kings (Martin 1997: 858; D. Stuart 2001). Nor can it be a coincidence that many kings take *k'inich*, a term for the Sun God, as part of their regnal names (Colas 2004: 250–63). The Sun God has an obvious centrality to daily life, the cynosure of everyday existence. In much the same way, queens had lunar associations, holding tenderly a rabbit linked in Maya thought to the moon (Schele 1981: 108, fig. 10). The menstrual connection to the moon is obvious because of the length of lunation at a month or so, variable much like the onset of menstruation. In more abstract terms, the pairing might also reflect an idealized notion of balance and dualism within a larger pattern of asymmetry: the play of two bodies in the sky, dominant at different times, yet fundamentally unequal in powers of brightness. Possibly this expressed some notion of the appropriate, internal disposition of Classic Maya royal families.

BECOMING AND BEING A KING

Ascending to the throne means that two matters have to be decided: determining who is eligible and making sure that ceremonies follow precedent or build on them in acceptable ways. An older comparative literature on divine kingship is still applicable in that it emphasizes accession as a process with several stages that serve to redefine identity and set the king apart from other beings (Fortes 1967; Goody [ed.] 1966; Richards 1961, 1969). This literature is also heavily functionalist, that is, willing to reduce cultural detail to part of a smoothly integrative system. It distinguishes, for example, between the "investiture" of kings with mystical duties and primordial covenants or contracts and the "installation" of rulers in substantive, read "practical," offices (Fortes 1967). In fact, Maya rituals blended both title and function by saying that rulers could "sit" (*chum*) as a lord (*ajaw*), as a person with the property of being a lord (*ajawil*) or as someone discharging a particular office (*ajawlel*, *kaloomte'l* (Fig. 5.6, Houston and Stuart 2001: 59–61). The emphasis on office as opposed to a title appears to be relatively late, either because of changes in the rhetoric of kingship or because of real changes in the functions and operation of kingship. "Sitting" explains the importance assigned by Classic Maya to thrones and benches (*teem*) in buildings of the time. The painted decoration of one such accession structure, House E at Palenque, suggests a metaphor of "flower-house" for these locations, buttressed by the statement, just under a throne, that a ruler of Tonina "sits in a flower-house" (*chumlaj nichte'naah*, Martin and Grube 2008: 188). The flowers here are richly positive in association, linked to fine fragrance, color, paradise, and the eloquence of high lords and their "flowery speech," a deeply rooted metaphor for formal rhetoric in Mesoamerica (Houston et al. 2006: 154).

Other expressions, present at an early date, place great attention on ritual treatment of the royal head, especially in the tying (*k'ahlaj*) of a headband (D. Stuart 1996). "Tying" and "wrapping" is often a sacred practice in Mesoamerican and beyond, the treatment accorded to sacred bundles or other holy objects (Houston et al. 2006: 83; Stenzel 1968). At a few sites in the western Maya region, nobles were key participants in these rituals of "tying," offering the headband to their king (Mathews 1980, fig. 9; Pérez Campa and Rosas Kifuri 1987: 768). The collective nature of this activity departs from

Figure 5.6. Royal accession at Bonampak, Panel 1 (drawing by Peter Mathews).

more impersonal references elsewhere, where the headband is simply tied on the forehead, as though no clear agent did the binding. The headband was often adorned with jade jewels, usually three in number, depicting a deity that embodied paper or ritual cloth, known at some sites as the *sak-hu'nal*. One such jewel was found in situ at Aguateca, precisely matching, down to the drill marks for beads, all elements of the royal *hu'n* shown on contemporary stelae (Fig. 5.7, Inomata et al. 2002, fig. 12). Some jewels may have been made for

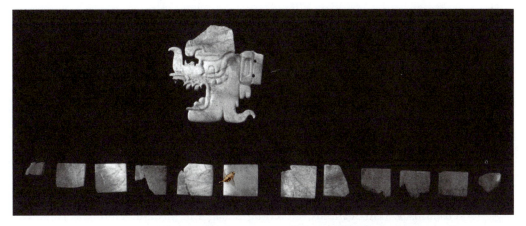

Figure 5.7. *Sak-hu'nal* royal diadem from Aguateca (photograph by Takeshi Inomata).

certain kings as part of their accession regalia, a supposition supported by the close match between the style-date of an object and the chronology of royal reign. Others descended from earlier kings in the form of sacred objects that imparted legitimacy through their very possession. The smattering of Middle Formative, Olmec-style jades with later Maya texts are likely to have been recycled fetishes of this sort, almost certainly not understood in their original meaning by the Maya but injected with new import (Chapter 3, e.g., Coe 1966). Not just regalia could be inherited. A cloak or tabard of *Spondylus* shell appears in one image of a king at Piedras Negras only to be buried, probably, with his successor, the shells long since dislodged from their perishable backing of textile or leather (M. Coe 1959, figs. 53–54; Houston et al. 2000, fig. 5).

What is known for the Maya is that few people could become kings, with overwhelming evidence that the father needed to be the holy lord. A few such heirs are depicted before their accession, all labeled the *ch'ok*-[place]-*ajaw*, "young lord of [such-and-such] a place" (D. Stuart and Houston 2001: 66–7). The surprising feature of these depictions, from Dos Pilas and Piedras Negras in particular, is that the heirs thus shown did not appear to have come to power. At Dos Pilas, on the Late Classic Panel 19, the heir dominates a scene where, presumably, he let blood for the first time, his parents standing nearby while a kneeling figure, stingray spine in hand, helps with this painful act (Houston 1993, fig. 4–19; Miller and Martin 2004, fig. 11). Yet the image was hacked to pieces and dumped in a small mound group on the outskirts of the site, as though especially noxious to the new, disruptive groups who came after (Palka 1995: 234–48). A post-hoc representation at Palenque of the complex negotiations behind succession – the site is rife with dynastic predicaments, brother following brother, nephew after uncle – may occur on a damaged stucco from Temple 18 (Houston et al. 2006, fig. 5.11; D. Stuart 2005: 152–3). As in most surviving statements of succession, the underlying concept was *tz'akbu*, "place in order," an expression with a highly concrete form of reference, as though rulers were likened to physical objects serried in neat sequence. Other heirs may have been known as the "head youth," *baah-ch'ok* (D. Stuart 2005: 38–40, 186, 187). Palenque is striking in that, alone among Classic sites, it shows secure evidence that when an elder brother came to the throne his younger brother, the *itz'iin-winik*, "younger brother person," could claim both the title of holy lord of Palenque and sit in the office of "head-youth-ship," *baah-ch'oklel* (Palace Tablet L12-K13). Nonetheless, that the heir himself commissioned the panel raises suspicions of a tendentious and self-serving narrative.

Once a lord became a king two modes of existence awaited him, one static, the other dynamic. When acceding, the lord was "tied" as though a revered object; he "sat" in office or perched, as at Piedras Negras, on jaguar cushions within scaffolds, clutching a bag for incense. Here the ruler was quiescent, sacred, seeing and approving through his physical presence, the

Figure 5.8. Royal sight and agency, *-ichnal* and *u-kabjiiy*: **(a)** Aguateca Stela 1: D6, AD 741, (after I. Graham 1967, fig. 3); and **(b)** Palenque Tablet of the 96 Glyphs: A3, AD 783.

-ichnal, but doing little more than encouraging with a gesture (Fig. 5.8a, Houston et al. 2006: 172–5). What the ruler saw, what lay in his field of vision, was what counted. That vision had power and influence nonetheless as part of a distinctive understanding of "sight" that emanated from human eyes and did not merely result from stimulation of the retina, as understood today (Houston et al. 2006: 163–70). The ruler's vision extended outwards to envelop and validate activities in front of him. In this, the Classic Maya departed considerably from such concepts among contemporary Maya, who did not see such vision as privileged or restrictive (Hanks 1990: 92; D. Stuart 1997: 10). Many references to Maya kings simply state that their "image" or "body" is present, *u-baah*, or record, in a large number of inscriptions, that he is paying due attention to priestly functions of scattering incense (*u-chokow-ch'aaj*).

The ruler who presided as a sacred being could also operate in a more active mode. This is exemplified by an expression read *u-kabjiiy*, whose verbal root is probably related to words for working in cornfields and means to cultivate or plow after plants have been burned to prepare the surface. More generally, the root refers to the act of governing or watching over (Fig. 5.8b, Laughlin 1975: 107; Laughlin 1988, I: 184; see D. Stuart 2005). The metaphor is revealing, for it compares in a direct way the work of kings with that of agricultural laborers. The ruler labors hard, one presumes, to public benefit, through a metaphor that would be broadly understood and appreciated. As a stratagem, the comparison of royal behaviour to the basic task of producing food recalls rhetoric in Madagascar, where kings root their exalted practices in common ones (Bloch 1985: 272; Houston et al. 2006: 7): whatever the Maya king did, he first prepared the "field" with an aim to "growing" and "harvesting his crops," namely, presiding over courtly rituals that were anything but agricultural. But there is a risk in this phrasing in that rulers needed to walk a line between suggesting the primary value of their labors and indicating that others could do it too (Houston et al. 2006: 6–7). Many people may have danced (*ak'taj*), for example, but few with the elaborate costuming of kings (Grube 1992).

It is likely also that only lords could impersonate deities, a theme peppered throughout Maya imagery of the Classic period (Houston et al. 2006: 270–2). Yet there remains a pronounced diffidence about much royal rhetoric, with relatively few instances in which kings do anything directly, even in their more active phases: warriors "are captured" (*chuhkaj*), places "get burned" (*puluyi*), sacred objects "acquire shape" (*patwani*), periods of time "get completed" (*tzutzuyi*), rulers "receive" objects (*ch'am*). Rulers appear both central and removed, and it is only in the vibrant imagery of conflict and ballplay that great exertion comes to the fore. There, the ruler grabs the hair of captives, a key violation of a warrior's body, and his body slides along surfaces to strike a large rubber ball.

QUEENS AND PRINCESSES

Royal women had titles much like kings but with gender tags: thus, not *k'uhul*-[place]-*ajaw*, but *ix*-[place]-*ajaw*, *ix*- meaning, in Classic texts, "lady," along with the general epithet of "lord," *ajaw*. There was another, stand-alone form, *ixik*, to which adjectives could adhere, including "holy." A very small number of females used the full emblem form. In these instances the likelihood is high that they were regarded as ruling queens, not just consorts (Martin and Grube 2008: 159–61). An example of this rare category is a woman from Dos Pilas, Guatemala, who appeared to have resuscitated the royal line of Naranjo after a gap that is only slowly being filled with dynastic information (Skidmore 2007). A great deal of emphasis is placed on her arrival; one finds a verb ordinarily associated with the "arrival" of new moons and the subsequent birth of the young king of Naranjo. The identity of the father is missing, a clue that this queen, shown standing on captives and holding a plate of sacrifice, may have governed in her own right. Yet this lady is an anomaly that proves the rule: ruling queens were exceedingly rare among the Classic Maya, salient only in circumstances of dynastic turbulence, when lines came to an end or needed rejuvenation.

An enigmatic quality of Maya imagery is that royal women, queens, consorts, and princesses, obviously central to maintaining society over time, achieved prominence only relatively late, with the first, unequivocal references appearing in the final decades of the Early Classic period (Fig. 5.9). Royal females may have become less visible on public occasions during the following Postclassic period. Bishop Landa noted, for example, that women did not take public stages and conducted their own ceremonies. This unique visibility of high-status women during the Late Classic can be interpreted literally as a hint that royal females were sequestered in harems prior to that date and that their "emergence into imagery and texts reflected a shift in gender roles" (R. Joyce 2000b: 73–82). Various figurines represent women with elaborate headdresses, the attire most likely reserved for public ceremonies (Triadan 2007). High-ranked

Figure 5.9. Royal lady from unknown site, probably in Chiapas, Mexico (drawing by Nikolai Grube).

women probably played active roles in mass spectacles in front of a large audience, although royal males took center stage (Inomata 2008). An alternative is suggested by the clear correlation between such visibility and increased references in Maya texts to royal parentage in both paternal and maternal lines. This may indicate a perceived need for impeccable genealogy on both sides, as though the pool of eligible candidates, enlarged by multiple lines of nobility descended from kings, required further restriction (Houston and D. Stuart 1996: 295). Several important cities, such as Copan and Tonina, are notable for their evident lack of interest in royal females, or at least in recording much notice of them, with only a small number of such references attested (e.g., Schele and Miller 1986: 81–2).

Yet structural explanations for the variable mention of royal women do little justice to the emotional resonances that seep out of Late Classic imagery. Royal females mattered deeply to the kings who commissioned sculptures, as can be gathered from the appearance of a lady offering a helmet to her son, Pakal the Great at Palenque (Martin and Grube 2008: 161); the paired stelae of rulers and consorts at Calakmul and El Perú, both usually in the guise of water-serpents (R. Joyce 2000b: 73–5; Ruppert and Denison 1943, pl. 49); and the many scenes on Maya polychrome pottery in which women sit close to the ruler on his throne, sometimes on the throne platform itself. Queens were, of course, necessary for the physical continuance of dynasties and created wealth for the dynasty through dowry and by making the textiles glimpsed in Classic imagery, as confirmed by the survival of weaving bones, *puutz'*, for certain queens (Houston and D. Stuart 2001: 64–6; see also Dacus 2005; R. Joyce 1993: 261; Kellogg 2005: 40). The clustering of weaving implements at large compounds within sites like Copan hints that these were collective activities, involving more than one royal or noble woman (McAnany and Plank 2001: 95–7). The bloodletting of royal ladies at Yaxchilan, in images redolent of pain and blood offering, confirms their role in central rituals of the dynasty (I. Graham and von Euw 1977: 43, 53, 55), as does their involvement in dressing kings for dance. At places like Bonampak, royal women seem to have been much concerned with bloody fluids, either in offering stingray spines to rulers or in collecting the blood of captives with *Spondylus* shells, as in Room 2 of the Bonampak murals. To a noteworthy extent, women at Yaxchilan were involved in acts of conjuring, not just of any deity but K'awiil, a being associated with dynasty and rule (Chapter 7). And unlike living kings, the women could be described outright as deities. The relative obscurity of women in Early Classic times changed to unique exaltation (Houston and D. Stuart 1996: 306; D. Stuart et al. 1999).

An affecting set of images and texts from Late Classic Piedras Negras shows the prominence of some queens and princesses (Fig. 5.10; D. Stuart 1985a, fig. 1; D. Stuart and I. Graham 2003: 18, 26). The texts are found on incised *Spondylus* shells from the tomb of Ruler 3 of Piedras Negras and in a series of

Figure 5.10. Queen and princess on Piedras Negras Stela 3 (D. Stuart and I. Graham 2003, *Corpus of Maya Hieroglyphic Inscriptions*, Vol. 9, Part 1: 26, reproduced courtesy of the President and Fellows of Harvard College).

stelae he commissioned for a platform in front of what is probably the burial pyramid of his father, Ruler 2. The queen, Lady "K'atun" Ajaw, was a princess from a site near the San Pedro Martír River, some fifty kilometers from Piedras Negras. Brought as a bride for the heir, she seems to have been "covered," perhaps a rite to signal or recognize the onset of menstruation. This happened under the supervision of her future father-in-law, Ruler 2 of Piedras Negras. There must have been some haste. The king died a short time later and, in his lifetime, had clearly wished to wed his son, Ruler 3, to a girl he found acceptable. (There is a hint that his wife also came from Lady "K'atun" Ajaw's home city.) Ruler 3 must have been pleased with his bride, for she received her own throne some years after giving birth to a young princess, Juun Tahn Ahk,

"Guarded Turtle." The image in which the child lovingly rests her arm on her mother's knee is one of the most touching in Classic imagery. The stelae that show the queen are at once public, on massive sculptures, and private, facing back to the royal palace where she may have spent much of her adult life. In one respect, however, these tender accounts differ little from other sites. The most desirable matches were often of princesses from foreign houses: Cancuen gave a bride to Dos Pilas, Dos Pilas to Naranjo, Calakmul to El Perú, and so on. Scholars have known for some time that the more important the site, the less likely it was to extol such connections: the treasured marital bond of one dynasty was another's *déclassé* necessity (see Flemming [1973] and Holmgren [1991] for comparative evidence). The calculations behind such links must have been carefully judged, with cost weighed against benefit. Only rarely, as at Piedras Negras, does an apparent depth of emotion enhance what must have been convenient arrangements of policy.

COURTLY SOCIETY AND AULIC CULTURE

Classic kings did not, of course, live in ether. Their physical and social setting lay at the core of Maya life as an aesthetic and political production (Fig. 5.11). A useful way of understanding this setting is in terms of a "court," a label that describes where kings live, called "palaces" after the Palatine Hill in Rome that housed the imperial family. "Court" also corresponds to a tangle of human relationships that existed within the physical court. An argument can be made that courts served as the primary units of rule and governance in Classic Maya society (Inomata and Houston 2001). They motivated the concentration of people that we call "cities" and orchestrated an elaborate tournament of competition, largesse, and consumption that played out around the king, his family, and his associates. Naturally, "courts" are not the only way to describe Maya polities. Others might speak, for example, of "states" or "archaic states," "chiefdoms" or "middle-range" societies, assigning a particular kingdom to one of these categories depending on the degree to which elites were entrenched and how such elites and their functionaries operated (Trigger 2003: 46–51). The terms are well-grooved in anthropological archaeology, with ardent exponents and many detractors (e.g., Yoffee 2005: 22–31).

Yet, to refresh discussion, Mayanists may need a slightly different emphasis. Kings are highly visible in the Classic period, as are their palaces. Focusing on them is a logical step that happens also to emphasize the personalities, motives, and aesthetics of rule (Adamson 1999a: 100–8; Duindam 1994; Wortman 1995, 2000). Wide study of kings, palaces, and the people and practices around them indicates that courts are, above all, about a monarch, a central human pivot, however he or she is described and however weak or strong that ruler might be. People we might call "courtiers" defer to, seek contact with, or attempt to control and influence that pivot according to elaborate rules of etiquette

Figure 5.11. View of courtly life, Bonampak Murals, Room 1 (painting by Heather Hurst with Leonard Ashby, courtesy of Mary Miller, Bonampak Murals Documentation Project, Yale University).

and expectation (Burke 1990). There must be something at stake in such strivings, whether prestige or tangible resources, along with a solid sense of hierarchy, both how to use it and how to flex it. The outer trappings of these maneuvers – the buildings, clothing, fragrances, and foods – are not simply stage furniture or theatrical space. In a sense, they participate in the flux of a court, marking meaning, channeling movement and sight, allowing people in, and keeping others out. But the degree of porosity changes from court to court, reign to reign: a presentable appearance allowed entrance to some courts, whereas that boundary hardened considerably in others, with elaborate vetting of petitioners. The Austrian dynasty in early modern Spain was particularly austere in this respect, much of it imitating the ceremonious standards of its ancestors in the Burgundian court (Armstrong 1977; Redworth and Checa 1999: 47–51). Trappings are important in another way in that they impress when they need to, which is often, and express in long-lasting form the values of the court (Brown and Elliott 1980: 31–40; Burke 1992: 18–37).

The degree of distinction between bureaucrats and courtiers varies from one society to another, with historic China representing an example of a marked division between their functions and spaces. In the Classic Maya court, this distinction was most likely blurred and in some aspects comparable to historic European courts and the Heian court of Japan (Inomata 2001c). So were administrative duties and the person and spiritual role of the ruler. As an analytic concept, court stresses the *human* dimension of rule: the family members, near, far, even fictive; courtiers, including "favorites"; servants and those generally in attendance; dwarves, fools, and the deformed, who played roles as friends and amusements for royalty; slaves and, in intermittent contact, purveyors of goods and services; allies of varying fidelity; and, in replications across the landscape, the smaller courts of magnates and lesser nobility or elites (Otto 2001). Whatever their scale, wherever they appear, courts function rather like households, where procreation, production, and consumption take place. In fact, the term "great household" has been used to describe precisely such sprawling establishments in Medieval Europe (Woolgar 1999: 8–14; also Elias 1983: 41–3; Neuschel 1988), with implications for some settlements in Mesoamerica, which seem to represent, in essence, large royal establishments (Sanders and Webster 1988: 524).

Courts are more than that, too. They celebrate marked, unusual forms of such activities – the downfall of rulership is its leveling with other kinds of existence (Geertz 1977). Consider that by general tendency, a monarch's activity typifies human action yet deviates from it. A royal birth, like any other, involves passage down the pelvic canal. But in hereditary systems the emergence of a potential heir has political implications, as does the introduction of a new royal being, a figure of promise and imminent expense. (By definition, monarchs and elites cost a great deal; that is, per capita they tend to consume a disproportionate share of resources.) When the king dies, he expires like other mortals. If a sacred personage, however, his death shakes society, inducing anxieties about change and continuity not prompted by other deaths (Houston and D. Stuart 1996: 289–90). Even food takes on a different significance: a monarch's meal or conversation with embassies resembles other suppers, other talk, but with large matters at stake, and with a need to distinguish such meals, through special dishes and servings, from those eaten by others (Houston et al. 2006: 103; Yang 1994). There is no clear way to reconstruct the orchestral arrangements of courtly musicianship beyond studies of the tones certain instruments could produce, yet the careful organization of such musicians points to elaborate productions and the use of people gifted in voice (Houston et al. 2006: 256–67; M. Miller 1988).

It is the conceit of most people that their own society functions smoothly, that rules, when established, are followed and that rule-breakers receive just chastisement. Yet, what is known historically of courts, regardless of setting, is that they were – and still are – places of paradox, tension, and dynamism. They embody order yet foment discord and competition. For example, the prudent ruler wants information from the outside world, as the isolation tends to deprive the monarch of the necessary background for momentous decisions. But he or she eschews open or unrestricted contact, which devalues the prestige of royal appearances (Adamson 1999b: 7). Scarcity breeds a sense of worth to the extent that most courts can be understood as engines for creating exclusivity. Nor do courtiers or servants necessarily want information to flow freely, which would thwart their own designs as they monitor and contest access to rulers (Boyden 1995; Elliott 1999; Loades 1986: 45). This is precisely what accounts for the outsized influence of certain servants, low-status in some respects, powerful in others (Adamson 1999b: 16; French 2003: 24). Courts are equally paradoxical in that they approximate the shape of families yet include many associates, even intimates, with no blood ties or affinal relationships to the ruler. Hemorrhaging resources, courts tend to attract or generate a sprawl of personnel, formally recognized or informally attached, some barely familiar or even unknown to the ruler (Loades 1986: 45). Such tissues of interaction would naturally differ by size of court: an estimate exists for about seventeen hundred people at the court of Philip IV of Spain, and, for the Austrian Hapsburgs, between five hundred persons in the time of Maximilian I to approximately twenty-five hundred under Charles VI (Duindam 1999: 168; Elliott 1989: 145).

Even wealth ebbs and flows. Most courts will hoard treasure and works of mystery and value – for Maya royalty, woven cloth, chocolate, greenstone, regalia, mirrors, and mosaics – but also ship them out as gifts to spread wealth among followers and eminent visitors. Strain arises from calibrating the need for gifts against the chance of depleting palace holdings. Making a good widely available will also reduce its value, so placing valuables in tombs or caches could, among other reasons, enhance their scarcity. In Classic society, outward flow needed to be offset by contributions of tribute from subordinate lords. In such a system, seldom tallied with any precision, corruption is likely to proliferate. Indeed, the chance of extracting benefit serves as an inducement to courtly service. In any case, "corruption" is a cultural concept, meaning that, in some places, it had a variable or even positive value, benefitting friends and family in ways thought appropriate (Peck 1990).

Perhaps the central paradox, though, is the reality that courts present both opportunity and danger. A courtier may rise and fall depending on the play of personalities and the extent to which the monarch remains a reliable fount of honor. All the while, the courtier must neutralize or co-opt others who seek similar benefit. The mutual surveillance can be uncomfortable at best, perilous at worst. To be noticed by the ruler could be useful but potentially destructive. Risk compounds with some breach of etiquette or expectation, or if a rival manages to perform some flanking maneuver. And the more rigid the protocol or codified the behavior or dress, the greater the chance of missteps in an atmosphere of harsh evaluation: heredity is important in the Maya case, but also honor, a constitution of "proper conduct, reflected in a reputation defended or enhanced" (Powis 1984: 3). Heightening the overall tension is the inevitable friction that comes from cabals, often centered on important figures, such as members of the royal family or high courtiers (Le Roy Ladurie 2001: 124, 149, 152). As the cabal changes over time, its actual workings often attain a high degree of complexity, being "polycentric" or "many-centered," with multiple collisions of interests, complicities, and secrets. In a form of social physics, the court affected by factionalism tends to follow "valences" of attraction and repulsion between participants (Le Roy Ladurie 2001: 53, 152). Contingent on the scale of the court, there may be "wagers" that a certain patron will ascend or fall. Comparative evidence indicates that marriage within and between courts almost always serves the interests of faction, as certain parties will favor a particular royal or aristocratic match over other possibilities (Flemming 1977).

An appropriate metaphor for a court involves doorways and passages towards and away from the ruler, or from figures that preside in his name. As physical and idealized thresholds, the doors imply incremental stages of exclusivity (Elias 1983: 74–7). Such arrangements protect the ruler from unwelcome intrusions but also limit him and, in their abuse, cede royal authority to a variety of gatekeepers (Baillie 1967: 198). The dictatorship of space matches a similar rigidity in the control of time. Fixed timing may affect unusual events, such as calendrical celebrations or the reception of embassies. The more usual settings, however, are the ceremonies of everyday life – dining, dressing, daily audience – each modeled on longstanding precedent and expressed with formalized movement and gesture, prior example, and decorous action being the essence of courtly etiquette: the palace scenes on Late Classic pottery exemplify "correct" movement and deference (Chapter 2, Reents-Budet 2001: 222–5). Subtle in use and hard to acquire, such encoded behavior and language present outward markers of suitability for court.

Another, cross-cultural feature of courts is their proclivity to replication. Grandiose examples will find their matches in smaller establishments around high nobles or "magnates" and lesser nobles (Fig. 5.12). It is by this means that court beliefs and practices diffuse through all levels of aristocracy; periodic attendance at royal courts allows courtly values to be updated in smaller, courtly centers or by loaning "memory artists" – scribes and sculptors – to subordinate courts, as occurred around Piedras Negras and Yaxchilan (Chapter 6; Warnke 1993). The series of traditions, venerable or self-consciously innovated, constitute what might be called "aulic" or "curial culture" (both from terms for "court" or "palace") for an imitative yet contrastive package of objectives, meanings, and routines (Smuts 1987: 4–5, 185–6). In a process of unwitting standardization, they mimic patterns at high-prestige courts yet seek to establish contrasts with foreign models, creating affinities alongside local differences (Cannadine 2001: xix). For courtly societies, imitations and reactions to them provide key sources of taste making, aesthetics, and patronage for

Las Palmitas

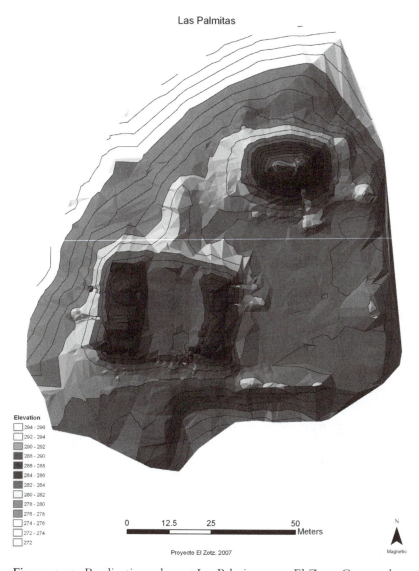

Elevation
294 - 296
292 - 294
290 - 292
288 - 290
286 - 288
284 - 286
282 - 284
280 - 282
278 - 280
276 - 278
274 - 276
272 - 274
272

0   12.5   25   50
                            Meters

N

Magnetic

Proyecto El Zotz. 2007

Figure 5.12. Replicative palace at Las Palmitas, near El Zotz, Guatemala.

sculptors and painters: the emphasis on beauty and exquisite sensation, particularly in relation to the king, explains many Classic images in which rulers sniff bouquets of flowers or gaze at their image in mirrors, sometimes supported by dwarves or dwarf effigies (G. Ekholm 1964; Houston et al. 2006: 45–8, 141; Miller and Martin 2004, pls. 4, 14, 16). The portable nature of these primers of aulic comportment spreads their influence far and wide. Change in curial culture arises from such copying and inevitable shifts during transmission, and from a variety of other historical events and mechanisms. These include the personality of a particular ruler; reactions to him or her in subsequent reigns, when attempts may take place to set a new tone; relative wealth or security of labor; movement up and down in systems of hierarchy; and redefinition of courtly roles as functions are taken away and others added (Baillie 1967: 169, 183, 191). A court that changes is a living court.

PALACES AND AULIC BEHAVIOR

Beyond their human dimension, courts were physical settings that enabled and constrained activity within them (Baillie 1967; Jarrard 2003; Webster 2001: 131–2; Winter 1993). That physical setting could be massive and, in most sites, became more so through time as buildings enveloped other buildings and, on the whole, routes of access became greatly restricted. At Piedras Negras, what had been a fairly open plan shifted radically by concentrating royal residences on a defensible and closed-off hill, with evidence of heightened distinctions between areas potentially visited by many and those frequented by few (Houston et al. 2003). Those in the northern part of the Yucatan Peninsula seem more accessible than those to south, at least to judge from the layout and routes of access; the suspicion, too, is that many were constructed over relatively short amounts of time, expressing overall, coherent planning more clearly than southern examples (Liendo Stuardo 2003, fig. 7.4).

Earlier scholars questioned whether "palace" was an appropriate term for such locales, finding it difficult to locate evidence of cooking or sleeping facilities (Satterthwaite 1935: 20; Webster 2001: 134). The many scenes on Maya pottery of rulers in open rooms with benches, porticos, and spaces in front of them for assembly underscores the need to understand these buildings on elevated platforms and galleried plans in quadrangles as the places where rulers lived and reigned. In themselves, they represent enduring, raised, grander versions of residences used by lower-ranking Maya, who lived in patio groups of roughly the same configuration, if smaller in investment (Kowalski 1987: 82). At the same time, the meanings of royal versions of those models must have acquired new shadings over time, as anything but facile appropriations of modest buildings (Kus and Raharijaona 2000: 101). In practical terms, the relatively small size of many Classic palaces and the general lack of domestic debris suggests that cooking could have been done elsewhere and was then transported to the palaces, and that servants, too, could have resided in separate locations (A. Chase and D. Chase 2001: 134; Inomata et al. 2001: 299–300). At Piedras Negras, the late appearance of such debris in the royal palace, often over collapsing buildings, hints at a reassignment of function, with occupants of reduced or altered status and changing notions of disposal (Golden 2002: 303–5). Nonetheless, not all palaces were created equal, as, in contrast to more modest structures, some enjoyed massive platforms that set them apart radically from surrounding space (Martin 2001: 184–5). The complex at Calakmul is singularly large, with multiple quadrangles (Fig. 5.13; May Hau et al. 1990) and, as at Tikal, matched by other, like complexes of only slightly smaller size: clearly, single palaces were not the norm at larger sites, and the chances are

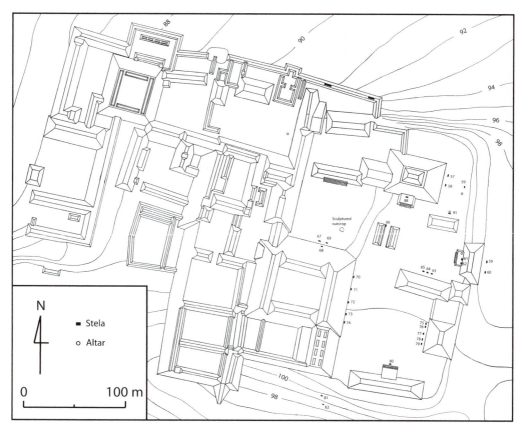

Figure 5.13. Principal palace at Calakmul, Mexico (Rupert and Denison 1941, pl. 61).

good that they represent cadet branches of the royal family or even alternative residences, depending on royal whim and comfort (Ball and Taschek 2001: 190).

A feature of royal palaces at Maya sites is that they both conform to general patterns – with the same attributes of patios, multiple rooms, restrictive access, epicentral location, monumental investment, spatial elevation – but also, in the particular, present different arrangements. Some do not require great effort to enter, others leave the visitor gasping from exertion, one stairway and plaza leading to another in ineluctable flow to a patio of reception. The Acropolis at Piedras Negras seems designed, in its last phase, to inflict discomfort on visitors who must traverse open, sweltering areas, pass through narrow entrances, neck craned up to the ruler on his throne. From texts and iconography, certain parts of the Palace at Palenque pertain to embassies and the receipt of captives and tribute (Robertson 1985, pl. 285), other sectors, such as the West Court, to the "young men's houses" known from ethnographic literature (Houston 2007b). Early ethnohistoric sources identify such locations as places where books were kept (Tozzer 1941: 113) and give a vivid description of their appearance: "in each town a large house, whitened with lime, open on all sides, where the young men came together for their amusements. . . . Almost always they all slept together here also until they married" (Tozzer 1941: 124).

The ubiquity of holes for perished wooden doorways or for suspension of textile coverings hints at variable concealment and privacy or the simple need to exclude vexing bugs or control ventilation. An enigmatic feature was also a set of subterranean rooms, some with benches but poorly illuminated, at sites like Oxkintok, Tonina, and Yaxchilan (García Moll 2003: 140–6, fig. 18; Šprajc 1990; Tate 1992: 182–5): their interpretation ranges from astronomical observation points to artificial "caves," or, more practically, areas for storage of valuables. Among the more unusual structures are a set of "condensed" palaces at sites of the Río Bec area of Campeche (G. Andrews 1999, III: 63, 73, 79). As though presenting notional distillations of all that makes a site royal– mortuary pyramids, godly residences, and abodes of royalty – they contain palace rooms, some with versions in stone of wall-hangings, and twin pyramids with spurious, unclimbable "stairways." Yet, as in all palatial buildings of the Classic period, the masonry rooms of the Río Bec can be understood through the imagination but without any real certainty of their shifting function or who, precisely, might have occupied them, for what exact purpose, or at what specified time (Kowalski 2003: 238–40). At some sprawling sites, such as Chunchucmil, Yucatan, the presence of dominant palaces is elusive at best in its center (Dahlin 2000: 284, fig. 2; Hutson et al. 2006: 79), perhaps because of comparatively thin chronology. Most interpretations of sectors, rooms or galleries of palaces are disappointingly indeterminate despite careful excavation and extensive survey (e.g., E. V. W. Andrews et al. 2003: 93–5; Nondedeo 2003, figs. 83, 85), and some royal facilities, such as thrones, occur in modest structures that would not seem inclined to impress or overwhelm visitors, although they might have permitted rulers to view larger spaces before them (Demarest et al. 2003: 128–32). At Aguateca, and in contrast to other elite residences that contained numerous objects, most rooms of the royal palace were swept clean at the time of abandonment. Still, valuables left in a sealed room for later retrieval allow a glimpse of the royal possessions that filled the palace (Fig. 5.14, Inomata et al. 2001: 302–3).

MORAL AUTHORITY AND RULERS

The role of rulers in the moral systems described so far and in Chapter 2 requires a modification in attitude from an agriculturalist's sense of debt and obligation to a belief that certain people held a special grip on moral authority, or that moral standards might adjust according to who or what kind of person was practicing them. This was not the authority held by fathers, mothers, uncle, aunts, or grandparents. Instead, it existed alongside and displaced such parental and kin-based dominion, involving people *born* to influence others. It is likely that Classic societies prioritized competing obligations, such as those

Figure 5.14. Palace at Aguateca, Guatemala, Structure M7–32 (photograph by Takeshi Inomata).

relating to kin, gods, and kings. In some spheres of behavior one duty might come to dominate others, such as the probable expectation that crops would first supply the needs of the farmer's extended family. But, presumably, the natural tendency of rulers was to exhort followers to favor the claims of royalty over those of other people in the community: *royal* bellies needed to be filled first, their conflicts serviced with able and willing warriors, their palaces and ancestral temples built and maintained.

According to one view, as Max Weber pointed out long ago, such forms of domination require an internal state of willingness before external compliance can take place (Chapter 2, Weber 1978, I: 226–8). There are many routes to this condition of willingness. The most important is to stress the "natural," or that which seems inevitable and normal. Maya and Mesoamerican comparisons of royal activity to mundane practices show, at least rhetorically, how the exercise of authority can come to seem "natural" and commonplace, much like the sowing of crops or the transportation of goods by tumpline (Houston and Cummins 2004): the labors of kings are likened to, and seem as necessary as, the raising of food or the movement of goods. Moreover, "authority" suggests a claim that someone was worth following, and that to do so made *another* person, the follower, feel virtuous and responsible. Morally, there may have been a shift in the observer's focus from good or bad acts, or good or bad conditions, to people who were transcendentally "good." In a sense, such beings would have been paradoxical. They participated in moral valuations by exemplifying "goodness" or "worthiness," yet, as in the "holy men" of India, may have remained outside such valuations by dodging the burdens of day-to-day accountability (Bailey 1981: 39). In Aztec belief, the ruler conducted metaphorical extensions of practical behavior, all the more resonant for being cast in terms of everyday actions: "He carries the load, he bears the burden. . . . He sows" but "he alone sits above others . . . [and] experiences nothing over him" (Maxwell and Hanson 1992: 176). The work of the world among modern K'ichee' Maya falls into different agricultural domains: God tends the cosmos, Jesus the world, the Apostles the community, the harvest being the end of current existence, when humans-as-crops were gathered (see below, Taube 2001; Warren 1989: 33).

What is not explained is how a ranking of values undergirded their strongly hierarchical societies. As moral authorities, royalty and elites were not, apparently, regarded with undiluted affection. One passage in Popol Vuh, although of much later date, describes an egregious figure who boasts, "I am great. I dwell above the heads of the people. . . . I am their sun. . . . I am surely their means of marking the passage of months," only to have his wealth stripped by the guile of the trickster twins (Christenson 2000: 34; see also Taube 1993: 17, and Shaw 1972: 56–7, for an ethnographic analogue). This was the bad ruler, someone who arrogated the attributes and privileges of gods. Depictions of his wrangling with the twins, especially the primordial Maya lord, Juun Ajaw, are found on monumental stucco sculpture at Tonina, Chiapas, and on several painted vessels (M. Coe 1989). A similar ambiguity about leaders characterizes the modern northern Lakandon, who seem to view such figures as violent and threatening (Boremanse 1998: 69). In contrast, the good ruler functioned, according to the integrative model of Maya society, as a moral object. The sacred kings of the Classic Maya served as such objects, as did deities, ancestors, and other beings, forces, and groups. People recognized their force and authority and internalized it to the extent that the ruler could extract labor and goods. Here, in a nutshell, was the glue of the Maya kingdom: no moral object, no moral community; no ruler, no polity. Beyond the primordial covenant of human existence – that involving maize and the body – other covenants structured the relation of ruler and ruled. The theological and practical challenge of Maya kingdoms was to devise a coherent, well-regulated system of moral foci that linked ideas of sanctity to ideas about the "naturalness" and "correctness" of inequality (Rappaport 1999: 426–7). A ruler who did not occupy the summit of a hierarchy of values lived in an unstable polity. Rightness might attach to other moral objects, placing the kingdom at risk through division and factionalism.

With a few exceptions, we can guess that this system was highly personal, that it did not develop the impersonal mechanisms of governance connected with empires or other kinds of states. One text from Tonina states that the ruler who supervised the opening of an ancestral tomb was a "wise lord" (*itz'aat-ajaw*) as well as a warrior of some prowess, with nine captives to his credit (Martin and Grube 2000: 188). The explicit emphasis on wisdom and knowledge is unusual for kings and perhaps stands in recognition of an achieved quality that lay beyond the formal language of conventional description. (The "wisdom" may also have been appropriate in the context of an ancestral rite, involving specialized knowledge available to few, including the precise location of ancient tombs.) Collective worship in Classic Maya cities helped cultivate a commitment to the ruler and gods as moral objects by making explicit a common orientation (Parish 1994: 21; see also Redfield and Singer 1954: 57). Joint celebrations created moods and dispositions, and made the Classic Maya aware of themselves as moral actors, choosing right behavior over wrong, responsible action over disinclination to duty.

Another view of internal willingness and external compliance is that expected behavior or unconscious routines of practice shape and maintain the authority and other social realities experienced by individuals (Chapter 2; Bell 1992: 197–223; Bloch 1974: 59–60). Some scholars even argue that the masses in many cases superficially comply while harboring internal dissents against dominant groups (Scott 1990: 2–19, 67–90). In these views, the authority is dependent on repetitive references to social norms. Such routine practices shape the feelings and experiences of the world, including power relations and social obligations, as given, acceptable, or tolerable. The emphasis on external compliance does not necessarily presuppose cynical subjects who consciously disguise revolutionary intent. Social reality is far more subtle and ambiguous. Classic Maya society, like any other, probably involved diverse attitudes, ranging from loyal, sincere followers of the dynasty to antagonists operating in various degrees of consciousness. Contradictory or ambivalent attitudes can coexist even within one individual. Royal authority, then, may not have been homogeneous through time and space. Many Maya probably felt episodic bonds with the dynasty and nobles during public ceremonies and construction projects sponsored by elites, but their recognition of the king may have been diluted when they returned to their daily routines in villages (Inomata 2007). Such inconsistency and fluidity may also have undergirded differences in royalty–subject relations between various regions and during the Classic period and beyond. Yet, the internal states of social agents are ultimately unknowable through archaeology, or even through the written record. Their ties to the more accessible dimensions of practice and discourse remain a perpetual problem for researchers.

CLASSIC MAYA ROYALTY

A difficulty with comparisons across societies is that they favor similarities over differences. To say that the Maya had kings and court societies runs the risk of focusing on general patterns rather than the historical idiosyncrasies and specific theologies of rule that operated over time and in varying ways. Every excavation of a palace in search of a court shows that royal stories, common on one level, diverge constantly in detail, in royal biography, and palatial setting. An apt metaphor is a collective tune played with different tone, emphasis, instrumentation, and, at times, sequence of notes and harmonies. But summations need to be made or the tale becomes too fragmentary. It loses sight of shared themes and of the nature of Maya courts as institutions "with a distinct nucleus but a vaguely defined periphery" at the intersection of kingship, courtiers, aesthetics, concepts of power, and practicalities of rule (Smuts 1987: 4; Winter 1993: 27, 38). Courtly attributes, where extractable from available textual, iconographic, and archaeological evidence, show that these notions and practices evolved over the course of the Classic period, from relatively open facilities for high lords to the restricted, thoroughly controlled settings used by sacred kings with their elaborate retinue and immediate family. In all cases, regardless of period, there is the probability that multiple stakeholders, not just rulers, focused on the court as place and institution for their own objectives. The intrigues and rich interplay known from courts in Europe and elsewhere become recognizable in the Late Classic period only, with earlier glimmerings at best in the form of a few murals, as at Uaxactun (A. Smith 1950, figs. 45–46). The dearth of texts to the north of the Maya region makes any discussion of kingship there speculative, although where they exist such glyphic accounts conform roughly to patterns attested in the south: why such texts should be so few prompts its own set of unanswered questions about royal rhetoric. Palaces, where discernible from elite residence by size and centrality, formed the core of courtly action, which nonetheless extended into the plazas, pyramids, and peripheries of Classic communities. Oscillating from coercive governance to the exercise of authority, kings existed in conditions of tension, paradox, and dilemma. Yet they found ways to harness the energies of people around them to create a court culture that failed, sometimes abruptly, at the end of Classic kingdoms in the ninth and tenth centuries AD.

CHAPTER 6

NOBLES

THE IMPORTANCE OF NOBLES

Along with royalty, the only Maya of the Classic period with known identities were members of the nobility. They lived grandly, took precious and varied goods with them to the grave, and inched into scholarly view because of their ostentation and access to the tools of record making and image making. Nonetheless, accounts of them are far more limited than for royalty, from whom some of them must have descended. A comprehensive report on Classic nobles builds on evidence from texts, imagery, and material residue in the form of subroyal palaces, opulent goods, and sumptuous burials. But, to sketch the range of possibilities for hierarchical action, it must first compare nobles and aristocracy as a general phenomenon. Attention can then shift to what the Classic Maya did, recorded, and made in commemoration of key actors in their world.

NOBLES AS A COMPARATIVE CATEGORY

Comparative evidence suggests that nobles can be understood in two ways (Powis 1984: 2–3). The first defines nobility as a condition of social and aesthetic refinement. Nobles show their station through a certain bearing, mode of speech, or way of life, behaving in ways that others do not, by codes difficult to master and expensive to perform (Fig. 6.1). Depending on region, they emphasize features that vary from fine delicacy of emotion to bold aggression, often blended in contradictory or illogical ways. Few can miss the ironies of troubadour culture in the Middle Ages, a language of love existing beside brutal conduct (Camille 1998; Schultz 2006). But mostly, as in early modern Europe, the quality of nobility emerges, it is asserted, because nobles can not help it. An inescapable legacy, refinement derives from a set of supposed inner qualities, present at birth. In ideological terms, the goal is transparent, namely, to justify inequality by stressing propensity to "rule" (Greek *arkhō*) by the "best" (Greek *aristos*, Powis 1984: 7). For greater effect, such differences must seem "natural," "routine," part of an unchanging, hereditary order. If, in fact, the differences are recent, they need to be wrapped in tradition to make them extend logically from what came before (Hobsbawm 1992).

With such ideas comes necessary consideration of descent, of finding the origins of noble essence through bloodlines. This accounts for pervasive aristocratic interest in genealogy, which serves to distinguish people with detailed charts of ancestors from those, the majority, who do not have such charts. Specific ancestors, lots of them, matter to nobles. Means are devised to preserve such sequences, from the memory aids of Polynesian rulers to the writing of the Old and New Worlds (Fenton 1983; Gaur 1992, 24–5, although, to be sure, this is not the only motivation for the origins of script [Houston 2004: 5–10]). A theory of intrinsic quality presumes that the education of a noble burnishes qualities received from parents and their predecessors. Passing off as a nobleman would, by this theory, prove difficult to sustain. In fact, anxiety about whether such claims were true – whether nobility was inherited or achieved – motivates much art and literature in aristocratic societies, especially at times of decline and redefinition (Cannadine 1999; Haynes 1990). Like royalty, which has similar pretentions, nobility tends to stimulate comment on how people differ from the lofty images they project. For the Maya, too: the epic Popol Vuh of the K'ichee' Maya describes with glee the downfall of a pretentious lord embodied as a bird (Christenson 2007: lines 985–1188). Rituals of inversion among ethnographic Maya jeer at Catholic bishops and overweening Ladinos of mixed heritage (Bricker 1973: 167–218).

The second way of looking at nobles is to focus on their relation with other people. This approach highlights not cultural notions of essence but the manner in which aristocrats interact with those above (the ruler or higher nobles), below (nonelites or lesser nobility), and sideways (persons of roughly comparable status, Powis 1984: 12–22). The overwhelming tendency is for noble relations to operate within systems of deference. One person always stands in hierarchical ties to another, as expressed by deferential language or gesture and overall disposition in ceremony and everyday life (Shils 1968). Codes of deference are formalized through titles and subject to continual testing. Yet their rigidity does not discourage nobles from probing for places of weakness and elasticity. It is in such spaces that nobles maneuver for advantage.

The other relational feature of nobles is that they do not create themselves. By definition, a noble cannot be self-declared other than as a poseur and fraud. There must be some fount of honor, some higher person, usually a ruler, to award or confirm nobility, often in relation to a peerage with similar privileges. Nor, in general, do nobles hold unique titles. As structural anomalies, singular, exalted ranks often lead to the death of the incumbent and an obvious reluctance to appoint others in their place (Mann 1976). Lazy or complacent, a few nobles do not strain upwards, closer to regal privilege. But

Figure 6.1. Nobleman, "he of 4 captives," with "Shield-Jaguar," king of Yaxchilan, Chiapas, Mexico, c. AD 730 (drawing by Peter Mathews).

most do. And if rulers can exert their will, they swat such people down or manipulate noble ambition to their own benefit. Once started, the machinery of inequality churns out tensions that are inevitable and never fully resolved. Traders may trade, craftspeople craft, but nobles and kings specialize in social and symbolic disparity, itself a stimulus to striving and conflict.

The reality of high preindustrial mortality, especially among warriors, means that new nobles need to be made. If nobility presumes an inherited essence, the paradox is obvious: how can a title be new when it relies on the possession of intrinsic, ancestral qualities? Again, comparative evidence indicates a range of possibilities. Recruitment usually takes place among those with wealth, or those who enjoy amity and intimacy with the ruler or who merit reward for military and civic service (Powis 1984: 20–2). For the ruler, recruitment is always a risky game. A peerage with too many members loses its very basis for existence. The relatively high numbers of nobles in early modern Spain, at around more than 10 percent of the population (cf. Sweden at around less than 1 percent), drove many in the lower nobility to seek fortunes in the New World. The ultimate source of distinction – the control of land, labor, and goods – can be watered down only so far before nobility loses its cachet or ability to impress and sway (Powis 1984: 24–6). The ruler cannot count on nobles for support if they are too impoverished to help. In much the same way, nobles who lack special training cannot dispense advice and offer productive service if their education varies little from nonelites.

Another challenge is the overmighty subject. Rulers wish to elevate their followers only so far. A tiny number of nobles, especially in smaller kingdoms, encourages competition with the king. For rulers, nobility cannot be so unusual as to rival the singular status of kings. The same risks come from magnates, nobles of soaring rank. Magnates are often recognized as such by special titles or position within the peerage and a prodigious, almost royal level of expenditure (Fragnito 1993; Woolgar 1999: 4–5). European history contains many such figures who vied with rulers and came too close to royal prerogative, seldom with harmonious consequences (Harriss 2006; Mann 1976). In Japan the Fujiwara house of the Heian period succeeded in overshadowing the emperor as regents and in establishing enduring control over sources of wealth and power (Otsu 2001).

Powerful subjects may also emerge through personal relations, as exemplified by "favorites," close friends of rulers that arise in the outer circles of court or even beyond (Eliott 1999). Favorites have their uses. Like pets, lovers, and court fools, they enrich the emotional life of the ruler (Fig. 6.2, Otto 2001). As royal creations, they stand opposed to entrenched noble families. In general, they have a diminished capacity or wish to usurp royal influence, although that can change with time. Yet their tenuous source of influence, mostly at royal whim, makes their position precarious. It is the rare favorite who escapes ignominy or death (Elliott 1999). They provide another lesson, too. Just as monarchs award titles, wise ones preserve the ability to remove them through demotion or attainder. If strong enough, rulers will strip nobility from followers who behave against royal interest. This is always easier with newfound favorites than with aristocrats of deep ancestry and wide affiliation.

The question is, why have nobles at all? In part, the answer is practical. Nobles discharge multiple functions, as landowners or landlords, tax collectors, judges, courtiers, scapegoats, patrons, proxies for royalty, ambassadors, and warriors. For the ruler, these are valued contributions, if accompanied by a tendency to incumbency and material acquisition (Powis 1984: 36–42). A Marxist would regard nobles as parasitic organisms, a dysfunctional evil in society (Gilman 2002). But nobles also provide protection, patronage, and

Figure 6.2. Dwarves and court buffoons, Late Classic period, area of Lake Peten Itza (K1453, copyright Justin Kerr).

material assistance for those in their network. Even in decline, nobility serve a role in local society, depending on their ability to retain wealth and dispense assistance (Cannadine 1999). One cannot simply be a noble but must work at it or the distinction becomes hollow.

As for setting, some nobles flourish and prosper today in circles close to royal courts – consider the "service families" of princely India or those in royal attendance at modern European courts (L. Rudolph and S. Rudolph 1983). Others develop in circumstances away from the royal person. As suggested in Chapter 5, the first are "curial" or "aulic" nobles, operating close to the ruler and his or her palaces. The latter correspond to "territorial" nobles with far-flung estates. They are of particular use in the insecure boundaries of polities or as local representatives of royal will. Yet the two categories overlap considerably. Courtly attendance facilitates the territorial aims of noble families; for those in close royal service, more distant bases of influence serve to hedge bets. In all of this, noble ladies play crucial roles, as physical transmitters of noble essence, channels for tangible inheritance, facilitators of alliance through marriage, and counselors educated to standards reached by few nonnobles (Fig. 6.3, B. Harris 2002; Powis 1984: 31–4).

Noble systems may rest on similar, resilient foundations of hereditary hierarchy. But to be a noble is to activate change through a quest for gain and through the exercise of patronage (Cohen 1974, 1981). Nobles receive wealth but need to distribute, often to lavish and ruinous extent, in partial reward to others (Powis 1984: 28–9). A noble outside a hierarchical, ramifying network is not a viable noble. A further key to understanding this play of prestige is the concept of "honor" as a notion of name or reputation. Although varied in meaning, and not always to rational benefit, honor induces much aristocratic action, as buttressed by largesse and magnificent works, and as defended by duels, vendetta, and feud (Billacois 1990; Byock 1982; Pitt-Rivers 1966). The multiple frictions of honor contribute to tensions between older and newer elevations to the aristocracy, with a possibility of factional split and accommodation in all cases. In much of this, nobles seldom engender affection, either from above or below. To rulers, nobles act as supporters and, in the negative, present the chance of insolent threat. To those of lower status and rank, nobles seem the harsh, extractive edge of inequality, far more so than the ruler, who usually absorbs bounty at greater remove from nonelites.

Comparative study of nobles thus emphasizes several features: (1) the station of nobility usually accords with rank; (2) rank depends on a ruler or other fount of honor; (3) honor comes from vigorous defense of hereditary rights and personal reputation in an unequal society; (4) noble rights help structure that inequality, in a scheme of deference and relative hierarchy; (5) rulers call on noble service at court and at a distance; (6) nobility involves finely honed ideas of refinement, with founding myths or ideologies to highlight those inherited qualities; (7) as a practice, nobility costs a great deal; and (8) as a system, nobility engenders tension at the same time it performs useful services. The plain truth, too, is that nobility evolves as an institution, wherever it appears, along with the residences, households of nobles, and their various investments, social and physical (Woolgar 1999: 197–204). Common across cultures, its basic principles endured for millennia and, in some places, persist today in modified form. But its emphases, participants, elaborations, and meanings differ between societies and shift within them. Nobility can appear, thrive, and perish, as it did among the Classic Maya.

NOBLES AS A CLASSIC MAYA CATEGORY

Later Maya sources contain many terms for nobles. Among the Yukatek Maya of the colonial period, nobles were people with "mother-fathers," *almehen* – probably in the sense of recognizable ancestors; they also had "names," *ah k'aba*, and the quality of being "good," *utz* (Chapter 2; Barrera Vásquez 1980: 14, 360, 901). In potent simile, colonial Tzotzil referred to lords as "penis persons," perhaps in allusion to their large families or other qualities associated with the male organ (Laughlin 1988, II: 428). A highland Mayan language, colonial Kakchiquel, emphasized that nobles had "renown" as one of their essential qualities, along with a link to seats or mats of authority, eloquent speech, and an overall, lustrous clarity to their person (Coto 1983: 272). But the more recent evidence shows some variety of meaning, in part because the early dictionaries passed through Spanish filters and systems of European rank.

For example, colonial Tzotzil and Tzeltal uses *aghau* [*ajaw*] for "noble," when the Classic evidence, presented in Chapter 5, links that title firmly to royalty (Ruz 1986: 241; 1989: 198, 206). This is most likely because the dictionary draws attention to the essence of nobility, not the status, in Spanish, of being a *hidalgo* or "son of someone." Other terms in colonial Tzeltal reveal that nobles are those who make themselves "first," that they are at the "head," "first person," "face person," that they are "good" or "straight," "generous," and that their homes, certainly those of kings, are "hot" (Calnek 1988: tables 13, 15, 18; Ruz 1986: 248; see Houston and Cummins 2004: 384–6). In general, they were not, it seems, people who had to farm for their daily *tamales*.

The presence of a peerage, as a vertical arrangement of distinct ranks, may be documented in some of the early historic evidence, reflecting the Postclassic period and perhaps before. Such titles have been interpreted as hierarchies with several levels, from royalty down to high lords, lower nobles, rich commoners, poor commoners, and the enslaved (e.g., Calnek 1988: tables 18–20; Miles 1957: 767). As ever with such indistinct evidence, problems arise in distinguishing inherited rank from occasional office or duty, a question the historic sources can only occasionally illuminate (e.g., Roys 1943: 62). This chain of hierarchy, with multiple bases of definition, resembles the abundant information from central Mexico, which emphasizes the aesthetic, fragrant, lustrous properties of nobles (López Austin 1961: 90–5; Sahagún 1950–1982, 10: 15–22). But little is known of these as a living system or the specific duties involved, beyond the reality that nobles, as a group, enjoyed great wealth, prestigious buildings, special access to supernatural beings, some possibility of social movement upwards, sumptuary privileges, and, for men, multiple wives (Calnek 1988: 38–9; Miles 1957: 766–7). Certain language may have been necessary to address nobles, as suggested by a special grammatical element in Ch'olti' Maya during the colonial period (Ringle n.d.: #932) and by deferential language used elsewhere in Mesoamerica

Figure 6.3. Noble lady, Room 2, Bonampak murals (painting by Heather Hurst, courtesy of Mary Miller, Bonampak Murals Documentation Project, Yale University).

(Terraciano 2001: 347). During the Classic period, the performance of these acts of deference probably took place in the courtyards or in front of the masonry benches of some noble groups (see Section titled "Setting").

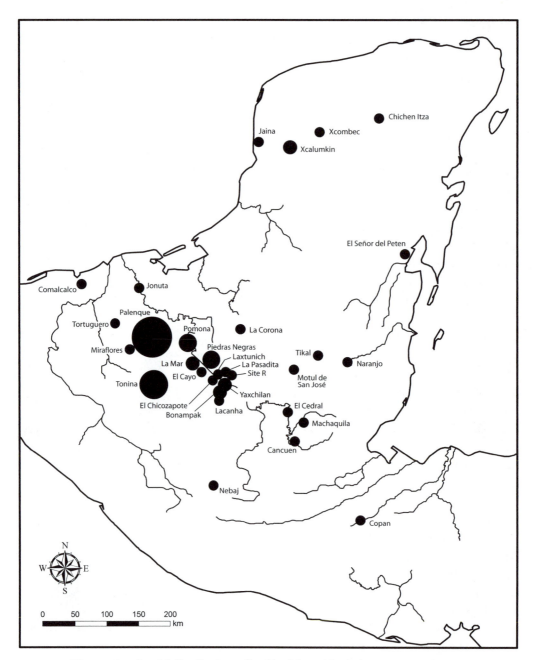

Figure 6.4. Spatial distribution of noble titles with circles corresponding proportionately to number of occurrences (redrawn from Jackson 2005, fig 3.5).

Varied evidence sparks much debate about extending such patterns to the Classic period. There is a stark divide between those who see multitiered systems (D. Chase and A. Chase 1992: 6) and others favoring the existence of rigid two-part systems, with elites and nonelites only and solid enforcement of endogamy or "in-group" marriage (J. Marcus 1992b: 221). As a social label,

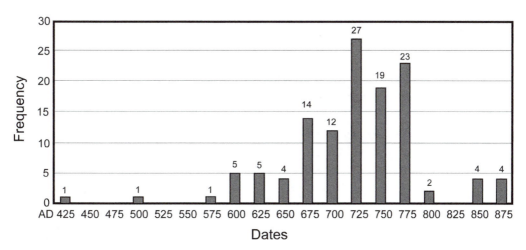

Figure 6.5. Temporal distribution of noble titles (redrawn from Jackson 2005, fig. 3.9).

"class," too, has filtered into scholarship, especially through the detection of a "middle class" thought to emerge during the final Early Classic period in and around the densely settled area of Caracol, Belize (A. Chase and D. Chase 1996a, b; see Bloch 1983: 18). The prosperity is evident at that site, with relatively large number of ceramics in graves. Yet "middle class" establishes an inevitable comparison with industrial-age bourgeoisie. This is of doubtful relevance to the Classic Maya, although it does raise the question of why some dynastic capitals were materially rich, whereas others were less so. A term like "elite," self-evident to some, also resonates with Western meaning, evoking industrial society and an explosion of class-based consumption and display that does not necessarily accord with formal rank (G. Marcus 1992: 295). It also treats a complex group as a single coherent whole and lumps royalty with nobles, not a desirable feature in describing Classic Maya society.

Glyphic titles and images are far less ambiguous, if variable. There is, for example, no one system across the Maya lowlands during the Classic period, or from earliest times to latest. The greatest puzzle is that nobility make a late appearance in texts and monumental imagery, a fact attracting comment by many scholars (Figs. 6.4 and 6.5; e.g., S. Jackson 2005, fig. 3.9). The Late Classic, with slow build-up after about AD 600 and clear acceleration after AD 650, contributes the most textual evidence of nobles, with an equally dramatic drop in references after AD 800 (Zender 2004b: table 9). The greatest visibility of nobles thus marks a span of only 150 years, give or take a generation, when populations peaked around the Classic Maya world. It is hard to overlook a correlation between this pattern and a burgeoning populace, the need to control or opportunity to exploit that surging population, the propagation of noble lines through multiple descent and inheritance from rulers, and greater difficulty in royal monopolization of text and image making (Houston and Stuart 2001: 59–61). Perhaps the new visibility of nobles is in part rhetorical. If they existed before, they only accessed the ability to memorialize themselves in stone and on pottery during the seventh century AD. Nobles could not have been new, to be sure. In early murals at Uaxactun, Guatemala, figures stand at the margins of presumed, royal events, but their noble, as opposed to royal, status, cannot be determined (A. Smith 1950, figs. 45–46).

Another oddity is that the number of references to noble titles occurs after the period of greatest friction between the two great hegemonic powers of the Classic Maya world, Calakmul and Tikal (Martin and Grube 2008: 20–1). It is as if this rivalry did not directly concern nonroyal nobles, who only asserted themselves afterwards. A notable feature of imagery from these, the largest Maya cities, is in fact this curious blind spot. On a few pots is heightened mention of nonroyal figures, but the contexts seem invariably of a tributary nature. Yet Calakmul and Tikal are also the sites with the greatest number of what are probable nonroyal palaces or outsized residences for magnates. The recent discovery of market scenes at Calakmul shows nonroyal personages but in strangely impersonal fashion, with generic, almost stock characters in place of tangible historical figures (Martin 2006). It may be that sumptuary codes and their enforcement were particularly strong at cities of this type. Nobles make an appearance where they are allowed to, where they can get away with it. In contrast, at sites with more complex arrangements, as evidently at Palenque or Copan, both, perhaps not coincidentally near the edge of the Classic Maya world, magnates made a louder show. This is reflected in titles like *ba[ah]-ajaw*, "head lord," known from Palenque, or by the figures who commissioned flamboyant displays in peripheral palaces at Copan (see Section titled "Setting").

The main feature to understand is that, like elsewhere, Classic Maya nobility were understood at the time as groupings, summoned for important acts of witness. At Dos Pilas in particular, there is mention of the "twenty-eight lords" or *ajaw-taak* who assemble for key events in royal lives, first-bloodlettings by heirs, even burials (David Stuart, personal communication, 1998; Houston 1993, figs. 4–14, 4–19). The ability to operate independently is only rarely apparent, as among the lords in and around Piedras Negras, some of whom had panels with their own portraits in distinction to similar nobles to the south, in the kingdom of Yaxchilan, where they almost always included the image of the ruler in such portrayals, in very different modes of interaction (Chinchilla Mazariegos and Houston 1993). In imitation of royal precedent, the texts of nobles near Piedras Negras trace an arc of biography; those around Yaxchilan display moments when nobles offer captives to kings or dance with rulers nearly, but not quite, in the role of coequals.

The most widespread noble title, evidently an office with priestly associations, is the *aj-k'uhuun*, with some remaining questions about the final part of the spelling (Fig. 6.6a, Houston 1993: 130–4; Houston and Stuart 2001: 71; S. Jackson and Stuart 2001: 219–22; Zender 2004b: 164–95). In some way, the title relates humans not of "holy lord status" – those who are not rulers – to

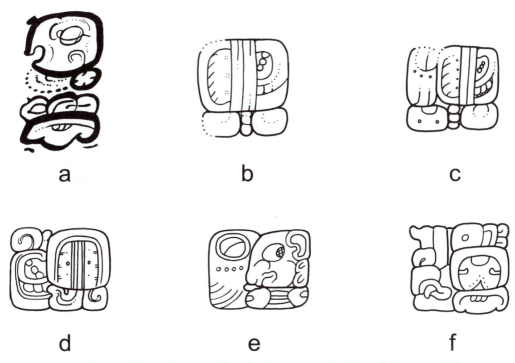

Figure 6.6. Titles used by noblemen: **(a)** *aj-k'uhuun* (K1728); **(b)** *sajal* ("Laxtunich" site, near Yaxchilan, Panel 1: E1); **(c)** *ba[ah]-sajal* ("Laxtunich" site, near Yaxchilan, Panel 1: G3); **(d)** *yajaw-k'ahk'* (Palenque Temple XIX pier, stone panel); **(e)** *ba[ah]-ch'ok* (Jonuta Stela 1: pA4); and **(f)** *ti'-sak-hu'n* (Pomona Panel 1, secondary text).

gods or *k'uh*. A few royal consorts use a female version of the title, but the vast majority appear with subordinate figures at court, often those wearing head-dresses with quills or folded paper (M. Coe and Kerr 1998: 92–6). Such figures tend to hover at the edges of royal imagery in simple, unadorned dress. One, a lady from the Usumacinta area, has in contrast her own stela and rich raiment; other royal consorts employ the title, too. Tonina makes it clear that the *aj-k'uhuun* attend and perform incensing at the conclusion of important cycles. Special altars could be dedicated to their memory. The same occurs in the area of Palenque, where such a noble has a censer stand, clear accounts of his death and passage into "roads" of the deceased, and fire rituals at or near his tomb, the *mukil* or "burial" (Miller and Martin 2004, pl. 122). Another sculpture at Palenque indicates the key roles of *aj-k'uhuun*. They could be "holy," "belong" to, or perhaps serve certain gods and have the rare honor of connecting *k'atun* (twenty-year) spans to their lifetimes. These chronological titles are ordinarily the prerogative of royalty. Even more telling is that Tonina pairs such figures in ritual, as though tandem attendance were useful to rulers. An indication that *aj-k'uhuun* accessed valued goods comes from at least two artifacts, both high-end productions. The first is an exquisitely incised alabaster bowl now in the collection of Dumbarton Oaks, Washington, D.C.; the second, from a private collection, is a finely molded vase from the area of Copan. It somehow ended up near Quirigua, a former vassal of Copan (Fig. 6.7, Kubler 1977).

Among the earliest representations of an *aj-k'uhuun*, also at Tonina, records that this figure was "seated," *chumjiiy*. "Seating" more often applies to an office like *ajaw*, but without, in this case, any implication of "essence" that came with the *ajawil* or *ajawlel* mentioned in royal accession (I. Graham et al. 2006: 118). The *-il* ending is crucial, for it indicates the quality of the title, not just its use. The *aj-k'uhuun* at Tonina holds a long knife of sacrifice and a bag of incense; around his forehead appears a royal jewel and headband. This last suggests that categories of title could overlap, with an *ajaw*, as signaled by the jewel and headband, holding another office at the same time. Glyphs confirm that the *aj-k'uhuun* belonged to certain kings or those of *kaloomte'* rank. At Copan, Honduras, in particular, those relations extended beyond the death of the ruler (Houston 1993: 134). The title, and whatever priestly functions it fulfilled, embodied a personal relationship between king and subject – it was not just a general set of duties. Whatever their specific roles, *aj-k'uhuun* accompanied the lord, at least in imagery, into the tomb. A set of them appears in vignettes, head and shoulders, perhaps an arm, within emblems for cavities or in stars (or vegetation?) on the sarcophagus at Palenque of Pakal the Great (Robertson 1983, pls. 159–62). A few of these figures appear to have been described as a kind of "bird" or messenger, *muut*. This is a term used for messengers in Maya society, who probably came with tribute to the royal palace from other, more distant nobles (Houston et al. 2006: 246–8). Other courtly scenes display a smattering of noble titles, many of the utmost opacity, but some perhaps related to tribute or priestly office (e.g., D. Stuart 2005: 113–36).

There is a suite of additional titles used by nobles. Nobles could use several at a time, confirming that the titles were not mutually exclusive. Unfortunately, they leave only a glimmer of their function or meaning. A group of figures was known as "the fire's lord," *yajaw-k'ahk'* (Fig. 6.6d). At Comalcalco, Tabasco, in close attendance on a lord, they encircle a Late Classic tomb in the shape of stucco figures in various poses (Zender 2004b: 196–210). At Palenque, one commemorative base for an incense burner shows only the head of such a person. He had other titles, too, including *aj-k'uhuun* and a second title probably read *ti'-sak-hu'n*, perhaps with the meaning of "speaker [of] the head-band, the *sak-hu'n*" or "white paper" (Fig. 6.6f, Zender 2004b: 219). In an important discovery, the urn burial of a *yajaw-k'ahk'* was recently found at Comalcalco, where the find proved to contain many exquisite stingray spines and bones with texts (Armijo Torres et al. 2000; Zender 2004b: 246–53). Along with his status as a *ba[ah]-ajaw*, "head lord," the interred noble gloried in specific ties to gods of the local dynasty. His actions took place in the "company of" (*-ichnal*) certain listed deities, and he was said to belong to a rain deity, Chak Xib Chahk. One text from the urn goes so far as to describe

Figure 6.7. Stone bowl belonging to *aj-k'uhuun*, reputed from area of Jaina, Campeche, Mexico, c. AD 718 (K4340, Dumbarton Oaks Collection, Harvard University, copyright Justin Kerr).

drought and famine, leaving the strong impression that the finds functioned in practical rites of prophecy and rain making, and in search of other benefits to local society. An enigmatic reference also records the seizing of what appears to be a foreign god, a *tz'ulba*, "stranger-image," to be placed under the noble's care (Zender 2004b, fig. 78). This recalls the Aztec practice of capturing the godly effigies of enemies and placing them in a special temple at Tenochtitlan, the imperial capital (Sahagún 1950–1982, 2: 168).

Yet the most salient title, especially in the region of the Usumacinta, is that of the *sajal* (Fig. 6.6b, Villela 1993, also Jackson 2005: 129–30, 233–76). It has two distributions, both of which, in a comparative sense, accord with the notion of a "magnate," a lord arching towards royal privilege, useful to holy lords yet also a potential source of threat. One kind of *sajal* is associated with people of second-tier status, nonroyal but with several references to their "seating" in office. Such figures appear at court and may even be known as the *ba[ah]-sajal*, "the head" *sajal*, as though set apart from others of this rank (Fig. 6.5c). They served as warriors for rulers, nonresident nobles who controlled smaller, more distant settlements under royal authority, if with relatively short genealogies. It is the rare site, such as El Cayo, Mexico, that attests to more than a generation or two. Does such brevity of ancestry suggest a struggle by kings to avoid entrenchment by *sajal*? Or was it a system devised by royalty for a particular place, at a particular time? In this instance that would be a hilly zone over which smaller kingdoms were attempting to assert territorial control during the middle and final years of the Late Classic period (Golden et al. 2008). The absence of recorded or reconstructible genealogies is surprising, for it was through hereditary status that nobles defined themselves in Mesoamerica and elsewhere. The absence of information can lead only to speculation. Nobles were invisible because, prior to their surge in the Late Classic period, they did not exist or were present in weak form, barely differentiated from others; or nobles were invisible in glyphs and images because rulers monopolized such physical devices for commemoration. Through speculative premises, a statistician might show that a small number of elites, the offspring or grandchildren of kings, became by Late Classic times a full set of people with provable descent from royalty. This would account for the evidence that only the offspring of rulers were *ajaw*, a necessary abridgement of a rank that many might claim to the detriment of its inherent value. Even worse than having too many nobles is having too many royals, costly and threatening as potential claimants to rule.

A second concentration of *sajal* is in the area of Xcalumkin, Campeche, far to the north of the Usumacinta zone, and one of the rare sites with legible texts in the northerly part of the Yucatan Peninsula (Fig. 6.8; e.g., I. Graham and von Euw 1992: 163, 169, 173). There is only a hint of an emblem glyph in this area, possibly used by an overlord at another site (I. Graham and von Euw 1992: 165, K4340). Such idiosyncrasy or redefinition, a noble title functioning much like an emblem glyph, underscores contrasts with titles in the southern lowlands. The clearer evidence at southerly sites, along with the suggestions of divergence to the north, emphasizes the danger of assuming common patterns of usage. This has led also to arguments that regions such as Río Bec in Campeche contain roughly equivalent sets of noble families living in cities without kings (Michelet et al. 2005). Perhaps the mechanisms in place there come closer to a pure definition of "aristocracy" or rule by nobles, and closer to the multiple, illustrious lineages known for Postclassic highland Guatemala (Braswell 2001). Such societies in the Yucatan Peninsula would need to be traced down to, or shown to depart from, those attested during Late Postclassic and colonial times. Those periods suggest more diffuse arrangements of control and a less developed theology of divine kings and of how nobles should relate to them (Restall 2001).

SETTING

The physical setting of nobles raises a number of questions. Several large residences were the probable dwellings of nobles (Fig. 6.9). Noncentral in location, middling in scale, the buildings are too large to be plausible residences for nonnobles and too small to be royal habitations. Yet, the challenges are many in proving occupancy by nobles. Ambiguities arise because of attempts to condense several dimensions of inequality, including rank, office or duty, and wealth, all of which intersected in intricate ways that can be baffling to

Figure 6.8. *Sajal* at Xcalumkin, Campeche, Mexico, Jamb 7 (I. Graham and von Euw 1992, *Corpus of Maya Hieroglyphic Inscriptions*, Vol. 4, Part 32: 169, reproduced courtesy of the President and Fellows of Harvard College).

archaeologists (Garraty 2000: 324). At Dos Pilas, Guatemala, varying investment in buildings and mound groups hints at graded differences between many levels of society; if such groups represented social units, variety might reveal disparities in access to labor for construction, although the excavator of these buildings recognizes the difficulties involved in such matches between mound groups and units of society (Palka 1997: 300–2). In mounds near Xunantunich, Belize, ceramics in supposedly "royal" groups differ from those in modest mounds (LeCount 1999: 250–4). But the pattern is temporal, and such contrasts diminish by the Terminal Classic period (LeCount 1999: 254).

At other communities, such as Aguateca, distinctions exist between noble and nonnoble households. Elite and royal buildings abound in figurines of distinctive theme and dress, whereas special objects and regalia rarely materialize in more modest buildings on the outskirts of the city (Triadan 2007). Caracol, too, presents evidence of variation in animal bone and ceramics during Late Classic and Terminal Classic times, the pottery in the center of the city having a wider variety of forms (D. Chase and A. Chase 2000: 73). Ritual ceramics, such as incense burners, diverged far less (D. Chase and A. Chase 2000: 74). Larger mound groups evinced heightened access to richer soils and greater hectarage but with relatively little proof of surplus for royalty or people other than those prosperous people living in such groups (Murtha 2002: 297–8, 301–2).

A murkier picture comes from Piedras Negras, were figurines and pottery occur in all manner of residences. Modeled figurines in a small mound resemble in all respects those found in or near palaces. Both emphasize richness of textiles, similar preoccupations with attributes of the face and markers of status, lavish use of exotic colorants like "Maya blue" (probably intended to make clay objects resemble precious jade), and a shared imagery of supernatural figures. Polychrome ceramics occur in the most modest buildings, although pieces with legible glyphs do cluster in the city center. Material impoverishment appears less to signal elite or nonelite status than, in a still-indeterminate correlation, distance from the site core. Humble structures in the center are appreciably richer in quality, quantity, and diversity of artifacts than buildings some hundreds of meters from the area of densest settlement. The difficulty is that archaeology bears only an indirect relation to the precise status and rank of people who commissioned dwellings and obtained goods, carried such abundance with them to the grave, and served nobles in close daily contact (S. Jackson 2005: 594). The probability is that no amount of statistics will elicit interactive subtleties of this sort from artifacts alone.

The best evidence comes from sites with thorough excavation and relevant inscriptions. At Copan, two substantial mound groups, both close to but not at the center, contain references to these figures on thrones of exceptional size and polish (Webster 1989). One, Group 9N-8, has been studied with great intensity and skill, confirming that subroyal figures such as *aj-k'uhuun* resided in or presided over buildings with multiple structures and a high complexity of occupation (Hendon 1991). Composing it are dozens of chambers, manifold courtyards, and corridors, many of fine finish, with other such groups nearby of comparable grandeur. The similarity to royal courts is clear, in careful replication of palatial layout. All are predicated on the modest patio grouping that extends far into the Maya past. The large number of these palaces around Copan and, indeed, at other Classic cities, points to a preponderance of nobles, at some places with recognizable "footprints," at others of reduced number, so few as to be, in the absence of texts, alternative palaces for the royal family (Plank 2004, figs. 5.52; 5.53, 5.59; Webster et al. 1998).

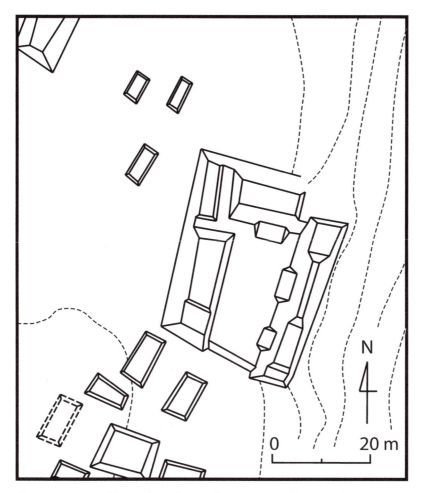

Figure 6.9. Possible *sajal* residence, the "C-Group," at Piedras Negras, Guatemala (redrawn from Weeks et al. 2005, 403).

Yet the likelihood is strong that all users of such buildings were not of noble station, hence the usefulness of concepts like the "house" (Chapter 2). Conceived by analogy with noble families in France, the "house" extends to social groupings organized according to metaphors of – and literal encasement within – dwellings of stone and mortar (e.g., Gillespie 2000c). Bonds derive from that association, by blood at times but mostly by conceptual ties to a unit that embraces all ranks in habitual contact and concerted action. Only the head of the "house" may, in fact, be noble. The speculative nature of such a concept is its weakness, however, in that only a few Maya inscriptions allude to "houses" in this way. One is at Tamarindito, Guatemala, in relation to the father and mother of a king (see Chapter 2); another is at Tonina, in reference to what may be actual buildings, as in a "person of the house of incense [?]," *aj-ch'a[aj?]-naah* (Houston 1993, fig. 4–17, Step V, A1-B1, Step VI, C1-D1).

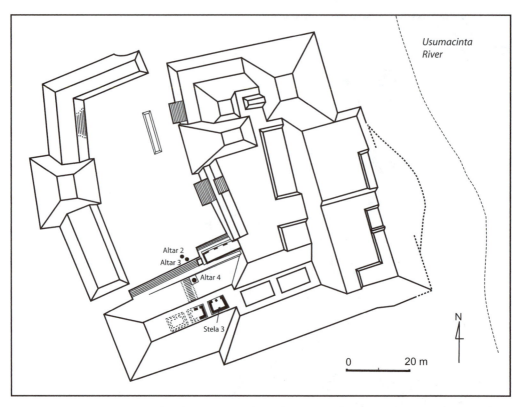

Usumacinta
River

Altar 2
Altar 3
Altar 4

Stela 3

N

0   20 m

Figure 6.10. *Sajal* palace, Acropolis, El Cayo, Chiapas, Mexico (redrawn from
Mathews and Aliphat Fernández 1997, fig. 11).

If truly central to Maya social order, the term would, it seems, appear with
greater frequency. It does not.

A separate set of evidence shows that *sajal* clustered not only within royal
cities but at some distance from the "holy lord." The strongest data are from El
Cayo, part of the kingdom of Piedras Negras. It consists of a diffuse settlement
highlighted by an acropolis of small temples, fine masonry steps, and enclosed
courtyard (Fig. 6.10, Mathews and Aliphat Fernández 1997, fig. 11). There is
a suggestion of high, more "private" areas, hinting at a seraglio or preserve
of noble ladies. At the high level, the Usumacinta River runs within twenty
meters of this palace, its highest area well equipped to monitor traffic along
this body of water and to look across to flat areas on the other side of the river.
In comparison to the vaulting Acropolis of Piedras Negras, this was a minor
investment, yet the features are similar, as though mimicking a royal palace.
Not far away, in what may be a planned settlement, a probable *sajal* at the site of
Tecolote, here under the sway of Yaxchilan, occupied a complex of buildings
on relatively low platforms but of exceedingly fine finish (Fig. 6.11, Golden
et al. 2008). The existence of buildings of such splendor yet isolated from
clusters of sustaining settlements may be a marker of noble residence, especially
for nobles fulfilling a territorial rather than a curial or aulic function. The

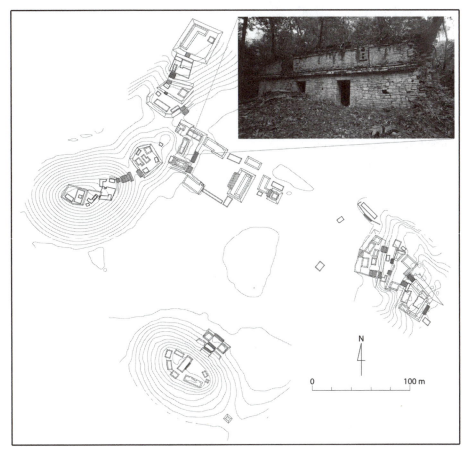

Figure 6.11. Noble palace, Structure D3-1, Tecolote, Guatemala, from kingdom of Yaxchilan (courtesy of Charles Golden, Brandeis University).

relative proximity of some such groups offers the real possibility of intermittent occupation, with territorial nobles changing roles as they shifted to courtly attendance and back again (Houston 1993, fig. 2–6).

A few of these magnates could have *ajaw* rank without, however, any hint of "holiness" (Fig. 6.12). Towards the end of the Piedras Negras dynasty, in the reign of its last, clearly identified king, such a magnate rose to be the main warrior of the ruler. The name of this figure was 1 May Mo' Chahk, the *ajaw* of what is now La Mar, Mexico. This lord attended court in his youth, as recorded by a carved panel at Piedras Negras, in close company with the royal heir. His record illustrates the advantages and predicaments of a magnate. Stela 12 at Piedras Negras is among the most complex compositions in Maya imagery, a jumble of captives between the columnar figures of victorious nobles. The main noble was Mo' Chahk of La Mar, the main captive a *sajal* from Pomona. The events leading up to this scene are rendered on a sculpture, now in the Los Angeles Museum of Art, in which the magnate pays no heed to his overlord, only to his own victory over the enemy. The rhetorical focus changes on

Piedras Negras Stela 12. The captive is now presented at court, in offering to the holy lord. The king thus insinuates himself into a conquest that appeared, from the vantage of La Mar, to form a relatively independent action. On the royal throne of Piedras Negras the name of Mo' Chahk marks the backrest of the king's throne. This is an impressive object positioned at the culmination of flow into the royal palace, in a building looking down on a courtyard for visitors, fronted by a megalithic stairway for the presentation of tribute (D. Stuart 1998, figs. 29–30; Thompson 1971, fig. 58). When sitting, the ruler would have rested against the magnate's name, a subtle reminder of the probable power behind the throne. Yet the sense of royal ineffectuality is belied by the ability of the holy lord to collect and commission work from the remarkable ateliers of sculptors (Montgomery 1995; see Section titled "What Nobles Did").

Noble burials, at least at places like Piedras Negras, differ notably from those of royalty, with their exclusive access to precious objects, and those of low station, who may have, at best, a prepared chamber for their repose (see Fig. 7.15 in Chapter 7). A tomb with a panel, now eroded but similar in size to mortuary slabs of *sajal*, consisted of a crypt with the body that could not, because of poor preservation, be sexed or aged (Houston et al. 2003, fig. 2; S. Jackson 2005: 548–90). The building with the crypt had cylindrical altars, suggesting rites of sacrifice to noble memory. Yet its contents, while rich in comparison to burials nearby, fell far short of royal mortuary finds at Piedras Negras. What is noteworthy is the ability of this figure, a probable *sajal* or nobleman, to trigger cults of sacrifice in formal ways, through an expensive structure dedicated to the noble's interment and subsequent remembrance.

WHAT NOBLES DID

The way to understand nobles is to see them in action, insofar as this is possible through controlled and restrictive texts and images. The principal distinction is between those attending the ruler at court and those in more energetic service, at places away from court or palace. The courtly noble is one who supported the throne or ruler as though an underworld supporter of upper surfaces, backs bent, arms lifted up in strain against an inconceivable weight. An idealized task as royal supporters found expression as a cosmic metaphor. The *ti'-sak-hu'n* could also grasp day signs, as participants in calendrical cycles that tended time itself in year-bearer rituals (Schele and Miller 1986, fig. III.12). Courtly life could involve more practical service, too. Nobles in palace scenes offered drink, food, and, in a crucial role, tribute. This could be brought in the form of war captives harvested in battle, for eventual delivery to rulers, or in other goods understood to be the labor of work and effort, *patan* (D. Stuart 1998, fig. 6). The fiction was of willing collaboration in the machinery and maintenance of the court. An entire set of unprovenanced vessels highlights the delivery of bloodied captives to overlords, by figures described as "head staffs,"

a

b

c

Figure 6.12. Portraits of magnate, 1 May Mo' Chahk, at various ages: **(a)** as youth, Piedras Negras Panel 3, in a scene dated to c. AD 749 (courtesy of Archives, University of Pennsylvania Museum); **(b)** La Mar Stela 3, AD 794 (now in Los Angeles County Museum of Art; drawing by Stephen Houston); **(c)** Piedras Negras Stela 12, AD 795 (D. Stuart and I. Graham 2003: 61).

ba-te', almost bailiff-like in their function (K6674). Not a few were specifically associated with the throne itself, as in a statement deciphered by Marc Zender as *ba-tz'am*, "head person of the throne," found in use by multiple people in the Bonampak murals of Mexico (Fig. 6.13, M. Miller 1986, figs. III:7, III:17).

Some such tributaries can be understood, according to a recent hypothesis, as lords or high commoners presiding over sectors of cities, perhaps coinciding with the clusters of mound groups seen in many Maya cities (Lacadena 2006). The title with such functions may have been, although rarely documented, *lakam*, from a term for "banner" or "standard" – perhaps to identify a social grouping – or from a Tzeltal term for "companion," *lak* (Ruz 1986: 316). In

baah took'   baah te'

baah pakal   baah tz'am

Figure 6.13. Noble titles related to objects, Bonampak murals building (drawing Stephen Houston, courtesy of Mary Miller, Bonampak Documentation Project, Yale University).

compensation, such lords were probably fed rich meals and drinks of chocolate, as in numerous depictions from Late Classic scenes. The reciprocal flow of service, attendance, and gifts is easier to discern than to break, on current evidence, into understandable rules. Skimpy and ill-prepared servings would compromise the honor of the host, however, as would failure to attend and offer appropriate deference. Visitors at such times might have been the *ebeet* or "messengers" from foreign courts. A few of these strangers, some possibly from Teotihuacan, Mexico, the capital of what was likely an early Mesoamerican empire, found their way as exalted personages into sites in central Peten, with supremely disruptive effects, perhaps even to the extent of prompting shifts in dynasties (D. Stuart 2000). The figure known as "Born from Fire," Sihyaj K'ahk', is in some respects the major historical personage of the Early Classic period, with references at several sites in northern Guatemala. Yet the Classic Maya generally found non-Maya or nonnobles beneath notice. Some of the few that appear are in the murals recovered from a market facility sponsored by royalty at Calakmul. The paintings feature a lady dressed in blue garments, almost erotic in presentation, along with a variety of vendors and, in one scene, a serving girl in drab gear (Martin 2006). From later evidence,

a

b

yebeet

chak ha'

ajaw

Figure 6.14. Messenger lord, Bonampak murals, Room 1, late ninth-century AD (painting Heather Hurst with Leonard Ashby, glyph drawing, Stephen Houston, courtesy of Mary Miller, Bonampak Documentation Project, Yale University).

slaves probably existed in Classic Maya society, but this may be the only such servant seen directly in imagery of the time.

The Bonampak murals, among the most grandiose portraits of court society in ancient America, demonstrates through its texts that the nobles in attendance were, in fact, emissaries from higher lords who chose not to attend in person (Fig. 6.14, Houston et al. 2006: 248–51). They came dressed in tribute – cotton mantles with distinctive bordering, *Spondylus* shells, bright plumes – stripping it when required, bundling it in neat packages at the throne of the lord.

They then shifted back to the comparatively plain dress of courtiers, with simple loincloths and forward-swept headdresses. Many are not even identified by glyphic labels but only by the name of the person they represent. In the final room of the murals, the labels are, as a cryptic touch, left blank, as though the relevant scribe did not finish the job for such nondescript figures. In contrast, across from these seated emissaries are dancing lords, each with full, labeling captions.

The presence of food and drink in many tableaux with nobles suggests that, like modern Maya, women or specialized chefs prepared such meals and in decided abundance. They are likely, too, to have woven the cotton tributary mantles seen in the Bonampak murals and other exemplifications of tribute (Chapter 5). The difficulty of detecting such females poses a challenge to scholarship. Some of these high-ranking figures must have been noble women, not just royalty. For example, excavations at Dos Pilas revealed a special "dower" house, with a throne commemorating royal deaths but especially that of a queen, whose probable tomb was found below the bench (Houston et al. 1991; also Haviland 1981: 115–7). Magnates of great wealth may also have commissioned similar buildings for widowed noble women, in part to distance them. Like queen mothers, dowagers are inclined to be a natural focus of faction in courtly societies, true forces to be reckoned with, and about whom ambivalent feelings swirl (F. Kaplan 1997: 100–1; Stoeltje 1997: 45–9). Little is known about the relation between older and younger women in noble households, although maidens were probably kept close until ready to marry. It is probable that headgear, especially twisted or elaborate wraps, differentiated instantly between married and unmarried women. Classic Maya pottery provides some evidence that the transition from married to unmarried involved transportation, at least metaphorically, by tumpline from natal to marital home (K5847). Overt sexuality may have been more closely linked with maidens or concubines than married women (K7268). Here, as with royalty, the existence of polygyny and concubinage was likely, for reasons of production, political alliance, and the burdensome demands of cousinage and client-patronage (Cohen 1981: 222). But it is not yet possible to identify these forms of marriage and affiance among Classic nobles with any certainty.

Another weakness of interpretation is the challenge of distinguishing those at court from those of actual noble status. The two are, from comparative information, unlikely to be the same (Chapter 5). Not a few palace scenes depict dwarves in attendance on rulers, without any overt markers of noble status. The dwarves often serve food, make sly comments in one case, and hold mirrors so the ruler can admire his appearance – the contrast of body types, beautiful lord with his opposite, must have been deliberate (Fig. 6.2). A dwarf is another mouth to feed, so some lords make do with wooden versions of them, holding mirrors at a good angle for royal view (Miller and Martin 2004, pls. 16–17). Musicians occur in some scenes, as in Late Classic Bonampak murals, characterized broadly as "singers," *k'ayoom*, worthy of personal names but no other epithets (Houston 1997). The skills must have been demanding. A vivid image on a Late Classic vessel shows only the hands and instrument, a trombone-like gourd with a sliding device allowing the player to extend the instrument's length and adjust its pitch; another musician modulates the tone of a conch trumpet, his hand covering its opening (K1453).

Noblemen could come to court as youths for training as pages (Chapter 5). This training, crucial in the dissemination of courtly knowledge and in forming bonds between king and noble, probably took place within special schools of the sort described for the Aztec (Sahagún 1950–1982, 2: 16, 60, 3: 49). A Classic vase shows a mythic template for such activities (Robicsek and Hales 1981: 53). Other than a ground line there is no architectural frame for the scene, but older gods speak to respectful pairs of youths. In obvious scenes of instruction, gods speak words and numbers that loop as thin speech lines from their mouths. There may have been corrosive factionalism between youths and their seniors, yet later sources describe, if anything, exceptional reverence for the elderly and, in Classic times, great esteem for the "wise," *itz'aat*, an attribute cherished by the *sajal* lords of Xcalumkin (D. Stuart 1989b). Guardians of royal youths represented another process by which important courts shipped nobles to inculcate values to heirs in subordinate dynasties. When shown, such guardians or tutors dress simply and lean over in the Maya gesture of deference, an arm placed on the shoulder (Houston 1993, fig. 4–19).

Figure 6.15. Sculptor loaned to Bonampak by Yaxchilan, Bonampak Stela 1, AD 780 (photograph by Michael Coe).

For a literate society, and one that prized image to high aesthetic refinement, scribes and sculptors would loom large (see Chapter 9; M. Coe and Kerr 1998; D. Stuart 1989, 1990). Many dozens of sculptors are known, and at least one was known as the "head" sculptor at Piedras Negras, perhaps the master of an atelier. Where the sculptors are well-documented, they appear to coincide in time as clusters of craftsmen working together, shifting to another set some twenty years later (Houston 2000: 154–6). Sculptors could be loaned from one dynasty to another, and such loans were called *anab*, perhaps meaning "person of the carving implement." Sculptures at Bonampak were, for example, shaped by carvers from Yaxchilan, and even Yaxchilan itself had sculptors loaned from elsewhere (Fig. 6.15, I. Graham 1979: 101; M. Miller 1986, fig. 12). If proof were needed, this confirms that image making was embedded in larger social relations. This makes all the more puzzling the spotty distribution of sculptors' labels at influential sites like Tikal, Copan, or Dos Pilas. One explanation may be that this reflects the variable sumptuary codes of those who could achieve recorded visibility. Notably, many such sculptors went by various forms of the name Chahk, a deity associated with an axe, a fitting device for carving. Yet sculptors are only in one case accorded *ajaw* rank, suggesting either an origin in vaguely noble status or meritocratic promotion from commoner families.

The calligraphers are known through mythic templates that connect such skills with dextrous figures like monkeys, particularly the howler monkey who wears, as a scribe, a distinctive fringed headdress of woven, almost basket-like material (Fig. 6.16; M. Coe 1977b; M. Coe and Kerr 1998, pl. 30). The fact that this figure appears as a substitute for the day sign *k'in* suggests a connection to the later title for calendar priest, *ah k'in*. Yet actual, named calligraphers are quite rare during the Classic period. Almost all of them are associated with the central lakes area of northern Guatemala, especially with the so-called Ik' kingdom, a polity with dominion over the western part of Lake Peten Itza (Houston 2000, fig. 4). Why these figures would have a prominence denied other scribes is not known, although it is a region characterized by vase painting of supreme finish and execution, along with experimentation in novel combinations of color (Houston et al. 2009). As with all nobles in the Classic world, such figures are visible in hieroglyphs and imagery only at a fairly late date, the first sculptor's labels coming to the fore in the later years of the Early Classic period.

For Classic nobles, it is easy to imagine the smooth play, if brutal undercurrents, of courtly interaction. The corridors, courtyards, and banqueting halls must have pulsed as arenas of competitive evaluation. Those who overlooked or failed to understand codes, or even the high language of court, would soon be exposed as buffoonish pretenders and excluded from royal society. But words may slash yet leave no bleeding wounds. That was not the case with another, principal role of nobles, which was to fight and to prepare for such conflict in conditions of controlled violence, ballplay, and hunting. These led eventually to the deadly serious games of seizing captives for heightened honor and to outright warfare, resulting in the burning and subjugation of cities and the submission and demise of foreign kings.

Ballplaying, known as *pitz* among the Classic Maya, occurred in a variety of settings, even against stairways, often with prodigiously large balls of rubber (Fig. 6.17; Taladoire 1981, 2001; Zender 2004a). Usually balls were thrown, to bounce and roll around ballcourts that consisted of parallel structures with sloping fields of play and vertical stops on the upper walls of the court. At Piedras Negras, these vertical walls displayed a panel with images of boxers, suggesting that courts had multiple uses for sport and contest (Taube and Zender 2005). Gladiatorial struggles are now thought to be more common than previously thought, and grim in the extreme. An incised vase from the

Figure 6.16. Monkey scribes, Late Classic period (M. Coe and Justin Kerr 1988, pl. 75, drawing by Diane Griffiths Peck).

Late Classic period depicts two youths assailing each other with sharpened weapons, perhaps of bone (K7749). One is close to gouging out the eyes of another, a bloody exhibit that recalls a captive on another vessel, his eyes removed, all that remains an ooze of body serum (K6674).

The physical setting of ballcourts is standardized yet divergent in detail. Some have markers in the court floor. These are often rounded, flush with the surface, and likely used in scoring systems that cannot now be interpreted. Scuffling movement, with players sliding hips and feet against the ball or striking it with a forearm, shunted the ball to the desired effect. A few Classic courts even have the ballcourt rings common in central Mexico, where the ultimate and tricky goal was to direct a ball through the circle (I. Graham 1980: 187). The links between ballplay, captives, decapitation, and symbolic cavities looking into the underworld, as at Copan, are deep and widespread, suggesting that this sport of kings prepared for or resulted from battle and war. More to the point here, several scenes on Classic pottery implicate lords, usually youths or *ch'ok*, in ballplay, or rulers and visiting lords of highest rank (K3814, I. Graham et al. 2006: 116). In preparation for play, trumpets sounded; when play was over, ballgear passed into storage within the palace, in one image just behind the royal throne (K2784). A long string of panels from Yaxchilan demonstrate that ballplayers included high-ranking nobles, even a "head *sajal*"

(I. Graham 1982: 163). The layering of meaning is dense. One lord strikes a ball, impersonates the wind god, and describes his prowess at war through a title of guardianship. The same set of sculptures injects metaphor into the display by showing ladies striking a ball at the same time they sit cross-legged, a position hardly conducive to this activity (I. Graham 1982: 156).

The aggressive action of such scenes and the occasional sculptures of captives in ballcourts ties in ballplaying, gladiatorial combat, and boxing with other forms of violence. Not a few images on Maya pots and even a few sculptures underscore the importance of the hunt, particularly of deer, to Maya royalty and nobles (Emery 2007). The coordination of activity, the weaponry, the bloody outcome, and the use of conch sounds to confuse and frighten prey all recall the special set of skills and equipment necessary for the hunting of more serious prey, namely, humans. Being warriors was probably the main role of nobles within a system that clearly prized bravery and direct contact with enemies – a title of royalty, expressive of this emphasis, is the count-of-captives by which lords reckoned their number of captives (D. Stuart 1985a). And with that duty came risks of becoming one of the many captives identified in Classic Maya texts and imagery. The copious images of misery after torture and humiliation may also have led to acts of stoicism and dignity in the competitive field of Maya honor. A tiny number are lords, but many, from lack of other titles, were likely nobles plucked in defeat from skirmishes or conflicts of greater scale and duration. A figure in the Bonampak murals is known as a "head-shield," *ba[ah]-pakal*; another was known as "head-flint," *ba[ah]-took'*, a title seen with a captive at Tonina (Fig. 6.13; I. Graham et al. 2006: 88; M. Miller 1986, fig. III:15, III:23). Expressions such as these, clearly attached to nobles of value, may have been allusions to a favored weapon or metonymic tokens of specific status within an armed force.

CLASSIC NOBLES

Aside from kings and their family, nobles are the people in clearest focus from the Classic period. Many of their names are known, in glory and defeat, as is their embedded state within Classic kingdoms. Comparative evidence and information from Maya sources expose them as figures in tense conditions, some of their own making. The more complete the data, the more transparent and intense the contest with royal will, the pretensions to honor and relative autonomy, and the regal responses to these maneuvers. Nobles were obvious conduits of tribute flowing up the system to kings and, in their palaces, channels of redistribution. Other functions, such as adjudication and landholding, are probable from a review of aristocrats in other parts of the world but hard to pin down given the available evidence. Nobles emerge into scholarly sight at a date far later than expected, but only to disappear once again as kingdoms and rulership veered into a decline from which few recovered. These remains, texts,

Figure 6.17. Ballplay against stairway and seated figure with conch, Drawings 21 and 22, Naj Tunich, Guatemala, Late Classic period (photograph courtesy of George Stuart).

and images afford, to positive effect, a sliver of vision within a restricted time, with especially strong information from the southern lowlands, where texts illuminate archaeology more fully than to the north of the Yucatan Peninsula. The view is only razor thin, however. A mystifying attribute of Classic nobles is their difficulty in creating legible, enduring memorials to the birthright claims behind most systems of aristocracy. Dependent on heredity, Maya nobles failed to leave much evidence of deep genealogy, deferring instead to royal appointment. In the future, the dimensions of noble life will attain greater legibility, not at all sites, but in those sites with promising leads already in place, especially those in the Usumacinta drainage and in select cities such as Palenque. Despite their importance and present-day accessibility, these settlements have yet to see much excavation beyond their royal cores. At the lower reaches of this core, barely rising above common status, nobility will provide a sustained focus for Mayanist scholarship to examine the people who articulated and bridged the highest reaches of society with the lowest.

CHAPTER 7

GODS, SUPERNATURALS, AND ANCESTORS

THE "SUPERNATURAL"

The Classic Maya perceived their world as a blend of physical matter and spirit vitality: bodies of water appeared as serpents, hills as creatures with faces, with caves for mouths; flints displayed bony heads in jagged outline; and storms danced as figures with axes in place of lightning. Expressing a distinctive understanding of sociality, the Maya assigned thought and action to a set of beings that would, by most present-day belief, exist apart from daily life. These personages included gods, supernaturals, and "ancestors" – that is, key humans who came before – all in categories that, to Maya faith, blurred and joined in their essence to commune in turn with humans. For the Classic Maya, this group of beings formed as much a part of society as any royals, nobles, farmers, artisans, or traders.

K'uh

"Supernatural" and "god" are words that risk a range of misleading connotations. The first suggests, for example, that there is a category of "natural" creature that contrasts with supernatural beings. As an existential claim, this departs greatly from what is known of essences and extendible spirits in Mesoamerica and the Maya region, where the natural and the supernatural can be hard to distinguish (Houston et al. 2006: 98–101). The second word, "god," evokes, at least potentially, a Western stream of theology, according to which deities intercede in human lives, save souls, and organize themselves as families. By common misconception, gods like this also lead in evolutionary progression towards monotheism, where a single deity replaces and subsumes other beings. These understandings may not capture the subtle interplay in Mesoamerica between transcendent and highly specific kinds of spiritual energy. For the Maya evidence, too, terms like "supernatural" and "god" prompt a set of claims and counterclaims, each of which purports to lie closer to indigenous belief.

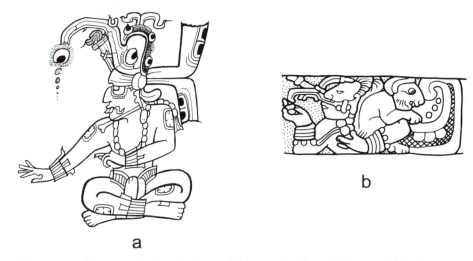

Figure 7.1. Maya gods, Sun Deity and Moon Goddess (Miller and Martin 2004, fig. 14c, and drawing by Stephen Houston, after rendering by Barbara Fash, Copan throne, Group 8N-11).

There have been three stages to scholarly discussion about intelligent, non-human or superhuman beings among the Maya. Early scholars, especially Paul Schellhas (1904), were the first to identify supernaturals by looking carefully at name glyphs and accompanying figures in a set of pre-Columbian codices widely assumed (but not proven) to come from Postclassic Yucatan. The beings identified by Schellhas were, in general, anything but human. In place of regular features, they had large eyes, now known to represent "eagle or raptor vision," aquiline noses, a consistent set of vestments and paraphernalia, and, in some cases, animal-like mouths (Fig. 7.1). Most were old, a Maya gloss on the power of the aged, wise with years, full of experience, and, for some such beings, laden with potent force described as "heat" by modern Maya (Guiteras-Holmes 1961: 71–3; Houston et al. 2006: 48–9; Vogt 1976: 32–3). Because Schellhas could not read the name glyphs, he assigned arbitrary labels like "God A," "God B," and so forth (Schellhas 1904: 7–8). The system is still used by Mayanists, with a number of additions and corrections (Taube 1992a: 5–7). Yet an unfortunate effect of the codical research was to emphasize the Postclassic period in most discussions of Maya religion, perhaps because the codices themselves dated to this later time (Vail and Bricker 2004). Even more recent, general books on the Maya refer to deities solely with respect to Schellhas and to enigmatic lists of deities from early colonial sources (e.g., Henderson 1997: 52; Morley 1947: 213, 221–31), skirting immense quantities of information from the Classic Maya themselves (e.g., M. Coe 1973, 1975, 1978). An analogy would be to study Christ from the vantage of post-Reformation views only, without attention to the beliefs from the early Christian period or the Middle Ages: not wrong per se, but incomplete.

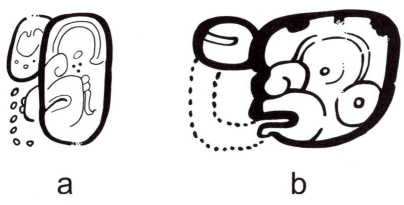

Figure 7.2. *K'uh* and *k'uhul*, for "god" or "holy": **(a)** Palenque Temple XXI bench:Z1, AD 736; and **(b)** Postclassic Dresden Codex, p. 5b.

A second wave of studies rejected the word "god" altogether or saw it as too compromised by Old World preconceptions. To this way of thinking, Maya "deities" were to be understood as impersonal forces of nature or apotheosized ancestors or heroes (J. Marcus 1978: 180; 1983b: 345, 349, 351; Proskouriakoff 1965: 470–1; 1978: 116–17). Related studies suggested that, if belief in gods existed, it had to be a late development, present among the Maya during the Postclassic but not earlier, with heavy borrowing from the doctrines of central Mexico (Baudez 2002; J. Marcus 1992b: 270–1). The first proposal had some limited truth. Chahk is a deity of rain and storms, K'inich a god of the sun, God "E" the personification of ever-resurgent maize; linked to the moon, a young goddess relates in an obvious manner to menstruation and cycles of fertility – her companion tends, not surprisingly, to be a rabbit. But the second claim was incorrect, its main flaw being that it perceived a strong divide between Classic and Postclassic supernaturals (Houston 2004: 446). This is contradicted by glyphs and iconography, which show overwhelming continuities across millennia, if in patterns that seem to be continually reshaped by transmission through different groups and periods (e.g., Taube 1992a: 22–3).

Yet there remains a legitimate question of definition. If gods are sentient, enduring beings with extraordinary powers and explanatory narratives, then surely the Classic Maya believed in these spirits. If all supernaturals are called "gods," however, there is a real difficulty, for the Classic Maya perceived other beings with unusual properties yet did not describe them as *k'uh* (Houston and D. Stuart 1996: 292–3). The distinction between different kinds of spirit leads to a third phase of study. This is Maya theology in its own framework, without naïve replications of Old World models or, in reaction, overstated rejections of religious comparisons.

For the Classic Maya, the fundamental term was *k'uh*, as spelled out syllabically in a number of texts, along with its adjectival form, *k'uhul* (Fig. 7.2). *K'uh* is an ancient word, going back to the beginnings of Mayan languages, with a range of meanings that includes, even today, "god," "day," and "blessing" (Kaufman 2003: 458–60). If certain suffixes are added, the term widens to mean "soul" or "spirit," a vital essence coursing through the blood (Houston and D. Stuart 1996: 292; Vogt 1969: 369–71). For some modern Maya groups, this more expansive term applies to the basis of human intelligence, language, and emotion (Pitarch Ramón 1993: 45). Other evidence from the wider setting of Mesoamerica indicates that spirit essence manifested itself as "a numinous, impersonal force diffused throughout the universe" (Townsend 1979: 28) or as a "divine principle . . . in multiple forms, some ambivalent, some expressing opposite principles in their different manifestations" (Burkhart 1989: 37).

In philosophy, a principle of this sort would accord with what has been described as "monism," the postulate that matter and mind neither divide nor separate from one another. But there is a necessary modification in the Maya case. What animated the material world was, according to a variety of sources, a vitalizing energy that could dissipate or shift to another location. The bond of things to inspiriting force was at least potentially dissolvable, although it seemed to attach more strongly to natural features, less so to portable objects or objects made by humans. In the Classic period, the idea of a shifting essence accounts for why portraits of rulers and others could be "switched off" or disabled by the expedient of scratching out sculpted eyes or by hacking at carved noses and ears (Houston et al. 2006: 76; Just 2005; Mesick 2006). If the portraits were mere stone, these actions would serve no purpose other than casual vandalism, an unlikely motivation given the precision and consistency of sculptural disablement. At death, human bodies, too, lost an energizing force that was conceptualized as wind or breath (Houston et al. 2006: 145–7). To create an image or build a structure became, in this notion of causality, a magical, potent act.

This was true also for certain acts of destruction, which could unmake or "kill" what were, for the Maya, vitalized objects or buildings. Perforations in the bottoms of bowls, especially those from Classic Maya burials, may have come from acts of "unmaking" a usable ceramic and disabling it as a firm-bottomed container by drilling a single hole in its base. Alternatively, the objects were transformed for inversionary use by the deceased, who might have consumed "food" that did not require a normal kind of pot. The intent is almost impossible to reconstruct, although the act of drilling, so often connected to fire making in Maya imagery, suggests that the creation of heat, perceived or real, played some part in these actions (D. Stuart and Houston 1994: fig. 89). The more important and general observation is that monism and its instabilities – energies in flux, attaching and detaching from the material world – probably explained to the Maya why inertia did not prevail and why the world ebbed and flowed, at times visibly but often imperceptibly. Not quite helpless, humans could channel and modulate that flow through specific action.

At this point an elite perspective comes to the fore, as it does with so much evidence from the Classic period. The bias is regrettable but inevitable,

Figure 7.3. Yaxchilan Stela 7, showing *k'uh* energy in blood, flowing over tributary, final quarter of eighth century AD (drawing by Stephen Houston).

and it would be counterproductive to ignore authentic, if skewed, voices from the time. Rich in detail, the data are also surprising. For example, royal imagery connected *k'uh* and *k'uhul* to kings and queens only or, in cases of deity impersonation, to a small group of nobles, as at Yaxchilan during the Late Classic period (D. Stuart et al. 1999: II-44). In contrast to the later evidence from the Maya that we presented earlier, these were concepts not connected in any detectable way to nonelites. In a few images, *k'uh* materialized as droplets with signs for color or shells, a likely borrowing from similar designs at Teotihuacan (A. Miller 1973: figs. 307–14, 324–14). Released by bloodletting, it coursed from the hands of kings onto tributaries and tribute, as though sacralizing such people or things (Fig. 7.3; D. Stuart 2005). Nonetheless, the energized substance was more than blood; it was also a vital element. Presumably, the many artifacts daubed with red pigments or colorants such as specular hematite or cinnabar evoked vital forces, not just effusions of blood. At Copan and Palenque, the use of red colorants marks certain royal tombs, as though expressing and preserving the spiritual intensities of people within (Bell 2007; López Jiménez 2005).

There is another nuance. As a basic noun in the inscriptions, *k'uh* refers to specific beings only. In this it appears to depart from the more abstract concept of a divine principle in all things. That is, imagery expands the frame of reference for *k'uh* and *k'uhul* by showing it oozing from royal palms. But texts restrict *k'uh* in particular to the kinds of personalities we might call "gods." This is evident when *k'uh* are possessed, as the owner was always a person and the *k'uh* always a named supernatural. An expression in several texts refers to the "eight thousand *k'uh*" or "gods," perhaps as some reference to an overwhelming number, and also describes the totality of gods as the *chanal k'uh*, *kabal k'uh*, the "celestial gods, the terrestrial gods," hinting, too, that deities had habitual abodes above and below, embracing the sum of the physical world (D. Stuart et al. 1999: II-43). Several texts and images show us that in remote time a selection of gods was assembled before the deity of traders and wealth, God L in the Schellhas system, to whom they offered tribute and submission (M. Coe 1973: pl. 49).

Indeed, many gods appear in multiples or pairs, or in fused depictions, as with God N and a celestial bird. Perhaps these mergers and fusions come about because the gods joined in tasks, such as rowing a canoe for the Maize God – these are the so-called "Paddler" Deities – or because they assembled to witness the accessions of rulers. Other fusions may have resulted from combinations of godly identity that stemmed from the customary movements and biographies of certain deities (Martin 2007; D. Stuart et al. 1999: II-48–50). Accordingly, the Sun God displayed fishlike properties because he had just emerged, as the sun does daily, from the eastern sea (Houston and Taube 2007). Other variants doubtless associated with world directions, as, in ethnographic evidence, a Chahk being connected to this or that sector of the universe (Hanks 1984: 138). Whatever their name or nature, gods were understood as necessary participants in certain rituals, not as those directly authorizing such events but as those whose company was deemed necessary. For example, an eagle-like being, the "Principal Bird Deity," occurs in the earliest Maya imagery, from Preclassic Izapa, Chiapas, and San Bartolo, Guatemala, and later swoops into royal lives as a messenger or harbinger of gods (Fig. 7.4, Houston et al. 2006: 236–41). For the Classic Maya, his presence signaled a high and holy event, particularly at moments of royal accession.

Maya deities can be seen to operate in sacred narratives portrayed on Classic Maya pottery, some with links to the colonial-era Popol Vuh of the K'ichee' Maya in highland Guatemala (Christenson 2000, 2003, 2007). Yet most such images, which are especially numerous in the Late Classic period, relate to accounts that have no known survivors among later Maya, although many

Figure 7.4. The Principal Bird Deity: **(a)** Late Preclassic, West Wall, Pinturas Sub-I, San Bartolo, Guatemala (painting by Heather Hurst, courtesy of William Saturno, San Bartolo Project); and **(b)** Late Classic vessel, ca. eighth-century AD, near Lake Peten Itza, Guatemala (after photography from Michel Quenon).

deities evolved into later versions: Chahk the Classic Rain God became the Yucatec Chak (Chac in many spellings), so well attested in ethnographic studies of Maya religion, and an elderly midwife goddess transformed into the Postclassic and colonial Ixchel (Gann 1917; B. Love n.d.: 10; Taube 1992a,

1994). Dominant narratives in the Classic sources refer to the Maize God on his journeys of growth, harvesting, and rebirth, or to courtly scenes with the Sun God, and even tricksterlike myths that involve rabbits seizing the head-dress of God L (Taube 1992a: fig. 43). Several accounts border on witty, almost folkloric ribaldry, as in elderly gods cuckolded by deer. Other offer presumed templates for royal behavior through the example of solemn and decorous gods in courtly settings (Taube 1992a: 31–41, 50–6).

Yet the sequences of narrative from pot to pot can be difficult to piece into an overall, coherent narrative. There are gaps in evidence and a strong likelihood of regional variations. A number of stories may have been codified or fixed, others varied according to the occasion, influenced by the precise setting in which they were told or presented. Idiosyncratic settings are elusive, naturally, but what is probable is that these narratives formed mythic templates for royal action and were to be retold or improvised as performances at court (Houston and D. Stuart 1996: 292). Familiarity with these stories reinforced their value as entertainment and, in their more refined form, as tokens of elite status. The fact that images of these narratives proliferate on drinking vessels indicates that they were designed to prompt some response, including a polished comment or recitation of narrative.

Humans had other relations to gods. The most obvious was the presence of "patron" deities at certain sites (Houston and D. Stuart 1996: 293–4). Dos Pilas and Aguateca had two such gods. These could be fused on occasion, as though the deities did not always possess absolutely discrete identities. For its part, Palenque possessed three patron gods, and even minor sites, like La Mar, itemized their own set of local supernaturals. Such gods were housed in special structures, known as *wahyib*, "sleeping places," that corresponded to some of the pyramids at Maya cities. The Temple of the Inscriptions at Tikal is one such building, situated at the end of a long causeway and at some distance, in a southwesterly direction, from other major structures at the site (A. Miller 1986: fig. 46a, b). Copan had these buildings in miniature, small, solid "structures" meant to resemble Maya dwellings, with doorways that contained the crouching god, always depicted in generic form (Fig. 7.5, Andrews V. and Fash 1992: figs. 16, 17). These gods were "seated" on the same day as the local king, in this case the final, well-known ruler of Copan (D. Stuart et al. 1999: II-59). Texts from Copan and Quirigua are especially informative, confirming that rulers had certain gods that belonged to them and, it seems, to them alone. The pattern continued into the Terminal Classic at Chichen Itza, where local lords had their own deities and housed them within the masonry rooms of single-story buildings (Plank 2004: 177; D. Stuart et al. 1999: II-61). Strangely, the architectural setting, although well made, was not especially impressive for such godly occupants.

The nature of Classic deities is likely to have been more than that of faces glimpsed or imagined in incense smoke. Instead, their presence may have been

Figure 7.5. *Wahyib* or "deity dwellings" from Copan, Honduras: **(a)**, **(b)**, and **(c)** Three sides of one house model; **(d)** a house model complete with roof. (Andrews and Fash 1992, fig. 16. Courtesy of the Middle American Research Institute and the Copan Acropolis Archaeology Project).

quite tangible. Small effigies appear in Maya imagery, and a number survive to the present, such as a series of Early Classic Rain Gods found in various public collections (Houston and Taube 2007). The sculptures of kings multiplied the royal presence, but so did the images of deities infused with the essence of gods (Houston et al. 2006: fig. 2.11). To have such an effigy of renown and might, to house it in a special facility, and, at times, to parade it in public view were, one presumes, rare privileges for a particular dynasty. As for the public, Maya kings could be seen maintaining and petitioning spirits. Rulership among the Maya clearly involved a role as pivotal intermediaries, to the extent, perhaps, of speaking for gods in oracular pronouncement, a feature noted for other

Figure 7.6. Yaxchilan Lintel 39, Structure 16, with summoning of K'awiil, ca. AD 763 (I. Graham 1979, *Corpus of Maya Hieroglyphic Inscriptions*, Vol. 3, Part 2: 85, reproduced courtesy of the President and Fellows of Harvard College).

parts of Mesoamerica (Pohl 1994: 117–18). There is no direct evidence of how such mediation took place – secluded spaces on temple summits were probable locations for some discourse between humans and deities. But later sources point to the necessity of appropriate preparation and comportment for the king and his courtiers, including fasting, abstinence, and other forms of abasement (Pharo 2007: 44).

A necessary step in this process was that of "conjuring" (*tzak*) particular gods who could materialize in Maya imagery in the form of figures in the maws of centipedes, as at Yaxchilan (Fig. 7.6; D. Stuart et al. 1999: II-51). The fact that, in colonial Yukatek, *tzak* also carries the meaning of "summon [weather] clouds" indicates that these royal actions were not just ethereal invocations of gods (Barrera Vásquez 1980: 850). Potentially, they had practical aims, such as rain making or ensuring material bounty for the people of the king. In the absence of secure evidence for the economic role of rulers, these may have been crucial royal functions, along with assembling tribute from underlings and offering feasts and other precious articles in return (see Chapter 5).

A valid question concerns the expectations of gods. The relevant term may be "phagiohierarchy," from Greek *phagos*, "eater of," and hierarchy, which pertains to beings that consume other creatures, as in deer that feed on plants, people who eat deer, gods who dine on people (Hunt 1977: 89; Monaghan 2000: 37–8). And always with a suggestion of cyclicity: farmers took food from the earth but ultimately offered their own bodies in return, as burials from which plants grew with earthy nourishment. Aztec deities could be represented by molded, edible seed or grain (Heyden 2005: 56–7), and the same may have been true of Maya god effigies, receiving offerings and then offering themselves, at least ritually or metaphorically. The overall system presents one model of what was at stake. Offered a quid pro quo, deities intervened in favor of human requests after receiving an appropriate payment of "food," from blood to incense, rubber, plants, even incense smoke and flowery fragrance (Houston et al. 2006: 122–7). The ultimate payment would have been human life, although, among the Classic Maya, there is no evidence for the great hecatombs known for the Aztec (Houston and Scherer 2007).

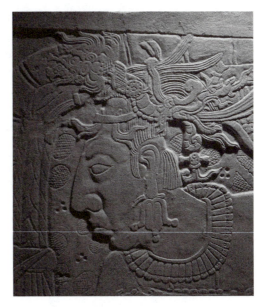

Figure 7.7. Impersonation of ancestors by Pakal, Temple XXI Platform, Palenque, AD 734 (photograph by David Stuart).

A palpable way of bringing gods into view was to dress and dance, inviting godly presences to inhabit the body and dress of the celebrant (Houston et al. 2006: 270–3). This was no fiction or conceit of performance, but a concurrence of human and divine essence in one, active shape. Gods came to earth as dynamic beings, combining their identity with the Sun God, deities of ballplay, even personages from Teotihuacan, and, in several cases, with earlier phases of a ruler's life, the events of which could be reenacted through dance (Houston 1993: 102–7, fig. 4–11). Tributaries, too, could impersonate gods while offering a cloth diadem to the ruler (D. Stuart 2005: 117–19). The doctrine of shared essence must have been quite complex, with different emphases on a site-to-site basis. Palenque, especially in the newly recovered bench of Temple XIX, conflated a mythic accession, as facilitated and supervised by an important deity, with that of a Late Classic ruler (D. Stuart 2005: 65–7). In this instance, a puzzling feature was the inversion of status between primordial deities and historical lords. Despite his theological importance, the presiding god on the bench was impersonated by a tributary lord of inferior status (Simon Martin, personal communication, 2001). Impersonations at Palenque can also be of key predecessors, as when Pakal embodied two ancestors at the same time (Fig. 7.7). In contrast, at Piedras Negras, rulers were seldom shown as gods. In accession-related imagery, or, rather, the first royal celebration of time after an accession (David Stuart, personal communication, 2006), the king sat within an icon for the sky, just below a swagged curtain and the Principal Bird Deity, as indicated earlier. The royal figure was motionless, depicted with a bag of incense but not using it. Because imagery tended to highlight frontal depiction and elevation, it transformed viewers from mere spectators to subordinates and petitioners. Kingship in all its pomp proved enough for local display, without the same call for godly impersonation.

Excavations at Aguateca reveal actual masks for dances of impersonation (Fig. 7.8). These were made of a light composite material consisting of textile layers soaked in clay and then shaped into the desired form. Maya plazas, generally of a size to accommodate a good share of any city's population, were designed for many purposes, but one was surely the enactment of such dances (Inomata 2006a: 814, table 1). For this reason, many stelae in plazas embody the royal presence in imperishable form, forever posed in the clothing and attitudes of dance (Grube 1992; Houston et al. 2006: 72–81). Generally, aside from rare finds like those at Aguateca, the apparel for impersonations is long gone. Yet glyphic texts record about fifty statements of specific acts of impersonation, underscoring the role of such rituals in establishing contact between gods and humans. The ubiquity of impersonations suggests that some of the chambers in Maya palaces were used for storing regalia, props, and sacred masks. Graffiti etched into the walls of Classic temples and palaces shows a vast inventory of paraphernalia in perishable materials, long since rotted away (e.g., Trik and Kampen 1983: figs. 48e, 58c).

To Maya belief, many blessings came from impersonation and close contact with the gods. One inscription labels the deities as the *koknoom*, "those who watch, attend," looking over the ruler during the course of his life in office; an alternative reading would have the ruler watching over the gods, but both alternatives signal close relations between patron gods and ruler (D. Stuart et al. 1999: II-59). A large number of local deities seem not to have been the major gods highlighted on Maya vases or in the codices. One, at Calakmul, was Yaman Ajaw, "the lord's trader" or "buyer" (?), others, at Dos Pilas, represent aspects of important deities, as in K'antuun Chahk, a variant of the Rain God. At present, there is little understanding of how these concepts of dynastic religion percolated down or drew from the rituals and beliefs of nonelites. Nor is it certain what relation existed between dynastic theology and domestic ritual. Contrasts such as between a "Great" and a "Little Tradition," or high religion as opposed to popular faith and practice, are helpful to some researchers but overly dualistic to others (McAnany 2002: 116–17). The important point is that rulers most likely "spoke" to particular deity in an exclusive manner, that they were the people who offered the right "food" and correct language of supplication. As in colonial Yucatan and elsewhere, the gods thus functioned as *abogados* or "advocates" in an intercessionary sense, but whether on behalf of some cause or in appeal to some higher godly authority remains unclear. The metaphor of lawyerly argument implied by "advocate" implies a spiritual judge or jury, neither of which is securely present among the Classic Maya (B. Love n.d.: 6–7; Nicholson 1971: 409).

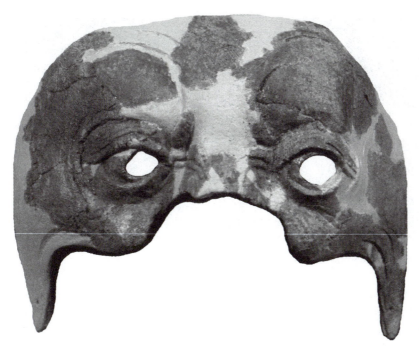

Figure 7.8. Dance or impersonation mask, Aguateca, Structure M7-22 (photograph by Takeshi Inomata).

Whatever the claims for exclusive intercession, rulers could not have monopolized the daily, countless negotiations between nonelites and spiritual beings. A common title, of varying interpretation and reading – the probable reading was *aj-k'uhuun* or *aj-k'uhu'n* – associates certain figures at court with gods, perhaps in service of deities or temple establishments (S. Jackson and D. Stuart 2001; Zender 2004: 371). Discourse with the supernatural was not a male privilege, it appears, as some *aj-k'uhuun* were high-ranking women (M. Coe and Kerr 1997: 94). Conversations between gods and humans may be what took place at the still-enigmatic but increasingly studied "geo-shrines" in caves, on hilltop summits, near streams, ponds, and other liminal features of the landscape, at places where earth, stone, water, and sky join or interact (Brady and Prufer 2005; Prufer and Brady 2005: passim).

With recent attention from archaeologists, along with unusual conditions of preservation, these places have proved among the richest sources for interpreting spiritual practice in Classic times. Unfortunately, the precise meaning of the deposits can be difficult to discern (Houston 2006). Their esoteric nature, extraordinary abundance, and mixture of objects from different periods make it hard to establish a single motive behind the elaborate placement of bone, ceramic, and other artifacts. Rituals expressed in this way may have been, at least in their details, highly ad hoc or improvised for the occasion, if guided by the broad aim of situating objects and animal or human remains in a sacred or

Figure 7.9. Whistles and figurines, Aguateca (photograph by Daniel Triadan).

enchanted location. But at least the full evidence from ethnographic Maya provides a suitable background for interpretation, a set of general attitudes about what such locations meant and how they were used (Brady and Prufer 1999).

Not all spiritual contact occurred in elite or remote settings. Modest structures and living spaces showed signs of "dedications" for house activation or "ensoulment" (the impartment of spirit to things), terminations or deactivations of the same, along with caching of a few precious objects (see Section titled "Ancestors"; Robin 2003: 323). At best, and somewhat loosely, these practices can be interpreted by reference to far later ethnography or the practices of central Mexico in the early colonial period. But a sense of enigma persists. For example, if offering platforms to deities existed, they are not easy to find, although there are some candidates at sites like Copan and Piedras Negras (Gonlin 2007: 91–3, 99–104). Moreover, many of the largest Maya cities, such as Calakmul and Yaxchilan, have been explored in their monumental districts but without the same attention to modest settlement (e.g., García Moll 2003; Kaneko 2003). At such sites, the ability to compare elite and nonelite spiritual practices is not yet possible. But there is hope for future interpretation. For example, the use of figurines, most of them opaque in meaning and function, no doubt contributed to the interventions sought from spirits (Hendon 2003: 33; Laporte et al. 2004). As whistles and ocarinas, most figurines could be made to "sing," triggering them as active "participants" in domestic ritual; the high-pitched sounds themselves would recall the calls of messenger birds and "creaky" and thin speech that present-day Maya link to sacred utterance (Fig. 7.9; Houston et al. 2006: 229–33). Yet the certainty that many figurines were traded raises a challenge in probing the intent behind them (Sears 2006: 394). Their use and meaning at their place of origin may have been quite different from such concerns at their final destination, where they ended up in graves or as refuse.

The interplay between broadly recognized gods and local instances of them was twofold. It allowed the Classic Maya to participate in a pan-lowland Maya system yet to express a unique status within that spiritual landscape. Consider, as a case in point, the deity K'awiil, among the most puzzling of Maya gods. Pictured as a male with reptilian skin, he seems as much an object and power fetish as a god with personality. Rulers "received" (*ch'am*) the deity and held scepters in his shape. But in some parts of the Yucatan Peninsula, K'awiil operates with more of an agricultural than a dynastic meaning. Several capstones or vault stones from buildings in the northern part of the peninsula emphasize his connection to kernels of maize and cacao (Jones 1975; Miller and Martin 2004: pl. 31). This may arise from a sacred narrative, in which lightning – K'awiil embodied a lightninglike celt – struck a deep repository to release maize for plant growth and eventual human consumption (Taube 1993: 39, 67). Rulers also name themselves after aspects of the god or invoke him in multiple shapes, as with a fishy deity at Dos Pilas (Colas 2004: 117–19). At Yaxchilan, rulers could summon K'awiil, but, just downstream, at Piedras Negras, he scarcely merited mention. Instead, rulers used bloodletting implements carved into the visage of the Rain God, Chahk, who appears to have been more important locally (Fitzsimmons et al. 2003: 458, fig. 11).

Figure 7.10. Ixchel, an aged goddess of creation, midwifery, and destruction (K5113, from Taube 1994: 650, copyright Justin Kerr).

Whatever their roles, Classic gods represented forces of considerable magnitude and danger. The aged Maya goddess known as Chak Chel or "Great Rainbow" could destroy by pouring forth a destructive flood from an upended vessel, at least in later sources, and could also assist as a curer or midwife, a figure of menace and transition that both obliterated and healed, and a postmenopausal woman, barren but wise (Fig. 7.10, Taube 1992a: 99–105; Taube 1994: 657–8, 662–3). In Ch'olti' Maya, "old woman" was used in tandem with terms of opprobrium and menace: "you are a dog, you are a wild animal, you are a devil . . . you are an old woman" (Houston et al. 2000: 11; *tzi et, bacat et, diablo et . . . ixcalel et*).

Similarly, Chahk, the god who brought rain for crops and released and nourished maize kernels with the blow of his thunderbolt axe, could also instigate
hurricanes and devastation (Taube 1993: 66–7). Gods contrived to deepen the
anxiety, insecurity, and ambiguity of human existence but also allowed people
to flourish: at Copan, the onset of the rainy season was the "new rainy Chahk"
(David Stuart, personal communication, 2003), a being who both controlled
and embodied rain.

INHUMAN "SUPERNATURALS"

A basic monograph on Maya deities refers to "major gods" (Taube 1992a).
The distinction is important, for there were other beings that the Maya did
not describe as *k'uh*. Among these were the *wahy* or "companion spirits" and
"co-essences" that exemplified the wild, nocturnal aspect of human existence
(Houston and D. Stuart 1989; Grube and Nahm 1994). The word *wahy* comes
form a pan-Mayan term for "sleep" or even "dream" (Kaufman 2003: 1258–
62). Weird, composite beings, often of sinister and skeletal mien, the *wahy*
attached to human beings by invisible but unbreakable bonds, pain or injury
to one resulting in the same damage to the other (Fig. 7.11). For the Maya,
the *wahy*, which are well attested among present-day groups, lived in forests,
on mountain tops, and in caves, places that could be harmful and amoral,
beyond the scope of the ordered human world (Guiteras-Holmes 1961: 26;
Hanks 1984: 134; Vogt 1976: 33). As such, the *wahy* were useful abettors of
witchcraft (Taube 2003), a reminder that malevolent intent lay behind some
Maya practices, not just benign acts of healing and mending (Hanks 1984: 134).
Fear of the forest might typify long-standing city dwellers, who, in the Classic
period, perceived in dark arboreal paths the chance of ambush and capture by
enemy dynasties.

   The appearance of *wahy* on the painted surfaces of some Maya pots implies
the routine invocation of such forces by people drinking from vessels. Several *wahy* depicted in this fashion may even involve terms for disease. Their
glyphic names, replete with terms for "fire," recall much later terms in Mayan
languages for a variety of fearsome, inflammatory afflictions, many leading to
death (independently noted by David Stuart, personal communication, 1999).
Fittingly, this community of spirits includes a being called "groan" or "moan,"
akan, a figure with deathlike associations linked to the consumption of alcoholic drinks (Grube 2004a). Modern Maya tend not to believe that death has
a "natural" cause, so that, in Classic times, the *wahy* might have provided a
persuasive etiology for disease and its fatal outcomes (Guiteras-Holmes 1961:
139; McGee 1990: 106; Vogt 1976: 22–3). Perhaps the use of vessels with these
images concerned notions of healing or apotropaic protection, a malignant
spirit displayed in such a way as to deflect and control its influence. But scholars simply do not know. The positioning of *wahy* in formal dance and gathered

Figure 7.11. A *wahy* of the ruler of Calakmul, Mexico (K5310, copyright Justin Kerr).

performance points to subtleties of meaning that elude us. There is no clear reason why particular *wahy* appear together and others do not, although there may be a faint correlation with where a pot was made and used. Pots from the area of Lake Peten Itza, for example, emphasize the birdlike *wahy* of a local ruler (Grube and Nahm 1994: 703–4).

The richness of ethnographical parallels is not always helpful, as in this instance, where the Classic notion of *wahy* differs in part from present-day concepts. For Classic Maya, the gods, too, were thought to have *wahy*, with a belief in the transformational nature of the co-essence, a deity sprouting, say, a snake leg in allusion to other aspects of its soul. Equally distinct from ethnography, the *wahy* of rulers were hereditary, often attached not to the names of particular rulers but to grand, impersonal titles, such as the emblem glyphs (Calvin 1997). The institutional character of the Classic-era *wahy* lies far from the almost shamanistic nature of similar spirits for present-day Maya. In fact, the religious specialists detectable in Classic sources, most of high elite status, clearly did not include *all* such specialists, healers, or shamanlike practitioners, although, regrettably, the ritualists of nonelites barely register in surviving evidence.

An option for scholars is to examine ethnographic evidence and extrapolate the likelihood of such practices and beliefs backwards to nonelite Maya of millennia before. Another option is to seek parallels in the wealth of evidence from early colonial Mexico, where there is great depth of information about healers and sorcerers (e.g., Pohl 2007: 28–37). This has worked in part for interpretations of the *wahy* and has also indicated what appear to be shifts or purely elite elaborations of basic concepts. Ethnography would suggest, for example, that the Classic Maya had, at all levels, people skilled at prognostication with special stones and talismans, specialists who healed through states of ecstasy, and persons who predicted, controlled, and subdued forces of nature (Guiteras Holmes 1961: 295–6; Tedlock 1982: 138–47). Perhaps such widespread, recent notions signal something about nonelite behaviors of the Classic period, particularly in matters of fleeting religious ideas at less visible strata of society. The little evidence that remains means, however, that this endeavor will always be speculative and, for some scholars, unconvincing. That certain ideas are likely to have existed does not mean they can be confirmed. Nonetheless, an intriguing observation is that some shamanistic ideas and attributes – pillars of centrality, gateways from one plane of existence to the next, divinatory objects – apply to royal or high-elite evidence from the Classic Maya (Schele and Freidel 1990: 72–88). Although institutionalized and rarified, these features may hint at ancient practices among nonelites, perhaps at the very point of origin for Maya spirituality (D. Stuart 2002: 411; Zender 2004: 46, 60–78). As such, they offer a glimpse of nonelite thoughts that otherwise elude us.

ANCESTORS

A final category of supernatural being in Maya society was the ancestor. By definition, an ancestor was a person who had died but, somehow avoiding oblivion, passed instead into a special, continuous relationship with the living. To understand this category of being presumes, however, a concept of what death meant to the Maya and what might await humans afterwards. Across cultures, the end of life is widely understood not as a moment, a matter of acute legal interest to Western medicine, but as a process (De Coppet 1981: 175; Van Gennep 1960: 146), a momentous course of events relating to a wide range of emotions and ideas, including loss and grief, concepts of the soul, rebirth, gender, pollution, danger, problems of succession, and even the negation of time (Bloch and Parry 1982: 7, 11; Huntington and Metcalf 1979: 153). For the Maya, it involved in particular a dissipation of animating breath. It could also be a journey along a road, an immersion in waters by a supernatural canoe – recalling Charon among the Greeks – and, to judge from evidence at Piedras Negras and surrounding sites, a sequence of events that could take several days (Houston et al. 2006: 142–7). Jade inserted into the mouth of the dead trapped the individual's essence or assured some promise of its future recovery.

One representation of the Maya soul is especially revealing. Shown in the act of floating away from the deceased on a bier, the soul combines a solar disk – a fatherly attribute, as in depictions of male ancestors at Yaxchilan – with a lunar crescent, a maternal one (Fig. 7.12; Tate 1992: figs. 46, 66, 86, 130). Hard and flintlike, much like a device for striking sparks, the solar disk emits beams of light in the form of centipedes, a standard convention in Classic Maya art (Taube 2002: fig. 4). Within the combined solar and lunar signs another glyph appears, one associated with the relation between father and sons. The presence of ethnographic terms for ancestral beings or divinities as a combination of "fathers and mothers" raises the possibility that the enduring

Figure 7.12. Souls of deceased parents, Yaxchilan Stela 4, AD 775 (courtesy of the President and Fellows of Harvard College).

essence of the Maya soul fused male and female principles. At the least, later Maya and Mesoamerican peoples labeled the dead as a whole as "fathers and mothers," a term found so widely as to indicate the high chance of antiquity (Craveri 2006: 146; Galinier 2004: 102; Guiteras-Holmes 1961: 342; Vogt 1976: 33). For the Tzotzil Maya, paternal and maternal qualities are still attributed to the sun and moon, respectively (Köhler 1977: 20). This is in clear linkage to the images carved a thousand or more years before at Yaxchilan.

The ability of ancestors to nourish the living, even to create life anew with their special energies, appears in a variety of sources, Maya and non-Maya (Galinier 2004: 106–7). The notion is found explicitly in the images of royal ancestors emerging as ingestible plants from the sarcophagus of Pakal the Great at Palenque (McAnany 1995: 75–6) or from a skeleton entombed within a pyramid on an Early Classic vase: it also sprouts chocolate and other valued plants (Grube and Gaida 2006: Abb.12.13). The belief in new growth as rebirth and transformation may account for the tendency in some dynasties for grandsons to take the name of grandfathers, as though in partial recycling of ancestral spirit and identity; the preference is particularly strong at sites in the western reaches of the Maya lowlands but is also documented at other cities (e.g., Martin and Grube 2008: 86, 88, 118, 120, 122, 128, 142, etc.). Indeed, the absence of such repetition at sites like Copan begs an explanation: did certain kingdoms emphasize the uniqueness of kings, others their spiritual continuities with past lords?

Still, despite such themes, researchers will look in vain for a single encapsulation of what death meant to the Classic Maya. A royal death, saturated with complex meanings and likely to have far-reaching implications in many lives, reverberated more widely than an infant's passing in an isolated farmstead. Even the afterlife involved different kinds of spiritual real estate. The belief in Mesoamerica that the mode of death determined the transit and eventual abode of the soul is likely to have existed among the Classic Maya, who saw the afterlife as a paradise, not always as the grim, malodorous Xibalba discussed in ethnographic sources – this last location, foul with the smell of urine, dark and menacing, may, in fact, have been the eventual home of nonelites in some models of the afterworld (Taube 2004a). Nonetheless, in broadest terms, the themes of movement, the abatement of breath and heat, and the distinctions between the energies of dead and living pervade the extant sources, allowing some general sense of death concepts among the Classic Maya, from the elite and royal to the nonelite. From a perspective many centuries later, the textual references seem cold and stripped of emotion. But there are representations, in Early Classic imagery, of mourners streaming tears, their limbs contorted in anguish (Grube and Gaida 2006: Abb. 12). The absence of young dead in the inscriptions suggests that elite accounts focused on lives that flourished into adulthood and on the people who mattered for dynastic motives (Houston et al. 2003: 114).

For the Classic Maya, ancestors tended to have several features (D. Stuart 2007b). In the first place, many show garments and headdresses that resemble the styles of Teotihuacan, the great center of Mexican civilization that would have gone up in flames by the time these images came into existence (e.g., Schele and M. Miller 1986: pl. 40a). In Western art, a comparison might be the depictions of figures in Roman togas to underscore their antiquity, or in the loose clothing of another time. Second, when shown in sculptures, Classic-era ancestors tend to be bearded, with the facial hair that takes some Maya years to grow (Fig. 7.13). Above all, the ancestors were old, mouths puckered from tooth loss, long hair covering their faces. The inscriptions, especially rich in such references during the Early Classic period, vary slightly in the precise description of these figures in that all are *mam* but sometimes with a more general meaning of "grandfather, ancestor," at other times with a narrower sense of "maternal grandfather." This was particularly true at Yaxchilan, where maternal ancestry mattered greatly to its Late Classic rulers (D. Stuart 2007b). A relevant feature of *mam*, too, is that the term can be reciprocal. A grandson can also be described as a *mam*, perhaps because of perceived recycling and replacement. In a world of limited longevity, the overlap between grandfather and grandson may not have been great.

The Classic Maya stressed the *mam* designation in most glyphic descriptions of such beings. It was the first feature worth mentioning, the first glyph in a string of names or titles. Several objects, heirlooms in all likelihood, were also inscribed with statements of ownership by *mam* or ancestors. Some are bowls of Early Classic date, especially from the area of Uaxactun (Grube and Gaida 2006: Abb.11.1); others take the form of shell pectorals that contained, to judge from the depictions on them, ancestral beings placed just over the chest (Houston et al. 2006: fig. 1.54; Houston and Taube 2007). On the whole, royal ancestors are shown floating in smoke, looking downwards as such celestial,

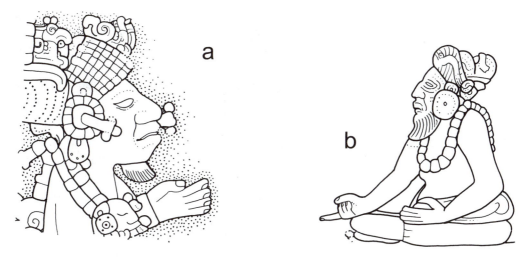

Figure 7.13. Depiction of ancestors: **(a)** a bearded man, wall panel, area of Bonampak, Mexico (after Emmerich 1984, pl. 49); and **(b)** ancestor on alabaster bowl, Palenque-area (after K4332, Dumbarton Oaks).

airy beings might. They appear in partial form, with only the head and, just below, a single arm in crooked position. The incomplete physical makeup of ancestors accords with the variably preserved bones the Maya might have seen and collected in reopened tombs. One such tableau, on an altar from Tikal, portrays the uncovering (*pas* in the text) of a burial with the bones of a noble lady. Her remains are shown synoptically by skull and long-bones alone, all other remains overlooked, presumably, as insignificant parts of the body (Jones and Satterthwaite 1982: fig. 23).

On Piedras Negras Stela 40, a similar image records an event in which a royal woman's tomb has been opened (Fig. 7.14, McAnany 1998: fig. 11). Her body is portrayed in fragmentary form. She waves a panache of feathers, but only her head, shoulders, and a single arm are visible. Above, the living ruler sprinkles incense into the tomb, from which the lady emits, through her nostrils, a winding cord of hot breath that arcs out of a crack in the ground, coursing to the sky and then descending towards the king. This is one of the clearest scenes in Classic imagery of interaction between the living and the dead, and of what reciprocal benefits were thought to accrue: incense given by the living as "food," hot energies emitted in return. A noteworthy feature of this interaction is that it tends largely to involve the immediate, personally known ancestors, not the remote founders of certain dynasties mentioned in the sequences of rulers (Schele 1992). But there is always an exception, in this case a monumental one: the sequence of buildings at Copan above the tomb of the dynastic founder, K'inich Yax K'uk' Mo' (Taube 2004b). Clearly, cults of founders played a strong role in some sites, less so at others, where, for unknown reasons, founders were not recorded in surviving evidence. In this,

Figure 7.14. Piedras Negras Stela 40, with incensing of royal tomb, AD 746 (drawing by David Stuart).

it is important to stress the distinction between, on the one hand, the generic dead, perhaps seen as no more than suffused energy, or people of low status lamented by only a small circle – and briefly at that – and, on the other hand, the "special dead" of specific memory, of biographies that could be elicited (Binski 1996: 21–2). It was for them that ancestor veneration could indeed be practiced (Houston et al. 2003: 123).

The connection with the sky, so evident in ancestral figures floating above kings in Early Classic imagery, stands opposed to ethnographic concepts, which place the *mam* in earthen fastnesses, rather like the royalty depicted at Piedras Negras (Taube 1992a: 92, 97, fig. 23; Thompson 1970: 297). A few places, such as Yaxchilan, acknowledge both settings. They situate deceased parents above, seated in elegant positions above bands that represent the sky, yet they also contain images on ballcourt markers, flush with the earth (Tate 1992: fig. 66). At Tonina, it is the nonroyal elites who sit in earthy spaces, some of it marked as the skin of cosmic crocodiles; they forever hold objects that appear, from their symbolism, to embody breath soul (Mathews and Graham 1996: 103). These seated images recall the relatively rare instances of such burials in the Maya lowlands, perhaps as mummy bundles in seated position, wrapped tightly in now perished cloth and rope (McAnany 1998: figs. 2, 3).

Of the greatest complexity, however, are royal burials. At Río Azul, Guatemala, they show on the four walls directional mountains, as though emphasizing the centrality of the burial within a sacred space defined by landscape (Adams 1999, figs. 3–17, 3–20); at Palenque, attendants are either painted or modeled in stucco on walls, not so much mourners as permanent attendants holding regalia of rule (Robertson 1983: pls. 234–331). The striking feature of such tombs is not only their elaborate physical setting, often within large pyramids, but their great variety,

even within single sites, such as Tikal.
There was no uniform equipage for the
royal dead. In a few places, youths could
be sacrificed for placement in the tomb
(Houston et al. 2003: 130); at others,
a panel was erected, as in the area of
Piedras Negras, to note the final fire
rituals for the interment of the dead (D.
Stuart 1998: 384–93; Tokovinine 2006:
12).

Comparative findings about death
make it clear that preparations for the
dead and subsequent treatment of them
conveyed two things: what awaited the
dead, who seldom died completely or
faded into utter oblivion; and how the
living continued to commune with and
categorize the deceased, as can be appreciated in exalted form on Stela 40 at
Piedras Negras or the placement of the
dead under the floors of humble Maya
dwellings, if not always in a consistent
way (Webster 1998: 10). (Evacuation of
buildings must have been a temporary
necessity, as the smell would have been
unbearable without embalming or some
other sort of mortuary palliation.) Maya
sites typically show evidence of scattered
human bones, perhaps from disturbed
burials or special deposits. The more
usual practice, however, was to adjust

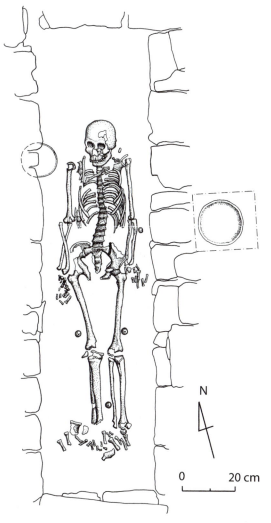

Figure 7.15. Piedras Negras Burial 45 (drawing
by Zachary Hruby).

the body into a variety of positions, mostly supine, rarely prone, usually
extended, and with often a paltry set of burial equipment. The offerings
most likely included objects thought to be useful to the dead, from vessels and
plates for future repasts to elaborate deposits for royal burials, which reflect
in death the opulence of elite lives and the ritual duties expected of them,
including bloodletting.

Metaphors abound in all burials, and perhaps as more than comforting fac-
similes of places for the living. To Maya thought, rather than just representing
dwellings, burials replicated houses and sleeping chambers by including "false"
doorways, alcoves for "storage," and continued residence just below the feet
of the living (Fig. 7.15). It is the rare Maya structure that does not contain
subsurface burials (Ruz 1968: 63; Welsh 1988: 27–34). Some have substantial

preparation, others are inserted with casual dispatch in garbage. By Late Classic times, the deposits in burials appear to concentrate in elite and royal burials, with some variety. At places like Piedras Negras, the poverty of nonelite burials is conspicuous in comparison to far richer deposits at sites like Caracol (Houston et al. 2003: 122; Laporte Molina 2003: 71): the constitution of the "special dead" is thus likely to have differed from site to the site. Moreover, houses could be reentered and so too could some tombs, especially those with stairways or, as at Caracol and surrounding regions in Belize, multiple interments in mausoleums. These could be opened and resealed as necessary (A. Chase and D. Chase 1996; Healy et al. 1998).

A few burials occasioned the construction of massive structures on top. Common in northern Guatemala, eastern structures in residential compounds frequently contain, as looters know all-too-well, important burials with marketable goods (Becker 1971, 1999). One argument has it that such structures interred the remains of key or apical ancestors, to be venerated and supplicated by living descendants. There is also a wide set of objects for ancestral commemoration: small altars at some sites, including portraits of nonroyal elites in death at places like Tonina; incense burners in evident service of nonroyal mortuary rites; and so-called "drum altars" from Edzna, Mexico, Piedras Negras, and La Joyanca, Guatemala (López Bravo 2004: fig. 89; M. Miller and Martin 2004: pl. 122; Schele and Mathews 1979: 281, 282, 303). These suggest that ancestors played a role from royal society down to that of nobles – here were the "special dead" of the Classic Maya, with biographies that, thanks to texts, persisted generations after the demise of particular individuals. The reduction in size from royal prototypes, some altars only twenty to thirty centimeters across in comparison to the large sculptures made for kings, reflect the probability of sumptuary understandings that allowed elite copying of royal models, but only to a certain extent and in restricted contexts. The meaning of larger numbers of burials in special facilities, as in the island of Jaina off the coast of Campeche, prompts a range of interpretation, from island necropolis to vigorous denial that such facilities exist (Benavides 2007: 51; Piña Chan 1968). The glyphically labeled objects from Jaina, many from sites inland, support the idea of a wide catchment for the island's burials; the counterargument that the burials simply occur under the houses of the deceased is not confirmed by excavations, which show instead a layering of deposits, not house foundations per se (cf. Benavides 2007: fig. 4).

WORSHIPPED AND FEARED

Maya society had many constituents, some of flesh and blood, some wraithlike, to be spied in smoke or clouds, or found in physical form as effigies or bones seen or extracted from burials. Others were detected only in dreams, perhaps expressing a notion of virulent diseases that the Classic Maya sought to control or appease. All deaths had some cause, and the *wahy* may have explained the etiology of human illness. Any attempt to understand the operation of society must incorporate these spirits as something other than figments of the imagination or delusions of the superstitious. In Maya thought, superhuman or inhuman entities contributed for good and ill to their communities. Supernaturals formed the multigenerational, enduring core of Classic communities, as attested in numerous artifacts, texts, images, and the disposition of all of elements in linked manner. Their company, physical or perceived, was omnipresent. Yet, as ever, the great variety of Classic sites betrays any effort at comprehensive summary. There are some common themes, to be sure: gods recognized universally but worshipped in distinctive local forms; supernaturals who affected the living, without, however, any grand degree of godly influence, and many of these recognized only in particular places; and, finally, as examples of what humans could become, ancestors as a general force, composed of humans who came before, but distinguished principally by the special dead who could be labeled truly as ancestors. These were the recognizable beings for whom stories were kept and consulted. No small part of the monumental landscape but often the product of high investment, certain sites housed such beings and signaled, through concentratetd attention, the importance of spirits to the Classic Maya.

CHAPTER 8

FARMERS

THE PEOPLE OF MAIZE

"Thus was found the food that would become the flesh of the newly framed and shaped people. Water was their blood. . . . Their flesh was merely yellow ears of maize and white ears of maize. Mere food were the legs and arms of humanity, of our first fathers. And so there were four who were made, and mere food was their flesh."

(Christenson 2007: lines 4822–61)

Popol Vuh reports that gods created the first humans from the flour of white and yellow corn. Maize and other food products formed the basis of Maya society both spiritually and economically. Like any society, the growth and maintenance of Classic Maya civilization hinged ultimately on those who produced and collected food: farmers, fishers, hunters, and gatherers. They supported the Maya economy not only by supplying food but also by producing various types of goods, such as ceramic vessels and stone tools (see Chapter 9), and by providing labor for the construction of civic and elite buildings. Agricultural workers and their families made up a significant portion of the population, perhaps as high as 90 percent or more of Maya society; many fishers and hunters may also have cultivated fields. The people we call farmers included diverse groups and individuals who engaged in overlapping, yet different, sets of activities and represented a wide range of social status, economic wealth, and political influence.

MAYA FOODS

The Classic Maya enjoyed a wide variety of food items, most of which are still used today in Mexico and Central America. After the Spanish conquest many cultigens were also adopted in other parts of the world, hence the polenta and tomato sauces of Italy or the chocolates of Belgium. Of all of such foods, maize (*Zea mays*) contributed the largest share, shaping society and beliefs profoundly. The French historian Fernand Braudel (1981, 1: 161) called maize a "miracle food," comparing it favorably to the productivity of European staples like wheat. One planted seed of maize yielded one hundred to two hundred grains in colonial Mexico, whereas European wheat during the same period produced a meager four to seven grains from one planted seed. Maize grows well in various conditions, and some types mature fairly quickly, leading after the conquest to rapid dispersal across the world. The high productivity of maize and its relatively short maturation, all without the need of significant agro-engineering, gave Maya farmers ample time to engage in tasks other than food production, such as the festivals, religious activities, and monumental construction commanded by elites.

In her analysis of Zapotec urns, some with molded shapes made of real corn, Mary Eubanks (Eubanks 1999: 185) identified as many as ten races of maize. These races probably showed a dazzling variety of colors – white, yellow, red, purple, and black – with cobs measuring five to fourteen centimeters in length. Their maturing time from planting to flowering also varied, from 70 to 140 days. It is likely that the Classic Maya used an equally abundant range of maize, giving them flexibility in cultivating diverse ecological zones. Such variety also made farmers less vulnerable to crop failure from drought and plant disease. A particularly important kind may have been the Nal Tel race, widely grown in Guatemala and Yucatan today. This early maturing maize, now measuring around eight centimeters in length, tolerates drought fairly well (Eubanks 1999: 174–77).

Maize, however, had one drawback, for all of its many benefits: it was deficient in the essential amino acids of lysine and tryptophan. To a certain extent, this problem was remedied by the use of lime. To prepare corn food, today's Maya – and most certainly their Classic-period predecessors – placed shelled maize in containers of water mixed with burned lime, leaving it to soak overnight. The next day, before grinding it, they washed the corn to rinse off any excess lime and indigestible outer shells. Lime not only ensures smooth dough; it adds calcium and increases the available amount of zinc and the deficient amino acids (FAO 1992: 117, 121). But unlike their modern descendants and contemporary highland neighbors, the lowland Maya made this maize dough into *tamales* and *atol* (porridge), not *tortillas* (Fig. 8.1, Taube 1989b). *Comales*, large flat griddles for *tortillas*, started to appear in lowland settlements during the Late and Terminal Classic periods (LeCount 2001: 944), and it was not until the Postclassic period that *tortillas* seem to have become common. The highland Maya, in contrast, have used *comales* – and presumably *tortillas* – since the Middle Preclassic period (Popenoe de Hatch 1997: 119).

A more fundamental solution to the nutritional deficiency of maize was to consume them with legumes (*Phaseolus spp.*). Although beans are sensitive to droughts and floods, they provide the essential amino acids that maize lacks. Modern nutritional studies show that a diet of 70 percent maize and 30 percent

Figure 8.1. Late Classic Maya *tamales*, on polychrome vessel (photograph by David Stuart).

beans provides balanced amounts of protein, carbohydrate, and fat, although, by adding foods like animal meat, the ratio of beans can be lowered. The cultivation of legumes had an additional advantage. When planted with maize, or in alternation with maize, legumes fertilized soil by fixing nitrogen (FAO 1992: 117, 121). Maize and beans made an ideal combination, the core of the Classic Maya diet, although there may still have been significant problems in diet, resulting in pellagra (David Webster, personal communication, 2008).

Farmers cultivated other crops, too, adding flavors and nutritional options, with implications for subsistence. Chiles (primarily *Capsicum annuum*) gave a piquant kick to meals and were rich in vitamins. As noted by Sophie Coe (1994: 62), the natives of Mesoamerica ate almost nothing without them. Many types of squashes (*Cucurbita spp.*) provided pithy food, edible seeds that could be dried and stored for long periods. The deep root systems of the squashes had the benefit of resisting drought (Rubatzky and Yamaguchi 1997: 614). Although tubers do not preserve well in the archaeological record, remains of manioc (*Manihot esculenta*) have been identified at Joya de Cerén, in present-day El Salvador, in an area close to, and perhaps part of, the Maya world (Lentz et al. 1996). Highly productive and drought resistant, manioc plants grew roots that could be stored underground for years (Latham 1997: 262). Fruit trees such as avocado (*Persea americana*), guava (*Psisium guajava*), papaya (*Carica papaya*), and nance (*Byrsonima crassifolia*) probably formed orchards around many houses. Palm trees (*Acronomia spp.*) provided foods such as nuts or hearts of palm, as well as construction materials (Lentz 1991); red seeds of achiote (*Bixa orellana*) were ground and mixed with many foods and drinks to impart a vivid flavor and color (S. Coe 1994: 143). Of special importance was cacao (*Theobroma cacao*), a delicate plant cultivated in limited areas that needed conditions of

yuk'ib   **[for *witik* and *koxoom mul*]**   **kakaw**

"his drinking vessel"   "chocolate"

Figure 8.2. Cacao (*kakaw*) mentioned on hieroglyphic text from Vessel 15, Río Azul Tomb 19, Early Classic period, in a couplet referring to two kinds of cacao, *witik* (top) and *koxoom mul* (bottom) (drawing by Stephen Houston after D. Stuart 2006, fig. 9.9).

high humidity and high temperature throughout the year (S. Coe and M. Coe 1996: 19). A frothed drink made of its ground seeds was highly appreciated by nobles, but its presence at Joya de Cerén suggests that nonelites also enjoyed the delicacy (Sheets and Woodward 2002: 189). Hieroglyphic texts on many elegantly painted vessels attest to their use as cacao vessels (Fig. 8.2). The Classic Maya may have enjoyed cacao drinks with the flavors of vanilla, chili, or maize porridge, in concoctions quite different from the "chocolate" of Europeans, who favored the addition of sugar and milk. More controversial to modern scholarship are the *ramón* trees (*Brosimum alicastrum*) that grow naturally in the forest (Fig. 8.3). Bearing edible fruits and seeds called "breadnuts," *ramón* prompted much heated discussions among scholars, some of whom identified it as a possible staple of the Classic Maya (Atran 1993; Puleston 1982). Yet its vestiges in the paleobotanical record are scarce, and indigenous peoples of Mesoamerica tend to view *ramón* as a famine food, palatable only when little else is available (Lentz 1999: 14). The *ramón* theory led to useful discussion, but, by current consensus, the fruit and seeds were unlikely to have been staples for the Classic Maya.

The Classic Maya also cultivated plants for fiber and other use. Cotton (*Gossypium hirsutum*) was worked into elaborate robes of the elites, perhaps woven by elite women into essential items of tribute (see Chapter 5); its seeds may have been used for cooking oil. Durable but less comfortable, coarser fibers of maguey (*Agave spp.*) may have been woven and worn primarily by lower-status people, along with bark cloth. Maguey fibers were also used for net bags and, in construction, for rope to tie roof beams and poles together. Various

Figure 8.3. *Ramón* fruits and a *tortilla* made of *ramón* (photograph by Takeshi Inomata).

types of gourds (*Crescentia spp.*) served as containers, and their young fruits and seeds could also be eaten, especially when toasted to release a pleasing flavor. Smoked as cigars or applied as a paste, tobacco (*Nicotiana tabacum*), known as *may* to the Maya, clearly had ritual and medicinal functions: one image shows a mythic scene in which a person daubs *may* or tobacco paste on the back of a toad, an early and effective patch that introduced nicotine into the bloodstream (Fig. 8.4a, David Stuart, personal communication, 2005). Some miniature ceramic vessels are likely to have been snuff bottles used in consuming and trading prepared tobacco; their holes are just large enough for a single human nostril (Houston et al. 2006: 114–16) (Fig. 8.4b). Depictions of nobles smoking in palace-meeting scenes or of deities holding cigars point to the social and religious importance of the plant. As for sweets, before the Europeans introduced sugar cane, the Maya favored honey, *kab*, understood by them to be a kind of excrement of bees: glyphs for "dirt" or "ordure" are indistinguishable, as is a Postclassic sign for "wax." During the contact period, honey was an important product of Yucatan, where many families kept hives of small stingless bees in hollowed-out tree trunks (Roys 1972: 42). They also used it to make an alcoholic drink called *balche*, in part from a special bark, although the main ritual drink of the Classic Maya seems to have been *pulque*, *chih*, made from agave plants and a liquid later beloved in central Mexico (Houston et al. 2006: 116–22). Sugar may also have come from maize plants and was brewed into a variety of drinks (Smalley and Blake 2003). But these were but a small part of the Maya food larder and medicine cabinet, as there were doubtless many other plants of value in the forest, probably, by Late Classic times, increasingly thinned by cutting and burning (Atran 1993).

Animal food was important, although the Maya did not have large domesticated animals (Fig. 8.5). Colonial documents mention domesticated turkey (*Meleagris gallopavo*) as a key component of feasts. The Maya also ate wild turkey (*Meleagris ocellata*) and muscovy ducks (*Cairina moschata*). Domesticated

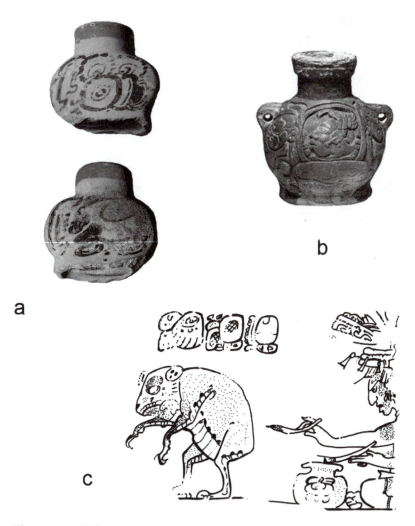

Figure 8.4. Tobacco in Maya imagery: **(a)** snuff container, Museo Nacional de Antropología e Historia, *yotoot umay*, "his snuff's dwelling" (photograph by Stephen Houston); **(b)** snuff container with tobacco leaves (M. Coe 1973, pl. 77, courtesy of Michael Coe, photograph by Justin Kerr); and **(c)** tobacco paste applied to the back of a mythic toad (courtesy of David Stuart, and personal communication, 2005).

dogs (*Canis familiaris*) were eaten, but dog bones account for only a small portion of excavated faunal materials (Emery 2004: Table 6.1; Wing 1981). Wild animals that the Maya often hunted and snared include peccaries (*Tayassu pecari* and *Tayassu tajacu*), white-tailed deer (*Odocoileus virginianus*), brocket deer (*Mazama americana*), armadillos (*Dasypuz novemcinctus*), iguanas (*Iguana iguana*), and various types of turtles. Although deer and peccaries were not domesticated, some may have been husbanded in pens (Hamblin 1980). The Maya in coastal areas appear to have extracted a wide variety of marine resources, including fish and shellfish, some of which may have been dried for trade and storage: most markets in highland Guatemala have baskets full of dried

Figure 8.5. Ceramic painting depicting a peccary and a turkey, by left-handed scribe (K1001, copyright Justin Kerr).

shrimp, to be reconstituted in broth. Inland habitants ate freshwater fish, such as *blanco* (*Centropomus spp.*), *mojarra* (*Cichilasoma guttulatum*), and various types of catfish. Small riverine snails called *jutes* (*Pachychilus spp.*) were useful as protein in some areas. What still eludes scholars is how activities related to plants and animals formed larger systems of scheduling and division of labor, or how lists of foodstuffs might yield up a cuisine of interacting flavors and culinary refinement.

LIFE AT HOME AND IN THE VILLAGE

By the end of the Classic period, a fairly large population was dispersed over wide areas of the Maya lowlands (see Chapter 1). The resulting pattern consisted of continuous settlements, leaving some open space between each group or cluster of residential structures (Fig. 8.6). Loose aggregations of residential buildings varied in size and form, but a common configuration comprised several buildings around a square patio. Most residential groups found both in centers and rural areas were probably occupied by farmers, with houses that were smaller and less elaborate than those of elites. The buildings themselves had wood frames, thatched roofs, and wattle-and-daub walls or partially masonry walls. Aside from differences in size and elaborateness, the spatial and physical settings of such houses resembled those of elites and vice versa. This applied also to the material possessions of farmers, which aside from the paucity of jade, shell ornaments, and elaborate polychrome ceramics did not differ widely from elites, at least in the goods that might remain for archaeologists to find (see Chapter 9). A word of caution, however: reading social station into such remains can be a circular process, a particular set of patterns assumed to correlate with position in society. Generally speaking, modest buildings were likely occupied by lower-status Maya, but each case must be evaluated on a site-by-site basis, by meticulous evaluation of archaeological

Figure 8.6. Reconstruction drawing of a patio group at Aguateca, Group M6–3 (drawing by Takeshi Inomata).

remains and their contexts. A more disturbing problem is that farmers remain silent to us, as opposed to elites who left texts and art that sometimes permit insights into personality, social and political role, and motivation (see Chapters 5 and 6). Yet it would be a mistake to see farmers as a faceless, homogeneous category. Only gradually, with additional excavation and agronomic research, is the diversity of Classic Maya food producers coming into focus.

Out of Volcanic Ash

Uniquely vivid views of farmers derive from the excavation of Joya de Cerén, El Salvador, by Payson Sheets and his colleagues (Fig. 8.7, Sheets 1992, 2002). It is not clear whether the residents of this small rural settlement in western El Salvador spoke a Mayan language, but their lifestyles were similar to those of many Maya farmers in the lowlands. Joya de Cerén was suddenly buried in three to five meters of ash emitted in a volcanic eruption of Loma Caldera around 600 AD. This resulted in an archaeological "time capsule" with remarkable assemblages of complete objects and extraordinary preservation of organic materials. Archaeologists even recovered the shapes of now-decomposed plants by pouring dental plaster in voids left in hardened ash (Fig. 8.8). Most buildings

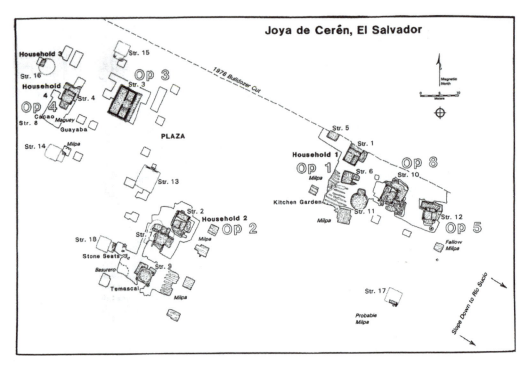

Figure 8.7. Joya de Cerén (Sheets 2002, fig. 1.1).

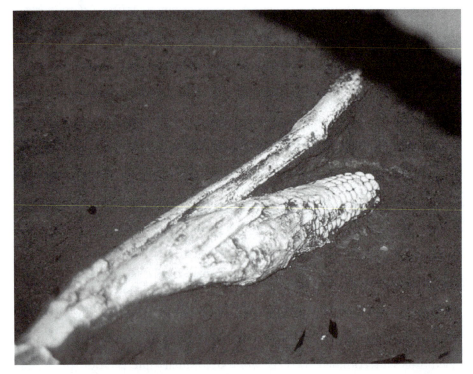

Figure 8.8. Plaster cast of maize from Joya de Cerén (courtesy of Payson Sheets).

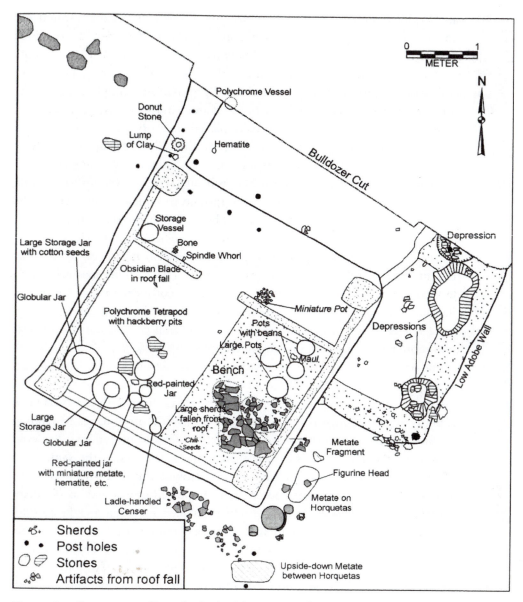

Figure 8.9. Structure 1 of Joya de Cerén (Sheets 2002, fig. 5.2).

at Joya de Cerén were relatively small, measuring around three-by-three and four-by-four meters, and consisted of wattle-and-daub walls and thatched roofs built on low platforms. Most domestic buildings had more roofed space outside the walls than inside, providing open air spaces for various activities and provisional storage of nonvaluables. Although only one residential group (Household 1) has been excavated completely, single households appear to have occupied several buildings, including domiciles, kitchen, storehouses, and workshops. Domiciles (Structures 1 and 2), which had benches, were the main living and sleeping spaces (Fig. 8.9). The presence of large storage jars, serving vessels, and painted gourds indicates that the residents stored and ate food in these buildings. Remarkably, a niche of Structure 2 contained a polychrome bowl, still showing finger swipes left by the person who ate from it. The residents stored obsidian blades in roof thatching, perhaps to avoid casual injury from sharp edges. Food preparation took place in separate kitchens (Structure 11), as well as in outdoor areas under the eaves of residences. *Metates* for corn grinding were usually placed on wooden supports at waist level. Some perforated spherical stones, generally called "donut stones," were found with wooden pestles and organic materials in their holes, suggesting use as grinding stones. Other donut stones probably served as weights for digging sticks, a device for making holes in the ground in which to sow seeds. The residents stored various food stuffs, such as beans and squash seeds, in numerous ceramic vessels in kitchens and storehouses. Inside Structure 4, which appears to have been a storage building, a circular corn crib measuring one meter in diameter was filled with husked corn cobs. These configurations at Joya de Cerén indicate that, as units of coresidence, collaboration, and property sharing, households consisted of a relatively small number of people, probably single nuclear families in most cases, but the overall picture remains unclear until more residential compounds are completely exposed.

The occupants of Joya de Cerén were clearly rural farmers or at least a group of people living in a small village, of relatively low status in their society. Yet the images of daily life from their community are far from a stereotypical view of poor, oppressed peasants. The richness of material inventories is striking, and Sheets (1992: 124) notes that the residents of Classic-period Joya de Cerén enjoyed richer material possessions than modern farmers in the same area. The most extensively excavated Household 1 owned more than seventy-five ceramic vessels, and villagers had access to imported goods such as obsidian, stone for axes, and shells. Locally produced objects included grinding stones and cotton threads. Their diet, including maize, legumes, squash, chili, manioc, avocado, gourds, cotton, palm, achiote, guava, hackberry, cacao, and nance, was as varied as that of the Maya nobility (Lentz et al. 1996: 259). To be sure, the occupants of Joya de Cerén had the advantage of fertile volcanic soil, but the prosperity of the site hints at similar patterns elsewhere in the Classic world.

The people of Joya Cerén had rich social lives, too. Structure 3, a long building with a substantially smaller number of objects than others, was probably a communal building where villagers met to discuss local affairs and to drink *chicha* (maize beer). Structure 10 appears to have been related to community festivals, with storage of ceremonial objects, including a painted deer skull headdress, and perhaps festival food and drink. Structure 9, a building with a domed room, served as a communal sweatbath. In the center of its interior floor was a fire box. Bathers probably entered the heated room after extinguishing the fire. Sweat baths are still common among the modern Maya, who use them not only for hygienic reasons but for medicinal purposes and ritual purification (Houston 1996; Child 2006). Structure 12 is interpreted as a place of ritual activity (Brown and Sheets 2000). Objects neatly stored in a niche – figurines, fragments of *Spondylus* shell, a pile of beans, and a deer antler – may have been used as ritual paraphernalia. Another pile of beans was found on the floor, which may have been used for divination, along with a collection of minerals atop an interior wall, as is common among the modern Maya.

Making Home and Community

The life of farmers was framed in terms of social organization. Particularly important settings for their daily life were nested domestic groups, each associated with certain rights and obligations for its members (see Chapter 2). For example, the social unit of food sharing may not have been the same as that of land holding (see Goody 1958). To archaeologists then, the task is not to find the "typical" composition of Classic Maya farming households but to analyze interrelations between various levels and types of social groups. Although these groups may have been fluid, variable, and socially porous, they still informed the perception and activities of people. It is likely that some patterns of social arrangements expressed themselves in the layout of buildings and the space within and around them.

Unlike Joya de Cerén, most Classic Maya sites lack in situ deposits on the floors, making inquiry into social relations difficult at best. Important data, however, are being provided by the analysis of soil chemistry (Barba and Manzanilla 1987; Terry et al. 2004). Concentrations of phosphate, metals, and other elements in soils and plaster floors reflect ancient activities. Their patterns are highly variable, but there often exist more than one area of high phosphate levels (Fig. 8.10). It appears that single patio groups commonly housed more than one unit of food preparation and consumption. This finding accords with patterns at Joya de Cerén. Such groups of people may have been economic units for the storage of food and possession of other movable materials. Patio groups found throughout the Maya area are generally interpreted as residences of extended families (Willey 1981). If so, these extended families may have comprised multiple economic units, as well as differences in wealth and status. We should also consider the possibility of great variety in the composition of domestic groups occupying patio compounds. It is suggestive that a significant portion of buildings at Joya de Cerén had functions other than residential ones. A patio group with small structures comparable to those at Joya de Cerén may have consisted of a single residence and additional nonresidential structures, perhaps housing a nuclear family.

Despite possible internal divisions, the occupants of a patio compound probably formed a significant focus of religious belief and practice. Aggregations of buildings often include a nonresidential structure of a roughly square plan, which may have served as a family shrine or storage structure. The social integration of occupants of a patio group appears to have been rooted in notions of kinship and local history. Excavations of such compounds often reveal a long sequence of architectural expansion and superimposition, as well as burials of former residents. Such bodies, viewed in part as those of "ancestors," were conceived in Maya thought as "active" interlocutors and key anchors of group identity among the living (McAnany 1995), although, to be sure, the emphasis on such personages varied strongly across the Maya region. As among modern Maya, daily activities of agriculture, cooking, and construction took place in constant dialogue and interaction with ancestors and deities. In Classic Maya houses, what Westerners would consider the sacred and secular merged inseparably (Monaghan 2000: 30).

Settlement surveys often find loose aggregations of patio groups and other buildings. Group identities, recruitment, and rights and duties associated with these buildings remain opaque. Yet it is reasonable to assume that the mere fact of spatial propinquity facilitated close interactions between and a certain level of coordination among inhabitants. The presence of a communal house and a building associated with ritual and feasts at Joya de Cerén, as well as the common occurrence of minor temple pyramids at other sites, points to an abiding sense of community, an entity that collectively discussed political matters and celebrated local festivals (Yaeger 2001). If farmers maintained agricultural fields close to their houses (see Section titled "Working in the Field"), negotiation and coordination of land tenure and rights of cultivation might have been a central concern (McAnany 1995: 159–62). Most occupants of such patio groups likely engaged in agricultural activities, shaping a feeling of shared identity, as well as the opportunity and need for cooperation. However, the internal heterogeneity, partially expressed in building sizes, material possession, and activities, is also evident at this level (Yaeger and Robin 2004). Besides agricultural work, some households engaged in different kinds of craft activities (Beaudry-Corbett and McCafferty 2002).

Another vexing problem is determining the division of labor within a household, whether by gender or age. Among most Maya groups, especially those known through ethnographic and ethnohistoric evidence, agricultural work is associated closely with males in both practice and ideology. Women are responsible primarily for work at home, particularly cooking, child rearing, and textile production. Among the contemporary northern Lakandon Maya, however, men, women, and children tend to collaborate in all agricultural tasks (Boremanse 1998; Robin 2006). Which case is closer to general practices among the Classic Maya? Those living in dispersed settlements with strong emphasis on intensive infield cultivation might have resembled the northern Lakandon; those who did not, perhaps, were the residents of aggregated towns

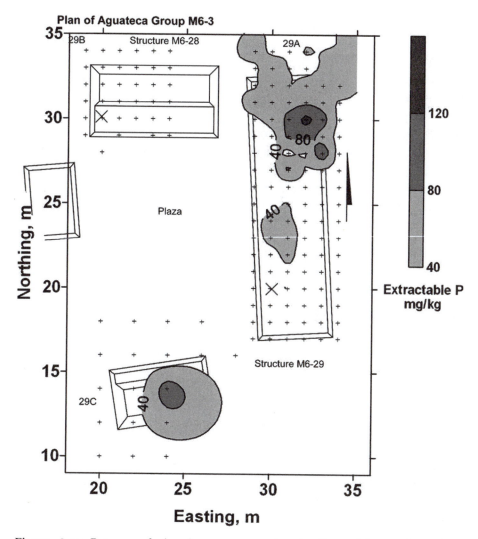

Figure 8.10. Patterns of phosphate concentration in Group M6–3 of Aguateca (courtesy of Richard Terry).

or villages, reliant on distant fields. An infield system lends itself to active participation of women in agricultural labor, especially when other traditional duties concentrate in and around the dwelling (Robin 2002). Yet centralized political systems might have conditioned such patterns to the extent that, as among modern Maya, rulers and elites interfered in the ownership and use of resources, a pattern quite dissimilar from traditional Lakandon. It is probable that in Classic times this political milieu contributed to a relatively clear division between a male's work in the field and a female's work at home. Such divisions, although often hard to discern archaeologically, need far more attention than they have received thus far.

WORKING IN THE FIELD

The Maya lowlands constitute a rich yet fragile ecosystem (see Chapter 1). Soils are generally thin, washed away easily by tropical rains once the natural vegetation is cleared. The lowland environment, particularly in the humid southern part, is characterized by biodiversity, nurturing a myriad of species but a limited number of any one kind at any one location. In Maya archaeology the successes and failures of local adaptations to ecosystem diversity have been central topics, especially when addressing the rise of centers during the Preclassic and Early Classic periods, along with their variable depopulation around the ninth century AD. Scholarly views have polarized in this matter. Some investigators assert that the Classic Maya relied on maize monoculture, which was highly destructive to the environment and vulnerable to pests and climatic changes. Such a practice is believed to have led to an inevitable environmental disaster, namely, the Maya collapse (see Chapter 10; e.g., Culbert 1988). Other archaeologists have challenged this view, proposing tree fruit or root crops as alternative staples (see Section titled "Maya Foods"; e.g., Puleston 1982). The truth probably lies between these perspectives.

Increasing data on human bone isotope and paleobotanical remains identify maize as the dominant staple of the Classic Maya (Lentz 1999; Wright and White 1996). Stable istotopic C4 signatures are estimated to show 50 to 80 percent of total caloric intake to be from maize, indicating a diet comparable to those of their modern descendants (Gerry and Krueger 1997: 202; Wright and Chew 1998: 932). Still, it is unwise to forget that the Classic Maya enjoyed a wide variety of plant and animal foods other than maize. There also existed significant regional variation in diet. Human bone chemistry suggests that populations in central Peten, the Pasión region, and at Copan relied more heavily on maize than the occupants of some Belizean settlements. Copanecos (those living at Copan) may have eaten less meat and fish than the inhabitants of Peten and Belize (Gerry and Krueger 1997: 204–5; Wright and White 1996: 175–6). Such variations reflected adaptation to the local environment, differences in cultural preference of food items, and the fluctuating impact of local and interregional politics.

Central to this inquiry is the problem of specific techniques of cultivation. Classic Maya farmers employed a relatively simple set of tools. Unlike farmers in many parts of the Old World, they had to cultivate lands without the help of large domesticated animals. Oval-shaped chipped stone axes were basic agricultural tools of multiple functions, handy for cutting trees and digging soils (Aoyama 1999; Lewenstein 1987; Rovner and Lewenstein 1997). We now know that, using such a tool kit, Maya farmers developed a wide repertoire of agricultural practices. What is not clear is how the Maya combined diverse methods and to what degree they relied on one technique over others.

Swidden or Intensive Agriculture?

One of the methods used was swidden agriculture. Colonial and modern Maya have also practiced this method extensively. The forest was cleared and burned before the rainy season. The ash of burned trees released nutrients to crops planted at the beginning of the rainy season. In drier northern Yucatan one crop a year was common, but double cropping was possible in more humid and fertile areas. The negative side to the high productivity of maize was that it quickly depleted the soil of nutrients. As yields in any one plot dropped, farmers let the land lie fallow and awaited the recovery of its fertility. Fallow periods varied widely by regions and soil types, ranging from a few years to twenty years. In some places with good soil fertility, such as Joya de Cerén, there was no need for fallow periods (Sheets, personal communication, 2008). Although freshly burned forests were generally more productive than fallowed lands, opening primary forests with stone axes meant significant investments of labor, particularly in the southern lowlands. Farmers may have preferred generally to return to fallowed plots unless there arose the need for new agricultural fields. It was possible to intensify production temporarily through shorter fallow cycles, but this would contribute in the long run to a depletion of soil nutrients and serious problems with pests and weeds. Another problem of swidden agriculture was the loss of soil through erosion. Early scholars believed that swidden agriculture was the only dominant agricultural method among the Classic Maya. As further settlement data showed fairly high population densities throughout the Maya lowlands, many wondered how the Maya could support a large number of people with swidden agriculture alone.

In the 1970s this picture changed drastically with the discovery of agricultural terraces and wetland cultivation. In terraces of the Río Bec region of Mexico, a series of small stone retaining walls along the contours of slopes helped prevent soil erosion, perhaps as a coping mechanism for environments already overpopulated and damaged (Turner 1974; see also Murtha 2002). Evidence of wetland agriculture came in the form of small patches recognized in flood plains of the Candelaria River in Campeche and along the Hondo and New Rivers in northern Belize (Fig. 8.11, Siemens and Puleston 1972). Researchers inferred that, long ago, Maya farmers had dug into ditches to remove soils rich in organic matter, piling the muck on small patches of land and thus creating agricultural fields of high productivity. Longer canals were then dug to drain excess water. A problem began to appear when scholars came to expect similar features across the Maya lowlands. They hypothesized that large centers of the southern lowlands, many at the edges of seasonal swamps or *bajos* (Chapter 1), relied heavily on wetland agriculture. Extensive lattice patterns detected by an airborne radar survey over wetlands seemed to support such a proposal (Adams et al. 1981).

Figure 8.11. Drained fields, Chan Cahal, Belize (Beach et al. n.d., courtesy of Timothy Beach).

Unfortunately, subsequent ground surveys in various parts of the Maya lowlands failed to meet the glow of initial expectation. To be sure, dense remains of terraces were found in central western Belize, where rolling terrain around the large center of Caracol was extensively modified into terraced hills (Fig. 8.12; A. Chase and D. Chase 1996). But surveys specifically focused on agricultural landscapes in the Puuc hills, the Petexbatun region, and northwestern Belize (Dunning 1992; Dunning and Beach 1994; Dunning et al. 1999), and in the upper Belize River Valley (Fedick 1994) found relatively scant evidence of terraces. Such remains appear to be scarce, too, in central Peten, Guatemala. Scott Fedick (1996b:128) suggests that the Maya built terraces only in patches of land that satisfied conditions appropriate to technologies of hand-tool cultivation – that is, areas with shallow, fertile, well-drained upland soils of the Mollisol order that developed over consolidated limestone bedrock. Nicholas Dunning and his colleagues (Dunning et al. 1998a; Dunning et al. 2003) believe that some terraces were constructed in response to anthropogenic changes in the environment. In the Petexbatun region and northwestern Belize, they found terraces primarily along the foot-slopes of hills. Soil cores taken from lakes of these regions, as well as those of central Peten, indicate that significant deforestation of upland areas, probably from agriculture, took place during the Preclassic period, causing the erosion of soils towards lower elevations

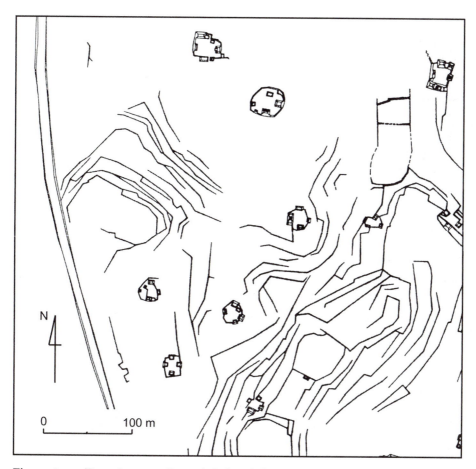

Figure 8.12. Terracing near Caracol, Belize (Chase and Chase 1994a, fig. 1.2).

(Brenner 1983; Curtis et al. 1998; Hillesheim et al. 2005). The resulting accumulations of soil probably became the primary focus of intensive cultivation during the Classic period; foot-slope terraces then served to preserve these premium agricultural lands. In addition, Dunning and colleagues (Dunning et al. n.d.), working in northwestern Belize, as well as a group led by Richard Hansen (Martínez et al. 1996) investigating the Preclassic site of Nakbe, found certain terraces had the characteristic signatures of swamp soils. These deposits hint that Maya farmers brought fertile wetland soils to terraces so as to enhance agricultural production, although this practice may have taken place primarily during the Preclassic period.

A key shift in scholarly thought began with additional survey in areas where lattice patterns were detected by airborne radar. These surveys consistently failed to reveal remnants of wetland agriculture (Dunning and Beach 1994; Pope and Dahlin 1989). Dunning (1996) argues that there existed a wide range of hydrological regimes in *bajos* of the Maya lowlands and that only limited areas were suited for wetland cultivation. Kevin Pope and colleagues (Pope et al. 1996) even suggest that some features interpreted as raised field in northern Belize resulted from natural processes, especially the violent shrinking and swelling of clay and the precipitation of carbonate and gypsum in raised hummocks. Pohl and others (Pohl et al. 1996: 366) reason, too, that wetland features with clear evidence of human modifications were used primarily during the Preclassic period. In their view, the Preclassic Maya cultivated edges of riverine wetlands of northern Belize during the dry season or as hedges against risk in dry years. Seasonal variation of the water table was no more than one meter, which kept the surface soil moist throughout the dry season. By contrast, water tables in the *bajos* of Peten dropped by over three meters during the dry season, making wetland cultivation improbable in that zone (Pope and Dahlin 1989). As the water level rose with the increase of sea level towards the end of the Preclassic period, Maya farmers of northern Belize found it necessary to drain wetland fields with ditches and canals, eventually abandoning them before the Classic period. Dunning and colleagues (Dunning et al. 1999), examining *bajos* near the site of La Milpa in northwestern Belize just upriver from the area where remnant wetland agricultural features have been found, contend that *bajos* in their study area, as well as those in Peten, were perennial wetlands at one time. Upland forest clearance and concomitant soil erosion during the Preclassic period transformed them into seasonal swamps. According to Dunning and his colleagues, cultivation in *bajos* became exceedingly difficult after this hydrological change because of high acidity and substantial shrinkage and hardening of soils during the dry season.

Peter Harrison (1996) counters these arguments by reemphasizing that the Pulltrouser swamp along the New River in Belize was indeed used for wetland cultivation, primarily during the Classic period. In much the same vein, Patrick Culbert and his coworkers (Culbert et al.1990) propose that many *bajos* of the Peten were used extensively for wetland cultivation. Their backhoe trenches in the Bajo Pedernal near Río Azul, Guatemala, revealed linear channels, which they interpreted as canals for wetland agriculture. Their survey of wetlands between Yaxha and Naranjo also recorded substantial settlements on islands and along the edges of *bajos*, perhaps reflecting intensive use of wetlands (Culbert et al. 1997). In response, Dunning and colleagues (Dunning et al. n.d.) suspect that canal-like features were naturally formed through the swelling and shrinkage of seasonal swamp clays, a suggestion likely to be correct. Alfred Siemens (Siemens 1996) similarly maintains that some of the impressive canals along the Candelaria River were used for fisheries. More recently, linear features were detected in high resolution IKONOS satellite images of *bajos* near Tikal and Calakmul (Sever and Irwin 2003). The carbon isotope analysis of soils of wetlands near Aguateca revealed a signature of maize cultivation (Richard Terry, personal communication 2008) or, alternatively, transplanted material from uplands. Thus, the debate on wetland cultivation continues.

Diverse Strategies

The true extent of Classic Maya intensive agriculture, particularly involving wetland cultivation, cannot be known without more research programs, some now underway. Nevertheless, intensive wetland agriculture does not seem to have been as prevalent as once thought. A large part of the northern lowlands, as well as the area around Copan, sustained substantial populations without the benefit of wetlands. Most scholars have recently come to emphasize diverse strategies as a key to understanding Classic Maya subsistence. At first glance, the tropical lowland environment seems homogenous in comparison to highland areas marked with valleys and ridges. A closer look, however, reveals a surprising degree of environmental heterogeneity. In addition to their biodiversity, marked by the coexistence of a variety of species, the lowlands are characterized by a mosaic of small patches of different ecological conditions, each shaped by different soil types, topography, and hydrological regimes (Fedick 1996a). In addition to the foot-slopes and edges of wetlands, premium agricultural lands included sinkholes that result from the erosion of limestone bedrock. Thick sediments at their bottoms usually retain moisture throughout the year, providing adequate conditions for the cultivation of cacao and other plants (Dunning and Beach 1994; Kepecs and Boucher 1996). The analysis of soil carbon isotopes in sinkholes of the Petexbatun region has detected signatures of maize cultivation (Johnson et al. 2007). In adapting to such conditions, Classic Maya farmers combined various subsistence strategies, choosing the most suitable technique for each microenvironment (Dunning et al. 1998b). Swidden agriculture, terracing, and wetland cultivation were just parts of a wide array of methods available to them – with, it seems, considerable impact in Preclassic times, when swidden was likely to have been the most significant initial system of cultivation.

A particularly important part of this system may have been intensive cultivation in relatively small plots near residences, generally called "infield agriculture" as opposed to outfield agriculture that involved more extensive use of land away from residences (Netting 1977; Sanders 1981: 362–3). At Joya de Cerén, plaster casts of decayed plants provide remarkable views of such practices. Maize fields were found close to residences. Neat ridges and furrows that facilitated water absorption and stabilized maize show that farmers carefully tended such fields (Sheets 1992: 59). Sheets and Michelle Woodward (Woodward 2000: 23) estimate that the maize yield of the Joya de Cerén field was, for the first planting, in volcanic soils of high fertility, some 5,280 kg per hectare, which is higher than the productivity of most traditional fields in the Maya area today, if, perhaps, a figure that may be overgenerous according some researchers (David Webster, personal communication, 2008). To the south of Structure 4 was a maguey garden and fields of manioc, and these and other features are unlikely to have been radically different from infields in other parts of the Maya lowlands. Even in a more urban setting, the results of intensive surface collection and soil chemical analysis at Sayil, Yucatan, have suggested to Thomas Killion and coworkers (Killion et al. 1989) that open areas between residential groups characterized with low sherd densities and high phosphate levels were used for agricultural production. To them, Sayil and probably many other Maya centers were "garden cities" with patches of agriculture filling areas between houses. Plots close to residences were probably intensively tended. Elevated phosphate levels appear to reflect fertilization with food refuse and the feces of household members and animals, along with organic mulches.

This agricultural strategy may have been closely tied to the relatively dispersed settlement patterns that the Classic Maya developed over wide areas of the lowlands. Robert Drennan (1988) has pointed out that compact settlements were more common during the Preclassic and Terminal Classic periods. The prevalence of dispersed patterns in Classic times suggests to him that Classic-period farmers relied heavily on intensive infield agriculture rather than extensive outfield swidden agriculture. Because of significant labor input in weeding and fertilization, the Maya probably preferred to live close to their agricultural fields, leading precisely to the dispersed pattern seen at many Classic sites. The dispersed pattern would also lend itself to tree crops. Like modern Maya houses in rural areas, Classic residences were probably surrounded by fruit trees. Related archaeological features may be the amorphous piles of stone rubble measuring two to four meters in diameter that are commonly found in Yucatan; these are nicknamed *ch'ich'* mounds. Susan Kepecs and Sylviane Boucher (1996: 76) note that modern Maya in the region commonly place stones around fruit trees so as to conserve moisture and support delicate trunks. They suggest that *ch'ich'* mounds reflected comparable practices among pre-Hispanic Maya.

It is equally probable that the Classic Maya actively managed forests away from their residences. Arturo Gómez-Pompa and others (Gómez-Pompa et al. 1987) note the presence of stone walls delimiting small patches of forest vegetation. According to local Maya, these features, called *pet kot*, were made by recent ancestors and by the "old" Maya for the cultivation and protection of useful trees. Gómez-Pompa and colleagues propose that the patches were artificial forests for the extraction of arboreal resources, which the pre-Hispanic Maya created by introducing and protecting desirable tree species. Scott Atran (1993) observes that the modern Itzaj Maya of Peten protect valuable trees in the forest, such as *ramón* and young mahoganies (*Swietenia spp.*), by selectively clearing areas around them. He suggests that the Classic Maya farmers employed similar strategies of forest management. The Classic Maya probably faced the shortage of fire wood, as is happening in many parts of the world today because of pressures from deforestation and increases in population. Selective thinning of forests might have been an effective strategy for ensuring a supply of fire wood while enhancing the growth of trees that provided fruits, medicine, incense, and construction materials. In some areas, the Classic Maya may have cultivated maize and other plants in forests, leaving a significant portion of trees uncut, as the Lakandon Maya did until recently (Nations and Nigh 1980: 20). Large parts of the Maya lowlands were probably deforested and filled with intermeshing patches of residential groups and agricultural fields. Yet, such animal species as jaguars (*Panthera onca*) and brocket deer, which require the presence of canopy forests for their survival, are relatively common in archaeological faunal assemblages, indicating that the Classic Maya preserved significant areas of forest (Emery 1997: 140–216). These forests were probably not so much untouched wilderness as carefully and actively managed sources of vital materials.

In sum, Classic Maya farmers devised various strategies, including intensive cultivation near the residences, orchards, terracing, wetland cultivation, swidden agriculture, and managed forestry. Their land use probably did not observe a marked differentiation between so-called infield and outfield or between the cultivated and the wild, but was characterized by a continuum from intensively tended plots close to home to managed forests at some distance away (McAnany 1995).

FARMERS AND POLITIES

The central authority of each Maya center obviously extracted tribute and services from farmers and other nonelites. This raises two related questions: How did elite and state or political institutions affect the life of individual farmers? And how did farmers cope with, resist, or benefit from those encounters?

Demography

The tension inherent in relations between elites and nonelites must have been aggravated by the trend of rapid population increase during the Classic period. The collapse of some polities and a probable population decline at the end of the Preclassic period left sparsely occupied, relatively open lands in many parts of the Maya area. Whereas large Early Classic settlements developed near rich agricultural lands, population levels in areas with lesser agricultural potential were relatively low. During the Late Classic period, however, the Maya expanded their settlements, filling less desirable lands. A particularly drastic case may be that of Dos Pilas and Aguateca, Guatemala, both situated at the edges of swampy lands. They grew from sparsely settled rural areas to densely occupied centers when an intrusive dynasty established twin capitals during the Late Classic period. By the end of the Late Classic period, the Maya lowlands were transformed into highly crowded landscapes. Patrick Culbert (1988) estimates the density of Late Classic rural population to be 168 persons/km^2 and, on average, the intrasite density to approximate 300 to 500 persons/km^2.

The numbers may have been smaller if the Maya maintained dual residences or if the occupancy rate per structure were lower. Still, many scholars, with some important dissenters, agree that the Classic Maya reached a remarkably high population density for a preindustrial agrarian society.

According to one theory, this demographic trend at least partially reflected incentives from the elite. Under the highly tense political climate of the Classic period, the main interest of competing dynasties was to attract an ever larger subject population so as (a) to secure labor for construction activities and (b) to gain economic and militaristic advantages over rivals. The elite may have strongly promoted population growth among their followers (Cowgill 1979), although the actual mechanism of such promotion is rather unclear. This theory would also imply competition and inequality among the farmers themselves. Under certain social and economic environments in such communities, larger households tend to enjoy economic advantages over smaller ones (Wilk 1983). By increasing family size, many Maya farmers might have tried to exploit economic and political opportunities that were embedded in the larger sphere of politics. As an alternative theory, generally large households might in fact have been poorer households, as suggested by David Webster (personal communication, 2008).

The Politics of Farming

Both polities and individual farmers needed to cope with demographic trends by intensifying agricultural production. A result was a dynamic agricultural system that expressed tensions between the conflicting interests of farmers and kingdoms. Three issues were critical in this precarious balance: the development and use of agricultural lands; the choice of specific crops; and land tenure. It could also be noted that the Maya dealt with "niche construction" and "niche inheritance" of particular opportunities for food production, with each successive generation of Maya adapting to anthropogenic niches of their own making. The problems facing Late Classic people were thus very different from those of their forebears.

In terms of agricultural land use, the primary strategy was, as seen already, the adoption of diverse agricultural techniques that responded to the mosaic-like, microenvironmental heterogeneity of the tropical lowlands, particularly by Late Classic times. This strategy required intimate knowledge of local environmental patches, which were most likely held by individual farmers rather than by elites. If so, decisions concerning agricultural landscapes might have been made primarily by individual farmers, as well as by small kin or local groups (see Netting 1993; Chayanov 1986, for the importance of decision making by individual farmers in the course of agricultural intensification and the ratio of producers to consumers in households, a strong influence on household economic prosperity). Agricultural fields developed through the direct involvement of the state tend to be highly standardized and at large scale. Evidence of such plots as developed by kingdoms is indeed scarce in the Maya lowlands, perhaps in itself a reflection of the nature of local political organization. Even highly productive wetland agricultural fields consisted of small, irregular patches of raised or ditched fields. Terraced fields also appear to have been amorphous and were generally associated with small residential groups. It is difficult to find any whisper of a master plan by state administrators in these agricultural landscapes. Such observations do not mean that the polities or kingdoms were uninterested in the direct development and management of agricultural lands. Many elites probably owned their own agricultural lands (see Section titled "Working in the Field"). In addition, Arlen and Diane Chase (1996a) argue that extensive terrace systems around Caracol were developed through the initiative of the elite, although this could also have been handled, as among the Ifugao in the Philippines, by small-scale organization (Conklin 1980). Large canals at Edzna may also have been constructed under the state supervision. Such examples, however, are uncommon.

We should remember that *comales*, the flat plates for cooking *tortillas*, were nearly absent at lowland Maya centers during the Classic period. In the Guatemalan highlands and Oaxaca, *comales* have been used since Preclassic times, and their appearance may, in some cases, correlate with significant state involvement in agricultural practice (J. Marcus and Flannery 1996: 146). *Tortillas* prepared on *comales* were more suitable for farmers who needed to work in distant agricultural fields than *atol* (porridge) and *tamales*, rather heavy, bulky foods, difficult to transport and easy to spoil. In other parts of Meso-america, the use of distant agricultural fields may have increased with the relocation of agrarian populations and the development of new maize fields under state supervision, especially in the Oaxaca Valley. In the Maya lowlands, however, *comales* became common only during the Postclassic period, when the Maya were under increasingly strong Mexican influence. Although food preferences cannot be explained by political factors alone, the scarcity of *comales* at lowland centers during the Classic period may be conditioned partly by the limited degree of elite involvement in agricultural practices.

Another piece of circumstantial evidence is that each Maya community appears to have been largely self-sufficient in most food items. Although some scholars have suggested that large centers, such as Tikal, exerted political control over wide areas and imported staples in a large quantity (Culbert 1988), there is in fact little evidence for this claim. The bone chemistry of skeletons suggests that the Classic Maya mostly ate locally acquired foods (Wright and White 1996: 174). Even settlements like Colha, which exported chert tools in significant quantity, also developed their own agricultural fields (Jacob 1995). A rare exception may be Chunchucmil, where the residents possibly depended on the import of food in exchange of salt, but the data are still inconclusive (Dahlin et al. 2005).

The political agenda of the elite and of polities was more strongly reflected in the choice of crops. There appears to have been a strong pressure toward a monoculture production, which runs counter to the biodiversity of the low-land environment. Is the mosaic, micromanaged interpretation wrong or feeble as an explanation, or was there constant tension between diversified strategy and an emphasis on maize? If diversified agricultural strategies were rooted in the local knowledge and practice of farmers, this standardizing demand may indeed have been exerted by polities (Pyburn 1996). In Classic Maya society, which lacked a well-developed, general-purpose money applicable to various types of transaction, a significant part of the state economy was based probably on "staple finance" sustained and mediated by tribute collected in the form of staple foods (See D'Altroy and Earle 1985). Maize, which could easily have been stored and transported, was most advantageous for taxation in this system. In addition, as James Scott (1998) forcefully argues, the state and other forms of centralized political institutions anywhere in the world tend to promote the homogenization of social practices. They encourage the standardization of language, currency, and measuring systems, and transform diverse natural land-scapes into homogenous agricultural fields. Such homogenized landscapes and standardized practices serve the needs of states by helping control population and resources. Although Classic Maya polities were neither highly successful nor interested in homogenizing agricultural land use, the promotion of maize cultivation could have been one area in which this tendency of the state could expressed itself.

The strong interest in maize on the part of polities was reflected in the ideological importance of this plant to elite Maya. The Maize God occupied a crucial place in the Classic Maya pantheon, and the rulers identified themselves closely with this agricultural deity (see Chapter 7). Royal iconography and performance were filled with maize symbolism. The states probably effected this heavy reliance on maize cultivation in an indirect manner. In other words, although kingdoms did not actively develop state-owned maize fields on a large scale, they may have specified the quantity of maize to be provided in tribute, as they certainly did in specifying tribute of cacao beans (D. Stuart 2006). The ideological emphasis on maize appears to have been a particularly important strategy for the indirect promotion of the monocultural tendency. At the same time, we need to pay attention to evidence that counters this hypothesis. Maya centers seem to have lacked large, centralized storage facilities, often associated with redistributive systems of grains as in the case of the Inka (D'Altroy and Earle 1985). In addition, tribute scenes in murals and ceramic paintings depict beans and other produce, but not maize.

Another critical issue would have involved land tenure. Landownership does not leave any clearly recognizable archaeological signature, and glyphic texts are mute on this matter. But we can reason thus: in an environmental mosaic with small patches of lands, all with diverse agricultural potentials, access to and possession of some premium lands, such as the bottoms of sinkholes and areas from foot hills to the edges of the *bajos* with thick sediments, would have been highly coveted. Or, to put this another way, Maya households would have experienced great variation in well-being, and hence much stress came from the bottom and worked upwards. It is probable that privileged groups, including old families within local groups, nobles, and royal families, owned or controlled desirable agricultural lands (McAnany 1995: 74). In colonial Yucatan, for example, elites owned sinkholes (Farriss 1984: 180). Intensive cultivation near residences also implies that the family or kin group possessed agricultural fields around their houses or at least controlled their use in a significant manner. Low stone walls found in probable agricultural fields in northern Yucatan, the Río Bec region, and the Petexbatun region may have represented property boundaries of just such lands (Kurjack and Garza 1981: 297; McAnany 1995: 94). In relation to land tenure, we should note that there existed large residential complexes scattered among smaller ones in areas outside monumental cores. In their feudal model of Classic Maya society, derived overtly from analogies from historical European, Japanese, and African societies, Richard Adams and Woodruff Smith (1981) have suggested that these large complexes were "country houses" of feudal chiefs who also kept temporary residences in centers. In this model, such mobile elites owned their agricultural lands and controlled peasant labor (see "house society" models in Chapter 2). Another possibility is that such large complexes were occupied by the heads of kin groups. For this reason, Patricia McAnany (1995: 95, 159) contends that the land tenure system of Classic Maya society was closely tied to the organization of kin groups, with their own internal inequalities of influence and wealth. Either way, land tenure was intertwined to a complicated extent with the agricultural practices and the power structures of society. There is also the possibility that the Maya concept of land ownership was not as clear-cut as that of modern capitalistic groups. It may have involved overlapping rights of access and control by individual farming households, larger kin groups, and central political authorities.

Centrifugal and Centripetal Forces

The relatively weak and indirect management of agricultural practices by polities, along with dispersed settlement patterns, fostered a centrifugal tendency in which farmers could potentially break away from control by central authorities. This tendency was behaviorally expressed through the high mobility of agrarian populations. Colonial-period Maya in Yucatan maintained considerable freedom of movement despite the efforts of the Spaniards to bind them to towns through the policy of *congregación*. Nancy Farriss (1984: 199) states that "the lowland Maya seem to have been uncommonly restless for a people defined as 'sedentary.'" Movements away from the reach of Spanish power indeed remained as an effective strategy of resistance to the colonial regime. Both Farriss (1984: 199) and Matthew Restall (1997: 174–5) conjecture that the high mobility of the colonial Maya had deep historical roots.

The mobility of nonelites during the Classic period appears to be reflected in the rapid growth and reduction in the size of centers (Inomata 2004). Arlen Chase and Diane Chase (1989), for example, argue that Caracol attracted a large number of people after the victory of its dynasty over Tikal, a matter probably linked more widely to power relations involving Calakmul and beyond (see Chapter 5). Whatever the location, farmers probably had the option of leaving oppressive or weak lords and moving on to the sphere of more appealing ones (see Chapter 2). A factor allowing the high mobility of Maya farmers was a relatively low degree of investment in the preparation of residences and agricultural fields. Structures with wattle-and-daub walls and thatched roofs, which Classic Maya farmers commonly used, can be built easily, and modern Maya frequently rebuild such houses. The initial labor investment for the preparation of agricultural fields may also have been modest, if the Classic Maya agriculturalists adopted the strategy of conforming to the natural environment on a relatively small scale rather than modifying topographies through large-scale agro-engineering. A relatively low level of investment in residential and productive capital meant that moving to a new locality became a viable option when local oppressions worsened or when new economic incentives beckoned at other places. In addition, colonial-period Yucatan patronymic groups were distributed over wide areas, cutting across local groups; those who visited new locations were assisted by locals of the same patronym (Roys 1943; Tozzer 1941: 99). If similar patterns of social organization existed in Classic times, they may well have facilitated movements of people. Moreover, the rapid population growth during the Classic period undergirded this tendency. As land shortage became an acute problem around old centers, some farmers needed to move to less crowded areas in search of new agricultural fields.

If centrifugal tendencies were so strong, what provided the counteracting centripetal forces that bound farmers to the elite and to centers in general? Two factors may be critical in this regard: the centralized control of water and the elite-sponsored public events of ceremonies and construction, underwritten by the covenant bonds described in Chapter 7. Water was one critical resource that the Classic Maya states did control, at least in some areas. Despite the commonly held image of perpetually humid tropical lowlands, rainfall is relatively scarce throughout the Maya area during the dry season. The seasonal low precipitation represented a serious problem, particularly in the central southern lowlands where significant bodies of surface water were absent and underground water indifferently accessible. The shortage of drinking water may have been exacerbated because stored water goes foul quickly in the tropics. The large centers of the central southern lowlands, such as Tikal and Calakmul, coped with this problem by creating substantial systems of water reservoirs,

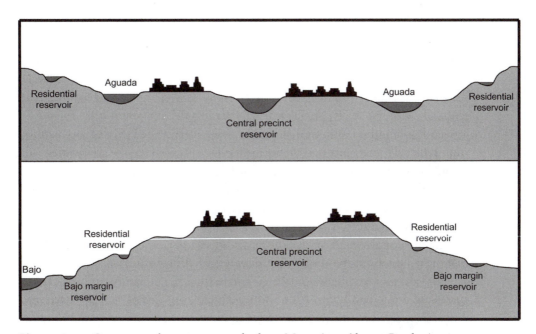

Figure 8.13. Concave and convex watersheds at Maya sites. Above: Preclassic concave watersheds. Below: Classic convex watersheds (redrawn from Scarborough 2003, fig. 4.24).

although it must be pointed out that Tikal's rural or outlying population maintained many *aguadas* that were probably not under centralized control. Vernon Scarborough (1993, 1994, 2003, 2006) has suggested that Late Preclassic centers managed water through channels and reservoirs constructed in gentle slopes of foothills and the edges of wetlands, creating "concave microwatersheds." During the Classic period, the focus of water storage shifted to "convex microwatersheds," with reservoirs built around the central precincts of centers that usually occupied hill tops (Fig. 8.13; see Chapter 3, however, for some doubts as to the categorical distinction between these watersheds). Dunning and colleagues (Dunning et al. 1999) suspect that this change in water management was a response to the transformation of perennial wetlands into seasonal ones at the end of the Late Preclassic period. Water stored in large upland reservoirs could be diverted to small ones downslope, near residential groups and agricultural fields. Lisa Lucero (1999) and Anabel Ford (1996) speculate that a significant number of farmers who were dependent on centralized water storage might have kept dual residences, living near agricultural fields during the rainy season and moving into centers during the dry season.

Water management, however, was far less centralized at centers on the Pasión River and other perennial bodies of water and at settlements in the northern lowlands. Although the northern part of the Yucatan Peninsula was drier than the southern lowlands, the water table in the area was closer to the surface and accessible through natural *cenotes*. In addition, the Classic Maya of northern Yucatan built numerous *chultun* (bell-shaped pits) in association with their residences (Fig. 8.14). These subterranean features were built specifically for water storage and were fundamentally different from the *chultun* in the southern lowlands, which were most likely used for storage. Households in northern Yucatan did not have to depend on central authorities for this vital resource.

Mass ceremonies and construction activities that took place at the centers under the sponsorship of the central authorities added to the force of centripetal impulses. Stone monuments and ceramic paintings commonly depict rulers and nobles performing public ceremonies: such acts represented and reinforced the core cultural values of the Maya elite (see Chapters 5, 6). The events were also the central media through which elite versions of beliefs gained currency among the populace (Demarest 1992), along with reciprocal influence on those beliefs by nonelites: the process is unlikely to have been one of passive brainwashing. Elites presumably presented themselves as mediators of supernatural powers like the Maize and Rain Gods, which were tied closely to the interests of farmers. The ideological effects of religion were rooted in the physical and sensory practice and experience of ritual. Although iconographic images and glyphic texts do not refer to nonelite participants of ceremonies, there are reasons to believe that extraordinary events held at centers involved the active participation of large numbers of farmers. Public rituals were political theaters where commonly held values were celebrated and conflicting interests negotiated through the physical copresence of diverse social groups and their embodied performance.

Colonial documents suggest that both elites and nonelites were deeply engaged in public ceremonies (Inomata 2006b). The same was probably true for the Classic Maya. Arrangements of ceremonial spaces at Classic Maya centers are telling in this regard (Inomata 2006a). Many large ceremonies took place in open plazas where stelae and other stone monuments were erected. The main plazas of relatively small centers, such as Aguateca and Quirigua, were spacious enough to contain nearly the entire population of the polity (see Chapter 2). Even at the medium-sized center of Copan, much of the local community could potentially have been accommodated in the adjacent spaces of the Great Plaza, Middle Plaza, East Plaza, and the Plaza of the Hieroglyphic Stairway. At large centers, simultaneous gatherings of the entire polity were increasingly difficult, but the planners of city spaces appear to have made their best efforts to include a large portion of the polity population in ceremonial events. At Tikal, for example, the primary public ceremonial space during the Early Classic period may have been the Great Plaza, at the core of the center. Along with the growth in population, the construction of Temples 1 and 2 during the early eighth century AD may have made this ceremonial space too small for plenum gatherings of the whole community. An important aim of subsequent construction projects at Tikal could have been to secure ample ceremonial

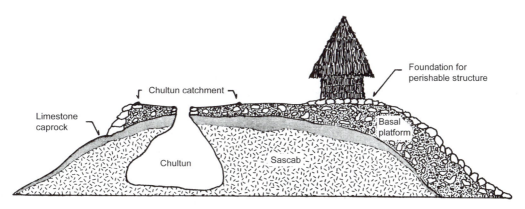

Figure 8.14. Water-storage pits, Puuc-region, Yucatan, Mexico (McAnany 1990, fig. 13.2).

space in less crowded areas. Extensive open areas were established in front of Temples 4 and 6 constructed during the mid-eighth century AD. Also built during this period were the extensive Twin Pyramid Complexes Q and R, as well as the Maler, Maudslay, and Mendez Causeways that connected Temples 4 and 6 with other areas (Harrison 1999: 158, 160). Spacious causeways measuring twenty to eighty meters in width most likely served as theatrical stages for parades and processions on the occasion of community rituals, and for the transport of elaborate tableaux or litters (see Chapter 7). Given their conspicuous width, these streets may also have permitted a large number of spectators along their edges. Such layouts and construction sequences at Classic Maya centers suggest that elite-sponsored public ceremonies and rituals were indeed mass spectacles in which a significant portion of the polity population participated. It would be surprising if Maya architects were unconscious of the theatrical qualities in the plazas, causeways, and surrounding temples that they designed.

Construction projects of temples, palaces, plazas, and causeways also presented occasions in which a large number of farmers engaged in activities coordinated by the elite. Construction projects were indeed closely tied to public theatrical events. The construction of certain buildings was planned for ceremonial occasions such as period ending and royal funerary rituals. In addition, edifices required dedication rituals before, during, and after their construction. In other words, temples, palaces, plazas, and causeways constituted theatrical spaces for public ceremonies, framing such events in spatial and social contexts and serving as mnemonic devices for proper behavior and shared, historic values. Theatrical events in turn attached narratives, memories, and meanings to buildings, giving them life and their own history. The symbolically and politically charged nature of theatrical spaces became particularly apparent at the time of social change and conflict. For example, when the Dos Pilas dynasty took over Aguateca, which was originally within the domain of the Tamarindito polity, the new ruling elite discontinued the ritual place used by the rival dynasty and constructed the Main Plaza as a new focus of community ritual (Inomata et al. in press). A similar process of ceasing the use of a traditional plaza and constructing a new ceremonial space also took place at the nearby settlement of Dos Ceibas, which was apparently incorporated in the Aguateca polity (Eberl 2007).

Participants in elite-sponsored construction projects probably overlapped significantly with those involved in concurrent acts of sacred theater. Construction workers were aware of ceremonies and rituals that would take place after the completion of buildings, and participants of spectacles remembered the process of construction to which they contributed: in this sense, "monumentality," both in physical mass and as quality of mind, expressed broader social and behavioral conditions. The larger the building project, the more likely to loom large in local lives (but see Webster and Kirker 1995, for more conservative estimates of the labor inputs). Construction work, then, may not always have been a burden that farmers accepted only grudgingly under the coercion of the dominant group. It was an integral part of the farmers' value system and imparted a satisfying meaning to their lives.

A FARMING PEOPLE

Beyond their bones and dwellings, individual farmers and other food producers in Classic Maya society remain largely invisible to archaeologists. Developments in settlement and landscape archaeologies, however, have provided significant clues to the lives of those who constituted most of Maya society. Farmers were primarily responsible not only for developing and maintaining complex agricultural knowledge that adapted to the diverse environmental mosaic of the tropical lowlands, but also, in basic terms, for producing children. Their subsistence strategy centered at first on the highly successful combination of maize and beans and incorporated a wide array of cultigens and nondomesticated resources. Their agricultural techniques were tailored to microenvironmental conditions with available choices of intensive infield cultivation, swidden agriculture, terracing, wetland cultivation, and the exploitation of resources from managed forests. Dispersed settlement patterns closely reflected such agricultural practices, with a heavy emphasis on intensive cultivation near residences. This was far from a stable agricultural system. Maya subsistence practices changed with political, economic, and demographic circumstances and with environment transformations for which Maya farmers themselves were responsible. Another critical factor that shaped the course of Maya agriculture and environment was the tension between diverse strategies rooted in the local knowledge of farmers and the pressure towards maize monoculture exerted by polities.

The lives of farmers were, according to some interpretations, deeply embedded in the broader politics and economics in which elites were prominent players. Although the nature of their agricultural practices, dispersed settlements, and high spatial mobility made the political control of farmers inherently weak, the vital resource of water was controlled by the elites in centralized storage systems, at least in some regions. Clearly, however, the nature of that storage will continue to be strongly debated. It may be that what bound farmers to polities and dynasties were mass spectacles and large construction projects that took place at centers. These were the occasions in which the communities focused on rulers and other elites, and social linkages were reconstituted and affirmed through the physical presence of most members of society. Thus, the term "people of maize" represents the central identity of Classic Maya nonelites. It was not, however, an identity rooted in farmers' independent existence. Rather, it emerged as a way of life through negotiations with higher-level forces, from kings to gods, and in the enduring interactions with a tropical environment.

CHAPTER 9

CRAFTSPEOPLE AND TRADERS

CREATORS AND NEGOTIATORS OF VALUES

The Classic Maya produced many works of skill and aesthetic refinement, including stone sculptures, polychrome ceramics, finely carved ornaments, and lavishly adorned buildings. They also devised a wide array of utilitarian tools, without, however, possessing more than a passing knowledge of metals (Bray 1977). The identity of Maya craftspeople and the means by which their products were made and traded explain much about Classic Maya society. Yet these systems of production and consumption do not yield their secrets easily. The Yukatek Maya in the early colonial period exchanged a variety of items in marketplaces, using cacao beans as money. But did their notion of "money growing on trees" exist during the Classic period? Did the Classic Maya even have marketplaces?

BASIC PERPLEXITIES: THE CASE OF MONEY AND MARKETS

Cacao beans and other prized goods, such as obsidian pieces, may have had certain levels of interchangeability with other items. However, this does not mean that they functioned in the same way as today's general-purpose money. Unlike coins or bills, Maya goods were not tied to any absolute standard of value. Their worth fluctuated according to local supply and demand or the intangibles of quality, some kinds of jade, obsidian, or cacao being favored over others. "Value" tends to elude archaeologists for the simple reason that such a variable concept cannot be accessed by applying present-day notions of worth. In many societies people's notions of value are indissolubly connected with their social relations: they esteemed certain objects according to *who* made them and *who* possessed them. To the Maya, the association of some stone statues and ornaments with certain individuals and historical events, as well as the fact that the stones were green, probably weighed more than any mineralogical evaluation – that is, whether the stone was true jade, a material from quarries or placer deposits in the Motagua River region of Guatemala, or any other stone of that color. The close tie to the legitimate producers or owners may even have given some objects a quality of inalienability (see Weiner 1992). Values were thus rooted in people's engagements with objects. Nonetheless, the presence of certain materials in special deposits, offerings destroyed by violent smashing and burning, as well as other burials and caches points strongly to the great value of those materials. The most important deposits merited the most exotic and rarest of goods, although the Maya and their neighbors sometimes made do with counterfeits, such as the clay "cacao beans" discovered in caches at Balberta, Guatemala (Bove 1991: 139). Maya valuables had another property, as consumable items: beans were ground into flavorings for drinks, and obsidian was employed for cutting and for use as ground mirrors. Such use and consumption, along with caching, burial offerings, or ritual destruction, diminished supply and increased the value of objects still in circulation, perhaps as an unintended secondary effect. Currency in Western society used to have the same, functional transformability, so that, for example, early American silverware was often marked "pure coin" to indicate its origin.

As for marketplaces, several scholars suggest that these trading fairs took place periodically in public plazas and other rectangular-shaped spaces, such as the East Plaza of Tikal (Jones 1996: 86). At first there was no clear proof of this, especially because of problems in showing how such marketplaces might be identified. Swept, broken goods? These would fill any deposit of trash. Multiple rooms and galleries? Such would occur in most palatial or administrative buildings. Others believe that marketplaces can be detected by examining the distribution of certain chemical traces in the soil, as at Chunchucmil, Yucatan (Dahlin et al. 2007), in an area much-disturbed by modern activity, or by ceramics, such as those around Tikal (Culbert in press). At Tikal the limited spatial distribution of certain pottery (see Section titled "Production and Distribution of Utilitarian Goods") conforms to what might be expected of local markets, the assumption being that goods radiate out from the markets where they were traded but then display rapid fall-off curves when approaching other networks of production and exchange. The strength of distributional studies is that they indicate the likely complexity of exchange systems among the Classic Maya. They suggest that major centers did not control the movement of utilitarian ceramics, which rather flowed along many other networks, whereas the circulation of obsidian and other goods may have been regulated to a certain degree by central authorities (Aoyama 1999; Fry 1980: 16). The defect of distributional studies is their inability to discount other possibilities, such as the presence of peddlers or of buyers walking directly to production centers. Until recently, large amounts of pottery were carried by tumpline *cacastes* (cargo containers suspended by the cords around the brow) from the central highlands to the Pacific Coast (Reina and Hill 1978: 208).

Another, deeper problem concerns the very notion of the "market." It is unclear, for example, why centers of production would be equivalent with markets. In the Maya region, scholarly understandings of them result largely from what was operating in Guatemala and adjacent countries over the last one hundred years, after centuries of colonial and plantation economies. We can assume that the social and political conditions leading to such marketplaces were not the same as those during the Classic period – basic human needs might remain the same, but not the means by which they were satisfied. If modern marketplaces are accepted as useful analogues, how, then, is the archaeologist to distinguish between the different types of people within them: the vendors (those who sell their own products), the middlemen (those who traffic locally in other people's work), and the itinerant merchants (those who move products over large areas) (Reina and Hill 1978: 207–8)?

Nonetheless, despite these caveats, many of which remain valid, there is evidence of some such facilities at Classic Maya sites. These complexes of buildings are of two types, both rare (Fig. 9.1). The first consists of galleries around a patio, close to the site center, as attested at Tikal and, in findings by a Mexican project at Calakmul, Mexico, of very similar galleries. These last appear around a tiered platform with extraordinary images of men and women serving or selling various foodstuffs, including tobacco, drink, and salt (Boucher and Quiñones 2007; Martin 2006). A strangely eroticized element intrudes into the murals, which feature a jeweled woman with gauzy bright blue dress, almost like the prostitutes known from marketplaces in late pre-Hispanic central Mexico. The dates of the complexes at Tikal and Calakmul may cluster in the eighth century AD, just at a time when these sites were locked in bitter rivalries (see Chapters 5 and 6). There is thus a possibility that part of that conflict involved the creation of competing, lavish market facilities so as to compete economically as well as politically: traders favoring one market over the other would yield benefits in prestige and from tangible forms of taxation or "skim" by the local royal family that commissioned the buildings. That the proposed marketplaces fell into apparent desuetude a short time afterwards – this remains to be proved by ceramics and stratigraphy, however – indicates a relatively short-lived concern with such matters by important dynasties. The other potential market facilities, discovered by Juan Pedro Laporte and his team at sites like Pueblito, Ixtutz, and Xa'an Arriba in the southeastern Peten, Guatemala (Juan Pedro Laporte, personal communication, 2007), are smaller-scale, but similarly positioned, at the axes of causeways and near palaces and temples. All of these facilities urgently need detailed, stripping excavations and chemical assays to confirm and extend the argument that they are market buildings.

EXPLORING THE MAYA "ECONOMY"

A critical question to ask is how what we might call "economic" activities overlapped and related to various aspects of Maya life. Instead of simply

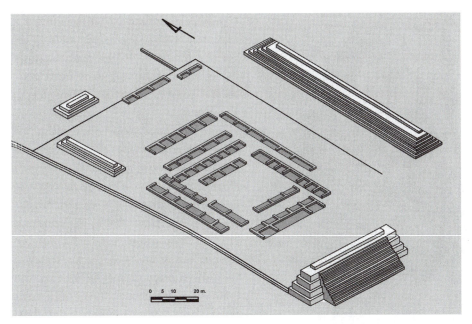

Figure 9.1. Possible market facilities at Pueblito, Guatemala (courtesy of Juan Pedro Laporte, Atlas Arqueológico de Guatemala, Instituto de Antropología e Historia de Guatemala).

wondering whether the Classic Maya had money or marketplaces, we need to examine how certain material media of values and spatial nodes of transactions were tied to a diverse array of actions, experiences, and ideas.

Three issues merit closer scrutiny. First, different modes of exchange appear to have coexisted. Some objects may have been exchanged at marketplaces, whereas others circulated through preexisting social ties among political allies or members of kin or local groups. Even transactions at marketplaces may have been quite different from the impersonal nature of the modern market system. The economic basis of the ruling elite hinged primarily on their ability to levy tribute in the form of human labor and material goods rather than money as an abstract unit of value. Others may have produced goods in payment of debts, as expressed in the colonial Yukatek label *ah sak bet*, "she who weaves for barter or debt" (Clark and Houston 1998: 42).

Second, the economic system was conditioned by modes of transportation. The Classic Maya did not have beasts of burden or wheeled carts, and most of the inland regions where they lived lacked navigable rivers or substantial bodies of water. Many goods must have been carried by human bearers with tumplines and rope backpacks. In some cases, they were combined with canoe transportation, following routes that probably looped in great circles rather than simply going up and down streams (Fig. 9.2; C. Shaw 2000: 105). The heavy reliance on human bearers restricted the ability to transport heavy goods over long distances. This makes the rare instances of large-scale

Figure 9.2. Maya backpack (K5451, copyright Justin Kerr).

transport all the more striking, such as a slate stela at Calakmul, Campeche. This slender, ungainly stone was obviously brought by arduous means from geological sources in Belize (Healy et al. 1995: 339).

The one exception to long-distance transport must have been the sea routes that went around the Yucatan Peninsula. Large canoes such as those encountered on Columbus' fourth voyage near the Bay Islands in Honduras could transport well over a ton in weight (las Casas 1951: 273–5), even though it now seems likely that the craft in question was traveling a relatively short distance when Columbus' crew interrupted its journey (Fig. 9.3; Edwards 1978: 203). At yet an earlier date, during the Archaic period, there is credible evidence that communication existed between the Yucatan Peninsula and islands in the Caribbean, despite the formidable barrier of the Yucatan Channel (Wilson et al. 1998: 351). Most water craft in Classic Maya imagery had flattened prow and stern with space for at least two standing people, one on either end of the dugout canoe (e.g., Hammond 1981b). They resembled the pirogue boat used in traditional Louisiana and parts of West Africa, even the punts of England. The inland Maya who created images of these boats were mostly familiar with river craft that could be beached easily or poled up shallow bodies of water. Dugouts served the Maya well, in that navigators probably preferred sheltered waters and daylong paddles from station to station along the shore; in all likelihood they rested at night (Edwards 1978: 207–8).

If one can trust site distribution maps from areas subject to geomorphological distortions, the number of coastal settlements in Belize increased from about AD 600 to 900 (McKillop 1989: 4). Sites to the north, such as Chunyaxche in Quintana Roo, Mexico, had elevated causeways and artificial canals leading to lagoons (Witschey 1988: 115; Romero 1998: 13). Although most of these settlements reached their full extension in the Postclassic period, there are

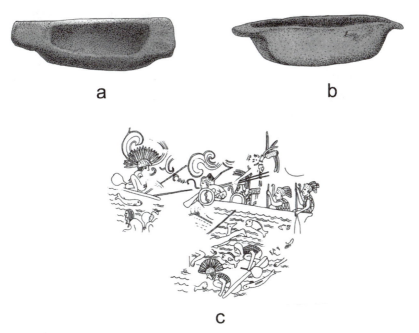

Figure 9.3. Classic Maya canoes: **(a)** manatee bone, Moho Cay, Belize, ca. 16 cm long (after Hammond 1981, fig. 7); **(b)** fired clay, Jaina, Campeche, Mexico, ca. 27 cm long (after photograph by Stephen Houston); and **(c)** on beaten gold disk, Chichen Itza, Yucatan, Mexico, Terminal Classic period (after Lothrop 1952, fig. 35).

suggestions of networks in which ports – namely, islands and coastal settlements (Canbalam, Campeche; Isla Cerritos, Yucatan) – were linked to communities about twenty kilometers inland or more (Chunchucmil, Campeche; Chichen Itza, Yucatan; Andrews 1990: 160; Dahlin et al. 1998: 12). In most cases, however, the coastal and island settlements principally served the needs of smaller inland catchments, with islands in the Belizean barrier reef and beyond mostly operating as small-scale fishing and conching stations (E. Graham 1994: 330). A few islands, such as Jaina, Isla Piedras, and Isla Uaymil, received visitors who never left (Piña Chan 1968; Andrews 1990: 163). They functioned as probable necropoli, a logical resting place for a people who saw the west as a place where the Sun God and a canoe-transported Maize God, a primordial and exemplary human being, entered the dark and watery voids of the underworld. Hieroglyphic links tie objects from the Jaina necropolis with dynasties from sites inland, such as Xcalumkin, Campeche.

A third point to be made about the Maya economy is that Classic centers apparently lacked large storage facilities for food and other commodities. Without efficient systems of transportation, the need for storage facilities was limited, although bulk valuables such as cacao and textiles might have been stored in palaces. There is more than a suspicion that such rooms varied in function according to the wishes of occupants: that is, they were not dedicated to a single, clear function but instead served as flexible spaces – this is precisely what makes them difficult for archaeologists to interpret. Most visitors to Classic cities soon notice the apparent inability of the Maya to engineer large covered areas of permanent form – the most capacious palace is still more a warren of angled corridors and narrow chambers than a cavernous Inka *qollqa* or similar storehouse (Protzen 1993: 134–5). At Aguateca, only one palace room of modest size was used as a sealed storage room when the royal family evacuated the center (Inomata et al. 2001). The lack of obvious storage buildings also implies that Classic Maya society did not have a large number of bureaucrats or merchants dedicated to the redistribution of goods. This is countered only by the evidence from especially large sites such as Calakmul, Campeche, a regional capital with a tightly integrated palace complex (Martin 2001: 175–6).

The Classic Maya economy should thus be viewed as a heterogeneous system that incorporated various modes of production and exchange. This very complexity means that most Maya economic activities remain opaque. A significant part of exchange took place among multiple agents of production and consumption, including single individuals, households, and other small groups. In this arrangement, Maya polities and smaller local groups within them probably retained a relatively high level of self-sufficiency, except for such materials as obsidian and volcanic rock. Another important feature of the Classic Maya economy is that most craftspeople and merchants did not constitute distinct social groups. Potentially, many of them were at once courtiers and carvers, warriors and painters, farmers and potters, or fishers and knappers. To judge from colonial evidence in Yucatan, identities did not result from exclusive association with particular activities. Labels attached to certain people merely reflected practices and products – "knowledgeable" or "informed doing" or "shaping," as expressed in the Yukatek terms *men* and *pat*, respectively – rather than any intrinsic, invariant identity of the maker (Clark and Houston 1996: 34, 42; Roys 1972: 46). Gendered activities most likely reflected those connected to tribute, intensive investments of labor, and tasks that involved "labor swaps and work bees" (Clark and Houston 1996: 38). The diffused nature of economic activities is indeed remarkable in comparison with such complex societies as ancient Egypt and Mesopotamia, both of which had distinct occupational classes (Algaze 2001: 35–6). To find artisans and merchants, then, we need to navigate various layers and sectors of Maya society. To understand them, we have to examine how their identities and roles as craftspeople and traders articulated with their social lives as, among other things, court officials, agriculturalists, and family members. The production, exchange, and consumption of various goods were not economic activities motivated solely by material needs. They were social actions through which individuals and groups forged or transformed mutual ties and systems of wealth and prestige.

CREATING CULTURAL AND AESTHETIC IDEALS
AT THE ROYAL COURT

In a pioneering work, Michael Coe (1977) suggested that Classic Maya scribes were also "artists," a term that is nonetheless outfitted with occidental meaning, as, for many of us, an "artist" has the connotation of dashing temperament and experimental individuality. In fact, Maya scribes can be better understood as craftspeople, admittedly ones of high social rank, who produced codices, painted ceramics, stone monuments, and various types of valuables. They took common materials – fig-tree bark, clay, pigment, limestone – and transformed them into objects of high value that were cherished as heirlooms, portraiture or, more precisely, embodiments of people, and articles of social exchange by royal families. Coe also noted that such scribes or artists were elites. Various studies now indicate that the most refined art objects were produced by important members of the royal court.

Elite Scribe-Artists

Some scribe-artists left their signatures on their masterworks. A delicately painted polychrome vase, for example, carries the name of Aj Maxam as the painter, and minutely carved and detailed stelae from Piedras Negras are incised with up to eight signatures of the carvers (Fig. 9.4; M. Coe 1973). These scribal signatures attest to the high visibility of these individuals and to the construction of new forms of personal identity in which labor input rather than mere possession began to play a more prominent role. The scribe was usually described as *aj-tz'ib*, literally meaning "he of the painting": for the Maya, *woj* referred to the glyphs themselves, but most of these signs were almost certainly painted on surfaces before they were carved (D. Stuart 1989). David Stuart (1987) has shown that scribes used the title of *itz'aat*, which can be translated as "sage," along with the rarer term of *miyaatz*. As the creators and possessors of esoteric knowledge, scribes were highly revered in Classic Maya society. It is likely that those who created vital images were perceived not only as clever artificers but as specialists who endowed objects with life. At once "admirable and dangerous," they were figures who could combine image making with theurgy, or the invocation of gods (Kris and Kurz 1979: 79, 90). One painted vessel uniquely displays what may be a gendered tableau of Promethean gifts to newly emerged humans (Fig. 9.5; M. Coe 1978, pl. 16). A man and woman, the former dressed with traveling by wearing a broad-brimmed hat – a common convention in Maya art – issue from a hole in the ground at the base of a world tree. A simian god associated with painted text and another with numbers offer their gifts to the man, as mediated by an elderly creator god, while an equally aged creator goddess appears to offer a stylized hearth or incense burner to the woman (Houston 2001: 337).

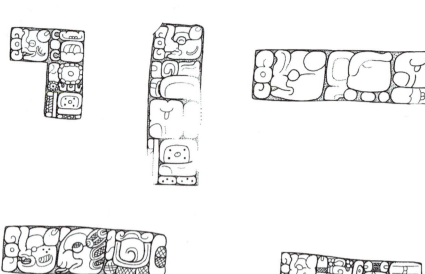

Figure 9.4. Sculptor's signatures, selection from Piedras Negras Stela 12 (D. Stuart and I. Graham 2003, *Corpus of Maya Hieroglyphic Inscriptions*, Vol. 9, Part 1: 63, reproduced courtesy of the President and Fellows of Harvard College).

Depictions of scribes facing codices with a paint brush and a shell ink pot in their hands are relatively common themes in ceramic painting. The characteristic attire of these scribes include net, spangled, and white cloth headdresses. In some cases, sticks that appear to be quills are stuck in the headgear, for ready paring or shaving to suitable widths. Other elements are almost certainly brushes, perhaps also of diverse width and softness (see the section titled The Work of Elite Scribe-Artists). Curiously, these costumes were not limited to the individuals conducting the scribal work of writing and painting but were worn also by those engaged in political and diplomatic interactions at court. Michael Coe (M. Coe and Kerr 1997: 91–7) argues that these courtiers were indeed scribes, who were also responsible for administrative, ceremonial, and diplomatic tasks. According to this hypothesis, many individuals in such paintings would have been scribes, including a few women. Nonetheless, the uniform in question might have been used by various types of court officials, including those who did not write or paint. In addition, some of the supposed scribal titles, especially *aj-k'uhuun*, are not securely deciphered and may refer to the concept of those who guard or keep precious goods (see Chapter 6; S. Jackson and D. Stuart 2001: 224).

Figure 9.5. Offerings of scribal skill to human pair emerging from stone cavity; scribal deities to upper left (drawing by Stephen Houston after M. Coe 1978, pl. 16).

Archaeology has also provided critical evidence of scribal work and its social setting, particularly through the excavation of possible "houses of writing" (*tz'ibal-naah*). A well-known example is Group 9N-8 of Copan, excavated by William Sanders, David Webster, and William Fash (Webster 1989). This was one of the largest and most elaborate residential compounds in the Copan Valley during the Classic period, and the presence of rich tombs dating to the Middle Preclassic period beneath the Classic-period constructions hints at the old roots and high prestige of the family who occupied this place (see Chapter 3). The most extensive and capacious of the more than fifty buildings in this compound was Structure 9N-82, which the excavators labeled the "House of the Bacab." At the last stage of elite occupation, around AD 800, it was an imposing vaulted building with a central bench recording the high status of the presumed occupant, Mak'an Kanal, who enjoyed a close relation, as *aj-k'uhuun*, with the sixteenth ruler of Copan, Yax Pahsaj Chan Yopaat. (In the main, such relationships were vested between two people rather than two offices, thus, one could continue in such a status after the death of the ruler, as shown by another throne at Copan, from Group 9M-18, which refers to just this kind of posthumous relationship.) The façade of the House of the Bacab was adorned with stone sculptures, and those flanking the central doorway were figures of scribes holding shell ink pots. Structure 9N-81, on the western side of the House of the Bacab, contained several pieces of ballgame paraphernalia. The scribe and courtier who presided over Group 9N-8 may have sponsored young ball players, or he may sometimes have exerted himself in the ballcourt.

A tantalizing piece of evidence comes from a smaller nearby group, 9M-22. Karl Taube (personal communication, 1998) has noted that a carving on

Figure 9.6. Sculptor's hand with double-hafted carving tool from Structure 195 in Group 9M-22, Copan, Honduras, Late Classic period (photograph by Karl Taube).

Structure 195 of this compound shows distinctive sculpting tools, apparently hafted rodent or peccary incisors, which may have marked this building as the house of a carver (Fig. 9.6). More-over, a midden with numerous marine shell ornaments and shell production debris was found in front of Temple 16, the tallest pyramid in the central precinct of Copan. The analysis of obsidian and chalcedony tools by Kazuo Aoyama (1995) found use-wear consistent with shell working. Shell ornaments were probably made in the elite core of this center, although the identity of the artisans remains unclear.

Even more vivid images of the lives of Classic Maya scribe-artists have emerged through excavations in the rapidly abandoned elite residential area at the center of Aguateca (Inomata et al. 2002; Inomata and Stiver 1998). Most of the buildings excavated in this area were elite residences, where people prepared their food, ate, slept, and presumably held meetings with other courtiers (see Chapter 5). Around the front bench of the center room of Structure M8–4, the "House of Mirrors," excavators found one stone pestle and seven stone mortars, each of which fits nicely in one hand (Fig. 9.7). These finely polished implements were probably

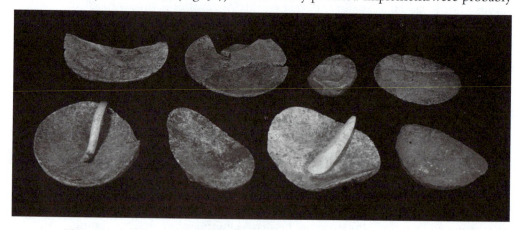

Figure 9.7. Artist tools from Structure M8–4, Aguateca, Guatemala, late ninth century AD (photograph by Takeshi Inomata).

used for the preparation of pigments. Along with twelve to fourteen unworked river clams found in the area, which may have served as ink pots, the tools suggest that a scribe worked on this bench. A remarkable find came from the south room of this structure. There, Daniela Triadan and her assistants painstakingly unearthed an alabaster ornament depicting an image of the Jester God, or *sak-hu'nal,* a symbol of rulership, together with eleven or twelve square plaques of the same material (Fig. 5.7). They were probably tied to a strip of cloth and formed a royal diadem. For the Classic Maya, the forehead represented a crucial seat of identity, so the diadem was more than a crown – it projected an essential attribute of the lord. Next to the alabaster ornament were numerous pieces of pyrite mosaic mirrors, rectangular pyrite artifacts reworked from mosaic pieces, and pyrite in the process of being reshaped. By recycling mosaic pieces, an artisan or artisans may have been making a headdress or other ceremonial gear with inlays, perhaps as part of a refurbished Jester God diadem (Inomata et al. 2002). Interestingly, Stela 19 of Aguateca, recently discovered in the Main Plaza by the Aguateca Archaeological Project, as well as Stela 7 from the same site, depicts Ruler 5, Tahn Te' K'inich – possibly the last king of this center – wearing a Jester God headband with a series of square plaques (Fig. 9.8). The depictions of the Jester God on the stelae are identical to the excavated piece, so the excavated alabaster ornament was very likely the same object. If so, the artist who lived

Figure 9.8. Aguateca Stela 19, AD 778 (photograph by Takeshi Inomata).

in the House of Mirrors was responsible for maintaining royal regalia, creating new costumes ensembles, or repairing old ones for the king. In this case, it was for a ceremony that, because of the violent collapse of Aguateca, never took place. Hints from a bench excavated recently in Temple XIX, Palenque, suggest that nonroyal elites had the privilege of guarding, storing, and presenting regalia (D. Stuart 2005, figs. 85, 87). Not far away, at Bonampak, Chiapas, a favored motif on inscribed and sculpted panels is the offering of the Jester God, with headband, to the ruler by an assembly of nobles (see Chapter 5, Fig. 5.6). No one like Archbishop of Canterbury invested the king, nor did a Napoleon seize the imperial crown: rather, the images emphasize the heightened, even central role of retainers in Late Classic acts of accession.

Structure M8–8 of Aguateca was named the "House of Axes" because of two concentrations of polished greenstone axes – five in front the north room and eleven in the north addition. Although polished stone axes are commonly found in other residences of Aguateca, this number is particularly high. The axes of Structure M8–8 came in various sizes, and one was chisel-like in shape. They appear to have been the tool kit of a carver. Use-wear analysis by Kazuo Aoyama (2007) indicates that these axes were used for carving stone, making it probable that a resident of the House of Axes was a stela carver. Nonetheless, stelae may well have been carved in situ after the blank was transported from a quarry to its eventual place of display. Relatively few stela sites have been carefully excavated or examined for signs of debris left by carvers, a problem compounded by the fact that the Maya are known to have shifted stela from their original locations. One monument from the site of Machaquila, Guatemala, states that thirty-five days after the dedication of a stela, "his image sees" (*ila ubaah*), implying that this amount of time was needed to sculpt a stela blank (or "preform" in technical jargon) into a fully realized, ritually activated image (David Stuart, personal communication, 1995).

Structure M8–10, the "House of the Scribe" at Aguateca, contained even clearer evidence of scribal activities. The central and north rooms of this building housed eight stone mortars and six stone pestles for pigment preparation, along with four halved conches and eleven unworked river clams that may have been used as ink pots. The north room also contained a shell ornament carved with a hieroglyphic text, which recorded a personal name and the Aguateca emblem glyph, followed by the scribal or consultative title *itz'aat* (a comparable sequence of titles in connection occurs with the name of a ruler at Tonina, Chiapas; see Fig. 9.9a). The other side of the shell shows the profile of a scribe wearing a headdress with a possible paint brush. This carved shell indicates that a resident of the House of the Scribe was indeed a scribe who either possessed the *itz'aat* title or carved the hieroglyphic text on the ornament for his patron. The building also contained various other carved bones and shells, including a shell ornament showing the face of monkey, which may represent a deity linked primordially

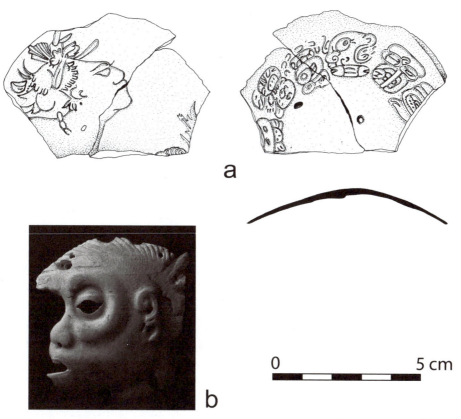

Figure 9.9. Shell artifacts from Structure M8–10, Aguateca, late ninth century AD: **(a)** image of scribe with text on reverse referring to heir as "wise person," *itz'aat* (drawing by Fernando Luin); and **(b)** image of monkey (photographs by Takeshi Inomata).

with scribes (Fig. 9.9b). The presence of refuse of cut bones and shells in a dense midden found next to the structure suggests that some of these ornaments were made by the residents of the House of the Scribe (Emery and Aoyama 2007).

These epigraphic, iconographic, and archaeological data are consistent. They show that some of the skilled scribe-artists were, because of their physical proximity to the royal palace and elegant setting, among the highest-ranking of courtiers. As suggested by the Aguateca emblem glyph on the shell ornament from the House of the Scribe, some scribes might have belonged to the royal family. The House of Mirrors of Aguateca also contained carved bones incised with the Aguateca emblem glyph. From this, it seems possible that many Classic Maya elites practiced scribal and artistic production, along with service as administrators and royal counselors (Inomata 2001a). It is also possible that some rulers engaged in scribal activities – or at least were purported to do so. Under Temple 1 of Tikal, excavators found the richly accoutered Burial 116, which housed the remains of the so-called "Ruler A," Jasaw Chan K'awiil.

Among numerous jade ornaments, carved bones, and polychrome ceramics was a ceramic paint container in the form of a halved shell and a carved bone depicting a scribe's hand holding a brush. At Copan, the body of a high-status personage, either a ruler or his close relative, was placed in Burial XXXVII-4 under Temple 26, one of the most extravagantly stocked tombs to be uncovered at this center (W. Fash 1991: 106–1). Ten small pots with pigments and a Copador polychrome depicting a profile with a net headdress point to the identity of the entombed personage as a scribe.

Most elite scribe-artists recorded in hieroglyphic texts and ceramic paintings appear to have been males. We should remember, however, that a colonial Aztec document, the Codex Telleriano Remensis, displays a possible female scribe in the employ of a ruler. This piece of evidence raises the question of whether there were female scribes in Classic Maya society. Closs (1992) argues that a hieroglyphic text on a polychrome bowl records the name of a female scribe. In the text, a female name, which may be read roughly as "Lady Writing-Sky," is followed by the *aj-tz'ib* (scribe) glyph. However, there are two problems with Closs's reading. First, the text is difficult to parse, with the possibility that the *aj-tz'ib* refers not to the female but another personage. Second, the spelling of the female name appears to contain a hand holding a brush, but the position of the hand differs from that used in the common scribal glyph. This glyphic element may indicate not the scribal role or status of the female but an attribute of the word that follows, "sky." Michael Coe (M. Coe and Kerr 1997: 89–110) notes that some female scribe-artists are rendered in ceramic paintings. These women wear what appears to be a bundle of short sticks, which Coe interprets as pens and markers of scribes. Yet, there are no known depictions of females engaged directly in scribal activities. Although depictions of women wearing a probable bundle of pens present an intriguing possibility, their identity as scribes – and thus as courtiers of a particular kind – needs to be examined further. Elsewhere in the ancient world, female literacy tended to be dramatically lower than that of males (W. Harris 1989: 329; Houston 1994: 42).

The Work of Elite Scribe-Artists

Finely wrought objects expressed a highly sophisticated knowledge of writing, history, religion, mathematics, the calendar, and astronomy. The scribe-artists who created such objects undoubtedly went through a long period of training. A vase painting that depicts apprentices learning from master scribes hints at the rigor of such apprenticeships (Fig. 9.10), the novices in rapt attention, the masters stern and hortatory. Scribe-artists were the "intellectuals" of Maya society, that is, they had the leisure to absorb and extend esoteric expertise. The detailed observations of linguistic forms in the script suggests a near-modern understanding of morphemics, and astronomical records point to a level of

Figure 9.10. Instruction of supernatural scribes by an elderly god (K1196, Kimbell Art Museum, Fort Worth, AP 2004.04, copyright Justin Kerr).

precision equal to that of much later European scientists (Bricker et al. 2001: 2110). This also means that, once scribe-artists mastered such arcane knowledge, they could apply it to various media (Inomata 2007b). The floor assemblages from the House of Mirrors and the House of the Scribe of Aguateca indicate that scribe-artists engaged in a variety of related work. A scribe who painted codices on one occasion may have carved shell ornaments on another – this by itself would have led to the cross-media consistency in iconography that is so clearly evident in Classic imagery. Hieroglyphs carved on stone monuments and shell ornaments show fluid calligraphic qualities rooted in painted media, perhaps, as noted before, because this was part of the carving process, or at least its planning and layout.

The elite residences of Aguateca also contained numerous musical instruments, such as ceramic drums and flutes. This pattern recalls 1 Batz and 1 Chowen in the K'ichee' Maya epic, Popol Vuh: they were flautists, singers, writers, carvers, and jewelers – cunning and dextrous, gifted in all manner of courtly accomplishments. Yet, the same epic casts doubt on the wisdom of such creatures, with more than a hint of their indolence and decadence. Popol Vuh in general conveys a generalized moral ambivalence about self-aggrandizers, just as the story of Wukub Kaqix in the same book describes in exemplary form the downfall of overmighty and egoistic kings (Christenson 2000: 58–9, 93–4). For the Classic Maya, as for their descendants, cleverness may have been viewed in a conflicted or even unsympathetic light. Artisanal or courtly skills could create objects of wonder and envy but also unsettle and destabilize, a novelty representing a marvel that could trigger anxiety about practices without precedent. Despite scribe-artists' ability to work in multiple media, we must acknowledge some division of labor among them – not all could reproduce in full the expertise of monkey gods, 1 Batz and 1 Chowen. Stone monuments of Piedras Negras are inscribed with signatures of carvers with various titles. Such titles imply a division of tasks, as well as hierarchical relations among them, one being described as the "head carver," probably the master of an atelier (Houston 2000; Martin and Grube 2008: 153). In addition, depictions of two supernatural scribes on a ceramic vase – one holding codices and the other with numbers on vegetation sprouting from his sides – may reflect the idealized division of labor among scribes specialized in glyphic writing and those in accounting or mathematical calculation (see the section titled Why Did Elites Become Scribe-Artists?; Houston 2000, fig. 2).

Archaeological and iconographic evidence afford a glimpse of the instruments and techniques that the scribe-artists used. As seen in the assemblages from Aguateca, they prepared pigments using stone dishes and pestles made of volcanic rock, sand stone, limestone, chert, and obsidian. Different textures of these stones may have reflected varying types of paints, some grittier than others. Pigments of hematite and mercury are often recovered archaeologically. The Maya artists probably used other mineral pigments as well, including manganese for black, limonite for orange and yellow, and copper-based minerals for green. Also used were organic paints, such as black carbon and blue indigo processed from plants. Some of these pigments required intensive labor for preparation, which may have been carried out by apprentices, assistants, or specialized workers rather than by master artists, a pattern that strongly recalls Italian painting of the fourteenth century AD. Paper was made from pressed bark strips, pounded in alternating layers by stone bark beaters striated with numerous parallel grooves. Some of this paper almost certainly went into headdresses and clothing or sacrificial offerings.

Dorie Reents-Budet (1994: 38–41) points out that Maya scribe-artists used at least three kinds of painting implements. One type of implement looks much like a Chinese calligraphy brush with fine hair bristles attached to a hollow shaft. The second kind consists of a larger flexible brush, which may have been consisted of plant fibers. These brushes probably allowed artists to paint a long, wide line in one stroke. A third type appears to have had a rigid end, rather like a stylus. Michael Coe (M. Coe and Kerr 1998: 148–9) argues that these were quill pens shaped from feathers. In some cases Maya scribes held these brushes with the thumb and forefinger as in European and Far Eastern traditions, but in others they placed their painting implements between the forefinger and middle finger. In either case they held up the fourth and fifth fingers elegantly, so as not to smear painted surfaces and to communicate a sense of exquisite, measured movement. As seen in the House of Axes of Aguateca, Maya sculptors used many kinds of axes for carving stone monuments. Details

Figure 9.11. Sculptor at work, Emiliano Zapata Panel 1, AD 702 (D. Stuart 1990).

of sculptures were probably made with finer carving tools applied in muscular, wedging motions. The Emiliano Zapata Tablet depicts a stone sculptor using an implement that on two ends has pointed pieces resembling claws or peccary tusks (Fig. 9.11; D. Stuart 1990). The Codex Vindobonensis from the Mixtec area of Mexico also shows similar carving tools, in which an agile carver could switch quickly between chisels of different width or hardness. It is unclear whether these tools consisted of hafted animal claws or tusks, or whether they were made of stone. Two pointed chert artifacts resembling claws or tusks found at Aguateca may have been used for this purpose. Artists also used various types of stones tools – obsidian blades, chert knives, and chert flakes – for carving shell, bone, and wood, along with sundry kinds of grit for polishing. The shaping of harder woods, such as the *chicozapote* (*Manilkara zapota*), which found its way into most surviving Maya lintels, would have involved almost unimaginable amounts of labor, close to that invested in polishing a greenstone adze but over a far wider expanse and with meticulous attention to glyphic and iconographic details.

The detection of production sites of elaborate polychrome ceramics is more difficult. It is likely that at least the firing of pots, with attendant smoke and noxious smells, took place somewhere away from elite residences: kilns are inherently difficult to find, in part because most were destroyed after a single firing (Prudence Rice, personal communication, 2001). Nonetheless, excavations in the elite core of Motul de San José, Guatemala, by Antonia

Foias have uncovered a secondary deposit of numerous fragments of misfired painted ceramics: this implies that they were fired somewhere relatively close to the central precinct (Foias 1999). On most other occasions, elite scribe-artists worked in their own residences or possibly in other palace-type buildings, as archaeological evidence from Aguateca suggests. The creation of art objects was usually a small-scale endeavor organized at the level of households or relatively small groups of masters and apprentices. Aside from exceptional circumstances, their archaeological signatures would be faint (Inomata and Triadan 2000).

Why Did Elites Become Scribe-Artists?

Elite scribe-artists of Classic Maya society differ in role and identity from scribes and artists in the Near Eastern and European traditions. Michelangelo and Leonardo, as well as scribes of Pharaonic Egypt, were respected figures in their societies, but they did not belong to the core elite who commanded political institutions and associated power structures. In most cases, controlling elites in Mesopotamia, Egypt, and Europe chose to sponsor master artists rather than apply their own hands to aesthetic creation. The European custom of sending second or third sons to monasteries or clerical vocations served to remove potential competitors from the sphere of power and to avoid the division of economic assets. In any case, most of these clerical elites did not spend their days in the scriptorium. Probably there were comparable practices among the Classic Maya, but we should reiterate that some accomplished scribe-artists remained at the crux of decision making in the Maya court.

Some terms thought to be of broad utility do not easily apply to Maya elite artists, one being "attached specialists," a label that gained wide popularity among archaeologists in the 1990s. According to Elizabeth Brumfiel and Timothy Earle (1987) and Cathy Costin (1991), attached specialists dedicate themselves to craft production under the patronage and command of political elites or governmental institutions. In contrast, "independent specialists" produced craft goods at their own initiative for a generalized market. Court artists of historic Europe may have been good examples of attached specialists, and it is the rare royal personage who created works of art, such as the lathe-turning King Christian IV of Denmark or the painting Prince Eugene of Sweden – both thought to be eccentric in their lifetimes. Maya elite artists devised objects for the ruler or other patrons, but on other occasions the same artists produced objects at their own will for their own use or for gift exchange. The more precise concept of attached production, then, applies only to specific acts of production, not to certain groups of people (Clark 1995; Inomata 2001b). In this sense, Maya elite artists engaged in both attached and independent production, the *practice* rather than the person being the distinguishing feature, just as, for example, homosexual acts failed to designate someone as fixedly homosexual (Houston et al. 2006: 210). Moreover, elite artisans were not powerless craftspeople attached to their masters but active players competing in court and polity.

Why did Maya elites invest their energy and time in the production of art objects rather than delegate such activities to others? Scholars have emphasized the role of craft production in imposing and spreading dominant ideologies through time, space, and social groups by the process of materializing abstract notions in conspicuous and portable forms (Costin 1991: 12–13; DeMarrais et al. 1996). According to Baines and Yoffee (1998: 235), the production and consumption of aesthetic items by craft work form an important component of the high culture maintained and used by the elite – it is a behavior that further sets them apart. From this, elites assemble "cultural capital," a Marxian concept devised by Bourdieu and Passeron (1990) that joins shadings of prestige with a notion of stored wealth. Although crafted objects can help sustain and communicate ideologies, the act of craft production itself carries ideological meaning. Mary Helms (1993) argues that, in many traditional societies, artisans draw not only on technical skills but supernatural or magical powers, a point made long before by Kris and Kurz in art historical studies from pre-World War II Vienna (1979). It may not be a coincidence that many Classic Maya sculptors were named after the axe-wielding Rain God, Chahk. According to Helms, rulers are, in a sense, skilled "craftspeople," creating cities, temples, and roads. In centralized and hierarchical polities, the separation of rulers and court artisans may originate in noncentralized antecedents, the expertise of master artisans contributing to his political success as well. Classic Maya society may have had relatively undeveloped divisions between political leaders and court artisans. Nonetheless, the Classic period provides little to no hieroglyphic evidence that the rulers took direct credit for building cities, temples, and roads. Supervision may have been acknowledged, but not outright agency (see Chapter 5). Elite engagement in craft production can also be seen in Hawaiian chiefdoms and among Northwest Coast groups of North America (Linnekin 1990: 232–7). Even in the more developed states of historic China and Japan, calligraphy was held to be the sine qua non of elite polish. Elite artists are also attested among other Mesoamerican groups such as the Aztecs and Mixtecs (D. Stuart 1989b).

The depiction of gods engaged in carving, painting, and scribal work is a common theme in Classic Maya imagery, which attests to the close connection between craft production and supernatural force. Reents-Budet (1998) further argues that the work of Maya artists is a metaphor for the act of the creator gods, who crafted the universe and human beings, as recounted in Popol Vuh. Unfortunately, there is little unequivocal evidence for this metaphor during the Classic period, when creator deities appear instead to have been aged and connected with acts of childbirth, emergence, and world destruction (Taube 1994: 658) – like demiurges elsewhere, they were less prominent than other gods. Even the act of "creation" is less-clearly mentioned than some scholars would argue (cf. Freidel et al. 1993).

Still, ritually "killed" ceramic vessels and other craft products, which are often found in archaeological contexts, imply that objects could be literally and magically disabled by fire, breakage, and perforation. According to Bishop Landa, wood carvers in contact-period Yucatan went through various rituals and prohibitions before making sculptures (Tozzer 1941: 159–60). For the pre-Columbian Maya, craft production was not simply an economic endeavor but an act freighted with ritual and supernatural invocation. Other groups in Mesoamerica shared similar concepts that linked skilled crafting with supernatural faculties. The Codex Vindobonensis of the Mixtecs depicts gods carving the world tree from which a human being emerges. For the Aztecs, the Toltecs represented the most highly skilled artisans, and Aztec rulers tried to enhance their legitimacy by claiming descent from the Toltecs (Chimalpahin 1965: 62). During the early colonial period, Bishop Landa wrote that the founder of the powerful Chel family attracted a large population because of learning acquired from his father-in-law, who was a high priest of Mayapan (Tozzer 1941: 40). The exclusivity of knowledge and the selective use of secrecy are worth noting here. The very ostentation of learning implies that such abilities were not held by all, nor were they to be widely shared. By the same token, rooms in temple summits or remote recesses of palaces contained that which was sensed, prized, even revered, but not seen.

WEAVING IDENTITIES AND PRESTIGE

Although most elite scribe-artists may have been males, elite females were also producers of valued objects, principally textiles. These organic materials rarely endure for very long in tropical conditions, but their depictions in ceramic paintings and stone carvings attest to their beauty and high degree of technical perfection. Many garments were decorated with intricate, colorful patterns, some of them reminiscent of modern Maya textiles (Fig. 9.12). Royal and noble women sometimes dressed in see-through wraps flung over their clothes: the nakedness of women in Maya art, particularly below the waist, suggests eroticism or, in men, humiliated or bestial status. Clothing was clearly seen as having a humanizing influence, and its removal was thus debasing or suggestive of immorality. In this, women's work played a "civilizing" role as the Maya would have understood this concept. The importance of textiles in the Classic political economy is suggested by frequent illustrations of these materials in tribute and gift-exchange scenes. In colonial and modern times, textiles were produced exclusively by females until the introduction of foot looms. This pattern of textile production may be traced back to the Classic period and beyond. Some figurines dating to Classic period depict females weaving with back strap looms (Schele and M. Miller 1986, pl. 51). At Aguateca,

Figure 9.12. Woman's clothing, a ceramic vessel from Mundo Perdido, Tikal, Guatemala, early ninth century AD (K2695, copyright Justin Kerr).

the distribution of spindle whorls was closely associated with the area of food storage and preparation, whereas in the central room and other areas, where males engaged in scribal work and courtly deliberation, the number of spindle whorls was significantly smaller. This evidence may point to gendered divisions of space and labor in elite households: males engaged primarily in scribal tasks, along with painting and carving, females responsible mainly for food preparation and textile production (Inomata 2008).

Rosemary Joyce (1993: 261) has suggested that Classic Maya monuments that depict females holding cloth bundles reflect the association of females with textile production as an ideal norm, thus underscoring their contributions to Maya political economy. As a general point, this is clearly the case. Yet, we have insufficient evidence to determine whether textiles were woven and embellished exclusively by females or whether a small number of males also participated. Homosexual men in present-day Santiago Atitlán, Guatemala, are known to embroider clothing of the highest quality, although their distinct status may be the exception that proves the rule; in other highland groups men may weave but only with distinctive fibers (Pancake 1992: 81). Ceramic paintings typically show offerings of textiles between males, hinting that these female products were in some cases appropriated by males who usually took front stage in courtly displays (Houston and D. Stuart 2001: 64–6). As for bundles, recent ethnographic evidence from Santiago Atitlán likens some bundles to wombs and rites of midwifery (Christenson 2001: 122). One unwrapped bundle in the iconography of Classic-period Palenque (Tablet of Temple XIV) shows an effigy of the K'awiil deity offered by a woman who is possibly dressed as the Moon Goddess. Nevertheless, the role of sacred bundles in Maya art is oversimplified by reducing such objects to mere emblems in a gendered political economy. Most stelae also seem to have been periodically "wrapped," sometimes literally (D. Stuart 1996), and doubtless, as suggested by the tokens of authority in Postclassic Maya bundles, the objects so enveloped by cloth were as important as the wrapping itself (Christenson 2001: 31, 171; Las Casas 1967 [1550], III.clxxx.2-8-222).

There are no indications of centralized facilities for textile production on a large scale, unlike the Inka Empire, where women chosen for state service (*aqllakuna*) made textiles (Rowe 1979). Excavations of residential structures at Aguateca and Copan unearthed numerous spinning and weaving tools, including spindle whorls, bone needles, and awls, which indicates that textile production was usually organized at the household level (Hendon 1997). This, however, does not mean that individual households – spatially restricted as most archaeologists, perhaps incorrectly, perceive them to be – were always distinct units of textile production. Bishop Landa noted that women in contact-period Yucatan often collaborated in weaving (Tozzer 1941: 127). It is likely that the Classic Maya also drew on networks of women whose activities cut across households.

Spindle whorls typically had a hemispherical shape and were made of stone or ceramic with a hole in the center where a wooden stick might pass (Fig. 9.13). Many whorls could also have been made of perishable materials, such as wood and unbaked clay. Some of the worked, round, and perforated

Figure 9.13. Selection of Terminal Classic Maya spindle whorls, Tonina, Mexico, largest ca. 4 cm in diameter; feathered serpents above, to lower left, bird with inverted head of captive; to lower right, scene of capture in war (after Becquelin and Baudez 1982, III, fig. 234a, b, m, r).

sherds – an artifact class common at Maya sites – might have served as spindle whorls. Other such sherds are not so well-rounded, nor are their holes always centered and straight; perhaps they served other functions, such as the weighting of fishing nets. The iconography of spindle whorls is largely unstudied, but examples from Tonina, Chiapas, are unexpected in their nondomestic imagery. Feathered serpents are common, as are birds with decapitated heads or warriors with captives (Becquelin and Baudez 1982: III, fig. 234). Could these images, as with the Aztec, have likened domestic labor to the rigors and rewards of battle (Burkhart 1992)? As is true today, Classic women might have used small ceramic or gourd bowls for their spinning, with the spindle partly inserted, to be whirled inside. These tools were highly portable, and spinning could be done almost any time, anywhere. As is true for modern Maya and other people living in traditional societies, Classic women might have spun in various places, at their convenience.

Most elaborate clothes for elites were probably made of cotton, but coarser agave fibers were also used. Some threads may have been worked in the natural cotton colors of white and brown; others were probably colored with various types of dyes, including indigo, cochineal, and tannin. Ephemeral blues are most likely to occur on figurines, perhaps as vague remembrances of Olmec-era jades or other heirlooms. Cochineal, or red dye taken from small insects that live on cactus, was an important industry of Guatemala during the nineteenth century. Archaeological evidence for such dyes, however, is virtually absent, and it is not clear whether threads were dyed by the same women who spun the threads. Certain processes of dying might have been carried out by more specialized workers. For example, until the early twentieth century the highland Maya imported yarns dyed with shell purple – the color also favored by Roman and Chinese emperors – from El Salvador and Costa Rica (Houston et al. 2009).

Weaving with back-strap looms produced relatively narrow widths of cloth that needed to be sewn together. Evidence at Palenque for curtains inside and outside certain temples suggests that these displays involved prodigious amounts of labor, and that the textiles were necessarily repaired with some frequency because of exposure to the elements, or perhaps they were exhibited only on special festival days (Robertson 1991: 24). In direct comparison, royal wealth in early modern Europe was signaled not by portraiture but by wall hangings. In the 1640s, a painting by van Dyck could be bought for £100, a suite of tapestries for £8,000, a range of values reflecting a world, much like that of the Classic Maya, in which labor contributed greatly to perceived worth (Adamson 1999b: 106) – after all, painting involved a few hours' application on thin canvas or wood, weaving many hundreds or more. Today, Maya women often weave on front porches or in patios where they have enough light, tying looms to posts or trees. The improvised and variable nature of this and other activities presents an inconvenience to archaeologists who wish for a rigid use of space, the better to interpret their excavations. The Classic Maya probably also worked on their textiles around their houses, as suggested by the presence of needles and awls in or near residential structures. Although the modern Maya use embroidery in some clothes, most designs are woven, as was probably the case for the Classic Maya. The production of robes with intricate designs, particularly of selvage, is highly labor intensive and time consuming, taking months to complete in the more elaborate examples. Classic Maya women might have collaborated in various stages of textile production, but each piece of textile was essentially the product of an individual weaver. Highly valued textiles were likely to have been sources of pride, prestige, and identity for weavers and cloth-workers.

As depicted in painted pottery, regional styles of textiles have yet to be studied systematically, although there are some initial efforts in this direction (Taylor 1983, 1992). Today, highland Maya produce and wear clothes that are distinctive to each municipality and closely associated with community identity (Holsbeke and Montoya 2003). But this may be a relatively recent phenomenon stimulated by the ready availability of yarns. In colonial times, clear distinctions in clothing existed between elites and nonelites rather than between communities, and some weaving activity may have been driven by Spanish tribute demands (Clark and Houston 1998: 38). Elites often used elaborate textiles, whereas nonelites wore simple clothes of white or blue colors. Among the colonial Lakandon, nobles wore fine attire, whereas commoners' clothes were made of bark fibers and coarse textiles. Until recently, bark-fiber clothes were also worn by the modern Lakandon. Similar patterns of use may apply to the Classic Maya. McAnany and Plank (2001: 96) note that spindle whorls were commonly associated with elite residences, whereas such objects are rare in nonelite structures, though it is still possible that some spindle whorls were made of perishable materials (see also Chase et al. 2008; Halperin 2008). It appears that elaborate textiles were mainly produced by elite females rather than by lower-class workers. Houston and David Stuart (2001) report a set of looted weaving bones inscribed with a queen's name – another is known from Dzibilchaltun, Yucatan (Karl Taube, personal communication, 1998) – suggesting that even a royal woman of the highest status could be a weaver, whether in truth or by normative expectation and claim is somewhat unclear. The problem with all such representations, whether textual or visual, is that we can access only that which was expected, not the real messiness of day-to-day life, work, and identity. For this reason, assertions about "gendered" crafts may be normatively or generally true but invalid in the case of certain women.

OTHER PRODUCERS OF SUMPTUARY GOODS

The foregoing discussion does not mean that all valued goods were made by elites. There were probably other types of court artisans who came from less honored groups. For example, in Group 9N-8 of Copan, where the House of the Bacab was located, Randolph Widmer excavated a relatively small building (Structure 110B) that appears to have collapsed in an earthquake. Sealed under the collapsed roof were tools, products, and debris related to the manufacturing of shell ornaments (Webster et al. 1993: 282–7). It is not clear whether artisans in this structure were kin of the person who occupied the House of the Bacab or whether they were of different affiliation. Either way, the artisans must have been less exalted socially than a master scribe. Unlike Copan and Aguateca, where certain shell ornaments were made in the central precincts, at Caracol evidence of shell working was found in the Mosquito Group one kilometer southeast of the monumental core. Diane and Arlen Chase (1992) suggest that these artisans formed an expanding "middle class" at this prosperous center.

At Aguateca, excavations in a small structure (Structure M8–3) next to the House of Mirrors uncovered a ball of specular hematite, still sparkling with brilliant red accents, and peculiarly long, flat limestone slabs, which might have been used for crafting activities (Fig. 9.14). The analysis of soil chemistry near this structure by Richard Terry and his team (Terry et al. 2004) also revealed high concentrations of iron and copper, probably related to the preparation and use of pigments. Given the location of this building next to the royal palace, whatever was made there was presumably for consumption by royalties and elites. The structure was poorly built, and its artifact assemblage lacked objects of high value. The artisans who worked in this structure were probably of lower status than the scribe-artists of the House of Mirrors, the House of Axes, and the House of the Scribe.

Joseph Ball (1993) unearthed a unique deposit of reconstructible polychrome vessels in the palace complex of the relatively small center of Buenavista, Belize. The ceramics were apparently painted by the same artist and were deposited near the locus of production during the Late Classic period. Paintings on those vessels lack the finesse of master scribes. In addition, they were embellished with pseudo-glyphs, and the artist may not have had the knowledge of hiero-glyphic writing. It is unclear whether a royal personage or a noble painted these vessels or a lower-class artisan working under elite patronage. Censers and cache vessels, which were essential for some rituals but coarsely made on occasion, might also have been made by lower-class artisans. Inherently, censers represent a certain "democratization" or broader dispersion of ritual practices. Each represents a portable device for communicating with deities. The results of excavations at Group 4H-1, a relatively small residential group located one kilometer east of the monumental core of Tikal, has suggested to Marshall Becker (1971) that it was a production locus of censers, simple polychrome vessels, and figurines. From their study of ceramic pastes in and around Palenque, Robert Rands and Ronald Bishop (1980) conjecture that censer supports and cache vessels were made in that center.

Classic Maya figurines are at the nub of these discussions. They usually show a high degree of participation in "high culture," including recondite under-standings of iconography. Yet, at some sites, such as Piedras Negras, figurines were produced in great quantities, often in combinations of freehand modeling and molded shapes, frequently slathered with blue pigment. The key in linking mass production with sophisticated imagery must be the molds, which could have been produced by comparatively few people yet were able to generate large numbers of artifacts. Similarly, Fine Orange ceramics from the Usumac-inta area between Mexico and Guatemala, although Terminal Classic in date, display a great, if formulaic, sophistication, at a time when graphic standards appear to be lapsing at many sites (Adams 1971, fig. 67). However, there is something of a paradox at work here: logically, molded objects promoted stan-dardization at the same time that they circulate a depleted, repetitive imagery, the net result being an impoverishment of designs for people to look at these objects and copy them in other media.

Figure 9.14. Grinding stones from Structure M8–3, Aguateca, Guatemala (photograph by Takeshi Inomata).

It is conceivable that nonelite artisans carried out certain labor-intensive tasks in the production of elite objects. The production of jade may be a case in point. The Classic Maya used a wide variety of greenstone, including serpentine and albitite, which are commonly known by a generic and misleading label of "jade." True jade, which consists mostly of the mineral jadeite, is quite resistant to scratching, measuring 6.5 to 7.0 on the Mohs scale. The area along the middle Motagua Valley is the only confirmed jade source in Mesoamerica (some few sources may lie in the lower portions of the valley [Zachary Hruby, personal communication, 2008]), and the archaeological site of Guaytan in this jade-bearing zone is known for its remains of jade workshops (Harlow 1993; Walters 1982). Refuse from jade working shows that artisans cut the hard stone with strings and hard-mineral sand as an abrasive. With the help of sand and water, holes were made with wooden or bone drills. The manufacturing of jade ornaments obviously required long, hard work. Recent excavations directed by Arthur Demarest at Cancuen on the Pasión River discovered a unique jade workshop outside the Motagua Valley, containing a jade boulder with cut marks and a large amount of production refuse. The building where this activity took place was near the royal palace compound but was of poor construction quality. It is probable that low-class artisans labored there under the supervision of elites. According to Brigette Kovacevich (2006, 2007), the workshop produced roughly cut pieces of jade, which may have been exported to other centers as blanks for jade ornament. Yet, there still remains the chance that elite scribe-artists were involved in the final stage of carving and polishing these jades, some of which show complex mythical themes and glyphic texts. This may have been equally true of stelae, which would have been finished by highly trained experts but quarried by relatively unskilled laborers, as in the limestone pit near Santa Amelia, Guatemala (Fig. 9.15; Beekman 1992).

EXCHANGE OF VALUED GOODS

Valued Craft Goods

Because of intensive labor and the need for unique knowledge, objects such as these were made in limited quantity, and their distribution was disproportionately among the elite. These goods probably changed hands through three modes of exchange: direct delivery to patrons from producers; tribute; and gift exchange. The three are largely overlapping modes in the sense that conceptual or behavioral distinctions between them might not have been cut and dried. Yet, in the first two, goods were usually transferred from individuals and groups of lower-status to higher-status ones, whereas the third mode involved people of varying differences in status. An important point is that most of the highly valued craft goods were probably not exchanged in the general market. Their exchange did not occur in simple economic transactions but in socially significant acts that led to the creation, confirmation, and negotiation of relations among the parties involved.

Delivery from producers to their patrons was often the first episode of exchange, to be followed by others kinds of transmission. Objects with the names of the owners on them were almost certainly commissioned by specific patrons, as in the large number of vessels linked to a particular ruler of Naranjo and other, nearly contemporary ones from Tikal, mostly in the beginning of the seventh century AD. Producers were probably compensated not only by economic means but also by strengthened political ties with patrons, higher status at court, and a suffusion of prestige. Scenes of tribute presentation and gift exchange are rendered in many paintings on ceramics (D. Stuart 1998). These kinds of exchange might have taken place on the occasions of visits by subordinates, meetings between political allies, royal audiences, and feasting by various individuals and groups, again underscoring the social setting of such actions. Whereas submission of tribute was primarily a political act implying

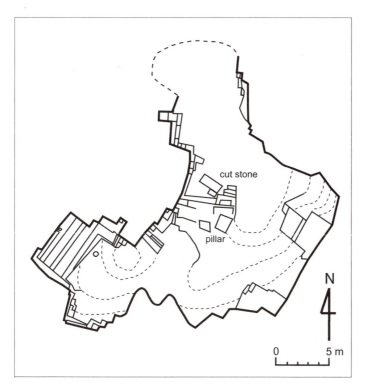

cut stone

pillar

N

0   5 m

Figure 9.15. Quarry near the Río Santa Amelia, Guatemala, Late Classic period (redrawn from Beekman 1992, fig. 2).

obligations of subordinates to superiors, gift exchange might have involved a broader range of motivations and relationships between givers and recipients.

Some objects inscribed with owner's names were probably bestowed as gifts. For example, Burial 30 of Dos Pilas, possibly the tomb of Ruler 2, "Itzamnaaj" K'awiil, contained an elaborate plate with the name of a ruler from the so-called "Ik, site" (Demarest et al. 1991); a bowl with the name of an early Late Classic ruler from Naranjo was excavated in a tomb from the outskirts of Tikal; and many other such objects are known, each with an enigmatic biography that must be fleshed out on a case-by-case basis. Such objects probably represent what Annette Weiner (1992) called "inalienable possessions," that is, when goods changed hands, they were still owned at least in part by their original holders. The objects were hubs around which social values, identities, and historical knowledge were created and negotiated. As Marcel Mauss (1954: 10) noted, the gifted object is in a sense an extension of a "person." To give something away is to give a part of oneself. Likewise, the display of such objects was a statement of the holders' status, power, networks, and identities. Some of these objects, like the Olmec jade ornaments kept by the Classic Maya or traded into Costa Rica, were passed down as heirlooms across the generations or might have represented the results of Classic-period excavations in earlier remains.

Valuables from a Distance

The Classic Maya placed great value on certain materials from distant places. They did so because the materials were rare, unique, or carried certain notions that are being teased out by scholars. There is strong iconographic evidence that an important deity, God L, was linked to trading in parts of Campeche and Yucatan, Mexico. He wore a broad-brimmed hat to evade the remorseless tropical sun, carried a walking staff and a trade bundle, and sometimes punted along in a trading canoe, as in the Dresden Codex (Taube 1992a: 81, fig. 40; see also Chapter 7; M. Miller and Martin 2004: 58–62). He is even depicted in the Late Classic murals of Cacaxtla, Puebla, Mexico, and parts of Veracruz, clearly a deity whose very nature as a trading god led to his broad dispersion in Mesoamerican iconography. The probable region of Tamoanchan, referred to in Mexican sources as the general area of Chiapas and Tabasco, might even include elements of his name (Taube 1992a: 85). The uncertainty of the trading life was underscored by a mythological narrative of trickster rabbits stealing God L's clothing, distinctive headdress, and trading bundle (Taube 1992a, fig. 43). Merchants without political protection must have walked warily.

Most of the Maya lowlands consisted of relatively flat limestone formations, and their occupants had to rely on long-distance trade for certain minerals and other natural products. These goods included obsidian from the Guatemalan highlands, jade from the Motagua Valley, quetzal feathers from the northern Guatemalan highlands, marine shells from the Pacific and Atlantic, and igneous rock from the Maya mountains and the highlands. The Classic Maya also traded various craft goods over long distances. As mentioned before, they had to carry most of these objects on human backs, a costly endeavor. The Aztec Empire had a class of long-distance traders called *pochteca*, but at the time of the Spanish contact the ruling elite of the Maya themselves engaged in long-distance trade (Berdan et al. 2003: 103). In the Classic period, the precise identity of traders is uncertain, yet a number of valuable materials, including jade and *Spondylus* shells, were most likely controlled or dominated by elites.

The exchange system of obsidian has been a subject of intensive study because it is ubiquitous at archaeological sites and can be securely traced back to a finite set of sources. A significant percentage of obsidian in the Classic period originated from the sources of El Chayal and Ixtepeque in the eastern Guatemalan highlands, but a small amount also came from San Martín Jilotepeque and Tajumulco (Nelson 1985). Green obsidian from the Pachuca source of central Mexico was imported in small quantities during the Early Classic period, probably through a connection with Teotihuacan (Spence 1996). Like other Teotihuacan-related goods, the value of green obsidian was more symbolic than economic, involving a hue closely associated with other precious exotics, jade and quetzal feathers. A large portion of El Chayal and Ixtepeque obsidian was brought in as roughly shaped macrocores or polyhedral cores almost ready for the detachment of fine prismatic blades (P. Rice 1987: 80). This was probably a more practical way of transporting obsidian on human backs than as bundles of fragile and sharp blades. Most green obsidian from central Mexico, however, was imported to the Maya area in the form of finished artifacts (Moholy-Nagy and Nelson 1990: 77).

Elites generally used a larger number of obsidian tools than nonelites, probably reflecting their control of trade in these items, although Prudence Rice (1987) observes that during the Late Classic period obsidian became more accessible to nonelites than in Early Classic times. Particularly important data were gleaned from the La Entrada region in western Honduras, which was located between the high-quality Ixtepeque obsidian source and the low-quality San Luis source. Analysis by Aoyama (1999: 145; Inomata and Aoyama 1996) demonstrates that the ratio of Ixtepeque obsidian to San Luis material dropped off sharply between the regional centers of Los Higos and Roncador. This distribution probably reflects the political boundary of the two centers and suggests that the distribution of Ixtepeque obsidian was politically controlled. Aoyama (1999: 181–95) also reports that, after the dynastic collapse at Copan at the end of the Late Classic period, the procurement and distribution of Ixtepeque obsidian macrocores at this settlement broke down. Unlike the Classic-period obsidian assemblage dominated by prismatic blades, Early Postclassic obsidian artifacts consisted mainly of percussion flakes made from small obsidian cobbles or scavenged polyhedral cores and macroblades. This drastic change in obsidian procurement suggests that during the Classic period the distribution of obsidian was administered by elites. At Piedras Negras, Zachary Hruby (2006: 325) also found it likely that a relatively small amount of obsidian was imported through the involvement of the ruling elite.

Fine paste ceramics were produced mainly along the Usumacinta drainage and were widely traded in the Maya lowlands and beyond from the Late Classic through the Early Postclassic periods (Bishop and Rands 1982; Foias and Bishop 1997; Forsyth 2005). Their mechanisms of production and exchange continue to be a vexing problem. At Piedras Negras, the presence of certain fine ceramics may have been dictated by political stability or lack thereof. Chablekal Fine Gray flowed along the Usumacinta drainage when the local dynasty was intact, Fine Orange ceramics when the dynasty fractured (Houston et al. 2001). Given the quantity of Fine Orange pottery at Yaxchilan, the historical antagonist and ultimate conqueror of Piedras Negras, the late appearance of Fine Orange at Piedras Negras may signal domination by an ancient enemy. Alternatively, this shift may reflect a change in broader exchange networks when Fine Orange was introduced at many other centers around the same time.

Another important material from the Guatemalan highlands and the Maya mountains was igneous rock for polished axes and grinding stones (Rathje 1972). The lowland Maya also used locally available materials, such as chert for axes and limestone, sandstone, and quartzite for grinding stones, but igneous

rock had unique qualities of hardness and strength. The transport of heavy
grinding stones was particularly costly, and these artifacts were likely to have
been highly valued. Inland inhabitants of the Maya area imported salt, which
was a vital nutrient in the hot, tropical climate. With their abundant sunlight,
northwestern and northern coasts of the Yucatan Peninsula were particularly
suited for salt production through solar evaporation and the controlled heating
of sea water. Remains of sea salt exploitation have been found at such sites as
Emal, El Cuyo, Celestun, and Xcambo (Andrews and Mock 2002). The large
centers of Dzibilchaltun and Chunchucmil near the northwestern Yucatan
coast, located in an agriculturally marginal zone, might have controlled some
part of the salt trade. Salt production was also conducted on the Belizean coast
(McKillop 2002, 2005) and from the inland salt deposit of Salinas de los Nueve
Cerros on the southern edge of the lowlands (Dillon 1977).

Some objects were traded over long distances for their symbolic and ideological value. The dredging of the Cenote of Sacrifice at Chichen Itza,
for example, uncovered a jade ornament in the Cotzumalhuapa style of the
Guatemalan Pacific Coast (Proskouriakoff 1974, pl. 78b). It is not clear whether
this object was brought to Chichen Itza through a series of gift exchanges,
by direct contact between distant centers, by pilgrimage, or through military
campaigns to foreign lands. A small quantity of crafted goods was brought
from Teotihuacan in central Mexico during the Early Classic period. These
include cylinder vases with slab-shaped tripod supports and the Thin Orange
Ware produced in Puebla, Mexico, and used widely at Teotihuacan (Rattray
2000). Whether these items were brought by migrations of Teotihuacanos or
were imported through the initiative of the local Maya elites is nearly impossible to sort out. At the least, they represent a prestigious, symbolically laden
connection with a distant and great metropolis.

PRODUCTION AND DISTRIBUTION OF UTILITARIAN GOODS

Ceramics

The Classic Maya, both elites and nonelites, used numerous ceramic vessels, including large jars for the storage of food and water, medium-sized jars
for carrying liquids and cooking, and bowls for cooking and soaking maize
(Fig. 9.16). Most of these vessels were simple in design, with decorations largely
limited to red or black slips, striation, simple incisions, or bands of stamped
impressions. Partly because of the lack of decorations and partly because of
fragmented and eroded states in which they are found archaeologically, we
tend to underestimate the skills and efforts of potters who made these objects.
Building large jars measuring nearly one meter in height with one-centimeter
thick walls, however, required significant practice and effort. When reconstructed, plain and striated jars show a certain austere elegance, sometimes

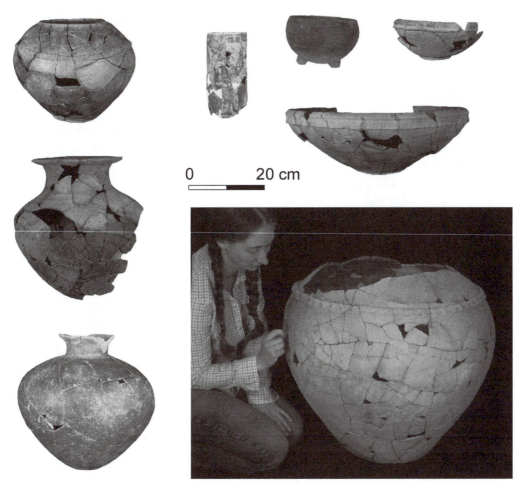

Figure 9.16. Array of vessels from late ninth-century Aguateca, Guatemala (photographs by Takeshi Inomata).

off-set by impressed designs that accentuated the break between the body of the vessel and its neck (Fig. 9.16). The styles of such utilitarian vessels as jars and bowls varied from one region to another, but they were fairly uniform within each area. This is an important observation, for it indicates that elites who occupied the ceremonial centers and others who lived in peripheries used similar kinds of vessels for storage and cooking. Many nonelites also had relatively simple polychrome plates and vases, and it is by now widely understood by Mayanists that such bright coloration on ceramics does not automatically indicate an elite occupation. Rather, the most conspicuous difference between elite and nonelite ceramic assemblages is in highly elaborate polychrome vessels painted by master artists, especially those who recorded nongeneric, historically specific scenes of courtly life.

Today, Maya potters usually fire their pots in open areas without kilns. Such practices would leave little evidence of ceramic production sites for archaeologists to find. Our knowledge of ceramic firing locations, and thus of those producing utilitarian vessels, is extremely limited. Important data have come from work by Andrés Ciudad Ruiz (2000) in the small community of Agua Tibia near Totonicapan in the Guatemalan highlands. Excavations revealed an open kiln for ceramics next to a small residential structure dating to the Late Classic period. The kiln measured 4.23 meters in length, 0.50 meters in width, and 0.5 to 0.8 meters in height, as defined by walls of pumice stones and clay. Potters fired vessels of common local types, including bowls and other neckless vessels. Probably they had to obtain large jars and *comales* that exceeded these dimensions from yet other potters. Another example comes from excavations at K'axob, Belize, directed by Patricia McAnany. Researchers identified pit features dug into limestone bedrock, holes most likely used as pottery firing kilns during the Late Classic period (López Varela et al. 2001). The potter at K'axob used sherds of various shapes for scraping, smoothing, and incising unfired ceramics (López Varela et al. 2002). It is still unclear whether these kilns are rare exceptions and the Maya potters generally preferred open firing. One influence on the scarcity of kilns may be the calcite temper commonly used in ceramics of the Maya lowlands. Although closed kilns achieve high firing temperature, calcite particles expand at high temperature, causing ceramics to spall or break (Shepard 1956).

Most information on ceramic production and exchange still derives from the study of ceramic paste types and their distribution. At Palenque, important evidence came from studies by Robert Rands and Ronald Bishop (1980; Bishop and Rands 1982), as supplemented by information obtained by Robert Fry for Tikal (1979; 1980). At Palenque most Late Classic utilitarian vessels appear to have been made in the Sierra and Plains zones up to twenty kilometers north of the site core. At Tikal, vessels of micaceous pastes that were found along the northern survey transect may have been produced roughly eight kilometers north of the ceremonial center. Reviewing these data, Prudence Rice (1987) suggests that most utilitarian vessels were produced by certain rural communities, each specializing in the production of specific forms of vessels, such as jars and serving vessels. The potters of Agua Tibia also appear to have specialized in certain forms. However, Joseph Ball (1993) argues that these ceramic-producing communities were not so specialized in specific vessels forms. Despite this disagreement, the lack of large-scale or highly concentrated production facilities hints to most scholars that, like the modern Maya, Classic-period potters made vessels on a part-time basis in their residential compounds. Ceramic production in modern Maya villages, as well as in many traditional societies, is the work of females. Presumably, this was also true in Classic times, although we have no way of proving this. Nor is there clear evidence that the production and distribution of utilitarian vessels were controlled by elites (Rice 1987: 84). Nonelite Maya probably exchanged jars, bowls, and other vessels often through kinship and other preexisting social ties without much elite interference.

Ceramics are a pyrotechnology that transforms one material, clay, into another. There is little evidence that the Classic Maya had much familiarity with another pyrotechnology, that of metalworking. Throughout the Classic period, metal was highly exotic, and tended to occur because of contact with Central America and, to a lesser extent, western Mesoamerica (Bray 1977: 397). The Maya collected liquid mercury, stable at room temperature, but probably did not have much experience with high-temperature technologies (Pendergast 1982).

Stone Tools

The Classic Maya, who did not use metal tools, made various implements necessary for their lives by chipping and grinding naturally occurring stones (see Chapter 4, Fig. 4.13). Important stone artifacts include chipped obsidian tools, chipped chert tools, polished stone axes, and grinding stones. Obsidian imported as macrocores or polyhedral cores was worked into blades or other cutting tools at many lowland settlements (see the section titled Valuables from a Distance). The prismatic blade technique was the most efficient way of producing large numbers of cutting tools from valuable imported stones. Experimental studies by Sheets and Muto (1972) and by Clark (1986) suggest that a knapper could have produced 100 to 150 blades from one core in roughly two hours. Although the amount of obsidian consumption varied from one region to another, blades taken from one core might have equated to a one-year supply for five to thirty families of about five people. Such blades were multipurpose tools for various craft activities, food preparation, and bloodletting. A set of blades excavated by Mark Child (2006) at Piedras Negras even suggests that some were used in sweatbaths to remove dirt and sloughed skin. Long, complete blades recovered from the central rooms of elite residences at Aguateca did not bear observable use-wear and may have been used in blood-letting rituals (Aoyama 2007).

The identity of obsidian workers remains enigmatic, not least because obsidian is sharp and dangerous, making it desirable to remove debris periodically from production sites. Although exhausted polyhedral cores occur in various contexts, they might have been recycled and traded after blades were removed. Secondary deposits of obsidian debitage in high concentrations have been found in the central precincts of such centers as Copan and Tikal, which may indicate that obsidian knappers worked in nearby areas (Aoyama 1999: 109, 161; Moholy-Nagy 1997). The scale of such production, however, was relatively small, and Aoyama (1999: 203) concludes that, at Copan, there was no evidence of obsidian blade production centrally controlled by elites, despite his suggestion of elite administration of obsidian procurement. At the same time, it is necessary to pay attention to the enormous quantity of obsidian debitage in the construction fills above tombs and in caches at various centers, including Tikal, Uaxactun, Río Azul, Caracol, Altun Ha, Lamanai, Dos Pilas, and Altar de Sacrificios. Hattula Moholy-Nagy (1997) estimates that the number of obsidian pieces from these contexts at Tikal was roughly 252,000, which makes up 96 percent of the total number of obsidian artifacts excavated at the site. This high concentration of obsidian debitage in elite ritual contexts implies that elites had at least a certain level of control over the knappers who produced a significant part of the obsidian tools used at Tikal (Moholy-Nagy 1997: 308). These deposits also indicate that the production of obsidian tools was, at some point in its cycle, a ritual process as well. At Piedras Negras, Zachary Hruby (2007) has discovered that the knappers who made flamboyant eccentrics for deposits in caches also worked other shapes. The large number of obsidian pieces in these centers does not necessarily show that full-time specialists made obsidian tools at specialized facilities. Given the efficiency of blade production, a relatively small number of knappers working part-time could supply enough tools for the entire community (Aoyama 2001: 353).

The evidence for chert tool production is, by contrast, ubiquitous. Chert nodules found naturally in limestone formations were available in many parts of the Maya lowlands. It appears that in many parts of the Maya lowlands chert was procured locally (Aldenderfer et al. 1989; Ford and Olson 1989). Relatively abundant chert was used mostly for core and flake tools, which did not require the level of technical training necessary for the production of obsidian blades. In addition, the damaged edges of these tools could be, and, indeed, had to be resharpened through further knapping by their users. Thus, most Classic Maya, elites and nonelites, were familiar with a certain level of chert knapping. Hruby's study (2006: 267) at Piedras Negras tends to confirm that chert tools were produced at numerous households.

Nonetheless, specialized production of chert tools did exist. A celebrated example of intensive production of chert tools is the small center of Colha, located on sources of high-quality chert in northern Belize. Remains of chert-tool production were found throughout the site. Mounds consisting almost purely of chert debris measured up to 1.75 meters in thickness, reflecting an extraordinary intensity of production (Shafer and Hester 1983). Although a significant fraction of the Colha community engaged in chert-tool production, these activities appear to have been organized primarily at the level of households or coresidential groups, near whose buildings most chert debris was found. Chert debitage at communities near Pulltrouser Swamp in northern Belize consisted predominantly of resharpening debris, which suggested to Patricia McAnany (1989) that their residents had imported finished chert tools from Colha. Thomas Hester and Harry Shafer (1994) have shown that, on the whole, chert tools made at Colha were distributed within sixty kilometers of the production center. Other remains of chert workshops have been found in El Pedernal near Río Azul and Becan. Daniel Potter (1993) contends that Chichen Itza, which did not have local chert outcrops, imported chert tools from the small center of Xkichmook or other settlements in the Puuc region.

The presence of secondary deposits of chert debitage in the monumental cores at Copan and Tikal indicates that a certain level of specialized chert-tool production was carried out in the central sectors of these centers. According to Moholy-Nagy (1997), the amount of chert debris in caches and above tombs of Tikal is roughly 122,000, which corresponds to 73 percent of the total number of excavated pieces of chert. Although this concentration is not as high as that of obsidian, it is still a significant quantity. It is probable that some portion of chert-tool production took place under the supervision of elites. Moholy-Nagy believes that the construction of monumental structures required a large quantity of stone tools. To guarantee that supply, central authorities needed, perhaps, to support specialists. In addition, producers of chert eccentrics, closely linked to elite ritual, most likely had close associations with the royal family (Hruby 2006: 332).

BETWEEN PRACTICES AND AGENTS

In a book that examines people, this chapter on craftspeople and traders has focused to a large and perhaps distressing extent on the residue left behind, and far less on the people themselves. For elite artisans, particularly scribes and sculptors, the problem is less acute, but for nonelites deeply so. Practices are visible but the likelihood is strong that a single person learned several skills as part of a diverse approach to survival: the potter might have woven, the obsidian knapper carved wood and stone – presumably, but not certainly, according to gender norms. Traders must have existed, but little is known of them for the reason that, in most places, they might have operated at the margins of dynastic societies. Motivation, notions of value, and the organization of labor all remain opaque for us and, for the ancient Maya, fluid. The pivotal observation here is that the behaviors discussed above cannot be separated from other dimensions of human life and from what made such life meaningful and productive during the Classic period.

CHAPTER 10

END OF AN ERA

THE MAYA COLLAPSE

Around the ninth century AD, numerous Maya centers in the southern low-lands ceased to erect stone monuments and suffered substantial, often catastrophic declines in population. This phenomenon, called the "Classic Maya collapse," has long fascinated scholars and the general public (Demarest et al. 2004; Webster 2002; and, most recently, Diamond 2005). Then and now, the question remains, how did the Maya live through this time of tumult and manage to endure to the present?

HISTORY OF DEBATE

Past Theories

Most arguments about the Maya collapse focus on scenarios that involve natural catastrophes, such as disease or earthquakes, or on ecological problems, social causes, or even some hybrid of these explanations (Sabloff 1973b; Sharer 1977). Ecological models have been perhaps the most influential, emphasizing long, vexed interactions between society and the natural environment. Early versions tended to attribute the collapse to the inherent limitations of slash-and-burn or swidden cultivation, suggesting that the excessive use of such methods led inevitably to soil exhaustion and erosion (Cooke 1931; Ricketson and Ricketson 1937: 10–1). Although later studies revealed evidence of intensive agriculture, such as terraces and wetland fields (Turner 1974), the extent of these practices and their ability to relieve stresses on the environment have continued to shape discussion (Chapter 8; Pope and Dahlin 1989). Today, ecological models are understood in relation to the population history of an area, and indeed, settlement pattern studies have confirmed rapid population growth during the Classic period, to the extent that, in most areas, population densities reached significant and unprecedented levels during the eighth century AD. Stimulated by such evidence, Sanders (1973), Culbert (1988), and others asserted that this increase imposed a heavy burden on the agricultural system. Demarest (1997) has responded by citing data from the Petexbatun region to show little evidence for ecological stress, underscoring the necessity of understanding the collapse on an area-by-area basis. Moreover, in addressing ecological models, researchers need to ask why pronounced population growth occurred in the Classic period and why the Classic Maya failed to overcome this problem.

Another school of thought focuses on social problems behind the collapse. One influential theory, developed by Thompson (1954), suggests that the increasing burden of tribute levied by elites led to peasant revolts against their oppressors. In similar vein, Kidder (in A. Smith 1950: 1–12) and Altschuler (1958) emphasized the internal weakness of Maya society, which comprised, they claimed, a class system churned and undone by Marxian pressures between classes. Nonetheless, recent developments in archaeology and epigraphy undermine Thompson's two-class society model of Maya society (Chapters 6 and 8). Most scholars perceive more complex forms of sociopolitical organization, including kings and various types of elites and other social groups, not all working in concert or class solidarity. In a more sophisticated version of the "class-conflict" theory, some archaeologists have gone on to propose that competition among elites itself triggered the collapse. At Copan, William Fash and David Stuart (1990) have argued that the power of nobles increased towards the end of the Late Classic period, destabilizing royal authority; this new set of conditions expressed itself as carved inscriptions in noble residences, involving skills formerly monopolized by kings. To Fash, the shift further resulted in an assertion of partial autonomy by nobles to the eventual detriment of centralized kingdoms. Increasing competition among elites also marks the Usumacinta region, which witnessed an increase in subsidiary titles during the Late Classic period (Chapter 6; D. Stuart 1993). The surge in multiple centers of power thus appears to have had a strong impact on society. But, at the same time, any ancient polity will show tensions between kings and nobles and conflicts between various sectors of society. The question continues to be, how did such pressures play a role in the unique conditions associated with the Maya collapse?

Yet another argument for the collapse emphasizes the influence of Maya concepts of time and cosmos. In a particularly extreme example, Dennis Puleston (1979) proposed that the Maya notion of cyclical history directly affected the course of social change. The Classic Maya collapse corresponded roughly to the end of an important *bak'tun* (*pih*) cycle, so that the Maya were quite simply "ready" to unravel socially, predisposed to collapse by their fatalistic understanding of the calendar. More recently, Prudence Rice (2004) has offered a variant of this model by proposing that the Maya rotated seats of authority among various cities according to the 256-year-cycle ritual calendar. For her, political change during the Terminal Classic was connected to the transfer of such a seat from Tikal to other centers. The proposal merits discussion, but, unfortunately, there is little evidence in the inscriptions that the Maya paid attention to such a cycle. Had it been so crucial the Maya would presumably have mentioned it in their inscriptions.

Another set of explanations addresses problems originating outside the Maya area, although these external-cause theories depend to a certain degree on interplay with internal forces (Sabloff 1973b: 39). One such model focuses on foreign invasion. Excavators of Altar de Sacrificios and Ceibal suggested that centers along the Pasión River in Guatemala were invaded by Mexicanized Maya or a non-Maya group, and that these intrusions disrupted Classic Maya society and economy (Fig. 10.1; Sabloff 1973a; Willey 1973). Later, however, Willey and Shimkin (1973) modified this proposal, asserting that invasion was a result rather than a cause of the collapse. With reason, others, too, have questioned the actual evidence for foreigners in the Pasión region (D. Stuart 1993). At present, many scholars dismiss foreign invasion as a primary cause of the collapse, but such movements cannot be ruled out entirely, especially in the northern part of the Yucatan Peninsula (see Section titled "Rise and Fall in the North").

According to some archaeologists, possible external problems included disruptions or changes in interregional patterns of trade. William Rathje (1971, 1973) has argued that competition between the central Peten core area and its surrounding buffer zones was crucial to the collapse. As the power of the buffer zone grew, the core area was cut off from vital resources supplied by the highlands. Malcolm Webb (1973) and David Freidel (1985a) have postulated that the Terminal Classic was a time of change from theocratic political systems to more secular ones, as well as a period that experienced new patterns of trade. The southern lowland Maya, who could not make this change, were outflanked by more successful rivals to the north. Although there are strong indications that such economic and political restructuring occurred throughout Mesoamerica, it is not clear how changes in trade patterns could so severely affect the southern region, where the economy was largely undergirded by local agricultural production. Nonetheless, many researchers believe that these diverse theories are complementary. Willey and Shimkin (1973) point out that the most promising course of inquiry is one that combines a wide variety of explanations. The Maya collapse appears to have been too complex to be elucidated by any one model (Webster 2002).

Revisions

Many such theories were proposed in the 1970s and 1980s. Although archaeologists have continued to tackle the issue of the Maya collapse, any clear answers to what happened, or when and how they occurred, remain as elusive as they were three decades ago. Except for proposals invoking warfare and climate change (Demarest 1997; Gill 2000), current discussions have concentrated primarily on critiques of previous assumptions and models, not on completely novel approaches.

Figure 10.1. Supposed "foreigner" at Ceibal, Stela 1, AD 869 (I. Graham 1996, *Corpus of Maya Hieroglyphic Inscriptions*, Vol. 7, Part 1: 13, reproduced courtesy of the President and Fellows of Harvard College).

A theory emphasizing the destructive effect of warfare is one of the few models to provide a fresh view. Early Maya scholars believed that the Classic Maya were largely peaceful, yet evidence of intense conflict began to accumulate from the 1940s on, with the discovery of the Bonampak murals and their view of a bloody battle and its aftermath (M. Miller 1986: 8–9). Like any society with centralized polities, the Classic Maya experienced numerous wars, some of which affected decisively the course of their history. One of the first theories to emphasize war came from Cowgill (1979), who claimed that escalated militarism led to population growth and environmental overexploitation, followed soon thereafter by collapse. More recently, Arthur Demarest and his team (Demarest et al. 1997) have documented intense conflicts in the Petexbatun region of Guatemala towards the end of the Classic period. These results led Demarest (1997) to argue that destructive warfare was the primary cause of the Maya collapse. He further suggested that the intensification of warfare at the end of the Classic period came not from ecological degradation but from social factors, namely, heightened rivalry among elite groups, as aggravated by an increase in elite population from the widespread practice of polygamy. Many anthropologists, however, view warfare as dynamic, resulting at times in destruction but also in the development of social inequality, the formation of the state, and the political unification of large areas. The issue here is how, in this area, at that time, warfare contributed to political disintegration rather than expansion and consolidation. In addition, virtually all cases of societal collapse, including those of Rome and various Chinese dynasties, involved intense warfare. War tends usually to be a symptom of social decline, not its primary cause.

A more recent trend in the study of the Maya collapse is to highlight changes in climate. The Maya region is subject to seasonal and yearly changes in atmospheric circulation. Air heated along the equator rises and actively forms tropical storms. This low pressure belt with heavy rain is called the Intertropical Convergence Zone (ITCZ). Areas to the north and south of the ITCZ, around 30° latitude, are in turn high-pressure belts with dry climates and, not coincidentally, the location of the world's most arid areas, including the Sonoran and Sahara Deserts. The Maya area, situated as it is between the equator and the dry regions, undergoes an annual cycle of wet and dry weather. In the summer, the ITCZ is positioned directly over the Maya region, bringing intense tropical rain. When the ITCZ migrates southward in the winter, the region passes into a dry season. The intensity and movements of these low and high pressure zones vary from year to year, resulting in fluctuations of rainfall in the Maya area. In addition, diminished solar activity and a lower global mean temperature correlate with less intensity in tropical air circulation and a southward displacement of the high pressure cell, causing droughts in the Maya area (Gill 2000: 131–90; Hodell et al. 2001).

In a key piece of evidence David Hodell and his colleagues (Hodell et al. 1995, 2001) examined core samples taken from Lake Chichancanab in Yucatan. Lake water is nearly saturated with gypsum, and under dry conditions this mineral precipitates at higher rates. Hodell and his group detected high concentrations of gypsum in sediments dating to the period between AD 800 and 1000, an observation that suggests a period of prolonged drought. The researchers also examined ratios of stable isotopes of oxygen, ^{18}O and ^{16}O, in snail shells. Because the $^{18}O/^{16}O$ ratio in a shell reflects that of lake water, and because water molecules containing lighter ^{16}O evaporate at a higher rate, the relative abundance of ^{18}O indicates less rain and greater evaporation. The analysis of oxygen isotopes of cores taken from Lake Chichancanab and Lake Punta Laguna, located near the center of Coba in Quintana Roo, corroborates the gypsum data, pointing to dry climate during the Terminal Classic period (Curtis et al. 1996).

Another crucial set of data comes from the Cariaco Basin in northern Venezuela (Haug et al. 2003). The basin may belong to the same climatic zone as the Maya region, in that both lie directly under the ITCZ during summer months. Researchers analyzed titanium concentrations in various cores extracted from the sea. For the most part, titanium is carried to the sea by ground water, with the result that lower concentrations of this element suggest reduced precipitation in the watershed. What makes these data unique is their chronological resolution. The cores obtained from the basin do not exhibit any signs of disturbance by living organisms because of its anoxic condition. Deposits appear as horizontal layers, each of which reflects annual fluctuations in ground water flowing into the basin. With a nearly bimonthy resolution, the data point to multiyear drought events that began in about AD 760, 810, 860, and 910, respectively. Nonetheless, a note of caution: the absolute dating of the layers derives from radiocarbon analysis of organic materials, meaning that dates are still subject to radiometric dating errors, which could easily exceed fifty years.

Maya scholars need to take seriously these compelling data on climatic change. Nowhere do global and regional climates remain stable over centuries, and the Maya most likely experienced a series of climatic changes over millennia, including severe droughts. Yet whether such droughts caused the Maya collapse must be understood as a separate question. We still need to evaluate whether the droughts correspond in time to the decline of centers and whether there is any causal relation between those events. Some disquiet arises from the lack of unequivocal evidence for droughts in the southern lowlands. The analysis of cores samples obtained from Lake Peten Itza (Curtis et al. 1998), Lake Salpeten in central Peten (Rosenmeier et al. 2002), and Lake Tamarindito in the Petexbatun region (Dunning et al. 1997) did not show clear indication of droughts at the end of the Classic period. A potential explanation for this pattern is that the southern lowlands underwent large-scale deforestation during the Late Classic period, resulting in an increased amount of water flow into these lakes. This human-induced change might have counteracted the effects of droughts on the chemistry of lake water – if, indeed, such droughts even took place to begin with (Brenner et al. 2002: 150).

A more serious problem comes from political and demographic trends in the Maya region, which appear to contradict the climatic data. The Classic Maya collapse is represented mainly by the decline of multiple centers in the southern lowlands. In contrast, the northern lowlands, particularly the Puuc region and the major center of Chichen Itza, exhibited vigorous construction activity and political expansion, all accompanied by population growth. The northern lowlands are substantially drier than the south, and may have been more susceptible to droughts. Richardson Gill (2000: 247–1) accounts for this disparity by highlighting the role of different sources of water in various regions. In the northern lowlands, underground fresh water, located relatively close to the surface, is accessible in many places through natural *cenotes*, which provide reliable year-round sources of drinking water. In the southern lowlands, by contrast, underground water may be more than one hundred meters deep, inaccessible in most places. Many centers had to rely on artificial reservoirs that collected rain water during the wet season. In prolonged droughts, reservoirs would not have contained enough water. The drawback of this explanation, however, is that the centers located along the Usumacinta-Pasión drainage, such as Piedras Negras and Yaxchilan, showed particularly severe and early symptoms of the collapse. Gill's suggestion that the Usumacinta River dried up at the height of drought is farfetched. Moreover, most Puuc centers, unlike their neighbors to the north and northeast, lacked *cenotes* and relied solely on rain water stored in *chultun* chambers, yet they still enjoyed prosperity during alleged periods of drought. Thus, although studies of climatic changes offer important data, their social implications are far from resolved.

Beside such models, an important development in the study of the Maya collapse is one of philosophy. Scholars place less emphasis on a search for the ultimate causes than on the very nature of social change. Although earlier studies viewed the collapse as a society-wide process, later studies revealed evidence of large regional variation in patterns of political change and depopulation. For example, various parts of Belize and Yucatan maintained substantial settlements during the Terminal and Postclassic periods. Even in the southern lowlands, where many elements of elite culture disappeared, a considerable inventory of utilitarian vessels and other nonelite artifacts persisted without significant stylistic or functional change. This evidence has persuaded some scholars that earlier theories reflect an ethnocentric, elitist view that privileges large buildings and royal imagery over more modest tokens of continuing prosperity or survival (D. Chase and A. Chase 2004). Some scholars go so far as to suggest that the degree of hardship, misery, or other negative implications of social change may have been exaggerated and that the very term "collapse" is inappropriate (Marcus 1993; P. Rice 2004: 151).

There is an emerging recognition that, even for a period of such drastic social change, human experience and behavior should be our target. Social changes are ultimately the expression of human action and inaction. In this respect, even the theory emphasizing climatic change is insufficient: instead of assuming a mechanistic relation between droughts and social collapse, scholars should analyze the vulnerability of society to climatic change and how the Maya dealt with, or failed to deal with, such natural disasters. Further, it may be naïve to believe that societies are inherently stable until upset by drastic events. The Maya, like any other society, struggled constantly with changing natural and social environments.

The following sections focus more on the question of how, rather than why, Maya society changed, paying attention to specific local histories in various regions. The picture that emerges, however, is not a random mosaic of unrelated regional patterning. Without question, there were sweeping changes over a wide area, devastating for many Maya, from elites to nonelites. Underneath such changes were diverse courses of action that helped the Maya cope with social upheaval or heightened its destabilizing effects.

THE ABANDONMENT OF AGUATECA

Aguateca provides a well-documented example of social changes among Maya at the end of the Classic period. Its abandonment, induced by warfare, was more drastic than the processes observed at many other sites (Inomata 2003b). The first clear sign of a problem emerged around AD 761. Aguateca was then a twin capital of Dos Pilas, both ruled by a strong, expansive dynasty. Its king, K'awiil Chan K'inich or "Ruler 4," was known for a series of successful war campaigns but ceased to erect monuments after this date. His fate is unclear, but inscriptions at the nearby center of Tamarindito suggest that he may have been defeated in battle or at least went into exile (Houston 1993: 117). Elite residents abandoned Dos Pilas yet remained at Aguateca, where the next king, Tahn Te' K'inich or "Ruler 5," continued to dedicate stone monuments. The ruler and his subjects chose Aguateca for several reasons, but the most important was probably its naturally defensible location surrounded by cliffs and steep slopes. The end came there, too, however. The decline of the Dos Pilas–Aguateca dynasty is first apparent in the rise of rival centers in the Pasión region. At Ceibal, the center that used to be under the control of Dos Pilas in the reigns of Rulers 3 and 4, a local ruler, Ajaw Bot, took the throne and began to use the Dos Pilas–Aguateca emblem glyph. A local chief employing the Dos Pilas emblem glyph also emerged at La Amelia. Tahn Te' K'inich of Aguateca maintained diplomatic and ceremonial relations with these rulers but no longer possessed the centralized power that his predecessors enjoyed (Fig. 10.2; Houston 1993: 119–21; Martin and Grube 2000: 64–7).

Tahn Te' K'inich and his courtiers tried to reestablish the glory of his dynasty. Their strategy was to follow the footsteps of previous kings through war and vigorous construction and ceremonial activity. At a rapid pace, Tahn Te' K'inich began to dedicate large stelae measuring four to five meters in height, in contrast to the monuments of Rulers 3 and 4 at Aguateca, which were relatively small (these kings did not hesitate to erect large stelae at their primary capital of Dos Pilas). Tahn Te' K'inich elevated the standing of Aguateca as his primary capital and the focus of his courtly life. Many of Tahn Te' K'inich's stelae depict the king as a glorious warrior, narrating his victories over enemies. Nonetheless, unlike his ancestors who fought such formidable enemies as Tikal, Ceibal, Yaxchilan, and the Ik' site, his captives do not include recognizable figures of great dynastic importance. His active construction programs probably included the pyramidal buildings around the Main Plaza, Structures L8–6 and L8–7. Whereas his predecessor's temples in the same area all had thatched roofs, Structures L8–6 and L8–7 appear to have had vaulted stone roofs, reflecting the pride and ambition of the new king (Inomata et al. in press). In addition, Tahn Te' K'inich commissioned the construction of Structure L8–8, which was meant to be the largest pyramid at Aguateca. As we will see, its construction was never completed. We can only speculate on its final shape, but the king and his architects may have planned a temple similar to Dos Pilas Structure L5–49, the largest pyramid at the Main Plaza of their former capital, or even a building comparable to the towering pyramids of Tikal.

Tahn Te' K'inich evidently pursued a traditional ideal of Maya kingship. Despite political problems, he still managed to muster labor for his campaigns and construction projects. Structure M8–10, an elite residence nicknamed the "House of the Scribe" by Inomata and his team, contained a carved human skull with a hieroglyphic text, which mentioned a ceremony attended by this ruler. Along with the *sak-hu'nal* diadem and other finds mentioned in Chapter 9, this skull signals that the courtiers of Tahn Te' K'inich remained loyal to their master and performed their courtly duties until the very fall of the center. Likewise, commoners maintained close affiliation with the king, participating in the construction of Structure L8–8 and other public projects led by the elite. Courtly lives and public ceremonies continued at least until AD 793, the date recorded on Stela 14, or possibly later, as other eroded monuments may have even more recent dates.

These efforts apparently did little to improve the fortunes of Aguateca. As threats of enemy attacks became imminent, the Aguatecans began to build a series of stone walls, probably supporting wooden palisades (Inomata 2008b). The hasty construction of these defensive walls marked a major disruption

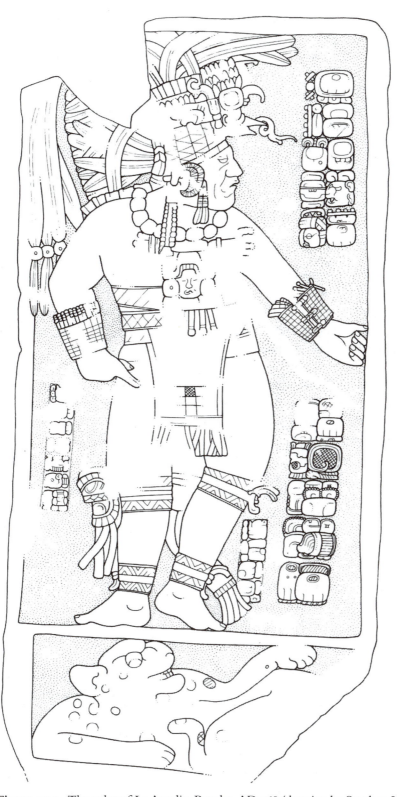

Figure 10.2. The ruler of La Amelia, Panel 2, AD 768 (drawing by Stephen Houston).

in the ceremonial and social lives of the center. The ambitious construction
of Structure L8–8 was suspended, and a defensive wall covered a corner of
the half-finished pyramid. The causeways where processions once paraded
were now blocked, and walls disfigured the middle of elite residential groups.
As frantic as the construction of defensive walls became, it sill maintained a
certain level of order, with supervision by the elite and participation by a
large number of commoners. Walls were placed in a concentric layout around
the royal palace, reflecting its main purpose of defending the king and his
family. The outermost walls surrounded a large part of the center to guard
its perimeters and many nonelite residential groups. In addition, hills around
the center were fortified with similar walls, and points of access along the
escarpments were blocked.

Eventually, Tahn Te' K'inich and his family appear to have left the center to
seek refuge elsewhere. Excavators found most rooms of the royal palace swept
clean. Only the easternmost room of Structure M7–22, the "House of the
Masks," contained numerous royal possessions, including the ceramic masks
mentioned in Chapter 5 (see Fig. 5.14), pyrite mirrors, and bone and shell
ornaments, all placed behind a sealed entrance (Fig. 10.3). The king probably
stored these objects in the hopes of returning to the center. The final fate
of Tahn Te' K'inich is not known. Despite the flight of the sovereign, most
other elites, and probably a large number of commoners as well, remained at
the center until the bitter end. They dismantled stone blocks from Structure
M7–32, the "House of the Bones," of the Palace Group, which was probably
the main throne building of the ruler, and built walls around the structure and
other elite residences.

The end of Aguateca was abrupt and swift. The enemy, whose identity
remains unknown, invaded the center and destroyed the elite residential area
in its epicenter. Courtiers who lived in the area had to flee or were taken
captive by attackers, leaving a large number of their possessions behind. The
invading army burned the elite residential area. Flaming roofs and walls collapsed over the many objects that the residents left, covering them for over a
thousand years until archaeologists found these frozen moments from a Maya
court. In all likelihood, the attack on Aguateca took place sometime around
9.19.0.0.0 (AD 810). This important period ending date was meant to be
commemorated on Altar M, placed on the front terrace of Structure L8–8.
The altar, like its associated temple, was never completed. The whole process
from the construction of defensive walls to the final attack probably happened
quickly, possibly in the range of several years or even a few months. The outermost walls of Aguateca end suddenly, in a flat location. The enemy probably
reached the center before the Aguatecans could complete this wall.

After securing their victory, the enemy conducted termination rituals, that
is, the ritual destruction of symbolically charged buildings. In the Palace Group,
they opened the sealed room of Structure M7–22, the House of the Masks,

Figure 10.3. Storage chamber in Aguateca Structure M7–22, the House of the Masks (photograph by Takeshi Inomata).

and destroyed some of its stored treasure. In Structure M7–32, the House of the Bones, a side niche and the nearby bench floor of the throne in the center room were destroyed. They then deposited a large quantity of broken objects, including ceramic vessels, grinding stones, chert and obsidian tools, jade ornaments, carved shells, figurines, and human and bones, inside the center room of Structure M7–32 and around Structures M7–22 and M7–32. In the climax of the ritual, the two buildings were burned and destroyed. Ritual destruction also took place in the Main Plaza. Structures L8–6 and L8–7, the temples most likely built or renovated by Tahn Te' K'inich, were robbed of cut stones. The enemy deposited yellow soil in front of Structure L8–6 and then a large amount of broken objects around the two buildings. Because other structures in the Main Plaza were left intact, the invaders appear to have selectively destroyed the buildings of Tahn Te' K'inich (Inomata et al. in press). These termination rituals in the Palace Group and the Main Plaza were probably public events, meant to be viewed by both the triumphant enemy and the defeated Aguatecans. The rituals symbolically destroyed the power and authority of the center's last ruler, handing a spiritual defeat to the Aguatecans, who had already been vanquished physically.

Buildings outside of the epicenter were not burned, and the residents had time to carry away their possessions. Still, the entire center seems to have been deserted soon after the destruction of the Palace Group and the elite residential area. The haste in which the Aguatecans left the center is suggested by human remains found around Structure L8–8. In one burial, a body was placed directly on the exterior floor against the back wall of the buildings, covered only by a few stones. Excavators also unearthed fragmentary skeletons on the exterior floor. Other bodies may have been left on the ground and soon damaged by animals and the elements. These exposed or cursorily buried human remains must have emitted an unbearable smell in the tropical heat. It is hard to imagine that people continued to live in this area long after the battle. Despite the numerous usable objects left in burned buildings, Aguatecans did not return to the center, and the residents of neighboring settlements, including Punta de Chimino and Ceibal, rarely visited the site. It is probable that the enemy prohibited them from returning to or visiting Aguateca. The enemy aimed at terminating Aguateca as a political and economic power. They achieved this goal with a suddenness and brutality that reflects the violence of the Maya collapse at some sites.

PROBLEMS AT THE END OF AN ERA

The fall of Aguateca may be unique in its abrupt and violent nature. At most other ruins, archaeologists have found patterns of gradual abandonment. But the collapse of Aguateca is certainly not an isolated event. An examination of other regions reveals a closely related process that took place in a relatively short span of time. Earlier scholars emphasized the gradual nature of the Classic Maya collapse, noting a wide temporal distribution of the last calendrical dates at various centers. It is true that the center of Dos Pilas fell silent after AD 761, whereas Tonina continued to erect monuments until 10.4.0.0 (AD 909); Ceibal enjoyed unprecedented prosperity after the fall of its neighbors. Many archaeologists have thus assumed that the collapse took place over a century, involving substantial regional variation. Some scholars attempted to discern a regional trend of the collapse by examining the spatial distribution of the last recorded dates (Bove 1981). Nonetheless, recent developments in epigraphic studies, along with more-detailed archaeological data, indicate a pattern not evident in the last recorded dates alone: a rapid social change affecting a wide area around 9.19.0.0.0 and 9.19.10.0.0 (AD 810 and 820), just before the end of a *bak'tun* cycle. Few centers recorded the important calendrical date of 10.0.0.0.0 (AD 830).

This upheaval at the beginning of the ninth century followed what may be called the heyday of Maya civilization. During the eighth century the population reached its highest level, and the number of centers erecting monuments was larger than ever. Numerous dynasties engaged in elaborate ceremonies and the construction of large buildings. Their rivalry often resulted in war. But in the midst of such activity we see early warning signs. The rapid population growth and concomitant moves of people to less-densely occupied regions must have heightened social and political tension. In many areas, particularly those with long occupation history, such as central Peten and Copan, deforestation had progressed to a dangerous level (Abrams et al. 1996). Dos Pilas was among the first centers to be abandoned. Altar de Sacrificios, another center in the southwestern lowlands, may also have suffered an early dynastic collapse, though the center is known to have ceramics from the Terminal Classic. At the least, it appears to have ceased monument erection after Stela 15 (AD 771), (Mathews and Willey 1991). The fall of Dos Pilas and Altar de Sacrificios might have resulted from emerging social problems, including waves of increasingly destructive warfare (Demarest 1997). As mentioned before, there might have been droughts, but evidence is lacking of serious environmental degradation or nutritional deficiency in the Pasión region (Dunning et al. 1997; Wright 2006). What is apparent is the emergence of new petty kingdoms claiming the Dos Pilas-Aguateca emblem glyph, all expressing a trajectory of political disintegration.

Southwestern Lowlands

Political problems probably lay behind the abandonment of various centers, including Aguateca, around 9.19.0.0.0 (AD 810). This process is most evident in the western lowlands. At Yaxchilan, "Itzamnaaj" Bahlam IV led active political and military activities in the late eighth century, defeating the Ik' site, Lakamtuun, Namaan, and Hix Witz (Martin and Grube 2008: 134–7). The next ruler, K'inich Tatbu Skull IV, followed this trend and vanquished Piedras Negras in AD 808, capturing its Ruler 7 (Houston et al. 1999). Nonetheless, Lintel 10, the carving recording this victory, did not have the elegance and sophistication of his ancestors' monuments and was the last sculpture dedicated at the center. Yaxchilan's elite rule collapsed soon after AD 808. Its rival, Piedras Negras, never recovered from the defeat and the loss of its ruler at the hands of Yaxchilan. Some of its palace buildings were burned and the magnificent Throne 1 was smashed, probably after the battle (Fig. 10.4). Following the dynastic collapse, elite occupation appears to have continued for some time, but the center was eventually deserted (Houston et al. 2001). The nearby center of Bonampak is famous for its murals, which depict the presentation of tribute in a throne room, dances, a battle, the torture and sacrifice of war captives, and an elaborate solar dance pageant (M. Miller 1986). Yet these spectacular paintings were the last monuments at the site and do not, in parts, appear to have been finished. Their last recorded date of AD 792 indicates that Bonampak experienced a sudden turn of its fortune around AD 800.

Further to the west, the last ruler of Palenque was inaugurated in AD 799 (Martin and Grube 2000: 175). We know little about his deeds and eventual fate, and the center soon fell silent. Its bitter enemy Tonina enjoyed a florescence under Ruler 8 in the late eighth century. This site, well-known for its late inscriptions, however, underwent a thirty-year hiatus in monument erection after the dedication of Monument 95 (AD 806, Martin and Grube 2000: 188–9). A similar pattern is found at Ceibal on the Pasión River. Its ruler, Ajaw Bot, with the Dos Pilas-Aguateca emblem glyph, erected his last monument on 9.18.10.0.0 (AD 800). After this date, Ceibal underwent a thirty-year hiatus in monument erection. Thus, Tonina and Ceibal, which would later show resurgence in political activities, were also part of a wave of widespread political disintegration around AD 810.

Central and Eastern Lowlands

The powerful center of Tikal experienced much the same. The eighth century witnessed the apogee of this center, in which Tikal enjoyed power unmatched in the Maya lowlands as its kings ordered the construction of a series of enormous temple pyramids. Its florescence, however, did not last long. Temple 3 was the last of the great construction projects, and Stela 24 at its base recorded a date of AD 810. The power of the ruling elite was already diminishing, and they did not honor the tradition of building a Twin Pyramid Complex to celebrate the *k'atun* ending, which had been in practice since AD 692. After 9.19.0.0.0, no monuments were erected for the next sixty years. Tikal's smaller neighbors had similar trajectories. At Yaxha the last monument, Stela 31, recorded a date of AD 796 (Grube 2000: 262–3), and Motul de San José's latest inscription probably dates to 9.19.0.0.0 (AD 810) (Proskouriakoff 1993: 150–1; P. Rice 2004: 145). Only Uaxactun recorded the late date of AD 830 on Stela 13 before it entered a hiatus (Valdés and Fahsen 2004).

Tikal's archenemy, Calakmul, could not take advantage of the fall of its rival. This center, once the most dominant power in the Maya area, lost its vigor after ruinous defeats at the hand of Tikal in AD 695 and in the early eighth century. Although it continued to erect stelae until around AD 810, the center underwent a lapse in monument dedication (Martin and Grube 2008: 115). Another large center, Naranjo, met a comparable fate. Its ruler, "Itzamnaaj" K'awiil, led successful military campaigns, and the next king, Waxaklajuun Ubaah K'awiil, erected Stela 32, with a date of AD 820. After this time, however, its activities diminished, although, in style, Stela 9 appears to date to the ninth century (Martin and Grube 2008: 83).

In southeastern Peten, Ixkun enjoyed a late prosperity in the late eighth century, only to decline abruptly. Its Stela 5, erected around AD 800, was the last monument at the center. Archaeologists found piles of stones in the central plaza, which may indicate unfinished construction activities like those of Aguateca. The abandonment of Ixkun, however, was not as drastic as that of Aguateca, and activities in residential areas continued into the next period. At another center in the region, Ixtonton, Stela 1 may have a date

Figure 10.4. Fragments of Piedras Negras Throne 1, when found, Structure J-6 (courtesy of Archives, University of Pennsylvania Museum).

of AD 825. If so, this represents the last recorded date in southeastern Peten (Laporte 2004). In northern Belize, the center of La Milpa appears to have experienced a rapid reversal of its fortune, probably in the early ninth century (Hammond and Tourtellot 2004). The construction of Structures 1 and 21, both temple pyramids, as well as a substantial portion of the Southern Acropolis ceased abruptly. The excavators, however, did not find evidence of warfare and destruction comparable to that of Aguateca.

Further to the southeast, the center of Quirigua could boast of the tallest stelae in the Maya area, but the monuments of the last ruler, "Jade Sky," dating to AD 800 and AD 805, were substantially smaller, indicating, presumably, its declining economic and political fortune. The façade of Structure 1B-1 recorded the last date at this center, AD 810, and Quirigua soon declined (Martin and Grube 2008: 225). This last text at Quirigua mentioned Yax Pahsaj Chan Yopaat, the ruler of Copan. This was the last reference to this Copan king, who did not erect monuments recording this date at his native center (Schele and Freidel 1990). At Copan, during the first fifteen years following his accession to the throne in AD 763, Yax Pahsaj actively engaged in monumental building projects, but construction activities declined visibly in the latter part of his reign. Other elites began to dedicate carved benches and other inscriptions in their residences in a process not dissimilar to the political fragmentation documented in the Pasión region, in which the high-ranked subjects of the sovereign were claiming larger autonomy (see the section titled Southwestern Lowlands; W. Fash and D. Stuart 1991). Stela 11, possibly a posthumous depiction of Yax Pahsaj, is one of the latest complete monuments at this center. The next ruler, Ukit Took', ordered the dedication of Altar L on which he is shown in conversation with, perhaps, a deceased Yax Pahsaj on his own accession ceremony at 9.19.11.14.5 (AD 822), but the monument was never completed (Grube and Schele 1987). The end of the Copan dynasty appears to have been rapid and violent. The residential complex of Yax Pahsaj, Group 10L-2, and probably many temples in the center, were burned and destroyed (W. Fash et al. 2004).

The pattern of demographic decline at Copan has been contested by scholars. Using obsidian hydration as a dating technique – a means of inferring absolute age by measuring the thickness of a water "rind" in obsidian – David Webster and AnnCorinne Freter (Freter 1992; Webster and Freter 1990) have suggested that a substantial population, including some elites, continued to live at and around Copan and to use Late Classic Coner ceramics after the dynastic collapse, possibly as late as AD 1250. In other words, the fall of Copan was gradual, taking place over several centuries. Others, however, have questioned the reliability of obsidian hydration methods (Braswell 1992). Research by Lawrence Anovitz and others (1999), in particular, have indicated problems with the hydration process and in the optical measurement of hydration layers. More recent investigations have shown that an extremely small population lived around the former ceremonial center for a short period around AD 1000. Their ceramics differed from Coner types and included such trade items as Fine Orange Ware, Tohil Plumbate, and Las Vegas Polychrome. They did not produce obsidian blade locally. Thus, these Postclassic occupants exhibited little cultural continuity with the Classic residents, indicating that the Terminal Classic abandonment of Copan was fairly rapid. Although a small population probably lingered on after the dynastic collapse around AD 822, as attested by a small number of Fine Orange vessels in elite residences, the area was completely abandoned by around AD 950. After a short lapse of time, the Postclassic population with distinct material culture reoccupied the area briefly (W. Fash et al. 2004; Manahan 2004).

In summary, many scholars once favored a gradualist view of the Classic Maya collapse, but data now point to more rapid social change just before the end of a *bak'tun* cycle. Only a few centers recorded what should have been an extremely important calendrical date of 10.0.0.0.0 (AD 830). Many centers in the southern lowlands suffered significant political disruption and population decline or even total abandonment. Underlying problems were already present during the late eighth century when construction activities diminished at Maya settlements.

CONTINUITY AND SHORT REVIVALS DURING THE TERMINAL CLASSIC PERIOD

The rapid deterioration in political organization around AD 810 does not mean that Maya society of the southern lowlands experienced a total collapse. There were a small number of centers that maintained vigorous activity through this troubled time, and others that rebounded from earlier setbacks. Scholars call this period after the first collapse the "Terminal Classic" (AD 830–950). The late resurgence, however, was limited and short-lived, only to end in more profound political disintegration and depopulation.

A powerful center that remained active was Caracol. After a hiatus in monument erection, triggered by a military defeat in AD 680 at the hand of its old foe, Naranjo, this center regained momentum at the end of the eighth century AD. Its king, K'inich Toobil Yopaat, led a successful battle in AD 800 against its neighbor, Ucanal. He and his successors continued to erect monuments, including an altar recording AD 830. Stela 10, a crude monument dating to AD 859, appears to be the last monument at the center (Martin and Grube 2000: 99). Relying on radiocarbon dates, Arlen and Diane Chase (2004) argue that occupations in elite residences and construction activities continued for forty years or so after this last inscribed date. In their view, the end of Caracol was drastic, somewhat similar to that of Aguateca. The palace buildings on top of the large Caana pyramid were burned, and archaeologists found complete and reconstructible artifacts as well as unburied bodies in the rooms. Some construction projects ended abruptly, leaving unfinished temple pyramids and piles of stone blocks nearby. Ucanal appears to have remained under the control of, or in a close affiliation with, Caracol after its defeat (Martin and Grube 2000: 98). Stela 4, dating to around AD 849, may be its last monument, but the occupation of the center continued into the Early Postclassic period (Laporte and Mejía 2002: 43–4). As discussed below, Ucanal, and possibly Caracol as its overlord, played an important role in the resurgence of Ceibal in the Terminal Classic period.

To the north of Caracol, on the Mopan River near the Guatemala-Belize border, Xunantunich grew into an imposing center around the time of the decline of the nearby major center of Naranjo. The prosperity of Xunantunich, however, was short-lived. By the end of the Terminal Classic period the center, as well as most of its hinterland settlements, was abandoned despite the richness of the riverine environment and the absence of evidence for ecological degradation (Ashmore et al. 2004). Further to the southwest, the rulers of Machaquila, Sihyah K'in Chahk and Juun Tzak Took', erected a series of stelae recording each of the five-year-period-ending events from AD 800 to AD 840 (I. Graham 1967). It is interesting to note that on his early monuments with the dates of AD 825 and AD 830, Juun Tzak Took' appears in typical Classic Maya ceremonial costume with feathered headdresses,

sak-hu'nal diadems, and pectorals. On his later stelae, however, he wears sim-
pler attire and a nose bar. Thus, such a change in costume does not necessarily
mean a dynastic takeover by foreigners; the same Maya ruler happened to adopt
new styles of attire. The later monuments are smaller, possibly indicating the
diminished power of the dynasty or at least reduced ambition in its image
making.

At Tikal, after sixty years of hiatus in monument erection, there may have
been a minor effort to reassert its past glory, as seen in the dedication of Stela
11 in AD 869 by Ruler Jasaw Chan K'awiil II. However, it does not appear
that any other late stelae were erected at the site. Only Stela 12 (AD 889) at the
nearby center of Uaxactun may have mentioned this king (Martin and Grube
2008: 53). By this time the former political domain of Tikal was fragmented.
Between AD 859 and AD 889 the minor centers of Ixlu and Jimbal in the same
region erected their own monuments using the Tikal emblem glyph. A process
similar to the fragmentation of the Dos Pilas dynasty one hundred years earlier
appears to have affected the central Peten. The pattern of final abandonment at
Tikal is not clear. Excavators found a large amount of trash accumulated in the
rooms of the Central Acropolis or the royal palace complex. Peter Harrison
(1999), who excavated the compound, believes that the palace was reoccupied
by squatters after the dynastic collapse, but there is the possibility that these
finds resulted from termination rituals.

The end of Calakmul was broadly similar. After a long interval in monument
erection, the Calakmul elite dedicated rather crude stelae on 10.3.0.0.0 (AD
899) or possibly on 10.4.0.0.0 (AD 909) (Fig. 10.5; Martin and Grube 2008:
115; Braswell et al. 2004). In a process of political fragmentation comparable
to that at Dos Pilas and Tikal, the minor centers around Calakmul, including
Oxpemul, Nadzcaan, and La Muñeca, began to dedicate their own monuments
around AD 830, a pattern continuing until AD 899 or even later (Martin and
Grube 2008: 115). Near the western margin of the Maya area, the Tonina
elite erected a monument around AD 839 after a thirty-year hiatus (Martin
and Grube 2008: 189). The momentum for a revival, however, was weak, and
Tonina stopped erecting monuments after AD 904 and 909, its last productions
done at a crude standard (Martin and Grube 2000: 189).

In comparison to these unimpressive attempts at recovery, the resurgence
of Ceibal was remarkable. The center became arguably the most dominant
power in the southern lowlands during the Terminal Classic period. The ruler
responsible for this revival was Aj Bolon Ha'btal Wat'ul K'atel, who was said
to have arrived at Ceibal on 9.19.18.17.15 (AD 829) under the auspices of a
person from Ucanal and, it seems, in the company of a previous king of Ceibal
(Martin and Grube 2008: 227; Schele and Mathews 1998: 183; D. Stuart
and Houston 1994: 20–1). Remarkably, this new king claimed the original
emblem glyph of Ceibal. Given the use of the Dos Pilas-Aguateca emblem
glyph by an earlier lord at Ceibal, along with the hiatus in monument erection

Figure 10.5. Calakmul Stela 50, Terminal Classic stela (Ruppert and Denison 1943, pl. 50b).

after 9.18.10.0.0 (AD 800), his accession may mark a break or renewal in the dynastic line. Nonetheless, his title, Aj Bolon Ha'btal, was comparable to those of the earlier Ceibal king, Ajaw Bot, and Dos Pilas-Aguateca rulers, signaling some continuity in royal tradition. It is not clear whether Wat'ul K'atel was a descendant of Ceibal royalty who went into exile after the defeat by Dos Pilas nearly a hundred years ago; he may also have been of very different descent.

The arrival of Wat'ul K'atel was obviously intended for the important calendrical ceremony on 10.0.0.0.0, but he apparently did not have the time or resource to dedicate monuments to commemorate that ceremony. He did, however, order the most ambitious monumental program in the Terminal Classic southern lowlands for the next *k'atun* ending (AD 849), positioning five finely executed stelae in and around a new temple, A-3, which was decorated with elaborate stucco sculpture. By that time, the dynastic power of Caracol and Machaquila was dwindling or had nearly collapsed. No other centers in the southern lowlands possessed the will or means to carry out comparable projects. The texts carved on these stelae also attest to Wat'ul K'atel's broad diplomatic connections. Stela 10 states that the rulers from Tikal, Calakmul, and the Ik' site attended the ceremony, although these individuals cannot be identified on the monuments of those centers, and they might have come from minor centers using the emblem glyphs of the old masters. Stela 9 records some connection to Lakamtun in modern Chiapas, Mexico, and Stela 8 mentions a visit of the *k'uhul ajaw* ("holy lord") of *puh* (Schele and Mathews 1998: 182–95). *Puh*, meaning a "cattail-reed place," was the Maya version of the central Mexican notion of *tollan* or primordial place of high culture; during the Classic period it generally referred to the great city of Teotihuacan (D. Stuart 2004b). In this case, it may have meant a central Mexican city such as Cholula, Cacaxtla, and Xochicalco – perhaps an unlikely possibility–or a large Maya center with Mexican connections, including Chichen Itza and Tikal (Schele and Mathews 1998: 182–95).

Ceibal has been the primary focus of the foreign invasion explanation for the Maya collapse (Sabloff and Willey 1967). Wat'ul K'atel's appearance with long hair, mustache, and a nose bar was interpreted as non-Maya (J. Graham 1973), but, as seen in the case of monuments from Machaquila, these traits do not necessarily signal a foreign identity. In addition, his association with Ucanal indicates Maya roots. Fine paste ceramics used also to be viewed as evidence for foreign invasions, but compositional analyses of ceramic pastes establish that these vessels were made within the Maya region along the Usumacinta and Pasión Rivers (Bishop and Rands 1982; Foias and Bishop 1997). More problematic is another set of Terminal Classic monuments at Ceibal, called "Facies B," which depict figures with even longer hair, simple costume, and snake belts. Some of them are carved with texts containing square day signs in a non-Maya calendar, and those figures are not identified as members of the Ceibal royal blood line. The figures are similar to ones carved on Fine Orange ceramics, and David Stuart (1993) has suggested that they can still be ethnic Maya, possibly commoners. Their appearance, however, represents a substantial break from the traditional Maya canons and shows a strong resemblance to figurines from the Gulf Coast area (Gutierrez and Hamilton 1977). Particularly intriguing is Ceibal Stela 17, which depicts a figure in precisely such nontraditional attire facing another person with typical Maya ceremonial gear, including mirrored belt sash, celts, and a feathered headdress. Although an outright conquest is unlikely, is it possible that the

Ceibal dynasty had close connections with non-Maya groups or even incorporated them in their administrative system. Either way, these monuments imply a new type of political alliance, whether with Maya commoners or non-Maya elites, an ultimately unsuccessful experiment devised by the elites of Ceibal.

A relevant point is that Terminal Classic Ceibal lacked defensive features comparable to the Late Classic sites of the Petexbatun region. Its focus of elite activities during the Late Classic period was in the naturally defensible Group D, located on top of a steep hill, but during the Terminal Classic it shifted to Group A, a place with easier access. In addition, Terminal Classic monuments of Ceibal appear to deemphasize militaristic themes (Tourtellot and González 2004). Another feature is the continuity of nonelite occupation. Although the Terminal Classic ceramic assemblage at Ceibal is characterized by fine paste ware, most utilitarian vessels exhibit strong continuity from the Late Classic period. It is virtually certain that the nonelite residents of Ceibal were Maya. Fine paste ceramics are found mostly around the ceremonial core of Ceibal, leading scholars to wonder whether the Terminal Classic Ceibal population concentrated in the central sector or whether a larger population continued to live in peripheries without using imported ceramics (Tourtellot and González 2004). The original Late Classic population may have continued without break. Alternatively, there could also have been a significant demographic collapse during the dynastic break from AD 800 to 830, and the population level may have rebounded with migrations from other Maya regions. The continuity in utilitarian ceramics, however, does not support this scenario. Ceibal eventually could not escape the same fate as other dynasties. The last recorded date is 10.3.0.0.0 (AD 889), although some stelae without calendrical dates may have been erected later. It appears that the center was largely abandoned by about AD 950. Structure A-16 of the East Court, decorated with elaborate stucco sculpture comparable to that of A-3, was most likely the residential-administrative building of the Terminal Classic Ceibal dynasty. The sculpture appears to have been intentionally destroyed at the time of dynastic implosion.

The Terminal Classic histories of other centers are highly varied. Various settlements, including Aguateca, never recovered from the collapse around AD 810. Along with dynastic tumult, population levels plummeted in general. At other centers, such as Piedras Negras, a smaller population lingered after the dynastic collapse. There also existed some places, including Altar de Sacrificios and Ixtonton, that showed construction and other activities despite the lack of sculptural commissions in the form of stelae. Many of those centers further declined in population by the end of the Terminal Classic period. In central Peten, the demographic focus after the decline of Tikal shifted to areas around a series of lakes, including Lake Peten Itza, though at a far smaller scale. Occupations in the lake region continued until the Spanish conquest.

One area that exhibited significant continuity to the Postclassic period was northeastern and central Belize. Although some centers such as Colha and Altun Ha declined at the end of the Classic period, others, including Lamanai, Barton Ramie, and settlements around Pulltrouser Swamp, maintained considerable levels of population and construction activity (Pendergast 1986; Willey et al. 1965). Caye Coco and other new settlements also developed during this period (Masson and Mock 2004). Many of the Terminal Classic and Postclassic sites are located near rivers or the coasts, benefitting from reliable water supplies, faunal resources, and high agricultural productivity. Their locations also facilitated their participation in maritime trade networks centered on Chichen Itza. An important factor for their prosperity appears to have been a successful transition from economic and political ties in Peten to northern Yucatan during Terminal and Postclassic times (Masson and Mock 2004; Pendergast 1986).

RISE AND FALL IN THE NORTH

While many southern cities were declining, the northern lowlands witnessed the florescence of various centers and the continuation of substantial populations into the colonial period. Various colonial sources referring to this period add rich detail unavailable in the southern lowlands, but they are highly confusing and difficult to use in writing any reliable sequence of events. The central issues among scholars are the chronology of major political centers and the nature of foreign relations. The more traditional view is one that posits a linear succession between centers and their associated ceramics (R. Smith 1971). According to this view, Puuc centers and the early Maya occupation at Chichen Itza with Puuc-style architecture and so-called Cehpech ceramics were disrupted by "Toltec" or "Mexicanized Maya" invasions into Chichen Itza, the latter characterized by Sotuta ceramics; this was then followed by the rise of Mayapan with Hocaba ceramics. In time, scholars began to suspect a partial overlap or total overlap of Cehpech and Sotuta ceramics, as well as prior growth at Chichen Itza (Ball 1979; Lincoln 1986). At present, most researchers recognize a certain degree of contemporaneity between Cehpech and Sotuta.

Cehpech and Sotuta ceramics are characterized by Slate Wares, so named after slatelike gray-brown slipped surfaces; they are distinguished by the prevalence of calcite temper in Cehpech Slate Wares and volcanic ash temper in Sotuta Slate Wares, as well as by different types and vessel forms (Fig. 10.6). Although scholars have traditionally associated the Cehpech and Sotuta complexes with Fine Orange imported from the Usumacinta drainage, and Sotuta with Plumbate wares from the Guatemalan Pacific coast, these trade wares are in fact found in limited quantities and contexts. The spread of Cehpech ceramics throughout the northern Yucatan Peninsula during the eighth century marked the emergence of a ceramic tradition distinct from the southern

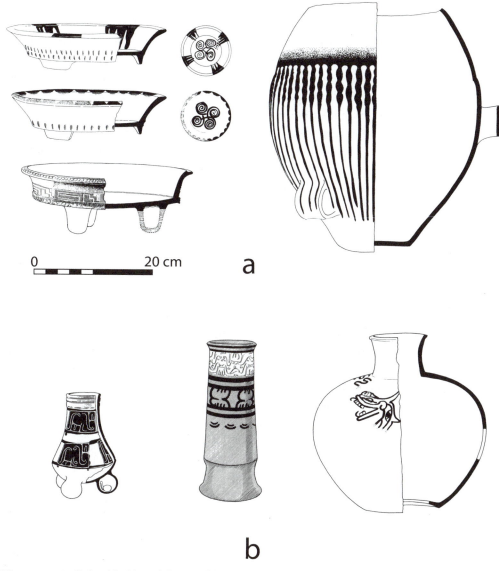

Figure 10.6. Cehpech (a) and Sotuta (b) ceramics (Brainerd 1958, fig. 35a, i, j, 58d, 77p, 78g, 76a).

lowlands. The beginning of the Sotuta complex is less clear, but it can be considered a minor variation of Cehpech centered on Chichen Itza (Bey et al. 1998; Robles and A. Andrews 1986).

Terminal Classic Florescence in the Northern Lowlands

Centers such as Dzibilchaltun, Ek Balam, Coba, Oxkintok, and Chunchucmil prospered during the eighth and ninth centuries. There is no clear indication of unrest or disruption that parallels the problems to the south around AD 810 and 820, with a possible exception of an apparent hiatus in monument erection at Oxkintok between AD 820 and 849 (García Campillo 1991). Coba was a large center with strong cultural ties to the southern lowlands, but in the late eighth century its erection of monuments ceased and a local Slate Ware tradition replaced Peten-style polychrome vessels. Still, Peten-style constructions continued into the ninth century (Robles and A. Andrews 1986). Coba wielded extensive political influence, attested by a long causeway built in the seventh century to connect the site with Yaxuna (Suhler et al. 2004). Ek Balam, with a probable dynastic connection to Coba, dedicated elaborate stucco façades, murals, and carved monuments in the Classic tradition from the late eighth to mid-ninth centuries (Vargas and Castillo 2006). Chunchucmil near the west coast was a populous city associated with salt production and trade, although it lacked ornate architecture and carved monuments (Dahlin and Ardren 2002).

In the late ninth century, the prosperity of Uxmal and Chichen Itza began to eclipse other centers. The early growth of Uxmal, with its Puuc-style architecture characterized by veneer stones and vaulted roofs, dates to around AD 700 (Carmean et al. 2004). The Books of Chilam Balam, colonial-period Maya accounts with often enigmatic chronicles and prophecies, tell us that the Tutul Xiw family established Uxmal after decades of migration. According to the Spanish friar Diego de Landa, the Tutul Xiw, one of the competing elite factions at the time of Spanish contact, were referred to as foreigners by their rivals (Tozzer 1941: 40). Archaeological remains at Uxmal, however, do not show prominent non-Maya elements, and some scholars consider the Tutul Xiw to have been nonlocal but still a branch of Maya speakers, possibly Cholan from the south or southwest. Suhler and his colleagues (2004) suggest that the appearance of Puuc architecture at Chichen Itza and Yaxuna during the eighth century reflects an expansion of political influence from the Puuc. It is at the beginning of the tenth century, during the reign of "Lord Chahk," or Chan Chahk K'ahk'nal Ajaw, that Uxmal reached the height of its prosperity. The buildings commissioned by him, including the House of Governor and the Nunnery Quadrangle, show elaborate mosaic and sculptural decorations on their façades, the very apex of Maya architectural polish and sophistication (Fig. 10.7). His stelae appear to show the last glow of royal symbolism in the Classic tradition. Other centers in the region, including Kabah and Sayil, also built elaborate structures in the late ninth and early tenth centuries. Uxmal and other Puuc centers declined soon after the reign of Lord Chahk. A smaller population remained at Uxmal after the dynastic collapse but engaged in less impressive construction.

The Expansion of Chichen Itza

Chichen Itza has been at the center of debates on northern chronology and its relation to foreign invasion. The traditional view divided Chichen Itza

Figure 10.7. Nunnery Quadrangle, Uxmal, early AD 900s (photograph by Takeshi Inomata).

chronology into two phases: the Terminal Classic component marked by Puuc architecture, hieroglyphic texts, and Cehpech ceramics, all contemporary with the Puuc centers; and the Early Postclassic component characterized by Sotuta ceramics and "Toltec" architecture, such as El Castillo, the Great Ballcourt, and the Temple of Warriors. Charles Lincoln (1986) has criticized this chronology, arguing that the two sets of elements are completely contemporaneous. The truth may lie between these extremes, with overlaps of different elements and a certain chronological trend. Glyphic inscriptions – a quintessential Maya element – date mostly to a period between AD 869 and 890, although isolated dates of AD 994 and 998 are recorded (Grube and Krochock 2007; Wren and Schmidt 1990). So-called "Toltec" elements increased during the tenth century (Cobo 2007; Bey and Ringle 2007). This was the time of the most vigorous construction activity at Chichen Itza. The cessation of carved texts thus represents, not the end of elite activities, but a fundamental change in modes of public political discourse (Krochock and Freidel 1994).

Early scholars suggested that nontraditional elements were brought by Toltec invaders from central Mexico, referring to remarkable similarities in architecture and sculpture between Chichen Itza and Tula, including colonnaded halls and "chac mool" (sculptures of a reclining figure; Fig. 10.8). They also cited curious parallels in the contact-period legends of K'uk'ulkan and Quetzalcoatl in the two regions. The central Mexican version affirms that a person or deity named Quetzalcoatl left Tula for the east, whereas the Yucatan version reports on a foreign ruler called K'uk'ulkan, the Maya version of the name Quetzalcoatl, who governed Chichen Itza. It is tempting to think that these legends refer to real historical events involving the same individual or group (Tozzer 1957). Other researchers focused on a group called Itza, who lived in Chichen Itza but were often referred to as foreigners in colonial documents. Descriptions of them as "those who spoke a broken language" may imply that they were speakers of a Maya language, but different from local Yukatek. Thompson (1970: 41–5) suggested that they were Chontal speakers, or "Mexicanized Maya," originating from Tabasco and southern Campeche. Schele and Mathews (1998: 201–4), however, propose that they migrated from the central southern lowlands. They note that a name somewhat like "Itzaj" is found in Classic-period monuments of Motul de San José near the Lake Peten Itza. When the Spaniards visited this lake region, it was home to a group called Itzaj. The Itzaj in Peten now speak a branch of the Yukatekan languages, not the Ch'olan or Ch'olti'an that formed the probable languages of the Classic period. As suggested by colonial accounts, this Yukatekan language may thus reflect a return migration to their ancestral land during the Postclassic period. The problem, unfortunately, is that the term in the inscriptions of the Peten is 'itza, not itzaj, and it likely refers simply to a local place name, not to an ethnic or language group per se (an -a ending, as on 'itza, probably signals a term for "water," common in Classic toponyms).

An important elite group at Chichen Itza was the Kokom family, which was found both in retrospective descriptions in colonial documents and in contemporary glyphic texts at the site. Despite the abundant indications of migrations related to the residents of Chichen Itza in colonial accounts, the Kokom claimed to be the "natural" lords of the area; in contrast, the Tutul Xiw of Uxmal were regarded as foreigners, further adding to a confused picture (Tozzer 1941: 26, 40). We should note that the Sotuta ceramics at Chichen Itza are essentially a variation of the local Slate Ware tradition, but Chichen Itza also received a considerable quantity of trade goods, including Fine Orange ceramics, Plumbate Ware, obsidian from central and western Mexico, and gold (Bey and Ringle 2007; Braswell et al. 2004). The quantity of imported materials was far smaller in the Cehpech sphere. Although the precise identities of the Chichen Itza residents still escape our understanding, it is safe to say that Chichen Itza was a multiethnic community, potentially including multiple nonlocal groups from Mexico and other parts of the Maya lowlands, as well as a large number of the local Maya.

The governmental organization of Chichen Itza has also been a subject of heated debate. Landa reported that the center was ruled by three brothers (Tozzer 1941: 19). Building on this account, Linda Schele and colleagues (Schele and Freidel 1990; Schele and Mathews 1998: 197) argue that the inscriptions of Chichen Itza mention multiple individuals as yitaj, "companions" or "brothers," and that the center was governed by multepal, or joint

Figure 10.8. "Chac mool" in the Temple of Warriors at Chichen Itza, Yucatan (photograph by Takeshi Inomata).

rule. David Stuart in particular (see Houston et al. 2000: 335) has countered that these texts involving the enigmatic *yitaj* glyph refer to acts of witness by deities, not brothers. Other scholars favor an organization similar to that of southern lowland centers during the Classic period, that is, a monarchy or single leader discharging disproportionate power over some kind of council (Kowalski 2007). This theory was inspired by the recognition of the name K'ahk'upakal in the inscriptions of Chichen Itza. Colonial documents mention an individual of the same name who was prominent in the affairs of Chichen Itza (Kelley 1968; Stanton and Gallareta Negrón 2001). In another theory, Lincoln (1994) has proposed that the opposition of the sun disk and the feathered serpent in Chichen Itza's iconography reflects dual rulership.

Drawing on ethnohistorical accounts on Cholula and other Mesoamerican groups, William Ringle (2004) suggests that the local government involved the coexistence of all of the features above. Councils were under the direction of dual leaders, with the political leader as a war captain enjoying supremacy over a religious figure. According to Ringle, Chichen Itza, like Cholula, was a pilgrimage center where investitures of leaders from various communities took place as part of a Quetzalcoatl cult that spread throughout Mesoamerica during this period (see Ringle et al. 1998). Whatever the validity of Ringle's proposal, councils and religious authorities distinct from monarchs were already present at Classic-period centers. Nonetheless, the political organization of Chichen Itza does indeed appear to represent a substantial shift from the Classic tradition in which the single ruler assumed supreme leadership in political, military, and religious affairs.

The decline of many northern centers appears to have been closely tied to warfare, in which Chichen Itza most likely played a central role. The monumental imagery of Chichen Itza emphasized militaristic themes, as seen in the battle scenes in the murals of the Upper Temple of the Jaguars, carvings of warriors in the Temple of Warriors, and sculptures of skulls in the Tzompantli (Fig. 10.9). Depictions of war captives are also common in sculptures of Uxmal and murals at the nearby site of Mulchic. The paintings of the Upper Temple of the Jaguars show a direct attack on an enemy settlement, and such battle practices are reflected in the construction of defensive walls at some centers, including Yaxuna, Dzonot Ake, Cuca, and Chacchob (Webster 1979). Although the primary function of the elaborate walls around the central part of Uxmal and Ek Balam may have been symbolic, they could also have served for defense (Ringle et al. 2004). By analyzing walls at Chunchucmil and other sites, Dahlin (2000) argues that enemy attacks resulted in the abandonment of these centers. In addition, Carmean and colleagues. (Carmean et al. 2004: 445) note that many Puuc centers, including Uxmal, Labna, and Oxkintok, have unfinished monumental buildings, which suggests the rapid fall of dynastic power, possibly triggered by military conflicts.

By means of war, Chichen Itza might have expanded its dominance over a wider area during the tenth century. It has been suggested that Lord Chahk of Uxmal was under the control of Chichen Itza, or that Uxmal was conquered by Chichen Itza after the reign of Lord Chahk (Kowalski et al. 1996; Suhler et al. 2004), but the evidence of this remains tenuous. Excavations at Yaxuna provided more convincing evidence of Chichen Itza's invasion, including ritually destroyed buildings (Freidel 2007; Suhler et al. 2004). The expansion of Chichen Itza was paralleled by the cessation of monumental construction and population decline at other centers in the northern lowlands (Robles and A. Andrews 1986: 88). The powerful centers of Ek Balam and Coba seem also to have been overshadowed by Chichen Itza, but Sotuta ceramics and other materials related to Chichen Itza are scarce at these centers (Ringle et al. 2004; Robles and A. Andrews 1986). The presence of Sotuta ceramics from Tabasco and western Campeche to coastal Quintana Roo, including El Meco and Cozumel, suggests that Chichen Itza expanded more direct control along the coast through its port of Isla Cerritos on the northern coast of Yucatan (Robles and A. Andrews 1986: 88; P. Rice and Forsyth 2004: 47). The presence of round buildings and iconographic similarities at Ceibal, Nohmul, and other sites, as well as the presence of a "chac mool" at Quirigua, has led some scholars to postulate that the influence of Chichen Itza reached distant centers in the southern lowlands (A. Chase 1985; Kowalski 1989; Sharer 1985). Chichen Itza may have devised the largest political hegemony in Maya history.

Figure 10.9. Battle scene in the Upper Temple of the Jaguars, Chichen Itza (de la Torre 1993: 135, rendering by Adela Breton, courtesy of Sue Giles, Bristol's City Museum and Art Gallery).

Anthony Andrews and colleagues. (Andrews et al. 2003) propose that the glory of Chichen Itza did not last long and that the center declined at the beginning of the eleventh century, whereas other scholars favor later dates for its fall. Our understanding of the process of its decline is limited, but various colonial accounts indicate that the Maya remembered the end of this powerful center as a time of political strife between rival groups.

THE MAYA COLLAPSE IN THE MESOAMERICAN SETTING

There are several key trends in the process of the Maya collapse. Towards the end of the eighth century, social problems in the southern lowlands might have worsened with the intensification of interdynastic conflict. This led to the collapse of numerous southern lowland centers at the beginning of the ninth century. Many western centers declined around AD 810, whereas the fall of cities in the central and southeastern lowlands may have taken place a decade or so later. Although the roughly simultaneous decline of various centers could support the drought theory of the Maya collapse, we should remember that this period of troubles in the south was a time of growth in the north, particularly in the Puuc region. The prosperity of the Puuc centers in areas lacking ground water is difficult to explain by a model stressing drought.

Some centers in the south, including Ceibal, Tonina, and Tikal, managed a short revival in the mid and late ninth century. Although these polities were still centered on traditional divine rulership, they, particularly Ceibal, might have been experimenting with new symbols and forms of political interaction. In the north, two prominent centers, Uxmal and Chichen Itza, enjoyed a florescence, whereas other centers, such as Ek Balam and Coba, gradually lost power. When the resurgence in the south ended at the beginning of the tenth century, the prosperity of Uxmal reached its height under Lord Chahk. He was the last powerful king fully committed to the aesthetics and symbolism of the Classic Maya tradition. His rival, Chichen Itza, was already adopting new sets of symbols and a new form of governmental organization during the ninth century. Chichen Itza abandoned the tradition of glyphic inscriptions at the beginning of the tenth century just in the midst of its political expansion. Whereas Ceibal in the south appears to have deemphasized militaristic themes, interpolity conflicts were primary concerns for the elites of Uxmal and Chichen Itza. Through military aggression during the tenth century, Chichen Itza further expanded its dominance at the expense of other centers.

This review shows that the Classic Maya collapse was not a random mosaic of localized events that occurred gradually over a century. We can recognize a series of turning points that affected a wide area. The process, however, was not a monolithic one that reflected a simple causal relation between droughts and societal tumult. Although ecological degradations and climatic changes might have been important factors in the Maya collapse, such processes also involved a complex interplay with human action. We need to examine further how the Maya dealt with environmental and social challenges and how their actions and inactions contributed to this decline.

Above all, the Maya collapse should be understood in a broad context involving social changes taking place in many parts of Mesoamerica. The Late and Terminal Classic periods represent a time of significant social change not only in the Maya area but throughout Mesoamerica, with movement of people and ideas. The rise of Uxmal and Chichen Itza in locations with little previous occupations might point to migrations within the Maya area, particularly from the southern lowlands, and perhaps beginning in the seventh and eighth centuries, as Schele and Mathews (1998) suggest. In central Mexico, significant population movement from the north might in turn have contributed to the collapse of Teotihuacan in the seventh century, although the chronology and social processes of this region are as confusing as those of the northern Maya area. The fall of this metropolis may have triggered another wave of migration towards the southeast. The subsequent rise of fortified centers, such as Cacaxtla, Xochicalco, and Teotenango, indicates the heightening of interpolity conflicts. Among those migrations, particularly significant ones appear to have been those involving Nahua speakers, whose descendants still live in various parts of Central America. Their moves from central Mexico to the southeast may have started as early as the seventh century. Yet, as seen in Maya-like iconography at Cacaxtla and Xochicalco, movements of people and ideas were not one-directional.

Earlier theories overemphasized migrations of a single group sweeping through the Maya area. Actual developments appear to have been far more complex, with multiple groups moving in diverse directions. Chichen Itza was a particularly active player in this new form of interregional interaction. Its wide network probably included direct contacts with Tula, Mexico. We should remember that no other pair of sites in Mesoamerica shows such striking similarities. Their contacts most likely involved bidirectional movements of people and ideas rather than a unidirectional conquest. Although many elements of the Tula-Chichen Itza complex do not have clear antecedents in both areas, colonnaded halls with flat roofs clearly had their roots in northern Mesoamerica, where there is less precipitation (Kristan-Graham 2007). The richer carving traditions of the Maya possibly provided a larger share of inspiration for sculptural innovations, including "chac mools" (M. Miller and Samoya 1998). If a migration serving as a model for the Quetzalcoatl-K'uk'ulkan legend took place, the voyage of such a prominent individual was probably based on previous contact between the two places.

Such active interregional interactions might have stimulated or accelerated the transformation of governmental organization and political ideologies away from ones highlighting divine rulership and a court culture of art and writing to the separation of political and religious authorities and an increased emphasis on secular leadership (Freidel 1985). Still, we should examine these broad patterns of interaction, not as direct causes of the collapse, but as part of a complex process that involved various other influences, including the tumult of environmental and ecological change.

EPILOGUE

After the end of the Classic period, Maya society and its many foci shifted to the northern part of the Yucatan Peninsula, to the highlands in the south, and to the coast, lakes, and rivers where their ancestors had first flourished millennia before. A much-reduced population remained in the central southern lowlands. During the Postclassic period and the ravages of the Spanish conquest, the Maya maintained their traditions, if in continuously evolving form and over periods of dramatic decline in population. The small Itzaj kingdom in the lake region of Peten resisted invasions of the Spaniards until the late-seventeenth century. Far into the twentieth century, some tiny groups even existed outside the direct control of nation states (Palka 2005).

The legacy of the Classic Maya is very much alive today. Archaeologists have been asked to interpret, display, conserve, and sometimes dispute and debate that heritage, often in complex circumstances. Houston and Inomata began to work in Guatemala during a horrific civil war. Because of its remoteness and covering canopy, the rain forest became the primary battlefield between government forces and guerrilla groups of Maya and displaced Ladino peasants. The Peace Accord of 1996 brought that period to an end. Thereafter, distant mortar blasts or machine gun fire were a remote, if chilling, memory. But Maya ruins soon attracted other kinds of conflict and change. Business-people and entrepreneurs saw revived economic opportunities for tourism in archaeological sites – a major source of foreign currency in Guatemala. Others wished to explore oil reserves in salt domes under the jungle. Increased drug trafficking on rivers and in isolated airstrips harvested new forms of wealth and violence, as did the traffic and transport of human beings across national boundaries. Leaders of indigenous groups, some connected to former guerrilla movements, sought to reclaim Maya sites as sacred ancestral places.

After the Peace Accord, Houston worked at Piedras Negras, the area controlled by one of the main guerrilla organizations, the *Fuerzas Armadas Rebeldes* (FAR). The FAR had discouraged looting but left caches of explosives and the occasional minefield. When the FAR departed, the area was soon hit by illegal settlement, despite its status as a national park, and increased activity by smugglers of drugs and people. At Aguateca, where Inomata continued his research, radical indigenous-rights groups agitated for control of the site, leading to illegal squatting and large-scale deforestation. Most of Inomata's workers were poor Q'eqchi' Maya farmers who had suffered during the civil war, caught between the army and the guerrillas. They distrusted both the government and radical groups associated with former guerrillas. Some opted for quick income through looting and land grabs. Yet, a small number explored initiatives to protect the site and forest and to seek sustainable development through community-based tourism. Today, attitudes towards archaeological sites remain as diverse and conflicted as the Maya themselves. That is unlikely to shift in the future.

The Classic Maya "speak" more broadly, too. When the destruction of rainforest became a worldwide concern, many people attempted to find guidance for modern policy by looking at the course of Classic society. Practical and moral lessons were drawn from the "failure" of Maya civilization or its "successful" adaptation to the tropical environment. Whatever the merit of these views, their existence shows that the study of the Classic Maya can not address just the distant past. The Classic Maya formed an important part of human experience, as documented in this book. But they endure yet more strongly in their relevance to living groups far and wide, as their contribution is pondered, studied, and reimagined a millennium after their demise.

REFERENCES

Abercrombie, N., Hill, S., and Turner, B. S. 1980. *The Dominant Ideology Thesis*. London, Boston: George Allen and Unwin.

Abercrombie, N., Hill, S., and Turner, B. S (eds.) 1990. *Dominant Ideologies*. London, Boston: Unwin Hyman.

Abrams, E. M., Freter, A., Rue D. J., and Wingard, J. D. 1996. The role of deforestation in the collapse of the Late Classic Copan Maya state. In Sponsel et al. 1996: 55–75.

Adams, R. E. W. 1971. *The Ceramics of Altar de Sacrificios, Guatemala*. Papers of the Peabody Museum of Archaeology and Ethnology, Harvard University Vol. 63, No. 1. Cambridge: Peabody Museum.

———. 1999. *Río Azul: An Ancient Maya City*. Norman: University of Oklahoma Press.

Adams, R. E. W., Brown, W., Jr., and Culbert, T. P. 1981. Radar mapping, archaeology, and ancient Maya land use. *Science* 213: 1457–63.

Adams, R. E. W. and Smith, W. D. 1981. Feudal models for Classic Maya civilization. In W. Ashmore (ed.), *Lowland Maya Settlement Patterns*, 335–50. Albuquerque: University of New Mexico Press.

Adamson, J. 1999a. The kingdom of England and Great Britain: The Tudor and Stuart courts 1509–1714. In Adamson 1999c: 94–117.

———. 1999b. The making of the ancien-régime Court 1500–1700. In Adamson 1999c: 6–41.

———. 1999c. *The Princely Courts of Europe: Ritual, Politics, and Culture Under the* Ancien *Régime 1500–1750*. London: Weidenfeld and Nicolson.

Agrinier, P. 2000. *Mound 27 and the Middle Preclassic Period at Mirador, Chiapas, Mexico*. Papers of the New World Archaeological Foundation 58. Provo, Utah: Brigham Young University.

Agurcia Fasquelle, R. 2004. Rosalila, temple of the sun-king. In E. E. Bell, M. A. Canuto, and R. J. Sharer (eds.), *Understanding Early Classic Copan*, 101–12. Philadelphia: University of Pennsylvania Museum of Archaeology and Anthropology.

Aimers, J. and Graham, E. 2007. Noble savages versus savage nobles: Gibson's apocalyptic view of the Maya. *Latin American Antiquity* 18(1): 105–06.

Aimers, J., Powis, T. G., and Awe, J. J. 2000. Preclassic round structures of the upper Belize River valley. *Latin American Antiquity* 11: 71–86.

Aimers, J. and Rice, P. M. 2006. Astronomy, ritual, and the interpretation of Maya "E-Group" architectural assemblages. *Ancient Mesoamerica* 17: 79–96.

Aldenderfer, M. S., Kimball, L. R., and Sievert, A. 1989. Microwear analysis in the Maya lowlands: The use of functional data in a complex-society setting. *Journal of Field Archaeology* 16: 47–60.

Algaze, G. 2001. The prehistory of imperialism: The case of Uruk period Mesopotamia. In M. S. Rothman (ed.), *Uruk Mesopotamia and Its Neighbors: Cross-Cultural Interactions in the Era of State Formation*, 27–83. Santa Fe: School of American Research Press.

Altschuler, M. 1958. On the environmental limitations of Mayan cultural development. *Southwestern Journal of Anthropology* 14: 189–98.

Alvarez, T. 1982. Restos de mamíferos recientes y pleistocenicos procedentes de las Grutas de

Loltún, Yucatán, México. *Cuaderno de Trabajo* 26: 7–35.

Anaya Hernández, A. 2002. The Pomoná kingdom and its hinterland. Report to FAMSI, http://www.famsi.org/reports/00082/index.html. Accessed April 15, 2008.

Anderson, B. 1991. *Imagined Communities: Reflections on the Origins and Spread of Nationalism.* New York: Verso.

Anderson, E. N. and Medina Tzuc, F. 2005. *Animals and the Maya in Southeast Mexico.* Tucscon: University of Arizona Press.

Andrews, A. P. 1983. *Maya Salt Production and Trade.* Tucson: University of Arizona Press.

———. 1990. The role of trading ports in Maya civilization. In F. S. Clancy and P. D. Harrison (eds.), *Vision and Revision in Maya Studies,* 159–67. Albuquerque: University of New Mexico Press.

Andrews, A. P., Andrews, E. W., and Robles Castellanos, F. A. 2003. Northern Maya collapse and its aftermath. *Ancient Mesoamerica* 14: 151–56.

Andrews, A. P. and Mock, S. B. 2002. New perspectives on the prehispanic Maya salt trade. In M. A. Masson and D. A. Freidel (eds.), *Ancient Maya Political Economy,* 307–34. Walnut Creek: Altamira Press.

Andrews, E. W., IV. 1965. *Progress Report on the 1960–1964 Field Seasons, National Geographic Society-Tulane University Dzibilchaltun Program.* Middle American Research Institute, Publication 31: 23–67. New Orleans: Tulane University Press.

Andrews, E. W. V. 1976. *The Archaeology of Quelepa, El Salvador.* Middle American Research Institute, Publication 42. New Orleans: Tulane University Press.

———. 1986. Olmec jades from Chacsinkin, Yucatan, and Maya ceramics from La Venta, Tabasco. In E. W. V. Andrews (ed.), *Research and Reflections in Archaeology and History: Essays in Honor of Doris Stone,* 11–49. Middle American Research Institution, Publication 57. New Orleans: Tulane University Press.

———. 1987. A cache of early jades from Chacsinkin, Yucatan. *Mexicon* 9: 78–85.

———. 1988. Ceramic units from Komchen, Yucatan, Mexico. *Cerámica de Cultura Maya* 15: 51–64.

———. 1990. Early ceramic history of the lowland Maya. In F. S. Clancy and P. D. Harrison (eds.), *Vision and Revisions in Maya Studies,*

1–19. Albuquerque: University of New Mexico Press.

Andrews, E. W. V., G. J. Bey III, and C. Gunn. 2008. Rethinking the early ceramic history of the northern Maya Lowlands: New evidence and interpretations. *Paper presented at the annual meeting of the Society for American Archaeology.*

Andrews, E. W. V. and Fash, B. W. 1992. Continuity and change in a royal Maya residential complex at Copán. *Ancient Mesoamerica* 3(1): 63–88.

Andrews, E. W. V., Johnson, J. L., Doonan, W. F., Everson, G. E., Sampeck, K. E., and Starratt, H. E. 2003. A multipurpose structure in the Late Classic palace at Copan. In J. J. Christie (ed.), *Maya Palaces and Elite Residences: An Interdisciplinary Approach,* 68–97. Austin: University of Texas Press.

Andrews, E. W. V. and Hammond, N. 1990. Redefinition of the Swasey Phase at Cuello, Belize. *American Antiquity* 55: 570–584.

Andrews, G. F. 1999. *Pyramids and Palaces, Monsters and Masks: The Golden Sage of Maya Architecture, Vol. 3: Architecture of the Rio Bec Region and Miscellaneous Subjects.* Culver City: Labyrinthos.

Anovitz, L. M., J. M. Elam, L. R. Riciputi, and Cole, D. R. 1999. The failure of obsidian hydration dating: Sources, implications, and new directions. *Journal of Archaeological Science* 26: 735–52.

Aoyama, K. 1995. Microwear analysis in the southeast Maya lowlands: Two case studies at Copán, Honduras. *Latin American Antiquity* 6: 129–44.

———. 1999. *Ancient Maya State, Urbanism, Exchange, and Craft Specialization: Chipped Stone Evidence from the Copán Valley and the La Entrada Region, Honduras.* University of Pittsburgh Memoirs in Latin American Archaeology No. 12. Pittsburgh: University of Pittsburgh Press.

———. 2001. Classic Maya state, urbanism, and exchange: Chipped stone evidence of the Copán Valley and its hinterland. *American Anthropologist* 103: 346–60.

———. 2006. Análisis de lítica. In E. Ponciano, T. Inomata and D. Triadan (eds.), *Informe del Proyecto Arqueológico Ceibal-Petexbatun: La Temporada de Campo 2006, 6.1–6.14.* Report presented to the Instituto de Antropología e Historia de Guatemala.

———. 2007. Elite artists and craft producers in Classic Maya society: Lithic evidence from Aguateca, Guatemala. *Latin American Antiquity* 18: 3–26.

Archer, M. S. 1988. *Culture and Agency: The Place of Culture in Social Theory*. Cambridge: Cambridge University Press.

Ardren, T. 2006. Is "Apocalypto" pornography? *Archaeology Online Reviews* http://www.archaeology.org/online/reviews/apocalypto.html. Accessed April 15, 2008.

Arellano Hernández, A., Ayala Falcón, M., de la Fuente, B., de la Garza, M., Stines Cicero, L., and Olmedo Vera, B. 1999. *The Mayas of the Classic Period*. Milan: Editoriale Jaca.

Armstrong, C. A. J. 1977. The Golden Age of Burgundy: dukes that outdid kings. In A. G. Dickens (ed.), *The Courts of Europe: Politics, Patronage, and Royalty, 1400–1800*, 55–75. London: Thames and Hudson.

Arnauld, M.-C. and Lacadena, A. 2004. Asentar su autoridad: Banquetas en el Grupo B de Río Bec (Campeche, México). *Journal de la Société des Américanistes* 90(1): 203–22.

Arnold, P. J. III. 2000 Sociopolitical complexity and the gulf Olmecs: A wiew from the Tuxtla mountains, Veracruz, Mexico. In J. Clark and M. Pye (eds.), *Olmec Art and Archaeology in Mesoamerica*, 117–35. National Gallery of Art, Washington DC.

Arroyo, B., Pereira, K., Cossich, M., Paiz, L., Arévalo, E., de León, E., Alvarado, C., and Quiroa, F. 2007. Proyecto de Rescate Naranjo: Nuevos datos del Preclásico en el Valle de Guatemala. In J. P. Laporte, B. Arroyo, and H. Mejía (eds.), *XX Simposio de Investigaciones Arqueologicas en Guatemala, 2007*, 861–74. Guatemala: Ministerio de Cultura y Deportes, Instituto de Antropología e Historia, and the Asociación Tikal.

Ashmore, W. and Sabloff, J. A. 2002. Spatial Orders in Maya Civic Plans. *Latin American Antiquity* 13: 201–15.

Ashmore, W., Yaeger, J., and Robin, C. 2004. Commoner sense: Late and Terminal Classic social strategies in the Xunantunich area. In A. A. Demarest, P. M. Rice, and D. S. Rice (eds.), *The Terminal Classic in the Maya Lowlands: Collapse, Transition, and Transformation*, 302–23. Boulder: University Press of Colorado.

Atran, S. 1993. Itza Maya Tropical Agro-Forestry. *Current Anthropology* 34: 633–700.

Aveni, A. and Hartung, H. 1986. *Maya City Planning and the Calendar*. Transactions of the American Philosophical Society 76(2). Philadelphia.

———. 1989. Uaxactun, Guatemala; Group E and similar assemblages: An archaeoastronomical reconsideration. In A. F. Aveni (ed.), *World Archaeoastronomy*, 441–61. Cambridge: Cambridge University Press.

Awe, J. J. 1992. *Dawn in the Land Between the Rivers: Formative Occupation at Cahal Pech, Belize, and Its Implications for Preclassic Development in the Maya Lowlands*. Ph.D. dissertation. University of London.

Awe, J. J., Campbell, M. D., Bill, C., and Cheetham, D. T. 1990. Early Middle Formative occupation in the Central Maya lowlands: Recent evidence from Cahal Pech, Belize. *Papers from the Institute of Archaeology* 1: 1–16. London: University of London, Institute of Archaeology.

Awe, J. J. and Healy, P. F. 1994. Flakes to blades?: Middle Formative development of obsidian artifacts in the Upper Belize River Valley. *Latin American Antiquity* 5: 193–205.

Awe, J. J., Griffith, C., and Gibbs, S. 2005. Cave stelae and megalithic monuments in western Belize. In J. E. Brady and K. M. Prufer 2005: 223–48.

Bachand, B. R. 2006. *Preclassic Excavations at Punta de Chimino, Petén, Guatemala: Investigating Social Emplacement on an Early Maya Landscape*. Ph.D. dissertation. University of Arizona.

Bachand, B. R., Inomata, T., and Castañeda Tobar, J. F. 2005. Excavación en La Plaza Sur de Ceibal: Operación 200A. In E. M. Ponciano, D. Triadan and T. Inomata (eds.), *Informe del Proyecto Arqueológico Aguateca Segunda Fase: La Temporada de Campo de 2005*, 19.1–19.8. Report presented to the Instituto de Antropología e Historia de Guatemala.

Bachand, B.R., Lowe, L.S., and Gallaga Murieta, E. 2008. Un reencuentro con Chiapa de Corzo: Rescatando y aumentando los datos de un centro mayor mesoamericano. Paper presented at the Simposio de Arqueología Guatemalteca.

Bailey, F. G. 1981. Spiritual merit and morality. In A. C. Mayer (ed.), *Culture and Morality: Essays in Honour of Christoph von Fürer-Haimendorf*, 23–41. Delhi: Oxford University Press.

Baillie, H. M. 1967. Etiquette and the planning of state apartments in baroque palaces. *Archaeologia* 101: 169–199.

Baines, J. and Yoffee, N. 1998. Order, legitimacy, and wealth in ancient Egypt and Mesopotamia. In G. M. Feinman and J. Marcus (eds.), *Archaic States*, 199–260. Santa Fe: School of American Research Press.

———. 2000. Order, legitimacy, and wealth: setting the terms. In J. E. Richards and M. Van Buren (eds.), *Order, Legitimacy and Wealth in Ancient States*, 13–17. Cambridge: Cambridge University Press.

Bakhtin, M. 1984. *Problems of Dostoevsky's Poetics*. Minneapolis: University of Minnesota Press.

Ball, J. W. 1977. The rise of the northern Maya chiefdoms: A socioprocessual analysis. In R. E. W. Adams (ed.), *The Origins of Maya Civilization*, 101–32. Albuquerque: University of New Mexico Press.

———. 1978. *Archaeological Pottery of the Yucatan-Campeche Coast*. Middle American Research Institute, Pub. 46. New Orleans: Tulane University.

———. 1979. Ceramics, culutre history, and the Puuc tradition: some alternative possibilities. In L. Mills (ed.), *The Puuc: New Perspectives*, 18–35. Pella, IA: Central College.

———. 1983. Teotihuacan, the Maya, and ceramic interchange: A contextual perspective. In A. G. Miller (ed.), *Highland-Lowland Interaction in Mesoamerica: Interdisciplinary Approaches*, 125–45. Washington DC: Dumbarton Oaks.

———. 1993. Pottery, potters, palaces, and polities: some socioeconomic and political implications of Late Classic Maya ceramic industries. In J. A. Sabloff and J. S. Henderson (eds.), *Lowland Maya Civilization in the Eighth Century A.D.*, 243–72. Washington DC: Dumbarton Oaks.

Ball, J. W. and Taschek, J. T. 2001. The Buenavista-Cahal Pech royal court: Multi-palace court mobility and usage in a petty lowland Maya kingdom. In T. Inomata and S. D. Houston (eds.), *Royal Courts of the Ancient Maya, Vol. 2: Data and Case Studies*, 165–200. Boulder: Westview Press.

———. 2003. Reconsidering the Belize Valley Preclassic: A case for multiethnic interactions in the development of a regional cultural tradition. *Ancient Mesoamerica* 14: 179–217.

———. 2007. 'Mixed Deposits,' 'Composite Complexes,' or 'Hybrid Assemblages?' A fresh reexamination of Middle Preclassic (Formative) ceramics and ceramic assemblages from the northern Maya lowlands. In L. S. Lowe and M. E. Pye (eds.), *Archaeology, Art, and Ethnogenesis in Mesoamerican Prehistory: Papers in Honor of Gareth W. Lowe*, 173–91. Papers of the New World Archaeological Foundation, 68. Provo: Brigham Young University.

Barba, L. A. and Manzanilla, L. 1987. Estudio de áreas de actividad. In L. Manzanilla (ed.), *Coba, Quintana Roo: Análisis de dos unidades habitacionales Mayas*, 69–116. Universidad Nacional Autónoma de Mexico, Mexico.

Barrera Vásquez, A. 1980. *Diccionario Maya Cordemex, Maya-Español, Español-Maya*. Mérida, Yucatán: Ediciones Cordemex.

Barrientos, T. 1997. Evolución tecnológica y sistema de canales hidráulicos en Kaminaljuyú y sus implicaciones sociopolíticas. In J. Pedro Laporte and H. L. Escobedo (eds.), *X Simposio de Investigaciones Arqueológicas en Guatemala, 1996*, 61–9. Guatemala: Ministerio de Cultura y Deportes, Museo Nacional de Arqueología e Etnología.

Barth, F. 1960. *Ethnic Groups and Boundaries*. Boston: Little, Brown.

Baudez, C.-F. 2002. *Une histoire de la religion des Mayas: Du panthéisme au panthéon*. Paris: Éditions Albin Michel.

Beach, T., Luzzadder-Beach, S., and Dunning, N. 2008. Human and natural impacts on fluvial and karst systems of the Maya lowlands. Paper presented at 39th International Binghamton Geomorphology Symposium, University of Texas, Austin.

Beach, T., Dunning, N., Luzzadder-Beach, S., Lohse, J., and D. Cook. 2006. Ancient Maya impacts on soils and soil erosion. *Catena* 66(2): 166–78.

Beach, T., Luzzadder-Beach, S., Dunning, N., Jones, J., Lohse, J., Guderjan, T., Bozarth, S. Millspaugh, S., and Bhattacharya, T. n.d. A review of human and natural changes in Maya lowlands wetlands over the Holocene. *Quaternary Science Reviews*.

Beard, M., North, J., and Price, S. 1998. *Religions of Rome: Volume I, A History*. Cambridge: Cambridge University Press.

Beaudry-Corbett, M. and McCafferty, S. 2002. Spindle whorls: household specialization at

Ceren. In T. Ardren (ed.), *Ancient Maya Women*, 52–67. Walnut Creek: AltaMira Press.

Becker, M. J. 1971. *The Identification of a Second Plaza Plan at Tikal, Guatemala, and Its Implications for Ancient Maya Social Complexity*. Ph.D. dissertation. University of Pennsylvania.

———. 1999. *Excavations in Residential Areas of Tikal: Groups with Shrines*. Tikal Report 21. Philadelphia: University Museum, University of Pennsylvania.

Becquelin, P., and Baudez, C. F. 1982. *Tonina: Une cite Maya du Chiapas (Mexique)*. Vol. III. Mexico: Centre d'études mexicaines et centraméricaines.

Becquelin, P., and Taladoire, E. 1990. *Tonina: Une cite Maya du Chiapas (Mexique)*. Vol. IV. Mexico: Centre d'études mexicaines et centraméricaines.

Beekman, C. S. 1992. A case of regional specialization in a quarry from the Río Santa Amelia Region, Guatemala. *Mexicon* 14: 98–102.

Beidelman, T. O. 1986. *Moral Imagination in Kaguru Modes of Thought*. Bloomington: Indiana University Press.

Beliaev, D. 2000. Wuk Tsuk and Oxlahun Tsuk: Naranjo and Tikal in the Late Classic in The Sacred and the Profane: Architecture and identity in the Maya lowlands. In P. R. Colas, K. Delvendahl, M. Kuhnert, and A. Schubart (eds.), 63–82. Acta Mesoamericana 10. Markt Schwaben: Verlag Anton Saurwein.

Bell, C. 1992. *Ritual theory, ritual practice*. Oxford University Press, Oxford.

Bell, E. E. 2007. *Early Classic Ritual Deposits within the Copan Acropolis: The Material Foundations of Political Power at a Classic Period Maya Center*. Ph.D. dissertation. Department of Anthropology, University of Pennsylvania.

Bell, E. E., Sharer, R. J., Traxler, L. P., Sedat, D. W., Carrelli, C. W., and Grant, L. A. 2004. Tombs and burials in the Early Classic acropolis at Copan. In E. E. Bell, M. A. Canuto, and R. J. Sharer (eds.), *Understanding Early Classic Copan*, 131–58. Philadelphia: University of Pennsylvania Museum.

Belting, H. 1994. *Likeness and Presence: A History of the Image Before the Era of Art*. Chicago: University of Chicago Press.

Benavides Castillo, A. 1997. *Edzná: A Precolumbian City in Campeche*. Mexico: Instituto Nacional de Antropología e Historia.

———. 2007. Jaina, Campeche: Panorama general en 2003. *Anales de Arqueología 2005*: 49–53.

Bender, T. 1978. *Community and Social Change in America*. New Brunswick: Rutgers University Press.

Becquelin, P. and Baudez, C. F. 1982. *Tonina, Une cité maya du Chiapas (Mexique)*. 3 vols. Paris: Editions Recherche sur les civilisations.

Berdan, F. F., Masson, M. A., Gasco, J., and Smith, M. E. 2003. An international economy. In M. E. Smith and F. F. Berdan (eds.), *The Postclassic Mesoamerican World*, 96–109. Salt Lake City: University of Utah Press.

Berlin, H. and Kelley, D. H. 1961. 819-day count and color-direction symbolism among the Classic Maya. In Archaeological Studies in Middle America, 9–20. Publication, 26. Tulane University, Middle American Research Institute, New Orleans.

Bey, G. J., III, Bond, T. M., Ringle, W. M., Hanson, C. A., Houck, C. W., and Carlos Peraza L. 1998. The ceramic chronology of Ek Balam, Yucatan, Mexico. *Ancient Mesoamerica* 9: 101–120.

Bey, G. J., III and W. M. Ringle. 2007. From the bottom up: The timing and nature of the Tula-Chichén Itzá exchange. In J. K. Kowalski and C. Kristan-Graham (eds.), *Twin Tollans: Chichén Itzá, Tula, and the Epiclassic to Early Postclassic Mesoamerican World*, 377–428. Washington DC: Dunbarton Oaks Research Library and Collection.

Billacois, F. 1990. *The Duel: Its Rise and Fall in Early Modern France*. New Haven: Yale University Press.

Binski, P. 1996. *Medieval Death: Ritual and Representation*. London: British Museum.

Bishop, R. L., Sears, E. L., and Blackman, J. M. 2005. A traves del río del cambio. *Estudios de cultura maya* 27: 17–40.

Bishop, R. L., and Rands, R. L. 1982. Maya fine paste ceramics: A compositional perspective. In J. A. Sabloff (ed.), *Excavations at Seibal: Analyses of Fine Paste Ceramics*, 283–314. Memoirs of the Peabody Museum of Archaeology and Ethnology, Vol. 15, No. 2. Cambridge: Harvard University Press.

Black, S. 1990. The Carnegie Uaxactún Project and the development of Maya archaeology. *Ancient Mesoamerica* 1(2): 257–76.

Blake, M. 1991. An emerging Formative Chiefdom at Paso de la Amada, Chiapas, Mexico. In W. L. Fowler (ed.), *The Formation of Complex Society in Southeastern Mesoamerica*, 27–46. Boca Raton: CRC Press.

Blake, M., Chisholm, B., Clark, J. E., Voorhies, B., and Love, M. 1992. Prehistoric subsistence in the Soconusco region. *Current Anthropology* 33: 83–94.

Blake, M. and Clark, J. E. 1999. The emergence of hereditary inequality: The case of pacific coastal Chiapas, Mexico. In M. Blake (ed.), *Pacific Latin America in Prehistory: The Evolution of Archaic and Formative Cultures*, 55–73. Pullman: Washington State University Press.

Blanton, R. E. 1994. *Houses and Households: A Comparative Study*. New York: Plenum Press.

Blanton, R. E., Feinman, G. M., Kowalewski, S. A., and Peregrine, P. N. 1996. A dual-processual theory for the evolution of Meso-american civilization. *Current Anthropology* 37: 1–14.

Blier, S. P. 1995. *African Vodun: Art, Psychology, and Power*. Chicago: University of Chicago Press.

Bloch, M. 1974. Symbols, song, dance and features of articulation. *Archives européenes de sociologie* 15: 55–81.

———. 1983. *Marxism and Anthropology*. Oxford: Clarendon Press.

———. 1985. The ritual of the royal bath in Madagascar: The dissolution of death, birth, and fertility into authority. In D. Cannadine and S. Price (eds.), *Rituals of Royalty: Power and Ceremonial in Traditional Society*, 271–97. Cambridge: Cambridge University Press.

Block, M. and Parry, J. 1982. Introduction: death and the regeneration of life. In M. Bloch and J. Parry (eds.), *Death and the Regeneration of Life*, 1–44. Cambridge: Cambridge University Press.

Blom, F. 1924. Report on the preliminary work at Uaxactun, Guatemala. *Carnegie Institution of Washington Year Book* 23: 217–219. Washington DC.

Blomster, J. P., Neff, H., and Glascock, M. D. 2005. Olmec pottery production and export in ancient Mexico determined through elemental analysis. *Science* 307: 1068–72.

Boone, S. A. 1986. *Radiance from the Waters: Ideals of Feminine Beauty and Mende Art*. New Haven: Yale University Press.

Boremanse, D. 1998. *Hach Winik: The Lacandon Maya of Chiapas, Southern Mexico*. Institute for Mesoamerican Studies, Monograph 11. Albany: The University at Albany.

Borhegyi, S. F. de. 1956. The development of folk and complex cultures in the southern Maya area. *American Antiquity* 21: 343–56.

Bottomore, T. B. 1964. *Elites and Society*. New York: Basic Books.

Boucher, S., and Quiñones, L. 2007. Entre mercadoes, ferias y festines: Los murales de la Sub 1–4 de Chiik Nahb, Calakmul. *Mayab* 19: 27–50.

Bourdieu, P. 1966. The sentiment of honour in Kabyle society. In J. G. Peristiany (ed.), *Honour and Shame: The Values of Mediterranean Society*, 191–241. Chicago: University of Chicago Press.

———. 1984. *Distinction: A Social Critique of the Judgement of Taste*. Cambridge: Harvard University Press.

———. 1990. *The Logic of Practice*. Stanford: Stanford University Press.

Bourdieu, P. and Passeron, J.-C. 1990. *Reproduction in Education, Society and Culture*. Sage: London.

Bourne, J. 2001. *Recollections of My Early Travels in Chiapas: Discoveries at Oxlahuntun (el Perro), Miguel Angel Fernandez, Bonampak, and Lacanhá*. http://www.mesoweb.com/publications/Bourne/Recollections.pdf. Accessed April 15, 2008.

Bove, F. J. 1981. Trend surface analysis and the lowland Classic Maya collapse. *American Antiquity* 46: 93–112.

Bove, F. J. 1991. The Teotihuacán-Kaminaljuyu-Tikal Connection: A view from the south coast of Guatemala. In V. M. Fields (ed.), *Sixth Palenque Round Table, 1986*, 135–42. Norman: University of Oklahoma Press.

Bove, F. J. and Medrano Busto, S. 2003. Teotihuacan, militarism, and pacific Guatemala. In G. E. Braswell (ed.), *The Maya and Teotihuacan: Reinterpreting Early Classic Interpretation*, 45–80. Austin: University of Texas Press.

Boyden, J. M. 1995. *The Courtier and the King: Ruy Gomez de Silva, Philip II, and the Court of Spain*. Berkeley: University of California Press.

Brady, J. E. 1997. Settlement configuration and cosmology: The role of caves at Dos Pilas. *American Anthropologist* 99: 602–18.

Brady, J. E., Ball, J. W., Bishop, R. L., Pring, D. C., Hammond, N., and Housley, R. A. 1998. The lowland Maya "Protoclassic": A reconsideration of its nature and significance. *Ancient Mesoamerica* 9: 17–38.

Brady, J. E., Cobb, A. B., Garza, S., Espinoza, C., and Burnett, R. 2005. An analysis of ancient Maya stalactite breakage at Balam Na Cave, Guatemala. *In Prufer and Brady* 2005: 213–24.

Brady, J. E. and Prufer, K. M. 1999. Caves and crstyalmancy: evidence for the use of crystals in ancient Maya religion. *Journal of Anthropological Research* 55: 129–144.

——— (eds.) 2005. *In the Maw of the Earth Monster: Mesoamerican Ritual Cave Use.* Austin: University of Texas Press.

Brady, J. E. and Rissolo, D. 2006. A reappraisal of ancient Maya cave mining. *Journal of Anthropological Research* 62(4): 471–90.

Brainerd, G. W. 1958. *The Archaeological Ceramics of Yucatan.* University of California Anthropological Records 19. Berkeley.

Braswell, G. E. Braswell, G. E. 1992. Obsidian-hydration dating, the Coner phase, and revisionist chronology at Copán, Honduras. *Latin American Antiquity* 3: 130–47.

———. 2001. Post-Classic Maya courts of the Guatemalan highlands: Archaeological and ethnohistorical approaches. In T. Inomata and S. D. Houston (eds.), *Royal Courts of the Ancient Maya, Vol. 2: Data and Case Studies,* 308–34. Boulder: Westview Press.

———. 2003. Introduction: Reinterpreting Early Classic interaction. In G. E. Braswell (ed.), *The Maya and Teotihuacan: Reinterpreting Early Classic Interaction,* 1–44. Austin: University of Texas Press.

Braswell, G. E., Gunn, J. D., del Rosario Domínguez Carrasco, M., Folan, W. J., Fletcher, L. A., Morales López, A., and Glascock, M. D. 2004. Defining the Terminal Classic at Calakmul, Campeche. In A. A. Demarest, P. M. Rice, and D. S. Rice (eds.), *The Terminal Classic in the Maya Lowlands: Collapse, Transition, and Transformation,* 162–94. Boulder: University Press of Colorado.

Braudel, F. 1981. *Civilization and Capitalism, 15th-18th Century.* New York: Harper & Row.

Bray, W. 1977. Maya metalwork and its external connections. In N. Hammond (ed.), *Social Process in Maya Prehistory: Studies in Honour of Sir Eric Thompson,* 365–403. London: Academic Press.

Brenner, M. 1983. Paleolimnology of the Petén Lake District, Guatemala, II: Mayan population density and sediment and nutrient loading of Lake Quexil. *Hydrobiologia* 103: 205–10.

Brenner, M., Leyden, B., and Binford, M. W. 1990. Recent sedimentary histories of shallow lakes in the Guatemala savanna. *Journal of Paleolimnology* 4: 239–52.

Brenner, M., Rosenmeier, M. F., Hodell, D. A., and Curtis, J. H. 2002. Paleolimnology of the Maya lowlands: Long-term perspectives on interactions among climate, environmental, and humans. *Ancient Mesoamerica* 13: 141–57.

Bricker, H. M., Aveni, A. F., and Bricker, V. R. 2001. Ancient Maya documents concerning the movements of Mars. *Proceedings of the National Academy of Sciences* 98(4): 2107–10.

Bricker, V. R. 1973. *Ritual Humor in Highland Chiapas.* University of Texas Press, Austin.

———. 1981. *The Indian Christ, the Indian King: The Historical Substrate of Maya Myth and Ritual.* Austin: University of Texas Press.

Bricker, V. R. and Miram, H.-M. 2002. *An Encounter of Two Worlds: The Book of Chilam Balam of Kaua.* Middle American Research Institute Publication 68. New Orleans: Tulane University.

Brown, J., and Eliott, J. H. 1980. *A Palace for a King: The Buen Retiro and the Court of Philip IV.* New Haven: Yale University Press.

Brown, L. and Sheets, P. 2000. Distinguishing domestic from ceremonial structures in southern Mesoamerica: Suggestions from Cerén, El Salvador. *Mayab* 13: 11–21.

Brumfiel, E., and Earle, T. 1987. Specialization, exchange, and complex societies: An introduction. In E. Brumfiel and T. Earle (eds.), *Specialization, Exchange, and Complex Societies,* 1–9. Cambridge: Cambridge University Press.

Bryant, D. D. and Clark, J. E. 1983. Los primeros mayas precolombinos de la cuenca superior del Río Grijalva. In L. Ochoa and T. A. Lee, Jr (eds.), *Homenaje a Frans Blom: Antropología e Historia de los Mixe-Zoques y Mayas,* 223–39. México, D.F.: Universidad Nacional Autónoma de México, Centro de Estudios Mayas.

Bryant, D. D., Clark, J. E., and D. Cheetham. 2005. *Ceramic Sequence of the Upper Grijalva Region, Chiapas, Mexico.* Papers of the New World Archaeological Foundation, No. 67. Provo, Utah: Brigham Young University.

Buber, M. 1949. *Paths in Utopia.* London: Routledge and Kegan Paul.

Buikstra, J., Price, T. D., Wright, L. E., and Burton, J. 2004. Tombs from the Copan acropolis:

A life history approach. In E. E. Bell, M. A. Canuto and R. J. Sharer (eds.), *Understanding Early Classic Copan*, 191–214. Philadelphia: University of Pennsylvania Museum of Archaeology and Anthropology.

Bujra, J. M. 1973. The dynamics of political action: A new look at factionalism. *American Anthropologist* 75: 132–52.

Burke, P. 1990. *The Fortunes of the Courtier: The European Reception of Castiglione's* Cortegiano. London: Polity Press.

———. 1992. *The Fabrication of Louis XIV*. New Haven: Yale University Press.

Burkert, W. 1996. *Creation of the Sacred: Tracks of Biology in Early Religions*. Cambridge: Harvard University Press.

Burkhart, L. M. 1989. *The Slippery Earth: Nahua-Christian Moral Dialogue in Sixteenth-Century Mexico*. Tucson: University of Arizona Press.

———. 1992. Mujeres mexicas en "el frente" del hogar: Trabajo doméstico y religión en el México azteca. *Mésoamerica* 23: 23–54.

Burridge, K. 1979. *Someone, No One: An Essay on Individuality*. Princeton: Princeton University Press.

Butler, J. 1999. *Gender Trouble: Feminism and the Subversion of Identity*. New York: Routledge.

Byland, B. E. and Pohl, J. M. D. 1994. *In the Realm of 8-Deer: The Archaeology of Mixtec Codices*. Norman: University of Oklahoma Press.

Byock, J. 1982. *Feud in Icelandic Saga*. Berkeley: University of California Press.

Calnek, Edward E. 1988. *Highland Chiapas Before the Spanish Conquest*. Papers, 55. Provo: Brigham Young University, New World Archaeological Foundation.

Calvin, I. 1997. Where the *Wayob* live: A further examination of Classic Maya supernaturals. In J. Kerr (ed.), *The Maya Vase Book: A Corpus of Rollout Photographs of Maya Vases*, Volume 5, 868–883. New York: Kerr Associates.

Camille, M. 1998. *The Medieval Art of Love: Objects and Subjects of Desire*. New York: Abrams.

Campbell, L. R. 1984. The implications of Mayan historical linguistics for glyphic research. In J. S. Justeson and L. Campbell (eds.), *Phoneticism in Mayan Hieroglyphic Writing*, 1–16. Institute for Mesoamerican Studies, SUNY, Publication 9. Albany.

———. 1988. Source on day names as anmes. In *Linguistics of Southeast Chiapas, Mexico*. New World Archaeological Foundation Papers, 50. Provo: Brigham Young University.

Campbell, L. R. and Kaufman, T. S. 1976. A linguistic look at the Olmecs. *American Antiquity* 41: 80–9.

Cannadine, D. 1999. *The Decline and Fall of the British Aristocracy*. New York: Vintage.

———. 2001. *Ornamentalism: How the British Saw their Empire*. Oxford: Oxford University Press.

Carlsen, R. S. and Prechtel, M. 1991. The flowering of the dead: An interpretation of highland Maya Culture. *Man* 26: 23–42.

Carmack, R. M. 1981. *The Quiché Mayas of Utatlán: The Evolution of a Highland Maya Kingdom*. Norman: University of Oklahoma Press.

Carmean, K., Dunning, N., and Kowalski, J. K. 2004. High times in the hill country: A perspective from the Terminal Classic Puuc region. In A. A. Demarest, P. M. Rice and D. S. Rice (eds.), *The Terminal Classic in the Maya Lowlands: Collapse, Transition, and Transformation*, 424–49. Boulder: University Press of Colorado.

Carrasco, D. 1995. Cosmic jaws: We eat the gods and the gods eat us. *Journal of the American Academy of Religion* 63(3): 429–63.

Carrasco Vargas, R. 2005. The sacred mountain: Preclassic architecture in Calakmul. In V. M. Fields and D. Reents-Budet (eds.), *Lords of Creation: The Origins of Sacred Maya Kingship*, 62–6. Los Angeles: Los Angeles County Museum of Art.

Cartwright Gerhardt, J. and Hammond, N. 1991. The community of Cuello: The ceremonial core. In N. Hammond (ed.), *Cuello: An Early Maya Community in Belize*, 98–117. Cambridge: Cambridge University Press.

de las Casas, B. 1951. *Historia de las Indias, tomo II*. México: Fondo de Cultura Económica.

Castañeda, Q. 1996. *In the Museum of Maya Culture: Touring Chichén Itzá*. Minneapolis: University of Minnesota Press.

Castillo, T (ed.) 1999. *Yaxhá: Laguna encantada: Naturaleza, arqueología y conservación*. Guatemala: Editorial de Fundación G y T.

Chase, A. F. 1985. Troubled times: The archaeology and iconography of the Terminal Classic southern lowland Maya. In M. G. Robertson and V. M. Fields, *Fifth Palenque Round Table, 1983*, 103–114. San Francisco: Pre-Columbian Art Research Institute.

Chase, A. F. and Chase, D. Z. 1989. Investigation of Classic Period Maya warfare at Caracol, Belize. *Mayab*: 5–18.

———. 1994a. Details in the archaeology of Caracol, Belize: An introduction. In D. Z. Chase and A. F. Chase (eds.), *Studies in the Archaeology of Caracol, Belize*, 1–11. Pre-Columbian art Research Institute Monograph 7. San Francisco.

———. 1994b. Maya veneration of the dead at Caracol, Belize. In V. M. Fields (ed.), *Seventh Palenque Round Table, 1989*, 53–60. San Francisco: Pre-Columbian Art Research Institute.

———. 1995. External impetus, internal synthesis, and standardization: E Group assemblages and the crystalization of Classic Maya society in the southern lowlands. In Nikolai Grube (ed.), *The Emergence of Lowland Maya Civilization: The Transition from the Preclassic to the Early Classic*, 87–102. Acta Mesoamerican 8. Markt Schwaben: Verlag Anton Saurwein.

———. 1996a. A mighty Maya nation: How Caracol built an empire by cultivating its middle class. *Archaeology* 49(5): 66–72.

———. 1996b. More than kin and king: Centralized political organization among the Late Classic Maya. *Current Anthropology* 37: 803–10.

———. 2001. The royal court of Caracol, Belize: Its palaces and people. In T. Inomata and S. D. Houston (eds.), *Royal Courts of the Ancient Maya, Vol.2: Data and Case Studies*, 102–37. Boulder: Westview Press.

———. 2004. Terminal Classic status-linked ceramics and the Maya collapse: De facto refuse at Caracol, Belize. In A. A. Demarest, P. M. Rice and D. S. Rice (eds.), *The Terminal Classic in the Maya Lowlands: Collapse, Transition, and Transformation*, 342–66. Boulder: University Press of Colorado.

Chase, A. F., Grube, N., and Chase, D. Z. 1991. *Three Terminal Classic Monuments from Caracol, Belize*. Research Reports on Ancient Maya Writing 36. Washington DC: Center for Maya Research.

Chase, A. F. and Rice, P. M. 1985. *Introduction*. In A. F. Chase and P. M. Rice (eds.), *The Lowland Maya Postclassic*, 1–8. Austin: University of Texas Press.

Chase, A.F., Chase, D.Z., Zorn, E., and Teeter, W. 2008. Textiles and the Maya Archaeological Record: Gender, Power, and Status in Classic Period Caracol, Belize. *Ancient Mesoamerica* 19: 137–42.

Chase, D. Z. and Chase, A. F. 1992. Mesoamerican elites: Assumptions, definitions, and models. In D. Z. Chase and A. F. Chase (eds.), *Mesoamerican Elites: An Archaeological Assessment*, 3–17. Norman: University of Oklahoma Press.

———. 1996. Maya Multiples: Individuals, entries, and tombs in structure A34 of Caracol, Belize. *Latin American Antiquity* 7(1): 61–79.

———. 1998. The architectural context of caches, burials, and other ritual activities for the Classic Maya period. In S. D. Houston (ed.), *Function and Meaning in Classic Maya Architecture*, 299–328. Washington DC: Dumbarton Oaks.

———. 2000. Inferences about abandonment: Maya household archaeology and Caracol, Belize. *Mayab* 13: 67–77.

———. 2002. Secular, sagrado y "revisitado": la profanación, alteración y reconsagración de los antiguos entierros mayas. In A. Cuidad Ruiz, M. Humberto Ruz Sosa, and M. Josefa Iglesias Ponce de Leó (eds.), *Antropología de la eternidad: La muerte en la cultura maya*, 255–78. Madrid: Sociedad Española de Estudios Mayas.

———. 2004. Hermeneutics, transitions, and transformations in Classic to Postclassic Maya society. In A. A. Demarest, P. M. Rice and D. S. Rice (eds.), *The Terminal Classic in the Maya Lowlands: Collapse, Transition, and Transformation*, 12–27. Boulder: University Press of Colorado.

Chayanov, A. V. 1986. *The Theory of Peasant Economy*. Madison: University of Wisconsin Press.

Cheetham, D. 1998. *Interregional Interaction, Symbolic Emulation, and the Emergence of Socio-Political Inequality in the Maya Lowlands*. M.A. thesis. University of British Columbia.

———. 2005. Cunil: A pre-Mamom horizon in the southern Maya lowlands. In T. G. Powis (ed.), *New perspectives on Formative Mesoamerican cultures*, 27–38. BAR International Series 1377. Oxford.

Cheetham, D. and Awe, J. J. 1996. The Early Formative Cunil ceramic complex at Cahal Pech, Belize. Paper presented at the 61st Annual Meeting of the Society for American Archaeology, New Orleans.

Cheetham, D., Forsyth, D. W., and Clark, J. E. 2003. La cerámica pre-Mamom de la Cuenca del Río Belice y del centro de Petén: Las correspondencias y sus implicaciones. In

J. P. Laporte, B. Arroyo, H. L. Escobedo, and H. E. Mejía (eds.), *XVI Simposio de Investigaciones Arqueológicas en Guatemala*, 615–34. Guatemala: Ministerio de Cultura y Deportes, Instituto de Antropología e Historia, and the Asociación Tikal.

Child, M. B. 2006. *The Archaeology of Religious Movements: The Maya Sweatbath Cult of Piedras Negras*. Ph.D. dissertation. Department of Anthropology, Yale University.

Chimalpahin Cuauhtlehuanitzin, D. F. de San Antón Muñón. 1965. *Relaciones Originales de Chalco Amaquemeca*. Silvia Rendón, trans. México: Fondo de Cultura Económica.

Chinchilla Mazariegos, O. 2005. Cosmos and warfare on a Classic Maya vase. *RES: Anthropology and Aesthetics* 47: 107–34.

Chinchilla Mazariegos, O. and Houston, S. 1993. Historia política de la zona de Piedras Negras: Las inscripciones de El Cayo. In *Simposio de Investigaciones Arqueológicas en Guatemala*, 63–70. Guatemala: Ministerio de Cultura y Deportes, Instituto de Antropología e Historia/Asociación Tikal.

Christenson, A. J. 2000. *Popol Vuh: The Mythic Sections–Tales of First Beginnings from the Ancient K'iche'-Maya*. Ancient Texts and Mormon Studies, No. 2. Provo: Foundation for Ancient Research and Mormon Studies.

———. 2001. *Art and Society in a Highland Maya Community: The Altarpiece of Santiago Atitlán*. Austin: University of Texas Press.

———. 2003. *Popol Vuh*. London: Allen Bell.

———. 2007. *Popol Vuh: Sacred Book of the Ancient Maya*. Provo: Center for the Preservation of Ancient Religious Texts, Brigham Young University.

Ciudad Ruiz, A. 2000. Después del fuego: El uso del espacio en una unidad habitacional del Clásico Tardío en Guatemala. *Mayab* 13:34–45.

Ciudad Ruiz, A. and Lacadena García-Gallo, A. 2006. La fundación de Machaquilá, Petén, en el Clásico Tardío maya. In M. J. Iglesias Ponce de León, R. Valencia Rivera, and A. Ciudad Ruiz (eds.), *Nuevas ciudades, nuevas patrias: Fundación y relocalización de ciudades en Mesoamérica y el Mediterráneo antiguo*, 149–80. Madrid: Sociedad Española de Estudios Mayas.

Clark, J. E. 1986. From mountains to molehills: A critical review of Teotihuacan's obsidian industry. In B. L. Isaac (ed.), *Economic Aspects of Prehispanic Highland Mexico*, pp. 23–74 Research in Economic Anthropology, 2 Greenwich: JAI Press.

———. 1987. Politics, prismatic blades, and mesoamerican civilization. In K. K. Johnson and C. A. Morrow (eds.), *The Organization of Core Technology*, 259–84. Boulder: Westview Press.

———. 1988. *The Lithic Artifacts of La Libertad, Chiapas, Mexico: An Economic Perspective*. Papers of the New World Archaeological Foundation 52. Provo, Utah: Brigham Young University.

———. 1991. The beginnings of Mesoamerica: Apologia for the Soconusco Early Formative. In W. R. Fowler, Jr. (ed.), *The Formation of Complex Society in Southeastern Mesoamerica*, 13–16. Boca Raton: CRC Press.

——— (ed.). 1994. *Los Olmecas en Mesoamerica*. Mexico: Equilibrista.

———. 1995. Craft specialization as an archaeological category. In B. L. Isaac (ed.), *Research in economic anthropology*, Vol. 16, pp. 267–94. Greenwich, CT: JAI Press.

———. 1997. The Arts of Government in Early Mesoamerica. *Annual Review of Anthropology* 26: 211–34.

Clark, J. E. and Blake, M. 1994. The power of prestige: Competitive generosity and the emergence of rank societies in lowland Mesoamerica. In E. M. Brumfiel and J. W. Fox (eds.), *Factional Competition and Political Development in the New World*, 17–30. Cambridge: Cambridge University Press.

Clark, J. E. and Cheetham, D. 2002. Mesoamerica's tribal foundations. In W. A. Parkinson (ed.), *The Archaeology of Tribal Societies*, 278–339. Archaeological Series 15. Ann Arbor: International Monographs in Prehistory.

Clark, J. E. and Gosser, D. 1995. Reinventing Mesoamerica's first pottery. In W. K. Barnett and J. W. Hoopes (eds.), *The Emergence of Pottery: Technology and Innovation in Ancient Societies*, 209–21. Washington DC: Smithsonian Institution.

Clark, J. E. and Hansen, R. D. 2001. Architecture of early kingship: Comparative perspectives on the origins of the Maya royal court. In T. Inomata and S. D. Houston (eds.), *Royal Courts of the Ancient Maya: 2. Data and Case Studies*. 1–45. Boulder: Westview Press.

Clark, J. E., Hansen, R. D., and Pérez Suárez, T. 2000. La Zona Maya en el Preclásico. In

L. Manzanilla and L. López Luján (eds.), *Historia antigua de México, 2da ed., Volumen I: El México antiguo, sus áreas culturales, los orígenes y el horizonte Preclásico*, 437–510. México: Instituto Nacional de Antropología e Historia.

Clark, J. E. and Houston, S. 1998. Craft specialization, gender, and personhood among the post-conquest Maya of Yucatan, Mexico. In C. L. Costin and R. P. Wright (eds.), *Craft and Social Identity*, 31–46. Archaeological Papers of the American Anthropological Association, No. 8. Washington DC.

Clark, J. E. and Pye, M. E. 2000. The pacific coast and the Olmec question. In J. E. Clark and M. E. Pye (eds.), *Olmec Art and Archaeology in Mesoamerica*, 217–51. Washington DC: National Gallery of Art.

Clark, J. E., Pye, M. E., and Gosser, D. C. 2007. Termolithics and corn dependency in Mesoamerica. In L. S. Lowe and M. E. Pye (eds.), *Archaeology, Art, and Ethnogenesis in Mesoamerican Prehistory: Papers in Honor of Gareth W. Lowe*, 23–42. Papers of the New World Archaeological Foundation, 68. Provo: Brigham Young University.

Clarke, J. R. 1998. *Looking at Lovemaking: Constructions of Sexuality in Roman Art, 100 B.C. – A.D. 250*. Berkeley: University of California Press.

Clendinnen, I. 1987. *Ambivalent Conquests: Maya and Spaniard in Yucatan, 1517–1570*. Cambridge: Cambridge University Press.

Clifford, J. 1988. *The Predicament of Culture: Twentieth-Century Ethnography, Literature, and Art*. Cambridge: Harvard University Press.

Closs, M. P. 1992. *I Am a kahal; My Parents Were Scribes (Soy un kahal; mis padres fueron escribas)*. Research Reports on Ancinet Maya Writing 39. Washington DC: Center for Maya Research.

Cobos, R. 2003. Ancient community form and social complexity at Chichen Itza, Yucatan. In W. T. Sanders, A. Guadalupe Mastache, and R. H. Cobean (eds.), *El Urbanismo en Mesoamerica; Urbanism in Mesoamerica. Vol. 1*, 451–72. Mexico: Instituto Nacional de Antropología e Historia; University Park: Pennsylvania State University.

———. 2007. Multepal or centralized kingship? New evidence on governmental organization at Chichén Itzá. In J. K. Kowalski and C. Kristan-Graham (eds.), *Twin Tollans: Chichén Itzá, Tula, and the Epiclassic to Early Postclassic Mesoamerican World*, 315–44. Washington DC: Dunbarton Oaks Research Library and Collection.

Coe, M. D. 1965. The Olmec style and its distribution. In G. R. Willey (ed.), *Handbook of Middle American Indians*, Vol. 3. Austin: University of Texas.

———. 1966. *An Early Stone Pectoral from Southeastern Mexico*. Studies in Pre-Columbian Art & Archaeology 1. Washington DC: Dumbarton Oaks.

———. 1973. *The Maya Scribe and his World*. New York: Grolier Club.

———. 1975. *Classic Maya Pottery at Dumbarton Oaks*. Washington DC: Dumbarton Oaks.

———. 1976. Early steps in the evolution of Maya writing. In H. B. Nicholson (ed.), *Origins of Religious Art and Iconography in Preclassic Mesoamerica*, 107–22. Latin American Studies Series 31. Los Angeles: UCLA Latin American Center.

———. 1977a. Olmec and Maya: A study in relationships. In R. E. W. Adams (ed.), *The Origins of Maya Civilization*, 183–95. Albuquerque: University of New Mexico Press.

———. 1977b. Supernatural patrons of Maya scribes and artists. In N. Hammond (ed.), *Social Process in Maya Prehistory: Studies in Honour of Sir Eric Thompson*, 327–47. New York: Academic Press.

———. 1978. *Lords of the Underworld: Masterpieces of Classic Maya Ceramics*. Princeton: Art Museum, Princeton University.

———. 1981. San Lorenzo Tenochtitlán. In V. R. Bricker and J. A. Sabloff (eds.), *Supplement to the Handbook of Middle American Indians, Vol. 1: Archaeology*, 117–46. Austin: University of Texas Press.

———. 1982. *Old Gods and Young Heroes: The Pearlman Collection of Maya Ceramics*. Jerusalem: Israel Museum.

———. 1989. The hero twins: Myth and image. In J. Kerr (ed.), *The Maya Vase Book, Volume 1: A Corpus of Rollout Photographs of Maya Vases*, 161–84. New York: Kerr Associates.

———. 1990. Next door to Olympus: Reminiscences of a Harvard student. *Ancient Mesoamerica* 1: 253–55.

———. 1993. From huaquero to connoisseur: The early market in pre-Columbian art. In E. H. Boone (ed.), *Collecting the Pre-Columbian Past*, 279–81. Washington DC: Dumbarton Oaks.

————. 1999a. *Breaking the Maya Code: The Last Great Decipherment of An Ancient Script*. Rev. ed. New York: Thames and Hudson.

————. 1999b. *The Maya*. 6th edition. London: Thames and Hudson.

Coe, M. D. and Diehl, R. S. 1980. *In the Land of the Olmec*. 2 vols. Austin: University of Texas Press.

Coe, M. D. and Flannery, K. V. 1967. *Early Cultures and Human Ecology in South Coastal Guatemala*. Smithsonian Contributions to Anthropology, Vol. 3. Washington DC: Smithsonian Institution.

Coe, M. D. and Kerr, J. 1997. *The Art of the Maya Scribe*. New York: Harry N. Abrams.

Coe, S. D. 1994. *America's First Cuisines*. Austin: University of Texas Press.

Coe, S. D. and Coe, M. D. 1996. *The True History of Chocolate*. New York: Thames and Hudson.

Coe, W. R. 1959. *Piedras Negras Archaeology: Artifacts, Caches, and Burials*. Philadelphia: University of Pennsylvania, University Museum.

————. 1965. Tikal, Guatemala, and emergent Maya civilization. *Science* 147(3664): 1401–19.

————. 1990. *Excavations in the Great Plaza, North Terrace and North Acropolis of Tikal*. Tikal Report, 14. Philadelphia: University Museum, University of Pennsylvania.

Coggins, C. C. 1979. Teotihuacan at Tikal in the Early Classic Period. *Actes du XLIIe Congrès international des américanistes*, Vol. 8, pp. 251–69. Paris: Congrès international des américanistes.

———— (ed.) 1992. *Artifacts from the Cenote of Sacrifice, Chichén Itzá, Yucatán*. Memoirs of the Peabody Museum, Vol. 10., No. 3. Cambridge MA: Harvard University.

Cogolludo, D. L. de. 1971 [1654]. *Los tres siglos de la dominación española en Yucatán o sea historia de esta provincia*. 2 vols. Graz: Akademische Druck- und Verlangsanstalt.

Cohen, A. 1974. *Two Dimensional Man*. Berkeley: University of California Press.

————. 1981. *The Politics of Elite Culture: Explorations in the Dramaturgy of Power in a Modern African Society*. Berkeley: University of California Press.

Cohen, A. P. 1985. *The Symbolic Construction of Community*. Chichester: Harwood.

Colas, P. R. 2004. *Sinn und Bedeutung klassicher Maya-Personennamen: Typologische Analyse von Anthroponymphrasen in den Hieroglypheninschriften der klassischen Maya-Kultur als Beitrag zur allgemeinen Onomastik*. Acta Mesoamericana 15. Markt Schwaben: Verlag Anton Saurwein.

Colby, B. N. and Colby, L. M. 1981. *The Daykeeper: The Life and Discourse of an Ixil Diviner*. Cambridge MA: Harvard University Press.

Conklin, H. C. 1980. *Ethnographic Atlas of Ifugao: A Study of Environment, Culture, and Society in Northern Luzon*. New Haven: Yale University Press.

Cooke, C. W. 1931. Why the Mayan cities of the Peten district, Guatemala, were abandoned. *Journal of the Washington Academy of Sciences* 21: 283–87.

Costin, C. L. 1991. Craft specialization: Issues in defining, documenting, explaining the organization of production. *Archaeological Method and Theory* 3: 1–56.

Coto, Fr. T. de. 1983. *[Thesavrvs Verborvm]: Vocabvlario de la lengua Cakchiquel v[el] Guatemalteca, nueumente hecho y recopilado con summo estudio, trauajo y erudición*. Mexico: Universidad Nacional Autónoma de México.

Cowgill, G. L. 1979. Teotihuacan, internal militaristic competition, and the fall of the Classic Maya. In N. Hammond and G. R. Willey (eds.), *Maya Archaeology and Ethnohistory*, 51–62. Austin: University of Texas Press.

————. 1988. Onward and upward with collapse. In N. Yoffee and G. L. Cowgill (eds.), *The Collapse of Ancient States and Civilizations*, 244–76. Tucson: University of Arizona Press.

————. 2000. 'Rationality' and contexts in agency theory. In M.-A. Dobres and J. Robb (eds.), *Agency in Archaeology*, 51–60. Routledge: London.

Craveri, M. E. 2006. La voz de los antepasados en la poesía K'iche'. In R. V. Rivera and G. Le Fort (eds.), *Sacred Books, Sacred Languages: Two Thousand Years of Ritual and Religious Maya Literature*, 141–57. Acta Mesoamericana 18. Markt Schwaben: Verlag Anton Saurwein.

Culbert, T. P. 1977. Early Maya development at Tikal, Guatemala. In R. E. W. Adams (ed.), *The Origins of Maya Civilization*, 27–43. Albuquerque: University of New Mexico Press.

————. 1988. The collapse of Classic Maya civilization. In N. Yoffee and G. Cowgill (eds.), *The Collapse of Ancient States and Civilizations*, 69–102. Tucson: University of Arizona Press.

————. 1993. *The Ceramics of Tikal: Vessels from the Burials, Caches, and Problematical Deposits*. Tikal Report No. 25, Part A. University

Museum Monograph 81. Philadelphia: University Museum, University of Pennsylvania.

————. In press. The ceramics of Tikal. Santa Fe: School of American Research Press.

Culbert, T. P., Fialko, V., McKee, B. M., Grazioso, L., Kunen, J. L., and Paez, L. 1997. Investigación arqueológica en la Bajo la Justa, Peten. In J. Pedro Laporte and H. L. Escobedo (eds.), *X Simposio de Investigaciones Arqueológicas en Guatemala, 1996*, 367–72. Guatemala: Ministerio de Cultura y Deportes, Instituto de Antropología e Historia, and Asociación Tikal.

Culbert, T. P., Cruz, L., and Levi, L. J. 1990. Lowland Maya wetland agriculture: The Rio Azul agronomy program. In F. S. Clancy and P. D. Harrison (eds.), *Vision and Revision in Maya Studies*, 115–24. Albuquerque: University of New Mexico Press.

Culbert, T. P., Kosakowsky, L. J., Fry, R. E., and Haviland, W. A. 1990. The population of Tikal, Guatemala. In T. P. Culbert and D. S. Rice (eds.), *Precolumbian Population History in the Maya Lowlands,* 103–22. Albuquerque: University of New Mexico Press.

Curtis, J. H., Hodell, D. A., and Brenner, M. 1996. Climate variability on the Yucatan peninsula (Mexico) during the past 3500 years, and implications for Maya cultural evolution. *Quaternary Research* 46: 37–47.

Curtis, J. H., Brenner, M., Hodell, D. A., Balser, R. A., Islebe, G. A., and Hooghiemstra, H. 1998. A multi-proxy study of Holocene environmental change in the Maya lowlands of Peten, Guatemala. *Journal of Paleolimnology* 19: 139–59.

Cyphers, A. 1999. From stone to symbols: Olmec art in social context at San Lorenzo Tenochtitlán. In D. C. Grove and R. A. Joyce (eds.), *Social Patterns in Pre-Classic Mesoamerica*, 155–82. Washington DC: Dumbarton Oaks.

Dacus, C. 2005. *Weaving the Past: An Examination of Bones Buried with an Elite Maya Woman*. M.A. thesis. Southern Methodist University.

Dahlin, B. H. 2000. The barricade and abandonment of Chunchucmil: Implications for northern Maya Warfare. *Latin American Antiquity* 11: 283–98.

Dahlin, B. H., Andrews, A. P., Beach, T., Bezanilla, C., Farrell, P., Luzzadder-Beach S., and McCormick V. 1998. Punta Canbalam in context: A peripatetic coastal site in northwest Campeche, Mexico. *Ancient Mesoamerica* 9: 1–15.

Dahlin, B. H. and Ardren, T. 2002. Modes of exchange and regional patterns: Chunchucmil, Yucatan. In M. A. Masson and D. A. Freidel (eds.), *Ancient Maya Political Economies*, 249–84. Walnut Creek: Altamira Press.

Dahlin, B. H., Beach, T., Lizzadder-Beach, S., Hixson, D., Hutson, S., Magnoni, A., Mansell, E., and Mazeau, D. E. 2005. Reconstructing agricultural self-sufficiency at Chunchucmil, Yucatan, Mexico. *Ancient Mesoamerica* 16: 229–47.

Dahlin, B. H., Jensen, C. T., Terry, R. E., Wright, D. R., and Beach, T. 2007. In search of an ancient Maya market. *Latin American Antiquity* 18(4): 363–84.

D'Altroy, T. N. and Earle, T. K. 1985. Staple finance, wealth finance, and storage in the Inka political economy. *Current Anthropology* 26: 187–206.

De Coppet, D. 1981. The life-giving death. In S. C. Humphreys and H. King (eds.), *Mortality and Immortality: The Anthropology and Archaeology of Death*, 175–204. London: Academic Press.

Deevey, E. S., Rice, D. S., Rice, P. M., Vaughan, H. H., Brenner, M., and Flannery, M. S. 1979. Mayan urbanism: impact on a tropical karst environment. *Science* 206: 298–306.

de la Torre, M. 1993. *Adela Breton: Una artista británica en México*. México: Smurfit Cartón y Papel de México.

de Jouvenel, B. 1959. *Sovereignty: An Inquiry into the Political Good*. Chicago: University of Chicago Press.

Demarest, A. A. 1976. A re-evaluation of the archaeological sequences of Preclassic Chiapas. *Middle American Research Institute Publication* 22: 75–107. New Orleans: Tulane University.

————. 1986. Archaeology of Santa Leticia and the rise of Maya civilization. *Middle American Research Institute Publication Publication*, 52. New Orleans: Tulane University.

————. 1989. Olmec and the rise of civilization in eastern Mesoamerica. In R. Sharer and D. C. Grove (eds.), *Regional Perspectives on the Olmec*, 303–44. Cambridge: Cambridge University Press.

————. 1992. Ideology in Acient Maya cultural evolution: The dynamics of galactic polities.

In A. A. Demarest and G. W. Conrad (eds.), *Ideology and Pre-Colombian Civilizations*, 135–58. Santa Fe: School of American Research Press.

———. 1997. Vanderbilt Petexbatun Regional Archaeological Project, 1989–1994: Overview, history, and major results of a multidisciplinary study of the Classic Maya collapse. *Ancient Mesoamerica* 8: 209–27.

———. 2004. *Ancient Maya: The Rise and Fall of a Rainforest Civilization*. Cambridge: Cambridge University. *Press*.

Demarest, A. A., Escobedo Ayala, H. E., Juan Antonio Valdés, J. A, Wright, L., Emery, K., and Houston, S. D. 1991. Arqueología, epigrafía y el descubrimiento de una tumba real en el centro ceremonial de Dos Pilas, Peten, Guatemala. *U tz'ib* 1: 14–28.

Demarest, A. A. and Fahsen, F. 2003. Nuevos datos e interpretaciones de los reinos occidentales del clásico tardío: Pasión/Usumacinta. In J. Pedro Laporte, B. Arroyo, H. L. Escobedo, and H. E. Mejía (eds.), *XVI Simposio de Investigaciones Arqueológicas en Guatemala, 2002*, 159–74. Guatemala: Ministerio de Cultura y Deportes, Instituto de Antropología e Historia, and Asociación Tikal.

Demarest, A. A., Morgan, K., Wolley, C., and Escobedo, H. 2003. The political acquisition of sacred geography: The Murciélagos complex at Dos Pilas. In J. J. Christie (ed.), *Maya Palaces and Elite Residences: An Interdisciplinary Approach*, 120–53. Austin: University of Texas Press.

Demarest, A. A, M. O'Mansky, C. Wolley, D. Van Tuerenhout, T. Inomata, J. Palka and Escobedo, H. 1997. Classic Maya defensive systems and warfare in the Petexbatún region: Archaeological evidence and interpretations. *Ancient Mesoamerica* 8: 229–54.

Demarest, A. A., Rice, P. M., and Rice, D. S. 2004. *Terminal Classic in the Maya Lowlands: Collapse, Transformation, and Transformation*. Boulder: University Press of Colorado.

Demarest, A. A., Sharer, R. J., Fowler, W., King, E., and Fowler, J. 1984. Las excavaciones: El Mirador. *Mésoamerica* 7: 14–52.

Desmond, L. G. and Messenger, P. H. 1988. *A Dream of Maya: Augustus and Alice Le Plongeon in Nineteenth-Century Yucatan*. Albuquerque: University of New Mexico Press.

DeMarrais, E., Castillo, L. J., and Earle, T. 1996. Ideology, materialization and power strategies. *Current Anthropology* 37: 15–31.

Devereaux, L. 1987. Gender difference and the relations of inequality in Zinacantan. In M. Strathern (ed.), *Dealing with Inequality: Analysing Gender Relations in Melanesia and Beyond*, 89–111. Cambridge: Cambridge University Press.

Diamond, J. M. 2005. *Collapse: How Societies Choose to Fail or Succeed*. New York: Viking.

Dietler, M. and Herbich, I. 2001. Feasts and labor mobilization: Dissecting a fundamental economic practice. In M. Dietler and B. Hayden (eds.), *Feasts: Archaeological and Ethnographic Perspectives on Food, Politics, and Power*, 240–64. Washington DC: Smithsonian Institution Press.

Dillon, B. D. 1977. *Salinas de los Nueve Cerros, Guatemala: Preliminary archaeological investigations*. Socorro: Ballena Press.

Dixon, B. M., Jones, D., and Dahlin, B. 1994. Excavaciones en el complejo Los Cruces, El Mirador, Guatemala. *Mayab* 9: 18–30.

Donadoni, S. (ed.) 1997. *The Egyptians*. Chicago: University of Chicago Press.

Drennan, R. D. 1988. Household location and compact versus dispersed settlement in Prehispanic Mesoamerica. In R. R. Wilk and W. Ashmore (eds.), *Household and Community in the Mesoamerican Past*, 273–94. Albuquerque: University of New Mexico Press.

Drucker, P. 1952. *La Venta, Tabasco: A Study of Olmec Ceramic and Art*. Bureau of American Ethnology Bulletin 158. Washington DC: Smithsonian Institution.

Drucker, P., Heizer, R. F., and Squier, R. J. 1959. *Excavations at La Venta, Tabasco, 1955*. Bureau of American Ethnology Bulletin 170. Washington DC: Smithsonian Institution.

Duindam, J. 1994. *Myths of Power: Norbert Elias and the Early Modern European Court*. Amsterdam: Amsterdam University Press.

———. 1999. The Archduchy of Austria and the kingdoms of Bohemia and Hungary: The court of the Austrian Habspurgs c.1500–1750. In J. Adamson (ed.), *The Princely Courts of Europe: Ritual, Politics, and Culture Under the Ancien Régime 1500–1750*, 164–87. London: Weidenfeld and Nicolson.

Dumont, L. 1986. *Essays on Individualism*. Chicago: University of Chicago Press.

Dunning, N. P. 1992. *Lords of the Hills: Ancient Maya Settlement in the Puuc Region, Yucatan, Mexico*. Monographs in world archaeology, No. 15. Madison: Prehistory Press.

———. 1996. A reexamination of regional variability in the pre-hispanic agricultural landscape. In S. L. Fedick (ed.), *The Managed Mosaic: Ancient Maya Agriculture and Resource Use*, 53–68. Salt Lake City: University of Utah Press.

Dunning, N. P. and Beach, T. 1994. Soil erosion, slope management, and ancient terracing in the Maya Lowlands. *Latin American Antiquity* 5: 51–69.

———. 2000. Stability and instability in Pre-Hispanic Maya landscape. In D. Lentz (ed.), *Imperfect Balance: Precolumbian New World Ecosystems*, 179–202. New York: Columbia University Press.

Dunning, N. P., Beach, T., Farrell, P., Luzzadder-Beach, S. 1998. Prehispanic agrosystems and adaptive regions in the Maya lowlands. *Culture and Agriculture* 20: 87–101.

Dunning, N. P., Beach, T., and David Rue, D. 1997. The paleoecology and ancient settlement of the Petexbatun region, Guatemala. *Ancient Mesoamerica* 8: 255–66.

Dunning, N. P. and Houston, S. D. 2006. *Chan Ik'*: Hurricanes as a destabilizing force in the prehispanic Maya lowlands. Paper presented at the 11th European Maya Conference, Ecology, Power, and Religion in Maya Landscapes, Malmö.

Dunning, N. P., Jones, J., Beach, T., and Luzzadder-Beach, S. 2003. Physiography, habitats, and landscapes of the Three Rivers region. In V. L. Scarborough, F. Valdez, Jr., and N. P. Dunning (eds.), *Heterarchy, Political Economy, and the Ancient Maya: The Three Rivers Region of the East-Central Yucatan Peninsula*. Tucson: University of Arizona Press.

Dunning, N. P., Luzzadder-Beach, S., Beach, T., Jones, J., Scarborough V., and Culbert, T. P. 2002. Arising from the bajos: The evolution of a neotropical landscape and the rise of Maya civilization. *Annals of the Association of American Geographers* 92: 267–83.

Dunning, N. P., Rue, D. J., Beach, T., Covich, A., and Traverse, A. 1998. Human-environment interactions in a tropical watershed: The paleoecology of Laguna Tamarindito, El Petén, Guatemala. *Journal of Field Archaeology* 25: 139–51.

Dunning, N. P., Scarborough, V., Valdez, Jr., F., Luzzadder-Beach, S., Beach, T., and Jones, J. G. 1999. Temple mountains, sacred lakes, and fertile fields: Ancient Maya landscapes in northwestern Belize. *Antiquity* 73: 650–60.

Durán, D. 1971. *Book of the Gods and Rites and The Ancient Calendar*. F. Horcasitas and Doris Heyden (trans). Norman: University of Oklahoma Press.

Durkheim, E. 1961 *Moral Education: A Study in the Theory and Application of the Sociology of Education*. E. K. Wilson and H. Schnurer (trans). New York: The Free Press.

———. 1965. *The elementary forms of the religious life*. New York: Free Press.

Dym, J. 2006. *From Sovereign Villages to National States: City, State, and Federation in Central America, 1759–1839*. Albuquerque: University of New Mexico Press.

Earle, D. M. and Snow, D. R. 1985. The origin of the 260-day calendar: The gestation hypothesis reconsidered in light of its use among the Quiche Maya. In V. M. Fields (ed.), *Fifth Palenque Round Table, 1983, Vol. VII*, 241–44. San Francisco: Pre-Columbian Art Research Institute.

Early, J. D. 1983. Some ethnographic implications of an ethnohistorical perspective of the civil-religious hierarchy among the highland Maya. *Ethnohistory* 30: 185–202.

Eberl, M. 2007. *Community heterogeneity and integration: The Maya site of Nacimiento, Dos Ceibas, and Cerro de Cheyo (El Petén, Guatemala) during the Late Classic*. Ph.D. dissertation. Tulane University.

Edmonson, M. S. 1993. The Mayan faith. In G. H. Gossen (ed.), *South and Meso-American Native Spirituality: From the Cult of the Feathered Serpent to the Theology of Liberation*, 65–85. New York: Crossroad.

Edwards, C. R. 1978. Pre-columbian maritime trade in Mesoamerica. In T. A. Lee, Jr. and C. Navarrete (eds.), *Mesoamerican Communication Routes and Cultural Contacts*, 199–209. Papers of the New World Archaeological Foundation, No. 40. Provo: Brigham Young University.

Ekholm, G. F. 1964. *A Maya Sculpture in Wood*. New York: Museum of Primitive Art.

Ekholm-Miller, S. 1969. *Mound 30a and the Early Preclassic Ceramic Sequence of Izapa, Chiapas, Mexico*. Papers of the New World Archaeological Foundation 25. Provo: Brigham Young University.

———. 1973. *The Olmec Rock Carving at Xoc, Chiapas, Mexico*. Papers of the New World Archaeological Foundation 32. Provo: Brigham Young University.

Elias, N. 1983. *The Court Society* [*Die höfische Gesellschaft*, 1969]. Trans. E. Jephcott. New York: Pantheon.

Elliott, J. H. 1989. *Spain and Its World, 1500–1700*. New Haven: Yale University Press.

———. 1999. Introduction. In J. H. Elliott and L. Brockliss (eds.), *The World of the Favourite*, 1–10. New Haven: Yale University Press.

Emery, K. F. 1997. *The Maya Collapse: A Zooarchaeological Inquiry*. Ph.D. dissertation. Cornel University.

———. 2004. Environments of the Maya collapse: A zooarchaeological perspective from the Petexbatún. In K. F. Emery (ed.), *Maya Zooarchaeology: New Directions in Method and Theory*, 81–96. Cotsen Institute of Archaeology, Monograph 51. Los Angeles: University of California Los Angeles.

———. 2007. Assessing the impact of ancient Maya animal use. *Journal for Nature Conservation* 15: 184–95.

Emery, F. K. and Aoyama, K. 2007. Bone, shell, and lithic evidence for crafting in elite Maya households at Aguateca, Guatemala. *Ancient Mesoamerica* 18: 69–89.

Emmerich, A. 1984. Masterpieces of Pre-Columbian art from the collection of Mr. and Mrs. Peter G. Wray, April 11 to May 12, 1984. André Emmerich Gallery, New York.

Escobedo, H. L. 1997. Arroyo de Piedra: Sociopolitical dynamics of a secondary center in the Petexbatun region. *Ancient Mesoamerica* 8: 307–20.

———. 2000. History of a Classic Maya court: The dynastic records of Arroyo de Piedras, Guatemala. Unpublished manuscript in possession of authors.

———. 2004. Tales from the crypt: The burial place of Ruler 4, Piedras Negras. In M. Miller and S. Martin (eds.), *Courtly Art of the Ancient Maya*, 277–80. New York: Thames and Hudson.

Escobedo, H. L., Urquizú, M., and Castellanos, J. 1996. Nuevas investigaciones en Kaminaljuyú: Excavaciones en los montículos A-V-II, A-VI-I y sus alrededores. In J. P. Laporte and H. Escobedo (eds.), *IX Simposio de Investigaciones Arqueológicas en Guatemala, 1995*, 419–37. Guatemala: Ministerio de Cultura y Deportes, Museo Nacional de Arqueología e Etnología.

Estrada-Belli, F. 2006. Lightning sky, rain, and the maize god: The ideology of Preclassic Maya rulers at Cival, Peten, Guatemala. *Ancient Mesoamerica* 17: 57–78.

Estrada-Belli, F., Tokovinine, A., Foley, J., Hurst, H., Ware, G. A., Stuart, D., and Grube, N. 2006. Two Early Classic Maya murals: new texts and images in Maya and Teotihuacan style from La Sufricaya, Petén, Guatemala. *Antiquity* 80(308). http://62.189.20.34/projgall/estrada-belli06/index.html. Accessed April 15, 2008.

Eubanks, M. W. 1999. *Corn in Clay: Maize Paleoethnobotany in Pre-Columbian Art*. Gainesville: University Press of Florida.

Evans-Pritchard, E. E. 1971. Reigning and ruling. *Man* 6: 117–18.

Fahsen, F. 2002. Rescuing the origins of Dos Pilas dynasty: A salvage of Hieroglyphic Stairway #2, Structure L5–49. Report to FAMSI, http://www.famsi.org/reports/01098/index.html. Accessed April 15, 2008.

FAO (Food and Agriculture Organization of the United Nations). 1992. *Maize in Human Nutrition. Vol. 25. Food and Nutrition Series*. Rome: Food and Agriculture Organization of the United Nations.

Farriss, N. M. 1978. Nucleation versus dispersal: The dynamics of population movement in Colonial Yucatan. *Hispanic American Historical Review* 58: 187–216.

———. 1984. *Maya Society Under Colonial Rule: The Collective Enterprise of Survival*. Princeton: Princeton University Press.

———. 1995. Remembering the future, anticipating the past: History, time, and cosmology among the Maya of Yucatan. In D. O. Hughes and T. R. Trautmann (eds.), *Time: Histories and Ethnologies*, 107–38. Ann Arbor: University of Michigan Press.

Fash, W. L. 1983. Deducing social organization from Classic Maya settlement patterns: A case study from the Copan Valley. In R. M. Leventhal and A. L. Kolata (eds.), *Civilization in the Ancient Americas: Essays in Honor of Gordon R. Willey*, 261–88. Albuquerque: University of New Mexico Press.

———. 1987. The altar and associated features. In D. C. Grove (ed.), *Ancient Chalcatzingo*, 82–94. Austin: University of Texas Press.

———. 1991. *Scribes, Warriors and Kings: The City of Copán and the Ancient Maya*. London: Thames and Hudson.

Fash, W. L., Andrews, E. W., and Manahan, T. K. 2004. Political decentralization, dynastic collapse, and the early Postclassic in the urban center of Copán, Honduras. In A. A. Demarest, P. M. Rice and D. S. Rice (eds.), *The Terminal Classic in the Maya Lowlands: Collapse, Transition, and Transformation*, 260–87. Boulder: University Press of Colorado.

Fash, W. L. and Fash, B. W. 2000. Teotihuacan and the Maya: A Classic heritage. In D. Carrasco, L. Jones and S. Sessions (eds.), *Mesoamerica's Classic Heritage: Teotihuacán to the Aztecs*, 433–63. Niwot: University Press of Colorado.

Fash, W. L. and Stuart, D. 1991. Dynastic history and cultural evolution at Copán, Honduras. In T. P. Culbert (ed.), *Classic Maya Political History: Hieroglyphic and Archaeological Evidence*, 147–79. Cambridge: Cambridge University Press.

Fedick, S. L. 1994. Ancient Maya agricultural terracing in the Upper Belize River area: Computer-aided modeling and the results of initial field investigations. *Ancient Mesoamerica* 5: 107–27.

———. 1996a. Conclusion: Landscape approaches to the study of ancient Maya agriculture and resource use. In S. L. Fedick (ed.), *Managed Mosaic: Ancient Maya Agriculture and Resource Use*, 335–47. Salt Lake City: University of Utah Press.

———. 1996b. Interpretive kaleidoscope: Alternative perspectives on ancient agricultural landscapes of Maya lowlands. In S. L. Fedick (ed.), *Managed Mosaic: Ancient Maya Agriculture and Resource Use*, 107–31. Salt Lake City: University of Utah Press.

———. 1996c. Introduction: New perspectives on ancient Maya agriculture and resource use. In S. L. Fedick (ed.), *The Managed Mosaic: Ancient Maya Agriculture and Resource Use*, 1–16. Salt Lake City: University of Utah Press.

Feinman, G. M. 2000. Corporate/Network: A new perspective on leadership in the American southwest. In M. W. Diehl (ed.), *Hierarchies in Action: Cui Bono?*, 152–80. Carbondale: Center for Archaeological Investigations.

Fenton, W. N. 1983. *The Roll Call of the Iroquois Chiefs*. Ohsweken: Iroqrafts.

Ferguson, T. 1956. Introduction concerning the New World Archaeological Foundation. In *New World Archaeological Foundation Publication No. 1*, 3–6. Orinda: New World Archaeological Foundation.

Fernandez, J. W. 1977. The performance of ritual metaphors. In J. D. Sapir and J. C. Crocker (eds.), *The Social Use of Metaphor*, 100–31. Philadelphia: University of Pennsylvania Press.

Fields, V. M. 1991. The iconographic heritage of the Maya Jester God. In V. M. Fields (ed.), *Sixth Palenque Round Table, 1986*, 167–74. Norman: University of Oklahoma Press.

Firth, R. 1957. Factions in Indian and overseas Indian societies, I: Introduction. *British Journal of Sociology* 8: 291–95.

Fischer, E. F. 2001. *Cultural Logics and Global Economics: Maya Identity in Thought and Practice*. Austin: University of Texas Press.

Fischer, E. F. and Brown, R. McK (eds.). 1996. *Maya Cultural Activism in Guatemala*. Austin: University of Texas Press.

Fisher, N. R. E. 1992. *Hybris: A Study in the Values of Honour and Shame in Ancient Greece*. Warminster: Aris and Phillips.

Fitzgerald, W. 2000. *Slavery and Roman Literary Imagination*. Cambridge: Cambridge University Press.

Fitzsimmons, J. 2006. *Kings of Jaguar Hill: Monuments and Caches at Zapote Bobal*. Report to FAMSI, http://www.famsi.org/reports/05047/section01.htm.

Fitzsimmons, J., Scherer, A., Houston, S. D., and Escobedo, H. 2003. Guardian of the acropolis: The sacred space of a royal burial at Piedras Negras, Guatemala. *Latin American Antiquity* 14: 449–68.

Flannery, K. V. and Marcus, J. 1994. *Early Formative Pottery in the Valley of Oaxaca*. Memoirs, 27. University of Michigan, Museum of Anthropology, Ann Arbor.

Flathman, R. E. 1980. *The Practice of Political Authority: Authority and the Authoritative*. Chicago: University of Chicago Press.

Flemming, P. H. 1973. The politics of marriage among non-Catholic European Royalty. *Current Anthropology* 14(3): 207–42.

Foias, A. E. (ed.) 1999. *Proyecto Arqueológico Motul de San José: Informe #2, temporada de campo 1999*. Report presented to the Institute de Antropología e Historia de Guatemala.

Foias, A. E. and Bishop, R. 1997. Changing ceramic production and exchange in the Petexbatun region, Guatemala: Reconsidering the Classic Maya collapse. *Ancient Mesoamerica* 8: 275–92.

Folan, W. J., Kintz, E. R., and Fletcher, L. A. (eds.) 1983. *Coba: A Classic Maya Metropolis.* New York: Academic Press.

Ford, A. 1996. Critical resource control and the rise of the Classic Period Maya. In S. L. Fedick (ed.), *Managed Mosaic: Ancient Maya Agriculture and Resource Use*, 297–303. Salt Lake City: University of Utah Press.

Ford, A. and Olson, K. 1989. Aspects of ancient Maya household economy: Variation in chipped stone production and consumption. In P. A. McAnany and B. L. Isaac (eds.), *Prehistoric Maya Economies of Belize*, 185–211. Greenwich: JAI Press.

Forsyth, D. W. 1993. The ceramic sequence at Nakbe, Guatemala. *Ancient Mesoamerica* 4: 31–53.

———. 1999. La cerámica preclásico y el desarrollo de la complejidad cultural durante el preclásico. In J. P. Laporte, H. E. Escobedo and A. C. Monzón de Suasnávar (eds.), *XII Simposio de Investigaciones Arqueológicas en Guatemala, 1998*, 51–63. Guatemala: Ministerio de Cultura y Deportes, Instituto de Antropología e Historia, Asociación Tikal.

———. 2005. A survey of Terminal Classic ceramic complexes and their socioeconomic implications. In S. L. López Varela and A. E. Foias (eds.), *Geographies of power: Understanding the nature of Terminal Classic pottery in the Maya lowlands*, 7–22. BAR International Series 1447. Oxford.

Fortes, M. 1967. Of installation ceremonies. *Proceedings of the Royal Anthropological Institute of Great Britain and Ireland*: 5–20.

Fox, J. G. 1996. Playing with power: Ballcourts and political ritual in southern Mesoamerica. *Current Anthropology* 37: 483–509.

Fragnito, G. 1993. Cardinal's courts in sixteenth-century Rome. *Journal of Modern History* 65: 26–56.

Freedberg, D. 1989. *The Power of Images: Studies in the History and Theory of Response.* Chicago: University of Chicago Press.

Freidel, D. A. 1985a. New light on the dark age: A summary of major themes. In A. F. Chase and P. M. Rice (eds.), *The Lowland Maya Postclassic*, 285–310. Austin: University of Texas Press.

———. 1985b. Polychrome façades of the lowland Maya pre-Classic. In E. Boone (ed.), *Painted Architecture and Polychrome Monumental Sculpture in Mesoamerica*, 5–30. Washington DC: Dumbarton Oaks.

———. 1986. The monumental architecture. In R. A. Robertson and D. A. Freidel (eds.), *Archaeology of Cerros, Belize, Central America, Vol. 1: An Interim Report*, 1–22. Dallas: Southern Methodist University Press.

———. 1990. The Jester God. In F. S. Clancy and P. D. Harrison (eds.), *Vision and Revision in Maya Studies*, 67–78. Albuquerque: University of New Mexico Press.

———. 2007. War and statecraft in the northern Maya lowlands: Yaxuna and Chichén Itzá. In J. K. Kowalski and C. Kristan-Graham (eds.), *Twin Tollans: Chichén Itzá, Tula, and the Epiclassic to Early Postclassic Mesoamerican World*, 345–76. Washington DC: Dunbarton Oaks Research Library and Collection.

Freidel, D. A. and Schele, L. 1988a. Symbol and power: A history of the lowland Maya cosmogram. In E. Benson and G. Griffin (eds.), *Maya Iconography*, 44–93. Princeton: Princeton University.

———. 1988b. Kingship in the late pre-Classic Maya lowlands: The instruments and places of ritual power. *American Anthropologist* 90: 547–67.

Freidel, D., Schele, L., and Parker, J. 1993. *Maya Cosmos: Three Thousand Years on the Shaman's Path.* New York: William Morrow.

French, A. 2003. Jesters, champions, and pipers. In G. Waterfield, A. French with M. Craske (eds.), *Below Stairs: 400 Years of Servant's Portraits*, 20–35. London: National Portrait Gallery.

Freter, A. 1992. Chronological research at Copan. *Ancient Mesoamerica* 3: 117–33.

———. 1993. Obsidian-hydration dating: Its past, present, and future application in Mesoamerica. *Ancient Mesoamerica* 4: 285–304.

Fried, M. 1967. *The Evolution of Political Society.* New York: Random House.

Fry, R. E. 1979. The economics of pottery at Tikal, Guatemala: Models of exchange for serving vessels. *American Antiquity* 44: 494–512.

———. 1980. Models of exchange for major shape classes of lowland Maya pottery. In R. E. Fry (ed.), *Models and Methods in Regional Exchange*, 3–18. Washington DC: Society for American Archaeology.

Furst, J. L. Mck. 1995. *The Natural History of the Soul in Ancient Mexico*. New Haven: Yale University Press.

Fürer-Haimendorf, C. von. 1967. *Morals and Merit*. London: Weidenfeld and Nicolson.

Gailey, C. W. 1987. *Kinship to Kingship: Gender Hierarchy and State Formation in the Tongan Islands*. Austin: University of Texas Press.

Gailey, C. W. and Patterson, T. C. 1987. Power relations and state formation. In C. W. Gailey and T. C. Patterson (eds.), *Power Relations and State Formation*, 1–26. Washington DC: American Anthropological Association.

Galinier, J. 2004. *The World Below: Body and Cosmos in Otomí Indian Ritual*. Boulder: University Press of Colorado.

Gann, T. W. F. 1917. Chachac, or rain ceremony, as practised by the Maya of southern Yucatan and northern British Honduras. *Proceedings of the International Congress of Americanists, Washington, DC, 1915*: 409–18.

Garber, J. F., Brown, M. K., Awe, J., and Hartman, C. J. 2004. Middle Formative prehistory of the Central Belize Valley. In J. F. Garber (ed.), *The Ancient Maya of the Belize Valley: Half a Century of Archaeological Research*, 25–47. Gainesville: University of Florida Press.

García Campillo, J. 1991 Edificios y dignitarios: La historia escrita de Oxkintok. In M. R. Dorado (ed.), *Oxkintok: una ciudad maya de Yucatán*, 55–78. Madrid: Misión Arqueológica de España en Mexicó.

———. 1992. Informe epigráfico sobre Oxkintok y la cerámica Chocholá. In *Oxkintok* 4, 185–200. Madrid: Misión Arqueológica de España en México.

García-Des Lauriers, C. 2007. *Proyecto Arqueológico Los Horcones: Investigating the Teotihuacan presence on the Pacific Coast of Chiapas, Mexico*. Ph.D. dissertation. University of California, Riverside.

García Moll, R. 2003. *La arquitectura de Yaxchilán*. Mexico: Instituto Nacional de Antropología e Historia.

———. 2005. *Pomoná: Un sitio del Clásico Maya en las colinas tabasqueñas*. Mexico: Instituto Nacional de Antropología e Historia.

Gardiner, M. 1992. *The Dialogics of Critique: M. M. Bakhtin and the Theory of Ideology*. London: Routledge.

Garraty, C. P. 2000. Ceramic indices of Aztec eliteness. *Ancient Mesoamerica* 11: 323–40.

Gaur, A. 1992. *A History of Writing*. Revised edition. New York: Cross River Press.

Geertz, C. 1977. Centers, kings and charisma: reflections on the symbolics of power. In J. Ben-David and T. N. Clark (eds.), *Culture and Its Creators: Essays in Honour of Edward Shils*, 150–71. Chicago: University of Chicago Press.

———. 1983. Common sense as a cultural system. In C. Geertz, *Local Knowledge: Further Essays in Interpretive Anthropology*, 73–93. New York: Basic Books.

Gella, A. 1971. The life and death of the old Polish intelligentsia. *Slavic Review* 30: 1–27.

Gerry, J. P. and Krueger, H. W. 1997. Regional diversity in Classic Maya diets. In S. L. Whittington and D. M. Reed (eds.), *Bones of the Maya: Studies of Acient Skeletons*, 196–207. Washington DC: Smithsonian Institution Press.

Giddens, A. 1984. *The Constitution of Society: Outline of the Theory of Structuration*. Berkeley: University of California Press.

———. 1994. Elites and Power. In D. Grusky (ed.), *Social Stratification: Class, Race, and Gender in Sociological Perspective*, 170–74. Boulder: Westview Press.

Gidwitz, T. 2002. Pioneers of the Bajo: Jungle surveyors in Guatemala uncover the breadbasket of the Maya world. *Archaeology* 55(1): 28–35.

Gifford, J. C. 1976. Prehistoric pottery analysis and the ceramics of Barton Ramie in the Belize Valley. *Memoirs, 18*. Cambridge MA: Harvard University, Peabody Museum of Archaeology and Ethnology.

Gill, R. B. 2000. *The Great Maya Droughts: Water, Life, and Death*. Albuquerque: University of New Mexico Press.

Gillespie, S. D. 2000a. Beyond kinship: An introduction. In R. A. Joyce and S. D. Gillespie (eds.), *Beyond Kingship: Social and Material Reproduction in House Societies*, 1–21. Philadelphia: University of Pennsylvania Press.

———. 2000b. Lévi-Strauss: *Maison* and *Société à Maisons*. In R. A. Joyce and S. D. Gillespie (eds.), *Beyond Kingship: Social and Material Reproduction in House Societies*, 22–52. Philadelphia: University of Pennsylvania Press.

———. 2000c. Maya 'nested houses': The ritual construction of place. In R. A. Joyce and S. D. Gillespie (eds.), *Beyond Kingship: Social and*

Material Reproduction in House Societies, 135–60. Philadelphia: University of Pennsylvania Press.

Gilman, A. 2002. Assessing political development in copper and bronze age southeast Spain. In J. Haas (ed.), *From Leaders to Rulers*, 59–81. New York: Kluwer Academic/Plenum Publishers.

Givens, D. R. 1992. *Alfred Vincent Kidder and the Development of Americanist Archaeology*. Albuquerque: University of New Mexico Press.

Golden, C. 2002. *Bridging the Gap between Archaeological and Indigenous Chronologies: An Investigation of the Early Classic / Late Classic Divide at Piedras Negras, Guatemala*. Ph.D. dissertation. University of Pennsylvania.

Golden, C., Scherer, A. K., Muñoz, A. R., and Vásquez, R. 2008. Piedras Negras and Yaxchilan: Divergent political trajectories in adjacent Maya polities. *Latin American Antiquity* 19: 249–274.

Gómez-Pompa, A., Flores, S., and Sosa, V. 1987. The "Pet Kot": A man-made tropical forest of the Maya. *Interciencia* 12: 10–15.

Gonlin, N. 2007. Ritual and ideology among Classic Maya rural commoners at Copán, Honduras. In N. Gonlin and J. C. Lohse (eds.), *Commoner Ritual and Ideology in Ancient Mesoamerica*, 83–121. Boulder: University Press of Colorado.

González Lauck, R. 1996. La Venta: An Olmec capital. In E. P. Benson and B. de la Fuente (eds.), *Olmec Art of Ancient Mexico*, 73–82. Washington DC: National Gallery of Art.

Goody, J. 1958. The fission of domestic groups among the LoDagaba. In J. Goody (ed.), *The Developmental Cycle in Domestic Groups*, 53–91. Cambridge: Cambridge University Press.

Gossen, G. H. 1993. On the human condition and the moral order: A testimony from the Chamula Tzotzil Maya of Chiapas, Mexico. In G. H. Gossen (ed.), *South and Meso-American Native Spirituality: From the Cult of the Feathered Serpent to the Theology of Liberation*, 414–35. New York: Crossroad.

Gossen, G. H. and Leventhal, R. M. 1993. The topography of ancient Maya religious pluralism: A dialogue with the present. In J. A. Sabloff and J. S. Henderson (eds.), *Lowland Maya Civilization in the Eighth Century A.D.*, 185–217. Washington DC: Dumbarton Oaks.

Graham, E. 1994. *The Highlands of the Lowlands: Environment and Archaeology in the Stann Creek District, Belize, Central America*. Monographs in World Archaeology No. 19. Madison: Prehistory Press.

Graham, I. 1967. *Archaeological Explorations in El Peten, Guatemala*. Middle American Research Institute, Publications 33. New Orleans: Tulane University.

———. 1979. *Corpus of Maya Hieroglyphic Inscriptions, Volume 3, Part 2: Yaxchilan*. Cambridge MA: Peabody Museum of Archaeology and Ethnology, Harvard University.

———. 1980. *Corpus of Maya Hieroglyphic Inscriptions, Volume 2, Part 3: Ixkun, Ucanal, Ixtutz, Naranjo*. Cambridge MA: Peabody Museum of Archaeology and Ethnology, Harvard University.

———. 1982. *Corpus of Maya Hieroglyphic Inscriptions, Volume 3, Part 3: Yaxchilan*. Cambridge MA: Peabody Museum of Archaeology and Ethnology, Harvard University.

———. 1992. *Corpus of Maya Hieroglyphic Inscriptions, Volume 4, Part 2: Uxmal*. Cambridge MA: Peabody Museum of Archaeology and Ethnology, Harvard University.

———. 1996. *Corpus of Maya Hieroglyphic Inscriptions, Volume 7, Part 1: Seibal*. Cambridge MA: Peabody Museum of Archaeology and Ethnology, Harvard University. 2002. *Alfred Maudslay and the Maya*. Norman: University of Oklahoma Press.

Graham, I. and von Euw, E. 1977. *Corpus of Maya Hieroglyphic Inscriptions, Volume 3, Part 1: Yaxchilan*. Cambridge MA: Peabody Museum of Archaeology and Ethnology, Harvard University.

———. 1992. *Corpus of Maya Hieroglyphic Inscriptions, Volume 4, Part 3: Uxmal, Xcalumkin*. Cambridge MA: Peabody Museum of Archaeology and Ethnology, Harvard University.

———. 1997. *Corpus of Maya Hieroglyphic Inscriptions, Volume 8, Part 1: Coba*. Cambridge MA: Peabody Museum of Archaeology and Ethnology, Harvard University.

Graham, I., Henderson, L. R., Mathews, P., and Stuart, D. 2006. *Corpus of Maya Hieroglyphic Inscriptions, Volume 9, Part 2: Tonina*. Cambridge MA: Peabody Museum of Archaeology and Ethnology, Harvard University.

Graham, J. 1973. Aspects of non–Classic presences in the inscriptions and monumental art at Seibal. In T. P. Culbert (ed.), *The Classic*

Maya Collapse, 207–19. Albuquerque: University of New Mexico Press.

Gramsci, A. 1971. *Selections from the Prison Notebooks of Antonio Gramsci*. London: Laurence and Wisehart.

Graña-Behrens, D. 2006. Emblem glyphs and political organization in northwestern Yucatan in the Classic Period (A.D. 300–1000). *Ancient Mesoamerica* 17: 105–23.

Grove, D. C. 1981. Olmec monuments: Mutilation as a clue to meaning. In E. P. Benson (ed.), *The Olmec and Their Neighbors: Essays in Memory of Matthew W. Stirling*, 49–68. Washington DC: Dumbarton Oaks.

———. 1996. Olmec horizons in Formative Period Mesoamerica: Diffusion or social evolution? In D. S. Rice (ed.), *Latin American Horizons: A Symposium at Dumbarton Oaks*, 1986, 83–111. Washington DC: Dumbarton Oaks Research Library and Collection.

———. 1997. Olmec archaeology: A half century of research and its accomplishments. *Journal of World Prehistory* 11: 51–101.

Grube, N. 1992. Classic Maya dance: Evidence from hieroglyphs and iconography. *Ancient Mesoamerica* 3: 201–18.

———. 1996. Palenque in the Maya world. In M. J. Macri and J. McHargue (eds.), *Eighth Palenque Round Table*, 1993. http://www.mesoweb.com/pari/publications/RT10/001grube/palenque_009.html#top. Accessed April 15, 2008.

———. 2000. Monumentos esculpidos e inscripciones jeroglíficas en el triángulo Yaxhá-Nakum-Naranjo. In W. W. Wurster (ed.), *El sitio maya de Topoxté: Investigaciones en una isla del lago Yaxhá, Petén, Guatemala*, 249–68. Mainz: Philipp von Zabern.

———. 2003. Archaeological reconnaissance in southeastern Campeche, México: 2002 Field Season Report, *Appendix 2: Epigraphic Analysis of Altar 3 of Altar de los Reyes*. Report to FAMSI, http://www.famsi.org/reports/01014/section14.htm.

———. 2004a. Akan – The god of drinking, disease, and death. In D. Graña Behrens, N. Grube, C. M. Prager, F. Sachse, S. Teufel, and E. Wagner (eds.), *Continuity and Change: Maya Religious Practices in Temporal Perspective, 5th European Maya Conference, University of Bonn*, December 2000, 59–76. Acta Mesoamericana 14. Markt Schwaben: Verlag Anton Saurwein.

———. 2004b. Ciudades perdidas mayas. *Arqueología Mexicana* XII (67): 32–7.

———. 2004c. La historia dinástica de Naranjo, Petén. *Beiträge zur Allgemeinen und Vergleichenden Archäologie* 24: 195–213.

Grube, N. and Gaida, M. 2006. *Katalog Ethnologisches Museum Berlin*. In N. Grube and M. Gaida (eds.), *Die Maya: Schrift und Kunst im Ethnologischen Museum Berlin*, 84–225. Berlin: SMB-DuMont.

Grube, N. and R. J. Krochock. 2007. Reading between the lines: Hieroglyphic texts from Chichén Itzá and its neighbors. In J. K. Kowalski and C. Kristan-Graham (eds.), *Twin Tollans: Chichén Itzá, Tula, and the Epiclassic to Early Postclassic Mesoamerican World*, 205–50. Washington DC: Dumbarton Oaks Research Library and Collection.

Grube, N. and Nahm, W. 1994. A census of Xibalba: A complete inventory of *way* characters on Maya Ceramics. In J. Kerr (ed.), *The Maya Vase Book: A Corpus of Rollout Photographs of Maya Vases, Volume 4*, 686–715. New York: Kerr Associates.

Grube, N. and Schele, L. 1987. U Cit Tok: The last king of Copán. *Copán Note 21*. Copan, Honduras: Copán Mosaics Project and the Instituto Hondureño de Antropología e Historia.

———. 1991. *Tzuk* in the Classic Maya inscriptions. *Texas Notes on Precolumbian Art, Writing, and Culture No. 15*. Unpublished manuscript in possession of authors.

Guenter, S. 2003. The inscriptions of Dos Pilas associated with B'ajlaj Chan K'awiil. *Mesoweb* www.mesoweb.com/features/guenter/DosPilas.pdf. Accessed April 15, 2008.

Guiteras-Holmes, C. 1961. *Perils of the Soul: The World View of a Tzotzil Indian*. Glencoe: Free Press.

Gutierrez Solana, N. and Hamilton, S. K. 1977. *Las esculturas en terracota de El Zapotal, Veracruz*. Mexico: Universidad Nacional Autónoma de México.

Halperin, C. 2008. Classic Maya Textile Production: Insights from Motul de San José, Peten, Guatemala. *Ancient Mesoamerica* 19: 111–125.

Hamblin, N. L. 1980. *Animal Utilization by the Cozumel Maya: Interpretation through Faunal Analysis*. Ph.D. dissertation. University of Arizona.

Hammond, N. 1981. Ancient Maya canoes. *International Journal of Nautical Archaeology and Underwater Exploration* 10(3): 173–85.

———. 1982a. A late formative period stela in the Maya Lowlands. *American Antiquity* 47: 396–403.

———. 1982b. *Ancient Maya Civilization*. New Brunswick: Rutgers University Press.

———. 1988. Cultura hermana: Reappraising the Olmec. *Quarterly Review of Archaeology* 9: 1–4.

——— (ed.) 1991. *Cuello: An Early Maya Community in Belize*. Cambridge: Cambridge University Press.

———. 1999. The genesis of hierarchy: Mortuary and offertory ritual in the pre-Classic at Cuello, Belize. In D. C. Grove and R. A. Joyce (eds.), *Social Patterns in Pre-Classic Mesoamerica*, 49–66. Washington DC: Dumbarton Oaks.

Hammond, N., Gerhardt, C., and Donaghey, S. 1991. Stratigraphy and Chronology in the reconstruction of Preclassic Developments at Cuello. In N. Hammond (ed.), *Cuello: An Early Maya Community in Belize*, 23–69. Cambridge: Cambridge University Press.

Hammond, N. and Tourtellot, G. 2004. Out with a whimper: La Milpa in the Terminal Classic. In A. A. Demarest, P. M. Rice, and D. S. Rice (eds.), *The Terminal Classic in the Maya Lowlands: Collapse, Transition, and Transformation*, 288–301. Boulder: University Press of Colorado.

Hanks, W. F. 1984. Sanctification, structure, and experience in a Yucatec ritual event. *Journal of American Folklore* 97(384): 131–66.

———. 1990. *Referential Practice: Language and Lived Space among the Maya*. Chicago: University of Chicago Press.

Hansen, R. D. 1990. *Excavations in the Tigre Complex, El Mirador, Peten, Guatemala*. Papers of the New World Archaeological Foundation, No. 62. Provo: Brigham Young University.

———. 1991. *An Early Maya Text from El Mirador, Guatemala*. Research Reports on Ancient Maya Writing 37. Washington DC: Center for Maya Research.

———. 1992a. *The Archaeology of Ideology: A Study of Maya Preclassic Architectural Sculpture at Nakbé, Peten, Guatemala*. Ph.D. dissertation. University of California, Los Angeles.

———. 1992b. El proceso cultural de Nakbe y el área del Petén nor-central: las épocas temporanas. In J. P. Laporte, H. L. Escobedo and S. Villagran de Brady (eds.), *V Simposio de Investigaciones Arqueologicas en Guatemala*, 81–96. Guatemala: Ministerio de Cultura y Deportes, Instituto de Antropología e Historia, Asociación Tikal.

———. 1994. Las dinámicas culturales y ambientales de los orígenes mayas: Estudios recientes del sitio arqueológico Nakbe. In J. P. Laporte and H. L. Escobedo (eds.), *VII Simposio de Investigaciones Arqueológicas en Guatemala, 1993, Museo Nacional de Arqueología e Etnología*, 369–87. Guatemala: Ministerio de Cultural y Deportes, Instituto de Antropología e Historia, and Asociación Tikal.

———. 1998. Continuity and disjunction: The pre-Classic antecedents of Classic Maya architecture. In S. D. Houston (ed.), *Function and Meaning in Classic Maya Architecture*, 49–122. Washington DC: Dumbarton Oaks.

———. 2005. Perspectives on Olmec-Maya Interaction in the Middle Formative Period. In T. G. Powis (ed.), *New perspectives on Formative Mesoamerican cultures*, 51–72. BAR International Series 1377. Oxford.

Hansen, R. D., Bozarth, S., Jacob, J., Wahl, D., and Schreiner, T. 2002. Climatic and environmental variability in the rise of Maya civilization: A preliminary perspective from northern Peten. *Ancient Mesoamerica* 13: 273–96.

Hansen, R., Hansen, E. F., and Rodríguez-Navarro, C. 1997. Incipient Maya lime technology: Characterization and chronological variations in Preclassic plaster, stucco, and mortar at Nakbé, Guatemala. In P. B. Vandiver, J. R. Druzki, J. F. Merkel and J. Stewart (eds.), *Material Issues in Art and Archaeology V, 207–16*. Material Research Society, vol. 462. Pittsburgh: Material Research Society.

Harlow, G. E. 1993. Middle American jade: Geologic and petrologic perspectives on variability and source. In F. W. Lange (ed.), *Precolumbian Jade: New Geological and Cultural Interpretations*, 9–29. Salt Lake City: University of Utah Press.

Harman, G. and Thomson, J. J. 1996. *Moral Relativism and Moral Objectivity*. Oxford: Blackwell.

Harris, B. J. 2002. *English Aristocratic Women, 1450–1550: Marriage and Family, Property and Careers*. Oxford: Oxford University Press.

Harris, W. V. 1989. *Ancient Literacy*. Cambridge MA: Harvard University Press.

Harriss, G. 2006. *Shaping the Nation: England 1360–1461.* Oxford: Oxford University Press.

Harrison, P. D. 1977. The rise of the Bajos and the fall of the Maya. In N. Hammond (ed.), *Social Processes in Maya Prehistory: Essays in Honor of Sir Eric Thompson,* 470–508. New York: Academic Press.

———. 1996. Settlement and land use in the Pulltrouser Swamp Archaeological Zone, Northern Belize. In S. L. Fedick (ed.), *Managed Mosaic: Ancient Maya Agriculture and Resource Use,* 177–90. Salt Lake City: University of Utah Press.

———. 1999. *The Lords of Tikal: Rulers of an Ancient Maya City.* London: Thames and Hudson.

Hartung, H. 1980. Certain visual relations in the Palace at Palenque. In M. G. Robertson (ed.), *Third Palenque Round Table, 1978, Part 2,* 74–80. Austin: University of Texas Press.

Hassig, R. 1988. *Aztec Warfare: Imperial Expansion and Political Control.* Norman: University of Oklahoma Press.

Hatch, M. P. de. 1997. *Kaminaljuyú / San Jorge: Evidencia arqueológica de la actividad económica en el Valle de Guatemala, 300 aC a 300 dC.* Guatemala: Universidad del Valle de Guatemala.

———. 2003. La cerámica del altiplano noroccidental de Guatemala, La Lagunita y la Tradición Cerámica Solano: Algunas comparaciones. In M. C. Arnould, A. Breton, M. Fauvet-Berthelot and J. A. Valdes (eds.), *Misceláneas – en honor a Alain Ichon,* 49–63. México and Guatemala: Centro Francés de Estudios Mexicanos y Centroamericanos and the Asociación Tikal.

Haug, G. H., Günther, D., Peterson, L.C., Sigman, D. M., Hughen, K. A., and Aeschlimann, B. 2003. Climate and the collapse of Maya civilization. *Science* 299: 1731–5.

Haviland, W. A. 1981. Dower houses and minor centers at Tikal, Guatemala: An investigation into the identification of valid units in settlement hierarchies. In Wendy Ashmore (ed.), *Lowland Maya Settlement Patterns,* 89–117. Albuquerque: University of New Mexico Press.

———. 1988. Musical hammocks at Tikal: Problems with reconstructing household composition. In R. R. Wilk and W. Ashmore (eds.), *Household and Community in the Mesoamerican Past,* 121–34. Albuquerque: University of New Mexico Press.

———. 1992. Status and power in Classic Maya society: The view from Tikal. *American Anthropologist* 94: 937–40.

———. 1997. The rise and fall of sexual inequality: death and gender at Tikal, Guatemala. *Ancient Mesoamerica* 9: 1–12.

Haynes, E. S. 1990. Rajput ceremonial interaction as a mirror of a dying Indian state system, 1820–1947. *Modern Asian Studies* 24(3): 459–92.

Healy, P. F., Awe, J. J., and Helmuth, H. 1998. An ancient Maya multiple burial at Caledonia, Cayo district, Belize. *Journal of Field Archaeology* 25(3): 261–74.

Healy, P. F., Awe, J. J., Iannone, G., and Bill, C. 1995. Pacbitun (Belize) and ancient Maya use of slate. *Antiquity* 69: 337–48.

Helms, M. 1993. *Craft and the Kingly Ideal.* Austin: University of Texas Press.

———. 1998. *Access to Origins: Affines, Ancestors, and Aristocrats.* Austin: University of Texas Press.

Henderson, J. 1997. *The World of the Ancient Maya.* 2nd ed. Ithaca: Cornell University Press.

Hendon, J. A. 1991. Status and power in Classic Maya society: An archaeological study. *American Anthropologist* 93: 894–918.

———. 1992. Hilado y tejido en la época prehispánica: Tecnología y relaciones sociales de la producción textil. In L. Asturias de Barrios y D Fernández García (eds.), *La indumentaria y el tejido mayas a través del tiempo,* 7–16. Guatemala: Ediciones del Museo Ixchel.

———. 1997. Women's work, women's space, and women's status among the Classic-Period Maya elite of the Copan Valley, Honduras. In C. Claassen and R. A. Joyce (eds.), *Women in Prehistory: North America and Mesoamerica,* 33–46. Philadelphia: University of Pennsylvania Press.

———. 1999. The pre-Classic Maya compound as the focus of social identity. In D. C. Grove and R. A. Joyce (eds.), *Social Patterns in Pre-Classic Mesoamerica,* 97–126. Washington DC: Dumbarton Oaks.

———. 2003. In the house: Maya nobility and their figurine-whistles. *Expedition* 45(3): 28–33.

Hermes, B. 1999. La cerámica y otro tipo de evidencia anterior al periodo Clásico en Topoxte,

Petén. In J. P. Laporte, H. L. Escobedo and A. C. Monzón de Suasnávar (eds.), *XII Simposio de Investigaciones Arqueológicas en Guatemala*, 3–49. Guatemala: Ministerio de Cultura y Deportes, Instituto de Antropología e Historia, and the Asociación Tikal.

Hermitte, M. E. 1964. *Supernatural Power and Social Control in a Modern Maya Village*. Ph.D. dissertation. University of Chicago.

Herrup, C. B. 1999. *A House in Gross Disorder: Sex, Law, and the 2nd Earl of Castlehaven*. New York: Oxford University Press.

Herzfeld, M. 2001. *Anthropology: Theoretical Practice in Culture and Society*. Oxford: Blackwell.

Hester, T. R. 1985. The Maya lithic sequence in northern Belize. In M. G. Plew, J. C. Woods and M. G. Pavesic (eds.), *Stone Tool Analysis: Essays in Honor of Don E. Crabtree*, 187–210. Albuquerque: University of New Mexico Press.

Hester, T. R., and H. J. Shafer. 1994. Ancient Maya craft community at Colha, Belize, and its external relationships. In G. M. Schwartz and S. E. Falconer (eds.), *Archaeological Views from the Countryside*, 48–63. Washington DC: Smithsonian Institution Press.

Heyden, D. 2005. The Bodies of the gods: As seen in cult images made of wood in the Pictorial Codices. In E. H. Boone (ed.), *Painted Books and Indigenous Knowledge in Mesoamerica: Manuscript Studies in Honor of Mary Elizabeth Smith*, 43–61. New Orleans: Middle American Research Institute.

Hill, J. H. 1992. The Flower World of Old Uto-Aztecan. *Journal of Anthropological Research* 48: 117–44.

Hill, R. M. II, and Fischer, E. F. 1999. States of the heart: An ethnohistorical approach to Kaqchikel Maya ethnopsychology. *Ancient Mesoamerica* 10: 317–32.

Hill, R. M. II and Monaghan, J. 1987. *Continuities in Highland Maya Social Organization: Ethnohistory in Sacapulas*. Philadelphia: University of Pennsylvania Press.

Hill, W. D. and Clark, J. E. 2001. Sports, gambling, and government: America's first social compact? *American Anthropologist* 103(2): 331–45.

Hillesheim, M. B., Hodell, D. A. Leyden, B. W., Brenner M., Curtis J., Anselmetti F. S., Ariztegui D., Buck D. G., Guilderson T. P., Rosenmeier M. F., and Schnurrenberger D. W. 2005. Climate change in Lowland Central America during the late deglacial and early Holocene. *Journal of Quaternary Science* 20(4): 363–76.

Hobsbawm, E. 1992. Introduction: The invention of tradition. In E. Hobsbawm and T. Ranger (eds.), *The Invention of Tradition*, 1–14. Cambridge: Cambridge University Press.

Hodell, D., Curtis, J. H., and Brenner, M. 1995. Possible role of climate in the collapse of the Classic Maya civilization. *Nature* 375(1): 391–94.

Hodell, D. A., Brenner, M., Curtis, J. H., and Guilderson, T. 2001. Solar forcing of drought frequency in the Maya lowlands. *Science* 292: 1367–70.

Holmgren, J. 1991. Imperial marriage in the native Chinese and non-Han state, Han to Ming. In R. S. Watson and P. B. Ebrey (eds.), *Marriage and Inequality in Chinese Society*, 58–96. Berkeley: University of California Press.

Holsbeke, M. and Montoya, J. (eds.) 2003. *"With Their Hands and Their Eyes": Maya Textiles, Mirrors of a Worldview*. Antwerp: Etnografisch Museum.

Houston, S. D. 1986. *Problematic emblem glyphs: Examples from Altar de Sacrificios, El Chorro, Río Azul, and Xultun*. Research Reports on Ancient Maya Writing 3. Washington DC: Center for Maya Research.

———. 1987a. *The Inscriptions and Monumental Art of Dos Pilas, Guatemala: A Study of Classic Maya History and Politics*. Ph.D. dissertation, Yale University.

———. 1987b. Notes on Caracol epigraphy and its significance. In A. Chase and D. Chase (eds.), *Investigations at the Classic Maya City of Caracol, Belize 1985–1987*, 85–100. PARI Monograph 3. San Francisco.

———. 1993. *Hieroglyphs and History at Dos Pilas: Dynastic Politics of the Classic Maya*. Austin: University of Texas Press.

———. 1994. Literacy among the pre-Columbian Maya: A comparative perspective. In W. Mignolo and E. H. Boone (ed.), *Writing Without Words: Alternative Literacies in Mesoamerican and the Andes*, 27–49. Durham: Duke University Press.

———. 1996. Symbolic sweatbaths of the Maya: Architectural meaning in the Cross Group at Palenque, Mexico. *Latin American Antiquity* 7: 132–51.

———. 1997. A king worth a hill of beans. *Archaeology* May/June: 40.

———. 1998. Finding function and meaning in Classic Maya architecture. In S. D. Houston (ed.), *Function and Meaning in Classic Maya Architecture*, 519–38. Washington DC: Dumbarton Oaks.

———. 1999. Classic Maya Religion: Beliefs and Practices of an Ancient American People. *BYU Studies* 38(4): 43–72.

———. 2000. Into the minds of ancients: Advances in Maya glyph studies. *Journal of World Prehistory* 14: 121–201.

———. 2001. Food, feast, and fast among the Classic Maya. Invited Paper, Opening Session, "Consumption and Embodied Material Culture: The Archaeology of Drink, Food, and Commensal Politics," organized by M. Dietler, 66th Annual Meeting, Society for American Archaeology, New Orleans.

———. 2004a. Review of *Une histoire de la religion des Mayas: Du panthéisme au panthéon*, by Claude-François Baudez. *Ethnohistory* 51(2): 445–8.

———. 2004b. Overture to the first writing. In S. D. Houston (ed.) *The First Writing: Script Invention as History and Process*, 3–15. Cambridge: Cambridge University Press.

———. 2006 Review of *Stones Houses and Earth Lords*, eds., K. Prufer and J. Brady. *Cambridge Archaeological Journal* 16(3): 356–8.

———. 2007a. Apasionado: Cities and monuments of the lower Pasión River. Paper presented at the 2007 Texas Maya Meetings, Austin.

———. 2007b. An Early Classic Cave Ritual. http://decipherment.wordpress.com/2007/12/11/an-early-classic-cave-ritual/. Accessed Sept. 6, 2008.

———. 2007c. Young Bloods: The nature and role of youths in Classic Maya society. Paper presented at the III International Copan Congress, The Art of Power in the Mundo Maya, Copan, Honduras.

———. 2008. A Classic Maya Bailiff? Maya Decipherment: A weblog on the Ancient Maya Script. http://decipherment.wordpress.com/2008/03/10/a-classic-maya-bailiff/. Accessed April 15, 2008.

Houston, S. D., Brittenham, C., Mesick, C., Tokovinine, A., and Warriner, C. In press. *Veiled Brightness: A History of Ancient Maya Color*. Austin: University of Texas Press.

Houston, S. D. and Cummins, T. 2004. Body, presence, and space in Andean and Mesoamerican rulership. In S. E. Evans and J. Pillsbury (eds.), *Palaces of the Ancient New World*, 359–98. Washington DC: Dumbarton Oaks.

Houston, S. D., Escobedo, H., Child, M., Golden, C., and Muñoz, R. 2001. Crónica de una muerte anunciada: Los años finales de Piedras Negras. In Andrés Ciudad Ruíz, M.a Josefa Iglesias Ponce de León, and M.a del Carmen Martínez Martínez (eds.), *Reconstruyendo la ciudad Maya: El urbanismo en las sociedades antiguas*, 65–93. Madrid: Sociedad Española de Estudios Mayas.

Houston, S. D., Escobedo, H., Hardin, P., Terry, R., and Stuart, D. 1999. Between mountain and sea: Investigations at Piedras Negras, Guatemala. *Mexicon* 21(1): 10–17.

Houston, S. D., Escobedo, H., Scherer, A., Child, M., and Fitzsimmons, J. 2003. Classic Maya death at Piedras Negras, Guatemala. In A. Ciudad, M. Humberto Ruz Sosa, and M. Josefa Iglesias Ponce de León (eds.), *La muerte en el mundo maya*, 113–143. Madrid: Sociedad Española de Estudios Mayas.

Houston, S. D., and Mathews, P. L. 1985. *Dynastic Sequence of Dos Pilas, Guatemala*. Pre-Columbian Art Research Institute, Monograph 1. San Francisco.

Houston, S. D., Mazariegos, C., and Stuart, D (eds.) 2001. *The Decipherment of Ancient Maya Writing*. Norman: University of Oklahoma Press.

Houston, S. D., Nelson, Z., Chiriboga, C., and Spensley, E. 2003. The acropolis of Kaminaljuyú, Guatemala: Recovering a "Lost Excavation." *Mayab* 16: 49–64.

Houston, S. D., Robertson, J., and Stuart, D. 2000. *Quality and Quantity in Glyphic Nouns and Adjectives*. Research Reports on Ancient Maya Writing, No. 47. Washington DC: Center for Maya Research.

Houston, S. D. and Scherer, A. K. 2007. La ofrenda máxima: El sacrificio humano en la parte central del área maya. Paper presented in *Nuevas Perspectivas Sobre el Sacrificio Humano entre los Mexicas*, Museo Templo Mayor, México.

Houston, S. D. and Stuart, D. 1989. *The Way Glyph: Evidence for "Co-Essences" Among the Classic Maya*. Research Reports on Ancient Maya Writing, No. 30. Washington DC: Center for Maya Research.

———. 1996. Of gods, glyphs, and kings: Divinity and rulership among the Classic Maya. *Antiquity* 70: 289–312.

———. 1998. The ancient Maya self: Personhood and portraiture in the Classic period. *RES: Anthropology and Aesthetics* 33: 73–101.

———. 2001. Peopling the Classic Maya court. In T. Inomata and S. D. Houston (eds.), *Royal Courts of the Ancient Maya*, 54–83. Boulder: Westview Press.

Houston, S. D., Stuart, D., Woolley, C., and Wright, L. 1991. A death monument: Dos Pilas Throne 1. Ms. in possession of authors.

Houston, S. D. and Taube, K. A. 2000. An archaeology of the senses: Perception and cultural expression in ancient Mesoamerica. *Cambridge Archaeological Journal* 10(2): 261–94.

———. 2007. The fiery pool: Water and sea among the Classic Maya. Ms. in possession of authors.

Houston, S. D., Taube, K. A., and Stuart, D. 2006. *The Memory of Bones: Body, Being, and Experience among the Classic Maya.* Austin: University of Texas Press.

Howell, W. K. 1989. *Excavations in the Danta Complex at El Mirador, Petén, Guatemala.* Papers of the New World Archaeological Foundation 60. Provo: Brigham Young University.

Hruby, Z. X. 2006. *The Organization of Chipped-Stone Economies at Piedras Negras, Guatemala.* Ph.D. dissertation. University of California Riverside.

———. 2007. *Ritualized chipped-stone production at Piedras Negras*, Guatemala. In Z. X. Hruby and R. K. Flad (eds.), *Rethinking Craft Specialization in Complex Societies: Archaeological Analyses of the Social Meaning of Production*, 68–87. Archaeological Papers of the American Anthropological Association 17. Arlington.

Hunt, E. 1977. *The Transformation of the Hummingbird: Cultural Roots of a Zinacantan Mythical Poem.* Ithaca: Cornell University Press.

Huntington, R. and Metcalf, P. 1979. *Celebrations of Death: The Anthropology of Mortuary Ritual.* Cambridge: Cambridge University Press.

Hutson, S. R., Magnoni, A., Mazeau, D. E., and Stanton, T. W. 2006. The archaeology of urban houselots at Chunchukmil, Yucatán. In J. P. Mathews and B. A. Morrison (eds.), *Lifeways in the Northern Maya Lowlands: New Approaches to Archaeology in the Yucatán Peninsula,* 77–92. Tucson: University of Arizona Press.

Hutson, S. R., Stanton, T. W., Magnoni, A., Terry, R., and Craner, J. 2007. Beyond the buildings: Formation processes of ancient Maya houselots and methods for the study of non-architectural space. *Journal of Anthropological Archaeology* 26: 442–73.

Hvidtfeldt, A. 1958. *Teotl and Ixiptlatli: Some Central Conceptions in Ancient Mexican Religion.* Copenhagen: Andreassen.

Iceland, H. B. 1997. *The Preceramic Origins of the Maya: The Results of the Colha Preceramic Project in Northern Belize.* Ph.D. dissertation. University of Texas, Austin.

Ichon, A. 1977. *Les sculptures de La Lagunita, El Quiche, Guatemala.* Guatemala: Editorial Piedra Santa.

Ichon, A. and Arnauld, M. C. 1985. *Le protoclassique á la Lagunita, El Quiché, Guatemala.* Paris: Centre National de la Recherche Scientifique.

Inomata, T. 2001a. The power and ideology of artistic creation: Elite craft specialists in Classic Maya society. *Current Anthropology* 42(3): 321–49.

———. 2001b. The Classic Maya royal palace as a political theater. In A. Ciudad Ruiz, M. Josefa Iglesias Ponce de León, and M. del Carmen Martínez Martínez (eds.), *Reconstruyendo la ciudad maya: El urbanismo en la sociedades antigua,* 341–362. Sociedad Española de Estudios Mayas, Madrid.

———. 2001c. King's people: Classic Maya royal courtiers in a comparative perspective. In T. Inomata and S. Houston (eds.), *Royal courts of the ancient Maya, Volume 1: Theory, comparison, and synthesis,* 27–53. Boulder: Westview Press.

———. 2003a. Aguateca: New revelations of the Maya elite. *National Geographic* 203(5): 110–19.

———. 2003b. War, destruction, and abandonment: The fall of the Classic Maya center of Aguateca, Guatemala. In T. Inomata and R. Webb (eds.), *The archaeology of settlement abandonment in Middle America,* 43–60. Salt Lake City: University of Utah Press.

———. 2004. The spatial mobility of non-elite populations in Classic Maya society and its political implications. In J. C. Lohse and F. Valdez, Jr. (eds.), *Ancient Maya Commoners,* 175–96. Austin: University of Texas Press.

———. 2006a. Plazas, performers, and spectators: Political theaters of the Classic Maya. *Current Anthropology* 47(5): 805–42.

———. 2006b. Politics and theatricality in Mayan society. In T. Inomata and L. S. Coben (eds.), *Archaeology of Performance: Theaters of Power, Community and Politics*, 187–221. Walnut Creek: Altamira Press.

———. 2007a. Classic Maya elite competition, collaboration, and performance in multi-craft production. In I. Shimada (ed.), *Rethinking Craft Production*, 120–35. Salt Lake City: University of Utah Press.

———. 2007b. Knowledge and belief in craft production by Classic Maya elites. In Z. X. Hruby and R. Flad (eds.), *Rethinking Production in Archaeological Contexts*, 129–41. Archaeological papers of the American Anthropological Association, No. 17. Arlington.

———. 2008a. Warfare and the fall of a fortified center: Archaeological investigations at Aguateca. Vanderbilt Institute of Mesoamerican Archaeology, Vol. 3, A. Demarest, series editor. Nashville: Vanderbilt University Press.

———. 2008b. Women in Classic Maya royal courts. In A. Walthall (ed.), *Servants of the dynasty: Palace women in world history*, 45–64. Berkeley: University of California Press.

Inomata, T. and Aoyama, K. 1996. Central place analyses in the La Entrada region, Honduras: Implications for understanding the Classic Maya political and economic systems. *Latin American Antiquity* 7: 291–312.

Inomata, T. and Houston, S. 2001. Opening the royal Maya court. In T. Inomata and S. Houston (eds.), *Royal courts of the ancient Maya, Volume 1: Theory, comparison, and synthesis*, 3–23. Boulder: Westview Press.

Inomata, T., Ponciano, E., Chinchilla, O., Román, O., Breuil–Martínez, V., and Santos, O. 2004. An unfinished temple at the Classic Maya center of Aguateca, Guatemala. *Antiquity* 78: 798–811.

Inomata, T. and Stiver, L. R. 1998. Floor assemblages from burned structures at Aguateca, Guatemala: A study of Classic Maya households. *Journal of Field Archaeology* 25(4): 431–52.

Inomata, T. and Triadan, D. 2000. Craft production by Classic Maya elites in domestic settings: Data from rapidly abandoned structures at Aguateca, Guatemala. *Mayab* 13: 57–66.

Inomata, T., Triadan, D., Ponciano, E., and Ayama, K (editors). In press. *La política de lugares y comunidades en la antigua sociedad maya de Petexbatun: Las investigaciones del Proyecto Arqueológico Aguateca Segunda Fase*. Guatemala: Ministerio de Cultura y Deportes, Dirección General del Patrimonio Cultural y Natural, and Instituto de Antropología e Historia.

Inomata, T., Triadan, D., Ponciano, E., Pinto, E., Terry, R. E., and Eberl, M. 2002. Domestic and political lives of Classic Maya elites: The excavation of rapidly abandoned structures at Aguateca, Guatemala. *Latin American Antiquity* 13: 305–30.

Inomata, T., Triadan, D., Ponciano, E., Terry, R. E., and Beaubien, H. F. 2001. In the palace of the fallen king: The royal residential complex at the Classic Maya center of Aguateca, Guatemala. *Journal of Field Archaeology* 28: 287–306.

Isendahl, C. 2002. *Common Knowledge: Lowland Maya Urban Farming at Xuch*. Studies in Global Archaeology, 1. Uppsala: Department of Archaeology and Ancient History, Uppsala University.

Jackson, S. 2005. *Deciphering Classic Maya Political Hierarchy: Epigraphic, Archeological, and Ethnohistoric Perspectives on the Courtly Elite*. Ph.D. dissertation. Department of Anthropology, Harvard University.

Jackson, S. and Stuart, D. 2001. The *Aj K'uhun* title: Deciphering a Classic Maya term of rank. *Ancient Mesoamerica* 12: 217–28.

Jackson, T. L. and Love, M. W. 1991. Blade running: Middle Preclassic obsidian exchange and the introduction of prismatic blades at La Blanca, Guatemala. *Ancient Mesoamerica* 2: 47–59.

Jacob, J. S. 1995. Ancient Maya wetland agricultural fields in Cobweb Swamp, Belize: Construction, chronology, and function. *Journal of Field Archaeology* 22: 175–90.

Jarrard, A. 2003. *Architecture as Performance in Seventeenth-Century Europe: Court Ritual in Modena, Rome, and Paris*. Cambridge: Cambridge University Press.

Joesink-Mandeville, L. 1970. *Comparative cultural statigraphy of Formative complexes in the Maya area: A re-appraisal in the light of new evidence from Dzibilchaltun, Yucatan*. Ph.D. dissertation. Tulane University.

Joesink-Mandeville, L. V. 1977. Olmec-Maya relationships: A correlation of linguistic evidence with archaeological ceramics. *Journal of New World Archaeology* 2: 30–9.

Joesink-Mandeville, L. V. and Meluzin, S. 1976. Olmec-Maya relationships: Olmec influence in Yucatán. In H. B. Nicholson (ed.), *Origins of Religious Art and Iconography in Preclassic Mesoamerica*, 89–105. Latin American Studies Series 31. Los Angeles: UCLA Latin American Center.

Johns, C. 1982. *Sex or Symbol? Erotic Images of Greece and Rome*. New York: Routledge.

Johnson, K., Wright, D. R., and Terry, R. E. 2007. Application of carbon isotope analysis to ancient maize agriculture in the Petexbatún Region of Guatemala. *Geoarchaeology: An International Journal* 22: 313–36.

Johnson, M. 1993. *Moral Imagination: Implications of Cognitive Science for Ethics*. Chicago: University of Chicago Press.

Johnston, K. J. 1994. *The "Invisible Maya": Late Classic Minimally-Platformed Residential Settlement at Itzán, Petén, Guatemala*. Ph.D. dissertation. Yale University.

Johnston, K. J. and Gonlin, N. 1998. What do houses mean? Approaches to the analysis of Classic Maya commoner residences. In S. D. Houston (ed.), *Function and Meaning in Classic Maya Architecture*, 141–85. Washington DC: Dumbarton Oaks.

Jones, C. 1969. *Twin-Pyramid Group Pattern: A Classic Maya Architectural Assemblage at Tikal, Guatemala*. Ph.D. dissertation. Department of Anthropology, University of Pennsylvania.

———. 1975. A painted capstone from the Maya area. In J. A. Graham (ed.), *Studies in Ancient Mesoamerica*, 83–110. Contributions of the University of California Archaeological Facility. Berkeley: Department of Anthropology, University of California.

———. 1996. *Tikal Reports No. 16: Excavations in the East Plaza of Tikal*. University Museum Monograph 92. Philadelphia: University Museum, University of Pennsylvania.

Jones, C. and Satterthwaite, L. 1982. *Tikal Report No. 33, Part A: The Monuments and Inscriptions of Tikal: The Carved Monuments*. University Museum Monograph 44. Philadelphia: University Museum, University of Pennsylvania.

Jones, G. D. 1982. Agriculture and trade in the colonial period southern Maya lowlands. In K. V. Flannery (ed.), *Maya Subsistence: Studies in Memory of Dennis E. Puleston*, 275–93. New York: Academic Press.

Jones, J. G. 1994. Pollen evidence for early settlement and agriculture in northern Belize. *Palynology* 18: 205–11.

Jones, T. 1985. Xoc, the sharke, and the sea dogs: An historical encounter. In V. M. Fields (ed.), *Fifth Palenque Round Table, 1983*, 211–22. San Francisco: Pre-Columbian Art Research Institute.

Joralemon, P. D. 1971. *A Study of Olmec Iconography*. Studies in Pre-Columbian Art and Archaeology 7. Washington DC: Dumbarton Oaks.

Josserand, J. K. and Hopkins, N. A. 1988. *Chol (Mayan) Dictionary Database*. 3 vols. Final performance report to the National Endowment for the Humanities, Grant RT-20643–86.

Joyce, A. and Winter, M. 1996. Ideology, power and urban society in prehispanic Oaxaca. *Current Anthropology* 37 (1): 33–86.

Joyce, R. A. 1993. Women's work: Images of production and reproduction in pre-Hispanic southern Central America. *Current Anthropology* 34: 255–74.

———. 2000a. A Precolumbian gaze: Male sexuality among the Ancient Maya. In R. A. Schmidt and B. L. Voss (eds.), *Archaeologies of Sexuality*, 263–283. London: Routledge.

———. 2000b. *Gender and Power in Prehispanic Mesoamerica*. Austin: University of Texas Press.

———. 2000c. High culture, mesoamerican civilization, and the Classic Maya tradition. In J. Richards and M. Van Buren (eds.), *Order, Legitimacy and Wealth in Ancient States*. Cambridge: Cambridge University Press.

Joyce, R. A. and Henderson, J. S. 2001. Beginnings of village life in eastern Mesoamerica. *Latin American Antiquity* 12: 5–23.

Just, B. R. 2005. Modification of Maya sculpture. *RES: Anthropology and Aesthetics* 48: 69–82.

Justeson, J. S. 1989. Ancient Maya ethnoastronomy: An overview of hieroglyphic sources. In A. F. Aveni (ed.), *World Archaeoastronomy*, 76–129. Cambridge: Cambridge University Press.

Justeson, J. S. and Kaufman, T. 1993. A decipherment of Epi-Olmec hieroglyphic writing. *Science* 259: 1703–11.

Justeson, J. S., Norman, W. M., Campbell, L., and Kaufman, T. 1985. *The Foreign Impact on Lowland Maya Language and Script*. Middle American Research Institute Publication 53. New Orleans: Tulane University.

Kaneko, A. 2003. *Artefactos líticos de Yaxchilán.* México: Instituto Nacional de Antropología e Historia.

Kaplan, F. E. 1997. Iyoba, the Queen Mother of Benin: Images and ambiguity in gender and sex roles in court art. *Annals of the New York Academy of Sciences* 810: 73–102.

Kaplan, J. 1995. The Incienso Throne and other thrones from Kaminaljuyu, Guatemala: Late Preclassic examples of a mesoamerican throne tradition. *Ancient Mesoamerica* 6: 185–96.

Karttunen, F. 1983. *An Analytical Dictionary of Nahuatl.* Austin: University of Texas Press.

Kaufman, T. S. 2003. A Preliminary Mayan Etymological Dictionary. http://www.famsi.org/reports/01051/pmed.pdf. Accessed April 17, 2008.

Kaufman, T. S. and Norman, W. M. 1984. An outline of Proto-Cholan phonology, morphology, and vocabulary. In J. S. Justeson, and L. Campbell (eds.), *Phoneticism in Mayan Hieroglyphic Writing*, 77–166. Institute for Mesoamerican Studies, Publication 9. Albany: State University of New York, Albany.

Keesing, R. M. 1987. Anthropology as interpretive quest. *Current Anthropology* 28(2): 161–76.

Kellogg, S. 2005. *Weaving the Past: A History of Latin America's Indigenous Women from the Prehispanic Period to the Present.* Oxford: Oxford University Press.

Kelley, D. H. 1968. Kacupacal and the Itzas. *Estudios de Cultura Maya* 7: 255–68.

Kepecs, S. and Boucher, S. 1996. Pre-Hispanic cultivation of Rejolladas and Stone-Lands: New evidence from northeast Yucatán. In S. L. Fedick (ed.), *Managed Mosaic: Ancient Maya Agriculture and Resource Use*, 69–91. Salt Lake City: University of Utah Press.

Kertzer, D. I. 1988. *Ritual, Politics, and Power.* New Haven: Yale University Press.

Killion, T. W., Sabloff, J. A., Tourtellot, G., and Dunning, N. P. 1989. Intensive surface collection of residential clusters at Terminal Classic Sayil, Yucatan, Mexico. *Journal of Field Archaeology* 16: 273–94.

Kirkby, A. V. T. 1973. *The Use of Land Water Resources in the Past and Present Valley of Oaxaca.* Memoirs of the Museum of Anthropology, University of Michigan 5(1). Ann Arbor.

Klass, M. 1995. *Ordered Universes: Approaches to the Anthropology of Religion.* Boulder: Westview Press.

Knauft, B. M. 1996. *Genealogies for the Present in Cultural Anthropology.* London: Routledge.

Köhler, U. 1977. *Čonbilal Č'ulelal: Grundformen mesoamerikanische Kosmologie und Religion in einem Gebetstext auf Maya-Tzotzil.* Wiesbaden: Franz Steiner Verlag.

———. 1995. *Chonbilal Ch'ulelal = Alma Vendida: Elementos fundamentales de la cosmología y religión mesoamericanas en una oración en maya-tzotzil.* Mexico: Universidad Nacional Aútonoma de México.

Kolb, M. J., and Snead, J. E. 1997. It's a small world after all: Comparative analyses of community organization in archaeology. *American Antiquity* 62(4): 609–28.

Kovacevich, B. 2006. *Reconstructing Classic Maya Economic Systems: Production and Exchange at Cancuen, Guatemala.* Ph.D. dissertation. Vanderbilt University.

———. 2007. Ritual, crafting, and agency at the Classic Maya kingdom of Cancuen. In E. Christian Wells and K. L. Davis-Salazar (eds.), *Mesoamerican Ritual Economy: Archaeology and Ethnological Perspectives*, 67–114. Boulder: University Press of Colorado.

Kowalski, J. K. 1987. *The House of the Governor: A Maya Palace at Uxmal, Yucatan, Mexico.* Norman: University of Oklahoma Press.

———. 1989. Who am I among the Itza? Links between northern Yucatan and the western Maya lowlands and highlands. In R. A. Diehl and J. C. Berlo (eds.), *Mesoamerica After the Decline of Teotihuacan A.D. 700–900*, 173–86. Washington DC: Dambarton Oaks Research Library and Collection.

———. 2003. Evidence for the functions and meanings of some northern Maya palaces. In J. J. Christie (ed.), *Maya Palaces and Elite Residences: An Interdisciplinary Approach*, 204–52. Austin: University of Texas Press.

———. 2007. What's "Toltec" at Uxmal and Chichén Itzá? Merging Maya and Mesoamerica worldviews and world systems in Terminal Classic to Early Postclassic Yucatán. In J. K. Kowalski and C. Kristan-Graham (eds.), *Twin Tollans: Chichén Itzá, Tula, and the Epiclassic to Early Postclassic Mesoamerican World*, 251–314. Washington DC: Dunbarton Oaks Research Library and Collection.

Kowalski, J. K., Barrera, R. A., Ojeda M. H., and Huchim H. J. 1996. Archaeological excavations of a round temple at Uxmal: Summary discussion and implications for northern

Maya culture history. In M. J. Macri and J. McHargue (eds.), *Eighth Palenque Round Table, 1993*, Vol. X, 281–96. San Francisco: Pre–Columbian Art Research Institute.

Kray, C. A. 1997. *Worship in Body and Spirit: Practice, Self, and Religious Sensibility in Yucatán*. Ph.D. dissertation. University of Pennsylvania.

Krejcki, E. and Culbert, T. P. 1995. Preclassic and Classic burials and caches in the Maya lowlands. In N. Grube (ed.), *The Emergence of Lowland Maya Civilization: The Transition from the Preclassic to the Early Classic*, 103–16. Acta Mesoamericana, 8. Berlin: Verlag von Flemming.

Kris, E. and Kurz, O. 1979. *Legend, Myth, and Magic in the Image of the Artist: A Historical Experiment*. New Haven: Yale University Press.

Kristan-Graham, C. 2007. Structuring identity at Tula: The design and symbolism of colonnaded halls and sunken spaces. In J. K. Kowalski and C. Kristan-Graham (eds.), *Twin Tollans: Chichén Itzá, Tula, and the Epiclassic to Early Postclassic Mesoamerican World*, 531–578. Washington DC: Dunbarton Oaks Research Library and Collection.

Krochock, R. and Freidel, D. A. 1994. Ballcourts and the evolution of political rhetoric at Chichén Itzá. In H. J. Prem (ed.), *Hidden Among the Hills: Maya Archaeology of the Northwest Yucatan Peninsula*, 359–75. Acta Mesoamericana, 7. Möckmühl: Verlag von Flemming.

Kubler, G. 1972. *Studies in Classic Maya Iconography*. Connecticut Academy of Arts and Sciences, Memoirs 18. New Haven.

———. 1977. *Aspects of Classic Maya Rulership on Two Inscribed Vessels*. Studies in Pre-Columbian Art and Archaeology, 18. Washington DC: Dumbarton Oaks.

Kurjack, E. B. 1974. *Prehistoric Lowland Maya Community and Social Organization: A Case Study at Dzibilchaltun*. Middle American Research Institute Publications 38. New Orleans: Tulane University.

Kurjack, E. B. and Garza Tarazona, S. 1981. Pre-Columbian community form and distribution in the northern Maya area. In W. Ashmore (ed.), *Lowland Maya Settlement Patterns*, 287–309. Albuquerque: University of New Mexico Press.

Kus, S. and Raharijaona, V. 2000. House to palaces, village to state: Scaling up architecture and ideology. *American Anthropologist* 102: 98–113.

Lacadena García-Gallo, A. 2000. Nominal syntax and linguistic affiliation of Classic Maya texts in The Sacred and the Profane: Architecture and identity in the Maya lowlands. In P. R. Colas, K. Delvendahl, M. Kuhnert and A. Schubart (eds.), 111–28. Acta Mesoamericana 10. Markt Schwaben: Verlag Anton Saurwein.

———. 2004. The glyphic corpus from Ek' Balam, Yucatán, México. Report to FAMSI, http://www.famsi.org/reports/01057/index.html. Accessed April 15, 2008.

———. 2006. El título Lakam: Evidencia epigráfica de la organización interna tributaria y militar de los reinos Mayas del Clásico. Paper presented at the 52nd International Congress of Americanists, Sevilla, Spain.

La Fontaine, J. S. 1985. Person and individual: Some anthropological reflections. In M. Carrithers, S. Collins and S. Lukes (eds.), *The Category of the Person: Anthropology, Philosophy, History*, 123–40. Cambridge: Cambridge University Press.

Lamont, M. 2000. *The Dignity of Working Men: Morality and the Boundaries of Race, Class, and Immigration*. Cambridge MA: Harvard University Press.

Laporte Molina, J. P. 2003. La tradición funeraria prehispánica en la región de Petén, Guatemala: Una visión desde Tikal y otras ciudades. In A. Ciudad, M. H. Ruz Sosa, M. J. Iglesias Ponce de León (eds.), *La muerte en el mundo maya*, 49–76. Madrid: Sociedad Española de Estudios Mayas.

Laporte, J. P. 1995. ¿Despoblamiento o problema analítico?: El Clásico Temprano en el sureste de Petén. In J. P. Laporte and H. L. Escobedo (eds.), *VIII Simposio de Investigaciones Arqueologicas en Guatemala, 1994*, 729–61. Guatemala: Ministerio de Cultura y Deportes, Instituto de Antropología e Historia, and the Asociación Tikal.

———. 2004. Terminal Classic settlement and polity in the Mopan Valley, Petén, Guatemala. In A. A. Demarest, P. M. Rice and D. S. Rice (eds.), *The Terminal Classic in the Maya Lowlands: Collapse, Transition, and Transformation*, 195–230. Boulder: University Press of Colorado.

Laporte, J. P. and Fialko, V. 1995. Un reencuentro con Mundo Perdido, Tikal, Guatemala. *Ancient Mesoamerica* 6: 41–94.

Laporte, J. P. and Mejía, H. E. 2002. Ucanal: Una ciudad del Río Mopan en Petén, Guatemala. *U Tz'ib* 1(2): 1–71.

Laporte, J. P., Reyes, M. A., and Chocón, J. E. 2004. Catálogo de figurillas y silbatos de barro del Atlas Arqueológico de Guatemala (F-001 – F191). In J. P. Laporte (ed.), *Reporte 18, Atlas Arqueológico de Guatemala*, 325–72. Guatemala: Instituto de Antropología e Historia.

Laporte, J. P. and Antonio Valdés, J. 1993. *Tikal y Uaxactún en el Preclásico*. México: Universidad Nacional Autónoma de México.

Larios Villalta, C. R. 2003. *Criterios de restauración arquitectónica en el área Maya*. Report to FAMSI, http://www.famsi.org/reports/99026es/index.html. Accessed April 15, 2008.

Las Casas, B. de. 1909. *Apologética historia de las indias*. 3 vols. Madrid.

———. 1951. *Historia de las Indias*. 3 vols. México: Fondo de Cultura Económica.

Latham, M. C. 1997. *Human Nutrition in the Developing World. Vol. 29. Food and Nutrition Series*. Rome: Food and Agriculture Organization of the United Nations.

Laughlin, R. M. 1975. *The Great Tzotzil Dictionary of San Lorenzo Zinacantan*. Washington DC: Smithsonian Institution.

———. 1988. *The Great Tzotzil Dictionary of Santo Domingo Zinacantán*. 3 vols. Smithsonian Contributions to Anthropology 31. Washington DC: Smithsonian Institution Press.

LeCount, L. J. 1999. Polychrome pottery and political strategies in Late and Terminal Classic lowland Maya society. *Latin American Antiquity* 10(3): 239–58.

———. 2001. Like water for chocolate: Feasting and political ritual among the Late Classic Maya at Xunantunich, Belize. *American Anthropologist* 103: 935–53.

Lee, T. A., Jr. 1989. Chiapas and the Olmec. In R. J. Sharer and D. C. Grove (eds.), *Regional Perspectives on the Olmec*, 198–226. Cambridge: Cambridge University Press.

Lee, T. A. and Hayden, B. 1988. *San Pablo Cave and El Cayo on the Usumacinta River, Chiapas, Mexico*. Papers of the New World Archaeological Foundation No. 53. Provo: Brigham Young University.

Leifer, T., Nielsen, J., and Reunert, T. S. 2002. *Det urolige blod: Biografi om Frans Blom*. Copenhagen: Høst & Søn.

Lenkersdorf, C. 1979. *B'omak'umal tojol ab'al – kastiya. Diccionario tojolabal – español. Volumen uno*. México: Editorial Nuestro Tiempo.

Lentz, D. L. 1991. Maya diets of the rich and poor: Paleoethnobotanical evidence from Copan. *Latin American Antiquity* 2: 269–87.

———. 1999. Plant resources of the ancient Maya: The paleoethnobotanical evidence. In C. D. White (ed.), *Reconstructing Ancient Maya Diet*, 3–18. Salt Lake City: University of Utah Press.

Lentz, D. L., Beaudry-Corbett, M. P., Reyna de Aguilar, M. L., and Kaplan, L. 1996. Foodstuffs, forests, fields, and shelter: A paleoethnobotanical analysis of vessel contents from the Cerén site, El Salvador. *Latin American Antiquity* 7(3): 247–62.

Le Roy Ladurie, E. 2001. *Saint-Simon and the Court of Louis XIV*. Trans. A. Goldhammer. Chicago: University of Chicago Press.

Lesure, R. G. 1997. Early Formative platforms at Paso de la Amada, Chiapas, Mexico. *Latin American Antiquity* 8: 217–36.

———. 2004. Shared art styles and long-distance contact in early Mesoamerica. In R.A. Joyce and J.A. Hendon (eds.), *Mesoamerican Archaeology*, 73–96. Oxford: Blackwell Publishing.

Leventhal, R. M. 1983. Household groups and Classic Maya religion. In E. Z. Vogt and R. M. Leventhal (eds.), *Prehistoric Settlement Patterns: Essays in Honor of Gordon R. Willey*, 55–76. Albuquerque: University of New Mexico Press.

Levi, L. J. 1996. Sustainable production and residential variation: A historical perspective on pre-Hispanic domestic economies in the Maya lowlands. In S. L. Fedick (ed.), *The Managed Mosaic: Ancient Maya Agricultural and Resource Use*, 92–106. Salt Lake City: University of Utah Press.

Lévi-Strauss, C. 1991. *Maison*. In P. Bonte and M. Izard (eds.), *Dictionnaire de l'ethnologie et de l'anthropologie*, 434–36. Paris: Presses Universitaires de France.

Lewenstein, S. M. 1987. *Stone Tool Use at Cerros: The Ethnoarchaeology and Use-Wear Evidence*. Austin: University of Texas Press.

Leyden, B. 1984. Guatemalan forest synthesis after pleistocene aridity. *Proceedings of the National Academy of Sciences* 81(15): 4856–9.

Liendo Stuardo, R. 2003. Access patterns in Maya royal precincts. In J. J. Christie (ed.),

Maya Palaces and Elite Residences: An Interdisciplinary Approach, 184–203. Austin: University of Texas Press.

——. 2007. The problem of political integration in the kingdom of Baak. In D. R. Marken (ed.), *Palenque: Recent Investigations at the Classic Maya Center*, 85–106. Lanham: Altamira Press.

Lienhardt, G. 1985. Self: public, private: Some African representations. In M. Carrithers, S. Collins and S. Lukes (eds.), *The Category of the Person: Anthropology, Philosophy, History*, 141–55. Cambridge: Cambridge University Press.

Lincoln, C. E. 1985. Ceramics and ceramic chronology. In G. R. Willey and P. Mathews (eds.), *A Consideration of the Early Classic Period in the Maya Lowlands*, 55–94. Institute for Mesoamerican Studies, Publication No. 10. Albany: State University of New York.

——. 1986. The chronology of Chichen Itza: A review of the literature. In J. A. Sabloff and E. W. Andrews V (eds.), *Late Lowland Maya Civilization: Classic to Postclassic*, 141–96. Albuquerque: University of New Mexico Press.

——. 1994. Structural and philological evidence for divine kingship at Chichén Itzá, Yucatan, México. In H. J. Prem (ed.), *Hidden Among the Hills*, 164–96. Acta Mesoamericana, 7. Möckmühl: Verlag Von Flemming.

Lindholm, C. 1990. *Charisma*. Cambridge: Blackwell.

Linnekin, J. 1990. *Sacred Queens and Women of Consequence: Rank, Gender, and Colonialism in the Hawaiian Islands*. Ann Arbor: University of Michigan Press.

Lizana, B. de. 1988. *Historia de Yucatán*. Madrid: Historia 16.

Loades, D. 1986. *The Tudor Court*. London: Batsford.

Lockhart, J. 1992. *The Nahuas After the Conquest: A Social and Cultural History of the Indians of Central Mexico, Sixteenth Through Eighteenth Centuries*. Stanford: Stanford University Press.

López, R. 1993. Un ensayo sobre patrones de enterramiento y evidencias de sacrificio humano en Kaminaljuyú, Guatemala. In J. P. Laporte, H. L. Escobedo and S. V. de Brady (eds.), *VI Simposio de Investigaciones Arqueológicas en Guatemala*, 391–99. Guatemala: Ministerio de Cultura y Deportes, Museo Nacional de Arqueología e Etnología.

López Austin, A. 1961. *La constitución real de México-Tenochtitlan*. México: Universidad Nacional Autónoma de México.

——. 1980. *The Human Body and Ideology: Concepts of the Ancient Nahuas*. Trans. T. Ortiz de Montellano and B. Ortiz de Montellano. Austin: University of Texas Press.

López Bravo, R. 2004. State and domestic cult in Palenque censer stands. In M. Miller and S. Martin (eds.), *Courtly Art of the Ancient Maya*, 256–58. London: Thames and Hudson.

López Jiménez, F. 2005. Quien es la Reina Roja? *Arqueología mexicana* 12(69): 66–9.

López Varela, S. L. 2004. Ceramic history of K'axob: The early years. In P. A. McAnany (ed.), *K'axob: Ritual, Work and Family in an Ancient Maya Village*, 169–91. Momenta Archaeologica, No. 22. Los Angeles: Cotsen Institute of Archaeology, UCLA.

López Varela, S. L., McAnany, P. A., and Berry, K. A. 2001. Ceramics technology at Late Classic K'axob, Belize. *Journal of Field Archaeology* 28: 177–91.

López Varela, S. L., van Gijn, A. L., and Jacobs, L. 2002. De-mystifying pottery production in the Maya lowlands: Detection of traces of use-wear on pottery sherds through microscopic analysis and experimental replication. *Journal of Archaeological Science* 29: 1133–47.

Lothrop, S. K. 1952. *Metals from the Cenote of Sacrifice, Chichen Itza, Yucatan*. Memoirs, 10(2). Cambridge MA: Harvard University, Peabody Museum of American Archaeology and Ethnology.

Lounsbury, F. G. 1978. Maya numeration, computation, and calendrical astronomy. In C. C. Gillispie (ed.), *Dictionary of Scientific Biography*, 759–818. New York: Charles Scribner's Sons.

——. 1983. Base of the Venus Table of the Dresden Codex, and its significance in the calendar-correlation problem. In A. F. Aveni and G. Brotherston (eds.), *Calendars in Mesoamerica and Peru: Native American Computation of Time*, 1–26. International Series, 174 British Archaeological Reports, Oxford, England.

Love, B. n.d. The gods of Yucatán from A.D. 1560 to 1980. Ms. in possession of authors.

Love, M. 1990. La Blanca y el Preclásico Medio en la Costa del Pacífico. *Arqueología* 3: 67–76.

——. 1999. Ideology, material culture, and daily practice in Pre-Classic Mesoamerica: A pacific coast perspective. In D. C. Grove and

R. A. Joyce (eds.), *Social Patterns in Pre-Classic Mesoamerica*, 127–54. Washington DC: Dumbarton Oaks.

Lowe, G. W. 1962. *Mound 5 and Minor Excavations, Chiapas de Corzo, Chiapas, Mexico*. Papers of the New World Archaeological Foundation, No. 12. Provo: Brigham Young University.

———. 1977. The Mixe-Zoque as competing neighbors of the early lowland Maya. In R. E. W. Adams (ed.), *The Origins of Maya Civilization*, 197–248. Albuquerque: University of New Mexico.

———. 1978. *Eastern Mesoamerica*. In R. E. Taylor and C. W. Meighan (eds.), *Chronologies in New World Archaeology*, 331–93. New York: Academic Press.

———. 1981. Olmec horizons defined in Mound 20, San Isidro, Chiapas. In E. P. Benson (ed.), *The Olmec and Their Neighbors: Essays in Memory of Matthew W. Stirling*, 231–55. Washington DC: Dumbarton Oaks.

———. 1989. The heartland Olmec: Evolution of material culture. In R. J. Sharer and D. C. Grove (eds.), *Regional Perspectives on the Olmec*, 33–67. Cambridge: Cambridge University Press.

———. 1995. Presencia maya en la cerámica del Preclásico tardío en Chiapa de Corzo. In *Memorias del Segundo Congreso Internacional de Mayistas*, 321–41. México: Universidad Nacional Autónoma de México.

Lowe, G. W., Lee, T. A., Jr., and Martínez, E. 1982. *Izapa: An Introduction to the Ruins and Monuments*. Papers of the New World Archaeological Foundation 31. Provo: Brigham Young University.

Lowe, G. W. and Mason, J. A. 1965. Archaeological survey of the Chiapas coast, highlands, and Upper Grijalva Basin. In G. R. Willey (ed.), *Handbook of Middle American Indians, Vol. 2: Archaeology of Southern Mesoamerica*, 195–236. Austin: University of Texas Press.

Lukes, S. 1990. *Individualism*. Oxford: Blackwell.

Lucero, L. J. 1999. Water control and Maya politics in the southern Maya lowlands. In E. A. Bacus and L. J. Lucero (eds.), *Complex Polities in the Ancient Tropical World*, 35–50. Archaeological Papers of the American Anthropological Association, No. 9. Arlington.

MacIntyre, A. 1979. Is understanding religion compatible with believing? In B. Wilson (ed.), *Rationality*, 62–77. Oxford: Blackwell.

MacNeish, R. S. 1964. Ancient mesoamerican civilization. *Science* 143: 531–7.

MacNeish., R. S., S. J. K. Wilkerson and Nelken-Terner, A. 1980. *First Annual Report of the Belize Archaic Archaeological Reconnaissance*. Andover: Robert S. Peabody Foundation for Archaeology.

Maler, K. H. 1984. *Maya Monuments: Sculptures of Unknown Provenance in Middle America*. Berlin: Verlag Karl-Friedrich von Flemming.

Manahan, T. K. 2004. The way things fall apart: Social organization and the Classic Maya collapse of Copan. *Ancient Mesoamerica* 15: 107–25.

Mandelbaum, S. J. 2000. *Open Moral Communities*. Cambridge MA: MIT Press.

Mann, G. 1976. *Wallenstein: His Life Narrated*. New York: Holt, Rinehart and Winston.

Mannheim, B. and Tedlock, D. 1995. Introduction. In D. Tedlock and B. Mannheim (eds.), *The Dialogic Emergence of Culture*, 1–32. Urbana: University of Illinois Press.

Manzanilla, L. (ed.) 1987. *Coba, Quintana Roo: Análisis de dos unidades habitacionales Mayas*. Mexico: Universidad Nacional Autónoma de Mexico.

Marcus, G. E. 1992. The concern with elites in archaeological reconstructions. In D. Z. Chase and A. F. Chase (eds.), *Mesoamerican Elites: An Archaeological Assessment*, 292–302. Norman: University of Oklahoma Press.

Marcus, J. 1976. *Emblem and State in the Maya Lowlands*. Washington DC: Dumbarton Oaks.

———. 1978. Archaeology and religion: A comparison of the Zapotec and the Maya. *World Archaeology* 10(2): 172–91.

———. 1983a. Lowland Maya archaeology at the crossroads. *American Antiquity* 48: 454–88.

———. 1983b. Topic 97: Zapotec religion. In K. V. Flannery and J. Marcus (eds.), *The Cloud People: Divergent Evolutions of the Zapotec and Mixtec Civilizations*, 345–51. New York: Academic Press.

———. 1992a. *Mesoamerican Writing Systems: Propaganda, Myth, and History in Four Ancient Civilizations*. Princeton: Princeton University Press.

———. 1992b. Royal families, royal texts: Examples from the Zapotec and Maya. In D. Z. Chase and A. F. Chase (eds.), *Mesoamerican Elites: An Archaeological Assessment*, 221–41. Norman: University of Oklahoma Press.

———. 1993. Ancient Maya political organization. In J. A. Sabloff and J. S. Henderson (eds.), *Lowland Maya Civilization in the Eighth Century A.D.*, 111–84. Washington DC: Dumbarton Oaks.

Marcus, J. and Flannery, K. V. 1996. *Zapotec Civilization: How Urban Society Evolved in Mexico's Oaxaca Valley*. London: Thames and Hudson.

Martin, S. 1996. Tikal's 'Star War' against Naranjo. In M. Macri and J. McHargue (eds.), *Eighth Palenque Round Table, 1993*, 223–36. San Francisco: Pre-Columbian Art Research Institute.

———. 1997. Painted king list: A commentary on codex-style dynastic vessels. In B. Kerr and J. Kerr (eds.), *The Maya Vase Book*, 5, 846–67. New York: Kerr Associates.

———. 2001. Court and realm: Architectural signatures in the Classic Maya southern lowlands. In T. Inomata and S. D. Houston (eds.), *Royal Courts of the Ancient Maya*, 168–94. Boulder: Westview Press.

———. 2003. In line of the founder: A view of dynastic politics at Tikal. In J. A. Sabloff (ed.), *Tikal: Dynastic, Foreigners, & Affairs of State: Advancing Maya Archaeology*, 3–46. Santa Fe: School of American Research Press.

———. 2004. A broken sky: The ancient name of Yaxchilan as Pa' Chan. *The PARI Journal* 5(1): 1–7.

———. 2005. Of snakes and bats: Shifting identities at Calakmul. *The PARI Journal* 6(2): 5–15.

———. 2006. Recently uncovered murals & facades at Calakmul. Paper presented at Symposium Mysteries of the Ancient Maya Murals, Beckman Center, National Academies of Sciences and Engineering, October 21.

———. 2007. Theosynthesis in ancient Maya religion. Paper presented at the 12th European Maya Conference, Geneva.

Martin, S. and Grube, N. 2008. *Chronicle of the Maya Kings and Queens: Deciphering the Dynasties of the Ancient Maya*. 2nd edition. London: Thames and Hudson.

Martínez Hidalgo, G., Hansen, R., Jacobs, J., and Howell, W. 1999. Nuevas evidencias de los sistemas de cultivo del Preclásico en la cuenca El Mirador. In J. P. Laporte, H. L. Escobedo, and A. C. Monzón de Suasnávar (eds.), *XII Simposio de Investigaciones Arqueológicas en Guatemala, 1998*, 327–36. Guatemala: Ministerio de Cultura y Deportes, Instituto de Antropología e Historia, and Asociación Tikal.

Martos, López, L. A. 2002. *Por las tierras mayas del oriente: Arqueología en el área de Calica, Quintana Roo*. Instituto Nacional de Antropología e Historia, México.

Masson, M. A. and Mock, S. B. 2004. Ceramics and settlement patterns at Terminal Classic-Period lagoon sites in Northeastern Belize. In A. A. Demarest, P. M. Rice, and D. S. Rice (eds.), *The Terminal Classic in the Maya Lowlands: Collapse, Transition, and Transformation*, 367–401. Boulder: University Press of Colorado.

Matheny, R. T. 1986. Early states in the Maya lowlands during the late Preclassic Period: Edzná and El Mirador. In E. P. Benson (ed.), *City States of the Maya: Art and Architecture*, 1–44. Denver: Rocky Mountain Institute for Pre-Columbian Studies.

Matheny, R. T., Gurr, D. L., Forsyth, D. W., and Hauck, F. R. 1983. *Investigations at Edzná, Campeche, Mexico*. Papers of the New World Archaeological Foundation, 46. Provo: Brigham Young University.

Mathews, P. L. 1980. Notes on the dynastic sequence of Bonampak, Chiapas, Mexico, part 1. In M. G. Robertson (ed.), *Third Palenque Round Table, 1978, Part 2*, 60–73. Austin: University of Texas Press.

Mathews, P. L. and Aliphat Fernández, M. 1997. *Informe de la temporada de campo 1992, Proyecto El Cayo*. Presented to the Consejo de Arqueología del Instituto Nacional de Antropología e Historia.

Mathews, P. L. and Graham, I. 1996. *Corpus of Maya Hieroglyphic Inscriptions, Volume 6, Part 2: Tonina*. Cambridge MA: Peabody Museum of Archaeology and Ethnology, Harvard University.

Mathews, P. and Willey, G. R. 1991. Prehistoric polities of the Pasion Region: Hieroglyphic texts and their archaeological setting. In T. P. Culbert (ed.), *Classic Maya Political History: Hieroglyphic and Archaeological Evidence*, 30–71. Cambridge: Cambridge University Press.

Mauss, M. 1950. *Sociologie et Anthropologie*. Paris: Presses Universitaires de France.

———. 1954. *The Gift: Forms and Functions of Exchange in Archaic Societies*. Glencoe, Illinois: Free Press.

———. 1985. A category of the human mind: The notion of the person; the notion of self.

In M. Carrithers, S. Collins and S. Lukes (eds.), *The Category of the Person: Anthropology, Philosophy, History*, 1–25. Cambridge: Cambridge University Press.

Maxwell, J. M., and Hanson, C. A. 1992. *Of the Manners of Speaking that the Old Ones Had: The Metaphors of Andés de Olmos in the TULAL Manuscript*. Salt Lake City: University of Utah Press.

May Hau, J., Cohouh Muñoz, R., González Heredia, R., and Folan, W. J. 1990. *El mapa de las ruinas de Calakmul, Campeche, México*. Campeche: Universidad Autónoma de Campeche.

Mayer, K. H. 1984. *Maya Monuments: Sculptures of Unknown Provenance in Middle America*. Berlin: Verlag Karl-Friedrich von Flemming.

McAnany, P. A. 1989. Stone-tool production and exchange in the eastern Maya Lowlands: The consumer perspective from Pulltrouser Swamp, Belize. *American Antiquity* 54: 332–46.

———. 1990. Water storage in the Puuc region of the northern Maya lowlands: A key to population estimates and architectural variability. In D. S. Rice and T. P. Culbert (eds.), *Precolumbian Population History in the Maya Lowlands*, 263–84. Albuquerque: University of New Mexico Press.

———. 1995. *Living with the Ancestors: Kinship and Kingship in Ancient Maya Society*. Austin: University of Texas Press.

———. 1998. Ancestors and the Classic Maya built environment. In S. D. Houston (ed.), *Function and Meaning in Classic Maya Architecture*, 271–98. Washington DC: Dumbarton Oaks Research Library and Collection.

———. 2002. Rethinking the great and little tradition paradigm from the perspective of domestic ritual. In P. A. Plunket (ed.), *Domestic Ritual in Ancient Mesoamerica*, 115–19. Los Angeles: Cotsen Institute of Archaeology, University of California.

McAnany, P. A. and López Verela, S. L. 1999. Re-creating the Formative Maya village of K'axob: Chronology, ceramic complexes, and ancestors in architectural context. *Ancient Mesoamerica* 10: 147–68.

McAnany, P. A. and Plank, S. 2001. Perspectives on actors, gender roles, and architecture at Classic Maya courts and households. In T. Inomata and S. D. Houston (eds.), *Royal Courts of the Ancient Maya, Volume 1: Theory,* *Comparison, and Synthesis*, 84–129. Boulder: Westview.

McAnany, P. A., Storey, R., and Lockard, A. K. 1999. Mortuary ritual and family politics at Formative and Early Classic K'axob, Belize. *Ancient Mesoamerica* 10: 129–46.

McCafferty, S. D., and McCafferty, G. G. 1998. Spinning and weaving as female gender identity in Post-Classic Mexico. In K. Hays-Gilpin and D. S. Whitley (eds.), *Reader in Gender Archaeology*, 213–30. London: Routledge.

McDonald, A. J. 1983. *Tzutzuculi: A Middle-Preclassic Site on the Pacific Coast of Chiapas, Mexico*. Papers of the New World Archaeological Foundation, 47. Provo: Brigham Young University.

McGee, R. J. 1990. *Life, Ritual, and Religion among the Lacandon Maya*. Belmont: Wadsworth.

McKillop, H. 1989. Development of coastal Maya trade: Data, models, and issues. In H. McKillop and P. Healy (eds.), *Coastal Maya Trade*, 1–18. Trent University Occasional Papers in Anthropology no. 8. Peterborough.

———. 2002. *Salt: White Gold of the Ancient Maya*. Gainsville: University Press of Florida.

———. 2005. Finds in Belize document Late Classic Maya salt making and canoe transport. *Proceedings of the National Academy of Sciences* 102: 5630–4.

———. 2006. *The Ancient Maya: New Perspectives*. New York: Norton.

McSwain, R., Johnson, J. K., Kosakowsky, L. J., and Hammond, N. 1991a. Craft technology and production. In N. Hammond (ed.), *Cuello: An Early Maya Community in Belize*, 159–91. Cambridge: Cambridge University Press.

McSwain, R., Kosakowsky, L. J., and Hammond, N. 1991b. External contacts and trade at Cuello. In N. Hammond (ed.), *Cuello: An Early Maya Community in Belize*, 192–203. Cambridge: Cambridge University Press.

Meade, M. 1977. *Eleanor of Aquitaine: A Biography*. Harmondsworth: Penguin Books.

Medina, L. K. 2003. Commoditizing culture: Tourism and Maya identity. *Annals of Tourism Research* 30: 353–68.

Medina Martín, C. and Sánchez Vargas, M. 2007. Posthumous body treatments and ritual meaning in the Classic Period northern Petén: A taphonomic approach. In V. Tiesler and A.

Cucina (eds.), *New Perspectives on Human Sacrifice and Ritual Body Treatments in Ancient Maya Society*, 102–19. New York: Springer.

Meillassoux, C. 1991. *The Anthropology of Slavery: The Womb of Iron and Gold*. Chicago: University of Chicago Press.

Mendelssohn, K. 1971. A scientist looks at the pyramids. *American Scientist* 59: 210–20.

Mesick, C. 2006. *The Modification of Maya Monuments: Towards a Local Theory of Sculptural Ontology*. M.A. thesis. Brown University.

Michelet, D., Nondedeo, P., and Arnauld, M.-C. 2005. Río Bec, una excepción? *Arqueología mexicana* 13: 58–63.

Miles, S. W. 1957. *The Sixteenth Century Pokom-Maya: A Documentary Analysis of Social Structure and Archaeological Setting*. American Philosophical Society, Transactions N.S. 47, Part 4: 733–81. Philadelphia.

Miller, A. G. 1973. *The Mural Painting of Teotihuacán*. Washington DC: Dumbarton Oaks Research Library and Collection.

Miller, D. and Tilley, C. 1984. *Ideology, Power, and History*. Cambridge: Cambridge University Press.

Miller, J. 1974. Notes on a Stela pair probably from Calakmul, Campeche, Mexico. In M. G. Robertson (ed.), *Primera Mesa Redonda de Palenque, Part I*, 149–61. Pebble Beach: Robert Louis Stevenson School.

Miller, M. E. 1986. *The Murals of Bonampak*. Princeton: Princeton University Press.

———. 1988. The boys in the bonampak band. In E. P. Benson and G. Griffin (eds.), *Maya Iconography*, 318–30. Princeton: Princeton University Press.

Miller, M. E., and Martin S. 2004. *Courtly Art of the Ancient Maya*. London: Thames and Hudson.

Miller, M. E., and Samoya, M. 1998. Where maize may grow: Jade, chakmools, and the maize god. *RES Anthropology and Aesthetics* 33: 54–72.

Moholy-Nagy, H. 2003. *Tikal Report No. 27, Part B: The Artifacts of Tikal: Utilitarian Artifacts and Unworked Material*. Philadelphia: University of Pennsylvania Museum of Archaeology and Anthropology.

Moholy-Nagy, H., Asaro, F., and Stross, F. 1984. Tikal obsidian: Sources and typology. *American Antiquity* 49: 104–17.

Moholy-Nagy, H. and Nelson F. W. 1990. New data on obsidian artifacts from Tikal, Guatemala. *Ancient Mesoamerica* 1: 71–80.

Monaghan, J. 1995. *The Covenants of Earth and Rain: Exchange, Sacrifice, and Revelation in Mixtec Sociality*. Norman: University of Oklahoma Press.

———. 1998a. Dedication: Ritual or production? In S. B. Mock (ed.), *The Sowing and the Dawning: Termination, Dedication, and Transformation in the Archaeological and Ethnographic Record of Mesoamerica*, 47–54. Albuquerque: University of New Mexico Press.

———. 1998b. The person, destiny, and the construction of difference in Mesoamerica. *RES* 33: 137–46.

———. 2000. Theology and history in the study of mesoamerican religions. In J. D. Monaghan (ed.), and V. R. Bricker (gen. ed.), *Handbook of Middle American Indians, Supplement 6: Ethnology*, 24–49. Austin: University of Texas Press.

———. 2001. Physiology, production, and gendered difference: The evidence from Mixtec and other Mesoamerican societies. In C. F. Klein (ed.), *Gender in Pre-Hispanic America*, 285–304. Washington DC: Dumbarton Oaks.

Mondloch, J. L. 1980. K'ezs: Quiche naming. *Journal of Mayan Linguistics* 2: 9–25.

Montejo, V. 1993. In the name of the pot, the sun, the broken spear, the rock, the stick, the idol, ad infinitum & ad nauseam: An exposé of Anglo anthropologists' obsessions with and invention of Mayan gods. *Wicazo Sa Review: A Journal of Native American Studies* 9(1): 12–6.

Montgomery, J. 1995. *Sculptors of the Realm: Classic Maya Artists' Signatures and Sculptural Style During the Reign of Piedras Negras, Ruler 7*. MA Thesis. Department of Fine Arts, University of New Mexico.

Moore, H. L. Ethics and ontology: Why agents and agency matter. In M.-A. Dobres and J. Robb (eds.), *Agency in Archaeology*, 259–63. Routledge: London.

Mora-Marín, D. 2001. *The grammar, orthography, content, and social context of late Preclassic portable texts*. Ph.D. dissertation. State University of New York, Albany.

Morley, S. G. 1947. *The Ancient Maya*. Stanford: Stanford University Press.

Morris, J. 2004. *Archaeological Research at the Mountain Cow Sites: The Archaeology of Sociocultural Diversity, Ethnicity, and Identity Formation*. Ph.D. dissertation. University of California at Los Angeles.

Morris, I. 1997. An archaeology of equalities? The Greek city-states. In D. L. Nichols and T. H. Charlton (eds.), *The Archaeology of City-States: Cross-Cultural Approaches*, 91–105. Washington DC: Smithsonian Institution Press.

Mosca, G. 1994. The ruling class. In D. Grusky (ed.), *Social Stratification: Class, Race, and Gender in Sociological Perspective*, 155–61. Boulder: Westview Press.

Murdock, G. P. 1949. *Social Structure*. New York: Macmillan.

Murdy, C. 1990. Tradiciones de arquitectura prehispánica en el Valle de Guatemala. *Anales de la Academia de Geografía e Historia de Guatemala LXIV*: 349–97.

Murtha, T. M. 2002. *Land and Labor: Classic Maya Terraced Agriculture at Caracol, Belize*. Ph.D. dissertation. Department of Anthropology, Pennsylvania State University.

Nations, J. D. 2006. *The Maya Tropical Forest: People, Parks, and Ancient Cities*. Austin: University of Texas Press.

Nations, J. D. and Nigh, R. B. 1980. The evolutionary potential of Lacandon Maya sustained-yield tropical forest agriculture. *Journal of Anthropological Research* 36: 1–30.

Neff, H., Blomster, J, Glascock, M. D., Bishop, R. L., Blackman, M. J., Coe, M. D., Cowgill, G. L., Diehl, R. A., Houston, S. D., Joyce, A. A., Lipo, C. P., Stark, B. L., and Winter, M. 2006. Methodological issues in the provenance investigation of Early Formative Mesoamerican ceramics. *Latin American Antiquity* 17: 54–76.

Nelson, F. W. 1985. Summary of the results of analysis of obsidian artifacts from the Maya lowlands. *Scanning Electron Microscopy* 11: 631–59.

Netting, R. McC. 1977. Maya subsistence: Mythologies, analogies, possibilities. In R. E. W. Adams (ed.), *Origins of Maya Civilization*, 299–333. Albuquerque: University of New Mexico Press.

———. 1993. *Smallholders, Householders: Farm Families and the Ecology of Intensive Sustainable Agriculture*. Stanford: Stanford University Press.

Neuschel, K. B. 1988. Noble households in the sixteenth century: Material settings and human communities. *French Historical Studies* 15: 595–622.

Nicholas, Linda M. 1989. Land use in prehispanic Oaxaca. In S. A. Kowalewski, G. Feinman, L. Finsten, R. Blanton, and L. Nicholas (eds.), *Monte Alban's Hinterland, Part II: Prehispanic Settlement Patterns in Tlacolula, Etla, and Ocotlan, the Valley of Oaxaca, Mexico*, 449–506. Memoir of Museum of Anthropology, University of Michigan, No. 23. Ann Arbor.

Nicholson, H. B. 1971. Religion in pre-hispanic central Mexico. In G. F. Ekholm and I. Bernal (eds.), *Handbook of Middle American Indians, 10: Archaeology of Northern Mesoamerica*, 395–446. Austin: University of Texas Press.

Nondedeo, P. 2003. *L'evolution des sites mayas du sud de l'etat du Campeche, Mexique*. British Archaeological Reports, International Series 1171. Paris Monographs in American Archaeology, 12. Oxford.

Ochoa Salas, L. 1974. Figurillas olmecas de las Tierras Bajas del área maya. *Boletín del Centro de Estudios Mayas* 1: 3–12.

———. 1977. Los olmecas y el Valle del Usumacinta. *Anales de Antropología* 14: 75–90.

———. 1982. Hachas olmecas y otras piezas arqueológicas del Medio Usumacinta. *Reivsta Mexicana de Estudios Antropológicos* 28: 109–22.

Ochoa, L., and Lee, T. A. Jr (eds.) 1983. *Homenaje a Frans Blom: Antropología e Historia de los Mixe-Zoques y Mayas*. México: Universidad Nacional Autónoma de México, Centro de Estudios Mayas.

Ohi, Kuniaki. 1994. *Kaminaljuyu (1991-'94)*. Tokyo: Tabako to Shio no Hakubutsukan.

Okoshi Harada, T. 1992. *Los Canules: Análisis etnohistórico del Códice de Calkini*. Ph.D. dissertation. Universidad Autónoma de México.

Olko, J. 2005. *Turquoise Diadems and Staffs of Office: Elite Costume and Insignia of Power in Aztec and Early Colonial Mexico*. Warsaw: Polish Society for Latin American Studies, University of Warsaw.

Ortega, E. R., Suasnávar Bolaños, J., Luis Velásquez, J., and Roldán, J. A. 1996. El Montículo la Culebra, Kaminaljuyu. In J. P. Laporte and H. Escobedo (eds.), *IX Simposio de Investigaciones Arqueológicas en Guatemala, 1995*, 68–91. Guatemala: Ministerio de Cultura y Deportes, Museo Nacional de Arqueología e Etnología.

Ortíz, C. P. and Rodríguez Martínez, M. del C. 2000. The sacred hill of El Manatí: A preliminary discussion of the site's ritual paraphernalia. In J. E. Clark and M. E. Pye (eds.), *Olmec Art and Archaeology in Mesoamerica*, 75–93. Washington DC: National Gallery of Art.

Ortíz C.P. and Rodriguez, M. del. C. 1999. Olmec ritual behavior at El Manatí: A sacred space. In D. C. Grove and R. A. Joyce (eds.),

Social Patterns in Pre-Classic Mesoamerica, 225–54. Washington DC: Dumbarton Oaks.

Ortner, S. and Whitehead, H. (eds.) 1981. *Sexual Meanings: The Cultural Construction of Gender and Sexuality*. Cambridge: Cambridge University Press.

Otsu, T. 2001. *Michinagato kyutei shakai* [in Japanese, *Michinaga and court society*]. Kodansha, Tokyo.

Otto, B. K. 2001. *Fools are Everywhere: The Court Jester Around the World*. Chicago: University of Chicago Press.

Overing, J. and Passes, A. 2000. Introduction: Conviviality and the opening up of Amazonian anthropology. In *The Anthropology of Love and Anger: The Aesthetics of Conviviality in Native Amazonia*, 1–30. London: Routledge.

Palka, J. 1995. *Classic Maya Social Inequality and the Collapse at Dos Pilas, Peten, Guatemala*. Ph.D. dissertation. Vanderbilt University.

———. 1997. Reconstructing Classic Maya socioeconomic differentiation and the collapse at Dos Pilas, Peten, Guatemala. *Ancient Mesoamerica* 8(2): 293–306.

———. 2005. *Unconquered Lacandon Maya: Ethnohistory and Archaeology of Indigenous Culture Change*. Gainesville: University Press of Florida.

Pancake, S. 1992. Gender boundaries in the production of Guatemalan textiles. In R. Barnes and J. B. Eicher (eds.), *Dress and Gender: Making and Meaning*, 76–91. Providence: Berg.

Paredes Maury, S. 1999. *Surviving in the Rainforest: The Realities of Looting in the Rural Villages of El Petén, Guatemala*. Report to FAMSI, http://www.famsi.org/reports/95096/index.html. Accessed April 15, 2008.

Parish, S. M. 1994. *Moral Knowing in a Hindu Sacred City: An Exploration of Mind, Emotion, and Self*. New York: Columbia University Press.

Parsons, L. A. 1981. Post-Olmec stone sculptures: The Olmec-Izapan transition on the pacific coast and highlands. In E. P. Benson (ed.), *The Olmec and their Neighbors*, 257–288. Washington DC: Dumbarton Oaks.

———. 1986. *The Origins of Maya Art: Monumental Stone Sculpture of Kaminaljuyu, Guatemala, and the Southern Pacific Coast*. Studies in Pre-Columbian Art and Archaeology 28. Washington DC: Dumbarton Oaks.

Patterson, O. 1982. *Slavery and Social Death: A Comparative Study*. Cambridge MA: Harvard University Press.

Peck, L. L. 1990. *Court Patronage and Corruption in Early Stuart England*. Boston: Unwin Hyman.

Pendergast, D. A. 1981. Lamanai, Belize: Summary of excavation results, 1974–1980. *Journal of Field Archaeology* 8: 29–53.

———. 1982. Ancient Maya mercury. *Science* 217: 533–5.

———. 1986. Stability through change: Lamanai, Belize, from the Ninth to the Seventeenth century. In J. A. Sabloff and E. W. Andrews V. (eds.), *Late Lowland Maya Civilization: Classic to Postclassic*, 223–49. Albuquerque: University of New Mexico Press.

———. 1990. *Excavations at Altun Ha, Belize, 1964–1970*. Vol. 3. Toronto: Royal Ontario Museum.

———. 2003. Teotihuacan at Altun Ha: Did it make a difference? In G. E. Braswell (ed.), *The Maya and Teotihuacan: Reinterpreting Early Classic Interaction*, 235–48. Austin: University of Texas Press.

Pérez Campa, M. and Rosas Kifuri, M. 1987. Dos nuevas piedras labradas de Bonampak. In *Memorias del Primer Coloquio Internacional de Mayistas: 5–10 de agosto de 1985*, 749–73. México: Centro de Estudios Mayas, Universidad Nacional Autónoma de México.

Peristiany, J. G. 1966. Introduction. In J. G. Peristiany (ed.), *Honour and Shame: The Values of Mediterranean Society*, 7–18. Chicago: University of Chicago Press.

Pharo, L. K. 2007. The concept of "religion" in Mesoamerican languages. *Numen* 54: 28–70.

Piña Chan, R. 1968. *Jaina: La casa en el agua*. México: Instituto Nacional de Antropología e Historia.

Piperno, D. 1989. Non-affluent foragers: Resource availability, seasonal shortages, and the emergence of agriculture in Panamanian tropical forests. In D. Harris and G. Hillman (eds.), *The Evolution of Plant Exploitation*, 538–54. London: Unwin and Hyman.

Piperno, D. and Pearsall, D. 1993. Phytoliths in the reproductive structures of maize and teosinte: Implications for the study of maize evolution. *Journal of Archaeological Science* 20: 337–62.

Pitarch Ramón, P. 1993. *Etnografía de las almas en Cancúc, Chiapas*. Ph.D. dissertation. Department of Anthropology, State University of New York at Albany.

Pitt-Rivers, J. 1966. Honour and social status. In J. G. Peristiany (ed.), *Honour and Shame: The*

Values of Mediterranean Society, 19–77. Chicago: University of Chicago Press.

———. 1970. Spiritual power in Central America: The Naguals of Chiapas. In M. Douglas (ed.), *Witchcraft: Confessions and Accusations*, 183–206. London: Tavistock.

Plank, S. E. 2004. *Maya Dwellings in Hieroglyphs and Archaeology: An Integrative Approach to Ancient Architecture and Spatial Cognition*. BAR International Series 1324. Oxford: British Archaeological Reports.

Pohl, J. M. D. 1994. *The Politics of Symbolism in the Mixtec Codices*. Nashville: Vanderbilt University Publications in Anthropology.

———. 2007. *Sorcerers of the Fifth Heaven: Nahua Art and Ritual of Ancient Southern Mexico*. Princeton: Program in Latin American Studies, Princeton University.

Pohl, M. E. D. and Pohl, J. M. D. 1994. Cycles of conflict: Political factionalism in the Maya lowlands. In E. M. Brumfiel and J. W. Fox (eds.), *Factional Competition and Political Development in the New World*, 138–57. Cambridge: Cambridge University Press.

Pohl, M. E. D., Pope, K. O., and Von Nagy, C. 2002. Olmec origins of Mesoamerican writing. *Science* 298: 1984–7.

Pohl, M. E. D., Pope, K. O., Jones, J. G., Jacob, J. S., Piperno, D., de France, S. D., Lentz, D., Gifford, J. A., Danforth, M. E., and Josserand, J. K. 1996. Early agriculture in the Maya lowlands. *Latin American Antiquity* 7: 355–72.

Ponciano, E. 2002. *Kaminaljuyú Archaeological Project: A Study of the Ancient City of the Southern Guatemalan Highlands: New Perspectives*. Report to FAMSI, http://www.famsi.org/reports/97031/index.html. Accessed April 15, 2008.

Pool, C.A. 2007. *Olmec Archaeology and Early Mesoamerica*. Cambridge: Cambridge University Press.

Pope, K. O. and Dahlin, B. H. 1989. Ancient Maya wetland agriculture: New insights from ecological and remote sensing research. *Journal of Field Archaeology* 16: 87–106.

Pope, K. O., Pohl, M. D., and Jacob, J. S. 1996. Formation of ancient Maya wetland fields: Natural and anthropogenic processes. In S. L. Fedick (ed.), *Managed Mosaic: Ancient Maya Agriculture and Resource Use*, 165–76. Salt Lake City: University of Utah Press.

Pope, K. O., Pohl, M. E. D., Jones, J. G., Lentz, D. L., von Nagy, C., Vega, F. J., and Quitmyer,

I. R. 2001. Origin and environmental setting of ancient agriculture in the lowlands of Mesoamerica. *Science* 292: 1370–3.

Popenoe de Hatch, M. 1997. *Kaminaljuyu/San Jorge: Evidencia arqueologica de la actividad economica en el Valle de Guatemala, 300 a.C. a 300 d.C.* Guatemala: Universidad del Valle de Guatemala.

Potter, D. R. 1993. Analytical approaches to Late Classic Maya lithic industries. In J. A. Sabloff and J. S. Henderson (eds.), *Lowland Maya Civilization in the Eighth Century A. D.*, 273–298. Washington DC: Dumbarton Oaks Research Library and Collection.

Potter, D. R., Hester, T. R., Black, S. L., and Valdez, Jr., F. 1984. Relationships between Early Pre-Classic and Early Middle Pre-Classic phases in northern Belize: A comment on "Lowland Maya Archaeology at the Crossroads." *American Antiquity* 49: 628–31.

Powell, B. B. 1991. *Homer and the Origin of the Greek Alphabet*. Cambridge: Cambridge University Press.

Powis, J. 1984. *Aristocracy*. Oxford: Basil Blackwell.

Prager, C. M. 2004. A Classic Maya ceramic vessel from the Calakmul region in the Museum zu Allerheiligen, Schaffhausen, Switzerland. *Human Mosaic* 35(1): 31–40.

Prechtel, M. and Carlsen, R. S. 1988. Weaving and cosmos amongst the Tzutujil Maya of Guatemala. *RES* 15: 122–32.

Prem, H. J. 2003. *Xkipché: Una ciudad maya clásica en el corazon del Puuc*. Bonn: Universidad de Bonn.

Price, S. 1999. *Religions of the Ancient Greeks*. Cambridge: Cambridge University Press.

Proskouriakoff, T. 1950. *A Study of Classic Maya Sculpture*. Washington DC: Carnegie Institution of Washington Publication, 593.

———. 1965. Sculpture and major arts of the Classic Lowlands. In R. Wauchope (ed.), *Handbook of Middle American Indians 2*, 469–497. Austin: University of Texas Press.

———. 1974. *Jade from the Cenote of Sacrifice, Chichen Itza, Yucatan*. Memoirs of the Peabody Museum, Vol. 10, No. 1. Cambridge MA: Harvard University.

———. 1978. Olmec gods and Maya godglyphs. *Codex Wauchope: A Tribute Roll, Human Mosaic* 12: 113–117.

———. 1993. *Maya History*. R. A. Joyce (gen. ed.) Austin: University of Texas Press.

Protzen, J.-P. 1993. *Inca Architecture and Construction at Ollantaytambo*. New York: Oxford University Press.

Prufer, K. M. and Brady, J. E. (eds.). 2005. *Stone Houses and Earth Lords: Maya Religion in the Cave Context*. Boulder: University Press of Colorado.

Puleston, D. E. 1979. An epistemological pathology and the collapse, or why the Maya kept the short count. In N. Hammond and G. R. Willey (eds.), *Maya Archaeology and Ethnohistory*, 63–71. Austin: University of Texas Press.

————. 1982. The role of Ramón in Maya subsistence. In K. V. Flannery (ed.), *Maya Subsistence*, 353–66. New York: Academic Press.

Puleston, D. E. and Puleston, O. S. 1971. An ecological approach to the origins of Maya civilization. *Archaeology* 24: 330–37.

Pyburn, K. A. 1996. The political economy of ancient Maya land use: The road to ruin. In S. L. Fedick (ed.), *The Managed Mosaic: Ancient Maya Agriculture and Resource Use*, 236–50. Salt Lake City: University of Utah Press.

Quintana, O. 2000. El programa de arquitectura. In W. W. Wurster (ed.), *El Sitio Maya de Topoxté: Investigaciones en una Isla del Lage Yaxhá, Peten Guatemala*, 24–7. Materialen zur Allgemeinen und Vergleichenden Archäologie, 5. Mainz: Verlag Philipp von Zabern.

Quirarte, J. 1973. *Izapán-Style Art: A Study of its Form and Meaning*. Studies in Pre-Columbian Art and Archaeology 10. Washington DC: Dumbarton Oaks.

————. 1976. The relationship of Izapan-style art to Olmec and Maya art: A review. In H. B. Nicholson (ed.), *Origins of Religious Art and Iconography in Preclassic Mesoamerica*, 73–86. Latin American Studies Series 31. Los Angeles: UCLA Latin American Center.

Ralph, E. 1965. Review of radiocarbon dates from Tikal and the Maya calendar correlation problem. *American Antiquity* 30(4): 421–7.

Ramos Gomez, J. 2006. *The Iconography of Temple 16: Yax Pasaj and the Evocation of a "Foreign" Identity at Copan*. Ph.D. dissertation. Department of Anthropology, University of California, Riverside.

Rands, R. L. 1977. The rise of Classic Maya civilization in the northwestern zone: Isolation and integration. In R. E. W. Adams (ed.), *The Origins of Maya Civilization*, 159–80. Albuquerque: University of New Mexico.

————. 1987. Ceramic patterns and tradition in the Palenque area. In P. M. Rice and R. J. Sharer (eds.), *Maya Ceramics: Papers from the 1985 Maya Ceramic Conference*, 203–38. BAR Publications 345(i). Oxford: British Archaeological Reports.

Rands, R. L. and Bishop, R. L. 1980. Resource procurement zones and patterns of ceramic exchange in the Palenque region, Mexico. In R. E. Fry (ed.), *Models and Methods in Regional Exchange*, 19–46. SAA Papers, 1. Washington DC: Society for American Archaeology.

Rappaport, R. A. 1999. *Ritual and Religion in the Making of Humanity*. Cambridge: Cambridge University Press.

Rapport, N. and Overing, J. 2000. *Social and Cultural Anthropology: The Key Concepts*. London: Routledge.

Rathje, W. L. 1971. Origin and development of Lowland Classic Maya civilization. *American Antiquity* 36: 275–87.

————. 1972. Praise the gods and pass the metates: A hypothesis of the development of lowland rainforest civilizations in Mesoamerica. In M. P. Leone (ed.), *Contemporary Archaeology: A Guide to Theory and Contributions*, 365–92. Carbondale: Southern Illinois University Press.

————. 1973. Classic Maya development and denouement: A research design. In T. P. Culbert (ed.), *The Classic Maya Collapse*, 405–54. Albuquerque: University of New Mexico Press.

Rattray, E. C. 2000. *Teotihuacan: Ceramics, Chronology and Cultural Trends*. University of Pittsburgh Memoirs in Latin American Archaeology, No. 13.

Read, K. A. 1998. *Time and Sacrifice in the Aztec Cosmos*. Bloomington: Indiana University Press.

Redfield, R. 1960. *The Little Community, and Peasant Society and Culture*. Chicago: University of Chicago Press.

Redfield, R. and Singer, M. 1954. The cultural role of cities. *Economic Development and Cultural Change* 2(1): 53–73.

Redworth, G. and Checa, F. 1999. The kingdoms of Spain: The courts of the Spanish Habsburgs, 1500–1700. In J. Adamson (ed.), *The Princely Courts of Europe: Ritual, Politics, and Culture Under the Ancien Régime 1500–1750*, 42–65. London: Weidenfeld and Nicolson.

Reents-Budet, D. 1994. *Painting the Maya Universe: Royal Ceramics of the Classic Period.* Durham: Duke University Press.

———. 1998. Elite Maya pottery and artisans as social indicators. In C. L. Costin and R. P. Wright (eds.), *Craft and Social Identity*, 71–89. Washington DC: Archaeological Papers of the American Anthropological Association, No. 8.

———. 2001. Classic Maya concepts of the royal court: An analysis of renderings on pictorial ceramics. In T. Inomata and S. D. H. Houston (eds.), *Royal Courts of the Ancient Maya*, 195–233. Boulder: Westview Press.

Reina, R. E. and Hill, R. M. II. 1978. *The Traditional Pottery of Guatemala.* Austin: University of Texas Press.

Renfrew, C. 1974. Beyond a subsistence economy: The evolution of social organization in prehistoric Europe. In C. B. Moore, *Reconstructing Complex Societies*, 69–85. Cambridge MA: American Schools of Oriental Research.

Restall, M. 1995. *Life and Death in a Maya Community: The Ixil Testaments of the 1760s.* Lancaster: Labyrinthos.

———. 1997. *The Maya World: Yucatec Culture and Society, 1550–1850.* Stanford: Stanford University Press.

———. 1998. The ties that bind: Social cohesion and the Yucatec Maya family. *Journal of Family History* 23(4): 355–81.

———. 2001. The people of the patio: Ethnohistorical evidence of Yucatec Maya royal courts. In T. Inomata and S. D. Houston (ed.), *Royal Courts of the Ancient Maya: Volume II*, 335–90. Boulder: Westview Press.

Rice, D. S. 1993. Eighth-century physical geography, environment, and natural resources in the Maya lowlands. In J. A. Sabloff and J. S. Henderson (eds.), *Lowland Maya Civilization in the Eighth Century A.D.*, 11–64. Washington DC: Dumbarton Oaks.

Rice, P. M. 1979. Ceramic and non-ceramic artifacts of lakes Yaxha-Sacnab, El Peten, Guatemala. Part I. The ceramics. Section A, Introduction and the Middle Preclassic Ceramics of Yaxha-Sacnab, Guatemala. *Cerámica de Cultura Maya* 10: 1–36.

———. 1984. Obsidian procurement in the central Peten lakes region, Guatemala. *Journal of Field Archaeology* 11: 181–94.

———. 1987. Economic change in the lowland Maya Late Classic Period. In E. M. Brumfiel

and T. K. Earle, *Specialization, Exchange, and Complex Societies*, 76–85. Cambridge: Cambridge University Press.

———. 2004. *Maya Political Science: Time, Astronomy, and the Cosmos.* Austin: University of Texas Press.

Rice, P. M. and Sharer, R. J. (eds.). 1987. *Maya Ceramics: Papers from the 1985 Maya Ceramic Conference.* BAR International Series 345. Oxford: British Archaeological Reports.

Rice, P. M. and Forsyth, D. W. 2004. Terminal Classic-Period lowland ceramics. In A. A. Demarest, P. M. Rice and D. S. Rice (eds.), *The Terminal Classic in the Maya Lowlands: Collapse, Transition, and Transformation*, 28–59. Boulder: University Press of Colorado.

Richards, A. 1961. African kings and their royal relatives. *Journal of the Royal Anthropological Institute of Great Britain and Ireland* 91(2): 135–50.

———. 1969. Keeping the king divine. *Proceedings of the Royal Anthropological Institute for Great Britain and Ireland for 1968*: 23–35.

Ricketson, O. G., Jr., and Ricketson, E. B. 1937. *Uaxactun, Guatemala: Group E – 1926–1931.* Carnegie Institution of Washington, No. 477. Washington DC.

Riesman, P. 1977. *Freedom in Fulani Social Life.* Chicago: University of Chicago Press.

Ringle, W. M. 1999. Pre-Classic cityscapes: Ritual politics among the early lowland Maya. In D. C. Grove and R. A. Joyce (eds.), *Social Patterns in Pre-Classic Mesoamerica. A Symposium at Dumbarton Oaks 9 and 10 October 1993*, 183–223. Washington DC: Dumbarton Oaks Research Library and Collection.

———. 2004. On the political organization of Chichen Itza. *Ancient Mesoamerica* 15: 167–218.

———. n.d. *Concordance of the Morán Dictionary of Ch'olti'.* Digital file in possession of authors.

Ringle, W. M. and Bey, G. J., III. 2001. Postclassic and Terminal Classic courts of the northern Maya lowlands. In T. Inomata and S. D. Houston (ed.), *Royal Courts of the Ancient Maya: Volume II*, 266–307. Boulder: Westview Press.

Ringle, W. M., Gallareta Negrón, T., and Bey, G. J., III. 1998. The return of Quetzalcoatl: Evidence for the spread of a world religion during the Epiclassic Period. *Ancient Mesoamerica* 9: 183–232.

Ringle, W. M., Bey, G. J., III, Freeman, T. B., Hanson, C. A., Houck, C. W., and Smith, J. G.

2004. The decline of the East: The Classic to Postclassic transition at Ek Balam, Yucatán. In A. A. Demarest, P. M. Rice, and D. S. Rice (eds.), *The Terminal Classic in the Maya Lowlands: Collapse, Transition, and Transformation*, 485–516. Boulder: University Press of Colorado.

Robertson, M. G. 1983. *The Sculpture of Palenque, Volume* I: *The Temple of the Inscriptions*. Princeton: Princeton University Press.

———. 1985. *The Sculpture of Palenque, Volume* III: *The Late Buildings of the Palace*. Princeton: Princeton University Press.

———. 1991. *The Sculpture of Palenque, Volume* IV: *The Cross Group, the North Group, the Olvidado, and Other Pieces*. Princeton: Princeton University Press.

Robicsek, F. and Hales, D. M. 1981. *The Maya Book of the Dead: The Ceramic Codex*. Charlottesville: University of Virginia Art Museum.

Robin, C. 1989. *Preclassic Maya Burials at Cuello, Belize*. BAR International Series 480. Oxford: British Archaeological Reports.

———. 2002. Gender and Maya farming: Chan Nòohol, Belize. In T. Ardren (ed.), *Ancient Maya Women*, 12–30. Walnut Creek: AltaMira.

———. 2003. New directions in Classic Maya household archaeology. *Journal of Archaeological Research* 11(4): 307–56.

———. 2006. Gender, farming, and long-term change: Maya historical and archaeological perspectives. *Current Anthropology* 47: 409–434.

Robin, C. and Hammond, N. 1991. Ritual and ideology: Burial practices. In N. Hammond (ed.), *Cuello: An Early Maya Community in Belize*, 204–25. Cambridge: Cambridge University Press.

Robles F. C. and Andrews, A. P. 1986. A review and synthesis of recent Postclassic archaeology in northern Yucatan. In J. A. Sabloff and E. W. Andrews (eds.), *Late Lowland Maya Civilization: Classic to Postclassic*, 53–98. Albuquerque: University of New Mexico Press.

Rodríguez Martínez, M. C., Ortíz Ceballos, P., Coe, M. D., Diehl, R. A., Houston, S. D., Taube, K. A., and Delgado Calderón, A. 2006. Oldest writing in the New World. *Science* 313: 1610–14.

Román, O. R. 1993. Hallazgo Preclásico medio en Kaminaljuyú. In J. P. Laporte, H. L. Escobedo, and S. V. de Brady (eds.), *III Simposio de Investigaciones Arqueológicas en Guatemala*, 209–18. Guatemala: Ministerio de Cultura y Deportes, Museo Nacional de Arqueología e Etnología.

Romero R., M. E. 1998. La navegación maya. *Arqueología mexicana* VI (33): 6–15.

Rosenmeier, M. F., Hodell, D. A., Brenner, M., Curtis, J. H., and Guilderson, T. P. 2002. A 3,500 year record of environmental change from the southern Maya lowlands, Peten, Guatemala. *Quaternary Research* 57: 183–90.

Rovner, I. and Lewenstein, S. M. 1997. *Maya Stone Tools of Dzibilchaltun, Yucatan, and Becan, and Chicanna, Campeche*. Middle American Research Institute, Publication 65. New Orleans: Tulane University.

Rowe, J. H. 1979. Standardization in Inca tapestry tunics. In A. Rowe, E. P. Benson and A.-L. Schaffer (eds.), *The Junius B. Bird Pre-Columbian Textile Conference, May 19th and 20th, 1973*, 239–60. Washington DC: Textile Museum and Dumbarton Oaks.

Roys, R. L. 1943. *The Indian Background of Colonial Yucatan*. Carnegie Institution of Washington, Publication 548. Washington DC.

———. 1957. *The Political Geography of the Yucatan Maya*. Carnegie Institution of Washington, Publication 613. Washington DC.

———. 1972. *The Indian Background of Colonial Yucatan. The Civilization of the American Indian series, v. 118*. Norman,: University of Oklahoma Press.

Rubatzky, V. E. and Yamaguchi, M. 1997. *World Vegetables: Principles, Production, and Nutritive Values*, 2nd edition. New York; London: Chapman & Hall.

Rudolph, L. I. and Rudolph, S. H. 1983. Oligopolistic competition among state elites in princely India. In G. E. Marcus (ed.), *Elites: Ethnographic Issues*, 193–220. Albuquerque: University of New Mexico Press.

Rudoph, R. L. 1992. The European family and economy: Central themes and issues. *Journal of Family History* 17: 119–38.

Ruppert, K. 1940. A special assemblage of Maya structures. In C. L. Hay, R. Linton, S. K. Lothrop, H. L. Shapiro, and G. C. Vaillant (eds.), *The Maya and Their Neighbors*, 222–31. New York: Appleton-Century.

Ruppert, K. and Denison, J. H. 1943. Archaeological reconnaissance in Campeche, Quintana Roo, and Petén. Publication 543,

Carnegie Institution of Washington. Washington DC.

Ruz Lhuillier, A. 1968. *Costumbres funerarias de los antiguos mayas*. México: Seminario de Cultura Maya, Universidad Nacional Autónoma de México.

———. 1973. *Palenque: el Templo de las Inscripciones*. Colección Científica, 7. Mexico: Instituto Nacional de Antropología e Historia.

Ruz, M. H. 1986. *Vocabulario de la lengua tzeldal segun el ordende Copánbastla de Fray Domingo de Ara*. México: Universidad Nacional Autónoma de México.

———. 1989. *Las lenguas del Chiapas colonial: Manuscritos en la Biblioteca Nacional de París*. México: Universidad Nacional Autónoma de México.

Ryder, J. W. 1977. Internal migration in Yucatán: Interpretation of historical demography and current patterns. In G. D. Jones (ed.), *Anthropology and History in Yucatán*, 191–231. Austin: University of Texas Press.

Sabloff, J. A. 1973a. Continuity and disruption during Terminal Late Classic times at Seibal: Ceramic and other evidence. In T. P. Culbert (ed.), *The Classic Maya Collapse*, 107–31. Albuquerque: University of New Mexico Press.

———. 1973b. Major themes in the past hypotheses of the Maya collapse. In T. P. Culbert (ed.), *The Classic Maya Collapse*, 35–40. Albuquerque: University of New Mexico Press.

———. 1975. *Excavations at Seibal: Ceramics*. Memoirs of the Peabody Museum, Vol.13, No.2. Cambridge MA: Harvard University.

Sabloff, J. A. and Willey, G. R. 1967. The collapse of Maya civilization in the southern lowlands: A consideration of history and process. *Southwestern Journal of Anthropology* 23(4): 311–36.

Sahagún, B. de. 1950–82. *The Florentine Codex: General History of the Things of New Spain*. Trans. J.O. Anderson and C.E. Dibble. Salt Lake City: University of Utah Press.

Saler, B. 1964. Nagual, witch, and sorcerer in a Quiche village. *Ethnology* 3(3): 305–28.

Sanders, W. T. 1973. Cultural ecology of the lowland Maya: A reevaluation. In T. P. Culbert (ed.), *The Classic Maya Collapse*, 325–65. Albuquerque: University of New Mexico Press.

———. 1981. Classic Maya settlement patterns and ethnographic analogy. In W. Ashmore (ed.), *Lowland Maya Settlement Patterns*, 351–69. Albuquerque: University of New Mexico Press.

———. 1989. Household, lineage, and state at eighth-century Copan, Honduras. In D. Webster (ed.), *The House of the Bacabs, Copan, Honduras*, 89–105. Studies in Pre-Columbian Art & Archaeology No. 29. Washington DC: Dumbarton Oaks.

Sanders, W. T. and Michels, J. W (eds.) 1977. *Teotihuacan and Kaminaljuyu: A Study in Prehistoric Culture Contact*. University Park: Pennsylvania State University Press.

Sanders, W. T., Parsons, J. R., and Santley, R. S. 1979. *The Basin of Mexico: Ecological Processes in the Evolution of a Civilization*. New York: Academic Press.

Sanders, W. T. and Webster, D. 1988. The mesoamerican urban tradition. *American Anthropologist* 90: 521–46.

Sartre, J. P. 1972. *The Psychology of Imagination*. New York: Citadel.

Satterthwaite, L., Jr. 1935. *Palaces Structure J-2 and J-6, with Notes on Str. J-6–2nd and Other Buried Structures in Court 1*. Piedras Negras Preliminary Papers, No. 3. Philadelphia: University Museum.

Saturno, W. A. 2006. The dawn of Maya gods and kings. *National Geographic* 209(1): 68–77.

Saturno, W. A., Sever, T. L., Irwin, D. E., Howell, B. F., and Garrison, T. G. 2007. Putting us on the map: Remote sensing investigation of the ancient Maya landscape. In J. R. Wiseman and Farouk El-Baz (eds.), *Remote Sensing in Archaeology*, 137–60. New York: Springer.

Saturno, W. A., Stuart, D., and Beltrán, B. 2006. Early Maya writing at San Bartolo, Guatemala. *Science* 311: 1281–3.

Saturno, W. A., Taube, K. A., and D. Stuart. 2005. The murals of San Bartolo, El Peten, Guatemala, Part 1: The north wall. *Ancient America* 7: 1–56.

Saturno, W. A., Taube, K. A., Stuart, D. S., Beltrán, B., and Román, E. 2006. Nuevos hallazgos arquitectónicos y pictóricos en la pirámide de Las Pinturas, San Bartolo, Petén. In J. P. Laporte, B. Arroyo, and H. Mejía (eds.), *XIX Simposio de Investigaciones Arqueológicas en Gautemala, 2005*, 571–88. Guatemala: Ministerio de Cultura y Deportes, Instituto de Antropología e Historia, Asociación Tikal, Fundación Arqueológica del Nuevo Mundo.

Scarborough, V. L. 1991. *Archaeology of Cerros, Belize, Central America, Vol. 3: The Settlement System in a Late Preclassic Maya Community*. Dallas: Southern Methodist University Press.

————. 1993. Water management in the southern Maya lowlands: An accretive model for the engineered landscape. In V. L. Scarborough and B. L. Isaac (eds.), *Economic Aspects of Water Management in the Prehispanic New World*, Vol. Supplement 7, *Research in Economic Anthropology*, 17–70. Greenwich: JAI Press.

————. 1994. Maya water management. *National Geographic Research and Exploration* 10: 184–99.

————. 2003. *The Flow of Power: Ancient Water Systems and Landscapes*. Santa Fe: School of American Research Press.

————. 2006. An Overview of Mesoamerican Water Systems. In B. L. Fash and L. J. Lucero (eds.) *Precolumbian Water Management: Ideology, Ritual and Power*, 223–36. Tucson: University of Arizona Press.

Scheffler, H. W. and Lounsbury, F. G. 1971. *A Study in Structural Semantics: The Siriono Kingship System*. Englewood Cliffs: Prentice-Hall.

Schele, L. 1981. Sacred site and world view at Palenque. In E. P. Benson (ed.), *Dumbarton Oaks Conference on Mesoamerican Sites and World Views*, 87–117. Washington DC: Dumbarton Oaks.

————. 1992. Founders of lineages at Copán and other Maya sites. *Ancient Mesoamerica* 3(1): 135–44.

Schele, L. and Freidel, D. 1990. *A Forest of Kings: The Untold Story of the Ancient Maya*. New York: William Morrow.

Schele, L. and Mathews, P. 1991. Royal visits and other intersite relationships among the Classic Maya. In T. P. Culbert (ed.), *Classic Maya Political History*, 226–52. Cambridge: Cambridge University Press.

————. 1998. *The Code of Kings: The Language of Seven Sacred Maya Temples and Tombs*. New York: Scribner.

Schele, L. and Miller, M. E. 1986. *The Blood of Kings: Dynasty and Ritual in Maya Art*. Forth Worth: Kimbell Art Museum.

Schellhas, P. 1897. *Die Göttergestalten der Maya-handschriften: Ein mythologische Kulturbild aus dem Alten Amerika*. Dresden: Verlag von Richard Bertling.

————. 1904. Comparative studies in the field of Maya antiquities. In C. P. Bowditch (ed.), *Mexican and Central American Antiquities, Calendar Systems, and History*, 591–622. Bureau of American Ethnology Bulletin 28. Washington DC.

Schlesinger, V. 2002. *Animals and Plants of the Ancient Maya: A Guide*. Austin: University of Texas Press.

Schieber de Lavarreda, C. and Orrego, M. 2001. Mil anos de historia en Abaj Takalik. *Utz'ib* 3(1): 1–31.

Schneider, D. M. 1984. *A Critique of the Study of Kinship*. Ann Arbor: University of Michigan Press.

Schultz, J. A. 2006. *Courtly Love, the Love of Courtliness, and the History of Sexuality*. Chicago: The University of Chicago Press.

Schwartz, N. B. 1990. *Forest Society: A Social History of Peten, Guatemala*. Philadelphia: University of Pennsylvania Press.

Schwendener, W. O. and Inomata, T. 2006. Sondeo enfrente de la Estructura A-24: Operación CB200A. In E. Ponciano, T. Inomata and D. Triadan (eds.), *Informe del Proyecto Arqueológico Ceibal-Petexbatun: La Temporada de Campo 2006*, 2.1–2.4. Report presented to the Instituto de Antropología e Historia de Guatemala.

Scott, J. C. 1976. *The Moral Economy of the Peasant: Rebellion and Subsistence in Southeast Asia*. New Haven: Yale University Press.

————. 1990. *Domination and the Arts of Resistance: Hidden Transcripts*. New Haven: Yale University Press.

————. 1998. *Seeing Like a State: How Certain Schemes to Improve the Human Condition Have Failed*. New Haven: Yale University Press.

Sears, E. L. 2006. Las figurillas mayas del clásico tardío de sistemas de los ríos de Usumacinta/Pasión. In *Los Investigadores de la cultura maya 14, tomo II*, 389–402. Campeche: Universidad Autónoma de Campeche.

Seitz, R., Harlow, G. E., Sisson, V. B., and Taube, K. E. 2001. Olmec Blue and Formative jade sources: New discoveries in Guatemala. *Antiquity* 75(290): 687–8.

Selby, H. A. 1974. *Zapotec Deviance: The Convergence of Folk and Modern Sociology*. Austin: University of Texas Press.

Sever, T. L. and Irwin, D. E. 2003. Landscape archaeology: Remote-sensing investigation of the ancient Maya in the Peten rainforest of northern Guatemala. *Ancient Mesoamerica* 14: 113–22.

Shafer, H. J. and Hester. T. R. 1983. Ancient Maya chert workshops in northern Belize, Central America. *American Antiquity* 48: 519–43.

Sharer, R. J. 1976. The Jenney Creek ceramic complex at Barton Ramie. In J. Gifford, *Prehistoric Pottery Analysis and the Ceramics of Barton Ramie in the Belize Valley*, 61–63. Memoir of the Peabody Museum of Archaeology and Ethnology, 18. Cambridge MA: Harvard University.

———. 1977. The Maya collapse revised: Internal and external perspective. In N. Hammond (ed.), *Social Process in Maya Prehistory: Essays in Honor of Sir J. Eric Thompson*, 532–52. New York: Academic Press.

———. 1985. Terminal events in the southeastern lowlands: A view from Quirigua. In A. F. Chase and P. M. Rice (eds.), *The Lowland Maya Postclassic*, 245–53. Austin: University of Texas Press.

———. 1989. The Olmec and the southeast periphery of Mesoamerica. In R. J. Sharer and D. C. Grove (eds.), *Regional Perspectives on the Olmec*, 247–76. Cambridge: Cambridge University Press.

———. 1994. *The Ancient Maya*. 5th edition. Stanford: Stanford University Press.

Sharer, R. J. and Sedat, D. W. 1987. *Archaeological Investigations in the Northern Maya Highlands, Guatemala: Interaction and the Development of Maya Civilization*. University Museum Monograph 59. Philadelphia: University of Pennsylvania.

Sharer, R. J. and Traxler, L. P. 2005. *The Ancient Maya*. 6th ed. Stanford: Stanford University Press.

Sharer, R. J., Traxler, L. P., Sedat, D. W., Bell, E. E., Canuto, M. A., and Powell, C. 1999. Early Classic architecture beneath the Copan acropolis: A research update. *Ancient Mesoamerica* 10: 3–23.

Shaw, C. 2000. *Sacred Monkey River: A Canoe Trip with the Gods*. New York: W. W. Norton.

Shaw, M. 1972. *Según nuestros antepasados: Textos folklóricos de Guatemala y Honduras*. Guatemala: Instituto Lingüístico de Verano.

Sheets, P. D. 1979. Environmental and cultural effects of the Ilopango eruption in Central America. In P. D. Sheets and D. K. Grayson (eds.), *Volcanic Activity and Human Ecology*, 525–64. New York: Academic Press.

———. 1992. *The Ceren Site: A Prehistoric Village Buried by Volcanic Ash in Central America. Case studies in archaeology series*. Fort Worth: Harcourt Brace Jovanovich College Publishers.

——— (ed.) 2002. *Before the Volcano Erupted: The Ancient Cerén Village in Central America*. Austin: University of Texas Press.

Sheets, P. D. and Muto, G. 1972. Pressure blades and total cutting edge: An experiment in lithic technology. *Science* 175: 632–4.

Sheets, P and Woodward, M. 2002. Cultivating biodiversity: Milpas, gardens, and the Classic Period landscape. In P. Sheets (ed.), *Before the Volcano Erupted: The Ancient Cerén Village in Central America*, 184–91. Austin: University of Texas Press.

Shepard, A. O. 1956. *Ceramics for the archaeologist*. Carnegie Institution of Washington, Publication 609. Washington DC.

Shils, E. 1968. Deference. In J. A. Jackson (ed.), *Social Stratification*, 104–32. Cambridge: Cambridge University Press.

Shook, E. M. 1998. *Incidents in the Life of a Maya Archaeology, as Told to Winifred Veronda*. San Marino: Southwestern Academy Press.

Shook, E. M., de Hatch, M. P., and Donaldson, J. K. 1979. Ruins of Semetabaj, Department of Solola, Guatemala. *Contributions of the Archaeological Research Facility* 41: 7–142. Berkeley: University of California.

Shook, E. M. and Heizer, R. 1976. An Olmec sculpture from the south (pacific) coast of Guatemala. *Journal of the New World Archaeology* 1(3): 1–8. Los Angeles: University of California.

Shook, E. M. and Kidder, A. V. 1952. *Mound E-III-3, Kaminaljuyú, Guatemala*. Contributions to American Anthropology and History, vol. 596, no. 11. Washington DC: Carnegie Institution of Washington.

Siemans, A. H. 1996. Benign flooding on tropical lowland floodplains. In S. L. Fedick (ed.), *Managed Mosaic: Ancient Maya Agriculture and Resource Use*, 132–44. Salt Lake City: University of Utah Press.

Siemans, A. H. and Puleston, D. E. 1972. Ridged fields and associated features in southern Campeche: New perspectives on the lowland Maya. *American Antiquity* 37: 228–39.

Sisson, E. B. 1970. Settlement patterns and land use in the northwestern Chontalpa, Tabasco, Mexico: A progress report. *Cerámica de Cultura Maya* 6: 41–54.

———. 1976. *Survey and Excavation in the North-western Chontalpa, Tabasco, Mexico.* Ph.D. dissertation. Harvard University.

Skidmore, J. 2007. An updated listing of early Naranjo rulers. *The PARI Journal* 7(4): 23–4.

Smailus, O. 1975. *El maya-chontal de Acalan: Análisis lingüístico de un documento de los años 1610–12.* Centro de Estudios Mayas, Cuaderno 9. México: Universidad Nacional Autónoma de México.

Smalley, J. and Blake, M. 2003. Sweet beginnings: Stalk sugar and the domestication of maize. *Current Anthropology* 44 (5): 675–703.

Smith, A. L. 1950. *Uaxactun, Guatemala: Excavations of 1931–1937.* Publication 588. Washington DC: Carnegie Institution of Washington.

———. 1982. *Excavations at Seibal: Major Architecture and Caches.* Memoirs of the Peabody Museum, Vol. 15, No.1. Cambridge MA: Harvard University.

Smith, K. 2004. Patterns in time and the tempo of change: A North Atlantic perspective on the evolution of complex societies. In J. Mathieu and R. Scott (eds.), *Exploring the Role of Analytical Scale in Archaeological Interpretation,* 83–99. Oxford: British Archaeological Reports.

Smith, M. E. 2003. Can we read cosmology in ancient Maya city plans? Comment on Ashmore and Sabloff. *Latin American Antiquity* 14: 221–8.

Smith, R. E. 1971. *The Pottery of Mayapan, Including Studies of Ceramic Material from Uxmal, Kabah, and Chichen Itza.* Paper of the Peabody Museum of Archaeology and Ethnology, Vol. 66. Cambridge MA: Harvard University.

Smuts, R. M. 1987. *Court Culture and the Origins of a Royalist Tradition in Early Stuart England.* Philadelphia: University of Pennsylvania Press.

Smyth, M. P. and Rogart, D. 2004. A Teotihuacan presence at Chac II, Yucatan, Mexico: Implications for early political economy of the Puuc region. *Ancient Mesoamerica* 15: 17–47.

Spence, M. W. 1996. Commodity or gift: Teotihuacan obsidian in the Maya region. *Latin American Antiquity* 7: 21–39.

Spinden, H. J. 1913. *A Study of Maya Art: Its Subject Matter and Historical Development.* Peabody Museum of American Archaeology and Ethnology Memoirs, 6. Cambridge MA: Harvard University.

Sponsel, L. E., Headland, T. N., and Bailey, R. 1996. *Tropical Deforestation: The Human Dimension.* New York: Columbia University Press.

Šprajc, I. 1990. El Satunsat de Oxkintok: Observatorio astronómico? In M. Rivera Dorado (ed.), *Oxkintok,* 87–97. Misión Arqueológico de España en México, Madrid.

———. 2003. Archaeological reconnaissance in southeastern Campeche, México: 2002 field season report. Report submitted to FAMSI, www.famsi.org/reports. Accessed April 15, 2008.

Stanton, T. W. and Ardren, T. 2005. The Middle Formative of Yucatan in context. *Ancient Mesoamerica* 16(2): 213–28.

Stanton, T. W., and Freidel, D. A. 2003. Ideological lock-in and the dynamics of Formative religions in Mesoamerica. *Mayab* 16: 5–14.

Stanton, T. W. and Gallareta Negrón, T. 2001. Warfare, ceramic economy, and the Itza: A reconsideration of the Itza polity in ancient Yucatan. *Ancient Mesoamerica* 12: 229–45.

Stark, B. L. 2000. Framing the Gulf Olmecs. In J. E. Clark and M. E. Pye (eds.), *Olmec Art and Archaeology in Mesoamerica,* 31–53. Washington DC: National Gallery of Art.

Steggerda, M. 1931. Results of psychological tests given to Maya Indians in Yucatan. *Eugenical News* 16: 120–25.

———. 1938. *Maya Indians of Yucatan.* Carnegie Institution of Washington Publication 501. Washington DC.

Stenzel, W. 1968. The sacred bundle in mesoamerican religion. In *Thirty-eighth International Congress of Americanists, Stuttgart-München, 1968,* 2: 347–52.

Stephens, J. L. 1841. *Incidents of Travel in Central America, Chiapas, and Yucatan.* 2 vols. New York: Harper and Brothers.

———. 1843. *Incidents of Travel in Yucatan.* 2 vols. New York: Harper and Brothers.

Stock, B. 1996. *Listening for the Text: On the Uses of the Past.* Philadelphia: University of Pennsylvania Press.

Stoeltje, B. 1997. Asante queen mothers: A study in female authority. *Annals of the New York Academy of Sciences* 810: 41–71.

Stone, A. J. 1989. Disconnection, foreign insignia and political expansion: Teotihuacán and the warrior stelae of Piedras Negras. In R. A. Diehl and J. C. Berlo (eds.), *Mesoamerica After the Decline of Teotihuacán, A.D. 700–900,* 153–72. Dumbarton Oaks Research Library and Collection. Washington DC.

———. 1992. From ritual in the landscape to capture in the urban center: The recreation of ritual environments in Mesoamerica. *Journal of Ritual Studies* 6(1): 109–32.

———. 1995. *Images from the Underworld: Naj Tunich and the Tradition of Maya Cave Painting.* Austin: University of Texas Austin.

Stuart, D. 1984. Royal auto-sacrifice among the Maya: A study in image and meaning. *RES* 7/8: 6–20.

———. 1985a. Inscription on four shell plaques from Piedras Negras, Guatemala. In E. P. Benson (ed.), *Fourth Palenque Round Table, 1980,* 175–83. San Francisco: Pre-Columbian Art Research Institute.

———. 1985b. "The count of captives" epithet in Classic Maya Writing. In Virginia M. Fields (ed.), *Fifth Palenque Round Table, 1983,* Vol. VII, 97–101. San Francisco: Pre-Columbian Art Research Institute.

———. 1989a. Hieroglyphs on Maya vessels. In J. Kerr (ed.), *The Maya Vase Book, A Corpus of Rollout Photographs of Maya Vases:* Volume 1, 149–60. New York: Kerr Associates.

———. 1989b. *The Maya Artist: An Iconographic and Epigraphic Analysis.* B.A. thesis. Department of Art and Archaeology, Princeton University.

———. 1990. *A New Carved Panel from the Palenque Area,* Research Reports on Ancient Maya Writing 32. Washington DC: Center for Maya Research.

———. 1993. Historical inscriptions and the Maya collapse. In J. A. Sabloff and J. S. Henderson (eds.), *Lowland Maya Civilization in the Eighth Century A.D.,* 321–54. Washington DC: Dumbarton Oaks.

———. 1996. Kings of stone: A consideration of stelae in ancient Maya ritual and representations. *RES* 29/30: 148–71.

———. 1997. Kingship terms in Maya inscriptions. In M. J. Macri and A. Ford (eds.), *The Language of Maya Hieroglyphs,* 1–11. San Francisco: Pre-Columbian Art Research Institute.

———. 1998. 'The fire enters his house': Architecture and ritual in Classic Maya texts. In S. D. Houston (ed.), *Function and Meaning in Classic Maya Architecture,* 373–425. Washington DC: Dumbarton Oaks.

———. 2000. 'Arrival of Strangers': Teotihuacan and Tollan in Classic Maya history. In D. Carrasco, L. Jones, and S. Sessions (eds.), *Mesoamerica's Classic Heritage: Teotihuacán to the Aztecs,* 465–513. Niwot: University Press of Colorado.

———. 2001. Earthquake! *Mesoweb.com:* www.mesoweb.com/stuart/notes/Earthquake.pdf.

———. 2002. Glyphs for 'Right' and 'Left'? *Mesoweb.com:* www.mesoweb.com/stuart/notes/RightLeft.pdf. Accessed April 15, 2008.

———. 2003. La identificacion de Hixwitz. Paper presented at the XV Simposio de Investigaciones Arqueologicas en Guatemala. Museo Nacional de Arqueologia y Etnologia de Guatemala.

———. 2004a. The beginnings of the Copan dynasty: A review of the hieroglyphic and historical evidence. In E. E. Bell, M. A. Canuto, and R. J. Sharer (eds.), *Understanding Early Classic Copan,* 215–48. Philadelphia: University of Pennsylvania Museum.

———. 2004b. A foreign past: The writing and representation of history on a royal ancestral shrine at Copan. In E. W. Andrews and W. L. Fash (eds.), *Copan: The History of an Ancient Maya Kingdom,* 373–94. Santa Fe: School of American Research Press.

———. 2005. Ideology and Classic Maya kingship. In V. L. Scarborough (ed.), *A Catalyst for Ideas: Anthropological Archaeology and the Legacy of Douglas Schwartz,* 257–86. Santa Fe: School of American Research Press.

———. 2006. The language of chocolate: References to cacao on Classic Maya drinking vessels. In C. L. McNeil (ed.), *Chocolate in Mesoamerica: A Cultural History of Cacao,* 184–201. Gainsville: University Press of Florida.

———. 2007a. A political transition at Palenque. http://decipherment.wordpress.com/2007/04/13/a-political-transition-at-palenque/. Accessed April 15, 2008.

———. 2007b. The mam glyph. http://decipherment.wordpress.com/2007/09/29/the-mam-glyph/. Accessed April 15, 2008.

Stuart, D. and Graham, I. 2003. *Corpus of Maya Hieroglyphic Inscriptions, Volume 9, Part 1: Piedras Negras.* Cambridge MA: Peabody Museum of Archaeology and Ethnology, Harvard University.

———. 2006. *Corpus of Maya Hieroglyphic Inscriptions, Volume 9, Part 1: Piedras Negras.* Cambridge MA: Peabody Museum of Archaeology and Ethnology, Harvard University.

Stuart, D. and Houston, S. D. 1994. *Classic Maya Place Names.* Studies in Pre-Columbian Art and Archaeology No. 33. Washington DC: Dumbarton Oaks.

————. 2001. Peopling the Classic Maya court. In T. Inomata and S. D. Houston (eds.), *Royal Courts of the Ancient Maya: Volume I, Theory, Comparison, and Synthesis, 54–83.* Boulder: Westview Press.

Stuart, D., Houston, S. D., and Robertson, J. 1999. *Recovering the Past: Classic Mayan Language and Classic Maya Gods.* Workbook for the XXII Maya Weekend, University of Texas, Austin.

Stuart, G. E. 1992. Quest for decipherment: A historical and biographical survey of Maya hieroglyphic investigation. In E. C. Danien and R. J. Sharer (eds.), *New Theories on the Ancient Maya*, 1–63. University Museum Monograph 77. Philadelphia: University Museum, University of Pennsylvania.

Suhler, C., Ardren, T., Freidel, D., and Johnstone, D. 2004. The rise and fall of Terminal Classic Yaxuna, Yucatán, Mexico. In A. A. Demarest, P. M. Rice and D. S. Rice (eds.), *The Terminal Classic in the Maya Lowlands: Collapse, Transition, and Transformation*, 450–84. Boulder: University Press of Colorado.

Sullivan, T. D. 1986. A scattering of jades: The words of Aztec elders. In G. Gossen (ed.), *Symbol and Meaning Beyond the Closed Community*, 9–17. Albany: Institute for Mesoamerican Studies, State University of New York.

Sykes, J. B. (ed.). 1976. *The Concise Oxford Dictionary of Current English.* 6th ed. Oxford: Clarendon Press.

Taladoire, E. 1981. *Les Terrains de Jeu de Balle (Mésoamerique et Sud-ouest des Etats-Unis).* Etudes mésoaméricaines: Série II(4). México: Mission Archéologique et Ethnologique Française au Mexique.

————. 2001. Architectural background of the pre-hispanic ballgame: An evolutionary perspective. In E. M. Whittington (ed.), *The Sport of Life and Death: The Mesoamerican Ballgame*, 96–115. New York: Thames and Hudson.

Tate, C. E. 1992. *Yaxchilan: The Design of a Maya Ceremonial City.* Austin: University of Texas Press.

Taube, K. A. 1983. *The Teotihuacan Spider Woman. Journal of Latin American Lore* 9(2): 107–89.

————. 1985. The Classic Maya Maize God: A reappraisal. In M. G. Robertson (ed.), *Fifth Palenque Round Table, 1983*, 171–83. San Francisco: Pre-Columbian Art Research Institute.

————. 1989a. Ritual humor in Classic Maya religion. In W. F. Hanks and D. S. Rice (eds.), *Word and Image in Maya Culture: Explorations in Language, Writing, and Representation*, 351–82. Salt Lake City: University of Utah Press.

————. 1989b. Maize tamale in Classic Maya diet, epigraphy, and art. *American Antiquity* 54: 31–51.

————. 1992a. *The Major Gods of Ancient Yucatan.* Studies in Pre-Columbian Art and Archaeology, No. 32. Washington DC: Dumbarton Oaks.

————. 1992b. The temple of Quetzalcoatl and the cult of sacred war at Teotihuacan. *RES* 21: 53–87.

————. 1992c. Uses of sport: Review of the mesoamerican ballgame. *Science* 256: 1064–5.

————. 1993. *The Legendary Past: Aztec and Maya Myths* London: British Museum Press.

————. 1994. The birth vase: Natal imagery in ancient Maya myth and ritual. In J. Kerr (ed.), *The Maya Vase Book, Volume 4: A Corpus of Rollout Photographs of Maya Vases*, 652–85. New York: Kerr Associates.

————. 1995. Rainmakers: The Olmec and their contribution to Mesoamerican belief and ritual. In J. Guthrie (ed.), *The Olmec World: Ritual and Rulership*, 83–104. Princeton: Art Museum, Princeton University.

————. 1996. The Olmec Maize God: The face of corn in Formative Mesoamerica. *RES: Anthropology and Aesthetics* 29/30: 39–81.

————. 1998. Jade hearth: Centrality, rulership, and the Classic Maya temple. In S. D. Houston (ed.), *Function and Meaning in Classic Maya Architecture*. 427–78. Washington DC: Dumbarton Oaks.

————. 2000. Turquoise hearth: Fire, self-sacrifice, and the Central Mexican cult of war. In D. Carrasco, L. Jones, and S. Sessions (eds.), *Mesoamerica's Classic Heritage: Teotihuacán to the Aztecs*, 269–340. Niwot: University Press of Colorado.

————. 2002. Maws of heaven and hell: The symbolism of the centipede and serpent in Classic Maya religion. In A. Ciudad Ruiz, M. Humberto Ruz Sosa, and M. Josefa Iglesias Ponce de León (eds.), *Antropología de la eternidad: la muerte en la cultura maya*, 405–42. Madrid: Sociedad Española de Estudios Mayas.

———. 2003. Ancient and contemporary Maya conceptions of the field and forest. In A. Gómez-Pompa, M. F. Allen, S. Fedick, and J. Jiménez-Moreno (eds.), *Lowland Maya Area: Three Millennia at the Human-Wildland Interface*, 461–94. New York: Haworth Press.

———. 2004a. Flower mountain: Concepts of life, beauty, and paradise among the Classic Maya. *RES: Anthropology and Aesthetics* 45: 69–98.

———. 2004b. *Olmec Art at Dumbarton Oaks*. Washington DC: Dumbarton Oaks.

Taube, K. A., Sisson, V., Seitz, R., and Harlow, G. 2004. The Sourcing of Mesoamerican Jade: Expanded Geological Reconnaissance in the Motagua Region, Guatemala, Appendix to Olmec Art at Dumbarton Oaks, Karl A. Taube, author: 203–20. Washington DC: Dumbarton Oaks.

Taube, K. A. and Zender, M. 2005. Ritual boxing among the Classic Maya. Paper presented at the 70th Annual Meeting of the Society for American Archaeology, Salt Lake City.

Taylor, D. 1983. *Classic Maya Costume: Regional Types of Dress*. Ph.D. Dissertation. New Haven: Yale University, Department of the History of Art.

———. 1992. Painted ladies: Costumes for women on Tepeu ceramics. In J. Kerr (ed.), *The Maya Vase Book, 3*, 513–25. New York: Kerr Associates.

Tedlock, B. 1982. *Time and the Highland Maya*. Rev. ed. Albuquerque: University of New Mexico Press.

Terracciano, A. et al. [98 co-authors] 2005. National character does not reflect mean personality trait levels in 49 cultures. *Science* 310 (5745): 96–100.

Terraciano, K. 2001. *The Mixtecs of Colonial Oaxaca: Nudzahui History, Sixteenth Through Eighteenth Centuries*. Stanford: Stanford University Press.

Terry, R. E., Fernández, F. G., Parnell, J. J., and Inomata, T. 2004. The story in the floors: Chemical signatures of ancient and modern Maya activities at Aguateca, Guatemala. *Journal of Archaeological Science* 31: 1237–50.

Therborn, G. 1980. *The Power of Ideology and the Ideology of Power*. London: Verso.

Thompson, J. E. S. 1930. *Ethnology of the Mayas of Southern and Central British Honduras*. Field Museum of Natural History Publication 274, Anthropological Series No. 2. Chicago.

———. 1940. Archaeological problems of the lowland Maya. In C. L. Hay, R. L. Linton, S. K. Lotrhop, H. L. Shaprio, and G. C. Vaillant (eds.), *The Maya and Their Neighbors: Essays on Middle American Anthropology and Archaeology*, 126–38. New York: D. Appleton-Century Company.

———. 1954. *Rise and Fall of Maya Civilization*. Norman: University of Oklahoma Press.

———. 1963. *Maya Archaeologist*. Norman: University of Oklahoma Press.

———. 1970. *Maya History and Religion*. Norman: University of Oklahoma Press.

Thompson, J. E. S., Pollock, H. E. D., and Charlot, J. 1932. *A Preliminary Study of the Ruins of Coba, Quintana Roo, Mexico*. Carnegie Institution of Washington, Publication 424. Washington DC.

Tokovinine, A. 2006. Art of the Maya epitaph: The genre of posthumous biographies in the Late Classic Maya inscriptions. In R. Valencia Rivera and G. Le Fort (eds.), *Sacred Books, Sacred Languages: Two Thousand Years of Ritual and Religious Maya Literature*, 1–19. Acta Mesoamericana 18. Markt Schwaben: Verlag Anton Saurwein.

Tokovinine, A. and Fialko, V. 2007. Stela 45 of Naranjo and the Early Classic lords of Sa'aal. *The Pari Journal* 7(4): 1–14.

Tomasic, J. and Fahsen, F. 2003. Exploraciones y excavaciones preliminares en Tres Islas, Peten. In J.P. Laporte, H. Escobedo and B. Arroyo (eds.), *XVII Simposio de Investigaciones Arqueologicas en Guatemala*, 819–32. Guatemala: Ministerio de Cultura y Deportes; Instituto de Antropologia e Historia.

Torres, R. A., Gallegos Gómora, M. J., and Zender, M. U. 2000. Urnas funerarias, textos históricos y ofrendas en Comalcalco. *Los investigadores de la cultura maya* 8, Tomo II: 312–23.

Tourtellot, G. 1988a. Developmental cycles of households and houses at Seibal. In R. R. Wilk and W. Ashmore (eds.), *Household and Community in the Mesoamerican Past*, 97–120. Albuquerque: University of New Mexico Press.

———. 1988b. *Excavations at Seibal, Department of Peten, Guatemala: Peripheral Survey and Excavation, Settlement and Community Patterns*. Memoirs of the Peabody Museum of Archaeology and Ethnology, Harvard University, Volume 16. Cambridge MA: Harvard University.

————. 1990. Population estimates for Preclassic and Classic Seibal, Peten. In T. P. Culbert and D. S. Rice (eds.), *Precolumbian Population History in the Maya Lowlands*, 83–102. Albuquerque: University of New Mexico Press.

Tourtellot, G. and González, J. J. 2004. The last hurrah: Continuity and transformation at Seibal. In A. A. Demarest, P. M. Rice, and D. S. Rice (eds.), *The Terminal Classic in the Maya Lowlands: Collapse, Transition, and Transformation*, 60–82. Boulder: University Press of Colorado.

Tourtellot, G., Wolf, M., Smith, S., Gardella, K., and Hammond, N. 2002. Exploring heaven on earth: Testing the cosmological model at La Milpa, Belize. *Antiquity* 76: 633–34.

Townsend, R. F. 1979. *State and Cosmos in the Art of Tenochtitlan*. Studies in Pre-Columbian Art and Archaeology No. 20. Washington DC: Dumbarton Oaks.

Tozzer, A. M. 1941. *Landa's Relación de las Cosas de Yucatan*. Papers of the Peabody Museum of American Archaeology and Ethnology, No. 18. Cambridge MA: Harvard University.

————. 1957. *Chichen Itza and its Cenote of Sacrifice: A Comparative Study of Contemporaneous Maya and Toltec*. Memoirs of the Peabody Museum of Archaeology and Ethnology, Vols. 11 and 12. Cambridge MA: Harvard University.

Triadan, D. 2007. Warriors, nobles, commoners and beasts: Figurines from elite buildings at Aguateca, Guatemala. *Latin American Antiquity* 18(3): 269–94.

Trigger, B. G. 2003. *Understanding Early Civilizations: A Comparative Study*. Cambridge: Cambridge University Press.

Trik, H. and Kampen, M. E. 1983. *Tikal Report No. 31: The Graffiti of Tikal*. University Museum Monograph 57. Philadelphia: University Museum, University of Pennsylvania.

Turner, B. L. 1974. Prehistoric intensive agriculture in the Mayan lowlands. *Science* 185: 118–24.

Turner, T. S. 1980. The social skin. In J. Cherfas and R. Lewin (eds.), *Not Work Alone: A Cross-Cultural View of Activities Superfluous to Survival*, 112–40. London: Temple Smith.

Ulrich, E. M. and de Ulrich, R. D. 1976. *Diccionario Maya Mopan/Español, Español/Maya Mopan*. Guatemala: Instituto Lingüístico de Verano.

Vail, G. and Bricker, V. R. 2004. *Haab* dates in the Madrid Codex. In G. Vail and A. Aveni (eds.), *The Madrid Codex: New Approaches to Understanding an Ancient Maya Manuscript*, 171–214. Boulder: University Press of Colorado.

Valdés, J. A. 1992. El crecimiento de la civilización maya en el área central durante el preclásico tardío: Una vista desde el Grupo H de Uaxactún. *U Tz'ib* 1(2): 16–31. Guatemala: Asociación Tikal.

————. 1995. Desarrollo cultural y señales de alarma entre los mayas: El preclásico tardío y la transición hacia el clásico temprano. In N. Grube (ed.), *The Emergence of Lowland Maya Civilization: The Transition from the Preclassic to the Early Classic*, 71–85. Acta Mesoamerican 8. Markt Schwaben: Verlag Anton Saurwein.

Valdés, J. A. and Fahsen, F. 2004. Disaster in sight: The Terminal Classic at Tikal and Uaxactun. In A. A. Demarest, P. M. Rice, and D. S. Rice (eds.), *The Terminal Classic in the Maya Lowlands: Collapse, Transition, and Transformation*, 140–61. Boulder: University Press of Colorado.

Valdés, J. A. and de Hatch, M. P. 1996. Evidencias de poder y conrol social en Kaminaljuyú: Proyecto Arqueológico Miraflores II. In Juan P. Laporte and Héctor Escobedo (eds.), *IX Simposio de Investigaciones Arqueológicas en Guatemala, 1995*, 377–96. Guatemala: Ministerio de Cultura y Deportes, Museo Nacional de Arqueología e Etnología.

Valdez, F., Jr. 1987. *The Prehistoric Ceramics of Colha, Northern Belize*. Ph.D. dissertation. Harvard University.

Varela Torrecilla, C. and Braswell, G. E. 2003. Teotihuacan and Oxkintok: New perspectives from Yucatan. In G. E. Braswell (ed.), *The Maya and Teotihuacan: Reinterpreting Early Classic Interpretation*, 250–71. Austin: University of Texas Press.

Vargas de la Peña, L. and Castillo Borges, V. 2006. Ek' Balam, un antiguo reino localizado en el oriente de Yucatán. In M. Josefa Iglesias Ponce de León, R. Valencia Rivera, and A. Ciudad Ruíz (eds.), *Nuevas ciudades, nuevas patrias: Fundación y relocalización de ciudades en Mesoamérica y el Mediterráneo antiguo*, 191–208. Madrid: Sociedad Española de Estudios Mayas.

Vargas Pacheco, E. 1994. Síntesis de la historia prehispánica de los mayas chontales de

Tabasco-Campeche. *América Indígena* 1–2: 15–61.

Velázquez, J. L. 1991. Replantamiento de la Fase Majada: Un componente Preclásico medio tardío. In J. P. Laporte, H. L Escobedo, and S. V. de Brady (eds.), *II Simposio de Investigaciones Arqueológicas en Guatemala, 1988*, 72–80. Guatemala: Ministerio de Cultura y Deportes, Museo Nacional de Arqueología e Etnología.

Velázquez Valadéz, R. 1980. Recent discoveries in the caves of Loltún, Yucatan, Mexico. *Mexicon* 2(4): 53–5.

Van Gennep, A. 1960. *The Rites of Passage.* Chicago: University of Chicago Press.

Veyne, P. 1988. *Did the Greeks Believe in Their Myths? An Essay in the Constitutive Imagination.* Chicago: University of Chicago Press.

Viel, R. 1993. *Evolución de la cerámica de Copán, Honduras.* Tegucigalpa: Instituto Hondureño de Antropología e Historia.

Villela, K. 1993. *The Classic Maya Secondary Tier: Power and Prestige at Three Polities.* M.A. thesis. Department of Art History, University of Texas, Austin.

Vogt, E. Z. 1969. *Zinacantan: A Maya Community in the Highlands of Chiapas.* Cambridge MA: Belknap Press, Harvard University Press.

———. 1976. *Tortillas for the Gods: A Symbolic Analysis of Zinacanteco Rituals.* Cambridge MA: Harvard University Press.

———. 1998. Souls. Unpublished manuscript in possession of authors.

Vogt, E. Z. and Stuart, D. 2005. Some notes on ritual caves among the ancient and modern Maya. In J. E. Brady and K. M. Prufer (eds.), *In the Maw of the Earth Monster: Mesoamerican Ritual Cave Use*, 155–85. Austin: University of Texas Press.

Wagley, C. 1949. *The Social and Religious Life of a Guatemalan Village.* Memoirs of the American Anthropological Association, No. 71. Menasha: American Anthropological Association.

Wagner, P. L. 1964. Natural vegetation of middle America. In R. C. West (ed.), *Natural Environment and Early Cultures.* Handbook of Middle American Indians, Vol. 1. Austin: University of Texas Press.

Walters, G. R. 1982. *The Pre-Columbian Jade Processing Industry of the Middle Motagua Valley of East Central Guatemala.* Ph.D. dissertation. University of Missouri.

Ware, G., Houston, S. D., Miller, M., Taube, K. A., and de la Fuente, B. 2002. Infared imaging of Precolumbian murals at Bonampak, Chiapas, Mexico. *Antiquity* 76(292): 325–6.

Warnke, M. 1993. *The Court Artist: On the Ancestry of the Modern Artist.* Cambridge: Cambridge University Press.

Warren, K. B. 1989. *The Symbolism of Subordination: Indian Identity in a Guatemalan Town.* 2nd ed. Austin: University of Texas Press.

———. 1998. *Indigenous Movements and their Critics: Pan-Maya Activism in Guatemala.* Princeton: Princeton University Press.

Watanabe, J. M. 1992. *Maya Saints and Souls in a Changing World.* Austin: University of Texas Press.

Waterson, R. 1995. Houses and hierarchies in island Southeast Asia. In J. Carsten and S. Hugh-Jones (eds.), *About the House: Lévi-Strauss and Beyond*, 47–68. Cambridge: Cambridge University Press.

Wauchope, R (ed.) 1964–1976. *Handbook of Middle American Indians.* 16 vols. Austin: University of Texas Press.

Webb, M. C. 1973. Peten Maya decline viewed in the perspective of state formation. In T. P. Culbert (ed.), *The Classic Maya Collapse*, 367–404. Albuquerque: University of New Mexico Press.

Weber, M. 1978. *Economy and Society.* 2 vols. Berkeley: University of California Press.

Webster, D. L. 1976. *Defensive Earthworks at Becán, Campeche, Mexico: Implications for Maya Warfare.* Publication 41. New Orleans: Tulane University, Middle American Research Institute.

———. 1979. *Cuca, Chacchob, Dzonot Ake: Three Walled Northern Maya Centers.* Occasional papers in Anthropology 11. Department of Anthropology. University Park: The Pennsylvania State University.

———. 1989. The House of the Bacabs: Its social context. In D. Webster (ed.), *The House of the Bacabs, Copan, Honduras*, 5–40. Studies in Pre-Columbian Art and Archaeology No. 29. Washington DC: Dumbarton Oaks.

———. 1998. Studying Maya burials. In S. L. Whittington and D. M. Reed (eds.), *Bones of the Maya: Studies of Ancient Skeletons*, 3–12. Washington DC: Smithsonian Institution Press.

———. 2001. Spatial dimensions of Maya courtly life. In T. Inomata and S. D. Houston (eds.), *Royal Courts of the Ancient Maya, Volume 1: Theory, Comparison, and Synthesis*, 130–67. Boulder: Westview.

———. 2002. *The Fall of the Ancient Maya*. London: Thames & Hudson.

Webster, D., Evans, S. T., and Sanders, W. T. 1993. *Out of the Past: An Introduction to Archaeology*. Mountain View: Mayfield.

Webster, D. L., Fash, B., Widmer, R., and Zeleznik, S. 1998. The Skyband Group: Investigation of a Classic Maya elite residential complex at Copán, Honduras. *Journal of Field Archaeology* 25: 319–43.

Webster, D. L. and Freter, A. 1990. Settlement history and the Classic Maya collapse at Copan: A redefined chronological perspective. *Latin American Antiquity* 1: 66–85.

Webster, D. L. and Kirker, J. 1995. Too many Maya, too few buildings: Investigating construction potential at Copán, Honduras. *Journal of Anthropological Research* 51(4): 363–87.

Weeks, J. M (ed.) 2006. *The Carnegie Maya: The Carnegie Institution of Washington Maya Research Program, 1913–1957*. Boulder: University Press of Colorado.

Weeks, J. M., Hill, J. A., and Golden, C. (eds.) 2005. *Piedras Negras Archaeology, 1931–1939: Piedras Negras Preliminary Papers; Piedras Negras Archaeology: Architecture*. Philadelphia: University of Pennsylvania Museum.

Weiner, A. B. 1992. *Inalienable Possessions: The Paradox of Keeping-While-Giving*. Berkeley: University of California Press.

Welsh, W. B. M. 1988. *An Analysis of Classic Lowland Maya Burials*. British Archaeological Reports, International Series 409. Oxford: British Archaeological Reports.

Wichmann, S. (ed.) 2004. *The Linguistics of Maya Writing*. Salt Lake City: University of Utah Press.

Wilk, R. R. 1983. Little house in the jungle: The causes of variation in house size among modern Kekchi Maya. *Journal of Anthropological Archaeology* 2: 99–116.

———. 1988. Maya household organization: Evidence and analogies. In R. R. Wilk and W. Ashmore (eds.), *Household and Community in the Mesoamerican Past*, 135–51. Albuquerque: University of New Mexico Press.

Wilk, R. R. and Netting, R. McC. 1984. Households: Changing forms and functions. In R. McC. Netting, R. R. Wilk, and E. J. Arnould (eds.), *Households: Comparative and Historical Studies of the Domestic Group*, 1–28. Berkeley: University of California Press.

Wilk, R. R. and Wilhite, H. L., Jr. 1991. The community of Cuello: Patterns of household and settlement change. In N. Hammond (ed.), *Cuello: An Early Maya Community in Belize*, 118–33. Cambridge: Cambridge University Press.

Willey, G. R. 1970. The Real Xe ceramics of Seibal, Peten, Guatemala. In W. Bullard (ed.), *Monographs and Papers in Maya Archaeology*, 313–55. Cambridge MA: Harvard University.

———. 1972. *The Artifacts of Altar de Sacrificios*. Papers of the Peabody Museum, Vol. 14, No. 1. Cambridge MA: Harvard University.

———. 1973. Altar de Sacrificios excavations: General summary and conclusions. *Papers*, 62(3). Cambridge MA: Harvard University, Peabody Museum of Archaeology and Ethnology.

———. 1978. *Excavations at Seibal: Artifacts*. Memoirs of the Peabody Museum Vol. 14 No. 1. Cambridge MA: Harvard University.

———. 1981. Maya lowland settlement patterns: A summary review. In W. Ashmore (ed.), *Lowland Maya Settlement Patterns*, 385–415. Albuquerque: University of New Mexico Press.

Willey, G. R., Bullard, W. R., Grass, J., and Gifford, J. 1965. *Prehistoric Maya Settlements in the Belize Valley*. Papers of the Peabody Museum, Vol. 54. Cambridge MA: Harvard University.

Willey, G. R., Culbert, T. P., and Adams, R. E. W. (eds.) 1967. Maya Lowland ceramics: A report from the 1965 Guatemala City conference. *American Antiquity* 32: 289–315.

Willey, G. R. and D. B. Shimkin. 1973. Maya collapse: A summary view. In T. P. Culbert (ed.), *The Classic Maya Collapse*, 457–501. Albuquerque: University of New Mexico Press.

Wilson, R. 1995. *Maya Resurgence in Guatemala: Q'eqchi' Experiences*. Norman: University of Oklahoma Press.

Wilson, S. M., Iceland, H. B., and Hester, T. R. 1998. Preceramic Connections between Yucatán and the Caribbean. *Latin American Antiquity* 9(4): 342–52.

Witschey, W. R. T. 1988. Recent Investigations at the Maya Inland Port City of Muyil

(Chunyaxche), Quintana Roo, Mexico. *Mexicon* 10(6): 111–17.

Winch, P. 1967. Authority. In A. Quinton (ed.), *Political Philosophy*, 83–111. Oxford: Oxford University Press.

Wing, E. S. 1981. A comparison of Olmec and Maya food ways. In E. P. Benson (ed.), *The Olmec and Their Neighbors: Essays in Memory of Matthew W. Stirling*, 20–8. Washington DC: Dumbarton Oaks.

Winter, I. 1993. 'Seat of kingship'/'A Wonder to Behold': The palace as construct in the ancient Near East. *Ars Orientalis* 23: 27–55.

Wisdom, C. 1940. *The Chorti Mayas of Guatemala*. Chicago: University of Chicago.

Wolf, E. R. 1955. Types of Latin American peasantry: A preliminary discussion. *American Anthropologist* 57(3): 452–71.

———. 1957. The vicissitudes of the closed corporate peasant community. *American Ethnologist* 13(2): 325–9.

Woodward, M. R. 2000. Considering household food security and diet at the Classic Period village of Cerén, El Salvador (A.D. 600). *Mayab* 13: 22–33.

Woolgar, C. M. 1999. *The Great Household in Late Medieval England*. New Haven: Yale University Press.

Wortman, R. S. 1995, 2000. *Scenarios of Power: Myth and Ceremony in Russian Monarchy*. 2 vols. Princeton: Princeton University Press.

Wren, L. H. and Schmidt, P. 1990. Elite interaction during the Terminal Classic Period: New evidence from Chichén Itzá. In T. P. Culbert (ed.), *Classic Maya Political History: Hieroglyphic and Archaeological Evidence*, 199–225. Cambridge: Cambridge University Press.

Wright, L. E. 2005. In search of Yax Nuun Ayiin I: Revisiting the Tikal Project's Burial 10. *Ancient Mesoamerica* 16: 89–100.

———. 2006. *Diet, Health, and Status among the Pasión Maya: A Reappraisal of the Collapse*.

Vanderbilt Institute of Mesoamerican Archaeology Series, Vol. 2. Nashville: Vanderbilt University Press.

Wright, L. E. and Chew, F. 1998. Porotic hyperostosis and paleoepidemiology: A forensic perspective on anemia among the ancient Maya. *American Anthropologist* 100: 924–39.

Wright, L. E. and White, C. D. 1996. Human biology in the Classic Maya collapse: Evidence from paleopathology and paleodiet. *Journal of World Prehistory* 10: 147–98.

Wuthnow, R. 1987. *Meaning and Moral Order: Explorations in Cultural Analysis*. Berkeley: University of California Press.

Yaeger, J. 2001. The social construction of communities in the Classic Maya countryside. In M. Canuto and J. Yaeger (eds.), *The Archaeology of Communities: A New World Perspective*, 123–42. London: Routledge.

Yaeger, J. and Canuto, M. 2001. Introducing an archaeology of communities. In M. Canuto and J. Yaeger (eds.), *The Archaeology of Communities: A New World Perspective*, 1–15. London: Routledge.

Yaeger, J. and Robin, C. 2004. Heterogeneous hinterlands: The social and political organization of commoner settlements near Xunantunich, Belize. In J. C. Lohse and F. Valdez, Jr., *Ancient Maya Commoners*, 147–74. Austin: Univeristy of Texas Press.

Yang, M. M. 1994. *Gifts, Favors, and Banquets: The Art of Social Relationships in China*. Ithaca: Cornell University Press.

Yoffee, N. 2005. *Myths of the Archaic State: Evolution of the Earliest Cities, States, and Civilizations*. Cambridge: Cambridge University Press.

Zender, M. 2004a. Glyphs for "Handspan" and "Strike" in Classic Maya ballgame texts. *The PARI Journal* 4(4): 1–9.

———. 2004b. *A Study of Classic Maya Priesthood*. Ph.D. dissertation. University of Calgary.

INDEX